Law, Peace, and Justice in Medieval and Early Modern Europe

Volume 1

Criminal Justice and Peace-making in Early Modern Italy

Law, Peace, and Justice in Medieval and Early Modern Europe

This series seeks to bring together work on 'peace-keeping' amongst medieval and early modern Europeans in the broadest sense: from criminal justice to transitional justice, from the resolution of interpersonal conflict within communities to treaty-making between states, from feud to refuge to reparations, from criminal trials to cultures of toleration. The series crosses conventional boundaries between medieval and early modern and welcomes work that crosses disciplinary boundaries, too, or that uses interdisciplinary approaches to subjects such as law, theology, art, political philosophy, social practice, etc. It aims broadly to promote work that helps us understand how law and justice were implicated in the ways in which people in the past imagined, implemented, and used 'peace', both within Europe and as Europeans moved out around the globe.

Monographs and coherent essay collections which explore the history of law, peace, and justice are welcome.

We are happy to consider both conventional and Open Access models of book publishing. Further information about the series and guidance on submitting a proposal can be found on the Durham University IMEMS Press website.

Other books in the series may be viewed on the Boydell & Brewer website

Criminal Justice and Peace-making in Early Modern Italy

Governing Hatred, c.1500–c.1700

Paolo Broggio

Durham University
IMEMS PRESS

First published 2025
A Durham University IMEMS Press publication
in association with
The Boydell Press
an imprint of Boydell & Brewer Ltd
PO Box 9, Woodbridge, Suffolk IP12 3DF, UK
and of Boydell & Brewer Inc.
668 Mt Hope Avenue, Rochester, NY 14620–2731, USA
website: www.boydellandbrewer.com
and with the
Institute of Medieval and Early Modern Studies
University of Durham

Any permissions requests, including translation requests, should be directed to Boydell & Brewer at the address above

Our Authorised Representative for product safety in the EU is Easy Access System Europe – Mustamäe tee 50, 10621 Tallinn, Estonia, gpsr.requests@easproject.com

ISBN 978-1-914967-18-4

A CIP catalogue record for this book is available from the British Library

Contents

Illustrations

The author and publisher are grateful to all the institutions and individuals listed for permission to reproduce the materials in which they hold copyright. Every effort has been made to trace the copyright holders; apologies are offered for any omission, and the publisher will be pleased to add any necessary acknowledgement in subsequent editions.

Acknowledgements

I would like to express my sincere gratitude to several individuals and institutions who, in various ways, contributed to the realisation of this research. First and foremost, Maria Pia Paoli, who many years ago suggested organising an international conference on the theories and practices of conciliation in early modern Europe. This conference resulted in a volume of proceedings that marked a significant milestone in my personal research journey in this field. My deepest gratitude goes to her, a distinguished scholar and friend, as well as to all the Italian and international colleagues who participated in the event held at the *Scuola Normale Superiore* in Pisa in May 2008 and contributed with written texts. I also extend my appreciation to Cecilia Palombelli for agreeing to publish the proceedings.

With Stuart Carroll, who was present in Pisa, I later organised two panels on Violence and Peace-making in Early Modern Europe: A Comparative Perspective in March 2015, as part of the Renaissance Society of America Annual Meeting in Berlin. I am thankful to Stuart for the always stimulating exchanges of views and knowledge. Special and affectionate thanks to Giancarlo Angelozzi, a man of extraordinary humanity and intellectual generosity, who provided me with not only his extensive historical and historiographic knowledge but also his invaluable knowledge of the archives of the *Torrone*'s Tribunal at the State Archives of Bologna. Without his guidance and precise instructions, my archival research in Bologna would have yielded much more modest results. Michele Di Sivo has been a careful guide for my research on the Governor of Rome's Tribunal at the State Archives of Rome. In the other archives of the former Papal States (Bologna, Perugia, Macerata, Ancona), I always found knowledgeable and helpful staff, to whom I am very grateful. A special mention goes to the staff of the Civic Library 'Romolo Spezioli' in Fermo and the Archiginnasio Library in Bologna, Dr Michele Moretti from the 'Biblioteca Interdipartimentale di Scienze Giuridiche – Storia del Diritto Italiano' at Sapienza University of Rome, and Luca Carboni from the Vatican Apostolic Archive. Without them, I would not have had access to certain documents during a period as challenging for research as the one marked by the SARS-CoV-2 pandemic.

I am also grateful to colleagues who provided me with the opportunity to present partial results of my research to an audience of experts and doctoral students, including Carlos Alberto González Sánchez (University of Seville),

Bruno Pomara Saverino (University of Valencia), Petra Bernardini (Lund University), Tommaso Caliò and Sandro Carocci (University of Rome 'Tor Vergata'), Xenia Von Tippelskirch and Matthias Pohlig (Humboldt University in Berlin), Maria Teresa Guerrini (University of Bologna), Andy Wood (Institute of Medieval and Early Modern Studies, Durham University), Sara Menzinger di Preussenthal and the group of colleagues who host the 'Historical-Legal Seminars' at my university (Roma Tre), among whom I would like to mention Emanuele Conte, Paolo Alvazzi del Frate and Italo Birocchi.

I owe heartfelt and sincere thanks to the Faculty of Arts and Humanities at Durham University for granting me a 'Holland Visiting Fellowship' in February–March 2020, which allowed me to benefit from the rich collections of the Durham Residential Research Library and Palace Green Library, as well as a productive period of peace and concentration. Durham has proven to be a special place for this research. My gratitude, therefore, goes to Stephen Taylor, General Editor of Durham University IMEMS Press, and to Krista Kesselring, General Editor of the series *Law, Peace, and Justice in Medieval and Early Modern Europe*, and of course to the Publisher, Boydell & Brewer; without their generous support, this book in its English version would not have seen the light of day.

For their valuable contributions, in the form of responses to my inquiries, a heartfelt thanks also goes to a series of colleagues, friends and mentors: Marco Bellabarba, Francesco Benigno, Giuseppe Capriotti, Tom Cohen, Gérard Delille, Jérémie Foa, Irene Fosi, Carlo Ginzburg, Tom B. Hamilton, James E. Kelly, Vincenzo Lagioia, Vito Loré, Jean-Claude Maire Vigueur, Martina Mampieri, Tomás Mantecón Movellán, Edward Muir, Ottavia Niccoli, Diego Pedrini, Claudio Povolo, Nicole Reinhardt, Domenico Rizzo, Francesco Trentini, Michaela Valente, Rafael Valladares, Massimo Vallerani, Andrea Vanni, Alfredo Viggiano, Flavia Tudini, Natalie Zemon Davis and Andrea Zorzi.

To Francesca Cantù, my heartfelt affection and perpetual intellectual debt.

ABBREVIATIONS

AAV	Archivio Apostolico Vaticano (Vatican City)
ASA	Archivio di Stato di Ancona
ASB	Archivio di Stato di Bologna
ASM	Archivio di Stato di Macerata
ASP	Archivio di Stato di Perugia
ASR	Archivio di Stato di Roma
BAV	Biblioteca Apostolica Vaticana (Vatican City)
BC	Biblioteca Casanatense (Rome)
BCF	Biblioteca del Comune di Fermo (Biblioteca Civica 'Romolo Spezioli')
BNE	Biblioteca Nacional de España (Madrid)
BNF	Bibliothèque Nationale de France 'François Mitterrand' (Parigi)

Pactum ... legem vincit, et amor judicium
Henry I of England

Les plus belles factions se font sur le maniement de la paix,
à savoir pour en avoir une meilleure
Christoph Besold (1624)

Un mauvais arrangement vaut mieux qu'un bon procès
Honoré de Balzac

Introduction

It is 27 April 2010. A small crowd, held back by a police cordon, waits in front of the entrance of the Reggio Calabria police headquarters for the exit of Giovanni Tegano and his transfer to prison. A *'Ndrangheta* boss and a fugitive since 1993, Tegano had been captured the previous day, in Terreti, along with five other individuals. Once outside, escorted by two police officers towards the patrol car, Tegano is greeted with a mixture of cheers and tears of despair by relatives, associates and supporters. Among the shouts, the voice of a woman becomes increasingly distinct as she angrily, repeatedly, yells, 'Man of peace! Man of peace! He has done good!'. The police car, with the boss on board, departs and the crowd's shouts gradually fade into silence, but the woman continues to shout that unsettling 'Man of peace!' for several tens of seconds, in an attitude of furious defiance towards the state and even some of those present, who were urging her to calm down.

The episode caused a sensation and no small amount of outrage in the public opinion, at both the local and national levels. Regardless of that woman's affiliation with criminal clans, how can a ruthless murderer at the helm of a *mafia* organisation be considered a 'man of peace'? How can a term ('peace') that evokes concepts such as harmony, concord and justice be associated with the ferocity of the struggle between criminal factions? The following year, it would be the turn of the informant Nino Lo Giudice to explain why Tegano could indeed be considered a 'man of peace' to those who are well-versed in the clan dynamics of the *'Ndrangheta*.[1] Lo Giudice explained that, during his time in hiding, the boss, in agreement with Pasquale Condello, another clan leader, would send envoys to prisons to prevent internal conflicts within the *'ndrine* (the criminal clans belonging to the *'Ndrangheta*) and to task individuals with ensuring peace. These actions were not born of a genuine moral desire, but because it would allow the criminal

[1] Regarding Cosa Nostra and the *'Ndrangheta* as organisations (brotherhoods) based on ritualistic affiliation mechanisms rooted in kinship and religious symbolism, aimed at political control within the community through the collection of tributes, see Letizia Paoli, *Fratelli di mafia. Cosa Nostra e 'Ndrangheta* (Bologna, 2000).

organisation to continue its illegal activities undisturbed, keeping it away from media scrutiny and law enforcement pressure.

This modern news event thrusts us into a dimension with an archaic flavour, where the concept of 'peace' is firmly embedded in a semantic field that, at first glance, might seem alien to it, bewildering the contemporary observer. Peace is undeniably and inseparably linked to violence as an integral part of the mechanisms of feuding. The history of Sicilian and Neapolitan mafia is also marked by peace agreements – reached for various reasons – which, albeit temporarily, put an end to clan wars, blood feuds and settling of scores; these *paci* ('peace deals') are sometimes sealed by marriages and celebrated with banquets.[2] Between the 1970s and 1980s, the Sicilian *Mafia* made agreements with the Calabrian *'Ndrangheta*. In 1974, the witness at the wedding of Totò Riina and Ninetta Bagarella was Domenico Tripodi, the boss of Sambatello, one of the highest-ranking figures in Calabrian organised crime. During the mafia war that, between 1985 and 1991, resulted in 966 deaths in Calabria alone, Totò Riina often travelled there to play the role of a peacemaker, with the particularly noteworthy detail that he was dressed as a priest.[3] The disguise served to conceal his fugitive status but also symbolically reinforced his peace-making role among the clans. Peace is a part of violence and, at the same time, draws from religious symbols. The relationship between the mafia, religion and devotion, after all, has long been the subject of historical, sociological and anthropological analyses, from initiation and passage rituals infused with Christian references to the ostentatious Marian devotion of many of its members.[4]

That peace is a part of the mechanisms of feuds is an established fact in anthropology and ethnology, at least since the works of Edward Evans

[2] See Ombretta Ingrasci, ''Ndrangheta Women in Contemporary Italy: Between Change and Continuity', in *The 'Ndrangheta and Sacra Corona Unita. The History, Organization and Operations of Two Unknown Mafia Groups*, ed. Nicoletta Serenata (Cham, Heidelberg, New York, Dordrecht and London, 2014), pp. 67ff.

[3] See Nicola Gratteri and Antonio Nicaso, *Fratelli di sangue. Storie, boss e affari della 'ndrangheta, la mafia più potente del mondo* (Milan, 2006).

[4] At the forefront of devotions cultivated in the Neapolitan *Camorra* environment is undoubtedly the Madonna of Pompeii. At least until the 1980s, the initiation ritual involved pricking the right fingertip of the candidate with a pin and letting the blood drip onto a small image of the Madonna of Pompeii. This image was then partially set on fire with a candle and passed from hand to hand among all the clan leaders. Only when all the affiliates had kissed the Madonna's image could the newly initiated individuals officially consider themselves part of the clan. See Roberto Saviano, *Gomorra. Viaggio nell'impero economico e nel sogno di dominio della camorra* (Milan, 2015), pp. 246–7.

Pritchard and Max Gluckman on the *Nuer* and other tribal societies in Africa.[5] However, this may be less evident in the dominant narratives told by Western European society about itself, building much of its self-understanding on the so-called 'civilising' process, ideologically relegating retaliatory systems to the barbarism of primitive, stateless societies or to explicitly anti-state phenomena such as mafia-style criminal organisations. According to the traditional historiographical approach, modernity is believed to have progressively limited interpersonal violence primarily by prohibiting the practice of revenge and by promoting behavioural models based on self-discipline. According to this same historiography, in modern Western societies the principle was progressively established that only the State holds the monopoly on the use of legitimate violence. Therefore, only judicial institutions controlled by the State are authorised to administer criminal justice. European society and its modern concepts and institutions continue to shape our interpretive frameworks for understanding pre-modern attitudes towards interpersonal violence and methods of conflict resolution.[6]

The direct correlation between the birth and consolidation of modern statehood, the gradual emergence of compulsory criminal proceedings, and the limitation of private violence seems too self-evident not to end up dominating the interpretive paradigms adopted by the late nineteenth- and early twentieth-century sociology and history of political institutions. An idea was concretely shaped: state justice does not admit different configurations; for this reason, pre-modern justice has been usually read through the lenses of modernity, with the result that scholars have been prevented from reaching a full understanding of it. Consequently, in many current debates on the restorative model of criminal justice, the main terms of comparison are the conflict resolution systems adopted in the so-called 'simple' societies. The pre-modern European judicial systems, characterised by not-so-dissimilar compositional methods, do not seem to be given due consideration, and, most importantly, not from the right perspective, by today's criminal justice

5 See Edward E. Evans Pritchard, *The Nuer. A Description of the Modes of Livelihood and Political Institutions of a Nilotic People* (Oxford, 1940); Max Gluckman, 'The Peace in the Feud', *Past & Present* 8 (1955), pp. 1–14. Of the same author, see also *Politics, Law and Ritual in Tribal Society* (Oxford, 1965), in particular chapters III ('Stateless Societies and the Maintenance of Order') and V ('Dispute and settlement').

6 See Norbert Elias, *Über den Prozeß der Zivilisation*, 2 vols (Basel, 1939). English edition: *The Civilizing Process*, vol. I: *The History of Manners*, vol. II: *State Formation and Civilization* (Oxford, 1969, 1982).

experts.[7] There is much to reflect upon regarding the connection between the main studies on justice reform in Italy, the research of a politically engaged sociologist like Boaventura de Sousa Santos on informal legal phenomena in the *favelas* of Rio de Janeiro as a tool of resistance against capitalist oppression,[8] and the broader debates on legal postmodernity, in which the present, marked by the dissolution of the 'modern' positivist monism, now weakened and no longer the sole subject producing law, increasingly resembles pre-modernity.[9] However, this certainly goes beyond the objectives of the present work.

The statist paradigm has also ensured that the functioning of justice in the early modern era was predominantly viewed in a teleological manner. Previously, historians with a liberal-positivist approach have been seemingly hesitant to study social violence stemming from enmities sparked by even trivial causes. This reluctance was influenced by an underlying moral binary, as political violence, especially in its revolutionary form, and to some extent violence with religious roots (consider the independence process of the United Provinces from Catholic Spain), has generally been celebrated as a vehicle for the progress of European civilisation. The tendency has been to label interpersonal violence as an uncivil, antisocial, anti-state and, therefore, primitive phenomenon. Consequently, the focus has been more on the tools of repression and limitation of violence, rather than on violence itself.[10]

7 See, for example, Marco Bouchard and Giovanni Mierolo, *Offesa e riparazione. Per una nuova giustizia attraverso la mediazione* (Milan, 2005); Grazia Mannozzi, *La giustizia senza spada. Uno studio comparato su giustizia riparativa e mediazione penale* (Milan, 2003). On her part, Marianna Pignata presents the proposal put forth by the jurist Camillo Borrelli through his *Commentaria super Pragmaticis Regis Ferdinandi primi* (1574) as a link between an ancient concept of arbitration and compromise, expressions of delegated justice, and a new concept in which the power of the state extended its protection and control over such institutions. Borrelli would, therefore, be a kind of precursor to modern forms of arbitration, which have been the focus of criminal science in recent years. See Marianna Pignata, *Spazi di giustizia negoziata nel* Regnum *della prima età moderna. I* Commentaria *di Camillo Borrelli* (Naples, 2018).

8 See Boaventura de Sousa Santos, *Law Against Law. Legal Reasoning in Pasargada Law* (New Haven and London, 1974); Boaventura de Sousa Santos, *Toward a New Legal Common Sense. Law, Globalization, and Emancipation* (London, 2002).

9 See, for instance, the recent *Percorsi giuridici della postmodernità*, ed. Roberto E. Kostoris (Bologna, 2017).

10 See Stuart Carroll, 'Introduction', in *Cultures of Violence. Interpersonal Violence in Historical Perspective*, ed. S. Carroll (Houndsmill and New York, 2007), pp. 1–43. See also the stimulating insights offered by Andrea Zorzi: 'I conflitti dell'Italia comunale. Riflessioni sullo stato degli studi e sulle prospettive di ricerca', in *Conflitti, paci e vendette nell'Italia comunale*, ed. A. Zorzi (Florence, 2009), pp. 7–41.

The same considerations can be made regarding enmity, on which we now have Stuart Carroll's powerful and innovative study. While much thought has been given in the past to the figure of the 'public' enemy, both within the State and as a threat from outside, much less emphasis has been placed on 'private' enmity during the early modern age, a phenomenon that disrupts some of the fundamental assumptions within Whig history.[11]

From this perspective, and starting with Max Weber, discipline has appeared as the very essence of the formation of the modern state, a precondition for its development. That acquired disposition, that ready and uncritical obedience to commands by a multitude of individuals achieved through non-repressive means, aimed – according to scholars who embraced and applied this successful paradigm directed towards the study of society and institutions in early modern Europe – at the gradual elimination of interpersonal conflicts. The judgement expressed by this historiographical strand on the phenomenon of peace-making is essentially ambivalent. On the one hand, it has highlighted the ability of certain instruments of education and acculturation, for both the masses and the noble elites, revolving around the concept of peace and the forgiveness of enemies, to implement mechanisms of social reintegration and to influence traditional behavioural codes centred on the system of revenge (pedagogical criteria used in seminaries for those of noble birth, the missions of religious orders, treatises on the prohibition of honour duels, etc.). On the other hand, some have not failed to emphasise that these conflict resolution systems would have acted to the detriment of the prerogatives of central powers, strengthening community-based dispute resolution systems and slowing the gradual but necessary establishment of state jurisdiction.[12]

Already in the 1970s, Michel Foucault, with his remarkable insight into power dynamics and the relationship between society and institutions in Western Europe, described, along with the birth of punishment and surveillance as cornerstones of discipline, the central role played by the modern

[11] See Stuart Carroll, *Enmity and Violence in Early Modern Europe* (Cambridge, 2023), especially pp. 5ff.

[12] This particular interpretation is quite common among those Italian historians who tackled peace-making from the perspective of Catholic pastoral care and the history of piety. See, for example, Giacomo Di Fiore, 'E tutti piansero. Perdonismo e impunità criminale tra Cinquecento e Settecento', in *Filosofia Storiografia Letteratura. Studi in onore di Mario Agrimi*, ed. Bernardo Razzotti (Lanciano, 2001), pp. 685–718; but see also Ottavia Niccoli, 'Rinuncia, pace, perdono. rituali di pacificazione della prima età moderna', *Studi Storici* 40, 1 (1999), pp. 219–61: p. 252; Alessandro Pastore, 'Inquisitori, confessori, missionari' *Rivista Storica Italiana* CX (1998), pp. 666–86: p. 680.

state in assuming functions of arbitration, pacification and mediation between competing and conflicting powers.[13] 'The slogan of this regime, *pax et iustitia*', writes Foucault, 'in keeping with the function it laid claim to, established peace as the prohibition of feudal or private wars, and justice as a way of suspending the private settling of lawsuits'.[14] The state's power, therefore, 'by combining the exemplary nature of a few cruel punishments with the gentleness of everyday life', would address its subjects 'in the reassuring guise of peacemakers'.[15] With this increased role of judicial action against infractions, along with the dominance of the inquisitorial method over the accusatorial one, confession emerged as one of the 'main rituals we rely on for the production of truth'.[16] We will examine how sacramental confession played a pivotal role in peace-making.

Discussions on discipline are still ongoing, although there is substantial agreement on the heuristic limits of a paradigm that, much like that of the state, does not sufficiently take into consideration the actual circumstances of communal living – circumstances from which arise the persistence and, above all, the degree of social legitimation of behaviour models that are far from disciplined. In the English-speaking world, the concept of 'social control' has gained greater popularity and success. It was primarily developed within the social sciences, starting with the studies of the American Edward Alsworth Ross from the late nineteenth to the first half of the twentieth century. It lent itself to diachronic analyses, primarily of a functionalist nature, which focused on the issue of social order, with the consequence of considering violence and disorder as exceptions to the rule.[17] There has been extensive discussion about identifying various agencies of social control beyond the law and state apparatus. In this regard, a common distinction has been made between formal and informal control tools in relation to the issue of consent, generally accepting the idea that order is the result of both 'top-down' and 'bottom-up' interactions.

Of particular interest for our study is the contribution of the sociologist Mark Cooney on the centrality of the intervention of 'third parties' in conflict

13 See Michel Foucault, *Surveiller et punir. Naissance de la prison* (Paris, 1975), English edition: *Discipline and Punish: The Birth of the Prison* (London, 1978).

14 Michel Foucault, *The History of Sexuality*, vol. 1 (*An Introduction*) (New York, 1980), p. 87.

15 Marco Bellabarba, *La giustizia nell'Italia moderna* (Rome and Bari, 2008), p. 79.

16 Foucault, *The History of Sexuality*, p. 58.

17 Edward Alsworth Ross, *Social Control. A Survey of the Foundations of Order* (New York and London, 1901).

dynamics involving two individuals or two groups. This intervention can either lead to the proliferation of violence or the resolution of the dispute.[18] These third parties are not only identifiable as individuals such as family members, acquaintances and friends, or individuals with special standing within the community, such as clergymen. They can also include judges and law enforcement officers when they decide to intervene (or not intervene) in a conflict. The difference in status between the third party and the disputants is certainly decisive and greatly influences the outcome of mediation, as well as the interaction between state coercion, which can potentially lead to resentment and resistance from social actors, and informal mechanisms for dispute resolution. These informal mechanisms, however, depend on the cooperation and consent of the same actors.[19]

On the field of 'disciplinamento' studies, even though historians like Pierangelo Schiera and Paolo Prodi managed to adjust their course in the face of increasingly tight objections about the shortcomings of a strictly 'top-down' model of rule diffusion, still tied to the paradigm of the civilising process, a teleological perspective remained rather evident. This perspective was subject to a radical re-evaluation, starting from the 1980s, by micro-historical research that focused on local dynamics of conflict management and power organisation. Osvaldo Raggio's work on a community in eastern Liguria (Fontanabuona), examining conflicts, kinships/alliances/exchanges, feuds and their local management, began with the awareness that studies based on the model of modern state formation, as elaborated for Italy by Federico Chabod for the State of Milan between the 1930s and the 1950s, had paid no attention to the 'concrete, daily articulations of power and authority, social practices and exchanges, group and individual relations, conflicts and the often close interweaving of processes of differentiation and social integration'.[20] By exclusively focusing on institutions and thus the 'growth of state organs and functions', Raggio continues, 'all cases that did

[18] Mark Cooney, *Warriors and Peacemakers. How Third Parties Shape Violence* (New York, 1998).

[19] Pieter Spierenburg, 'Social Control and History: An Introduction', in *Social Control in Europe*, vol. I, *1500-1800*, ed. Herman Roodenburg and Pieter Spierenburg (Columbus, 2004), pp. 8–9.

[20] 'articolazioni concrete, quotidiane, dei rapporti di potere e autorità, alle pratiche e agli scambi sociali, alle relazioni tra gruppi e individui, ai conflitti e all'intreccio spesso molto stretto tra i processi di differenziazione e di integrazione sociale', Osvaldo Raggio, *Faide e parentele. Lo stato genovese visto dalla Fontanabuona* (Turin, 1990), pp. IX–X.

not seem to contain elements of modern state anticipation, were judged from time to time as archaic or marginal'.[21]

The tendency to label seemingly dysfunctional phenomena in relation to the construction of modern statehood as remnants of the medieval past has affected both feuds and retaliatory mechanisms, as well as conflict resolution methods that appeared to elude state jurisdiction and courts of justice.[22] This trend has remained unchanged even in the face of clear evidence of the persistence of such phenomena throughout the early modern period. For much of the historiography, the privatistic nature and archaism continue to be characteristic features of phenomena that, by their nature, escape essentially dualistic explanatory models. This is despite scholars – as demonstrated by Giorgio Chittolini in a now-classic essay – having long rejected a rigid dichotomy between the public and the private and emphasised the various forms that modern statehood could assume: the pluralism of bodies, social strata and political centres; the existence of privileges, immunities, exemptions; arbitrary interventions in the realm of justice, *sospensiones causarum*, letters of grace, conflict resolution strategies that judicial systems often recognised and even promoted; 'all elements that are intimately interconnected and complementary, in a difficult-to-unravel connection, in a unified *Verfassung*, acknowledged not only by a political theory that tends to emphasise a new concept of sovereignty but also by a legitimate and widespread rule practice'.[23]

The problem also lies in disciplinary divisions: while medieval studies have more easily shed interpretative burdens of an evolutionary nature that have none the less persisted until at least forty years ago (a clear example being the classical interpretation of the Italian communal experience, understood in a strongly publicist sense as an incubator of public experiences and a stage in the formation of the modern state and public criminal justice),[24] his-

21 'crescita degli organi e delle funzioni dello Stato', op. cit., p. IX. 'tutti i casi che non sembravano contenere elementi di anticipazione dello Stato moderno sono stati giudicati di volta in volta arcaici o marginali', op. cit., p. X.

22 For the High Middle Age see *The Settlement of Disputes in Early Medieval Europe*, ed. Wendy Davies and Paul Fouracre (Cambridge, 1986).

23 'tutti elementi che risultano fra loro intimamente legati e complementari, in un nesso difficilmente districabile, in un'unitaria *Verfassung*, riconosciuta, se non da una teoria politica che tende piuttosto a insistere su un nuovo concetto di sovranità, da una legittimata e diffusa pratica di governo', Giorgio Chittolini, 'Il privato, il pubblico, lo Stato', in *Origini dello Stato. Processi di formazione statale in Italia fra Medioevo ed età moderna*, ed. Giorgio Chittolini, Anthony Molho and Pierangelo Schiera (Bologna, 1994), p. 569.

24 Zorzi, *I conflitti nell'Italia comunale*.

torians of the early modern period have had more difficulty in overcoming a fundamental unease regarding phenomena that, if fully recognised, would reinforce the idea of a pre-modern *Ancien Régime*, of a long if not very long Middle Ages. This idea would irreparably weaken the strong notion of political modernity that, according to the traditional image, permeates European history in the sixteenth and seventeenth centuries.[25]

From the 1980s onward, for Italian early modern historiography a fundamentally important contribution in this regard has certainly come from scholars, some of whom were associated with the journal *Quaderni Storici* and the microhistory movement, proponents of a new way of conducting social and socio-political history, and therefore, the history of justice. Historians such as Edoardo Grendi[26] and Osvaldo Raggio[27] on local communities in the Republic of Genoa, Angelo Torre in the Langhe region of Piedmont,[28] Marco Bellabarba in the episcopal principality of Trento,[29] Claudio Povolo[30] and Alfredo Viggiano in the Veneto region[31], and even Marco Gentile in

25 In this regard, the words of Claudio Donati regarding a conference organised in 2008 by the author of the present book and Maria Pia Paoli on the theories and practices of conciliation in early modern Europe are particularly significant. See Paolo Broggio and Maria Pia Paoli, 'Introduzione', in *Stringere la pace. Teorie e pratiche della conciliazione nell'Europa moderna*, eds Paolo Broggio and Maria Pia Paoli, (Rome, 2011), p. 9.

26 See Edoardo Grendi, 'Introduzione all'analisi storica delle comunità liguri: Cervo in età moderna', in *Studi di micro-analisi storica (Piemonte-Liguria secoli XVI-XVIII)* = 'Miscellanea Storica Ligure', VII, 2 (1977), pp. 135–211; Edoardo Grendi, 'Il sistema politico di una comunità ligure: Cervo fra Cinquecento e Seicento', *Quaderni storici* XVI, 46 (1981), pp. 92–129; Edoardo Grendi, 'Stato e comunità nel Seicento genovese', in *Studi in memoria di Giovanni Tarello*, I, *Saggi storici* (Milan, 1990), pp. 243–82.

27 See Raggio, *Faide e parentele*.

28 See Angelo Torre, 'Faida, fazioni e partiti: la ridefinizione della politica nei feudi imperiali delle Langhe tra Sei e Settecento', *Quaderni Storici* 63 (1986), pp. 775–810.

29 See Marco Bellabarba, *La giustizia ai confini. Il Principato vescovile di Trento agli inizi dell'età moderna* (Bologna, 1996).

30 See Claudio Povolo, *L'intrigo dell'onore. Poteri e istituzioni nella Repubblica di Venezia tra Cinque e Seicento* (Sommacampagna, 1997).

31 Alfredo Viggiano, *Governanti e governati. Legittimità del potere ed esercizio dell'autorità nello Stato veneto della prima età moderna* (Treviso, 1993); Alfredo Viggiano, 'Giustizia, disciplina, ordine pubblico', in *Storia di Venezia dalle origini alla caduta della Serenissima*, VI, *Dal Rinascimento al barocco*, ed. Gaetano Cozzi (Rome, 1994), pp. 825–57.

Parma (although with reference to a chronological span that does not extend beyond the mid-sixteenth century),[32] to name just a few, have extensively explored, through various approaches, the significance of factions – and peace-making – in the social and political dynamics of early modern Italy. They have also revealed the richness of judicial sources in understanding conflict management methods and engaged in a fruitful dialogue with legal historians, with Mario Sbriccoli being one of the prominent figures.[33] A generally deconstructionist spirit has prevailed, and certainly a non-essentialist approach to modern statehood, albeit sometimes with possibly excessive accents, facilitated by the choice of the micro-analytical scale, which had some difficulty relating to the macro dimension. From these studies, which intentionally neglected intellectual constructs and, more generally, cultural aspects (and therefore treatises and narrative sources), they have nevertheless provided a significant contribution to the analysis of interpersonal violence in Italian society during the early modern period. The same cannot be said for peace, considered at best as a kind of taken-for-granted outcome of feud mechanisms, not deserving a specific focus. The concept of 'peace' is polysemic, as has been observed, difficult to circumscribe, and by its nature it eludes precise categorisations, insinuating itself through a multitude of channels into the deeper social, political, legal and cultural structures of early modern Europe.[34]

The greatest challenge lies in finding the right balance between a perspective entirely centred on discipline, obedience and the internalisation of norms, and the opposite perspective, solely focused on indiscipline and conflict, which tends to regard the grand intellectual constructs (especially in the field of morality) as little more than frills. The two levels of theory and

32 Marco Gentile, *Fazioni al governo. Politica e società a Parma nel Quattrocento* (Rome, 2009); Marco Gentile, 'La vendetta di sangue come rituale. Qualche osservazione sulla Lombardia fra Quattro e Cinquecento', in *La morte e i suoi riti in Italia tra Medioevo e prima Età moderna*, ed. Francesco Salvestrini, Gian Maria Varanini and Anna Zangarini (Florence, 2007), pp. 209–41.

33 See the debate between Mario Sbriccoli and Edoardo Grendi published in the journals *Studi Storici* and *Quaderni Storici* between the late 1980s and the early 1990s: Edoardo Grendi, *Premessa*, in *Quaderni Storici*, monographic issue on *Fonti criminali e storia sociale*, 66 (1987), pp. 695–700; Mario Sbriccoli, 'Fonti giudiziarie e fonti giuridiche: riflessioni sulla fase attuale degli studi di storia del crimine e della giustizia criminale', *Studi Storici*, 29 (1988), pp. 491–501; Edoardo Grendi, 'Sulla "storia criminale": risposta a Mario Sbriccoli', in *Quaderni Storici* 73 (1990), pp. 269–75.

34 See Maria Clara Rossi, 'Polisemia di un concetto: la pace nel basso medioevo. Note di lettura', *Quaderni di storia religiosa* 12 (2005), pp. 9–45.

practice cannot be separated in any way because both played a fundamental role in shaping a culture of conflict resolution on a continental scale. Culture, Santo Burgio asks, 'should not be seen as that dynamic meta-field in which different obediences, *widely accepted* values, and factors and forces of change constantly seek their own balance?'.[35] It is precisely for this reason that, in this study, the analysis of concrete social dynamics that came into contact with the actions of the judicial apparatus should not be disconnected from religious and devotional representations, as well as from intellectual constructs – especially in the spheres of political theory and moral theology – that contributed to shaping the concept of peace in relation to equally central issues for the early modern European culture, foremost among them being matters of honour and public reputation, typically – and erroneously – considered relevant only to aristocratic classes and limited to Mediterranean societies, perpetuating a stereotype that is hard to eradicate not only in historical and anthropological studies but also in common perception.[36] The challenge lies precisely in considering these dimensions together: norms, doctrine and practice alone cannot provide a comprehensive view of historical reality through a simple summation of these elements. Thus, an integrated analysis becomes necessary, achievable only through careful consideration of the contexts.

The bibliography on what is commonly referred to as 'private peace-making' in the Anglo-Saxon world is now quite extensive. Recently, at least two studies have focused on the Italian context in the late medieval period. On one hand, there is Katherine L. Jansen, who studied the interplay between peace, confession and penitential practices in the communes of central Italy, especially in Florence, between the thirteenth and fourteenth centuries.[37] On the other hand, Glenn Kumhera conducted comprehensive research on conciliation practices in late medieval Italy.[38]

35 'non va pensata come quel meta-campo dinamico nel quale sia le differenti obbedienze, sia i valori affermati e *diffusi*, sia i fattori e le forze produttive di mutamento cercano incessantemente il proprio equilibrio?', Santo Burgio, *Appartenenza e negozio. La crisi della teologia barocca* (Soveria Mannelli, 2004), p. 15, italics in the original.

36 *Honour and Shame. The Values of Mediterranean Society*, ed. John G. Peristiany (Chicago, 1966); *Onore e storia nelle società mediterranee*, ed. Giovanna Fiume (Palermo, 1989); *Honor and Grace in Anthropology*, ed. John G. Peristiany and Julian Pitt-Rivers (Cambridge, 1991); *L'anthropologie de la Méditerranée*, ed. Dionigi Albera, Anton Blok and Christian Bromberger (Cahors, 2001).

37 See Katherine L. Jansen, *Peace and Penance in Late Medieval Italy* (Princeton and Oxford, 2018).

38 See Glenn Kumhera, *The Benefits of Peace. Private Peace-making in Late Medieval Italy* (Leiden and Boston, 2017).

For the early modern period, the theme of peace-making has been addressed mostly tangentially and in a sectoral manner, almost always in connection with the phenomenon of factional or aristocratic violence, without systematic attempts at definition. An exception is a recent collective volume edited by Stephen Cummins and Laura Kounine, which, from a broad perspective, raises the fundamental question of the decline of retaliatory mechanisms in early modern Europe. The essays contained in it seek to answer this question well beyond the Eliasian paradigm of the civilising process, drawing from the so-called 'anthropological turn' in the study of conflict and its resolution systems, which, as rightly noted by the two editors, are 'far from always a positive and consensual act. Instead, it is often a product of domination and the reinforcement of inequality'.[39]

Ottavia Niccoli, on her part, has provided stimulating and highly interesting insights into peace in her study on forgiveness practices in early modern Italy, primarily based on documentation from Bologna.[40] However, renunciations and pardons are just one aspect of a complex mechanism, not always – indeed, rarely – initiated by the parties themselves, which made peace one of the pivotal axes of the overall justice systems and practices in the early modern period, operating according to criteria quite different from what we consider characteristic of modernity. Moreover, John Bossy's proposed model for describing and analysing the various systems of peaceful conflict resolution operating in the post-Reformation period has not proven to be particularly suitable or useful. The English historian argued that, following the religious reforms of the sixteenth century, the widespread diffusion of a 'moral tradition' rooted in Christianity played a predominant role in limiting recourse to individual violence:

> Moral tradition [...] joins together three items: the notion or practical instinct that to be a Christian means to love your neighbour, and in particular your enemy; the fact that in these times and places it was very likely that people might be in a state of enmity towards others, which would call for arrangements of peace-making if it was to be resolved; and the historical or perhaps archaic connection between these arrangements and the sites, rites and persons of the Church.[41]

39 Stephen Cummins and Laura Kounine, 'Introduction: Confronting Conflict in Early Modern Europe', in *Cultures of Conflict Resolution in Early Modern Europe*, eds Stephen Cummins and Laura Kounine, (Farnham and Burlington, 2016), p. 6.

40 See Ottavia Niccoli, *Perdonare. Idee, pratiche, rituali in Italia tra Cinque e Seicento* (Rome and Bari, 2007).

41 John Bossy, *Peace in the Post-Reformation. The Birkbeck Lectures* (Cambridge, 1998), p. 2.

Ottavia Niccoli raised in this regard a very convincing objection, stating that 'it is not possible to package a quantity of deeply different moral attitudes, practices and behaviours into a single container titled 'moral tradition', and they should be evaluated considering highly differentiated legal traditions, statutory legislation and other factors'.[42] What heuristic value can a paradigm like that of the 'moral tradition' have, for example, when confronted with the phenomenon of truces between mafia clans? A *'Ndrangheta* boss might even be personally convinced of the compatibility of his criminal conduct with the Gospel's teachings, but it is highly unlikely that he would be moved to make peace because he believes that 'to be a Christian means to love your neighbour'. For him, peace is not the result of a 'conversion' to good. What remains outside the Bossyan paradigm is the central issue of the concrete circumstances and motivations that led individuals to make peace, what underlies the decision to reconcile, which could also be the simple willingness to postpone (and thus continue) the feud and criminal activities or a response to the very real threat of retaliation that would be carried out by public authorities in case of refusal to reconcile – a mechanism that could apply to Giovanni Tegano as well as to the anonymous criminal sought and brought to make peace with his victim by the officials of the Governor of Rome's Tribunal in the late sixteenth century.

Tracing the organising criteria of social relationships and exchanges is a daunting task, nearly impossible if one remains confined within disciplinary boundaries. Anthropology and the history of law have taught us a great deal about gift-giving and non-legal obligations underlying the social dynamics of early modern Europe, from Marcel Mauss[43] to Natalie Zemon Davis,[44] and up to Giovanni Levi,[45] Bartolomé Clavero[46] and Antó-

[42] 'non è possibile imbustare in un unico contenitore intitolato "tradizione morale" una quantità di atteggiamenti morali, di pratiche, di comportamenti profondamente diversi e che vanno valutati tenendo conto di tradizioni giuridiche e legislazioni statuarie e di altra sorta profondamente differenziate', Ottavia Niccoli, 'Giustizia, pace, perdono. A proposito di un libro di John Bossy', *Storica* 25–26 (2003), pp. 195–207: p. 203.

[43] See Marcel Mauss, 'Essai sur le don. Forme et raison de l'échange dans les sociétés archaïques', in *L'Année Sociologique*, 1923–4.

[44] See Natalie Zemon Davis, *The Gift in Sixteenth Century France* (Oxford, 2000).

[45] See Giovanni Levi, *L'eredità immateriale. Carriera di un esorcista nel Piemonte del Seicento* (Turin, 1985); Giovanni Levi, 'Reciprocidad Mediterránea', *Hispania* 60, 204 (2000), pp. 103–26; Giovanni Levi, '*Aequitas* vs *fairness*. Reciprocità ed equità fra età moderna ed età contemporanea', *Rivista di Storia Economica* XIX, 2 (2003), pp. 195–204.

[46] See Bartolomé Clavero, *Antidora. Antropología católica de la economía moderna* (Milan, 1991).

nio Manuel Hespanha.[47] Remunerative donation, non-legal obligation, the concept of reciprocity, as well as disciplining agencies other than the State (the Church, the family), non-legal knowledge – foremost among them moral theology – have become a primary field of reflection in recent years. However, this has overshadowed the presence of elements of coercion, which relied on a sphere that is essentially juridical in the classical sense, as pointed out by Giorgia Alessi. This era of legal historiography, especially in the Iberian context, thus faced the risk of:

> bracketing the particular ability of legal systems to configure space and act upon bodies, institutional projection, the compelling persuasive capacity, distinct from the purely performative nature of discourses: that is, the elements of strength and coercion. The 'natural' arrangement of social relationships within overlapping and potentially harmonious normative spheres is not immune to a strong organicist temptation, nor, most importantly, to the denial of the inescapable connection between 'incurable' conflict and law. It is precisely from the failure of other normative reference points – love, friendship, religion, disciplinary precepts – that law assumes space and meaning.[48]

The present research aims to scrutinise how peace, in its various meanings, has been able to exert its influence on the social and political dynamics of early modern Italy through unquestionable 'elements of strength and coercion', stemming from specific legal institutions, which should by no means be considered incompatible with concepts such as peace, harmony and forgiveness. In fact, one of the key points I wish to emphasise is the connection between a series of legal instruments typically used by the *Ancien Régime*'s tribunals (*sicurtà*, injunctions, guarantees, petitions) and peace as both a concept and an institution. Private peace agreements should not be relegated solely to the study of pastoral and religious experiences, as has

[47] See António M. Hespanha, *La gracia del derecho. Economía de la cultura en la edad moderna* (Madrid, 1993).

[48] 'di porre tra parentesi la particolare capacità degli ordinamenti giuridici di configurare lo spazio e di intervenire sui corpi, la proiezione istituzionale, la cogente capacità persuasiva, ulteriore e diversa dall'azione pur performante dei discorsi: ossia gli elementi di forza e di coazione. La "naturale" sistemazione delle relazioni sociali entro sfere normative sovrapposte e tendenzialmente armoniose non si sottrae né ad una forte tentazione organicista né, soprattutto, alla rimozione del nesso ineliminabile esistente tra conflitto "insanabile" e diritto. Proprio dal fallimento degli altri riferimenti normativi – amore, amicizia, religione, precetti disciplinari – il diritto assume spazio e senso', Giorgia Alessi, 'Giustizia pubblica, private vendette. Riflessioni intorno alla stagione dell'infragiustizia', *Storica* 39 (2007), pp. 91–118: p. 98.

often been the case, especially in the early modern period. For this very reason, in the sequence of chapters I have chosen not to highlight the more religious aspect, not to diminish its importance but as a deliberate critical and historiographic choice. Is it possible to craft a 'history of peace' in reference to a world governed by conflict and violence? This was the question posed by Gregory Hanlon in his study of Layrac (Aquitaine) in the seventeenth century, a context marked by religious division and the search for models of peaceful coexistence.[49] I have opted to conduct a study on 'peace' within a context not marked by confessional schism but, like any other, characterised by social and political divisions and tensions.

The scope of this research is the Papal States, and it is in this environment that I have attempted to immerse peace agreements in the actual contexts that gave rise to them, both at the local level and in the relationships between the centre and the peripheries. The perspective will be then expanded in order to capture, in a comparative manner, an image of a European culture of peace-making. The intention is to demonstrate how the concept of peace eludes fixed characterisations, how it lends itself to different, sometimes conflicting, and even opposing interpretations, and how it is necessary to consider all aspects connected to the functionality of the concept itself (social, political, judicial, cultural, religious).

Peace was not just a tool in the hands of communities to defend themselves from the encroachment of state jurisdiction, nor was it solely, on the contrary, the factual and ideal weapon that allowed the central power to curb private violence by taking control of the equally private mechanisms for dispute resolution, enabling the State to play a pacifying role in social conflicts, as previously discussed in Michel Foucault's insight. This study operates on the premise that there is no 'pure' negotiated/community justice untouched by the intrusion of public, state or seignorial institutions, whose traces can essentially be found in notarial sources, distinct from a hegemonic, institutional (state or feudal) justice that is equally pure and unaffected.[50]

49 See Gregory Hanlon, *Confession and Community in Seventeenth Century France. Catholic and Protestant Coexistence in Aquitaine* (Philadelphia, 1993).

50 Simona Cerutti's methodological reflections seem more than reasonable: 'Per ricostruire la pluralità delle concezioni di giustizia che potevano coesistere in queste società non è necessario e forse non è neppure utile procedere alla ricerca delle fonti 'dirette', nel senso di poco contaminate e poco istituzionalizzate. [...] Nel corso degli ultimi anni, la storia sociale ha contribuito a dissolvere la distanza tra istituzioni e società, attraverso analisi attente ai modi di funzionamento delle prime. Istituzioni e società sono fatte della stessa materia (il che non significa, ovviamente, che siano la stessa cosa); la loro opposizione è politica (nutre i discorsi dei politici), piuttosto che analitica' ('To reconstruct the plurality of

The parallel tracks schema proposed by Mario Sbriccoli – negotiated justice/hegemonic justice – not only fails to fully capture the complexity of a judicial reality in constant interaction and dialogue with social conflict resolution practices, but it also makes it difficult to understand the ways in which one could influence the other.[51] Peace emerges as a component of an integrated system of coercion exerted by judicial institutions on communities and of control mechanisms relying on the constant interaction between power and society, between justice and social actors. In order to test this initial hypothesis, I have chosen to employ a deliberately non-local or microhistorical investigative scale. My aim is not to illustrate how various centres of power sought to govern, in the sense of disciplining, hatred as an emotional drive; instead, I will attempt to identify the roots of conflict and the methods of its resolution, factors that an emotion-centric historical approach would be incapable of revealing.

In recent decades, the Papal States have been at the centre of lively discussions regarding the emergence of modern statehood, starting at least with Paolo Prodi's essay on the *Sovrano Pontefice* (Sovereign Pontiff).[52] An object of detailed research, and also of the excellent synthesis by Irene Fosi on the administration of justice, the Papal States serve as a case study exceptionally well suited for the analysis of the mechanisms (social, judicial and political) and the meanings of everything related to practices and models

conceptions of justice that could coexist in these societies, it is not necessary, and perhaps not even useful, to seek 'direct' sources, in the sense of being less contaminated and less institutionalised. [...] Over recent years, social history has contributed to dissolving the distance between institutions and society through careful analyses of how the former function. Institutions and society are made of the same material (which does not mean, of course, that they are the same thing); their opposition is political (nourishing political discourse), rather than analytical'), Simona Cerutti, *Giustizia sommaria. Pratiche e ideali di giustizia in una società di Ancien Régime (Torino, XVIII secolo)* (Milan, 2003), p. 19.

51 In a similar vein, Marco Bellabarba states, 'Non è detto che queste procedure penali a doppio binario escludessero in modo reciso, quasi per principio, di collaborare tra loro. Infatti, un modello "autoritativo" e uno a base "comunitaria" potevano coincidere senza che ciò desse origine a particolari imbarazzi' ('It is not a given that these dual-track criminal procedures categorically excluded collaboration between them. In fact, an "authoritative" model and a "community-based" one could overlap without causing any particular complications'), Bellabarba, *La giustizia nell'Italia moderna*, p. 90. See also Giovanni Tocci, *Le comunità in età moderna. Problemi storiografici e prospettive di ricerca* (Rome, 1997), p. 116.

52 See Paolo Prodi, *Il sovrano pontefice. Un corpo e due anime: la monarchia papale nella prima età moderna* (Bologna, 1982).

of pacification and reconciliation.[53] Legal institutions that, since Antiquity and the High Middle Ages, had aimed to govern feuds through truces and peace agreements were progressively and increasingly accompanied by rituals, gestures and religious symbolism. These latter aspects eventually became more prevalent than the definition of the bond established by the peace agreement.[54] For this very reason, a political reality where the governance of secular justice was the domain of the ecclesiastical personnel, who could, when necessary, employ the power of inflicting spiritual penalties and granting absolution from censures, reflects the peripheral manifestation of the dual nature – temporal and spiritual – of papal authority. This perspective provides extremely intriguing insights.[55]

The primary sources forming the foundation of this research are mainly judicial, produced by the bodies operating in various territories of the Papal States. This approach necessitated an institutional perspective and, at the same time, required a critical examination of these sources when reconstructing phenomena, circumstances, contexts, and assessing their significance within the framework of the complex relationship between official judicial machinery and social practices for regulating violence and conflicts. Given that the Governor of Rome's Tribunal operated along very similar lines to that of the Senator in terms of conflict containment through the use of transactive legal instruments, the focus has been directed towards the actions of the former as a direct expression of papal authority. It was in the second half of the sixteenth century that the papal authority completed a process of strengthening central judicial prerogatives at the expense of municipal institutions in the city of Rome. In addition to the city of Rome, the Governor's Tribunal (similar to the Senator's) extended its jurisdiction to

[53] See Irene Fosi, *La giustizia del papa. Sudditi e tribunali nello Stato pontificio in età moderna* (Rome and Bari, 2007).

[54] See Kiril Petkov, *The Kiss of Peace. Ritual, Self, and Society in the High and Late Medieval West* (Boston, 2003), pp. 109–34. Petkov notes an increase in the involvement of ecclesiastical personnel in performing the rituals that substantiated the agreement (increasingly over written or oral oaths) and the prominence of canon law compared to civil law.

[55] For example, see the briefs issued by Gregory XIII during the fight against banditry, which were later imitated by Sixtus V: *Breve di Gregorio XIII a favore di cardinali deputati ad assolvere e comporre in materia di banditi* (AAV, Arm. V, t. 44, n. 242, f. 33); *Indulto di Gregorio XIII nel quale si dà per un anno la facoltà alli confessori di poter assolvere dalle censure quelli che haveranno conversato con banditi* (ivi, Arm. V, Misc., t. X, n. 208, f. 101), both cited in Irene Polverini Fosi, *La società violenta. Il banditismo dello Stato pontificio nella seconda metà del Cinquecento* (Rome, 1985), p. 147, footnote 24.

the vast surrounding territory. Commissioners were often sent to this region with the task of pacifying conflicts, both factional and non-factional. The study will also concentrate on the activities of various peripheral courts with jurisdiction over different territorial divisions of the Papal States: Umbria (Perugia), Marca (Macerata and Ancona) and Bologna, where the *Torrone*'s Tribunal was active and highly protective of its traditional autonomy from Rome. The chronological framework aligns roughly with the post-Tridentine reorganisation of the Papal States, the golden age of the disciplinary process whose prerequisites and, above all, outcomes have long been discussed from both a cultural and a factual perspective.

1.

Vendetta, justice, peace: definitions and contextualisations

1. Eighteenth-century perspectives on judicial modernity

It is always an interesting exercise to observe how the Enlightenment culture projected its idea of modernity onto European institutions – political, legal and social – of preceding centuries, an idea to which we are still deeply attached. The administration of justice, and thus the governing of violence and conflict, concerns the most fundamental dynamics of communal living, and the Enlightenment was able to grasp the centrality of peace in laying the foundations of legal institutions arising from the dissolution of the ancient world. In the eighteenth-century debate, from France to Scotland, the formation of Roman–barbarian realms, with the consequent emergence of feudal institutions, was generally identified as the birth of Europe, as is well known.[1]

In the XXXth book of the *Esprit des lois* (*The Spirit of Laws*), in chapter XIX, when addressing the issue of the *Compositions chez les peuples barbares* (*On Compositions among the Barbarous Nations*), Montesquieu provides very precise coordinates useful for conceptually placing peace in the development of European civilisation. Just before, in the XXVIIIth book, the great French philosopher had outlined the main differences between Salic law and the laws of other barbarian peoples regarding compositions (financial settlements), the judicial evidence required (such as duelling), and the point of honour. Now, drawing on Tacitus, Montesquieu reminds us that among the Germans hatred was quenched through a composition, as only two types of criminals were punished with death: traitors (by hanging) and cowards (by drowning). The exercise of *vendetta*, except in very rare cases, was not left entirely free, and the custom of imposing a fair price for the composition due to those who had suffered wrong or offence gradually spread. In other words, it was the 'wise men' who 'thought of determining by themselves what would have been too long and too dangerous to expect from the mutual agreement

[1] See Marcello Verga, *Storie d'Europa. Secoli XVIII-XXI* (Rome, 2004), pp. 25ff.

of the parties'.[2] In this way, 'the law substitutes itself in the place of the person injured and insists upon the same satisfaction as he himself would have demanded in cold blood'.[3] Compositions were fixed in money, but in money's absence they could be paid in various types of goods; those who sought revenge after receiving satisfaction committed a serious offence, of both a public and private nature, an act of contempt for the law. At first, not wanting to give or receive satisfaction was also considered a serious offence, but this was later mitigated by the 'wise men' in the sense that compositions ceased to be an obligation at a certain point, becoming instead something to be strongly desired.

But it is in the next chapter that Montesquieu explains the Germanic institution of *Fredum* as the foundation of feudal jurisdiction. He emphasises that, even in his time, the word *Fred* in Swedish means 'peace'; *Fredum* consists of the 'recompense for the protection granted against the right of vengeance'.[4] In the Germanic world, dispensing justice

> was nothing more than granting to the person who had committed an offence a protection against the vengeance of the party offended, and obliging the latter to accept the satisfaction due to him: insomuch that among the Germans, contrary to the practice of all other nations, justice was administered in order to protect the criminal from the injured party.[5]

The culprit had to pay the *Fredum* to ensure peace and security, which had been compromised by their violent actions. But who was it paid to? It was a local right owed to those who administered justice in that territory. For this reason, Montesquieu saw the genesis of feudal jurisdiction here: the lord had the right to various emoluments, with the most important undoubtedly being

2 'faire par eux-mêmes ce qu'il était trop long et trop dangereux d'attendre de la convention réciproque des parties', *OEuvres de Montesquieu, avec les remarques des divers commentateurs, et des notes inédites, seule édition complète, dirigée par M. Collin de Plancy* (Paris, Louis Duprat Duverger Editeur, 1823), p. 326; the English version is Thomas Nugent's translation dated 1752, republished as *The Spirit of Laws* (Kitchener, 2001), p. 644.

3 'la loi se met à la place de celui qui est offensé, et demande pour lui la satisfaction que, dans un moment de sang-froid, il aurait demandée lui-même', ibid.

4 'récompense de la protection accordée contre le droit de vengeance', op. cit., p. 327 (p. 646).

5 'n'était autre chose qu'accorder à celui qui avait fait une offense sa protection contre la vengeance de celui qui l'avait reçue, et obliger ce dernier à recevoir la satisfaction qui lui était due: de sorte que, chez les Germains, à la différence de tous les autres peuples, la justice se rendait pour protéger le criminel contre celui qu'il avait offensé', op. cit., p. 328 (p. 646).

judicial profits (*Freda*). Those who held the fief also administered justice, 'the exercise of which consisted of the compositions made to the relatives, and of the profits accruing to the lord; it was nothing more than ordering the payment of the compositions set by the law, and demanding the legal fines'.[6] The right to dispense justice exclusively within the fief – royal judges no longer had the opportunity to enter it, and they were even prohibited from requiring parties to post bail to appear before them – was, therefore, a profitable right: 'jurisdictions are patrimonial in France'.[7] Churches also had the right to collect settlements in their territories and demand the *Fredum*; this right to administer justice was called 'immunity'.

To a right of feuding (*Fehde*) recognised by Germanic law, which consisted of the possibility of engaging in a private war that involved the entire extended family of the wronged or offended party and the entire extended family of those considered responsible, corresponded a proto-feudal and then feudal justice. This justice involved obtaining protection from the lord against the retaliation of the offended party or the offended party's relatives, in exchange for a predetermined sum of money that varied depending on the status of the victim. *Fehde* was intimately connected to *Friede*: the feud only ceased when the wrong, as judged by the relatives of the offended party, was fully avenged; the payment of compensation served as revenge and could put an end to the vicious circle of violence.[8]

Even in these few lines, it is clear how the philosophical-legal culture of the eighteenth century recognised the intimate correlation between peace and revenge, between settlements and retaliatory systems, within the framework of an overall evaluation of pre-modern justice, and especially with a view to its final demise. Germanic legal institutions had overlapped with Roman law, which distinguished between crimes for which a settlement (*transactio*) was possible and those that required the intervention of a judge (as found in the VIIIth book of Ulpian's *Disputationes*, later incorporated into Justinian's *Corpus Juris Civilis*). Agreements were allowed based on the nature of the potential penalty: if the accused faced a risk to life or physical well-being (*poena sanguinis*), then they had the right to seek a settlement

6 'qui ne s'exerçait que par des compositions aux parens et des profits au seigneur. Elle n'était autre chose que le droit de faire payer les compositions de la loi, et celui d'exiger les amendes de la loi', ibid (pp. 647–8)

7 'les justices sont patrimoniales en France', op. cit., p. 329 (p. 648).

8 On ritual, see Gerd Althoff, *Spielregeln der Politik im Mittelalter. Kommunikation in Frieden und Fehde* (Darmstadt, 1997). In general, on justice in the German Empire during the Ottonian dynasty, see the recent Laura E. Wangerin, *Kingship and Justice in the Ottonian Empire* (Ann Arbor, 2019).

with the victim (in other words, they could 'corrupt the accuser'). A famous phrase stated that one must pardon someone who seeks to redeem their own blood ('It was decreed by the Emperors that where capital crimes were involved, he who corrupts his adversary is not liable to punishment, except in such cases as incur the penalty of death; for it was their opinion that they who desire to save the life of a blood relative by any means whatever should be excused').[9] This was an explicit acknowledgment of the right to revenge in compliance with the principle of the sacredness of kinship bonds.

The eye of the *Philosophes* focused on the Germanic origins of feudal justice in order to emphasise the substantial difference between the past and a modern conception of justice that rejected its private and patrimonial character, underpinned by compositions, instead exalting its public nature. Cesare Beccaria, a reader and admirer of Montesquieu, also recalls, in his *Dei delitti e delle pene*, the times when 'the crimes of the subjects were the inheritance of the prince', as most penalties were monetary, reaffirming that 'crimes were tried, at that time, in a court of Exchequer, and the cause became a civil suit between the person accused and the crown. ... The judge was rather a collector for the crown, an agent for the treasury, than a protector and minister of the laws'.[10] The work is entirely based on the distinction between the private and public dimensions of justice, where the prevalence of the latter becomes tangible evidence of a modernity firmly rooted in the rejection of private and state revenge and the impersonal rule of law, as the chapters on honour, duels and pardons clearly demonstrate. An efficient public justice system proportionately measures punishments according to the seriousness of the crime, in the belief that 'crimes are more effectually prevented by

9 'In capitalibus criminibus a principibus decretum est non nocere ei qui adversarium corrupit, sed in his demum, quae poenam mortis continent: nam ignoscendum censuerunt ei, qui sanguinem suum qualiter redemptum voluit', *Le pandette di Giustiniano riordinate da R.G. Pothier*, vol. VI (in Venezia, co' tipi di Antonio Bazzarini, e C., 1835), p. 672 (Lib. XXVIII *Pandectarum*, Art. 2). English edition: *The Civil Law*, ed. Samuel Parsons Scott, vol. XI, *The Digest or Pandects*, Book XLVIII, tit. 21, 1 (Ulpianus, *Disputations*, Book VIII) (Cincinnati, 1932).

10 'i delitti degli uomini erano il patrimonio del principe', 'l'oggetto delle pene era [...] una lite tra il fisco (l'esattore di queste pene) ed il reo; un affare civile, contenzioso, privato piuttosto che pubblico [...] Il giudice era [...] un avvocato del fisco piuttosto che un indifferente ricercatore del vero', Cesare Beccaria, *Dei delitti e delle pene, nuova edizione corretta e accresciuta* (Harlem and Paris, Dal Molini Librajo rue du Jardinet près la rue du Paon, 1780), p. 174. English edition: *An Essay on Crimes & Punishments, translated from the Italian with a Commentary, attributed to M. de Voltaire* (Philadelphia, William P. Farrand and Co., 1809), p. 60.

the *certainty*, than the *severity* of punishment';[11] it is for this reason that 'As punishments become more mild, clemency and pardon are less necessary.'[12] In the ideal society imagined by Beccaria, where justice functions perfectly because it is flawless in applying laws that prescribe moderate penalties, not only would the clemency and pardons of the prince be unnecessary, but also the forgiveness granted by individuals:

> A small crime is sometimes pardoned, if the person offended chooses to forgive the offender. This may be an act of good nature and humanity, but it is contrary to the good of the public. The right of punishing belongs not to any individual in particular, but to society in general, or the sovereign. He may renounce his own portion of this right, but cannot give up that of others.[13]

Beccaria applies the same treatment to two other central tools of pre-modern justice, namely, bans and confiscations, which were parts of a complex system that also included peace-making and settlements, as will be explained.[14] It is with the legal rationalism of the eighteenth century that peace-making, settlements, transactions, oaths, as well as duels and private wars, began to be classified as symbols of an archaic medieval past, identified with the increasingly intolerable and anachronistic aristocratic ideology that modernity would leave behind.[15] If any traces remained, a desired reform

[11] 'uno dei più grandi freni dei delitti non è la crudeltà delle pene, ma la infallibilità di esse', op. cit., p. 101 (p. 80).

[12] 'a misura che le pene divengono più dolci, la clemenza ed il perdono divengono meno necessari', op. cit., p. 102 (p. 134).

[13] 'Alcuni liberano dalla pena di un piccolo delitto, quando la parte offesa lo perdoni: atto conforme alla beneficenza e alla umanità, ma contrario al bene pubblico; quasi che un cittadino privato potesse egualmente togliere colla sua remissione la necessità dell'esempio, come può condonare il risarcimento dell'offesa. Il diritto di far punire non è di un solo, ma di tutti i cittadini, o del sovrano. Egli non può che rinunziare alla sua porzione di diritto, ma non annullare quella degli altri', ibid (p. 135).

[14] Op. cit., pp. 92–3.

[15] Intriguing reflections on the limits of anti-Enlightenment and nostalgic reconstructions of medieval (and early modern) legal pluralism and the preference for legal practice over the impersonal rule of the state and state law, which finds its most emblematic example in the work of Paolo Grossi, *L'ordine giuridico medievale* (Rome and Bari, 1995), can be found in Vincenzo Ferrone, *La società giusta ed equa. Repubblicanesimo e diritti dell'uomo in Gaetano Filangieri* (Rome and Bari, 2008), cap. I. See also Rodolfo Savelli, 'Tribunali, 'decisiones' e giuristi: una proposta di ritorno alle fonti', in *Origini dello Stato. Processi di formazione statale*

of justice would have to promptly eliminate them. Political thought moved along the same lines as legal thought. Rousseau notes that in the state of nature, relationships between men 'were not sufficiently durable to constitute a state either of peace or war; so that men cannot be naturally enemies',[16] since 'it is the relation subsisting between things, and not between men, that gives rise to war; which arising thus, not from personal, but real, relations cannot subsist between man and man'.[17] For this reason, duels and private wars are to be considered abuses of the feudal government, absurd phenomena contrary to natural law. The state of war is conceivable only in the context of relations between states, not between individuals.[18]

Almost a century earlier, John Locke had written that life in society, in which all parties are equally subject to the determination of the law, presupposes the existence of a common judge to appeal to in case of unjust aggression. The existence of a third-party judge is the only antidote to the perpetuation of a state of war.[19] From these brief hints, which anticipate a vast subject that will necessarily need further exploration, one can clearly understand why the common understanding of the words 'peace' and 'war' underwent a profound change, albeit in a still embryonic form, starting with the elaborations of seventeenth-century natural law theorists on crime and punishment, and then fully through the utilitarianism of the eighteenth

in Italia tra medioevo ed età moderna, ed. Giorgio Chittolini, Anthony Molho and Pierangelo Schiera (Bologna, 1994), pp. 397–421.

16 'n'ont point entr'eux de rapport assez constant pour constituer ni l'état de paix ni l'état de guerre, ils ne sont point naturellement ennemis', Jean-Jacques Rousseau, *Du contrat social* (Paris, 2001), p. 51, English version: *The social contract: or, principles of political law. Also, a project for perpetual peace, by Jean-Jacques Rousseau, citizen of Geneva* (New York, Peter Eckler, 1893), p. 17.

17 'c'est le rapport des choses et non des hommes qui constitue la guerre; et l'état de guerre ne pouvant naître des simples relations personnelles, mais seulement des relations réelles', op. cit., p. 52 (p. 18).

18 'La guerre n'est donc point une relation d'homme à homme, mais une relation d'État à État, dans laquelle les particuliers ne sont ennemis qu'accidentellement, non point comme hommes, ni même comme citoyens mais comme soldats; non point comme membres de la patrie, mais comme ses défenseurs', op. cit., p. 52, ('War is not, therefore, any relation between man and man, but a relation between state and state; in which individuals are enemies only accidentally, not as men or even as citizens, but as soldiers; not as members of their particular community, but as its defenders', p. 18).

19 See John Locke, *Two Treatises of Government* (London, Whitmore and Fenn-C. Brown, 1821), pp. 200–5.

century.[20] Not that their polysemy has been impoverished, but it is beyond doubt that the immediate meaning we commonly associate with these terms nowadays pertains to relations between states, not between individuals.[21] It is precisely on the basis of the Enlightenment view that, until very recently, vendettas and peace-making were conceptualised: remnants, vestiges of a Middle Ages reluctant to die out in the face of the progress of state justice. According to this view, public justice could, at least, tolerate these remnants, but always with a view to their total eradication, as in the case of aristocratic behaviour, since noblemen continued throughout the early modern period to assert vengeance as a class attribute, as its exclusive prerogative.[22] Not by chance, even at the beginning of the eighteenth century, Ludovico Antonio Muratori felt the need to revisit the question of the legality of resorting to duels and the preference for peace-making through *professori d'onore*.[23]

A century after the composition of the dense pages of *The Spirit of Laws*, Alexis de Tocqueville would dismantle the image of an absolutist-era state

20 See Francesco Forzati, 'Il diritto penale dell'obbedienza fra fondamento etico-religioso dell'offesa e funzione potestativa della pena', *Archivio Penale* 3 (2017), available online at http://www.archiviopenale.it/il-diritto-penale-dellobbedienza-fra-fondamento-etico-religioso-delloffesa-e-funzione-potestativa-della-pena/articoli/15245.

21 'War and peace cannot be made for politic societies, but by the supreme power of such societies; because war and peace, giving a different motion to the force of such a politic body, none can make war or peace, but that which has the direction of the force of the whole body, and that in politic societies is only the supreme power. In voluntary societies for the time, he that has such a power by consent, may make war and peace, and so may a single man for himself, the state of war not consisting in the number of partisans, but the enmity of the parties, where they have no superior to appeal to', Locke, *Two Treatises of Government*, p. 148.

22 See Michel Porret, 'Lumières et droit de punir: l'impossible vengeance', in *La vengeance en Europe, XIIe-XVIIIe siècle*, ed. Claude Gauvard and Andrea Zorzi (Paris, 2015), pp. 307–17. About the trajectory of noble ideology between the Middle Ages and the early modern period, the obligatory reference is to Claudio Donati, *L'idea di nobiltà in Italia. Secoli XIV-XVIII* (Rome and Bari, 1988). For the treatises aimed at disciplining noble behaviour, see especially for the Bolognese case, Giancarlo Angelozzi and Cesarina Casanova, *La nobiltà disciplinata. Violenza nobiliare, procedure di giustizia e scienza cavalleresca a Bologna nel XVII secolo* (Bologna, 2003).

23 The *professori d'onore* were men from various social backgrounds who were asked, based on their education and skills, to provide opinions useful for resolving a dispute concerning honour, more specifically the violation of honour, based on principles of equity. See Ludovico Antonio Muratori, *Introduzione alle paci private, composta, e dedicata, all'Altezza Serenissima di Rinaldo I, Duca di Modena, Reggio & c.* (in Modena, per Bartolomeo Soliani Stamp. Ducale, 1708).

law ready to ruthlessly strike down wrongdoers through the machinery of justice. On the lifeless body of the *Ancien Régime*, his pen captured a salient point: 'The Ancien Régime is there in its entirety: rigid rule, loose practice; such is its character.'[24] Subsequent historiography struggled to break free from a dichotomous pattern that, from the broader level of pairs like theory/practice, public/private, descended to a particular level where two types of justice confronted each other: the hegemonic, state-administered justice, and the communal, local justice managed autonomously by individuals and communities, a realm from which public institutions were largely excluded. For a long time, historians have failed to understand the transactional dimension that dominates the whole judicial reality of early modern Europe. The persistent attempt, characteristic of a historiographical era highly focused on the privileged relationship with anthropology, to isolate 'popular' (or 'subaltern') culture, with its full array of practices and values, from the hegemonic one, led scholars to concentrate almost exclusively on horizontal relationships at the expense of vertical ones, thereby sharply distinguishing negotiation practices – seen as essentially popular attributes – from the world of official justice.[25] This resulted in a way of conceptualising interpersonal violence that tends to elude the foundational element of violence itself: legitimacy. Against any form of essentialism, social sciences now agree on defining violence as a judgement: what is stigmatised and condemned as such in a given culture and historical period is considered illegitimate and, hence, violent. For this reason, violence and criminality cannot be considered overlapping phenomena at all. The same act that might be defined as offensive and deserving of punishment could, for example, be socially judged as a form of reparation and reintegration. Legitimacy, therefore, appears as the central element in defining violence, an aspect that risks escaping from socio-anthropological analyses that do not give due weight to the diachronic dimension.[26] The process of

[24] 'L'Ancien Régime est là tout entier : une règle rigide, une pratique molle ; tel est son caractère', Alexis de Tocqueville, *L'Ancien Régime et la Révolution* (1856), cited by Eric Wenzel, 'La paix par la justice. Les modes alternatifs de règlement des conflits dans la France d'Ancien Régime', in *Stringere la pace. Teorie e pratiche della conciliazione nell'Europa moderna*, ed. Paolo Broggio and Maria Pia Paoli (Rome, 2009), pp. 509–19: p. 509.

[25] See Francesco Benigno, *Parole nel tempo. Un lessico per pensare la storia* (Rome, 2013), pp. 126–31.

[26] Compared to David Riches's definition of violence as 'intentional rendering of physical hurt', Pieter Spierenburg suggests considering violence as any 'intentional encroachment upon the physical integrity of the body', further emphasising that

legitimisation operates not only at the popular level but is in continuous interaction with powers and institutions. What is socially legitimised must always contend with what is institutionally legitimised.

2. Forms of conflict and its resolution in early modern Italy

Context is a foundational element for the forms that conflict and violence can assume.[27] When engaging in the description and analysis of the mechanisms that lead individuals, or groups of individuals, into conflict and violent confrontation, it is customary to distinguish the urban world from the rural one, with the awareness that these are not entirely separate and non-communicating contexts, and the deep connections between cities and their surrounding areas, albeit on an unequal footing, inevitably reflect on conflict phenomena. It is precisely through the prism of conflict that it has been possible to shed new light on the points of intersection between social action and legal-institutional frameworks that are crucial for a deep understanding of the historical development of European societies between the Middle Ages and the early modern era. From this perspective, the adoption of tools from social anthropology by historians has proven to be crucial.[28] In recent decades, studies have also highlighted the various types of conflict that have characterised European history, especially in village communities: endemic rebellions (*jacqueries*), revolts against fiscal intrusiveness, cyclical conflicts stemming from particular socio-environmental conditions, struggles arising

'definitions should be compatible with (long-term) historical developments'. See Pieter Spierenburg, 'Violence: Reflections about a Word', in *Violence in Europe. Historical and Contemporary Perspectives*, ed. Sophie Body-Gendrot and Pieter Spierenburg, (New York, 2009), pp. 13–25.

27 For a classification of the forms of interpersonal violence, see Xavier Rousseaux, 'La violence dans les sociétés pré-modernes: sources, méthodes et interprétations. Nivelles, une cité brabançonne à travers cinq siècles', in *Violence, conciliation et répression. Recherches sur l'histoire du crime, de l'Antiquité au XXIe siècle*, eds Aude Musin, Xavier Rousseaux and Frédéric Vesentini (Louvain-la-Neuve, 2008), pp. 263–88.

28 See Angelo Torre, 'Antropologia sociale e ricerca storica', in *La storiografia contemporanea. Indirizzi e problemi*, ed. Pietro Rossi (Milan, 1987), pp. 206–39; Renata Ago, 'Gli storici italiani e le fortune dell'antropologia. Il dibattito sulla storia sociale in Italia', in *Orientamenti marxisti e studi antropologici italiani. Problemi e dibattiti* (Milan, 1980), pp. 223–9.

from unique social dynamics and configurations (factional conflicts, feuds, familial antagonisms).[29]

In the European sixteenth century, the culture inherited from the late medieval period led to a profound reflection on the nature and causes of conflict and violence, which were generally seen as the seeds of political dissolution. In Italy, the establishment of the *popolo* regimes in Italian city-states between the thirteenth and fourteenth centuries was characterised by the widespread dissemination of political discourses and programmes entirely centred around the ideal of achieving peace and social harmony. This was considered an indispensable condition for political, social and economic prosperity.[30] Consequently, in the realm of discourse, often inspired by republican ideals, a distinct, if not exclusive, aristocratic character was attributed to violence among individuals and groups. This was in stark contrast to a reality marked by the extreme complexity of both horizontal and vertical fault lines (and reconciliations) that ran through the communal socio-political fabric and frequently gave rise to extremely bloody conflicts. As Andrea Zorzi has emphasised on numerous occasions, it was from the mature experience of *popolo* regimes in the central and northern Italian city-states that social harmony (and the associated delegitimisation of feuding) emerged as a rational aspiration advocated by a specific social rank. This was done in a practical manner with regard to the development of trade and in opposition to an ideology of the aristocracy and the magnates that was characterised by the legitimisation of retaliatory practices – a veritable culture of hatred whose perpetuation, according to the publications endorsed by the *popolo* regimes, would lead to the dissolution of the political body.[31] However, it is evident that this rhetoric was not entirely divorced from reality. These very same regimes undertook a reform of communal judicial systems

[29] See Sandro Lombardini, 'Rivolte e ribellismo contadino nel Monregalese del Seicento: ipotesi di ricerca', *Bollettino storico-bibliografico subalpino* 80 (1982), pp. 645–57.

[30] See, in general, Alma Poloni, 'Il comune di popolo e le sue istituzioni tra Due e Trecento. Alcune riflessioni a partire dalla storiografia dell'ultimo quindicennio', *Reti Medievali Rivista* 13, 1 (2012), pp. 3–25.

[31] Andrea Zorzi, 'I conflitti nell'Italia comunale. Riflessioni sullo stato degli studi e sulle prospettive di ricerca', in *Conflitti, paci e vendette nell'Italia comunale*, ed. Andrea Zorzi (Florence, 2009), pp. 7–42. Regarding the systemic violence amongst aristocratic lineages, typical of the twelfth-century communal regimes, dominated by the *militia*, see Jean-Claude Maire Vigueur, *Cavalieri e cittadini. Guerra, conflitti e società nell'Italia comunale* (Bologna, 2004), pp. 388–98; original edition: *Cavaliers et citoyens. Guerre, conflits et société dans l'Italie communale, XIIe-XIIIe siècles* (Paris, 2004).

characterised by an expansion of the criminal sphere. This expansion was based on the progressive generalisation of *ex officio* and inquisitorial procedures, the dissemination of political bans, and the issuance of measures against the magnates, aimed at excluding certain individuals from political positions and the protection offered by the city, with the precise goal of assigning central value to their potential reintegration in political dynamics through truces, concords and peace agreements.[32]

Between the fifteenth and early sixteenth centuries, the processes of forming territorial state entities and the rise of princely regimes were accompanied by profound changes in socio-economic structures. The distinctly urban character of late medieval society in the central and northern regions of the Italian peninsula was at least partially mitigated by social developments that affected areas previously characterised by relatively undifferentiated structures. Smaller urban centres and large towns began to emerge alongside traditionally dominant cities, which now served as regional capitals, increasingly focused on consuming agricultural rents and carrying out governmental and financial–speculative activities, primarily due to the growth of manufacturing.[33] In rural areas, the erosion of small peasant ownership in favour of large landowners (often rooted in cities), common property and traditional community social structures led to a growing subordination of rural society to market and urban-based ownership dynamics. This also gave rise to a new movement of people, typically poor and marginalised, towards the cities.[34] At the dawn of the early modern era, influenced initially by disruptions stemming from the Italian Wars and subsequently by the establishment of Spanish monarchic

32 Andrea Zorzi, 'Politica e giustizia a Firenze al tempo degli Ordinamenti antimagnatizi', in *Ordinamenti di giustizia fiorentini. Studi in occasione del VII centenario*, ed. Vanna Arrighi (Florence, 1995), pp. 107–47; Andrea Zorzi, 'Negoziazione penale, legittimazione giuridica e poteri urbani nell'Italia comunale', in *Criminalità e giustizia in Germania e in Italia. Pratiche giudiziarie e linguaggi giuridici tra tardo medioevo ed età moderna / Kriminalität und Justiz in Deutschland und Italien. Rechtspraktiken und gerichtliche Diskurse in Spätmittelalter und Früher Neuzeit*, ed. Marco Bellabarba, Gerd Schwerhoff and Andrea Zorzi (Bologna, 2001), pp. 13–34. Regarding the centrality of the political reintegration of the excluded subjects, see Christiane Klapisch-Zuber, *Retour à la Cité. Les magnats de Florence (1340-1440)* (Paris, 2006); Italian edition: *Ritorno alla politica. I magnati fiorentini 1340-1440* (Rome, 2009).

33 See Franco Angiolini, 'La società', in *Storia degli antichi stati italiani*, ed. Gaetano Greco and Mario Rosa (Rome and Bari, 1997), pp. 309–10.

34 For a broad European comparative perspective on the urban–rural relationship see Marino Berengo, *L'Europa delle città. Il volto della società urbana europea tra Medioevo ed Età moderna* (Turin, 1999), pp. 111–70.

power over much of the peninsula, which substantially redefined the internal structures of regional ruling classes, the causes of social conflict potentially became more complex than in the past. This explains why one of the primary concerns of Italian rulers in the sixteenth century was to find the most suitable means to quell both indiscipline of the nobility and the restlessness of segments of the population driven to criminal behaviour due to the loss of their traditional means of sustenance and social protection.[35] The result was a dynamic socio-political landscape in the sixteenth century, underpinned by rapidly changing economic structures compared to the late medieval period, although with significant differences between the southern part of the peninsula including the islands, dominated by feudal baronies, and the central and northern regions, where the prestige and wealth inherited from the communal past of major urban centres were never entirely overshadowed by an evident process of ruralisation.

In early modern Italy, there were no major peasant uprisings like those that plagued the regions beyond the Alps, a genuine source of fear for rulers across Europe.[36] The resistance of rural inhabitants to the worsening of their living conditions took on various forms, including banditry, smuggling, theft and disobedience regarding crop cultivation and land use practices.[37] This was a conflict and violence that could be described as being of low (compared to full-scale revolts) but constant intensity. It stemmed from difficult neighbourly relations or took on the shape of what Edward P. Thompson studied as "anonymous crime" some forty years ago. In this context, the line between civil and criminal action blurred, and it represented one of the few available resources for peasants who, had they openly protested, would have exposed themselves to reprisals from landowners.[38] Violence in rural areas, therefore, assumed diverse forms. It was influenced, on one hand, by the generally harsh living conditions of the peasants, which heightened tensions and made it easier for individuals to resort to personal violence. On the other hand, it was influenced by the attitude of a feudal nobility that served as a crucial channel of communication between the rural and urban worlds. This was due to their patron–client relationships with residents of both cities

[35] See Marco Bellabarba, *La giustizia nell'Italia moderna* (Rome and Bari, 2008), pp. 40–59.

[36] See Oscar Di Simplicio, *Le rivolte contadine in Europa. I grandi movimenti che scuotono le campagne nell'epoca moderna* (Rome, 1986).

[37] See Angiolini, La società, p. 315.

[38] See Edward P. Thomson, *Società patrizia, cultura plebea. Otto saggi di antropologia storica sull'Inghilterra del Settecento* (Turin, 1981).

and rural communities. While they combat social deviance through their own criminal jurisdiction, they could simultaneously provide protection to bandits as a method of anti-absolutist resistance.[39]

In the urban world, the factional divisions, which were the essence of order – and disorder – in the social and political systems of late medieval Italy, did not dissolve but had to adapt to the policies pursued by the new princely regimes.[40] In theory, these regimes were strongly opposed to the idea of local political life based on *partes* (factions), in line with foundational principles of modern statehood such as territorial sovereignty and the dominance of state law. However, in practice, they actively participated in those same factional dynamics. The tensions between the common people and the nobility were not confined within the city walls; they had the ability to draw rural inhabitants into the fray, as rural communities could be brought to support their feudal lords. What is now established is that, like peace-making, factional conflict in the early modern era was by no means a medieval relic but rather 'one of the fundamental dimensions of political action, which evolved and transformed in parallel with the growth of the state apparatus'.[41]

Only an awareness of the substantial lack of homogeneity within the ruling and subordinate classes, as well as the absence of one-dimensionality in the conflict, can help us understand the socio-political dynamics in the early modern era. The aristocratic order was far from uniform, and the wider population was equally diverse. Urban political life was by no means the exclusive domain of the nobility, and, as such, 'any factional strategy aimed at controlling municipal power had to include the popular sphere'.[42] Factions were structured along vertical lines and were in a state of constant aggregation and disaggregation based on various types of loyalty and interest. In the south, as well as in the Duchy of Milan, local factional dynamics had to relate to both the local government institutions of the Spanish monarchy and the

[39] See Irene Polverini Fosi, *La società violenta. Il banditismo nello Stato pontificio nella seconda metà del Cinquecento* (Rome, 1985).

[40] Among the most recent contributions, see Marco Gentile, *Fazioni al governo. Politica e società a Parma nel Quattrocento* (Rome, 2009). Also focused on Parma, but centred on the thirteenth century and justice as seen through the lens of municipal statutes, is Gabriele Guarisco, *Il conflitto attraverso le norme. Gestione e risoluzione delle dispute a Parma nel XIII secolo* (Bologna, 2005).

[41] 'una delle dimensioni fondamentali dell'agire politico, venutasi strutturando e modificando in parallelo alla crescita dell'apparato statuale', Francesco Benigno, 'Conflitto politico e conflitto sociale nell'Italia spagnola', in *Nel sistema imperiale. L'Italia spagnola*, ed. Aurelio Musi (Naples, 1994), pp. 115–46: p. 124.

[42] Op. cit., p. 127.

court factions in Madrid, of which they were an integral part.[43] It is easy to imagine how the violent clashes and ensuing peace-making between these groups, far from diminishing once the sixteenth century began, continued to be a central aspect of the political and social life in both urban and rural areas of the ancient Italian states.

The image of the Italian Cinquecento to which we have been accustomed is that of a century divided in two between the 'fire' of the Italian Wars – the political, social and religious instability of the early decades connected to international political disturbances – and the 'calm' resulting from the Spanish monarchy's control over the Italian peninsula and policies of social and political stabilisation (as well as the Catholic Reconquest and a harsh anti-heretical struggle) starting from the 1540s and 1550s, if not even earlier, from the Peace of Cambrai (1529). Even the political vocabulary reflected the repercussions of this change, as the words that had been used to describe social dynamics and the functioning of political institutions, both central and local, gradually changed in usage and meanings. Terms such as 'faction', 'amity', 'enmity', 'revenge', which explained the possible sources of violence, took on different meanings in opposing narratives: those of social actors, as well as those of the governing and controlling institutions. But what becomes macroscopically evident from the political stabilisation in the mid-century is, in political and legal literature, the rhetoric of the rule of law (and the law of the prince in particular) and the necessity of limiting the arbitrariness of judges and officials as the only antidotes to the proliferation of conflict and violence. This rhetoric has profoundly influenced our interpretation of the transition from the 'fire' of the early Cinquecento to the 'calm' at the century's end. We tend to imagine a weakening of factional cohesion that led to a substantial reduction in revenge systems, aided by the deployment of coercive tools – as in the case of the vigorous military actions launched in the course of the Cinquecento to bring the rebellious (and factious) peripheral aristocracies into obedience[44] – and tools of

[43] See in general *L'Italia degli Austrias. Monarchia cattolica e domini italiani nei secoli XVI e XVII*, ed. Gianvittorio Signorotto, monographic issue of *Cheiron*, fasc. 17–18 (1993).

[44] For example, consider the career of Bernardino Castellari, who held numerous positions in the service of the popes between the 1520s and the 1540s. These positions included that of vice legate in the Marche and governor of Bologna, where his work stood out for its effectiveness and, above all, its severity towards city authorities and noble prerogatives. See Anna Foa, 'Castellari (Castellaro), Bernardino (Bernardino della Barba)', in *Dizionario Biografico degli Italiani*, vol. 21 (Rome, 1978), pp. 652–6.

discipline aimed at influencing education, individual behavioural models and reference ideologies.[45]

It was not so long ago that ferocious violence, endowed with extraordinary symbolic significance as seen, for example, in Friuli in 1511 during the *Crudel zobia grassa* (Cruel fat carnival), the last peasant revolt in renaissance Italy (and perhaps even the only one in terms of scale and intensity), was considered something no longer repeatable in the socio-political context of a few decades later, that of territorial states striving to establish organisational forms and territorial control based on absolutist criteria.[46] Edward Muir's study partly reflects this perspective, following Weberian and Eliasian paradigms. As the author himself writes, in the late sixteenth century the reality of Friuli appears to have changed entirely from the early part of the century concerning the spirit of faction and revenge: 'the obsession with the collective honor of families and clans faded as concerns arose about preserving individual honor, which depended less on ancient lineage than on good manners'.[47] An approach overly focused on mental and emotional aspects runs the risk of reinforcing the distinctly evolutionary assumptions that make the establishment of modern statehood, the decline of factional dynamics in local political life, and self-control and passions (anger, wrath, hatred, desire for revenge) the characteristic features of the transition to modernity.[48]

45 In the vast bibliography, see at least *Disciplina dell'anima, disciplina del corpo e disciplina della società tra medioevo ed età moderna*, ed. Paolo Prodi (Bologna, 1994). Regarding the Papal States see, inside the just mentioned volume, Umberto Mazzone, '"Evellant vicia ... aedificent virtutes": il cardinal legato come elemento di disciplinamento nello Stato della Chiesa' (ivi, pp. 691–731); Angelozzi and Casanova, *La nobiltà disciplinata*.

46 See Furio Bianco, *1511. La'crudel zobia grassa'. Rivolte contadine e faide nobiliari nel Friuli tra '400 e '500* (Pordenone, 1995).

47 Edward Muir, *Mad Blood Stirring. Vendetta in Renaissance Italy* (Baltimore and London, 1998), p. XXVII.

48 'In Friuli [Muir writes] the system of Patronage embodied in two mutual antagonist factions collapsed in the years after the Cambrai wars, leaving the citizens of the region in a state of collective anomie. After the demise of the factions, through which peasant and artisan commoners had built bonds of clientage with the great feudal lords, the classes separated in various ways. Villagers achieved a modest form of representation with the institution of a peasant parliament, and nobles escaped into a fantasy world of aristocratic exclusivity, epitomized by their emulation of courtly manners. By the 1560s the traditions of vendetta, which had once bonded Friulans from all social levels in a common culture of revenge killing, dissolved as aristocrats took up dueling to settle old grievances and to counter new insults', op. cit., pp. XX–XXI.

Sources, and not just judicial ones, nevertheless speak to us about a different reality, highlighted by a now well-established historiography that has chosen a local scale of investigation and perspective, thus paying more attention to the concreteness of the actions of social actors and the plurality of agencies responsible for controlling and mediating conflicts within communities, rather than doctrinal constructs, general legal and institutional frameworks and the intentions of central organs of power, whose effectiveness is always difficult to verify. In recent years, rather than a history of communities, a history *starting from* communities, understood as organised forms of power, has emerged.[49] This perspective is not limited to the analysis of the local dimension but looks at the interdependencies with other organised forms of power (major urban centres, the central power of the State), also – but not only – in terms of the progressive loss of autonomy of these communities.[50] In the last decades, historical research has demonstrated how important it is to integrate traditional methods of social history with the tools of anthropology (social, political, legal) and ethnology, especially when used to unravel the intricate networks of kinship structures and family alliances, and how arbitrary it is to separate social conflict from political dialectics, at both local and supralocal levels, in their mutual interactions, and the internal conflict within dominant cities from that of subject territories, mostly rural, composed of more or less large villages, towns and fiefdoms. Similarly, it is not possible to isolate urban and communal dynamics from the broader international political events.

Conflict was the prevailing dimension of life in *Ancien Régime* communities, both internally and in their interaction with the external world. This is not just a factual observation: as has been extensively demonstrated, in the early modern era conflict institutionalises and legalises itself, despite a formal legal and political discourse that tends to obscure, if not erase, its significance. In reality the factional structuring of the community fabric does not clash with the centralising policies of the new territorial states, as it

49 Legal doctrine since the Middle Ages has grappled with the precise definition of what a community, understood as a territorial-based *universitas*, was, as disputes often arose regarding the very existence, in legal terms rather than in fact, of a given community. Typically, it was seen as an 'original entity' relative to any higher authority and, therefore, did not require any sovereign recognition. In cases of doubt, jurists would verify the existence of certain indicative elements: the presence of written statutes, the administration of a common heritage and the existence of a land registry. See Luca Mannori, *Il sovrano tutore. Pluralismo istituzionale e accentramento amministrativo nel Principato dei Medici (Secc. XVI-XVII)* (Milan, 1994), p. 25.

50 See Giovanni Tocci, *Le comunità in età moderna. Problemi storiografici e prospettive di ricerca* (Rome, 1997), p. 25.

might seem from the discursive production of central governing institutions. With very significant differences from one context to another, central powers sometimes acknowledged the existing factions in cities and communities, sometimes fought against them, even with grand declarations of intent, and sometimes even created them from scratch, considering them useful interlocutors, as in the case of the Savoyard Piedmont.[51] In the face of an official political discourse that could do nothing but condemn the existence of factions as a source of disorder and subversion, we find ourselves confronted with a reality in which this model of aggregating and disaggregating forces continued to constitute the essence of the social and political life of communities, with highly important ceremonial and religious implications.[52]

As Osvaldo Raggio has pointed out, the feud 'constitutes the privileged mechanism for regulating these conflicts and a form of social organisation: it defines the quality and intensity of relationships and delimits the human and territorial boundaries of groups'.[53] However, what is increasingly evident is that, within communities, not all possible explanatory keys for the conflicts that take place there are exhausted. It is necessary, therefore, to make a continuous effort to connect local realities with supralocal ones because the resonance of conflict is broad and transcends the boundaries of communities. In the case of papal Romagna studied by Cesarina Casanova, multiple and profound connections were established between prominent local families and legates or presidents; this resulted in a political dialectic that certainly cannot be represented by the 'centre vs periphery', 'state vs community' schema, where the centre often delegated functions to the periphery, and the periphery itself sought links and agreements with the centre.[54]

51 See Angelo Torre, 'Faide, fazioni e partiti, ovvero la ridefinizione della politica nei feudi imperiali delle Langhe tra Sei e Settecento', *Quaderni Storici*, 63 (1986), pp. 775–810.

52 From the consideration of factions as an element of order, albeit alternative or different from the state's order, the research of several students of Giorgio Chittolini began. We recall Marco Gentile, Massimo della Misericordia, Andrea Gamberini.

53 'costituisce il meccanismo privilegiato di regolazione di questi conflitti e una forma di organizzazione sociale: definisce la qualità e l'intensità delle relazioni e delimita i confini umani e territoriali dei gruppi', Osvaldo Raggio, 'La politica nella parentela. Conflitti locali e commissari in Liguria orientale (secoli XVI-XVII)', in *Conflitti locali e idiomi politici*, ed. Sandro Lombardini, Osvaldo Raggio and Angelo Torre, monographic issue of *Quaderni Storici* XXI, 63 (1986), pp. 721–57: p. 736.

54 See Elena Fasano Guarini, 'Centro e periferia, accentramento e particolarismi: dicotomia o sostanza degli Stati in età moderna?', in *Origini dello Stato*, pp. 147–76, republished in English as 'Geographies of Power: the Territorial State in Early

The fundamental political dialectic of early modern state organisms is characterised by a continuous negotiation of arenas of power and a dense series of interactions between elements of the social body and institutional elements.[55] It is for these reasons that there can be no rupture or opposition between 'community' methods and 'institutional' methods of conflict resolution, as per the well known distinction that has developed in the ongoing debate between Benoît Garnot and Mario Sbriccoli.[56] Communities cannot be seen as non-communicating monads with central authorities; and the two judicial systems, one formal and the other informal, were not alternatives to each other. One did not activate only when the other had failed in its task, or was considered unsuitable due to the nature of the crime in question, or when one of the parties suddenly decided to change strategy and seek, in the presence of a 'third' authority, the recognition of violated rights.[57] It tends to be forgotten, in fact, that social actors did not have complete freedom of initiative, and often it was the judiciary itself that pushed the conflict in one direction or another.

Communities faced a 'two-headed law', consisting of on the one hand the law as perceived by the group, and on the other hand the law imposed from above.[58] Just as in the socio-political realm, the local judiciary was intimately intertwined with the supralocal one, in the sense that community systems were connected to institutional systems. Similarly, the ways of labelling the 'enemy' were deeply interconnected: the extent and nature of the punishment for a crime depended greatly on how the perpetrator of the unlawful action was perceived, at both the community and central levels, with a pronounced tendency to be harsher in the case of marginalised/excluded individuals and anyone who could not rely on a strong network of social solidarity, primarily of a familial nature and secondarily of a neighbourly nature. This social capital became indispensable when facing a legal process. In essence, the justice system targeted anyone perceived as a potential threat to social, communal and/or general order.

Modern Italy', in *The Renaissance. Italy and Abroad*, ed. John J. Martin (London, 2003), pp. 89–103.

55 See Cesarina Casanova, *Comunità e governo pontificio in Romagna in età moderna* (Bologna, 1981).

56 See Introduction, p. 16 in this volume.

57 As Nicole Castan, among others, claims: 'The Arbitration of Disputes under the "Ancien Régime"', in *Disputes and Settlements. Law and Human Relations in the West*, ed. John Bossy (Cambridge, 1983), p. 220.

58 See Tocci, *Le comunità in età moderna*, p. 106.

If especially Osvaldo Raggio and Angelo Torre have emphasised the idiomatic nature of the feud, understood not as the 'automatic outcome of a kinship structure but as the choice of a language to forge binding relationships',[59] it is important to understand whether a language of peace and negotiated settlement also may have constituted a similarly decisive element in the processes of both factional aggregation and disaggregation, and in the dialectic between communities and between these and central authorities. Imposed peace agreements legitimise the intervention of central powers in the life of the community, but, as Raggio observed for the Genoese state, they 'strengthen local forms of political organisation'.[60] The subtle ways in which this occurred represent an aspect that may have received less attention from historiography, which has tended to focus on the analysis of moments of conflict eruption and perpetuation over those of reconciliation, which are seen rather as recurrent and at the same time inevitable outcomes of factional dynamics than as equally significant symbolic and idiomatic turning points. To bring this about, it is essential to connect community dynamics with external centres of power, as it is through this connection that the effectiveness of conflict resolution is achieved. 'In reality, it is a matter of considering – as Sandro Lombardini has written – not only the development of a revolt, but also the methods of its absorption and pacification'.[61]

It was believed that one could extract from notarial sources the essence of community justice, untainted by incursions from institutional justice. The problem is that behind a peace agreement, at least one that appears spontaneous or at most encouraged by the actions of the community's elders or the clergy, there might be hidden pressure exerted by a court of justice or a representative of central power. In principle, it is not excluded that the community could have 'the strength to independently resolve the dispute without resorting to the coercive means of formal justice',[62] but the pressure

[59] 'esito automatico di una struttura della parentela, bensì [come] scelta di un idioma per forgiare rapporti vincolanti', Torre, *Faide, fazioni e partiti*, p. 804.

[60] 'rafforzano le forme locali di organizzazione politica', Raggio, *Faide e parentele*, p. 29.

[61] 'Si tratta in realtà di prendere in considerazione non soltanto lo sviluppo di un movimento di rivolta, ma anche le modalità del suo riassorbimento e della sua pacificazione', Sandro Lombardini, 'Le premesse ecologiche di una rivoluzione contadina. Agricoltura e demografia nel Monregalese all'epoca delle Guerre del sale', *Bollettino della Società per gli studi storici, archeologici ed artistici della Provincia di Cuneo* 89 (1983), 2, pp. 107–89: p. 176.

[62] 'la forza di ricomporre in modo indipendente il dissidio, senza ricorrere ai mezzi coercitivi della giustizia formale', Michelangelo Marcarelli, 'Pratiche di giustizia in età moderna: riti di pacificazione e mediazione nella Terraferma veneta',

exerted by external agents often does not emerge from the source and must be established through perusal of other types of document.

It is now widely accepted that the 'calm' brought about by the stabilisation of the international political framework and the centralisation policies pursued by the various territorial states on the Italian peninsula did not lead to the gradual disappearance of *vendetta* practices and outbreaks of raw violence, whether individual or collective. Rather, it represented a process of adaptation of the mechanisms of violence – and its representations and narratives – to a social, political and institutional context in continuous and nonlinear transformation. Once again, it is necessary to focus on the processes of self-legitimisation of local elites and the legitimisation of revenge practices.

3. The boundaries of discipline between legislative production, political–legal thought and negotiation practices

Early modern Italy is a complex mosaic of highly diverse political realities, in terms of both the forms of power and bureaucratic-administrative organisation, and their territorial extent. From small states whose borders coincided with those of the surrounding county, we move to regional states such as the Duchy of Milan or the Savoyard Piedmont, and to multi-regional states like the Papal States and the Kingdom of Naples. For all these realities, the primary goal in the mid-sixteenth century was to assert, consolidate and, in some cases, extend their dominion over the subject territories, which were also characterised by extreme fragmentation, even on a purely jurisdictional level. The case of the Grand Duchy of Tuscany, and the image of Cosimo I de' Medici that propagandists sought to promote, is exemplary in this regard. Marked by the deep divisions generated between the late fifteenth century and the 1530s by republican experiences and the harsh repression of anti-Medici dissent, both within and outside the boundaries of the Grand Duchy, from 1537, the Tuscan state embarked on a powerful effort of princely-style state-building. Its foundations lay in the administration of justice and the achievement of order, harmony and social peace. These results were to be obtained through a skilful combination of coercion and gentle, paternal ways capable of erasing hatred, enmity and *vendettas*. Phenomena that, according to Vincenzo Fedeli, the first ambassador sent by

in *L'amministrazione della giustizia penale nella Repubblica di Venezia, secoli XVI-XVIII, vol. II, Retoriche, stereotipi, prassi*, ed. Giovanni Chiodi and Claudio Povolo (Sommacampagna, 2004), pp. 259–309: p. 262.

the Serene Republic of Venice to Florence in 1561 after the establishment of the principality, had cast a shadow over the (albeit in some respects admired) previous oligarchic regime.[63] Upon investiture, the grand duke was tasked with a mission of an almost divine nature: to put an end to the abuses and injustices of the previous oligarchic republican regime, heal the divisions in the social body, pacify disorders and seditions, and enforce his own law, albeit respecting traditional autonomies and privileges. According to Filippo Cavriani, the author of an unpublished biography of Cosimo I, the new laws issued by the first grand duke were conceived specifically to 'repress night-time extortionists and assassins, prohibit smuggling, moderate excessive luxury and decrease the multitude of lawsuits'.[64] The moralising intentions of this policy are clear, at least in the eyes of observers: the pursuit of internal order and peace was combined with a language, both legal and theological, that deliberately blurred the lines between crime and sin and contributed to the paternalistic dissemination of behavioural models in line with the new political and cultural climate.

The areas that required particular attention were certainly the legislative and judicial domains, which were closely interconnected and embodied the sovereignty itself.[65] In ancient Italian states, legislative reforms (especially through the creation of collections) and judicial procedure reforms never reached the breadth and organisational structure of those accomplished, with the partial exception of Savoyard Piedmont, from the early sixteenth century in France, Spain or the Holy Roman Empire. Nevertheless, the Italian peninsula was by no means static, and responded in diverse ways to the challenges posed by the new political and institutional structures and the needs of consolidating territorial states, which still had to contend with a dense network of legal entities endowed with their own robust statutory legislation.

The problem was, therefore, to unravel the tangle resulting from the intersection of the *iura propria* of local statutes with the *ius commune* constituted by both Roman law and 'state' law, and, especially for the Papal States, by canon law. It is well known that a legal and formal perspective entirely focused on the goals of legislative, administrative and judicial centralisation has led scholars in the past to outline the emergence of a more imaginary

63 See Elena Fasano Guarini, 'Produzione di leggi e disciplinamento nella Toscana granducale tra Cinque e Seicento (spunti di ricerca)', in *Disciplina dell'anima*, pp. 659–90, republished in Fasano Guarini, Elena, *L'Italia moderna e la Toscana dei principi. Discussioni e ricerche storiche* (Florence, 2008), pp. 105–24: p. 106.

64 'reprimere grassatori notturni e sicari, proibire il contrabbando, moderare il lusso eccessivo, nonché diminuire la *litium multitudinem*', op. cit., p. 108.

65 See Vincenzo Piano Mortari, *Gli inizi del diritto moderno in Europa* (Napoli, 1980).

than real state, starting from the sixteenth century.[66] Detailed research on individual territorial realities has shown all the significant limitations of the centralisation projects carried out by the ancient Italian states during the early modern period, at the expense of local autonomies and seigniorial powers. Even based on innovative perspectives of inquiry into normative and doctrinal sources produced in the early modern era, the political–institutional reality of the *Ancien Régime* appears much less as a precedent, albeit incomplete, of the nineteenth-century state and much more as a distinct model with its own features, characterised by elements of strong continuity rather than rupture with the late medieval structures. It was a sort of mosaic of highly diversified territorial realities held together by a central power that had no choice but to come to terms with pre-existing local autonomies and vibrant urban patriciates. It was, if anything, a matter of devising renewed mechanisms of interference, certainly not of undermining the recognition of historical identities, corporate powers and normative authorities stemming from tradition.[67] The jurisdictional domain was polymorphic, marked by contamination resulting from the intersection of social dynamics and political struggle, both internal and external to the communities. Its exercise could only be characterised by pragmatism, compromise and negotiation, given the tensions arising from the coexistence of multiple rights and powers (statutory legislations, privileges of the nobility and clergy, and the expanding rights of sovereign intervention and interference).[68]

Legal language is a reflection of a constitutional reality that is very different from that of the State conceived as a sovereign entity, as the centre of attribution of general interests, or as a legal person identified based on territory, population and government.[69] In Medicean Tuscany, as well as in the Papal States and other Italian territorial entities, legal doctrine described the various principalities as the outcome of successive aggregations of minor and differently sized and articulated legal systems 'held together by a dense

[66] The debates that have been ongoing for several decades on the emergence of modern statehood have generated an extensive bibliography. In addition to the previously mentioned volume *Origini dello Stato*, subsequent reference points include the insights provided by Francesco Benigno, 'Ancora lo "stato moderno" in alcune recenti sintesi storiografiche', *Storica*, VIII, 23 (2002), pp. 119–43; Francesco Benigno, 'Stato moderno', in Francesco Benigno, *Parole nel tempo. Un lessico per pensare la storia* (Rome, 2013), pp. 163–84.

[67] See *Comunità e poteri centrali negli Antichi Stati Italiani. Alle origini dei controlli amministrativi*, ed. Luca Mannori (Naples, 1997).

[68] See Tocci, *Le comunità in età moderna*, p. 104.

[69] See Mannori, *Il sovrano tutore*, p. 17.

web of contractual bonds',[70] and which maintained their legal individuality almost unchanged throughout the early modern period, at least until the Napoleonic invasions if not beyond. Without delving too deeply into a complex subject, it is enough to bear in mind that, even in the early modern era, there was a prevailing Aristotelian view of the 'state' as a 'pyramid of *consociationes* of different radii, but of identical structure, each constituted by the aggregation of those of lower rank and in turn participating in the higher-level entities'.[71] It was a hierarchy of corporate entities in which, according to Bartolus de Saxoferrato's doctrine, full jurisdiction (*iurisdictio*) and legislative authority (*ius statuendi*) were attributed to the larger *universitates* or *civitates*, while the subordinate communities were left with *administratio*, i.e., the management of property and income through a sort of private-law statute.[72] As Luca Mannori has succinctly summarised, what stands out in the early modern era is

> the further significant compression experienced by community autonomy. Indeed, that entire realm of 'private' self-administration, which medieval jurists still perceived as a space free from the interference of higher powers, was also removed from the control of the *civitas* due to the gradual development of an entirely unfamiliar administrative control system, which jurists were gradually forced to acknowledge.[73]

It is interesting to note, furthermore, that post-Bartolian doctrine largely sided with the regulatory capacities of subordinate entities. This allowed municipal law to thrive in the early modern period despite the undeniable centralising efforts of territorial states and despite also a heated debate aimed at questioning the legitimacy of the very *ius statuendi* (the right to legislate) of subject communities. This occurred for several reasons. First, jurists, whose

70 'tenuti insieme da una fitta trama di vincoli pattizi', ibid.

71 'piramide di "consociationes" di raggio diverso, ma di identica struttura, ciascuna delle quali costituita dall'aggregazione di quelle di grado inferiore ed a sua volta partecipe degli organismi di livello più elevato', op. cit., p. 37.

72 See Francesco Calasso, '"Iurisdictio" nel diritto comune classico', *Annali di storia del diritto* IX (1965), pp. 89–110; Mario Sbriccoli, *L'interpretazione dello statuto. Contributo allo studio della funzione dei giuristi nell'età comunale* (Milan, 1969).

73 'la forte compressione ulteriore a cui andò incontro l'autonomia comunitativa [...]. Tutto quel settore di autoamministrazione "privata", infatti, che il giurista medievale vedeva ancora come uno spazio libero dalle interferenze dei poteri superiori, venne sottratto anch'esso alla disponibilità della *civitas* a seguito del graduale sviluppo di un sistema di controlli amministrativi del tutto sconosciuto all'esperienza precedente, di cui i giuristi furono costretti poco a poco a prendere atto', Mannori, *Il sovrano tutore*, p. 100.

prestige and social influence were distinctive features of late medieval and early modern Italian society, could thereby carve out an irreplaceable role in interpreting the inevitable conflicts between municipal statutory regulations and laws issued by the ruler.[74] Second, the intensification of statutory normative production did not necessarily imply a strengthening of local autonomies but was rather the result of the integration of statutes into the legislative system of Italian territorial states. Municipal legislation, with the necessary variations depending on whether it concerned major urban centres or small rural communities dependent on them, continued throughout the early modern era to be the primary legal source for Italian territorial states, the one initially referred to for the resolution of cases, both civil and criminal, without, however, envisioning a modern hierarchy of legal sources.[75]

Contrary to what one might think, in the early modern period states did not simply tolerate the autonomy of territorial communities; they depended on that autonomy in order to exercise sovereignty. The strengthening of traditional community powers, especially those of smaller communities, served to maintain corporate balances, onto which – and here is the innovation – progressively stricter control mechanisms were grafted starting in the late Middle Ages: in the regulatory sphere (approval of statutes), in the judicial sphere (dispatch or appointment of magistrates from the centre, albeit bound by the *ius proprium* of the community;[76] introduction of new districts aimed at fragmenting, from a jurisdictional standpoint, the pre-eminence

74 See Sara Menzinger, *Giuristi e politica nei comuni di Popolo. Siena, Perugia e Bologna, tre governi a confronto* (Rome, 2006).

75 Cardinal Giovanni Battista De Luca shared this view, as evidenced by his *Theatrum veritatis et iustitiae*, cap. XV. See Alessandro Dani, 'Gli statuti comunali nello Stato della Chiesa in Antico Regime: qualche annotazione e considerazione', *Historia et ius* 2 (2012), paper 6, available online at http://www.historiaetius.eu/uploads/5/9/4/8/5948821/dani.pdf

76 For ordinary cases, the judges sent from the centre would have had to operate based on the *ius proprium* of the subject community. However, for extraordinary cases, the margin of discretion expanded significantly. In the ordinances imposed on Arezzo in 1384, for instance, the captain, a Florentine citizen chosen by Florence, had the authority to 'condemn at his discretion and without any formalities those who disturbed the "peaceful state" of the city and its surrounding territory or aimed to subvert the dominion of Florence' ('condannare a suo arbitrio e senza alcuna "solennità" chi turbasse il "pacifico stato" della città e del suo contado o mirasse a sovvertire il dominio di Firenze'), Elena Fasano Guarini, 'Gli statuti delle città soggette a Firenze tra Quattrocento e Cinquecento: riforme locali e interventi centrali', in *Statuti città territori in Italia e Germania tra medioevo ed età moderna*, ed. Giorgio Chittolini and Dietmar Willoweit (Bologna, 1991), pp. 69–124, republished in Fasano Guarini, Elena, *L'Italia moderna*, pp. 69–104: p. 78.

of cities gradually subjected to the dominant city's authority),[77] and in the management of communal assets (administrative controls).[78] This resulted in the extreme care with which central authorities collected, organised and preserved the statutory regulations of subject communities. As noted by Elena Fasano Guarini in the case of the Grand Duchy of Tuscany, the presence in Florentine archives of a vast wealth of documentary material consisting of the statutory regulations of cities, towns, lands and castles subject to Florence testifies, first and foremost, to the eminently practical function of these records as daily working tools for auditors and clerks who needed to prepare for their activities in outlying areas. It also represents the path – towards the capital – that any local provision usually would have had to follow to gain recognition as having the status of a statute.[79]

Among the most important testing grounds in this balance between attempts at centralisation and the preservation of traditional corporate bonds with local communities were, on the one hand, statutory reforms – periodic occasions for selecting the individuals destined to govern local authorities and the approval of statutes themselves; and on the other hand, there was the moment of their jurisprudential application and interpretation, through both annotations and glosses.[80] To evaluate this, it is necessary to cross-reference normative sources with administrative and judicial sources.[81] To quell the hatred and discord that characterised the life of subject communities, a new figure emerged in sixteenth-century Medicean Tuscany: the commissioner, directly dependent on the Florentine government (while the rectors were still subject to local scrutiny) and endowed with extraordinary powers. This occurred in varying ways within the Italian regional states, but the trend was

77 One of the focal points of conflicts between the ruling authority and subject cities was the transformation of the ancient bonds of subordination between the latter and their surrounding territories. See Giorgio Chittolini, 'Ricerche sull'ordinamento territoriale del Dominio fiorentino agli inizi del secolo XV', in Giorgio Chittolini, *La formazione dello stato regionale e le istituzioni del contado. Secoli XIV e XV* (Turin, 1979), pp. 292–351: pp. 292ff.

78 See Dani, *Gli statuti comunali.*

79 See Fasano Guarini, *Gli statuti delle città soggette*, p. 72.

80 Typically, through reforms, the local elites ensured control over local political life, and conversely the dominant – by appointing the *riformatori* – carved out an arbitral role between the opposing factions in the struggle. Over time, local reformers also emerged alongside those appointed by the dominant city. See op. cit., p. 89.

81 See Sbriccoli, *L'interpretazione dello statuto*; Daniele Edigati, 'Le annotazioni agli statuti come genere di letteratura giuridica nell'età del diritto comune', *Archivio Storico Italiano* 170, 4 (2012), pp. 653–704.

to intervene, often very harshly, in the periphery to pacify communities and assert central authority without completely emptying the *potestas statuendi et judicandi* (the authority to legislate and judge) of subject communities. The new regimes derived their *raison d'être* from their ability to maintain peace and tranquillity within the communities, but they had every interest in respecting, if not strengthening, local prerogatives. This is evident in the case of smaller municipalities, as doing so prevented the excessive dominance exerted over them by larger cities. Rather than being a supreme legislator, the prince had a role as a supreme guarantor of justice and peace through, and not despite, the *iura propria*, whose observance visitors were obliged to oversee.[82]

The legislative production of Italian princes, on the one hand, strongly emphasised the equality of subjects before the law, apparently granting no exceptions to local privileges and statutes, and combating excessive discretion on the part of judges; on the other hand, it focused on specific categories of crime related to moral conduct and state security: blasphemy, sodomy, usury, vagrancy, possession of weapons, murder, sedition, *lèse-majesté*, heresy. The rhetorical–political significance of such an operation is clear: for the prince, it was a matter of asserting and legitimising his sovereign authority, which depended on achieving 'peace' and 'prosperity' within the *respublica*. It is very challenging to verify the actual application of princely legislation compared to the *ius commune* and the *iura propria* of local communities on a case-by-case basis. What is certain is that the situation in Italy was characterised by a unique prominence of legal experts, jurists who claimed – and mostly obtained – a leading role in interpreting the law for the princes and harmonising it not only with municipal legislation but also with customs, natural laws and divine laws. For example, Pietro Cavallo from Pontremoli, a legal consultant, minister to Ferdinand I de' Medici, auditor of the *Consulta*, and author of *Resolutionum criminalium centuriae duae*, in recognising the prince's full legislative power, emphasised that he could indeed grant pardon in cases of murder, and 'even when peace has not been obtained from the offended party'.[83] The custom of negotiated procedures was, anyhow, able to substantially limit what the sovereign could do.

The jurists extolled the role of the law as an antidote to disorder and were called upon to provide empirical responses tailored to the times, starting

[82] See Maura Piccialuti, 'I controlli del Buon Governo sulle comunità negli anni del Prefetto Giuseppe Renato Imperiali (1701-1737)', in *Comunità e poteri centrali*, pp. 183–209.

[83] 'licet pace non obtenta a parte offensa', cit. in Fasano Guarini, *Produzione di leggi*, p. 123. See Pietro Cavallo, *Resolutionum criminalium ... centuriae duae* (Venetiis, apud Bertanos, 1644).

from a theoretical legal knowledge perceived, however, as something fixed and timeless, and therefore in need of continuous updating.[84] The remarkable pages of *Dottor volgare*, by Giovanni Battista De Luca, perhaps the most authoritative and influential Italian jurist of the seventeenth century, shed light on this matter.[85] In various parts of his perhaps most famous work – in chapters on trusts, benefits, pensions and so on – De Luca reiterates that 'this is not a subject capable of a certain and general rule';[86] everything depends 'on the particular circumstances of each case, to be considered with the prudent discretion of the Judge'[87] – a judge to whom the modifications in criminal procedure had granted enormous discretionary powers, which only the eighteenth-century reforms were able to limit. The jurist is the one who has nourished himself with texts, glosses and 'ancient repeaters, and also [with] those modern ones who have maintained a good style of pure theorists or scholastics',[88] but who then has appropriately 'digested' this essential nourishment in the courts. University categories, writes De Luca, 'are eaten and swallowed in schools, but then they are digested in the courts'.[89] This is a science of the particular, a research methodology not so much for truth but for the probable and practicable, an art of accommodation and flexibility, a casuistry that invades all fields of normativity, but also of administration and government.[90] The guiding idea is the exception, and the 'doubt' takes on a

84 See Bellabarba, *La giustizia nell'Italia moderna*, p. 141.

85 See Alessandro Dani, *Giovanni Battista De Luca divulgatore del diritto. Una vicenda di impegno civile nella Roma barocca* (Rome, 2012). Still very useful is Aldo Mazzacane, 'De Luca, Giovanni Battista', in *Dizionario Biografico degli Italiani*, vol. 38 (Rome, 1990), pp. 340–7.

86 'questa non è materia capace di regola certa, e generale', Giovanni Battista De Luca, *Il dottor volgare, ovvero il compendio di tutta la legge civile, canonica, feudale, e municipale, nelle cose più ricevute in pratica*, vol. IV (Colonia [Köln], a spese di Modesto Fenzo Stampatore in Venezia, 1740), p. 97.

87 'dalle circostanze particolari di ciascun caso, da considerarsi con il prudente arbitrio del Giudice', ibid.

88 'repetenti antichi, ed anche [di] que' moderni, li quali abbiano tenuto un buono Stile di puri teorici, o Scolastici', op. cit., vol. VI, p. 496.

89 'si mangiano e s'inghiottiscono nelle scuole, ma poi si digeriscono ne' tribunali', op. cit. (in Roma, nella Stamperia di Gioseppe Corvo, 1673), p. 51.

90 A recent and significant contribution on the centrality of the casuistic method from Antiquity to the Contemporary era and from a global cultural perspective is provided by the volume *A Historical Approach to Casuistry. Norms and Exceptions in a Comparative Perspective*, ed. Carlo Ginzburg and Lucio Biasiori (London, Oxford, New York, New Delhi and Sidney, 2018). For the legal field, see the fundamental works of Yan Thomas on the *fictio* and the state of exception, also

heuristic status hitherto unknown. Those who find themselves operating in the field, and therefore having to apply a rule, are constantly prompted by circumstances, by the specific case.[91] But even those who govern – the prince himself, or specific institutions – are often inclined to intervene not through laws but through rescripts, which therefore have limited validity in the particular case, appended to applications and supplications, often in derogation of laws, statutes and customs.[92]

To understand the reasons for the extensive use of rescripts in the *Ancien Régime*, several factors must be considered. The theory of the State as it had been evolving during the late Middle Ages was alien to the principle of the separation of 'public functions', such as legislating, judging and administering. Except for the right to wage war against an external enemy, public activity was perceived as a homogeneous space in which the sole function was jurisdiction. This was because the primary task of the sovereign, as well as of all of his officials (not dissimilar to the sovereign in terms of the essence of the power they held), was to maintain the balance of the order and resolve social conflicts through a reference (in the sense of preservation) to a pre-existing law inscribed in the nature of things and the world. By the sixteenth century, the theoretical framework began to change towards the

along the line drawn by Carl Schmitt, from which Giorgio Agamben, among others, drew inspiration: Yan Thomas, 'Fictio legis. L'empire de la fiction romaine et ses limites médiévales', *Droits* 21 (1995), republished as *Les opérations du droit* (Paris, 2011); Yan Thomas, *L'exception dans tous ses états*, ed. Yan Thomas (Paris, 2007). For an historical perspective, see 'Sistemi d'eccezione', monographic issue of *Quaderni Storici*, ed. Massimo Vallerani, XLIV, 2 (2009).

91 A heated debate has developed on the theological–moral or juridical–Romanistic origin of the casuistic procedure, which held such significance in European culture between the Middle Ages and the early modern era, sparked in part by the publication of Carlo Ginzburg's book *Nondimanco. Machiavelli, Pascal* (Milan, 2018). Critical remarks on the theory put forward by Ginzburg, see Gabriele Pedullà, 'Machiavelli secondo Carlo Ginzburg', *Storica* 71 (2018), pp. 9–86 (Ginzburg's reply: 'Gabriele Pedullà e la carta della Cina', *Storica* 72 (2018), pp. 193–8).

92 Cosimo I de' Medici was a frequent issuer of rescripts, to the point that, realising the misuse often made by judges, he had to affirm the difference between law and rescript on several occasions. As he wrote in 1561 to Francesco Vinta, an auditor of the *Riformagioni*, 'In this way, we will remedy many tricks that are played, and six times out of ninety-six times, they make [us] say things we never thought of, divert rescripts, and commit many injustices and a thousand tricks and rogueries' ('per questa via rimedieremo a molti berlingozzi che si fanno e delle sei volte le 90sei fan dire quello [che] mai pensavamo, stornan li rescritti e fanno molte iniustizie e mille furfanterie e ribalderie', cited in Fasano Guarini, *Produzione di leggi*, p. 110, n. 23.

separation of certain functions, deemed to belong to the prince, from those of jurisdiction, considered instead appropriate to the institutional apparatus of the State. However, a certain degree of osmosis between administration and jurisdiction would last for much of the early modern era. Jurisdiction remained a polymorphic field, characterised by a significant contamination of the tasks assigned to different offices due to social power relationships, political dynamics and economic structures and contingencies. The process of differentiation between princely functions and the functions of the institutional apparatus pivoted on the sovereign's ability, as *legibus solutus*, to derogate from objective law. It is the derogation that allows for the daily regulation of the complexities of the legal system, and the rescript – the principal legislative instrument of pre-modern states – embodies this true art of exception.[93]

In addition to being a legislative tool, from a general perspective the decree fully belongs to the category of writings, which, between the Middle Ages and the early modern era, acquired a previously unknown status, as evidenced by the development and widespread use of notaries throughout Europe.[94] These writings substantiate social practices (as in the case of *chartae pacis*, which we will discuss) and administrative practices, without assuming a sharp division between these two categories, in an important phase of statehood construction that underwent a process of standardisation

93 'Naturalmente refrattario alla vocazione uniformizzante e livellatrice propria dell'atto legislativo, [il rescritto] guarda invece al centro come ad un'istanza di mediazione tra le esigenze confliggenti delle sue singole cellule costitutive. [...] il sovrano pone il proprio "imperium absolutum" al servizio di interessi settoriali, dietro specifica domanda di singoli corpi o persone: assumendo una posizione non poi molto diversa da quella del giudice a cui ricorriamo per ottenere soddisfazione di una qualche pretesa. La "grazia" certo, va *oltre* la giustizia, in quanto consiste proprio nell'attribuire al suddito qualcosa che non gli è giuridicamente dovuto; ma il fine che essa persegue è sempre legato all'appagamento di un interesse particolare' ('Naturally resistant to the uniformising and levelling inclination inherent in legislative acts, the decree instead views the centre as a mediating instance between the conflicting needs of its individual constituent elements. The sovereign places their "imperium absolutum" at the service of sectoral interests, upon specific requests from individual groups or individuals, assuming a position not very different from that of a judge to whom we turn to seek satisfaction of a certain claim. "Grace", of course, goes *beyond* justice, as it precisely involves granting the subject something that is not legally owed to them; however, its aim is always connected to the fulfilment of a particular interest'), Mannori, *Il sovrano tutore*, p. 412, italics in the original.

94 See *Écritures grises. Les instruments de travail des administrations (XIIe–XVIIe s.)*, ed. Arnaud Fossier, Johann Petitjean and Clémence Revest (Paris, 2019).

or modelling. Think of the formularies of acts and letters, which began to be used in the fields of diplomacy as well as in secular and ecclesiastical governance: it was in this way that judicial and administrative institutions were able to group similar cases and determine the appropriate treatment for a given type. However, as Arnaud Fossier noted, the formularies did not teach their users the norm but, on the contrary, 'the art of the exception'. Each document, classified typologically, also served as an example of 'annulment, suspension or derogation from the rule of law'.[95] The quest for accommodation did not entirely disappear in the transition to the nineteenth-century modernity but was the characteristic feature of an *Ancien Régime*, both legal and political, where social mediation and the maintenance of corporate balance were far more important than the abstract assertion of state jurisdiction.

4. Peace and vendetta as instruments and practices

In the process of consolidating the political leadership of Italian city-states between the late thirteenth and the early fourteenth centuries, the renewal of judicial instruments served the purpose of fighting political projects alternative to that of the faction that had managed to rise to power. This leadership became the source of political legitimacy; to survive, it had to strike against the opposing front, automatically identified as subversive of the established order. The instrument of banishment was precisely used to exclude from the political community the members of the opposing faction to those in power; the latter, in fact, ceased to consider themselves a faction, identifying themselves with the same municipal institutions.[96] The ordinary criminal process with inquisitorial procedure, built on charges unrelated to faction membership but referring to the disturbance of public peace (rebellion, treason, conspiracy, etc.), became the means through which political adversaries could be expelled: the rate of contumacy in these proceedings was very high, and one of the most common penalties was indeed banishment *in absentia*.[97] The expansion of the criminal system witnessed since the mature phase of

95 'annulation, de suspension ou de dérogation à la règle de droit', Arnaud Fossier, 'L'exemple ou la norme? De l'art d'administrer par formulaire (XIIIe-XIVe)', in *Pouvoir des formes, écriture des normes. Brièveté et normativité (Moyen Âge/Temps Modernes)*, ed. Laurence Giavarini (Dijon, 2017), pp. 21–40: pp. 25–6.

96 See Giuliano Milani, *L'esclusione dal comune. Conflitti e bandi politici a Bologna e in altre città italiane tra XII e XIV secolo* (Rome, 2003).

97 See Glenn Kumhera, *The Benefits of Peace. Private Peace-making in Late Medieval Italy* (Leiden and Boston, 2017), pp. 93–6.

the communes of *popolo* must, therefore, be linked to the ongoing political conflict and, above all, should not be considered as at odds with the negotiable dimension that characterises, as noted above, pre-modern political systems. The aim was the negotiated reintegration of the excluded.

Judicial instruments, even those seemingly more 'hegemonic', thus adhered to purely negotiable logic. In fact, the severity of the procedure was in large part oriented to the negotiated outcome of the proceedings rather than on the imposition of a harsh sentence. There were few exemplary convictions, and everyday administration was made up of satisfactory transactions and the reintegration of the excluded. This holds true for political trials, but it is equally true for the entire field of criminal justice, where the pressure exerted by the courts on social actors and their kinship networks, as we will see more clearly in the next chapter, did nothing but drive the parties towards renunciations, truces or peace agreements, outcomes stemming from a strong social dimension, as well as a ritual aspect in religious terms. As demonstrated by quantitative estimates, the incidence of settlements and peace-making was very high in the total number of cases, but the relevant point is that the percentage of those conducted with an inquisitorial procedure that ended in an agreement with the injured party was higher than those conducted with an accusatorial procedure. The case of Perugia studied by Massimo Vallerani serves as an example, where one can observe – compared to the period of the *podestà* courts – a more widespread use of renunciation and the instrument of peace by the *Capitano del Popolo* (Captain of the People). As is well known, he implemented a significant reorganisation of public justice but also an initial flexibility in inquisitorial procedures, in which the margins of action (and therefore discretionary evaluation) left to the parties remained considerable, even though doctrine attributed a predominant role to the judge's *ex officio* initiative.[98] In late

[98] See Massimo Vallerani, *La giustizia pubblica medievale* (Bologna, 2005), pp. 181–3. 'Dal libro delle inquisizioni del capitano del Popolo del 1279 sono venuti risultati sorprendenti: su 96 processi iniziati, 50 sono terminati in assoluzione e di questi ben 38 sono conclusi dalla pace raggiunta tra le parti. Un'incidenza altissima, riscontrata in un registro posteriore di un ventennio al primo libro esaminato (del 1258), redatto da un magistrato di grandi capacità come Federico Manuelis de' Maggi, nello stesso anno della revisione statutaria (1279)', op. cit., p. 181 ('From the book of inquisitions by the *Capitano del Popolo* of 1279, surprising results have emerged: out of 96 cases initiated, 50 ended in acquittal, and, of these, a remarkable 38 were concluded through a peace agreement reached between the parties. This high incidence was also found in a subsequent register from the first book examined (from 1258), compiled by a highly capable magistrate, Federico Manuelis de' Maggi, in the same year as the statutory revision (1279').

thirteenth-century Perugia, there were several cases where the injured party in an act of violence, even a serious one, chose to discontinue legal action for various reasons, well aware of the prerogatives effectively accorded to them by the judicial system, despite a doctrine and statutory regulations that tended to exclude the effect *erga omnes* (of the peace agreement) and fully suspensive effects of negotiated peace, at least for crimes considered more serious (*effusio sanguinis*, permanent injuries, death), on the proceedings and on the assessment of evidence.

A careful analysis of the legal proceedings reveals, first of all, the presence of repeated and intersecting trials, indicating that the inquisitorial process could become an arena of conflict where vengeance could be ritualised and resorted to at more or less regular intervals. What is certain is that the severity of the inquisitorial procedure is by no means incompatible with the extensive use of renunciation and conciliation. In fact, there is a 'directly proportional relationship between the frequency of peace and the expansion of the municipal judicial structure'.[99] Throughout the early modern era, the judges' activities were essentially directed towards mending the fabric of social relationships disrupted by the crime or the trail of

[99] 'emerge un rapporto direttamente proporzionale tra la frequenza della pace e l'espansione della struttura giudiziaria comunale', Vallerani, *La giustizia pubblica medievale*, p. 197. 'Contrariamente a quanto si potrebbe credere, l'alto numero di concordie non prelude a una procedura inquisitoria debole, minata da un'apertura eccessiva verso l'intervento delle parti. [...] Il ricorso massiccio alla pace coesiste, quindi, con un uso severo dei meccanismi inquisitori. Ne è una conferma la struttura dei processi terminati con la pace, che sono quasi tutte inquisizioni complete nelle fasi principali: la denuncia-deposizione della vittima, spesso accompagnata da una fideiussione, l'interrogatorio dell'incolpato, la menzione o forse l'audizione dei testi e infine l'atto di concordia', op. cit., p. 192 ('Contrary to what one might believe, the high number of settlements does not suggest a weak inquisitorial procedure, undermined by excessive openness to the intervention of the parties. The extensive use of peace-making, therefore, coexists with a rigorous application of inquisitorial mechanisms. This is confirmed by the structure of cases concluded with a peace agreement, which are almost all complete in the main phases of the inquisition: the victim's complaint-statement, often accompanied by a surety, the interrogation of the accused, the mention or perhaps the hearing of witnesses, and finally, the peace agreement itself'). Vallerani also highlights 'la natura composita del processo: un'arena di confronto a più livelli dove gli atti di procedura disposti dal giudice "integrano" le decisioni dei litiganti, se queste dimostrano di avere rilevanza processuale sufficiente a trovare una soluzione accettabile al conflitto', op. cit., p. 193 ('the composite nature of the process: a multi-level arena where the procedural acts ordered by the judge "integrate" the decisions of the disputants, provided these demonstrate sufficient procedural relevance to find an acceptable resolution to the conflict').

crimes committed. To do this, they relied on a range of figures, guarantors and mediators, especially legal experts who played a fundamental role. Peace continued to be an act of explicit procedural relevance, all the more so when the trial concerned conflicts deeply rooted in the community's kinship networks. In such cases, it was essential to maximise the reintegration of the offender into the family and neighbourhood; criminal courts primarily served the function of generating the set of documents and information that would enable political authorities to intervene and seek to bring the case to a negotiated solution.[100] Legal knowledge was shaped by this specific negotiative or arbitrative function of criminal justice, which operated according to highly flexible criteria and was directed towards creating systems of penalty reduction or suspension. In many cases, legal expertise served precisely this purpose: the numerous 'criminal practices' published in the sixteenth and seventeenth centuries attest to the central role played by practical jurists in regulating conflicts through the legal process. This process is understood as a meeting point between 'living law' and 'state (or official) law', following the distinction proposed by Eugen Ehrlich, one of the founders of legal sociology, with whom Hans Kelsen, at the beginning of the twentieth century, entered into a debate.[101]

In the opinion of a sector of the historiography, the transition from the Middle Ages to the early modern period was characterised by the gradual integration of state justice in the management of criminal matters in cities and subject communities. This occurred through a process of delegitimising city magistracies, previously managed with significant autonomy by the ruling elites, often, if not primarily, through extensive use of negotiative procedures. It was in this way that the mechanisms of *vendetta* could be dismantled and deprived of internal legitimacy, transforming into a series of episodes of futile private revenge.[102] Already in his celebrated essay of 1939,[103] Otto Brunner, like other German scholars of *Verfassungsgeschichte*, described this transition, which was already occurring in the Middle Ages, due to the

[100] See Stuart Carroll, *Enmity and Violence in Early Modern Europe* (Cambridge, 2023), p. 30 and *passim*.

[101] See Eugen Ehrlich, *I fondamenti della sociologia del diritto*, ed. Alberto Febbrajo (Milan, 1976); original edition: *Grundlegung der Soziologie des Rechts* (München and Leipzig, 1913). See also Bellabarba, *La giustizia nell'Italia moderna*, pp. 85–8.

[102] See Claudio Povolo, *L'intrigo dell'onore. Poteri e istituzioni nella Repubblica di Venezia tra Cinque e Seicento* (Sommacampagna, 1997), pp. 158–63; James Casey, *The History of the Family. New perspectives on the Past* (Oxford, 1989), p. 58.

[103] See Otto Brunner, *Land und Herrschaft. Grundfragen der territorialen Verfassungsgeschichte Südostdeutschlands im Mittelalter* (Baden bei Wien, 1939).

progressive disregard for the rules inscribed in the aristocratic code of conduct. These rules included the confidentiality of challenges and the rejection of arbitrators. As a result, there was a shift from predominantly spontaneous peace-making, stemming from the distrust and fear communities had for the courts, governed by principles of self-governance by the communities and local aristocracies, to predominantly state-imposed peace-making by the early modern absolute states of the fifteenth and sixteenth centuries.[104] This interpretative framework undoubtedly requires some refinement, as it risks leading to an undervaluation of the influence and role of both local and central authorities in the medieval era, and conversely, an overestimation of that same influence and role in the early modern period.[105]

Among the conflict resolution systems, revenge, *vendetta* and peace-making should be considered on a par. The fundamental difference lies in the fact that, while the former two practices were progressively condemned in official public discourse, both civil and religious, and gradually restricted and prohibited in the legislations of various municipalities and later states (although at the beginning of the early modern era, some degree of legitimacy and tolerance still existed), the latter emerged as the principal tool for eradicating these retaliatory practices, especially in the realm of aristocratic behaviour. The latter can be gleaned and analysed primarily from judicial documentation, but, of course, they were not, and could not be, subject to legislative and judicial regulation. Peace, truce, provisions not to harm, etc., on the other hand, were the subject of meticulous legal definition, if only because they constituted one of the areas with the greatest overlap between municipal and communal *iura propria* and *ius commune*.

'Private' peace agreements, between individuals or groups, have always possessed a distinctly public character, from the thirteenth-century municipalities to the seventeenth-century regional states. Courts have always played a role in the genesis and validation of the bilateral agreement that substantiates peace-making. Furthermore, as we have seen earlier, even with

[104] Also Marcarelli shares this opinion (*Pratiche di giustizia*).

[105] Even in the medieval era, many peace agreements were imposed from above, and at times, with particular severity, as in the case of Charles of Anjou, the Duke of Calabria, taking control as the lord of Florence. The provision of 1326 stipulated that the new lord had the authority to enforce peace-making in cases of violent crimes. Specifically, in cases where the offender had caused bloodshed, they could not seek pardon and peace until the victim had obtained symmetrical revenge. The duke held the power to decide the type and extent of this reparation. See Klapisch-Zuber, *Retour à la cité*, pp. 145–192.

the rise of the inquisitorial procedure, an active role was recognised for the parties in seeking a way out of the conflicts intercepted by the court.[106] It is a shared view that the princely ideology that emerged in the sixteenth century led to 'a more pronounced and active involvement of public authorities in self-regulatory conflict mechanisms'.[107] This is especially visible in the frequency with which individuals or groups could be compelled to make peace, a tool that 'risked conflicting with the progressive inquisitorial commitment undertaken by the judicial authority first in the communal era and subsequently in the age of lords and princes'.[108] The evolution of the institutions of peace-making and truce over time is a complex and elusive matter, and the path that culminated in the ascendance of the inquisitorial system over the triadic-accusatorial one was not always straightforward. The paradigm of the progressive imposition of mandatory criminal justice, and hence the need for public repression of offences regardless of agreements between parties, as well as the increasingly intrusive role of sovereign justice in communal negotiation practices, is not always applicable to the judicial reality of the *Ancien Régime*. The fully public dimension of peace-making is more than evident in the regulation, both legislative and doctrinal-legal, of the rupture of peace, which we will revisit on several occasions.

The Italian princes of the sixteenth century generally identified the *rupta* or *fracta* peace as the sensitive point at which it was opportune to intervene in order to assert their jurisdiction.[109] In 1513, shortly after being reinstated in Florence following the end of Pier Soderini's republican regime, the Medici issued a provision stating that a case involving the breach of peace initiated before the *Otto di Guardia e Balia* or before a Rector

[106] Vallerani, *Giustizia pubblica medievale*, pp. 167–8.

[107] 'una più marcata e attiva partecipazione della pubblica autorità nei meccanismi autoregolativi dei conflitti', Carmelo Elio Tavilla, 'Paci, feudalità e pubblici poteri nell'esperienza del Ducato estense', in *Duelli, faide e rappacificazioni. Elaborazioni concettuali, esperienze storiche*, ed. Marco Cavina (Milan, 2001), pp. 290–1.

[108] 'rischiava di cozzare contro il progressivo impegno inquisitorio assunto dall'autorità giudiziaria d'età comunale prima e signoril-principesca dopo', ibid. Michelangelo Marcarelli, in reference to the Venetian *Terraferma*, emphasises the difference between a justice system based on informal mechanisms of mediation when expressed through the accusatorial procedure, and a late sixteenth-century modern justice system that, through the inquisitorial procedure, 'deprived the accused of the favourable conditions they had previously enjoyed' ('privava gli imputati delle condizioni favorevoli delle quali avevano goduto precedentemente'). Marcarelli, *Pratiche di giustizia*, p. 260.

[109] See Valerio Antichi, 'Giustizia consuetudinaria e giustizia d'apparato nello Stato pontificio: *la ruptura pacis* (1550-1600)', in *Stringere la pace*, pp. 229–75.

should be transferred to the Council of Justice. The Council was to provide the judge *a quo* with a binding *consilium*. However, the result, which soon became clear, was an extension of the time it took to resolve these cases. For this reason, the following year, the law on the 'modo di procedere nelle cause delle tregue e paci rotte' ('procedure in cases of breached truces and peace') returned the competence for *ruptura pacis* to the *Otto di Guardia* and the Rectors. This decision was based on the fact that the high costs of this type of legal case, the helplessness and discomfort of the disputing parties, and the endless quibbles of the defence lawyers had precluded the judicial path.[110] Furthermore, a register of peace and truces was established to record the names of both the parties and all the guarantors involved, to be kept in the lower courts. Forty years later, in 1548, it would be Duke Cosimo I who would revisit the matter, regulating it through a law and explicitly referring to the provisions contained in another legislative measure more than a century earlier, the *Cum fuerit assertum* of 1423, the 'modo di ammettere il beneficio della pace' ('manner of granting the benefit of peace'). The motivation was to clarify the legal aspects of a complex matter largely dependent on practice and to standardise the actions of the Rectors, which were sometimes so contradictory that they risked undermining the validity of statutory legislation itself.[111]

The same desire for standardising practices and, above all, for rigorously penalising the breach of peace had prompted Alfonso I d'Este to issue an *Ordine et declaratione ducale contra coloro che romperanno le paci o le tregue* ('Ducal order and declaration against those who will break the peace or truce') in 1531. Noting the 'contentions, difficulties and disputes ... that occur concerning instruments of peace and truce concluded among our subjects, and regarding the executions and collections to be made either against the principals or against the sureties of the penalties stipulated in those instruments',[112] also because of notaries who, owing to their limited experience

[110] See Daniele Edigati, *La pace nel processo criminale. Il caso toscano in età moderna*, in op. cit., pp. 369–409: p. 375.

[111] *Legislazione toscana raccolta e illustrata dal dottore Lorenzo Cantini socio di varie accademie*, vol. II (Florence, nella Stamperia Albizziniana da S. Maria in Campo per Pietro Fantosini e figlio, 1801), pp. 41–7.

[112] 'contentioni, difficultadi et disputationi [...] che accadono sopra instromenti di paci et tregue celebrati tra nostri sudditi et sopra le essecutioni et essazioni che si hanno da fare o contra li principali o contra li fideiussori delle pene stipulate in essi instrumenti', 'Ordine et declaratione ducale contra coloro che romperanno le paci e le tregue', in *Gride ducali, provisioni, gratie et ragioni della città di Modona* (Modena, 1575), pp. 47–9, cited in Tavilla, *Paci, feudalità*, p. 308.

or ignorance, fail to include in the agreements 'everything that would be necessary for the purpose for which they are made',[113] the Duke believed it was necessary to ensure that in cases of non-compliance with the obligations undertaken, 'justice should be the one to exact appropriate revenge, so that the offended parties need not seek it through the multiplication of scandals'.[114] The objective of this intervention was to ensure that penalties, whether penal or financial, would be enforced without fail and in full against both the signatories of the peace agreement and their guarantors, regardless of whether they were expressly named in the document:

> In all instruments of peace, truce and *sicurtà* not to harm [...] it shall be understood to be expressly stipulated that the sentences and condemnations that will be issued and carried out are intended to harm not only the principal wrongdoers included in the peace and truce and promises, even if they were not named and had not ratified said peace, but also the principals who have made the peace or truce and their sureties. We also intend that outlaws for any crime be considered included in the peace and truce agreements.[115]

The enforcement of the pecuniary penalty would have been immediate, while any legal proceedings against the offender of the breach of the peace could have been conducted through inquisition. With an additional provision, Duke Alfonso also foresaw the retroactive effect of the measure, sparking a long series of protests. In Medicean Tuscany, it was further emphasised that those who would suffer the consequences prescribed for the breach of peace were not only the principal parties and guarantors but also all the 'other relatives, adherents, accomplices or followers' who had violated the agreed terms.[116] Even the principal parties and sureties were granted a right of recourse against the violators of the peace agreement, who could

[113] 'tutto quel che saria necessario all'effetto per lo qual si fanno', ibid.

[114] 'la giustizia sia quella che ne faccia conveniente vendetta, acciò che gli offesi non habbiano a pensar di farla con moltiplicationi di scandali', ibid.

[115] 'in tutti gli istromenti di pace, tregua e *sicurtà* di non offendere [...] si intenda d'esservi apposta per ispresso sempre che le sententie et condemnationi che si daranno et si faranno habbiano a nuocere non solamente alli principali delinquenti compresi nella pace e tregua et promissioni, etiam se non fossero nominati et che detta pace non avessero ratificata, ma anchora alli principali che havranno fatta la pace o tregua et alli loro fideiussori, et volemo che nelle paci et tregue si intendano esser compresi gli banditi per qualunque delitto', op. cit., pp. 308–9.

[116] 'altri parenti, aderenti, complici, o seguaci', *Pratica universale del dottor Marc'Antonio Savelli, Auditore della Rota Criminale di Firenze, compendiosamente estratta per alfabetto dalle principali leggi, bandi, statuti, ordini, e Consuetudini, massime*

not 'plead ignorance of the truce or peace'.[117] These references indicate that public authority could be present in many different ways in the genesis of peace agreements and, above all, looked for a severe judicial punishment against those who had reneged on their word by resorting to violence, injuring or killing the person with whom peace or truce had been established or in favour of whom the court had imposed a *sicurtà di non offendere* (provision not to harm one another).

Peace, an agreement between two or more individuals promising to set aside the causes of discord and not offend each other in the future, could take on various forms depending on the circumstances and the timing in which it occurred. It could be the conclusive act of a feud between noblemen or private wars between aristocratic clans,[118] a judicial authority's imposition originating from a request by someone who felt threatened by an adversary's behaviour (usually taking the form of a *cautio* or *sicurtà* to prevent future offences), a legal instrument collectively signed or imposed on a plurality of individuals involved in ongoing legal disputes or in bloody factional struggles. On the other hand, peace could be initiated by the offender, either outside of a process – perhaps one that was never initiated – or during a trial as an outcome of a specific strategy pursued by one of the parties, aimed at exerting pressure on the opposing party through the use of the legal system itself. Peace with the offended party, furthermore, was generally referred to as a condition for obtaining a royal pardon, lifting of banishment, or even a reduction in the penalty, including pecuniary penalties.

The range of possibilities and circumstances was therefore very broad, and in this context peace played a central role in exiting, even if only temporarily, from a situation of violent conflict or in easing the tension caused by acts of violence or the legal pressure exerted on the involved family groups. One of the most significant aspects is the provision for the involvement of other individuals, in addition to the protagonists of the criminal act, in the negotiation of *sicurtà* not to harm, truce or peace agreement: guarantors, to be identified with extreme caution within family networks and based on rather clear and codified rules, committed to enforcing the agreement under penalty of payment of a usually substantial sum of money. What is certain is that legal doctrine took a keen interest in peace and other related legal institutions.

---

criminali, e miste, che si osservano nelli Stati del Serenissimo Gran Duca di Toscana (Venice, presso Paolo Baglioni, 1697), p. 239.

117 'allegare ignoranza delle tregue, o paci', ibid.

118 See Marco Bellabarba, *La giustizia ai confini. Il principato vescovile di Trento agli inizi dell'età moderna* (Bologna, 1996), pp. 13–65.

Among the issues that were most debated in doctrinal discussions at the beginning of the early modern period were the suspensive effects of the legal process originating from the peace agreement between the parties. Did a peace agreement reached before the pronouncement of the verdict prevent the judge from proceeding with the trial? Similarly, could peace prevent a third party from accusing the offender who had been granted remission? Giulio Claro, a sixteenth-century jurist educated in Spanish Lombardy and generally very attentive to customs and practices,[119] noted a discrepancy between theory and practice in this specific context, ultimately recognising the suspensive effects of peace only for crimes that, according to the law, did not trigger a judicial procedure *ex officio*.[120] However, it was the jurists of central Italy, and thus variously linked to the power of the popes, who produced treatieses specifically dedicated to peace and other related institutions.[121] These strictly legal treatises should not be considered separate from the contemporary production in the moral, philosophical, theological and pastoral–homiletic spheres. Despite their specific technical function, legal treatises were an integral part of a broader culture of mediation with a European scope, which we will explore further. This doctrinal production is usually linked, on the one hand, to the period that saw the implementation of *disciplinamento* policies addressed to the nobility carried out by the Italian states from the mid-sixteenth century, and, on the other hand, to the

[119] See Aldo Mazzacane, 'Claro, Giulio', in *Dizionario Biografico degli Italiani*, vol. 26 (Rome, 1982), pp. 141–6.

[120] 'Sed punctus est, nunquid possit transigi super crimine antequam sit super eo instituta accusatio; nam, de iure loquendo, videtur quod non, et quod sit facta si transactio, nihil valet [...] Sed certe de consuetudine contrarium servatur, nam quandocunque fiunt paces et transactiones super criminibus, semper valent et sunt observandae'. 'Et ideo in casibus in quibus non potest procedi nisi ad querelam partis, crederem quod remissio partis superveniens tolleret omnem processum et quod accusatus esset omnino absolvendus', Giulio Claro, *Sententiarum receptarum liber quintus* (Venice, apud Altobellum Salicatium, 1601), cited in Tavilla, *Paci, feudalità*, pp. 291–2 ('But the question arises, whether it can be settled regarding a crime before an accusation has been brought against it; for, from a legal perspective, it seems that it cannot, and that if a settlement is made, it is of no value [...] However, certainly the opposite is observed by custom, for whenever peace agreements and settlements are made concerning crimes, they always hold and must be observed'. 'Therefore, in cases where proceedings can only be initiated upon the complaint of a party, I would believe that the subsequent pardon of the party would nullify the entire process, and the accused should be completely acquitted').

[121] See below, Chapter 2.

anti-duelling literature that flourished around the same period.[122] The use of the typical tools of peace and renunciation, however, is so pervasive across social strata that it is necessary to avoid labelling instruments designed for a population that, in all its ranks, was affected by revengeful phenomena in a univocal manner.

In general, the legal doctrine of the sixteenth and seventeenth centuries adhered to the principle, established by Roman law, that the pursuit of a settlement with the victim was allowed specifically for those types of crime that carried a penalty of bloodshed; Sebastiano Guazzini makes this very clear in his treatise on peace and truce: 'The rule is that, in every crime for which a penalty of blood is imposed, a peace and settlement are permissible'.[123] The validity of this principle could pose a real hindrance to a doctrine that aimed, instead, to restrict the opportunities of applying remissions to lesser crimes, especially those for which there was no *ex officio* initiation of the judicial proceedings.[124] The statutes of Ferrara from 1567 excluded that an agreement between the parties reached before the verdict could preclude the issuance of a sentence. Peace, or the offender's confession, was reserved for the sole effect of reducing the prescribed pecuniary penalty by half or a quarter (thus only for offences for which pecuniary sanctions were provided). The reduction was completely excluded for offences that entailed severe afflictive penalties or the death penalty.[125] Although the Modenese statutes did not, in principle, rule out the possibility of a peace agreement before the verdict even for blood crimes, the Italian states in the second half of the sixteenth century adopted a common approach: to consider peace as equivalent to a remission of the statutory penalty but incapable of granting full impunity to

[122] See Giancarlo Angelozzi and Cesarina Casanova, *La nobiltà disciplinata. Violenza nobiliare, procedure di giustizia e scienza cavalleresca a Bologna nel XVII secolo* (Bologna, 2003).

[123] 'Regula est, ut in omni crimine, pro quo poena sanguinis irrogatur licita sit pax, & transactio', *Sebastiani Guazzini Jurisconsulti & in Curia Romana advocati, ac Petri Pauli Guazzini [...] Opera omnia juridica et moralia* (Coloniae Allobrogum, sumptibus Marci-Michaelis Bousquet & Sociorum, 1738), p. 14.

[124] See Antonio Padoa Schioppa, 'Delitto e pace privata nel pensiero dei legisti bolognesi. Brevi note', *Studia Gratiana* 20 (1976), pp. 271–86.

[125] *Statuta urbis Ferrariae nuper reformata* (Ferrariae, Giovan Battista Pigna, 1567), lib. III, cap. 19 (*Quòd de rixis, et iniurijs pace facta Potestas Ferrariae, vel alius Iudex nullam faciat condemnationem*). See Tavilla, *Paci, feudalità*, p. 294. In the 1930s, Tancredi Gatti equated peace-making with instruments of repentance, including the confession of the offender. See Tancredi Gatti, *L'imputabilità, i moventi del reato e la prevenzione criminale negli statuti italiani dei sec. XII-XVI* (Padua, 1933), pp. 381–8.

the offender, especially in cases of homicide. Even the statutes of Rome had conformed to this criterion, defining peace – in the case of homicide – as necessary for the rehabilitation of the offender (re-admission to the community after banishment or exile) but excluding any suspensive effects on the legal process. This rule applied particularly when the homicide was committed against blood relatives (with the exception of the killing of an adulterous wife caught in the act). Here too, for offences for which a pecuniary penalty was stipulated, peace obtained by the aggrieved party within ten days from the day of the crime had the effect of halving the amount.[126]

In the late seventeenth century, Marc'Antonio Savelli's *Pratica universale*, based on the legislation, both statutory and ducal, of the Medici Tuscany, acknowledged this predominant nature of peace, providing specific guidelines on who could legitimately grant it, which was a necessary condition for the offender (with exceptions for thugs and prostitutes) to benefit from a reduction in the penalty:

> Peace, for it to be effective, must be obtained from the offended party, if they are alive, and if not, from the father and blood brothers, and if none of them exist, then from their uncles or paternal aunts; in their absence, from male cousins, and those who grant peace must be at least 15 years of age. If all of these individuals are missing, peace can be obtained from the mother or from the widow of the offender, and in the absence of these, from blood sisters of the same age, or from the nearest male relative if all the previously mentioned individuals are unavailable. If peace cannot be obtained from the first group, a declaration from the local court of the offended party's place of residence must be presented, confirming the absence of closer relatives as described above. If the offended party is a Florentine or resides in Florence, the affirmation of the three neighbours where they live, examined by the Notary of the Uffizio del Monte, will suffice, as mentioned above. However, if the offended party is a foreigner, obtaining peace from the Lords and Colleges on their behalf is sufficient.[127]

126 *Statuta Almae Urbis Romae Auctoritate Gregorii Papae XIII, a Senatu Populoq. Rom. Reformata, & Edita* (Romae, in Aedibus Populi Romani, 1590), p. 83.

127 'Pace acciocché giovi si deve avere dall'offeso proprio vivendo, se non dal Padre, e da' fratelli carnali, e da tutti loro avendoli, o da quelli avesse, e non avendo questi dal zio, o zij paterni, in loro mancanza da' cugini per linea masculina, e quelli che rendono la pace devono esser almeno d'età d'anni 15, e mancando tutti questi dalla madre, e dalla moglie sendo vedova, e doppo dalle sorelle carnali di detta età, o dal più prossimo per linea masculina in mancamento di tutti gli altri suddetti, e suddette nominati; e non si avendo dalli primi, si deve produr fede della Corte di quel luogo di dove era l'offeso, che non avesse altri congiunti più prossimi come sopra, et essendo l'offeso fiorentino, o abitante in Firenze di tre

The clear predominance of the agnatic line in determining the individuals entitled to grant forgiveness and, consequently, peace, corresponds, as we will see more clearly later, to the criteria followed by the judicial authority in the search for sureties and guarantors at the time of imposing *cautiones de non offendendo*. Savelli continued by stating that the settlement with the offended party, although 'reasonably indicating an investigation and torture for crimes for which it is not lawful to settle',[128] owing to the 'general custom throughout all of Italy, *being allowed to settle for every crime*, not only does not provide any indication or lead to a confession of the crime but also helps to reduce the penalty'.[129] Even for the most serious crimes, in the late seventeenth century, according to Savelli's words, custom allowed judges not to consider the settlement with the offended party as an admission of guilt, and therefore not a confession. Hence, peace-making was attributed exceptional efficacy in reducing the penalty, compared to the ordinary legal principles that had by then become established in the judicial procedure. This was accomplished through a system, particularly invoked in the event of *fractio*, firmly rooted in the network of kinship and friendships of social actors.

5. Peace and vendetta as concepts and rhetorical devices

> In the succession of parties that have, in turn, vied for power, the theatre has often resounded with unwarranted insults for the defeated and sycophantic flattery for the victors. The current government renounces and disdains the resources of factions; it wants nothing for them and will do everything for the Republic. Let all French citizens rally behind this will, and let the theatres support its influence. Let the sense of harmony, the principles of moderation and wisdom, and the language of noble and generous passions alone be honoured on the stage. Let nothing that can divide

testimoni della vicinanza, dove abitava esaminati per mano del Notaio dell'Ufizio del Monte, affirmanti come sopra; ma se fusse forestiero basta in luogo de' congiunti aver la pace da' Signori, e Collegi per lor Partito', *Pratica universale del dottor Marc'Antonio Savelli*, p. 239. See Daniele Edigati, *Una vita nelle istituzioni. Marc'Antonio Savelli giurista e cancelliere tra Stato pontificio e Toscana medicea* (Pisa, 2005).

128 'di ragione faccia indizio ad inquisizione, e tortura sopra li delitti, de' quali non è lecito transigere', *Pratica universale del dottor Marc'Antonio Savelli*, p. 239.

129 'consuetudine generale di tutta l'Italia, *essendo lecito transigere sopra ogni delitto*, non solo non fà indizio alcuno, né induce confessione nel delitto, ma anco giova a diminuire la pena', ibid, italics mine.

minds, fuel hatred, or prolong painful memories be tolerated there. It is time for there to be nothing but French citizens in the French Republic.[130]

So read a provision dated 26 Brumaire of the year VIII (17 November 1799), bearing the signature of the Minister of Police, Joseph Fouché, but most likely drafted by the First Consul, Napoleon Bonaparte, and addressed to all theatre directors. The context certainly goes beyond the chronological limits of this study, but the wording of the provision is emblematic of the persistence, over the long and very long term, of the way in which those in power have narrated political dynamics and, consequently, the conflict and violence that result. The disdain and criminalisation of factions and the spirit of faction ('The current government renounces and disdains the resources of factions') is a constant feature of political regimes regardless of their nature. This is based on the mechanism by which the faction that manages to seize power ceases to describe itself as a faction, identifying itself as the sole source of political legitimacy and branding all opposition forces to the regime as 'factious', automatically labelled as seditious. Hence, the tendency of those in power to present themselves as bearers of ideals of harmony and peace, even in the form of, as happened during the Consulate era in France, strict control over the performances staged in theatres, especially in Paris, which were social venues central to the formation of public opinion and consensus. Here, only a 'a sense of harmony' ('sentiment de concorde'), a 'language of great and generous passions' ('langage des passions grandes et généreuses'), should have been represented, while everything that could 'divide minds, fuel hatred, prolong painful memories' ('diviser les esprits, alimenter les haines, prolonger les souvenirs douloureux') had to be kept away.

[130] 'Dans la succession des partis qui se sont tour à tour disputé le pouvoir, le théâtre a souvent retenti d'injures gratuites pour les vaincus et de lâches flatteries pour les vainqueurs. Le gouvernement actuel abjure et dédaigne les ressources des factions; il ne veut rien pour elles, et fera tout pour la République. Que tous les Français se rallient à cette volonté, et que les théâtres en secondent l'influence. Que le sentiment de concorde, que les maximes de modération et de sagesse, que le langage des passions grandes et généreuses soient seuls consacrées sur la scène. Que rien de ce qui peut diviser les esprits, alimenter les haines, prolonger les souvenirs douloureux, n'y soit toléré. Il est temps qu'il n'y ait plus que des Français dans la République française', Louis-Henry Lecomte, *Napoléon et le monde dramatique. Étude nouvelle sur des documents inédits* (Paris, 1912), pp. 34–5, cited in Franco Piva, 'Le cadre historique et normatif du théâtre français sous le Consulat et l'Empire', in *Théâtre, identité, et politique culturelle sous le Consulat et l'Empire*, ed. Vincenzo De Santis, Paola Perazzolo and Franco Piva, *Studi Francesi* 191, LXVII, II (2020), pp. 258–68: p. 259.

A veritable peace-making mission of political power: this is the underlying idea expressed since Antiquity – albeit with different nuances – both in philosophical reflection and in the discursive production emanating from power itself. Peace and violence, peace and revenge can easily be seen as two sides of the same coin. We describe and aspire to social harmony and peace, always with revenge as a reference, even if implicit. Political bodies and social groups have always employed discursive mechanisms to attribute precise connotations to interpersonal violence and social conflict. Claudio Povolo, in particular, studying feuds and vendettas through the procedural sources from the Venetian area in the late sixteenth century, has highlighted how important it is to consider the 'evocative power of words, their expressive strength, and their ability to encompass memory, to reshape and transform lived reality' in this context.[131] The meanings of conflict, Povolo continues, go well beyond its essence: 'The conflict represented by such a process [to Paolo Orgiano] was, above all, a conflict *narrated* in light of the relationships between the various powers that clashed in the field of criminal justice administration and in the especially decisive field of judicial procedure'.[132] In relation to the trial itself, there is a context of kinship relationships and communal power structures that 'exerted great force to favour the outcome of the judicial proceeding in their own interest'.[133] Conflict thus ends up becoming a 'conflict of values' ('conflitto di valori'). However, political and non-political conflict and revenge can be narrated not only by social actors but also by public authorities and, more generally, by the agencies that, over the course of the centuries-long history of European institutions, have sought to govern these phenomena.

The concepts of *vendetta* and peace evolved in a meeting ground between political theory and practice, something that often took place within the courts of justice, mainly because the line of demarcation between political conflict and social conflict can rarely be clearly drawn. The discursive production that flourished from the thirteenth century, primarily rooted in Aristotelian–Thomist philosophy, worked to disseminate the idea at all

[131] 'potere evocativo della parola, la sua forza espressiva e la sua capacità di inglobare la memoria, per riplasmare e trasformare la realtà vissuta', Povolo, *L'intrigo dell'onore*, p. 355.

[132] 'Il conflitto rappresentato da tale processo [a Paolo Orgiano] fu dunque, soprattutto, un conflitto *raccontato* alla luce dei rapporti intercorrenti tra i diversi poteri che si affrontarono sul terreno dell'amministrazione della giustizia penale e su quello, oltremodo decisivo, della procedura giudiziaria', ibid, italics in the original.

[133] 'premevano, con grande forza, per volger a loro favore l'esito del procedimento giudiziario', ibid.

levels that the primary task of political power is the defence of the common good and, therefore, the limitation of violence for the establishment of peace and harmony. This, as previously mentioned, was the core of the political programme of the so-called *popolo* regimes. At that time, new actors emerged in public life, generally of modest origins but who had established themselves through mercantile, financial, manufacturing activities and even the exercise of liberal professions. They claimed the right to participate in government. From a political perspective, 'from power understood essentially as "the capacity for coercion and dominance", nourished by an *ethos* of chivalry whose courteous aspects should not overshadow its original function of subjugation, the transition in the *popolo* age tends to the idea of power that must operate within a network of constraints and must primarily manifest as a capacity for governance'.[134] This is, therefore, the 'choice to operate within the institutional framework, identified as the designated place for political activity'.[135]

From this perspective, revenge and feuds, considered as the natural outcome of factional struggles, are depicted as a social ill to be remedied. It is true that a jurist such as Bartolus de Saxoferrato had acknowledged the existence of 'good' factions for the defence of the common good against the dangers of establishing a tyrannical government. However, what prevailed in the late Middle Ages and the Renaissance was a profoundly negative view of feuds and *vendetta*, both on the part of the city or community faction that had gained power and on the part of princely authority that had little tolerance for local political dynamics based on the struggle between *partialitates*. In general, even as the Middle Ages waned, the overwhelmingly dominant trend was to relegate feuds and revenge systems to the realms of the pathological or the non-political.[136] In the early modern age, the practice of structuring local politics around narrow *partes* based on bonds of amity was definitively condemned by public authorities and largely recognised by

[134] 'da un potere inteso essenzialmente come "capacità di costrizione e dominio", nutrito di un *ethos* cavalleresco i cui eventuali aspetti cortesi non devono far dimenticare l'originario nucleo di sopraffazione, si transita nell'età di "popolo" verso l'idea di un potere che deve muoversi all'interno di una rete di condizionamenti e deve esplicarsi soprattutto in una capacità di governo', Enrico Artifoni, 'I governi di 'popolo' e le istituzioni comunali nella seconda metà del secolo XIII', *Reti Medievali*, 4, 2 (2003), available online at http://www.rmojs.unina.it/index.php/rm/article/view/urn%3Anbn%3Ait%3Aunina-3304/5085 [pp. 3–4].

[135] 'scelta di operare sul terreno istituzionale, individuato come il luogo deputato dell'attività politica', ibid.

[136] See Stuart Carroll, 'From Feud to Enmity', *Acta Histriae* 25, 2 (2017), pp. 43–4.

legal and political science as the source of disorder and conflicts, which, in turn, could lead to open warfare.[137]

The direct causal relationship between internal sedition and war was a recurring theme in humanistic literature. Nevertheless, concurrently and at least until the fourteenth century, revenge continued to be recognised by public authorities as a right.[138] And even when mandatory public justice began to supplant community-based reconciliation procedures, and the impartiality of the judge became an established principle in Western judicial systems, revenge did not completely vanish from the social and cultural landscape of European populations, although it became absorbed by the concept of justice itself. Revenge becomes lawful when it is enacted by the state, the sole holder of legitimate violence. From the perspective of social actors, resorting to official justice, as we have seen, can be a part, a segment, of the feuding mechanism or reconciliation process. However, on the other hand, the criminal process itself can be a tool of revenge in the hands of social actors. According to this thesis, the increase in recourse to courts between the Middle Ages and the early modern period was not solely due to the increasing ability of the state to assert its jurisdiction in conflict resolution, but also, if not primarily, because social actors increasingly wanted to use the courts as a means to achieve a form of emotional satisfaction in relation to their adversaries, regardless of the outcome of such recourse. This would be a 'judicial revenge' and a public acknowledgment of one's position in relation to the dispute.[139] The court could become a stage where the feud was ritual-

[137] See Bellabarba, *La giustizia nell'Italia moderna*, p. 59. It is significant that, at the end of the fifteenth century, Bishop Pietro Barozzi of Bergamo felt it necessary to publish the treatise *De factionibus extinguendis*, in which he analysed the political situation in Bergamo, following in the footsteps of Bartolus de Saxoferrato's *De Guelphis et Gibellinis*. See *Il vescovo Pietro Barozzi e il trattato 'De Factionibus Extinguendis'*, ed. Franco Gaeta (Florence, 1958). The same condemnation of *factiones* is evident in the writings of Francesco Guicciardini regarding his own experience of governance in papal Romagna between 1521 and 1523, as discussed in Carlo Baja Guarienti, *Il bandito e il governatore. Domenico d'Amorotto e Francesco Guicciardini nell'età delle guerre d'Italia* (Rome, 2014).

[138] See Aude Musin, *Sociabilité urbaine et criminalisation étatique. La justice namuroise face à la violence de 1360 à 1555* (Turnhout, 2017); Aude Musin, 'Le droit de vengeance et son déclin dans les Pays-Bas (XIVe-XVIe siècles)', in *Krypton. Identità, potere, rappresentazioni* V–VI (2015), available online at http://romatrepress.uniroma3.it/wp-content/uploads/ 2019/05/Le-droit-de-vengeance-et-son-d%C3%A9clin-dans-les-Pays-Bas-XIVe-XVIe-si%C3%A8cles.pdf

[139] Daniel L. Smail, *The Consumption of Justice. Emotions, Publicity and Legal Culture in Marseille, 1264-1423* (Ithaca and London, 2003), p. 243.

ised, and feelings of hatred, anger and the desire for revenge were channelled and displayed, allowing them to have their appropriate public expression. According to this perspective, the civilising process is not configured as a process of containing emotions but rather as a process of expressing those very emotions differently. In late medieval Marseille, the area of research chosen by Daniel L. Smail, social actors chose not to repress their emotions, but to use the court as a stage.[140]

Western philosophical thought has always sought to place *vendetta* and the desire for revenge in the territory of human passions. In doing so, *vendetta* has gradually been disconnected from its social and, above all, political motivations, paving the way for a process of psychologisation that was anything but accidental and unconscious. The most immediate connection has always been, from ancient times, with anger. Aristotle incorporated revenge and anger into the theory of human passions, emotions that cannot be eradicated but must be tempered in harmony with rational will and desire for a good end. Anger, understood as a just reaction to an unjust offence received, is not inherently good or bad; it becomes good if the rational soul directs it towards moderation and vicious if irrational behaviour leads us to unhappiness.[141] A noteworthy aspect is that the Stagirite identifies a deep connection between anger, revenge (as its consequence), and amity, in the sense that anger is especially unleashed in relationships with friends, from whom we do not expect betrayal, much more so than in relationships with enemies.[142]

Seneca marks a turning point that will pave the way for Christian thought, especially as articulated by Saint Augustine: anger becomes an enemy to be defeated, something with which right reason cannot and should not compromise. In polemics with Aristotle, in his work *De Ira*, Seneca seeks to demonstrate the detestability of anger and its opposition to human nature; it is not a passion (*affectus*) to be directed, as in the case of Aristotle, but always a vice, a disease to be wholly overcome. One cannot be angry and

[140] This thesis, however, clashes with those who have argued, such as Mario Sbriccoli, that within communities the resort to official justice was considered by social actors as 'interim and of last resort' ('interinale e di ultima istanza'), to be implemented when community methods proved ineffective or unusable. See Mario Sbriccoli, 'Giustizia negoziata, giustizia egemonica. Riflessioni su una nuova fase degli studi di storia della giustizia criminale', in *Criminalità e giustizia in Germania e in Italia*, p. 349.

[141] *The Nicomachean Ethics of Aristotle*, translated by F. H. Peters (London 1884), Book III, 10, pp. 91–3.

[142] See Stefano Berni, Giovanni Cosi, *Fare giustizia. Due scritti sulla vendetta* (Milan, 2014), p. 30.

good at the same time; passions must be eradicated from the realm of reason, and anger must be forever expunged.[143] For Seneca, revenge (the desire to punish) is linked to a sense of justice and, therefore, to the law. However, to prevent this desire from turning into uncontrolled violence, which inevitably involves the avenger himself, it must not be accompanied by anger. Anger, on the other hand, should be accompanied by reason, which guides revenge in the search for a more neutral and objective justice. Where there is passion, there is no reason; where there is anger and revenge, there is no justice; passions are destructive. Augustine will only reaffirm Seneca's thought by arguing that revenge derives from the passion of anger, the most ferocious, diabolical and brutal part of the human soul. It must be annihilated and uprooted; passions must disappear, and the vengeful person must suppress his anger and model his behaviour on the peace-making example of Christ. In his work *De libero arbitrio*, Title I, the Bishop of Hippo lists cases in which killing can be considered lawful (soldiers in war, self-defence, etc.), but in doing so he places at the centre of the analysis the passion understood as 'guilty desire' or 'reprehensible desire', which becomes the real evil. For the late Antique and early medieval Christian culture, humans must await God's revenge; they cannot carry it out themselves, just as Saint Paul had stated in the famous passage from the Letter to the Romans.[144]

143 'An secundum naturam sit manifestum erit, si hominem inspexerimus. Quo quid est mitius, dum in recto animi habitus est? Quid autem ira crudelius est? Quid homine aliorum amantius? quid ira infestius? Homo in adiutorium mutuum genitus est, ira in exitium; hic congregari vult, illa discedere, ic prodesse, illa nocere, hic etiam ignotis succurrere, illa etiam carissimos petere, hic aliorum commodis vel inpedere se paratus est, illa in periculum, dummodo deducat, descendere', Seneca, *De Ira*, libro I, par. 5, §2 ('Whether it is in accord with nature will be evident if we consider the human person closely. What is milder, when its mental condition is not warped? What, on the other hand, is crueller than anger? What is more inclined to love others than a human? What is more hostile than anger? The human is born to give and receive assistance – anger to destroy. The one wants to form associations, the other to secede; the one wants to be of benefit, the other to do harm; the one wants to aid even strangers, the other, to assault even the nearest and dearest. Human beings are prepared even to sacrifice themselves for the sake of other's advantage; anger is prepared to plunge into danger, provided it drags the other down'), Lucius Annaeus Seneca, *Anger, Mercy, Revenge*, translation by Robert A. Kaster and Martha C. Nussbaum (Chicago, 2010), p. 18.

144 'Render to no one harm for harm. Provide good things, not only in the sight of God, but also in the sight of all men. If it is possible, in so far as you are able, be at peace with all men. Do not defend yourselves, dearest ones. Instead, step aside from wrath. For it is written: "Vengeance is mine. I shall give retribution, says the Lord". So if an enemy is hungry, feed him; if he is thirsty, give him a

However, the focus seems to be increasingly on the emotional elements: the issue does not lie in the murder itself but in the struggle against vengeful passions. Christian thought merely criminalised anger, believing hatred and the desire for revenge as passions inherent to animals, not rational beings. In the Middle Ages, authors such as the Anglo-Saxon philosopher and theologian Alcuin of York (735–804), Abbot Smaragdus of Saint-Mihiel (760–840), the erudite Carolingian, Saint Rabanus Maurus (780–856), up to Saint Peter Damian (1007–72) had no doubt that passions were something negative and harmful, to be contained at all costs, as they were the source of violence.[145] However, it was only in the thirteenth century that Thomas Aquinas would settle the matter by discussing, in the *Secunda Secundae*, the concept of 'vengeful intent', which ended up forming the basis for much of the Catholic theological–moral reflection on the legitimacy of *vendetta* in the late medieval and early modern ages:

> I answer that, Vengeance consists in the infliction of a penal evil on one who has sinned. Accordingly, in the matter of vengeance, we must consider the mind of the avenger. For if his intention is directed chiefly to the evil of the person on whom he takes vengeance and rests there, then his vengeance is altogether unlawful: because to take pleasure in another's evil belongs to hatred, which is contrary to the charity whereby we are bound to love all men. Nor is it an excuse that he intends the evil of one who has unjustly inflicted evil on him, as neither is a man excused for hating one that hates him: for a man may not sin against another just because the latter has already sinned against him, since this is to be overcome by evil, which was forbidden by the Apostle, who says (*Romans* 12:21): 'Be not overcome by evil, but overcome evil by good'. If, however, the avenger's intention be directed chiefly to some good, to be obtained by means of the punishment of the person who has sinned (for instance that the sinner may amend, or at least that he may be restrained and others be not disturbed, that justice may be upheld, and God honored), then vengeance may be lawful, provided other due circumstances be observed.[146]

drink. For in doing so, you will heap burning coals upon his head. Do not allow evil to prevail, instead prevail over evil by means of goodness' ('Si fieri potest, quod ex vobis est, cum omnibus hominibus pacem habentes. Non vosmetipsos defendentes charissimi, sed date locum iræ. Scriptum est enim: Mihi vindicta: ego retribuam, dicit Dominus. Sed si esurierit inimicus tuus, ciba illum: si sitit, potum da illi: hoc enim faciens, carbones ignis congeres super caput eius. Noli vinci a malo, sed vince in bono malum'), *Rom*, 12, 17–21.

[145] See *Vengeance in Medieval Europe. A Reader*, ed. Daniel L. Smail and Lyn Gibson Kelly (Toronto, 2009), pp. 88–93, 177–83.

[146] *The Summa Theologiæ of St. Thomas Aquinas*, second and revised edition, literally translated by Fathers of the English Dominican Province, *IIa–IIae, quaestio* 108,

Between the fourteenth and fifteenth centuries, especially in religious literature, there was an increasing discourse regarding the moral imperative to restrain and control emotions that could lead to vindictive actions, such as anger, rage, envy and hatred, among others. Think of the sermons by the Franciscan San Bernardino of Siena in Italy or the Dominican San Vicente Ferrer in Aragon, which emphasised the need to achieve inner peace and gain control over one's violent emotions. They unequivocally condemned the desire for vengeance as sinful, much like carnal desire. However, as Ferrer pointed out, this does not mean that peace is inherently and necessarily good, because its goodness depends on the end it serves. There can be peace even among thieves, criminals and wrongdoers.[147]

During the same period, when mendicant friars travelled thousands of kilometres on foot to preach the beauty of inner peace and the Christian's need to abandon vindictive desires, humanists such as Leonardo Bruni proposed different interpretations of anger and revenge. Reviving the debate between Stoics and anti-Stoics (*apatheia* as freedom from emotions vs *metriopatheia* as the control or moderation of emotions), Bruni, in particular, argued that in certain circumstances anger serves a positive function in contrast to *apatheia*, which he saw as harmful and unproductive. The relationship between the individual, inner dimension and the social and political dimension of expressing hatred and anger, potentially leading to revenge, was not always straightforward. Renaissance political thought had a uniform and negative view of conflict, to the extent that it shaped a paradigm: that

---

art. 1 (London, 1920; online edition 2017) ('Respondeo dicendum quod vindicatio fit per aliquod poenale malum inflictum peccanti. Est ergo in vindicatione considerandus vindicantis animus. Si enim eius intentio feratur principaliter in malum illius de quo vindictam sumit, et ibi quiescat, est omnino illicitum, quia delectari in malo alterius pertinet ad odium, quod caritati repugnat, qua omnes homines debemus diligere. Nec aliquis excusatur si malum intendat illius qui sibi iniuste intulit malum, sicut non excusatur aliquis per hoc quod odit se odientem. Non enim debet homo in alium peccare, propter hoc quod ille peccavit prius in ipsum, hoc enim est vinci a malo, quod apostolus prohibet, Rom. XII, dicens, *noli vinci a malo, sed vince in bono malum*. Si vero intentio vindicantis feratur principaliter ad aliquod bonum, ad quod pervenitur per poenam peccantis, puta ad emendationem peccantis, vel saltem ad cohibitionem eius et quietem aliorum, et ad iustitiae conservationem et Dei honorem, potest esse vindicatio licita, aliis debitis circumstantiis servatis', *S. Thomae Aquinatis Secunda Secundae partis Summae Theologicae Sancti Thomae Aquinatis. De virtutibus omnis et vitiis in speciali*, Antverpiae, ex Officina Christophori Plantini, 1569, p. 321).

[147] See Rosa Maria Dessì, *Pratiques de la parole de paix dans l'histoire de l'Italie urbaine*, in *Prêcher la paix et discipliner la société. Italie, France, Angleterre, XIIIe-XVe siècle*, ed. Rosa Maria Dessì (Turnhout, 2005), pp. 245–78.

of civic concord as the ultimate goal for which politics should aim. This humanistic paradigm was first challenged by Niccolò Machiavelli, who paved the way for a positive evaluation of conflict as the true engine of political action and history.[148]

In his *Istorie fiorentine*, Machiavelli criticises Leonardo Bruni and Poggio Bracciolini for having neglected in their works the 'civil discord' and the 'intrinsic enmities' that characterised the history of Florence. He argues that 'the grave and natural enmities that exist between the men of the people and the nobles, caused by the wish of the latter to command and the former not to obey, are the cause of all evils that arise in cities. For from this diversity of humors all other things that agitate republics take their nourishment'(Book III, 1).[149] In his *Discorsi sopra la prima deca di Tito Livio*, written only a few years earlier, Machiavelli had dedicated an entire chapter to the analysis of tumult as a factor in the development and greatness of political entities (specifically, *That the Disunion of the Plebs and the Roman Senate made That Republic Free and Powerful*). In this chapter, he commented that

> I say that to me it appears that those who damn the tumults between the nobles and the plebs blame those things that were the first cause of keeping Rome free, and that they consider the noises and the cries that would arise in such tumults more than the good effects that they engendered. They do not consider that in every republic are two diverse humors, that of the people and that of the great, and that all the laws that are made in favor of freedom arise from their disunion, as can easily be seen to have occurred in Rome.[150]

148 See Gabriele Pedullà, *Machiavelli in tumulto. Conquista, cittadinanza e conflitto nei 'Discorsi sopra la prima deca di Tito Livio'* (Rome, 2011).

149 'le gravi e naturali nimicizie, che sono intra gli uomini popolari e i nobili, causate dal volere questi comandare, e quelli non ubbidire, sono cagione di tutti i mali che nascono nelle città; perché da questa diversità di umori tutte le altre cose che perturbano le republiche prendono il nutrimento loro', Niccolò Machiavelli, *Historie fiorentine*, libro III, in *Opere istoriche e politiche di Niccolò Machiavelli, Segretario e Cittadino fiorentino*, vol. I (Filadelfia, nella Stemperia delle Provincie Unite, 1818), p. 137; *Florentine Histories*, a new translation by Laura F. Banfield and Harvey C. Mansfield Jr (Princeton, 1988), p. 105.

150 'coloro che dannano i tumulti intra i Nobili e la Plebe mi pare che biasimino quelle cose che furono prima cagione del tenere libera Roma, e che considerino più a' romori ed alle grida che di tali tumulti nascevano, che a' buoni effetti che quelli partorivano; e che e' non considerino come e' sono in ogni republica duoi umori diversi, quello del popolo, e quello dei grandi; e come tutte le leggi che si fanno in favore della libertà, nascono dalla disunione loro, come facilmente si può vedere essere seguito in Roma', Niccolò Machiavelli, *Discorsi sopra la prima deca*

These tumults cannot be considered harmful because, as Machiavelli notes, 'in so much time [the Republic] sent no more than eight or ten citizens into exile because of its differences, and killed very few of them, and condemned not many more to fines of money'.[151] A politically managed and controlled conflict, therefore, is something beneficial, and this perspective leads Machiavelli to extend the reasoning to the sphere of individual behaviours, not necessarily tied to political dialectics. In another part of the same *Discourses*, he criticises Christian morality precisely because it had only made people less fond of liberty, less manly, and weaker compared to the ancient world. This is because it teaches endurance of insults received, rather than seeking vengeance. Avenging an offence represents a behaviour that is certainly more 'politically' oriented than forgiveness:

> Thinking then whence it can arise that in those ancient times peoples were more lovers of freedom than in these, I believe it arises from the same cause that makes men less strong now, which I believe is the difference between our education and the ancient, founded on the difference between our religion and the ancient. [...] This mode of life thus seems to have rendered the world weak and given it in prey to criminal men, who can manage it securely, seeing that the collectivity of men, so as to go to paradise, *think more of enduring their beatings than of avenging them*.[152]

With Machiavelli, a new path emerges, sharply contrasting with the humanistic culture of the thirteenth and fourteenth centuries, which, by exalting political concord and stigmatising factional dynamics, had relegated conflict (and hence political dialectics) to an exclusively unpolitical dimension.

---

di Tito Livio, commentati da Giuseppe Piergili (Firenze, Successori Le Monnier, 1893), p. 33; *Discourses on Livy*, translated by Harvey C. Mansfield and Nathan Tarcov (Chicago and London, 1996), p. 16.

[151] 'in tanto tempo per le sue differenzie non mandò in esilio più che otto o dieci cittadini, e ne ammazzò pochissimi, e non molti ancora ne condannò in danari', Niccolò Machiavelli, *Discorsi sopra la prima deca di Tito Livio*, p. 33 (*Discourses on Livy*, p. 16).

[152] 'Pensando dunque donde possa nascere, che in quegli tempi antichi, i popoli fussero più amatori della libertà che in questi; credo nasca da quella medesima cagione che fa ora gli uomini manco forti: la quale credo sia la diversità della educazione nostra dalla antica, fondata nella diversità della religione nostra dalla antica. [...] Questo modo di vivere, adunque, pare che abbi renduto il mondo debole, e datolo in preda agli uomini scellerati; i quali sicuramente lo possono maneggiare, veggendo come l'università degli uomini, per andare in Paradiso, *pensa più a sopportare le sue battiture, che a vendicarle*', Niccolò Machiavelli, *Discorsi sopra la prima deca di Tito Livio*, p. 131, italics mine (*Discourses on Livy*, pp. 240–1).

Inspired by a careful reading and modernisation of a specific strand of Latin culture (including Appian and Cicero, among others), Machiavelli demystifies Renaissance political thought rooted in the ideal of uniform concord. He envisions society as driven by 'humours', set in motion by individuals who are not 'apathetic' (in the Stoic sense of the term) and groups that necessarily come into conflict with each other. This physiological conflict needs to be properly regulated, not suppressed or eradicated. These are energies that require an outlet and, when appropriately managed, keep a society alive, as long as they do not escalate into bloodshed and spirals of destructive violence.[153] Starting with Machiavelli, an idea took root that would traverse, albeit in different forms, late Renaissance and Baroque thought, ultimately reaching figures like Hobbes, Spinoza, Locke and Montesquieu.[154]

The relationship between the theory of passions and political theory in the strict sense is not straightforward and deserves further exploration, which is not possible in this context. It is worth highlighting that in, the early modern era, various authors, including Spinoza, focused on passions as 'passivity', as indispensable elements that can, however, be transformed into 'affections', active forces that do not conflict with reason and can enhance the *vis existendi* and *vis agendi* of individuals. The same confidence in the possibilities for humans not only to control but to use passions constructively, based on the insights of scientific thought, can be found in Descartes's *Traité des passions de l'âme*. In general, the Horatian concept of 'concordia discors' (*Epistles* I, 12, 19), the discordant harmony of things, an idea derived from the philosophy of Empedocles and connected to Aristotelian *medietas*, seems to continue to exert a significant influence on views not only of the universe and the world but also of society and the State (which are modelled on the former). This is especially true during the zenith of an ideal of 'discipline' that goes hand in hand with attempts by rulers to centralise power. Virgilio Malvezzi had already expressed this idea in his *Discorsi su Cornelio Tacito* (1622), a thought commonly found in Baroque political philosophy. A few

[153] Marie Gaille has retrospectively linked Machiavelli's thought on political and social conflict to the notion of a 'société chaude', coined by Claude Lévi-Strauss. 'Hot societies are those in which "caste and class distinctions are incessantly milked to extract energy and a future". [...] Far from preserving in simply being, they are in a constant state of flux. The core of their history is a conflict which operates as a motor, driving civic life. Like the "hot societies" identified by Claude Lévi-Strauss, Machiavelli's insights emphasise "differential gaps between power and the opposition, majority and minority, exploiters and exploited"'. Marie Gaille, *Machiavelli on Freedom and Civil Conflict. An Historical and Medical Approach to Political Thinking* (Leiden and Boston, 2018), p. 1.

[154] See Pedullà, *Machiavelli in tumulto*, pp. 41–80.

decades later the Jesuit Daniello Bartoli, a highly respected clergyman and writer of his time, published *La ricreazione del savio* (1659), a work intended to provide the reader with models of behaviour derived from the observation of the natural world and the social world. When discussing the harmony of the world's parts through natural discord leading to natural concord and consonance, Bartoli seems to conceive an ideal of order that does not require the eradication of dis-order (read: conflict). Instead, he suggests that the 'private contrast' ('privato contrasto') among the parts composing the universe tends, not without wonder, towards the 'public peace' ('pace del pubblico'):

> Do these natures, so relentlessly hostile, not oppose each other? Yes, they do, and this is the wonder: that their private opposition is the public peace. They do not destroy each other because of balance, that is, having forces counterpoised, where one's resistance is as strong as the other's opposition. And from the continual clashing and mingling of their opposing qualities arises the production of mixtures, in which the excess of those that were too extreme is rebuffed, and thus reduced to a suitable moderation, they harmoniously blend.[155]

For the Ferrarese Jesuit Bartoli, the marvellous 'order' is the result of a supernatural intervention that eludes human comprehension. Nevertheless, it remains significant that this harmony, this peace, does not necessarily coincide with absolute uniformity but, if anything, with a kind of acceptance of conflict, maintained by the ruler – inspired by divine law – within a certain threshold of tolerance, as an intrinsic and ineliminable aspect of human societies. A typical characteristic of Baroque literature is an unprecedented perception and awareness of mutability, instability, continuous transformation, movement and transience in both nature and social and political reality.

[155] 'E nature sì implacabilmente nimiche, non si contrastano elle? Sì: e questa è la maraviglia, che il lor privato contrasto sia la pace del pubblico. Non si distruggono insieme, per cagione dell'equilibrio, cioè, dell'aver le forze contrappesate, essendo l'una al resistere sì gagliarda, come l'altra al contrastare. E in tanto dal continuo azzuffarsi e permischiar che fanno le contrarie lor qualità, ne nasce il producimento de' misti, ne' quali rintuzzato il soverchio di quelle, che di troppo eccedevano, e così ridotte a convenevole mezzanità mirabilmente s'accordano', *La ricreazione del savio in discorso con la natura e con Dio, del padre Daniello Bartoli della Compagnia di Gesù*, vol. I (Venezia, dalla Tipografia di Giuseppe Gattei, 1831), pp. 111–12. Michele Olivari was the first to hypothesise a connection between a non-negative conception of conflict expressed by Bartoli and the work of pacification of enemies carried out in the pastoral activities of his affiliated order. See Michele Olivari, *Lettura 'politica' dei resoconti missionari di Pedro de León, gesuita andaluso (1580-1620)*, in *Rivista di Storia e Letteratura Religiosa* XXII, 3 (1986), pp. 475–91: p. 475.

Therefore, the fundamental issue becomes the preservation of power in the face of an inherently restless society, as was clear to the entire Baroque culture.[156] Some years before Bartoli, an author like Diego de Saavedra Fajardo could describe, in the commentary on the hundred emblems that make up his *Idea de un Príncipe político christiano* (1640), the justice of the prince as exclusive, pervasive, exemplary and functional for achieving harmony in a world irreversibly dominated by conflict. The problem for those in power is to reconcile social order with the individual's aspiration for freedom, which cannot be suppressed.

Reflection on the State necessarily connects with moral literature, since models of governance must grapple with models of individual behaviour, towards the formation of what José Antonio Maravall called 'moral de acomodación' ('moral of accomodation').[157] For Saavedra, the art of governing lies in maintaining an unstable balance: the pursuit of absolute uniformity risks transforming the ideal prince into a tyrant. Just as water putrefies in perfect stillness, society needs to keep its conflicts alive – both internal and external, and this is the interesting aspect – as vital forces for the body politic: 'Waters are preserved within their movement; if it is lacking, they corrupt, but it is not necessary for them to flow; it is enough for them to move within themselves, as happens to waters stirred by the winds'.[158] Based on that same pessimistic anthropology that would have inspired Thomas Hobbes's *Leviathan*, Saavedra recommends, both to the prince and to individuals in their relations with others, a model of behaviour marked by dissimulation and adaptation to a reality of relationships – both interstate and interpersonal – inevitably marked by the spirit of domination. Reality should not be interpreted 'solely with the staff of reason but also with that of the malice of the ordinary injustices and tyrannies of the world'.[159] Gabriele

[156] See Rosario Villari, *Politica barocca. Inquietudini, mutamento e prudenza* (Rome and Bari, 2010), p. 98.

[157] José Antonio Maravall, 'Saavedra Fajardo: moral de acomodación y carácter conflictivo de la libertad', in José Antonio Maravall, *Estudios de historia del pensamiento español*, serie tercera (Madrid, 1984), pp. 223–54: p. 228.

[158] 'Las aguas se conservan dentro de su movimiento; si falta, se corrompen, pero no es necessario, que corran, basta, que se muevan en si mismas, como sucede a las aguas agitadas de los vientos', *Idea de un principe politico christiano, representada en cien empresas, dedicada al Principe de las Españas, nuestro Señor, por Diego de Saavedra Fajardo* (en Amberes, en casa de Ieronymo y Iuan Bapt. Verdussen, 1655), p. 487.

[159] 'con la vara de la razón solamente, sino con la de la malicia de las ordinarias injusticias y tiranías del mundo', op. cit., p. 267.

Pedullà wrote that, 'in contrast to Machiavelli, Baroque authors' conflictualism does not preserve any autonomous role for the people, which becomes a mere instrument in the hands of those wielding power',[160] but it is equally undeniable that, in the seventeenth century, a reflection entirely centred on the State gave rise to an unprecedented focus on conflict that was no longer political (understood as political dialectics between the oligarchy and subordinate classes) but essentially social.

6. Amity and enmity

In ancient societies, humans needed to establish bonds that could ensure support and protection. Kinship is the primary bond through which basic needs can be satisfied, and bonds of friendship – a concept with much more varied meanings than we commonly attribute to it today – arise when kinship ties are absent or insufficient. In classical theories, at least from Greco-Roman culture onwards, the terms 'friendship' or 'amity' were used to define a metasocial bond capable of encompassing other types of relationships not based on consanguinity, from more socially dense relationships such as marriage and affinity to weaker ones such as godfatherhood, neighbourly connections and modern-day friendship. For all these reasons, the concept of friendship has provided excellent elements for historical and anthropological investigations into the mechanisms of social aggregation and disaggregation through alliances between kinship and non-kin groups;[161] symmetrically, the concept of enmity – strictly political and not necessarily synonymous with hatred – has also been central to research on social conflict, interpersonal violence, as well as the dynamics of reconciliation.[162]

Since ancient Rome, the term 'amicitia' referred to an objective relationship (although not yet legally binding) that obligated the parties to adopt a certain attitude (referred to as *benevolentia*) and entailed a set of duties (*officia*) aimed at enhancing the *dignitas*, which is the social and political

[160] Gabriele Pedullà, *Machiavelli in Tumult. The Discourses on Livy and the Origins of Political Conflictualism* (Cambridge, 2018), p. 230.

[161] See *Kinship in Europe. Approaches to Long-term Developments (1300-1900)*, ed. David Warren Sabean, Simon Teuscher and Jon Mathieu (New York and Oxford, 2007); Gérard Delille, *Le maire et le prieur. Pouvoir central et pouvoir local en Méditerranée occidentale (XVe-XVIIIe siècle)* (Rome and Paris, 2003); Marco Gentile, 'Giustizia, protezione, amicizia: note sul dominio dei Rossi nel Parmense all'inizio del Quattrocento', *Reti Medievali Rivista* V, 1 (2004), available online at http://www.rmoa.unina.it/2275/1/gentile.pdf

[162] See Carroll, *Enmity and Violence*.

prestige of the 'friend'. In Germanic law, friendship based on a contract (*Schwurfreundschaft*) involved specific behaviours on the part of the parties: *consilium* and *auxilium*. Other features of friendship included loyalty (*fides*) and love (*caritas*). All of these aspects contributed to shaping a relationship that excluded judicial dispute in case of disagreement, in favour of a peaceful resolution. The conceptual pairs were, therefore, 'fides et caritas', but also 'pax et caritas'. The goal of these well-defined procedures was to proactively express consent to reaching an agreement outside the courtroom, as well as a commitment not to abruptly end the friendship or settle any disputes through the use of violence.[163]

António Manuel Hespanha, drawing from the pioneering works of Marcel Mauss, has analysed the 'gift economy' and the complex system of power relations that giving, receiving and reciprocating create. The situation of imbalance that arises when the act of generosity is performed, especially between individuals who were already in a situation of inequality, is typically referred to as 'friendship'. Aristotle had already reflected on this concept, one of the fundamental pillars of political bonds, in the *Nicomachean Ethics* and, more importantly, in the *Politics*.[164] This 'unequal friendship' is how Aristotle describes the relationships of patron and client that underlie the structure of political socialisation. Aristotle's *philia* is intimately associated with at least two other concepts central to defining the ethical foundations of political association.[165] First, *homonoia*, the harmony among citizens, is crucial because, without a sense of mutual friendship and affection in the *polis*, not only can political stability not be achieved, plunging the community into factional strife, but moral rectitude, which represents the very purpose of the political community, cannot be attained either. The relationship between the *potentior* (more powerful) and *humilior* (less powerful) constitutes a case of 'voluntary servitude', a relationship of subordination aimed at mutual

[163] See Reinhard Schneider, 'Politische Freundschaft', in *Il concetto di amicizia nella storia della cultura europea / Der Begriff Freundschaft in der Geschichte der Europäische Kultur*, Atti del XXII Convegno Internazionale di Studi Italo-Tedeschi (Merano, 9–11 maggio 1994) (Merano, 1995), pp. 372–94.

[164] On the 'relative' distinction that Aristotle establishes between ethics and politics, see Günther Bien, *La filosofia politica di Aristotele* (Bologna, 1985), pp. 189–254. For a fascinating analysis of the role of the 'gift' in shaping a 'Catholic anthropology of the modern economy', closely connected to the concept of 'friendship', see Bartolomé Clavero, *Antidora. Antropología católica de la economía moderna* (Milan, 1991).

[165] For example, see the dated but still useful Thomas A. Sinclair, *A History of Greek Political Thought* (London, 1952).

benefit. Through meticulous regulation of the codes of conduct for such a relationship, not only can abuses of power be prevented, but a basic and well-ordered form of hierarchy can also be established at the microscopic level, serving as a model for collective life as a whole. Friendship, moreover, is a kind of harmony that does not rest on the identity of opinions but rather, like the harmony of cities, on the concordance of practical attitudes. This is why political harmony is also called 'political friendship'.[166] Justice is closely linked to friendship as well, because, for Aristotle, 'it seems [...] that the subject-matter and occasion of friendship and of justice are the same. Every community or association, it is thought, gives some occasion for justice, and also for friendship'.[167] Everything ultimately leads to order, as the friendship that makes relationships between different individuals fruitful must be based on the identity of the individuals in question and, ultimately, on the moment of *discriminatio* (in the sense of legal *interpretatio*), through which it is possible to treat different subjects and different realities differently and treat equal subjects and equal realities equally.[168]

With the rise of Christianity, Aristotle's and Seneca's notions of 'liberality' underwent a process of marginalisation in comparison to the concept of 'charity'. Charity is considered inherently superior to liberality, as it is born not out of love for one's neighbour but out of love for God. This shift diverted attention away from the external publicity of the act of giving and the worldly retribution/reward of the act itself. According to Saint Augustine, the agreement at the core of a friendship (consent) is identified with an agreement with God. Since true love is based on the love of God, there can be no true friendship except in God.[169] Thomas Aquinas addresses friendship in his commentary on the *Nicomachean Ethics* and in the second part of the *Summa*, explaining that friendship is exercised in otherness and differs from justice in that the latter creates equality among unequals, whereas equality is the necessary prerequisite of friendship. Equality is the endpoint of the justice process, while in friendship, it constitutes the starting point. Friendship involves reciprocity, unlike justice. In a mutually defined friendship, three

[166] 'Unanimity, then, seems to be, as it is called, the kind of friendship that prevails in states; for it has to do with what is for the common interest, and with things that have a considerable influence upon life', *The Nicomachean Ethics of Aristotle*, translated by F. H. Peters (London, 1884), Book IX, 6, p. 300.

[167] Op. cit., Book VIII, 9, p. 269. See Gianfrancesco Zanetti, *La nozione di giustizia in Aristotele* (Bologna, 1993).

[168] See Paolo Grossi, *L'ordine giuridico medievale* (Rome and Bari, 1995).

[169] See Luigi Franco Pizzolato, 'L'amicizia in S. Agostino e il 'Laelius' di Cicerone', *Vigiliae Christianae* 28 (1974), pp. 203–15.

different types of exchange can be distinguished: the useful, the pleasant and the virtuous. The first two are based on the benefits that can be derived from mutual companionship; virtuous friendship, on the other hand, is a mutual relationship in which one person loves the true good of the other, i.e., virtue, which, as defined by Aristotle and Thomas, makes both the individual and their actions good. Virtuous friendship, unlike the other two concepts, which endure only as long as usefulness or pleasure last, is as enduring as virtue itself; virtue is inherently permanent. Aquinas recognises the high value of political friendship, which aims to provide citizens with the benefits necessary for a complete and honourable existence. Political utility must be based on justice governed by good laws, implemented by right reason and organised to promote the common good; individual well-being stems from the common good, following the rules of distributive justice. Political friendship requires harmony in its pursuit of the common good; thus, the law is established to create and preserve civil friendship, one that is honest and constant. This type of friendship is not based on an arbitrary or coercive rule but on right reason directed towards the common good.[170]

Medieval philosophical and theological thought paid special attention to these concepts, which were central not only in the development of the definition of the Greco-Roman-derived *politeia* but also in one of the key questions concerning the relationship between human action and the afterlife: the efficacy of deeds for individual salvation. Saint Thomas Aquinas, in *Quaestio* 106 of the *Secunda Secundae*, takes up Seneca's view, according to which the balance between action and reward is essentially based on intentions (*affectus*), and thus the demonstration of gratitude is already inherently compensatory for the received gift. Aquinas argues that the enduring debt that exists between the benefactor and the beneficiary is resolved through the adoption of a 'reverential attitude, like the gratitude that flows from friendship among equals, [which] knows no bounds'.[171] For Thomas, the debt/gratitude of the *humilior* towards the *potentior* is, therefore, *interminabilis*, a moral duty that almost becomes a legal obligation.[172]

170 See Enrico Di Rovasenda, 'L'amicizia nel Commento di Tommaso d'Aquino all'Etica a Nicomaco di Aristotele e nella *Summa Theologiae*', in *Il concetto di amicizia nella storia della cultura europea*, pp. 538–43.

171 'actitud reverencial, como la gratitud que fluye de la amistad entre diseguales, [que] no conoce límites', Hespanha, *La gracia del derecho*, p. 168.

172 On the Aristotelian–Thomistic category of 'friendship' and its revival in early modern times concerning the political dynamics of the court and families of the first rank, see the insights of Paolo Pissavino, 'Il *De officiis* del Della Casa e alcuni raffronti metodologici', in *'Famiglia' del principe e famiglia aristocratica*, ed. Cesare Mozzarelli (Rome, 1989), pp. 51–145.

Building on these doctrines, late medieval and early modern legal thought developed a matter of fundamental importance in political discussions about the feudal system: whether or not the king had an obligation to confirm past donations, privileges and benefits, or conversely, whether the monarch could repossess the assets granted.[173] However, other strands of early modern thought on friendship concerned both civic and political friendship and the distinction between friendship based on utility and self-interest, and 'true' friendship, as described by Erasmus of Rotterdam in his *Adagia*. This concept gained ground in the sixteenth century through the famous works of Jean Bodin and Michel de Montaigne.[174] Both of these areas of reflection fall squarely within the general question of the nature of relationships between individuals and that of relationships between subjects and those in authority, closely correlating with a series of other concepts, such as gift, liberality, concord and peace.

A thorough understanding of a world dominated by the 'culture of hatred' would certainly be impossible without taking into account the fundamental mechanism of social relations within the dominant elites in the traditional European world: the system of alliances between kinship groups, implemented through marital strategies, which inevitably generated conflicts and feuds. In the era of the Italian communes (*Comuni*), these alliances between lineages, forming the basis of a complex and cyclical system of feuds and reconciliations that structured the mechanism of political and social dominance of the *milites* class, changed when there was a substantial polarisation of the alliance system. This shift led to the transition from the consular regime to the *podestà* regime, thereby marking the decline of the predominance of the *militia*.[175] Furthermore, for the *podestàs*, the elimination of conflicts and the achievement of peace and justice were central to their governance programme, as clearly stated in municipal statutes and the formulas of oaths.[176] In the late Middle Ages, through the

[173] In this regard, a perfect correspondence can be observed between the legal production of the sixteenth and seventeenth centuries and the development of moral theology, especially flourishing, as is known, in the Iberian Peninsula. Portuguese jurists resolved the issue in favour of the donees, as the *debitum morale* (moral obligation) was considered to take precedence over the legal obligation, thereby deducing that the donation cannot be revoked, not even on the grounds of ingratitude. See Hespanha, *La gracia del derecho*, p. 173.

[174] See Natalie Zemon Davis, *The Gift in Sixteenth-Century France* (Oxford, 2000), p. 32.

[175] See Maire Vigueur, *Cavalieri e cittadini*, pp. 359–425.

[176] See Enrico Artifoni, 'Boncompagno da Signa, i maestri di retorica e le città comunali nella prima metà del Duecento', in *Il pensiero e l'opera di Boncompagno da Signa*. Atti del convegno nazionale (Signa, 23–4 febbraio 2001), ed. Massimo

instrumentum super pace et concordia drawn up by notaries, private individuals could settle their disputes using concepts, images, gestures and ceremonies deeply rooted in the Christian message.[177]

The omnipresence of hatred, conflict and enmity between lineages or factions constitutes a fundamental feature of the mechanisms of local power management (especially in terms of access to public offices) and of relations between local power and central authority until very recent times, regardless of the profound differences between different eras and institutional structures.[178] Even when peace and civic harmony were elevated to a true ideology of power, as eloquently demonstrated by Ambrogio Lorenzetti's fresco of the *Allegory of Good Government* in the Hall of Peace of the *Palazzo Pubblico* in Siena (1338–9), violence, vendettas and hatred would continue to structure not only social relationships but also the political dynamics of Italian city-states. Without delving into a description of the changes that occurred in this context between the fourteenth and eighteenth centuries, it is worth noting that the implementation of such changes aimed to control violence within communities, reduce the influence of factions, and ensure the circulation of public offices among those entitled to access them.[179] From a theoretical standpoint, the concern of political thinkers of the sixteenth and seventeenth centuries to provide conceptual and doctrinal foundations for sovereign power significantly influenced the conception of political friendship. Understood in social terms rather than individual ones, the common good was identified as the constant reference point for any reflection on friendship.[180] In the *De Regno et Regis Institutione* by Sienese author Francesco Patrizi, Bishop of Gaeta, chapter VIII of the eighth book is dedicated to friendship.

Baldini (Signa, 2002), pp. 23–36; Maria Clara Rossi, 'Polisemia di un concetto: la pace nel basso medioevo. Note di lettura, in La pace fra realtà e utopia', in *Quaderni di Storia Religiosa* (2005), pp. 9–45: p. 15.

[177] On private peace-making in Verona during the fifteenth century, see Vito Rovigo, 'Le paci private: motivazioni religiose nelle fonti veronesi del Quattrocento', in *La pace fra realtà e utopia*, pp. 201–33.

[178] The literature on the issue is extensive. In this context, see Delille, *Le maire et le prieur*, along with its comprehensive bibliography.

[179] Op. cit., p. 358.

[180] Francesco Patrizi, *De Regno et regis institutione libri IX. Ad Alphonsum Aragonium inclitum ac celeberrimum Calabriae Ducem scripti* (Argentinae, Impensis Lazari Zetzeneri, 1594). On Patrizi see Felice Battaglia, 'Francesco Patrizi politico senese del Quattrocento', in *Annuario della Regia Università di Pisa*, 1933/4, but ample insights on this important figure in humanistic culture are in Pedullà, *Machiavelli in tumulto*, *passim*.

Some concepts there assume unquestionable centrality: union (*coniunctio*), harmony, charity.[181]

Patrizi's conceptualisation of friendship is indicative of a still embryonic stage in the theoretical construction of the State, especially when compared to that contained in Jean Bodin's *Six Livres de la République*, which appears to be much more institutional. For Bodin, friendship/amity is an *instrumentum regni*, a fundamental factor of social cohesion, unity and harmony. Bodin introduces the concept of 'harmonic justice': the task of the State (and, therefore, of the sovereign) should be to ensure not only geometric justice (a concept derived from Plato) and geometric–arithmetic justice (a concept derived from Aristotle) but also this particular form of justice, which must be considered the highest and most desirable, in so far as it can reconcile the nobles with the commoners, the powerful with the humble, the rich with the poor, the worthy with the unworthy, the honest with the corrupt, the good with the evil. At the heart of his argument lies a metaphysical principle: beautiful music cannot be played without some dissonance.[182] This theme of equality and inequality among the parties bound by friendship recurs here. For Bodin, the perfect state is a pyramid formed by the projection of a triangle, with its sides made up of Order, Harmony and Justice, while its apex consists of Sovereignty. However, Sovereignty alone is not sufficient for maintaining the State in perfect unity. A further and deeper bond is required; man, variously placed within families and intermediate bodies, becomes the privileged point of observation: '[empires and kingdoms have] no more surer foundation wherupon to rest (next unto God) than the love and amitie of one of them towards another'.[183] For Bodin, friendship is a spiritual quality

[181] See Pierangelo Schiera, 'L'amicizia politica in Francesco Patrizi, senese', in *De amicitia. Scritti dedicati a Arturo Colombo*, ed. Giovanna Angelini and Marina Tesoro (Milan, 2007), pp. 61–72.

[182] See Diana Thermes, 'L'amicizia cosmica e cosmopolitica di Jean Bodin', in *De amicitia. Scritti dedicati a Arturo Colombo*, pp. 73–82: p. 77. See also Sara Miglietti, 'Amitié, harmonie et paix politique chez Aristote et Jean Bodin', *Astérion. Philosophie, histoire des idées, pensée politique* 7 (2010), available onlione at https://journals.openedition.org/asterion/1660

[183] *The six bookes of a commonweale. Written by I. Bodin, a famous Lawyer, and a man of great Experience in matters of State, out of the French and Latin copies, done into English, by Richard Knolles* (London, Impensis G. Bishop, 1606), p. 379, original edition: '[les republics] n'ont point de fondement plus seur après Dieu, que l'amitié & bienveuiallance des uns envers les autres', *Les Six Livres de la Republique par I. Bodin Angevin* (à Lyon, par Iacques du Puy Iuré à l'Université de Paris, 1580), p. 345.

that states receive from families through intermediate bodies. We will have the opportunity to revisit this question.[184]

The ecclesiastical culture of the Counter-Reformation contributed to the gradual detachment of the concept of friendship from the world of associational bonds and solidarity, both vertically and horizontally. It is a process of individualisation of friendship, which found an extraordinary laboratory of reflection in France during the civil wars, as evidenced by the writings of Michel de Montaigne, Pierre Charron, Antoine Hotman and Étienne de la Boétie. Ludovico Zuccolo, active in the court of the Dukes of Urbino but culturally influenced by the Venetian environment, and in particular by the figure of Paolo Sarpi, is the author of *Il Molino, o vero della amicizia scambievole fra' cittadini*, a brief treatise in which the following question takes centre stage, echoing the recurring theme of discordant harmony in the culture of the time: 'Whether friendship is more likely to arise among the similar or the dissimilar is not easy to judge [...] From unequal strings, dissimilar voices and different times, a sweet and gentle harmony is drawn. Humours that are not uniform come together to produce the good balance of human and animal bodies'.[185] Zuccolo provides a clear solution to the dilemma: 'For the unity and tranquillity of citizens, both types of friendship are needed, but the second one is much more necessary. Because the first, by keeping each order in harmony by itself, almost makes more cities within one city. But the second, by uniting them all together, constitutes a single body with diverse members'.[186]

The most important form of friendship, which takes the shape of cooperation (quite different from dominion), is thus that among 'dissimilars'. Cooperation should be achieved through the functional harmonisation of differences of rank. The ideal is the right agreement between the two types of friendship. An important role, in Zuccolo's reasoning, is attributed to the education of the young: the state must instruct its subjects in conviviality,

[184] See below, Chapter 4.

[185] 'Se l'amicitia più nasca tra i simili, o tra i dissimili, non è facile giudicarlo [...] Da corde diseguali, da voci dissimili, e da tempi dispari si trahe dolce, e soave armonia. Humori non uniformi convengono a produrre la buona temperie de' corpi degli huomini e degli animali', Ludovico Zuccolo, 'Il Molino o vero della amicizia scambievole fra' cittadini', in Ludovico Zuccolo, *Dialoghi* (in Venetia, appresso Marco Ginammi, 1625), pp. 174–85: p. 174.

[186] 'Per l'unione, e per la tranquillità de' Cittadini serve l'una, e l'altra amicitia, ma più la seconda assai. Perché quella col tenere concorde ciascun ordine da per sé, vien quasi a fare più Città d'una sola Città; ma questa unendogli tutti insieme, di più membri difformi costituisce un corpo uniforme', op. cit., p. 175.

exchange and friendship, among both similar and dissimilar individuals. In ancient Rome, adds the Faenza scholar, the Spartan ideal underwent a transformation, leading to the concept of *clientela*: 'To this same end, it was introduced in Rome that the poorest and most humble lived under the protection of the nobles and the most powerful: where, as these nobles did good to the former and were compensated by them with service and homage, unity and concord were maintained among all'.[187]

The excellent prince 'dispenses rewards and penalties, distributes severity and kindness according to merits and demerits, and in accordance with the quality of individuals, without showing partiality to anyone, because he desires the good of all and lives securely in the public affection, seeking the public happiness'.[188] However, the city, 'which aims to live free from revolutions and civil wars, and secure from the insults of enemies, needs to keep its citizens united by mutual love. This will not be achieved unless it well preserves the equality among equals and the inequality among the dissimilar with equal retribution of benefits and homage'.[189] How should the prince operate if he wants to prevent discord and turmoil within his State?

> By preventing or diverting competitions and rivalries that can divide each class into factions; by being vigilant that no one excessively surpasses others of their class in wealth or the honour of ranks; by foreseeing that one class does not usurp what belongs to others, such as the nobles taking the benefits of the commoners, and the commoners taking the honours of the nobles, everyone will be satisfied and content with their own status, and the city will remain peaceful and tranquil.[190]

[187] 'A questo medesimo fine fu introdotto in Roma, che i più poveri, e i più vili vivessero sotto la protettione de' più nobili, e più potenti: dove, mentreché questi facevano beneficio a que' primi, e venivano da essi compensati con servitio, e con ossequio, mentenevasi unione e concordia tra tutti', op. cit., p. 177.

[188] 'dispensa i premi, e le pene, comparte il rigore, e la dolcezza, secondo i meriti, e demeriti, e conforme alla qualità delle persone, senza mostrarsi partiale a nissuno, perché vuole il bene di tutti, e vive sicuro della pubblica affettione, procurando egli la pubblica felicità', op. cit., p. 179.

[189] 'la qual pensi a vivere discosto da rivolutioni, e da guerre civili, e sicura dagli insulti de gli inimici, ha bisogno di tenere uniti i suoi Cittadini di scambievole amore: né questo le verrà fatto, mentre non ben conservi la parità tra i pari, e la disuguaglianza tra i dispari con egual retributione di beneficii, e d'ossequio', op. cit., p. 182.

[190] 'Col prevenire, o divertire le concorrenze, e le gare, che possono far dividere ciascun ordine in sette e in fattioni; con lo stare avvertito, che nissuno ecceda di soverchio gli altri del suo ordine in seguito, o in facoltà, o in honorevolezza di gradi; con prevedere, che uno ordine non usurpi quello, ch'è proprio degli altri,

Peace, harmony and unity – necessary conditions for the preservation of political entities – cannot be achieved through an egalitarian levelling of citizens. Similarly, Zuccolo asserts that it is wrong and illusory to think that social cohesion can be strengthened by waging wars against external enemies.[191] But it is interesting to note that even representatives of the Catholic *Ragion di Stato*, faithfully aligned with the dictates of post-Tridentine culture, contributed to the definition of this friendship among dissimilars, which had obvious implications for reciprocity. This contribution undoubtedly leaned towards the verticalisation of social bonds in contrast to a traditional culture that promoted the creation of networks of relationships that moved both towards dependency (vertical) and solidarity among equals (horizontal). The culture of the Counter-Reformation proposed its unique model of friendship, closely connected to the ideal model of society pursued by ecclesiastical hierarchies in collaboration with secular powers.

The *Sacri ragionamenti* by Cardinal Federico Borromeo, published in four volumes between 1632 and 1648, are illuminating from this perspective, especially where they offer insight into the social and even political significance of auricular confession. According to the Archbishop of Milan, the confessor should be considered a genuine public official. Similar to Johannes Eck before him, confession was a powerful tool in Borromeo's view for the Church and public authorities to promote discipline and obedience. However, in comparison to the times of Eck, the term 'discipline' had taken on different nuances of meaning, as it had evolved from the humanistic sense of self-control to a more modern sense, primarily referring to social and political cohesion.[192] Giovanni Botero, in his work *Della Ragion di Stato*, polemicising with Machiavelli, presented the Christian religion as the best and most suitable for the birth and preservation of political entities: 'Among all the laws, there is none more favourable to Princes than the Christian one; according to which not merely the bodies and possessions but even the souls and consciences of [the ruler's] people are subject to him: their affections

come per esempio i nobili gli utili de' plebei, e questi le honorevolezze de' nobili, rimarrà ciascuno soddisfatto e contento dell'esser suo, e la città quieta, e tranquilla', ibid.

[191] This is a very interesting example of how the line of *Ragion di Stato* could conceal, almost Nicodemus-like, traces of libertinism and genuine scepticism, which contact with the intellectual circles of Venice undoubtedly helped to reinforce. See Carlo Ginzburg, 'Una testimonianza inedita su Ludovico Zuccolo', *Rivista Storica Italiana* LXXIX, fasc. IV (1967), pp. 1122–8.

[192] See Wietse De Boer, *The Conquest of the Soul: Confession, Discipline, and Public Order in Counter-Reformation Milan* (Leiden and Boston, 2001), p. 133.

and thoughts are bound, as well as their hands'.[193] Religion is an *instrumentum regni*, and Borromeo, an avid reader of Botero, drew from this conception.[194] In his mature years, the cardinal came to a reevaluation of the relationship between politics and religion, as previously expressed by the ex-Jesuit Botero. In the *Sacri Ragionamenti*, he wrote: 'We must consider not just worthy of the greatest reprehension but foolish those people who, when speaking about religion, speak at the same time about reason of state, whether it be good and laudable, or treacherous and unjust'.[195] The prince, he continued, cannot manipulate religion for his own purposes; he can only use it to pursue the common good, but in any case, such usage represents an illicit intrusion of the secular sphere into spiritual and ecclesiastical affairs. The context is the Milanese jurisdictional controversy, a very tense atmosphere in which the Church showed impatience towards the increasing encroachment of secular authorities.[196] On another occasion, Borromeo launched an attack on the so-called *Ragion di Stato*, even going so far as to call it the 'perverse reason', the origin of tyranny, which arises when the 'true reason', enlightened by God, is defeated by arbitrariness. In these cases, the Church has a duty to resist. Balance is restored when civil power submits to religious power, as happened in the days of Theodosius when Saint Ambrose, Bishop of Milan, imposed public penance on the Roman Emperor for ordering the massacre of thousands of Thessalonians in response to the murder of the local governor. It was only through his repentance that Theodosius could be readmitted to the Holy Roman Church, and this was achieved through the ritual of confession.

Borromeo agreed with Botero that confession was a potent and legitimate political tool, necessary for influencing the consciences of subjects for the purpose of governance. However, for the Cardinal, auricular confession was

[193] 'Tra tutte le leggi non ve n'è più favorevole a Prencipi, che la Cristiana; perché questa sottomette loro, non solamente i corpi, e le facoltà de' sudditi, dove conviene, ma gli animi ancora, e le coscienze; e lega non solamente le mani, ma gli affetti ancora, e i pensieri', cited in op. cit., p. 134.

[194] See Blythe Alice Raviola, *Giovanni Botero. Un profilo fra storia e storiografia* (Milano, 2020).

[195] 'non solo degni di grandissime riprensioni, ma sciocchi ancora estimar si debbono coloro, i quali, della religione parlando, parlano insieme di Ragione di stato, o sia essa buona e laudevole, overo ingannevole ed ingiusta', cited in De Boer, *The Conquest of the Soul*, p. 135.

[196] See Flavio Rurale, 'Clemente VIII, i gesuiti e la controversia giurisdizionale milanese', in *La corte di Roma tra Cinque e Seicento. "Teatro" della politica europea*, ed. Gianvittorio Signorotto and Maria Antonietta Visceglia (Rome, 1998), pp. 323–66.

an alternative to human justice, a superior alternative capable of penetrating territories of human behaviour otherwise inaccessible, exerting a subtle influence over them. Borromeo contended that if the governance of the body politic is based on religion, the concerns of the prince should not only encompass the external aspects of human behaviour; the formation of good subjects must be one of the cornerstones of governance. In this context, the confessor played an absolutely central role. Already in the Roman Catechism of 1566, he appears as 'the prudent and faithful friend, who can help them [the penitents] in word and deed'.[197] However, the political utility of confession did not presuppose a friendly and confidential relationship between confessor and penitent. In contrast to the classical concept of friendship derived from Aristotle, seen as a tool for strengthening social cohesion, Borromeo proposed a more vertical concept characterised by a relationship of subordination. The confessor became a 'friend' of the penitent, but a friend endowed with sovereign power, a power that is not human but divine. Confession thus took shape as a genuine power relationship, as Michel Foucault has aptly pointed out,[198] and the confessor as a 'superior friend' whose role was to exert influence over the intimate sphere of individuals, that of conscience. An authority connected to a public office was essential to support this unique relationship of 'unequal friendship'.

[197] De Boer, *The Conquest of the Soul*, p. 138.

[198] See Michel Foucault, *The History of Sexuality*, vol. 1 (*An Introduction*) (New York, 1980), p. 61ff.

2.

Governing violence and conflict in the Papal States

1. Not just repression: a 'conditional' judicial system for violence prevention

> I, the undersigned Priest, testify and affirm on behalf of Antonio Capodanni, that he forgives and pardons any harm, injury, or offence, whether in deeds or words, received from Nicola Papa. He declares to do this sincerely, from the heart, for the love of God, and for no other reason, in the presence of the undersigned witnesses.
>
> I, Sebastiano Pier Cassini, by commission of this sacred apostolic mandate.
>
> Cross † of the aforementioned Antonio Capodanni, as he does not know how to write.
>
> Cross † of Lorenzo Verroni, who stated he does not know how to write.
>
> Cross † of Filippo Iosa, as he does not know how to write.[1]

In Macerata, on 23 September 1777, a scene that had been part of the daily life of the population for centuries, regardless of social rank, was repeated. A priest, Sebastiano Cassini, took on the role of mediator and guarantor for the granting of forgiveness and the renunciation of pursuing future offences received by Antonio Capodanni in favour of his adversary, Nicola Papa, in the

1 'Io infrascritto Sacerdote attesto, e faccio fede per Antonio Capodanni, che nel commette, com'egli rimette, e condona qualunque danno, ingiuria, ed offesa tanto in fatti che in parole da Nicola Papa ricevuta, e questo si dichiara di farlo di cuore per amor di Dio, e non altrimenti, alla presenza dei sottoscritti testimoni. Io Sebastiano Pier Cassini di commissione q.to s.a m.o pp.a. Croce † del sudetto Antonio Capodanni per non saper scrivere. Croce † di Lorenzo Verroni che disse non saper scrivere. Croce † di Filippo Iosa per non saper scrivere', ASM, *Curia Generale della Marca di Ancona*, vol. 391.

presence of two witnesses, Lorenzo Verroni and Filippo Iosa. All, except for the priest, were illiterate. A few days later, on 28 September, again in Macerata, Luigi, son of Giuliano Pannelli, known as Aurelio, who had previously lodged a complaint against Sebastiano Pagnanelli, Pasquale Scarponi and Giuliano Menchini for a stone thrown directly at his face, also granted forgiveness: 'having considered that being a Christian requires forgiving all injuries', 'for the love of God, he absolves and forgives all the affronts received from them, both in deeds and in words, and willingly consents to have the complaint filed against them withdrawn'. Luigi, too, did not know how to write and for this reason had entrusted his parish priest, Giovanni Antonio Bottoni, to draft and sign the renunciation on his behalf.[2] Unfortunately, we do not know the occupations of any of them, or the reasons that led to their enmity, or whether it was long-standing or merely incidental. They were simple people, dealing with a difficult daily life, full of neighbourhood tensions.

Years later, in November 1791, it would be the outcome of a game of 'fossette'[3] that triggered the quarrel between Domenico Tesori and Francesco Pantanari. Both claimed to have won and demanded that the other honour his gambling debt. According to Tesori's deposition, it was Pantanari who had pelted him with stones and threatened him with an arquebus; according to one of the witnesses, however, it was a full-blown brawl, which escalated from hand-to-hand combat to mutual threats with raised sticks and guns. 'I accuse him', Domenico Tesori had the Chancellor of the General Curia of the Marca write, 'so that Justice may take its course, and he may not be acquitted without my consent'.[4] Consent that would, in all likelihood, soon come in the form of a withdrawal of the complaint, considering the nature of the crime, although no record of this remains.

The examples could multiply infinitely, in their serial repetitiveness. These types of pardon, peace agreement and renunciation remained intact

2 ibid. The peace agreements are collected in a dossier titled *Illustrissimo et Reverendissimo Domino Emerico de Marchionibus Bolognini, Patricio bononiensi. Praefecto Brevium, utriusque Signaturae Referendario S.D.N. Praesuli Domestico, Protonotario Apostolico, & Provinciae Marchiae Gubernatori Generali. Paces.* Emerico Bolognini was appointed Governor of the March of Ancona on 10 December 1753. See *Legati e governatori dello Stato pontificio (1550-1809)*, ed. Christoph Weber (Rome, 1994), p. 118. Other volumes from the same collection gather late eighteenth-century pardons and renunciations (for example, volume 397, which contains bundles of reconciliations signed under the governors Giovanni Francesco Arrigoni, from Mantua, and Angelo Altieri, from Rome).

3 'Fossette' is a game, similar to 'Nine men's morris' (played in ancient Rome), in which marbles were used on a playing board dotted with shallow indented holes.

4 ASM, *Curia Generale della Marca di Ancona*, vol. 397.

until the revolutionary era, the era of legal rationalism and the great reforms of criminal procedure; the era in which Cesare Beccaria wrote about them, as we have seen, as if he were writing about archaic and now unacceptable institutions. Contrary to the usual assumption that peace-making was a remnant of medieval private judicial practices, mostly limited to chivalric honour disputes, and that by the seventeenth century they had already declined in presence and real effectiveness, they were instead deeply rooted in the social, judicial and religious reality of the mid- and late eighteenth century.[5] Peace-making had gradually assumed rather standardised characteristics: first of all, the religious reference, omnipresent and stereotypical, which was supposed to guarantee the absence of coercion in granting the renunciation or reaching an agreement with the opposing party, and which found its complete realisation in the intervention of ecclesiastics, particularly members of the parish clergy; second – and this for more serious crimes – the close connection with the system of petitions, sometimes for the granting of sovereign pardon but much more often to obtain a review or annulment of the sentence by the same court.[6] An ideal type has ended up being constructed on peace-making that has been projected, in its timelessness, onto the past and that, however, has generally not taken into account that system of measures underlying renunciations and peace-making itself, whose purpose was always to push social actors towards that type of solution, strongly desired, if not imposed, by judicial apparatus.

Let us take a leap back nearly two centuries and immerse ourselves in the reality of Montalto di Castro, a territory granted in fief to the Farnese family since 1535. In 1600, Alessandro Barlocci addressed a memorial to the governor of Rome to plead for his intercession with the *Sacra Consulta*, the only institution capable of annulling a *sicurtà* not to harm (*sicurtà de non offendendo*) previously signed and imposed by the local feudal court. Barlocci's son had been killed, and Almonte Santucci, a relative, was accused

5 See Nicole Castan, 'The Arbitration of Disputes under the Ancien Régime', in *Disputes and Settlements. Law and Human Relations in the West*, ed. John Bossy (Cambridge, 1983), pp. 219–60; Rosa Maria Dessì, *Justice et répression en Languedoc à l'époque des Lumières* (Paris, 1980); Rosa Maria Dessì, *Les criminels de Languedoc. Les exigences d'ordre et les voies du ressentiment dans une société prérévolutionnaire (1750–1790)* (Toulouse, 1980).

6 See Natalie Zemon Davis, *Fiction in the Archives. Pardon Tales and Their Tellers in sixteenth-century France* (Stanford, 1987); *Grazia e giustizia. Figure della clemenza fra tardo medioevo ed età contemporanea*, ed. Karl Härter and Cecilia Nubola (Bologna, 2011); *Suppliche e* gravamina. *Politica, amministrazione, giustizia negli Stati italiani e nel Sacro Romano Impero (secc. XIV–XVIII)*, ed. Cecilia Nubola and Andreas Würgler (Bologna, 2002).

of the murder. The suspect was taken prisoner to Rome, but his innocence was soon proven, leading to his release. However, before his release, he was forced to issue a *sicurtà* not to harm against Alessandro Barlocci, the victim's father, which Barlocci then reciprocated. Meanwhile, a peace agreement had been reached between the two; for this reason, Barlocci requested the annulment of the *sicurtà* he had given but wanted to maintain the one that Santucci had signed to secure his release from prison. Evidently, he did not feel safe from a possible vendetta by Santucci, likely because he had been the accuser, despite the peace agreement reached between them. We will have the opportunity to analyse in detail what the *sicurtà* or *cautio de non offendendo* entailed; suffice it here to briefly recall that it was a measure issued by the judge in which the subject committed to not offending, or having others offend, their adversary in the future, under penalty of paying a sum of money, whose amount was defined in advance and guaranteed by the surely. Generally, such sworn promises involved not only the subjects but also their entire families up to the third degree. The subsequent peace agreement did not automatically resolve the *sicurtà*, but it gave the parties the opportunity to request its annulment, thus freeing themselves from the threat of a potential collection of the *sicurtà* by the authorities.

Two years later, in another territory of the Papal States, the governor of Rome asked the chancellor of the Criminal Chamber of Spello whether there was a *sicurtà* up to the third degree between Don Papiniano Angelini and Giovanni Maria Mancino, son of Vincenzo, and whether the two were within the aforementioned degree of kinship.[7] The dean responded meticulously, first confirming the existence of the *sicurtà* document, preserved in the archives of the criminal chancellery,[8] and then transmitting to Rome the verification of the degrees of kinship between the parties involved in the dispute, based on direct testimonies and archival evidence:

> In response, I state that in this Criminal Chamber there is an instrument of *sicurtà* involving Alfio Thonio, amounting to one hundred *scudi*, promising to keep the peace with Vincenzo Mancino and his relatives up to the third degree, and Vincenzo, amounting to two hundred *scudi*, promising for his not so offending the said Alfio and his relatives up to the said third degree, from the year 1599, as Your Most Illustrious Lordship will

7 The documents are signed by the 'Dean of Imola', who evidently held that position in the Criminal Chamber of Spello.

8 A copy of the '*sicurtà*' instrument (*sicurtà* not to harm) given by Vincenzo Mancino and his son Giovanni Maria, promising for his not so offending Papiniano Angelini and his nephew Giulio, is in ASR, *Tribunale Criminale del Governatore, Atti di Cancelleria, Lettere*, vol. 49, ff. 108–11.

see from the certificates of these instruments extracted by the current Chancellor. Moreover, it is presumed that the said Vincenzo and Alfio are cousins of Don Papiniano, born of two full sisters, as attested by two citizens whose testimonies are sent to Your Most Illustrious Lordship, and consequently, the said *sicurtà* includes the said Papiniano and Giovanni Maria. Your Most Illustrious Lordship may judge if this suffices, and if anything else is needed, please command me, and I will promptly execute everything. Finally, I kiss your hands.[9]

Vincenzo Mancino and Don Papiniano were thus direct cousins, sons of two biological sisters, which is why Giovanni Maria, son of Vincenzo, and Don Papiniano were bound by a kinship tie contemplated by the *sicurtà*. Copies of the instruments were sent to Rome, specifying that Giovanni Maria Mancino had not provided *sicurtà* because he was currently elsewhere (in Rome) and that Vincenzo (his father) had not reciprocated the *sicurtà* given by Papiniano Angelini, probably because he claimed the validity of a *sicurtà* already granted in 1599 to Alfio Tonio, his cousin; none the less, due to the refusal to reciprocate the *sicurtà*, the Mancino family was fined 100 *scudi* each, while Papiniano, along with his nephew Giulio, provided another *sicurtà* not to harm at the request of Captain Teodoro Munaldi and Giuseppe Massaro (and son), who feared retaliation. The peace agreement had not been reached, although the authorities strongly desired it: 'it would be good, indeed necessary, to conclude the Peace for the quiet of these citizens, and the preservation of moods'.[10] Statutory legislations usually listed the cases in which it was possible to request a *sicurtà* not to harm. In the statutes of Rome, for example, a distinction was made between offences inflicted 'with arms, and bloodshed, or bone fracture',[11] in which case the *sicurtà* could not be requested against the offenders 'unless first proceedings had been initiated

9 'Per risposta dico che in questa Camera Criminale si trova un instrumento de *sicurtà* fra Alfio Thonio di scudi cento di non offendere Vincenzo Mancino, et suoi fino al terzo grado, et esso Vincenzo di scudi 200 di non offendere detto Alfio, e suoi sino al detto terzo grado di l'anno 1599 come vedrà Vostra Signoria Illustrissima dalla fede di detti Instrumenti cavata dal moderno Cancelliero et perché detto Vincenzo et Alfio me si presuppone che sia filio consubrino di Don Papiniano nati di due sorelle carnali, come fanno fede dui cittadini che si manda a Vostra Signoria Illustrissima e che conseguentemente detta *sicurtà* comprehenda detto Papiniano, e Gio. Maria. Potrà Vostra Signoria Illustrissima giudicar lei se questo li basta, et occorrendo altro si degni comandarmi, che con prontezza esseguirò il tutto et per fine le bacio le mani', op. cit., f. 52.

10 Op. cit., f. 57.

11 'cum armis, & sanguinis effusione, aut fractura ossis', *Statuta Almae Urbis Romae Auctoritate Gregorii Papae XIII, a Senatu Populoq. Rom. Reformata, & Edita*, Romae, in Aedibus Populi Romani, 1590, p. 86.

against him for the effective execution of the penalty by the Court, or the penalty had been voluntarily paid or deposited by him',[12] and those without bloodshed, for which it could instead be requested, 'upon satisfaction of the injury at the discretion of the Peacekeepers, and *sicurtà* [...] provided, and the penalty paid'.[13]

In those same years in Cori, a city a few miles to the south of Rome, a local judge, Fausto Dionisio, had received from the governor of Rome the order to compel Evangelista Pomice, Svetonio Boccabella and Marsilio Marzellone on one side, and Agostino and Antonio Candelli on the other, to provide *sicurtà* not to harm. The order, however, proved difficult to execute. In May 1600, Dionisio replied to the governor that he had not been able to compel Antonio Candelli to provide *sicurtà* because he was no longer in Cori but in Rome, and that Svetonio Boccabella had also fled. For this reason, the judge had ordered the imprisonment of Agostino Marsilio Scariolta and Albanio Meluzza on one side, and Evangelista, father of Ludovico Paolo Pomice, and Marsilio Boccabella, brother of Svetonio, on the other. Marsilio Marzellone had escaped arrest, but the judge was confident of recapturing him within a couple of days. Most importantly, Dionisio assured that the 'prisoners will not be released until they have all provided *sicurtà* in accordance with the order of Your Most Illustrious Lordship'.[14] Once burdened with *sicurtà*, a significant economic weight for the family groups, the machinery of peace negotiations would most likely be set in motion. The *modus operandi* of the apostolic commissioner is clear: in the absence of the directly interested parties, the imprisonment of the closest relatives was carried out without hesitation, a necessary measure to force the subjects to sign the *sicurtà* not to harm.

It goes without saying that the act of forgiveness, renunciation or peace, considered in isolation, tells us little or nothing about the complex, articulated, conflictual dynamics dominated by power relations that were, by definition, asymmetric, which induced social actors to reach an agreement. Elusive and very difficult to reconstruct in its entirety, this dynamic becomes visible to the scholar only through documentary traces that allow the historical reconstruction of only certain parts of it; power was almost always playing its part, and the room for manoeuvre available to the actors was generally very limited, sometimes reduced to zero. The same agreement could be imposed not necessarily by judicial authority but by circumstances,

[12] 'nisi prius contra eum ad effectualem executionem poenae per Curiam processum, vel per ipsum sponte dicta poena soluta, aut deposita fuerit', ibid.

[13] 'facta satisfactione iniuriae arbitrio Paceriorum, & cautione [...] praestita, & poena soluta', ibid.

[14] ASR, *Tribunale Criminale del Governatore, Atti di Cancelleria, Lettere*, vol. 47, f. 356.

which the social actors themselves could use to force their adversaries to sign a peace agreement. In the mid-seventeenth century, in the Sabina of the Borghese fiefs, a violent assault provoked by an unpaid loan resulted in a peace agreement, but it is interesting to understand how this was achieved. Andrea da Vallepietra from Palombara Sabina had gone to Moricone, a nearby village, to claim his credit, but the debtor responded by hitting him on the head with a stone. To make matters worse, the debtor's relatives started beating him, and Andrea was saved from lynching only thanks to the intervention of some villagers. Having to stay in Moricone to get his wounds treated, Andrea was approached by his attackers, who implied that if he wanted the freedom to return to Palombara, he would have to sign a peace agreement with them. Under threat of seizure, Andrea was forced to accept, but once back in Palombara, he turned to the feudal court to file a complaint against his debtor, who was then arrested. At this point, with the aggressor in prison, the auditor could implement the usual strategies to conclude a new peace, this time under the auspices of the feudal court.[15] What difference was there between the seizure and threat carried out by social actors and the imprisonment aimed at obtaining a peace agreement (or possibly *sicurtà*) arranged by judicial authorities? In fact, none. But in adherence to the principle that only public power institutions hold the monopoly on the legitimate use of violence, it was made clear that this monopoly extended to include specific and well-codified instruments of persuasion, not free from aspects of particular harshness. We will soon see how such instruments were borrowed from the civil field, contributing to blurring the line between civil and criminal, but also between persuasion and coercion.

More interesting than the peace itself are the behind-the-scenes dynamics, the succession of contacts and negotiations prompted by specific actions undertaken by the judicial power, to which social actors had to respond – whether by acceptance, negotiation or refusal, the latter exposing them to the sanctions normally prescribed. What lay behind the peace agreements? Can we discern differences between the renunciations of the late eighteenth century and those of the second half of the sixteenth century or the early seventeenth century? There are at least two different factors to consider: the nature of the crime, and the social rank of the actors involved. In the late eighteenth century, it was rare for a case of homicide to be resolved through a renunciation or peace. It almost always involved minor crimes: insults, public affronts, threats, beatings, assaults without bloodshed, offences generally provoked by occasional altercations or small civil disputes (encroachments, unpaid debts, neighbourhood quarrels, or

[15] The episode, which occurred in 1656, is reported by Bertrand Forclaz, *La famille Borghese et ses fiefs. L'autorité négociée dans l'État pontifical d'Ancien Régime* (Rome, 2006), p. 151.

contested testamentary successions). What likely changed the most, however, was the attitude of public authorities towards the aristocrats' claim not only to manage their own conflicts autonomously – through feuds, vendettas and reconciliations – away from the interference of the courts but also to govern the conflicts of their subjects, who were inclined to turn first to their 'patrons' to settle disputes long before approaching the dangerous and especially expensive official justice system.

If non-factional conflicts were mostly horizontal, meaning they involved individuals of equal social status, their resolution was usually the prerogative of a higher judgement instance – even if of an arbitrary type. Between the late seventeenth and early eighteenth centuries, what the political authority began to tolerate less and less was the arrogance with which aristocrats and citizens forced the humble, especially those from the countryside, to accept certain compromise solutions decided at their discretion. In the collective imagination and the evaluation of the papal power, these were real 'private courts': to avoid the delays and exorbitant costs of public justice, or perhaps because they were forced by the patrons, to resolve a dispute, one would go to the lord's palace and rely on his decision, which was only ostensibly arbitrary and negotiable. In Bologna during that period, such practices were called 'filata' or '*concussione*', terms indicating the act of forcing someone, through violence or threats, to act against their will. Prohibited by several general edicts, starting with that of Cardinal Benedetto Giustiniani in 1610, these 'overbearing actions' were tolerated at least until the early eighteenth century, when the legates decided to turn the page, no longer allowing such a significant portion of their jurisdiction to be eroded by dubious characters – of violent, quarrelsome, arrogant temperament – who effectively controlled other people's assets and decided people's fates, even to the point of forcing girls into marriage and imposing peace agreements.[16] In the 1680s, a memorial was sent to Rome, signed by several heads of Bolognese families, denouncing the unsustainability of a situation characterised by knights who 'hold courts in their own homes'[17] and 'want things by force'.[18]

[16] See Giancarlo Angelozzi and Cesarina Casanova, *La giustizia criminale a Bologna nel XVIII secolo e le riforme di Benedetto XIV* (Bologna, 2010), pp. 43–51. If the breaking of a marriage promise was often the cause of conflict between families, the celebration of intermarriages between warring families was equally often the main instrument of reconciliation, based on the maxim 'there is no true friendship without kinship'. However, the type of sources consulted for this research did not allow for detailing the matrimonial agreements contained in the peace agreements signed in the Papal States during the period under examination.

[17] 'fanno tribunali in casa sua', cited in op. cit., p.45.

[18] 'vogliono le cose per forza', cited in ibid.

In 1685, in his correspondence with Rome, the legate Antonio Pignatelli reported the deplorable conduct of the Marquis Felice Montecuccoli, a member of the Bolognese senatorial aristocracy, who 'had reached such a level of audacity and arrogance that he deemed it permissible to hold what amounted to an open tribunal, forcibly arranging marriages, settling debts, imposing peace, and other similar extortions'. In December 1686, however, the prosecutor Marco Marabini filed a complaint against Senator Carlo Rodolfo Fantuzzi for attempting to have him killed by one of his servants. Previously, Fantuzzi had repeatedly invited Marabini to his palace to settle a dispute between an apprentice he sponsored and an apothecary who had sought the good offices of the influential senator, but the former had always refused the invitation because he feared Fantuzzi's deceitful behaviour. Following Marabini's complaint, the *Torrone* indicted Fantuzzi for attempted murder and 'filata', with every intention of applying the severity that was becoming the cornerstone of Legate Pignatelli's government programme. The sentence was intended to be exemplary: capital punishment, confiscation of property and deprivation of senatorial dignity. The senators' reaction in defence of a member of their class was swift, initiating the usual *j'accuse* against the ministers of the *Torrone* and the legate, whom they accused of granting clemency for serious crimes too easily just to raise funds, and the equally customary pressure on influential figures in the Roman curia. Fantuzzi, having become a fugitive, never returned to Bologna,[19] but in July

[19] 'Il senatore Carlo Rodolfo Santuzzi fu gonfaloniere per la seconda volta nel 3° bimestre 1680 [...]. Al principio dell'ottobre 1685 il senatore Fantuzzi entrò in quistione col procuratore Marabini e, riscaldandosi, lo caricò di minaccie e d'improperii. L'indomani il medesimo procuratore se ne querelò ed ottenne l'esilio di lui dalla legazione. Il Fantuzzi deliberò allora di farne vendetta ed inviò per mandatari un suo servo ed un suo contadino di nome Cavallina. Questi aspettarono il procuratore Marabini al suo ritorno dalla predica dei Servi e mentre egli voleva entrare in casa sua nella Seliciata di Strada Maggiore il contadino gli sparò contro un'archibugiata, ma non lo colpì. Il servo allora si avventò contro il Marabini e lo ferì leggermente con un coltello. Accorsi altri in aiuto, l'attentato andò a vuoto; ma si processò il Fantuzzi in contumacia. Lì 20 dicembre 1685 fu gridato il bando penale in tutta la legazione, con cui fu condannato l'esule Fantuzzi al taglio della testa, alla confisca dei beni e alla privazione del senatorato. Egli si recò fuggiasco a Venezia; ma anche colà si rese intollerabile pel suo naturale inquieto ed agitatore e ne fu bandito. Finalmente morì contumace alla Polesella nella notte del sabato venendo alla domenica 18 ottobre 1698' ('Senator Carlo Rodolfo Santuzzi was gonfaloniere for the second time in the 3rd bimester of 1680 [...]. At the beginning of October 1685, Senator Fantuzzi had a dispute with Prosecutor Marabini and, in the heat of the moment, loaded him with threats and insults. The next day, the same prosecutor filed a complaint and obtained his exile from the

1687 Marabini decided to grant peace to Fantuzzi, which was followed by the annulment of the decrees issued against his relatives. Compared to a century earlier, the atmosphere was changing; Rome was increasingly less willing to accede to the continuous protests of the Bolognese Senate regarding alleged violations of privileges, whether they were exemptions from fines and confiscations or autonomy in settling conflicts through compositions and adjusted peace agreements.

What immediately stands out is the dual nature of the system: citizens and aristocrats took it upon themselves to settle the conflicts of their subordinates and affiliates, but this activity could in turn provoke quarrels, disagreements and violent clashes among themselves, which the Tribunal of the *Torrone* would have to address. In any case – as Legate Pignatelli wrote with reference to Marquis Montecuccoli – these peace agreements could indeed be considered, along with forced marriages and debt settlements, as extortion, in the sense of 'an act aimed at coercing a person's free will or preventing them from seeking justice'[20] – an extraordinary and absolutely realistic consideration, which we must apply not only to the peace agreements imposed by the 'private tribunals' of the nobles, according to the legate's perspective, but also (as paradoxical as it may seem) to those obtained by the supreme judicial court of Bologna. If the lords imposed peace agreements by preventing their subordinates from seeking justice, the judiciary did not behave differently when it imprisoned or conducted the hated deployments of soldiers and constables to seize the properties of those involved in criminal acts to force them to sign a *sicurtà* not to harm.[21] By combating the 'filata', the official justice system was merely

legation. Fantuzzi then decided to take revenge and sent his servant and a farmer named Cavallina as his agents. These men waited for Prosecutor Marabini to return from the preaching of the Servi, and while he was about to enter his house on the Seliciata di Strada Maggiore, the farmer fired a shot from an arquebus at him but missed. The servant then attacked Marabini and slightly wounded him with a knife. Others rushed to his aid, and the attempt failed; however, Fantuzzi was tried in absentia. On 20 December 1685, a criminal edict was proclaimed throughout the legation, condemning the exiled Fantuzzi to beheading, confiscation of his property and deprivation of his senatorial status. He fled to Venice; but even there, his naturally restless and agitating nature made him intolerable, and he was banished from there as well. He finally died in absentia in Polesella on the night of Saturday to Sunday, 18 October, 1698'), Giuseppe di Giovanni Battista Guidicini, *I Riformatori dello stato di libertà della città di Bologna dal 1394 al 1797* (Bologna, 1876), pp. 36–7.

20 Angelozzi and Casanova, *La giustizia criminale a Bologna*, p. 44, n. 45.

21 'L'invio *ad standum* [...] consisteva nell'inviare un numero variabile di sbirri o soldati, a seconda della ricchezza e pericolosità dell'individuo colpito dalla misura,

attempting to reclaim a portion of jurisdiction that rightfully belonged to it and that the lords had effectively usurped, but it was certainly not in a position to contest the method used, as it was still a form of coercion.

Yet the outcome of these dynamics was always identical to itself: peace writings modelled on a language that had to convey freedom, spontaneity, a desire to conform to the Christian dictate of forgiveness, and living in friendship and harmony; the exact opposite of the language of hatred. In these writings, it is almost invariably stated that only for the love of God, out of devotion to the Virgin or a saint, without any other aim and only out of a desire to live as a Christian, the complainant forgave the injury, renounced legal actions, agreed to a sincere peace and also promised not to harm or have their adversary harmed. This does not necessarily mean that all peace agreements were the result of coercion, and the writings or ceremonies mere stage fiction, but it certainly makes us understand that the rule was quite different from what appears at first glance. And the rule tells us that the outcome of a significant and quite substantial number of judicial proceedings was constituted by peace. As for the Tribunal of the Governor of Rome, it is also possible to proceed with a statistical sampling thanks to the documentary series of the Registrations of Acts. We know, for example, that between the months of February and October 1576, out of about 350 outcomes other than condemnation, ninety-one were peace agreements, that is, about 25% of the cases. Condemnations remained the outcome that involved the largest number of people, as in the same period there were 145 proceedings noted in the section of condemnations, and we know that the number of people involved in those proceedings was greater than 700.[22] However, the Registrations of Acts do not intercept either the peace agreements signed after the condemnation for the purpose of obtaining a revision or an acquittal, nor those that the apostolic commissioners sent to various outlying areas of the territory subject to the governor's jurisdiction *de facto* imposed after appropriate pressures, especially of an economic nature, and outside of regular processes. For this reason, the source cannot provide us with an exact picture of the capacity of this judiciary to widely apply legal instruments based on obligations and oaths.

---

a soggiornare sui beni o in casa di quest'ultimo e a sue spese, fino a che non avesse obbedito agli ordini del legato' ('The deployment *ad standum* consisted of sending a variable number of constables or soldiers, depending on the wealth and danger posed by the individual subjected to the measure, to stay on their property or in their house at their expense until they complied with the legate's orders'), Giancarlo Angelozzi and Cesarina Casanova, *La giustizia criminale in una città di antico regime. Il tribunale del Torrone di Bologna (secc. XVI–XVII)* (Bologna, 2008), p. 261, n. 187.

[22] ASR, *Tribunale Criminale del Governatore, Registrazioni di Atti*, vols 67–8.

Peace continued to be the main condition for obtaining sovereign pardon even in cases of capital banishment, subject to the release of *sicurtà* and following a settlement. Francesco Guicciardini provides us with a testimony related to his mandate as President of Romagna, a land particularly plagued by feuds amongst the nobility. Once several members of the Rasponi family were banished from those lands, on 21 August 1525, Guicciardini wrote from Faenza to Cesare Colombo, his agent in Rome:

> To the Rasponi, although they have not yet provided *sicurtà*, the supplication was signed, not only concerning their property but also for capital penalties, provided that peace is achieved; that is, when they make peace, they will be assured of grace without further expedition; and when they are cleared by the Treasurers, they will come to confirm it to Our Lord. It seemed to me that this was the intention of His Holiness when he said he wanted it to be expedited in such a way that they would be assured that once peace was made, no further settlement would be needed for grace; and this assurance could not be obtained in any other way, especially since it is uncertain when they will achieve peace, nor did they otherwise agree: we are now dealing with those from Forlì, and their matter will be resolved for two thousand ducats.[23]

In this circumstance, the governor announced his intention, according to his understanding of the pope's will, to pardon the Rasponi, who were capital exiles, on the condition that they make peace with their enemies and pay a settlement of two thousand ducats, even though they had not previously signed any *sicurtà*. Peace with the victim or the victim's relatives could nullify even capital sentences or life imprisonment, and this continued to be the case for a long time and at all levels of jurisdiction. Indeed, it is true that almost a century and a half later in Montefortino, now modern Artena, a possession of the Borghese family, one of the participants in a shootout between rival gangs on Shrove Tuesday in 1655, which left several wounded

[23] 'A' Rasponi, benché ancora non hanno dato *sicurtà*, si segnò la supplicazione, non solo della roba ma etiam delle pene capitali, habita pace; cioè che quando aranno le paci, restino sicuri della grazia sanza nuova espedizione; e loro quando saranno espediti da' Tesorieri, verranno a fare confirmarla a Nostro Signore. Mi parse così fussi la intenzione di Sua Santità, quando vi disse voleva si espedissi in modo che restassino sicuri, che fatte le paci non li bisognassi altra composizione per la grazia; e questa *sicurtà* non si poteva avere per altro modo, sendo massime incerti a che tempo aranno le paci, né loro concordavano altrimenti: siamo ora alle mani con questi di Furlì, e si risolverà la cosa loro in due mila ducati', *Opere inedite di Francesco Guicciardini illustrate da Giuseppe Canestrini e pubblicate per cura dei conti Piero e Luigi Guicciardini*, vol. VIII (Firenze, presso M. Cellini e Comp., 1866), p. 306.

and one dead, was captured, sentenced to life imprisonment, but then pardoned after making peace with the victim's family and paying a settlement of twenty-five *scudi*.[24]

Starting from the mid-sixteenth century, coinciding with the first systematic attempts at centralising and increasing institutional powers, the governance of violence became a top concern for the popes.[25] Specific socio-cultural and economic structures could be at the root of a dynamic of violence, which was very difficult to confront. This is the case of the legations north of Rome, characterised by endemic factional conflicts, and also of the southern provinces, Campagna and Marittima, deeply marked by feudal structure. Additionally, there was an intensification of the phenomenon of banditry, certainly not new but reaching such proportions that it became the real test for the governance and territorial control capabilities of the popes from Paul IV to Clement VIII. It was precisely with the generalisation of the use of banishment and exile as punishments for the most serious crimes that the punctual episodes of violence in rural and mountainous areas, as well as in feudal territories, against peasants and travellers, transformed into the formation of numerous armed bands. These bands saw the active participation of noble elements previously condemned to exile for various types of violence and insubordination. This occurred in conjunction with the establishment of the new post-Tridentine climate, and the measures adopted by the popes were consequently increasingly marked by the concern to obtain from the population, and particularly from the restless and rebellious nobility, the morality and discipline of customs and individual behaviours that constituted the cultural ideal of the Counter-Reformation.[26]

In such a context, what role was assigned to arbitral justice, negotiations and peace as instruments for resolving interpersonal conflicts? Since the second half of the fifteenth century, the popes' 'solution' was to toughen the penalties against offenders and their accomplices, but – as mentioned earlier – the harshness of the law ended up exacerbating the phenomenon, given that the penalty often resorted to was banishment from the territory where the crime had been committed. Faced with the objective increase in crime, on

[24] The episode is reported in Forclaz, *La famille Borghese et ses fiefs*, pp. 154–6.

[25] See in general Mario Caravale, Alberto Caracciolo, *Lo Stato pontificio. Da Martino V a Pio IX*, 'Storia d'Italia' directed by Giuseppe Galasso, vol. XIV (Turin, 1991). On the Pontificate of Sistus V, particularly, see Michele Di Sivo, 'Le costituzioni e i bandi di Sisto V: l'amministrazione della giustizia tra accentramento e crisi dello Stato pontificio', *Archivi per la Storia* IV (1991), pp. 137–48.

[26] See Irene Polverini Fosi, *La società violenta. Il banditismo dello Stato pontificio nella seconda metà del Cinquecento* (Rome, 1985).

28 January 1461, Pope Pius II Piccolomini issued a bull *Contra homicidas* that established that 'all those who have been condemned for the crime of homicide, may not return to the city or district at any time, or remain in them or either of them, even having made peace with the heirs or relatives or children of the deceased'.[27] Moreover, the causes of homicide could no longer be appealed, and perpetual interdiction from any public office was introduced for those affected by the ban. But what did it mean exactly that the condemned could not return to their cities and towns 'even having made peace with the heirs or relatives or children of the deceased'?

Since the twelfth century, the statutes of Italian communes had provided for the penalty of banishment for those who had committed crimes harmful to public peace, foremost among them homicide, but with the important exception of those who had obtained peace from the victim's family.[28] It has been hypothesised that, with this bull, Pius II intended to 'nullify the custom of pacification between the offender and the victim's family, a practice that until then had allowed, especially in rural society, a "private" composition of discord, a resumption of broken relationships for the spirit of vendetta'.[29] But a comprehensive look at both the papal legislative production issued throughout the following century and the concrete actions of legates, commissioners and presidents reveals a different reality, as the case of Guicciardini previously mentioned demonstrates. First of all, because since the fourteenth century legal doctrine had established that perpetual banishment, unlike ordinary banishment, could not be revoked through peace with the offended party, as in the latter case the injured party was considered the commune, not the personal victim of the crime.[30] Moreover, in that same papal legislation, remissions and peace agreements were continuously referenced and carefully regulated, occupying a significant space in the overall normative framework. The refusal to make peace, as well as the criminal offence of *fractio pacis*, gradually became configured as increasingly serious crimes, on a par with the *crimen laesae maiestatis*, as evidenced, for example, by the bull of Leo X *Contra homicidas, bannitos & c. Communitates et Dominos eos non capientes, aut auxiliantes faventes & receptantes*, from February

[27] 'omnes illi qui pro delicto homicidii fuerint condemnati, non possint ad civitatem seu districtum huiusmodi quocumque tempore redire, seu in eis vel eorum altero moram trahere, etiam habita pace ab haeredibus vel consanguineis seu filiis ipsius occisi', cited in op. cit., p. 34.

[28] See Giuliano Milani, *L'esclusione dal comune. Conflitti e bandi politici a Bologna e in altre città italiane tra XII e XIV secolo* (Rome, 2003), p. 4.

[29] Polverini Fosi, *La società violenta*, p. 35.

[30] See Milani, *L'esclusione dal comune*, p. 100.

1519, addressed to 'homicides, banished persons, outlaws, rebels, or those condemned for any capital crime, as well as troublemakers, those refusing to make peace, violators of truces or ceasefires, and peacebreakers'.[31] The equating of *ruptura pacis* with capital crimes was regularly reaffirmed in the provisions of the following decades, but it was with the bull of Pius IV on 12 June 1562 that the motivations behind such a tightening were definitively made explicit.

Breaking a peace agreement meant openly defying God, before whom one had sworn to abandon vengeance. However, reality showed – according to the bull – that man's obstinacy had reached the point of using that very oath as a tool of deception: believing themselves protected by peace, people were more easily exposed to indirect vendettas; convinced that it would be easier to strike their adversary during a period of peace or truce, malicious individuals might be driven to sign a peace agreement to then have greater ease of action. For this reason – the bull continued – if men had begun no longer to fear divine judgement, they should start to fear the severity of the law:

> And moreover, since the obstinacy of men has reached such a point that those who plan to commit homicide or some other misdeed first seek to deceive those they consider enemies under the pretext of truce or peace, thereby making the commission of the crime easier later, it is therefore expedient that those whom the fear of God does not restrain should be deterred and controlled by the severity of punishments, to ensure the tranquillity of the people and to suppress the criminal daring of murderers and troublemakers.[32]

31 'homicidas, bannitos, exititios, rebelles, aut pro quocunque crimine capitali poena damnatos, necnon brigosos, pacem facere recusantes, treguarum sive induciarum violatores, seu fractores', *Bullarum privilegiorum ac diplomatum Romanorum Pontificum amplissima collectio cui accessere Pontificum omnium Vitae, Notae, & Indices opportuni. Opera et studio Caroli Cocquelines,* tomus tertius, par tertia (ab Eugenio IV ad Leonem X, scilicet ab anno 1431 ad 1521), (Romae, typis et sumptibus Hieronymi Mainardi, 1743), pp. 472–3.

32 'Et insuper quoniam eo hominum protervitas devenit, ut hi, qui homicidium vel maleficium aliquod committere deliberarunt, prius quaerant eos, quos pro hostibus habent, treguae vel pacis praetextu assecurando, decipere, quo facilior postea delicti perpetratio reddatur, expeditque propterea, ut quos Dei timor non retinet, poenarum rigor deterrendo coerceat, populorum quieti consulere et flagitiosos sicariorum ac scandalosorum ausus deprimere', 'De homicidis aliisque reis poenae capitalis vel sanguinis, etiam non condemnatis vel in contumaciam condemnatis, et infra sex menses non sponte se in carceribus constitutis non audiendis, appellationibusque condemnatorum in poenam fisco et Camerae Apostolicae applicatam non admittendis, nisi facto deposito. Ac de poenis fractae pacis vel treguae, et allegatione novae causae vel minoritatis, et legitimae filiorum confiscatione', in

Breaking a peace or a truce meant simultaneously betraying both God and the established power; it meant reneging on the pact of civil coexistence based on maintaining order and tranquillity – but, as the papal bulls made clear, only if the peace had been signed under the aegis of the central power. There were too many uncertainties in the peace agreements concluded within communities, too many circumstances that could undermine the validity and certainty of the bond established by the agreement, too many variables to consider, as well as too frequent inaccuracies or errors made by negligent notaries ('notariorum imperitia'), making it difficult to correctly interpret the writing and thus its actual observance. This was particularly the case – as the bull noted – with the *sicurtà* not to harm, through which the parties 'promise not only on their own behalf but also on behalf of their associates that they will not offend nor cause offence',[33] but in whose instruments drafted by the notary 'distorting the sense and intention, they happen to write that the parties promise for his not so offending by themselves and others, where it should have been written "on behalf of themselves and others"'.[34] This was a significant difference ('on behalf of' versus 'in favour of'), capable of causing confusion in cases of offences inflicted on relatives included in the *sicurtà* and making life easier for its violators.

What was thus being affirmed was the certainty of the law, the certainty of the penalty, the centralisation of the powers of pardon, but also the centralisation of the economic benefits of the *sicurtà* not to harm 'system'. This is because it was finally established that the amounts corresponding to the *sicurtà* had to be paid to the Apostolic Chamber and not to the coffers of the communities. This was followed by a careful treatment of the collection systems for the *sicurtà*, even in the frequent cases of contumacy of the offender, the *sicurtà* and their relatives. The prohibition of the return of criminals to the places of residence of the victim's relatives – established by papal power in the time of Pius II – even if peace had been obtained, must be understood from this precise perspective. It should be noted that a century after Pope Piccolomini, Pius IV reversed the provision, stipulating as follows: 'We none the less decree and order perpetually that he must be exiled from the place

---

Bullarum, diplomatum et privilegiorum sanctorum romanorum pontificum taurinensis edito, locupletior facta collectione novissima plurium brevium epistolarum decretorum actor umque S. Sedis a S. Leone Magno usque ad praesens …, vol. VII (Augustae Taurinorum, Seb. Franco et Henrico Dalmazzo editoribus, 1862), p. 191.

33 'promittunt non solum pro seipsis, sed etiam pro aliis eorum coniunctis, quod non offendent neque offendi facient', ibid.

34 'sensum et intentionem pervertente, contingit eos scribere quod partes promittunt non offendere per se et alios, ubi scriptum oportuisse pro se et aliis', ibid.

where the heirs of the deceased reside until he has obtained peace from them, and that he cannot return to that place otherwise, except by having obtained peace from them',[35] despite the fact that only the previous year, in 1561, the same Pope Medici had reaffirmed the prohibition 'even having obtained peace from the heirs'.[36] In any case, it was not about completely disempowering or delegitimising the practices of negotiation and pacification, but rather asserting once and for all the superiority of the composition systems managed by the centre over those controlled by communities and aristocratic elites. The pope intended in this way to affirm his role as the supreme guarantor of peace and justice and to establish a centrally controlled system based on the mechanism of exclusion/reintegration capable of acting as a deterrent to those involved in bloody feuds. Only in this way would the breaking of peace or truce certainly entail grave consequences.

The tightening of criminal legislation did not automatically mean the weakening of the system of compositions, peace agreements and mechanisms of pardon. Quite the opposite. In fact, the tightening resulted in a reorganisation of the system and its valorisation, perceptible in the unprecedented criminalisation of *fractio pacis*. Regarding peace agreements in particular, it was essentially a process of substitution: not the central power at the expense of the spontaneity of egalitarian composition systems, considered typical of community justice, but the central power at the expense of equally asymmetrical and coercive relationships within the community or in relations between rural communities and urban centres. As for the powers of grace, one cannot help but notice a certain parallelism between the measures adopted starting around 1560 in combating the scourge of banditry and the instruments deployed in the fight against the spread of heretical ideas, which centred on the promise of mercy and absolution, provided that those who confessed – both for themselves and any accomplices – of having committed the crime of heresy did so voluntarily before the inquisitor. During the pontificate of Paul IV Carafa, this system extended to the use of confessors, a dense network intended to intercept heretical dissent *in foro conscientiae* and direct it towards external justice, always based on the promise of absolution.[37]

35 'Eum nihilominus a loco, in quo haeredes occisi commorantur, quousque ab illis pacem obtinuerit, exulare debere, neque ad eum locum aliter, nisi pace ab illis habita, remitti posse, perpetuo statuimus et ordinamus', op. cit., vol. VII (1862), p. 188.

36 'etiam habita pace ab haeredibus', op. cit., p. 103.

37 There has been a wide and lively historiographical debate on the connection between the internal forum (sacramental and otherwise) and the external forum, with positions that are often diametrically opposed, which cannot be fully addressed here due to space constraints. It is sufficient to mention the volume

Just as the spread of the 'heretical plague' required agile and effective instruments, so too did the intensification of violent episodes and the rise of armed gangs prompt the popes to abandon the delays of ordinary criminal procedure in favour of publishing edicts aimed at targeting the supporters and collaborators of bandits. Alternatively, they adopted the policy of bounties, attempting to break the bonds of solidarity and complicity with bandit groups within communities in exchange for monetary rewards. It was no longer the time for the 'cavillationes' (quibbles) and 'disputationum subtilitates' (subtleties of disputes) of ordinary procedure. In 1554, Julius III, through a bull, made it clear that it was his will that,

> in any process against such cited persons, it should proceed summarily, simply and plainly, without clamour and the form of judgement, with no regard for the terms, which are called substantial in the Curia, nor any other judicial observance intervening, but only the truth of the fact and the contravention of the aforementioned letters being inspected.[38]

Based on the same underlying philosophy, a few years later, still addressing the fight against banditry, Gregory XIII and then Sixtus V decided to complement temporal justice with the instrument of spiritual justice, offering the absolution from censures for those who confessed to a priest that they had been accomplices or supporters of bandits. This offence – like the *ruptura pacis* – was elevated to the rank of reserved cases, fully qualifying as *crimen laesae maiestatis*/heresy.[39] The absolution would not be limited to the internal forum but

---

that undoubtedly initiated the discussion, that is Adriano Prosperi, *Tribunali della coscienza. Inquisitori, confessori, missionari* (Turin, 1996), and the main subsequent contributions, which vary in approach and purpose: Giovanni Romeo, *Ricerche su confessione dei peccati e inquisizione nell'Italia del Cinquecento* (Reggio Calabria, 1997); Paolo Prodi, *Una storia della giustizia. Dal pluralismo dei fori al moderno dualismo tra coscienza e diritto* (Bologna, 2000); Elena Brambilla, *Alle origini del sant'Uffizio. Penitenza, confessione e giustizia spirituale dal medioevo al XVI secolo* (Bologna, 2000).

[38] 'in quilibet processu contra sic citatos faciendo procedatur *summarie, simpliciter, & de plano sine strepitu, & figura judicii*, nulla terminorum, qui in Curia substantiales appellentur, aut alias judiciaria observatione interveniente, sed sola facti, & contraventionis literarum praedictarum veritate inspecta', 'Contra homicidas, Brigosos, Duellantes, & alia gravia crimina patrantes, Bannitosque, & eorum complices, receptatores, & fautores', in *Bullarum privilegiorum ac diplomatum*, tomus quartus, pars prima (ab Hadriano VI ad Paulum IV, scilicet ab Anno 1521 ad 1599) (Romae, typis et sumptibus Hieronymi Mainardi, 1745), p. 313, italics mine.

[39] 'I nemici dell'ordine pubblico sono stigmatizzati con l'appellativo di eretici e "Lutherani" che da solo, quest'ultimo, sintetizzava ed evocava paurosi ricordi,

would have the effect of annulling any ongoing judicial proceedings, without the need for a monetary settlement. Anyone who had come into contact with bandits, providing them with assistance, food, money, clothes, weapons or ammunition, and who sincerely repented for having done so, even if already charged or under trial for those same crimes, and even if a fugitive, could spontaneously present themselves, or through a proxy, within six months of the publication of the edict, to an authorised confessor to obtain complete remission, avoiding both the infamy of condemnation and the confiscation of goods. An extraordinary period of grace, useful for breaking bonds of solidarity and obtaining information useful for the capture of bandits. However, the measures did not produce the desired effects.

There is a direct link between the extraordinary resort to periods of grace and valorisation, in the name of centralisation, of the system based on *sicurtà* and peace agreements, which will be detailed in the following pages. It was not so much an attempt at 'privatising' the adopted solutions, an unequivocal sign of the incompleteness of the modernisation coherent process of the judicial and government structures of the Papal States,[40] but rather a policy aimed at consciously mixing the temporal and spiritual planes, intervening swiftly in the search for the guilty 'sine strepitu, et figura judicii' ('without clamour and the form of judgment'), and impacting the kinship and community networks of both criminals and potential criminals, to the extent that they were fully involved in conflict dynamics, as well as their supporters, breaking solidarities and complicities, creating bonds, constraints and burdens, with a perspective more of prevention than repression.

secondo le metafore ed i simboli già inaugurati durante il pontificato di Sisto V' ('The enemies of public order are stigmatised with the appellation of heretics and "Lutherans", the latter alone synthesising and evoking fearful memories, according to the metaphors and symbols already inaugurated during the pontificate of Sixtus V'), Polverini Fosi, *La società violenta*, p. 202. These are the briefs proclaiming the periods of grace: *Breve di Gregorio XIII a favore di cardinali deputati ad assolvere e comporre in materia di banditi*, AAV, Armadio V, t. 44, n. 242, f. 33; *Indulto di Gregorio XIII nel quale si dà per un anno facoltà alli confessori di poter assolvere dalle censure quelli che haveranno conversato con banditi*, op. cit., Armadio V misc., t. X, n. 208, f. 101 (both cited in Polverini Fosi, *La società violenta*, p. 147, n. 24); *S.D.N. Sixti papae V absolutio et gratia generalis iis, qui aut cum bannitis versati fuerint, aut iisdem auxilium praestiterint concessa* (Romae, apud haeredes Antonij Bladij Impressores Camerales, 1586).

[40] Thesis supported in Polverini Fosi, *La società violenta*, p. 203 and *passim*.

2. Prevention of crime and *potestas oeconomica*: imposing *sicurtà* 'to avoid future evils'

The process of homogenisation and centralisation of the legal system of the Papal States, especially from the perspective of the articulation between canon law and civil law, has been – well known – one of the main pillars of Bolognese historian Paolo Prodi's successful (and much-debated) thesis on the formation and consolidation of the papal monarchy between the fifteenth and seventeenth centuries. Also well known is the phase delineation of the phenomenon identified by Prodi: a first phase, beginning in the second half of the fifteenth century, where the dual nature of papal power facilitated the path towards absolutism and centralism at the expense of local municipal powers and magistrates (and even episcopal tribunals), followed by a second phase in the late seventeenth century, witnessing a reverse degenerative process that, already starting from the Counter-Reformation, saw the prevalence of ecclesiastical privileges, supported by some Roman congregations.[41] This is not the place for a detailed examination of Prodi's theses on justice, anticipated by *Il sovrano pontefice* of 1982 and culminating in his extensive work specifically dedicated to this theme.[42] However, it is useful to recall these 'strong' theses to verify, from the very specific angle of interpersonal conflict resolution systems, the validity of the many critical observations that have been raised in recent years against the thesis of the presumed precocity, specificity and ultimately greater completeness of the process of constructing modern statehood by the Roman popes between the Renaissance and the Counter-Reformation compared to other peninsular and non-peninsular contexts.

The very extension of the Constitutions of Cardinal Egidio Albornoz for the governance of the March of Ancona to the entire structure of the Papal States (bull of Sixtus IV *Etsi de cunctorum* of 30 May 1478, later confirmed by Paul III and strengthened by Sixtus V) was not without strong resistance and difficulties of all kind. For example, in the case of the Bologna legation, which never ceased to send to Rome, through its own embassy, the vibrant protests of the Senate for the lack of respect for the prerogatives it claimed (although difficult to prove legally and jurisprudentially) and which asserted that it was not willing to be treated by Rome like Romagna and the March.[43]

41 See Paolo Prodi, *Il sovrano pontefice. Un corpo e due anime: la monarchia papale nella prima età moderna* (Bologna, 1982), pp. 129–63.

42 See Prodi, *Una storia della giustizia*.

43 See Angela De Benedictis, *Repubblica per contratto. Bologna: una città europea nello Stato della Chiesa* (Bologna, 1985); Andrea Gardi, *Lo Stato in provincia.*

At least on paper, however, with Sixtus V, a precise hierarchy of norms regarding the criminal field was definitively established: at the top were the papal constitutions, followed by the city statutes that had received papal approval starting from Paul IV, and only residually could locally approved bans and edicts be considered valid.[44]

This legislative centralising effort – setting aside for now the issue of its effectiveness and efficiency – heavily, preferentially, and certainly not marginally, affected the systems of controlling interpersonal violence, which only partly passed through ordinary criminal procedure. To centrally govern the violence marking the daily life of both urban and rural populations, it was necessary to set up a mechanism for intercepting cases of transgression capable of neutralising the functions of city-appointed officials and, above all, centralising the decision-making process that defined the line between serious and minor crimes. In the Bologna legation, this was achieved through the generalisation of the practice of 'cavalcades', itinerant sections of the Tribunal of the *Torrone* composed of a subauditor, a notary and some constables, tasked with conducting preliminary investigations and identifying witnesses. It also involved the recruitment by the *Torrone* of community *massari*, who were to ignore the city-appointed officials of the countryside and report directly and exclusively to the notaries of the supreme legatine tribunal all criminal acts occurring in the communities, regardless of their severity. Contrary to the Senate's requests, which demanded from Rome – through its ambassador – a declaration distinguishing once and for all between atrocious crimes and minor ones, and asked that only the most serious cases be reported to the *Torrone*, the popes gradually sought to impose the practice whereby it would be the task of the supreme tribunal of the legate, once all cases were reported, to sort them, reserving lighter cases for precepts, *sicurtà* and decrees centred on peace between enemies (e.g., the decrees *non molestari secuta reconciliatione*).

The legate would thus decide autonomously in which cases to intervene more incisively; the *ruptura pacis*, along with murders, bloodshed, major thefts and serious insults leading to bloody conflicts, was among these.[45] The rapacity

L'amministrazione della Legazione di Bologna durante il regno di Sisto V (1585-1590) (Bologna, 1994). For aspects specifically related to criminal justice, the fundamental reference remains the volume by Angelozzi and Casanova, *La giustizia criminale*.

[44] See Prodi, *Il sovrano pontefice*, p. 149.

[45] On the rupture of peace see Valerio Antichi, 'Giustizia consuetudinaria e giustizia d'apparato nello Stato pontificio: *la ruptura pacis* (1550-1600)', in *Stringere la pace. Teorie e pratiche della conciliazione nell'Europa moderna (secoli XV-XVIII)*, ed. Paolo Broggio and Maria Pia Paoli (Roma, 2011), pp. 229–75.

of the *Torrone* notaries, who travelled throughout the legation territory to intercept and resolve non-capital cases, was the subject of frequent complaints. For example, in December 1579, the *Assunti di Torrone* wrote to the ambassador in Rome that these notaries, during their cavalcades, demanded a pay of half a scudo per day, whereas, according to the constitutions, they should not have received anything. For the imposition of *sicurtà* not to harm, they demanded twenty *bolognini* instead of the seven provided.[46]

Depending on the circumstances, even for major crimes, the use of tools of repression or prevention was not forbidden, as evidenced by many cases of murder, often resulting from vendettas, for which *sicurtà* not to harm were imposed on a large number of individuals following regular sentences of exile or banishment, or waves of imprisonments or deployments of soldiers *ad standum*. The preferred type of intervention by the Criminal Tribunal of the *Torrone*, as well as the Tribunal of the Governor of Rome and tribunals controlled by legates and governors in other areas of the Papal States, lay somewhere in between total repression and prevention. In cases of murder, the holding of a trial and the issuance of a sentence (capital banishment, confiscation of goods, galley slavery) were not guaranteed outcomes. In case of conviction, especially if the accused belonged to the local elites, it was common to initiate a request for revision or annulment of the sentence terms through an appeal, which presupposed reaching peace with the victim's relatives and included the imposition of a *sicurtà* not to harm against the convicted/pardoned individual.[47] But in many other cases, even before a trial began, a judicial mechanism would come into play, aimed at laying the foundations for a coercive process to prevent the actors from reoffending in the future. In both cases, as well as in the granting of sovereign grace, reaching peace with the opposing party was an indispensable precondition.

Pardoning a murderer without having achieved peace with the victim's family was, in the eyes of local government institutions, an execrable practice, as the Bologna Senate pointed out to Pius IV in January 1565 regarding the pardon he granted to Giovanni Bonasoni, condemned to capital banishment for the murder of a member of the Aldrovandi circle, a particularly heinous murder due to the circumstances in which it was committed: at night, in cold blood, and with premeditation. The pope justified himself by asserting that he had been erroneously informed that peace had actually been reached,

46 ASB, *Ambasciata Bolognese a Roma, Lettere all'Oratore*, reg. 12 (the Assunti di Torrone to the Ambassador, 5 December 1579).

47 Regarding the Jesi Episcopal tribunal see Diego Pedrini and Lucia Dubbini, *Il prezzo del perdono. Il Tribunale episcopale di Jesi in età moderna (1530-1730)* (Fermo, 2020).

but the Senate did not hold back its protests: it felt damaged by a pardon 'so unusual and new and prejudicial in the future',[48] both because it was a vendetta – compromising on this point would have set a dangerous precedent – and because the *Torrone* had imposed a *sicurtà* not to harm on the Aldrovandi, the injured party, whose legitimacy was pending a ruling from the *Sacra Consulta*.[49] The pope ultimately had to partially backtrack by not decreeing the complete annulment of the pardon but the continuation of the prohibition for Bonasoni to return to the lands of the legation.[50] Even in 1591, this time in Umbria, the authorities had to acknowledge the impossibility of peace in the request for grace in favour of Benedetto di Pasquale from Cascia, guilty and condemned to exile for the murder of a man from Valentano, a possession of the Farnese, but committed in Soriano, a fief of the Altemps. The appeal requested the annulment of the exile but, of course, excluding Valentano, 'where the heirs of the dead are',[51] and also Soriano, 'the place of the crime'.[52]

To fully define this coercive mechanism, legates and apostolic commissioners widely resorted to their authority to impose monetary penalties, fines, confiscations and *sicurtà* not to harm on a multitude of individuals involved in criminal acts, with this action often not following regular trials but imposed as a preventive measure. One of the defining elements of this system was precisely targeting not only the author of the offence (lethal or otherwise) and their direct accomplices but an entire network of relatives and kin. As can be imagined, this provoked strong protests in the Bologna legation, whose special status within the Papal States was continuously reaffirmed and proudly claimed by the senatorial oligarchy, causing considerable irritation in the curia. In the late seventeenth century, it was the jurist and legal scholar of Abruzzese origin, Giovan Domenico Rainaldi, who defined the economic power (*potestas oeconomica*) of the legate, as necessary as the purely judicial one for the good governance of the territories under his jurisdiction and the containment of violence from a preventive

48 'tanto insolita et nova et pregiudiciale nel tempo avvenir', ASB, *Senato, Lettere*, series III, reg. 10 (The Senate to the Ambassador, 3 January 1565).

49 On the origins of the Congregation of the Sacred Consulta see Giampiero Brunelli, *Il Sacro Consiglio di Paolo IV* (Rome, 2011).

50 ASB, *Senato, Lettere*, series VII, register 40 (the Ambassador to the Senate, 21 February 1565).

51 'onde sono li heredi del morto', ASR, *Tribunale Criminale del Governatore, Atti di Cancelleria, Lettere*, vol. 43, year 1591, f. 15.

52 'luogo del delitto', ibid.

perspective. Protected by Pope Clement X, Rainaldi was the criminal lieutenant in Fermo, in the Marche, and an auditor of the Criminal Tribunal of the *Torrone* between 1671 and 1676, before finally settling in Rome. In his most famous work, *Observationum criminalium, civilium et mixtarum*, Rainaldi portrayed the figure of the legate as a perfect reflection of that of the prince, operating at the periphery of the state and necessarily endowed with the same prerogatives. After clarifying that legates can legitimately 'judicare, gratiare, leges condere' (judge, grant pardon, establish laws), the jurist goes on to ask whether the judicial power includes the economic power, and the answer is undoubtedly affirmative:

> And indeed, all unanimously agree that contentious and economic, or political, jurisdiction resides with the supreme Prince. For where offenses cannot be judicially punished due to the power of the delinquent, the fear of witnesses, or because they are in the process of being committed, and thereby public tranquillity is disturbed or feared to be disturbed, in such a case, it is necessary that the Prince, as the Head and parent of the Republic, from his economic and political authority, can intervene without process, based on just suspicion and informed conscience, and provide as is most expedient, as many modern authorities affirm.[53]

The purpose of the *potestas oeconomica*, used 'sine processu ex justa suspicione' (without trial by just suspicion), and together with the *potestas politica*, is to lead 'to the public peace, and the political and economic preservation of the Provinces, Kingdoms, and towns subject to the same'.[54] The prince, through his legate, can not only impose monetary penalties to punish crimes but also has full authority to issue injunctions, always under monetary

[53] 'Et quidem apud supremum Principem contentiosam, ac oeconomicam, seu politicam residere Jurisdictionem omnes unanimi consensu fatentur, nam ubi delicta nequeunt judicialiter puniri ob potentiam delinquentis, timorem testium, vel quia in fieri consistunt, & inde quies publica turbatur, aut turbare timetur, eo casu necesse est, ut Princeps, tanquam Reipublicae Caput, & parens ex ejus oeconomica, & politica auctoritate sine processu ex justa suspicione, & informata conscientia possit succurrere, & prout magis expedit providere, ut pluribus ex modernioribus firmant', *Jo. Dominici Raynaldi, Sacrosanctae Basilicae Principis Apostolorum de Urbe canonici, Observationum criminalium, civilium, & mixtarum, liber primus, in quo rariores quaestiones in foris tum ecclesiasticis tum saecularibus disceptari solitae, & ad regimen politicum accommodatae, plenèdiscutiuntur... cum additionibus, ac suppletionibus seorsim anteà impressis, congruis nunc locis distributis ... necnon votis ejusdem authoris noviter emanatis* (Venetiis, apud Paulum Balleonium, 1699), p. 11.

[54] 'ad quietem publicam, & conservationem politicam, & oeconomicam Provinciarum, Regnorum, & oppidorum eidem subjectorum', ibid.

penalty, 'not to leave the house, not to pass through a certain part of the city, and not to commit an offence',[55] with the purpose not 'ad crimina punienda' (in order to punish crimes) but 'to avoid future harm and to maintain and defend public quiet and peace'.[56] Rainaldi was merely providing a theoretical basis for a practice always in use in the Papal States, as well as elsewhere; we are facing the very heart of the repression/prevention system mentioned earlier, whose foundations are constituted by economic impositions aimed at striking the patrimonies of lineages involved in feuds and criminal dynamics.[57]

Not only *sicurtà* (not to harm or for appearing before a judge), and not only monetary penalties properly so-called or confiscations, but also imprisonments and the dispatch of soldiers to the properties of relatives of criminals up to the third degree, were to be considered legitimate based on the *potestas oeconomica*. The *sicurtà* for appearing before a judge were, like those to prevent an offence, secured by a bail, and could also prove decisive in the investigative phase of an ongoing trial. This was the case, for example, in 1596, when the commissioner of Rieti, Francesco Tutini, wrote to the heads of the Tribunal of the Governor of Rome that he was carrying on the trial against Antonio Nobili and his companions and that, from the interrogation of a prisoner, he had come to know of the latter's contacts and associations with other suspects. Against the standard-bearer Giuseppe Angelozzi, also suspected of harbouring

55 'de non exeundo de domo, de non transeundo per certam partem civitatis, de non offendendo', ibid.

56 'ad futura damna vitanda et quietem et pacem publicam tuendam et defendendam', [Giovan Domenico Rainaldi], *Syntaxis rerum criminalium, cum adnotationibus ad bannimenta generalia civitatis, et legationis bononiae* (Romae, Ex Typographia Dominici Antonij Herculis, 1688), cited in Angelozzi and Casanova, *La giustizia criminale*, p. 198, n. 32. On the *potestas oeconomica* see op. cit., pp. 198–205, and also Angelozzi and Casanova, *La nobiltà disciplinata. Violenza nobiliare, procedure di giustizia e scienza cavalleresca a Bologna nel XVII secolo* (Bologna, 2003), pp. 164–89.

57 Cf. Osvaldo Raggio, *Faide e parentele. Lo stato genovese visto dalla Fontanabuona* (Torino, 1990), pp. 10–12, p. 29 and *passim*. 'L'impegno a rispettare la pace e a tener lontani i banditi – sancito dalla cerimonia della pacificazione una domenica mattina dopo la messa alla presenza del commissario, di un notaio e di due notabili del borgo di Rapallo come testimoni – l'adesione "in solidum" e un'ipoteca sui beni costituiscono i legami più forti che, in questo come in altri casi, si instaurano tra la società locale e la Repubblica' ('The commitment to maintaining peace and keeping bandits away – sanctioned by the ceremony of pacification one Sunday morning after mass in the presence of the commissioner, a notary and two notables of the village of Rapallo as witnesses – the adhesion *in solidum* and a mortgage on the goods constitute the strongest bonds that, in this and other cases, are established between the local society and the Republic'), p. 29.

various criminals, and who had meanwhile fled, the commissioner ordered an inventory of goods as a prelude to confiscation, and instructed any measure to be proportionate to the economic capabilities of the subjects. During the process, Tutini also learned that another strongly suspected character, Ippolito Vicentino, also in flight, was burdened by a *sicurtà* for appearing before a judge of 200 *scudi*. The commissioner then asked that Rome be informed as soon as possible 'not only whether the aforesaid *sicurtà* was given there or elsewhere, but also of the name and surname of the same so that if he was from Rieti, he could be cited before the act of his capture'.[58] The citation of the guarantor could present a twofold advantage to the judicial authority: the refusal to collaborate would result in the collection of the bail by the Apostolic Chamber, but otherwise, the citation could prove a very useful tool in securing the recapture of the suspect burdened by the *sicurtà* and suddenly gone into hiding. Indeed, faced with the possibility of having to pay the fixed equivalent, the guarantor – necessarily a relative of the burdened subject – would very likely mobilise the network of familial solidarities to trace the suspect and convince (or force) him to present himself before the commissioner.

To fully understand peace in the judicial system of the *Ancien Régime*, one must not analyse it in its extrinsic aspects but as part of a mechanism whose centre of gravity did not lie so much in the now-established obligatory criminal trial, characterised by the inquisitorial procedure, but rather in the judicial bodies' ability to insert themselves at the intersection between the application of preventive measures provided by the prince's *potestas oeconomica* (delegated to his representatives in the outlying areas), aimed at placing aristocratic families in a condition of hardship and thus exerting pressure, and the community mechanisms of governing retaliatory violence. These 'socially compatible' procedures, according to the interpretation provided by Chris Wickham regarding Tuscany in the eleventh and twelfth centuries,[59] indebted – among others – to British legal anthropology and the studies of Simon Roberts in particular, aimed to match intervention strategies to the power relations present in society.[60]

58 'non solo se la *sicurtà* predetta fu data costì overo altrove, ma anco il nome et cognome di essa acciò se fusse de Riete se possa citare prima che se venghi al atto della cattura sua', ASR, *Tribunale Criminale del Governatore, Atti di Cancelleria, Lettere*, vol. 45, f. 183.

59 See Chris Wickham, *Legge, pratiche e conflitti. Tribunali e risoluzione delle dispute nella Toscana del XII secolo* (Rome, 2000); English edition: *Courts and Conflict in Twelfth-Century Tuscany* (Oxford, 2003).

60 See Simon Roberts, *Order and Dispute. An Introduction to Legal Anthropology* (London, 1979).

3. The bond between *sicurtà* not to harm and peace agreement as the fulcrum of the system

In the second half of the sixteenth century, the key phase of the popes' fight against rampant violence – especially factional and bandit violence – there are various examples of communities reconciled through the conclusion of general peace agreements. A well-known case, although not studied in detail, is represented by the peace agreements concluded in the Bolognese legation under the pontificate of Gregory XIII, between 1573 and 1579, among the relatives of the Righi of Villa d'Aiano, belonging to the 'Ghibelline' faction, and the Menzani of Montetortore, an Estense *podesteria* of the Guelf faction. An interesting documentary trace of these peace agreements remains, the *Liber pacis et gratiarum*, preserved in the archives of the Tribunal of the *Torrone* at the State Archives of Bologna. We are in the countryside south of the legation, in a predominantly mountainous area on the border with the Estense Duchy, where the phenomenon of banditry and factional struggles had reached worrying levels. Specifically, a papal-leaning Guelf faction tied to noble Bolognese families, especially the Pepoli, opposed a Ghibelline party that represented the autonomist aspirations of the local feudal lords, particularly close to the Tanari of Gaggio.[61] The leaders of the factions initially appeared before the General Auditor of the *Torrone*, the Umbrian Sertorio Petrucci, on 17 June 1573, after the legate had granted amnesty to all the signatories of the peace, around ninety people of both sexes, the previous month 'da qualunque loro delitti' (from all their crimes).[62] For the peace to be lasting, 'in tal gratia' (in the case of such a pardon), the Apostolic Protonotary of Bologna, Lattanzio Lattanzi, who had previously been the governor of Rome, 'reserved six days to all those who claimed to be offended and not to have peace with the said pardoned, to be able within the said six days to speak against such pardoned'.[63] Within this period, anyone could have submitted in writing to the notary, Gaspare Faberio, the names of the pardoned with whom they were still in a state of enmity, and the reasons for it, so that the *Torrone* could include those offenses in the pardon to be granted. After that term, and 'not having appeared before His Most Illustrious

[61] See Claudia Evangelisti, 'Angela Vallerani, vedova (1559-1600 ca.)', in *Rinascimento al femminile*, ed. Ottavia Niccoli (Rome and Bari, 1998 (1st edn 1991)), p. 213.

[62] 'da qualunque loro delitti', ASB, *Tribunale Criminale del Torrone, Registri*, vol. 886, ff. 19^{v}–20^{r}.

[63] 'ha riservato sei giorni à tutti quelli che si pretendessero offesi, et non haver pace con detti gratiati di poter fra detti sei giorni dir contra di tali gratiati', ibid.

and Reverend Lordship and submitted to the acts of the said Messer Gaspare Faberio the said names and causes in writing [...] imposes perpetual silence upon such peace and renunciations, and wills that everyone understands and is as if they had legitimately made peace and renounced'.[64]

Among the beneficiaries of the amnesty appears a Matteino di Nicolò from Creda, in the countryside around Bologna, a short distance from Castel D'Aiano and Montetortore, and in the series of appearances and petitions that follow there is that of Battista di Olivari, also from Creda, who explains why Matteino, banished for having killed Battista's father, did not deserve to be pardoned. Matteino had indeed committed the murder despite a peace agreement having been signed between him and the victim:

> It has not even been three years to limit such absolution when, if you indeed decide to absolve him, it must be that he should observe exile for at least ten years and ten miles from his place of residence, which is in the same place and village where Battista lives, from whom he has no peace, nor can Battista think of making peace and being secure, having had his father killed by his adversary after making another peace. This violation of peace brought with it, according to the statutes, a very severe ban, and thus, may that appearance be considered for the petitioner Battista in said manner or otherwise as it shall seem and please you best.[65]

If Matteino had no qualms about killing Battista's father despite the existing peace, how could Battista himself feel safe if Matteino were to return to live in Creda, even protected by the eventual signing of another peace agreement? Beneath the surface of an extraordinary instance of the sovereign's mercy and the pacification between enemy factions emerges all the complexity, and also the fragility, of the dynamic of making and enduring settlement in a challenging situation of conflict. In fact, this general peace was destined to have a short life: in 1580, a bloody clash occurred between

64 'non essendo comparsi avanti Sua Signoria Illustrissima e Reverendissima et dimesso alli atti del detto messer Gaspare Faberio gli detti no[m]i e cause in iscritto [...] impone perpetuo silentio sopra tal pace e rinuntie, e vole che ognuno si intenda, e sia, come se havesse legittimamente pacificato, e rinuntiato', ibid.

65 'non sono anco tre anni di limitar tal'absolutione, quando pur deliberi di absolverlo cioè di dover servar l'essilio almeno per dieci anni et per dieci miglia dall'habitatione sua quale ha nel medesimo luoco e villa dove habita Battista dal quali non ha pace ne sa Battista pensar di far pace et essere sicuro havendoli l'avversario morto il padre fatto un'altra pace; la quale violatione di pace portò seco secondo gli statuti bando molto grave e così si voglia degnare quella comparitione ad esso oratore Battista in detto o in altro modo secondo che ad essa più parerà et piacerà', op. cit., ff. 32^{v}–33^{r}.

the two gangs during which Giulio Cesare Menzani killed Andrea Martini, a *massaro*, and his son Pompeo, a double homicide that was then pardoned by the legate, who was not new to connivance with the Menzani in an anti-Ghibelline function.[66]

Behind the surface of the peace agreements, it is not difficult to see the fragile balances between people, families and factions in a state of enmity, always close to the breaking point, and also the complex interactions between social actors and judicial authorities. Although they struggled significantly to overcome widespread criminality and the insubordination of the small and medium feudal aristocracy, they repeatedly intervened through a series of measures inspired by the logic of prevention. The peace between Villa d'Aiano and Montetortore is just one of many such peace agreements that, in the same period and in different areas of the Papal States, involved groups of varying size in feuds. On 4 April 1564, about ten people, all citizens of the municipality of Offida, a centre of some importance that had experienced bloody factional clashes fuelled by the rivalry between Ascoli Piceno and Fermo, met before Bonfilio Colluccio da Fermo, the ordinary judge of Offida, the notary Niccolò Girardini, and some witnesses. On one side were four people from two families: Pompeo and Cesare Angelozzi, Ascanio and Felice Bracogni; on the other side were six people from different families: Pasquale Melchiorre, Cruciano and Mauro Ziantoni, Luca, son of Cruciano (represented by proxy), Prospero Migni and Micone Radicotice. All 'called, and asked, unanimously, and concordantly, voluntarily, of their own free will, not seduced, nor suborned, nor persuaded by anyone else',[67] stipulated a general remission, absolution, peace and perpetual concord for all the injuries, insults, beatings and wounds received and inflicted up to that moment, 'with the kiss of true peace intervening'.[68]

[66] See Claudia Evangelisti, *Roffeno: ricerche su una comunità montana di fine Cinquecento* (Verona, 2010).

[67] 'vocati, et rogatis, unanimiter, et concorditer, sponte, motu proprio non seducti, nec subornati, minusquam à quovis alio persuasi', ASM, *Curia Generale della Marca di Ancona*, vol. 423 (4 April 1564).

[68] 'osculo verae pacis interveniente', ibid. The type of research undertaken, as well as the types of source consulted, did not allow for the identification, case by case, of the social status of those who signed the peace agreements – an essential data point if one aims to trace the mechanisms of factional division, and the vertical type of aggregation and disaggregation within individual communities. On these aspects, as well as on the equally important aspect of family alliances achieved through marriages included in the same peace agreements, the obligatory reference is to the fundamental study by Gérard Delille, *Le maire et le prieur. Pouvoir central et pouvoir local en Méditerranée occidentale (XVe–XVIIIe siècle)* (Rome and

Regarding the peace of Offida, we do not know how many and which judicial measures had previously been taken against the signatories of the agreement, but, like any other, it did not arise from nothing. Like peace itself, these measures were well regulated by doctrine, to which not only the most widespread criminal practices of the time devoted ample space, but which, starting from 1560 and up to the early years of the following century, became the subject of specific treatises by jurists from the periphery of the Papal States. These jurists interpreted the project of governing hatred and violence carried out by the Roman popes.[69] At least four authors from central Italy identified peace agreement, truce and the *sicurtà* not to harm as subjects worthy of targeted treatment, serving the many jurists who daily had to deal with doubts about the application of legal institutions with a long tradition to concrete cases. From this perspective, the University of Perugia seems to hold a unique record: three of these jurists obtained their doctorates in both civil and canon law (*in utroque iure*) in the Umbrian capital. Niccolò Moroni, from Gualdo Tadino, born around 1520 and died in 1591, was a jurist and also a politician in his home town, where he worked as a lawyer and held important public offices, including those of standard-bearer, municipal lawyer and auditor of *Rota* in Perugia and later in Florence.[70] Francesco Ercolani, a native of Panicale who died young in 1569, was the author of a treatise solely dedicated to the *cautio de non offedendo*, published in Venice in the year of his death.[71] A few decades later, and better known,

Paris, 2003). On peace agreements and marriages in early modern Corsica, see Antoine-Marie Graziani, *La violence dans les campagnes corses du XVIe au XVIIIe siècle* (Ajaccio, 2011), pp. 131–5.

69 On the relationship between legal experts and power that developed after the communal era, see Sara Menzinger and Massimo Vallerani, 'Giuristi e città: fiscalità, giustizia e cultura giuridica tra XII e XIII secolo. Ipotesi e percorsi di ricerca', in *I comuni di Jean-Claude Maire Vigueur. Percorsi storiografici*, ed. Maria Teresa Caciorgna, Sandro Carocci and Andrea Zorzi (Rome, 2014), pp. 201–34. On pp. 225ff., there is an emphasis on the provision of legal knowledge in 'nameless trials', that is, on the practices of conflict resolution not based on recourse to judicial bodies (feuds, vendettas, peace agreements, arbitrations), also drawing on the fundamental contribution offered by Wickham's book, *Courts and Conflict*.

70 *Tractatus aureus, de Fide, Treugua, & pace. Clarissimi Iuriconsulti D. Nicolai Moroni Patricij Gualdensis. In quo omnia fère continentur, quae in civilibus & criminalibus iudicijs frequentius in controversiam venire solent* ... (Venetiis, apud Damianum Zenarum, 1574) (first edn 1570), later published as volume XI of the *Tractatus illustrium in utraque tum pontificii, tum Caesarei iuris facultate iurisconsultorum* (Venetiis, s.e., 1584).

71 *Tractatus Francisci Herculani Perusini Iureconsulti & Equitis Lauretani. De Cautione de non offendendo* (Venetiis, apud Io. Andream Valvassorem cognomine Guadagninum, 1569).

is Sebastiano Guazzini, born in Città di Castello in 1559, who was appointed criminal lieutenant of the general auditor of the Apostolic Chamber in 1606, and later governor of Terni.[72] Known for being an opponent of Prospero Farinacci, from whom he received a defamation lawsuit that led to a trial resulting in his removal from Rome, Guazzini was a prolific author who also dealt with confiscations and inquisitorial procedures.[73] If we add to these jurists the theologian Ludovico Carbone from Costacciaro, whom we will encounter later,[74] one can truly hypothesise a sort of Umbrian supremacy in the doctrinal definition of peace, truce and the *cautio de non offedendo*, along with other related institutions such as the *promissio* and the *fide*. Active always in central Italy but outside the machinery of the papal government is Ottaviano Volpelli, born at an unknown date in Sant'Angelo in Vado, in the Duchy of Urbino, and active as a jurist under Guidobaldo II and the early years of the reign of Francesco Maria II della Rovere.[75]

The subject matter treated in these works is not perfectly classifiable within the tradition of sixteenth-century Italian criminalistics, which in its development had nevertheless relied on common law 'according to orientations clearly directed towards practice'.[76] In the late sixteenth century and throughout the seventeenth, 'practical' jurists, especially those trained in the peripheries of the Italian regional states and who found career prospects in the major appellate courts, mostly focused their attention on criminal procedure, playing a fundamental role in streamlining and accelerating the phases of the trial as defined by classical penal law, all to the advantage of the judge's authority, also through the enhancement and expansion of the *processus informativus*.[77]

72 *Sebastiani Guazzini I.C. de Civitate Castelli nuper Supremi Tribunalis Illustriss. et Reverendiss. D. Auditoris Camerae Locumtenentis Criminalis, & Causarum Criminalium Advocati in Urbe primarij. Tractatus de Pace, Treuga, Verbo dato aliqui Principi, vel alteri personae nobili, & de cautione de non offendendo per Quaestiones divisus. Omnibus Iudicibus, Advocatis, et aliis in Foro versantibus, nedum utilis, sed per quam necessarius* ... (Romae, ex Typographia Guillelmi Guacciotti, 1610).

73 See John Tedeschi, 'Guazzini, Sebastiano', in *Dizionario Storico dell'Inquisizione*, ed. Adriano Prosperi, with the collaboration of Vincenzo Lavenia and John Tedeschi, vol. II (Pisa, 2010), pp. 740–1.

74 See below, Chapter 5.

75 *Octaviani Vulpelli a Sancto Angelo Metaurense Tractatus de Pace, Indutiis, et Promissionibus de non offendendo. In quo Sex, & centum quaestiones ad forensem praxim pertinentes, examinantur* ... (Venetijs, ex Typographia Guerraea, 1573).

76 'secondo orientamenti nettamente orientati verso la prassi', Italo Birocchi, *Alla ricerca dell'ordine. Fonti e cultura giuridica nell'età moderna* (Turin, 2002), p. 255.

77 See Marco Bellabarba, *La giustizia nell'Italia moderna, XVI-XVIII secolo* (Rome and Bari, 2008), p. 136.

From an eminently 'practical' viewpoint, our authors instead turned their gaze not to criminal procedure but to legal institutions that, although applicable to criminal matters – and, in fact, usually occupying substantial parts of the most widespread criminal law practices of the time – contained various elements of the private law discipline of contracts and obligations, as well as succession law, in addition to topics proper to the *ius gentium* (especially concerning peace and truce). It is thus a borderline subject, as evidenced by the fact that Prospero Farinacci, a famous and controversial Roman jurist active between the late sixteenth century and the early seventeenth, in his *Praxis et Theorica Criminalis*, deals with the *ruptura pacis* from both a criminal and a civil perspective.[78] The fact that some jurists, who certainly do not occupy a prominent place in the history of late sixteenth-century Italian criminalistics, dedicated themselves to the composition and publication of specific treatises on peace and related institutions, and were able to capture the attention of authors of much greater diffusion and prestige (they were often cited in the criminal practices of a Farinacci or – later – of a Savelli), and precisely during the focal phase of the Roman popes' efforts to ensure peace and order within a state ravaged by violence, is not at all coincidental. It testifies to the centrality of the use of such instruments by a judicial power that was called to disseminate a dense series of measures against a very extensive network of individuals, involved in criminal activities in various ways. It is probably not a coincidence either that these authors commonly hailed from central Italy, 'a large "traverse" region between the feudalism of the Po-Emilian area and that of Rome–southern Italy',[79] endowed with common characteristics from the perspective of the sociopolitical factors underlying the reproduction of interpersonal violence.

At the centre of the functioning of this system, constituted by the series of interlinked measures mentioned earlier, was the connection between the *sicurtà* (*sicurtà* not to harm) and the peace agreement. Let us first understand

[78] See *Prosperi Farinacii Iurisconsulti Romani Praxis et Theoricae Criminalis Amplissimae, Pars Tertia* (Prodit e Collegio Paltheniano, quod est in nobili Francofurto, 1605). In particular, see for example the *Argumentum* of *Quaestio* CVII, part II, art. XVII, concerning the possibility that theft may be the origin of a breach of peace or a bond *de non offendendo*, where Farinacci questions the *fractio* caused by false testimony given during a criminal or civil trial (p. 544). For more on the controversial Roman criminalist, see Niccolò Del Re, 'Prospero Farinacci giureconsulto romano (1544-1618)', *Archivio della Società Romana di Storia Patria* 98 (1975), pp. 135–220; Aldo Mazzacane, 'Farinacci, Prospero', in *Dizionario Biografico degli Italiani*, vol. 45 (Rome, 1995), pp. 1–5.

[79] 'una grande regione "traversa" tra il feudalesimo dell'area padano-emiliana e quello romano-meridionale', Stefano Calonaci, *Lo spirito del dominio. Giustizia e giurisdizioni feudali nell'Italia moderna (secoli XVI-XVIII)* (Rome, 2017), p. 46.

the difference between these two legal institutions, using the words not of a pure jurist but of a literate and political writer who nevertheless had received legal training: Bonifacio Vannozzi from Pistoia, who lived between the second half of the sixteenth century and the early seventeenth century among the courts of Turin, Rome and Florence; a man with multifaceted interests, 'jurist and literate, secretary and diplomat, clergyman and tutor'.[80] In the three books *Della suppellettile degli avvertimenti politici, morali e christiani,* published in Bologna respectively in 1609, 1610 and 1613, Vannozzi precisely delineates the distinction that interests us here. After discussing the difference between peace and truce from the perspective of their violation, the Pistoian writer clarifies that 'the promise not to offend is different from peace and truce in several respects; but in particular, because those are voluntary and free actions; and the promise not to offend is forced and necessary: the judge can proceed in this either at the instance of others or *ex officio*, and compel the parties to give it'.[81] For this reason, 'one commits a lesser fault who breaks the promise not to offend than one who breaks the peace or the truce; and one's own honour is more compromised by breaking the truce or the peace than by failing to comply with the *cautio de non offendendo*'.[82]

Peace, being an agreement, a contract, must by definition be free and voluntary, to the extent that any coercion of the will can be recognised as a cause of nullity; the *cautio de non offendendo*, on the other hand, is a measure imposed by judicial authority, *ex officio* or at the request of third parties.[83] Breaking

80 'giureconsulto e letterato, segretario e diplomatico, uomo di chiesa e precettore', Marzia Giuliani, 'Il segretario e l'arte del "particolarizzamento". Bonifacio Vannozzi e le corti di Torino, Roma e Firenze', in *Essere uomini di'lettere'. Segretari e politica culturale nel Cinquecento*, ed. Antonio Geremicca and Hélène Miesse (Florence, 2016), pp. 189–99: p. 190.

81 'la promessa, de non offendendo, è diversa dalla pace, e dalla tregua, in più cose; ma in particolare, perché quelle sono attioni volontarie & libere; & la promissione de non offendendo, è sforzata, & necessaria: potendo in ciò il giudice procedere, ò ad instanza d'altri, overo ex officio, & necessitar le parti à darla', *Della suppellettile degli avvertimenti politici, morali, et christiani di Mons. Bonifatio Vannozzi, Dottor Pistoiese, & Protonotario Apostolico*, vol. III (in Bologna, appresso gli Heredi di Giovanni Rossi, 1613), p. 599.

82 'commette minor fallo, chi rompe la promessa de non offendendo, che chi rompe la pace, ò la tregua; & manca più all'honor proprio, chi rompe la tregua, ò la pace, che chi manca alla cautione de non offendendo', ibid.

83 Ottaviano Volpelli defines the *promissio de non offendendo* in this way: 'The promise to prevent offence is a legitimate protection, which, to one justly fearing injury to himself, is customarily granted at his instance or by the official authority; to prevent the parties from proceeding to arms and brawl' ('Promissio de non

peace or truce means reneging on one's word, not only to one's adversary but also to God; it consequently means gravely tarnishing one's honour. For these reasons, the breach of peace or truce is considered more serious than the breach of *sicurtà*, by virtue of the same difference that exists between disobedience to the order of a single judge, even if reflecting the prince's power, and the breach of a politico-religious pact that constituted the very foundation of the constitutional order of the *Ancien Régime* states.[84] Due to the almost sacrosanct importance of the bond that peace and truce, as well as the caution, create, Vannozzi emphasises that in many places the allegation of a 'new cause' to escape the application of penalties provided for in case of breach of the *sicurtà* is not allowed, as it 'can be a palliated and affected pretext, and can give rise to many scandals and inconveniences, and multiply enmities'.[85] It is better, therefore, to preclude this possibility, 'because those who want to break peace or truce will always find some way to allege having done so for a new cause'.[86] And in the case of a breach, 'if it is not clear which party was the first to break it; the fiscal authority proceeding to the penalty against all, should not take the entire penalty from each one, but from all collectively'.[87]

Within a work of political precepts, Vannozzi deemed it necessary to include passages on peace, truces and the *sicurtà* not to harm, indicating that the relevance of these institutions in the ordinary practice of conflict, violence and crime management went far beyond the technicalities of criminal practices. However, when moving from theoretical formulations to reality, when delving into the complex dynamics of interaction between private and public, between communities and judicial powers, the difference – apparently so clear – between *sicurtà* and peace blurs in quite an unexpected manner, just as the image of peace always being signed on completely free and voluntary bases

offendendo est legitimum praesidium, quod iuste timenti, iniuriam sibi inferri, ad ipsius instantiam, vel ex officio praesidis; ne partes ad arma & rixam procedant; praestari solet'), *Tractatus de Pace, Indutiis, et Promissionibus de non offendendo*, p. 146.

84 The obligatory reference is Paolo Prodi, *Il sacramento del potere. Il giuramento politico nella storia costituzionale dell'Occidente* (Bologna, 1992).

85 'può essere pretesto palliato, & affettato, & può dar'occasione à di molti scandali, & inconvenienti, & moltiplicar le nemicizie', *Della suppellettile degli avvertimenti politici*, p. 600.

86 'perché chi vorrà romper pace, ò tregua, troverà sempre qualche via, da allegar d'haverlo fatto, per nuova cagione'.

87 'non constando quale delle parti sia stata la prima, à romperla; il fisco procedendo alla pena contro à tutti, non hà da levar l'intero di detta pena da ciascheduno, ma da tutti in solido', ibid.

becomes clouded. Let us return to Offida, just two months after the general peace of April 1564. In June, the priors and consuls of the Marche town drew up a record of the reconciliation between Maurizio Filoteri and Cesare de Mostacci, using the terms *sicurtà* and peace almost as if they were synonyms:

> Having given each other *sicurtà* not to harm, through the intercession and work of our community this present month in Ascoli, before the Most Illustrious and Excellent Lord Gabrio Serbeloni, and the Most Reverend Lord Paulo Odescalchi, the said Captain Maurizio and Cesare have reconciled and settled their differences with each other through the contemplation of the said Lords, and at present live peacefully and quietly together. And for the confirmation of the said peace made between them, as a testimony to the truth, we have had these documents drawn up by the hand of our Public Chancellor with the impression of our Public seal.[88]

We are not dealing with just any peace agreement. Filoteri and Mostacci were two military men, and their reconciliation took place before the Governor General of the Marche, Paolo Odescalchi,[89] and the Captain General of the Papal Guard and superintendent of the papal fortresses, Gabrio Serbelloni.[90] The formulation is ambiguous, as it is unclear whether the peace proper followed the *sicurtà* not to harm, as was usually the case. The confusion is aggravated by the fact that these *sicurtà* do not seem to have been imposed by a judge but concluded thanks to the mediation of the community of Offida and then formally sealed in Ascoli. Perhaps these *sicurtà* were equivalent to a peace, a sufficient legal basis to ensure their living peacefully and quietly? A few decades later in Cerchiara, in the contado of Rieti, Berardino d'Antonio, a *massaro* of the community, explained to the papal commissioner that nothing prevented the return of the exiled Berardino di Francesco, because 'between him and the offended party there is the *sicurtà* not to harm, also

88 'essendosi tra loro date le sigortà di non offendersi, per intercessione, et opera della nostra comunità del presente mese in Ascoli, avanti all'Illustrissimo et Eccellentissimo Signor Gabrio Serbeloni, et Monsignor Reverendissimo Paulo Odescalchi, li detti Capitan Mauritio, et Cesare se sono riconciliati, et quietati insieme fra loro a contemplatione delli detti Signori et al presente vivono pacifacamente (sic) et quietamente: et per fede della detta Pace seguita tra di loro in testimonio della verità, havemo fatto far le presenti per mano del nostro Publico Cancelliere con l'impressione del nostro Publico sigillo', ASM, *Curia Generale della Marca di Ancona*, vol. 423 (22 June 1564).

89 See Massimo C. Giannini, 'Odescalchi, Paolo', in *Dizionario Biografico degli Italiani*, vol. 79 (Roma, 2013), available online at https://www.treccani.it/enciclopedia/paolo-odescalchi_(Dizionario-Biografico)

90 See Fabrizio Biferali, *Serbelloni, Gabriele (Gabrio)*, in op. cit., vol. 92, 2018, pp. 66–8.

because the brothers of Hipolito Pamphilio, who was killed, have granted him peace, and also because the said Berardino has his residence in our castle of Cerchiara, and the said brothers of Hipolito live in Ornaro and do not frequent each other's territories'.[91] Here too, the terms peace and *sicurtà* not to harm (*sicurtà*) seem to be used interchangeably, and indeed a certain similarity between the two institutions can be found in theory, especially when one examines instances of their effects and violations, at least judging by Farinacci's *Responsorum criminalium*, where the formula 'Pax, seu cautio de non offendendo' often recurs.[92]

The documentation clearly shows that, in the event of criminal acts, judicial authorities imposed *sicurtà* not to harm in large numbers and even indiscriminately, without distinguishing the aggressors from the victims. Sometimes, moreover, such imposition was not consequent to a crime but concurrent with the achievement of peace, as happened in the Bolognese legation again in the context of the feud between the Menzani (subjects of the dukes of Ferrara) and the Tanari, subjects of Bologna. In February 1547, the Senate asked the legate, cardinal Giovanni Morone, to release a series of individuals from Toledo, Sassomolare, and Liserna, of the Menzani faction, from the *sicurtà* not to harm of thirty *scudi* that they had been forced to sign on the occasion of a peace concluded years earlier between the two factions. The same request was addressed to Ercole II d'Este, Duke of Ferrara, specifying that the *sicurtà* had been promised at the time of the peace agreements (the use of the plural is not accidental) and that due to the breaking of one of these by the Menzani, the latter had 'been compelled by justice to pay the conventional penalties'.[93] Thus, the instruments of peace were more than one, linked to *sicurtà* not to harm, whose breach had resulted in the demand for payment of the sums.

More legal instruments, more agreements, more breaches intertwined and, above all, added up, making the debt exposure of the subjects unsustainable. Indeed, the letter continues, 'being newly demanded the same penalty for

[91] The village of Ornaro, also in Sabina, is approximately twenty-five kilometres from Cerchiara. 'tra esso et la parte offesa vi è la securtà di non offendere, si anco perché li fratelli d'Hipolito Pamphilio morto gl'han data la pace, come anco perché detto Berardino hà l'habitatione nel nostro castello della Cerchiara, et li detti fratelli d'Hipolito habitano nell'Ornaro et non praticano nelli territorij l'uno dell'altro', ASR, *Tribunale Criminale del Governatore, Atti di Cancelleria, Lettere*, vol. 50, fasc. 5, f. 5 (29 March 1613).

[92] *Prosperi Farinacii I.C. Romani Responsorum Criminalium Liber secundus* ... (Lugduni, sumptibus Horatii Cardon, 1616), pp. 135ff.

[93] 'stati astretti dalla giustitia pagar le pene conventionali', ASB, *Senato, Lettere*, series I, reg. 8, f. 238 (to the Duke of Ferrara, 9 February 1547).

another homicide that followed',[94] these poor mountain people were no longer able to meet their commitments. The Bolognese Senate then asked the duke 'that his subjects have to keep them indemnified from such surety bonds as justice requires, and likewise the form of the peace contract',[95] especially because 'the poor fellows [...] were forcibly made to enter into these surety bonds',[96] and therefore it must be ensured that they do not 'remain ruined by such payments'.[97] What had happened exactly? The Senate explains in the letter sent to the legate: 'having certain individuals from that faction committed homicide on one from the Tanari faction, these poor men, although they excused themselves for not having broken the peace through their fault, nor that of the faction for which they had promised, were compelled to pay the conventional penalty by which they were gravely injured';[98] the men of the Menzani faction, 'believing themselves to be unburdened for the future'[99] and convinced 'that these penalties were not like those of hell, eternal',[100] 'have been tolerating the damage as best they could in peace',[101] but now 'it happens again that they are harassed by the *Torrone* for another case and homicide followed in wanting them to pay the penalties, so that these poor men find themselves desperate, and in a very bad situation seeing that these things are never to have an end'.[102]

At least three aspects of interest emerge in the case of the peace agreements between the Menzani and Tanari signed in the 1540s. First, the fact that individual peace instruments were linked to the *sicurtà* not to harm,

94 'sendo novamente per un'altro homicidio seguito dimandata la medesima pena', ibid.

95 'che quelli suoi sudditi habbino da conservarli indenni da tali fideiussioni segondo che ricerca la giustitia, et parimente la forma del contratto della pace', ibid.

96 'li poverini [...] per quanto ne vien detto furono sforzatamente fatti intrar in dette fideiussioni', ibid.

97 'rimangano ruinati da tali pagamenti', ibid.

98 'havendo certi di quella parte commesso homicidio in uno della parte delli Tanari, essi poverij homini, benché si scusassero non esser rotta la pace per colpa loro, ne della parte per quale havevano promesso furono astretti a pagar la pena conventionale di che ne rimasero gravissimamente lesi', ibid.

99 'credendosi esser disobbligati per l'avenir', ibid.

100 'che dette pene non fossero come quelle dell'inferno eterne', ibid.

101 'si sono andati tollerando il danno al meglio che hanno potuto in pace', ibid.

102 'accade di novo sono molestati dal Torrone per un altro caso et homicidio seguito in volerli far pagar le pene, onde che li poverij homini si ritrovano disperati, et à malissimo partito vedendo che queste cose, non siano per haver mai fine', op. cit., f. 239*v* (to the Cardinal legate, 12 February 1547).

a circumstance mostly omitted in the majority of sources, which typically mention the *sicurtà* (with guarantee) as coercive acts imposed by the judge on the suspect or the accomplice relative of the culprit, as a condition for the cessation of pressure (imprisonment or summons), but otherwise unconnected to the achievement of peace, which at most was considered a prerequisite for the subsequent request to annul the *sicurtà* not to harm themselves. This connection between peace and *sicurtà*, however, is made explicit in a normative source such as the statutes of Rome reformed under Gregory XIII, where the death penalty or capital ban provided for those who broke the peace was accompanied by the enforcement of the surety bond amount, 'si poena fuerit in instrumento apposita', in addition to the prohibition of rehabilitation.[103] Another noteworthy aspect is the Bolognese Senate's assertion that the *sicurtà* possessed a temporary validity, that is, once broken and once the corresponding penalties had been paid, these should dissolve into nothing. Finally, the emphasis on the coercion of the will of the subjects as a reason for the invalidity of the *sicurtà* signed, when instead we know that such coercion was a constant characteristic of the imposition of *sicurtà*. In general, the Bolognese Senate never ceased in the following years to protest to the legate, and also directly to Rome, about the massive imposition of *sicurtà* not to harm, considered a surreptitious introduction of monetary penalties and, above all, confiscations in a territory that deemed itself exempt from such measures by virtue of its specific statute.[104]

One characteristic of this institution was reciprocity: once a *sicurtà* was imposed on one subject, it was expected that his adversary would sign one of the same type and amount, even if the latter was the victim. The rationale of this practice is easily understood, as burdening the victim with *sicurtà* dissuaded him from seeking revenge against his aggressor. If we consider that these *sicurtà* were imposed on all relatives up to the third degree, it becomes clear how, in small and particularly violent communities, it became practically impossible to be exempt from them. For commissioners from Rome, it was necessary to constantly request information about the degrees of kinship among the subjects involved in a criminal event and about the existence or non-existence of *sicurtà* and peace agreements signed between them. In April 1564, the commissioner of Monterubbiano, near Fermo, certified to the auditor Vincenzo Bellucci both that Berardo di Pierdomenico and Marchitto di Battista were related within the third degree to Cecco di Giovanni, known as Ciarrullo, and therefore also to his brothers, and the existence of

[103] *Statuta Almae Urbis Romae*, p. 84.

[104] See Angelozzi and Casanova, *La giustizia criminale*, pp. 185–289.

a peace instrument made between Cecco and Domenico di Marchese, later ratified by Matteo and Berardo, brothers of Cecco, and Marcone and Giovanni, sons of Domenico di Marchese. The commissioner added that he had heard from Marchitto and Vincenzo, son of Berardo, 'that they are content if the *sicurtà* given for Cecco di Giovanni, known as Ciarrullo, and his brothers are cancelled, since peace has been achieved for the death of their relative Antonio, for which Your Lordship may freely cancel the *sicurtà*'.[105] The tangle of measures affecting the extensive networks of kinship and community was difficult to handle and untangle. From this fragment we learn, for example, that, just as the *sicurtà* not to harm had to be firmly anchored to the kinship of the culprits, especially through the instrument of the *sicurtà*, similarly peace was sometimes ratified, as an additional guarantee, by close relatives of the contracting parties. We also learn of a consolidated practice of requesting the cancellation of *sicurtà* by virtue of achieving peace. Peace was sought to free oneself from *sicurtà*, although the effect of cancellation was not automatic and the doctrine was far from unanimous on the point.[106]

Officially not forced, by definition free, spontaneous, the result of the unanimous will of the contracting parties, the phenomenon of peace agreements intertwined with that of arbitration, but their conclusion was constantly solicited by public authorities through rather severe pressure tools. Pressure was exerted on all types of arbitration procedures, where we might have expected autonomy of action and symmetry of interpersonal relationships. In the Umbrian area, for example, documentary traces are particularly rich in references to the action of the vice-legates towards local governors (and judges) to ensure that arbitrators quickly reached the resolution of disputes in which criminal and civil matters were mixed. Solutions were to go in the direction desired by the authorities and imposed on the aggressor the due compensation, of a monetary nature, to the victim. In June 1555, the vice-legates wrote to the governor of Todi that once the reciprocal *sicurtà* not to harm had been imposed on one side by Marco di Pier Nofrio and his son, on the other by Giovanni Maria, Jacomo, and Giulio, so that 'no other scandal may occur',[107] the latter should elect an arbitrator, a 'huomo dabene' (good man), to quantify

[105] 'che loro se accontentino se cassino le sigurtà date per Cecco de Giovanni detto Ciarrullo et fratelli sendo che ce sia seguita la pace per la morte d'Antonio loro parente, perilché Vostra Signoria potrà farli cassar' liberamente le sigurtà', ASM, *Curia Generale della Marca di Ancona*, vol. 423 (22 April 1566).

[106] Guazzini, *Tractatus de Pace, Treuga, Verbo dato aliqui Principi*, pp. 98–100.

[107] 'non habbia da succedere altro scandalo', ASP, *Governo Pontificio*, Sezione I, Classe I, n. 1, f. 55$^{v.}$

the damages, expenses and interests suffered and to be suffered, resulting from the 'crippling of the son of the said Marco'.[108] Once the amount was established, they should 'be compelled to repay it immediately'.[109] Just a couple of months earlier, Jacomo Sellaro and his apprentice, both from Foligno, claimed money from Cristofaro Sellaro 'for the injuries received from him';[110] the vice-legates wrote to the governor that he should 'compel the said master Cristofaro to repay all that they had suffered due to the said injuries'.[111] The recurring final formula in such communications between vice-legates and commissioners was: 'having removed the cavillations and subterfuges'.[112] The aim of the strongly desired arbitration solutions by the authorities was to avoid trials, by definition the place of cavillation and subterfuge, to give space to procedures based on equitable criteria, which none the less required close supervision. This confirms the reflection on judicial practice of a religious-cultural *topos* that enjoyed wide fortune in Europe, as we will have the opportunity to verify later, and which was the basis of the so-called summary procedure in civil and commercial matters.[113]

If the *sicurtà* were explicitly extorted through waves of incarcerations, deployments *ad standum*, or pecuniary penalties, family groups were similarly compelled to make peace to escape an unbearable pressure – the imminent danger of the demand for the collection of the *sicurtà*. The scheme could certainly vary depending on the specific contexts. It is, then, possible that in July 1599 the governor of Assisi ordered the incarceration of Giovanni Maria di Giuseppe 'so that he might give *sicurtà* not to harm'[114] Francesco Maria Ballante, but that immediately a supplication was made to inform the vice-legate that Ballante 'due to poverty cannot give reciprocal *sicurtà* nor the said *sicurtà* of a lesser amount',[115] and also that 'the parties have already agreed to make peace'.[116] The order addressed to the governor of Assisi was

108 'storpiamento del figliolo di detto Marco', ibid.

109 'astringerli a refarli subbito', ibid.

110 'per le ferite ricevute da lui', op. cit., f. 28r.

111 'astringere il suddetto m[ast]ro Christofaro à refarli tutto quello che havessero patito per causa di dette ferite', ibid.

112 'remosse le cavillationi et sutterfugij', ibid.

113 See Simona Cerutti, *Giustizia sommaria. Pratiche e ideali di giustizia in una società di Ancien Régime (Torino, XVIII secolo)* (Milan, 2003).

114 'perché desse securtà de non offendere', ASP, *Governo pontificio*, Section I, Class I, n. 3, f. 38v.

115 'per povertà non può dar reciproca né di minor somma detta securtà', ibid.

116 'di già le parti sono concordi à far pace', ibid.

clear: 'Your Excellency can order his Chancellor to receive this peace in the usual form, send an authentic copy, and then release the said prisoner, which I am content with notwithstanding any other order to the contrary'.[117]

At the time of the incarceration of the perpetrator of an assault or offence, intense negotiation began between the individual, his family group, that of the opposing party, and the judicial authorities. Poverty was continually invoked to try to relieve the burden of the *sicurtà*, and certainly the economic disparity between the parties constituted a problem for the reciprocation of *sicurtà*. In Montefalco, near Foligno, the nobleman Altinate Clarignano was forced to give *sicurtà* not to harm for 300 scudi, 'for himself and his up to the 3rd degree',[118] towards Donna Tarquinia di Giovanni Maria, who, despite being poor, was still required to sign a corresponding *sicurtà*. Considering the lesser economic means, Tarquinia was imposed a *sicurtà* of a lower amount, that is, 100 scudi instead of 300, 'but of reciprocal tenor'.[119] On 24 May 1600, the vice-legate authorised the *Podestà* of Montefalco to have the said *sicurtà* signed on the spot and not in Perugia, 'not having the convenience to give them at this court',[120] with the recommendation that they be 'suitable, and stipulated with the clauses of the *Motu proprio*, and the *Consulta*'.[121] Only four days later, on 28 May, the vice-legato wrote again to the *Podestà* of Montefalco to communicate that:

> Because it is clearly discernible that the intention of Captain Altinato is neither to offend nor to cause offense to Donna Tarquinia di Giovanni Maria or her family, since he offers to make peace. I am satisfied that when this peace is not achieved, the said Captain will give the same *sicurtà* that Tarquinia will give, that is, the same amount of 100 scudi notwithstanding anything to the contrary [...] provided that he, as he has promised, makes peace and that it does not fail on his account.[122]

We do not know what kind of offence had been inflicted on Donna Tarquinia and to what extent her immediate family members (typically, her male children) were involved in the incident; we do not know if the woman

[117] 'Potrà Vostra Signoria ordinar al suo Cancelliere che riceva essa pace in forma solita con rimetterne copia authentica, et far relassar poi detto carcerato, che di tanto mi contento nonostante altro ordine che vi fosse in contrario', ibid.

[118] 'per se et suoi sino in 3° grado', op. cit., f. 147.

[119] 'ma di tenore reciproco', ibid.

[120] 'non havendo loro commodità di darle in questa corte', ibid.

[121] 'idonee, et stipulate con le clausole del Moto proprio, e della Consulta', ibid.

[122] Op. cit., f. 148.

had been given the opportunity to act alone before the governor, or if she needed a male representative, as was often the case; finally, we do not know if, being a noble, Altinato's word was deemed sufficient without the need for a guarantor. What we do know, however, is that the judge's action was highly influenced by the attitude shown by the prisoner from the outset. The transition from the *sicurtà* to the peace agreement could indeed be immediate: if the disposition from the beginning was inclined towards pacification and non-repetition of the offence, the imposition of the *sicurtà* could even be entirely avoided for the purpose of release. At the judge's discretion, release could occur even in the absence of both *sicurtà* and peace, as was granted in April 1600 to Bartolomeo, known as Sbrozzino, and his son Vincenzo, from Spello. The two, called to give *sicurtà* to benefit from the grace granted to them, 'due to poverty could not find such *sicurtà*, and peace could not be made as their adversaries were absent';[123] for these reasons, the *Podestà* considered it sufficient that father and son only 'gave their word to some person of rank'.[124] In Bologna, on the other hand, in 1562 Count Ascanio Leoni had promised at the *Torrone* to make peace, but then, once cited, fled, placing himself in contempt of court; the vice-legate Pier Donato Cesi then ordered that an inventory of his assets (and those of his mother-in-law, which he would inherit upon her death) be made to demand a fine of 1,000 scudi for connivance with bandits, sparking the usual protests from the Senate.[125] The simple promise to make peace thus had to be evaluated very carefully by the judicial authority, as deceit was always lurking. Sometimes, however, the situation was difficult from the start. Inveterate hatreds and hearts hardened by years of revenge and retaliation could suggest to the judicial authority – especially in the presence of persons with economic means – to impose *sicurtà* without delay, but it was known that the path from these to peace would soon come to an end, and that the *sicurtà* would likely soon be broken. In other cases, the same precepts initially issued by the judicial authority could be the subject of explicit resistance, with violent and armed aggression against the constables sent to carry out an arrest or the stationing on the assets of those precepted.

[123] 'per la povertà non trovano tal *sicurtà*, e la pace non può farsi per trovarsi assenti detti loro avversari', op. cit., f. 129.

[124] 'la parola costì a qualche persona di grado', ibid.

[125] ASB, Senato, Lettere, series I, reg. 11, ff. 130r–v (the Senate to the ambassador, 18 March 1562). Ascanio Leoni was the son of the philosopher and physician Ludovico Leoni. See Angelozzi and Casanova, *La giustizia criminale*, pp. 198ff.

4. Contumacy, exile, banishment

In governing criminality, the states of the early modern period had to continually deal with the phenomenon of the absence of offenders, both because the latter often chose to flee to escape prosecution, and because judicial authorities themselves systematically used exile and banishment as instruments of condemnation, adhering to a punitive criterion very different from those adopted in today's judicial systems. The contumacy of suspects and offenders was the norm, as, immediately after a criminal event occurred, a whole series of individuals, affected by a citation from the judge or aware that they would be because of their degree of kinship or social proximity to the offender, would flee. Local judges and pontifical commissioners then had to act decisively and harshly against the few who remained within the communities, through stringent, almost ruthless, recourse to measures derived from the *potestas oeconomica*, whose purpose was to put pressure on family groups not necessarily in view of the trial against the offenders but for the restoration of the social fabric through peace.

The first objective of the commissioner, once he arrived at the place where the crimes had been committed, was to compel the involved parties to release a *sicurtà* not to harm up to the third degree of kinship, which, naturally, the adversaries would have to reciprocate. To do this, one operation was imposed before any other: the inventory of the assets of the subjects. The imposition of *sicurtà* with a guarantor has its proper place within a judicial policy that made pecuniary sanctions and confiscations the main weapon in the fight against all criminality, not just banditry. The doctrine was very clear and unanimous on this point: *sicurtà* without a guarantor was in no way effective in preventing violence, and the sum of money essentially equated to the confiscation of all the obligor's assets in the event of the breach of the *sicurtà* itself, at which point the judicial authority could proceed 'summarily and executively as required by the obligation in forma Camerae' ('sommarie et executive secondo richiede l'obbligatione in forma Camerae').[126] The

[126] 'Nelle cause delle *sicurtà* rotte, come sa Vostra Signoria, si procede sommarie et executive secondo richiede l'obbligatione in forma Camerae tanto più in questa che vien rotta dui volte non ch'una, Vostra Signoria dunche non manchi astringere la *sicurtà* di Chiavilloni à pagare, et in tanto ritenerlo priggione come si deve, acciò se ne cavi le mani, et non possendosi haver la persona si faccia l'esecutione nelli beni più atti a farne ritratto ch'intendo non ci manca modo, che siccome in questo sta il verbo principale per servitio della Reverenda Camera così Io come procuratore d'essa ne desidero et aspetto esito' ('In cases of broken bonds, as Your Excellency knows, proceedings are summary and executive as required by the obligation in forma Camerae, especially in this instance where it has been

reference to cameral obligations opens a very interesting perspective for understanding the precise legal form assumed by the *sicurtà* not to harm in the context of the Papal States. Originating in the thirteenth century as a particular type of executive clause attached to a public instrument (usually money loans), cameral obligations evolved over time in some aspects but remained a particularly solid form of guarantee enjoyed by creditors, to the extent that upon the subscription of the cameral obligation, the obligor, in addition to confessing the debt before the judge or notary, swore to comply, renouncing from the outset any exception or appeal and immediately accepting the pronouncement of an excommunication with *ex tunc* effect in case of non-compliance. Particularly relevant is certainly the form of the oath, but especially the mingling of the temporal and spiritual planes. The effects of non-compliance fell not only on the debtor's patrimonial sphere but also on his personal and spiritual one. The cameral obligation contained vexatious aspects, which unsurprisingly raised numerous protests from the Gallican clergy at the beginning of the fifteenth century, who resented the arrogance of the Apostolic Chamber in collecting the debts contracted by their clergy; furthermore, the application of the cameral formula was normally prohibited in contracts between laypeople, highlighting its coercive nature, which only a public institution could use.[127]

The imposition of the *cautio de non offendendo*, reinforced by cameral clauses, also attested in the activities of the Criminal Tribunal of the Senator, can in many respects be considered an application in the field of criminal justice of those instruments of guarantee that were originally conceived for patrimonial obligations.[128] It had the effect of supplementing the jurisdictional

broken twice, not just once. Your Excellency should therefore not fail to compel Chiavilloni's bond to pay, and in the meantime, hold him prisoner as required, so that he cannot escape, and if the person cannot be apprehended, execution should be made on the assets most suitable for recovery, which I understand are not lacking. Since in this matter lies the principal action for the service of the Reverenda Camera, I, as its procurator, desire and expect an outcome'), ASR, *Tribunale Criminale del Governatore, Atti di Cancelleria*, vol. 40, *filza* 179 (from Rome, the procurator of the Reverenda Camera Apostolica Felice Salviati to the apostolic commissioner sent to Rieti, August 18 1576).

127 See Cf. Antonia Fiori, *Espropriare e scomunicare. L''executio parata' delle obbligazioni camerali (secoli XIV-XIX)* (Naples, 2018), pp. 7ff. On the Tribunal of the *Auditor Camerae* see the recent Andrea Cicerchia, *Giuristi al servizio del papa. Il tribunale dell'auditor Camerae nella giustizia pontificia di età moderna* (Vatican City, 2016).

128 See Michele Di Sivo, 'Il tribunale criminale capitolino nei secoli XVI-XVII: note da un lavoro in corso', *Roma moderna e contemporanea* 3 (1995), pp. 201–16: p. 213.

powers of the *Reverenda Camera Apostolica*, through the intervention of the Tribunal of the *Auditor Camerae*, with those of the Tribunal of the Governor of Rome, the tribunals dependent on the legates and governors, as well as other Roman tribunals. The obligation subscribed to demanded that the subject neither offend nor re-offend a specifically identified person, and if one did so, one subjected oneself to a regime that, in case of non-compliance, provided for the impossibility of appeal, allowing the court to proceed 'sommarie et executive' (summarily and executively), in addition to – an aspect of certain relevance when connected with the efforts of confessors to achieve peace and renunciations – the imposition of excommunication. Without delving into a technically very complex matter, it is noteworthy that modern states tried to reduce this excessive use of the oath in contractual matters in order to prevent the intervention of the ecclesiastical courts. This was achieved by 'on the one hand, trying to limit the custom of strengthening contracts (*or even commitments of behaviour*) with the oath, while on the other hand, multiplying the tactics aimed at suppressing the intervention of ecclesiastical courts, even in the presence of sworn contracts, giving precedence to the substance of the contract over the attached oath assurance'.[129] For the Papal States, the issue did not arise, or at least not in the same terms, mainly because of the blending of temporal and spiritual spheres that characterised it, making it possible – a unique feature in the context of modern European states – to impose excommunication in case of non-compliance with credit obligations. That same possibility was widely used in imposing obligations concerning the conduct of the contracting parties in interpersonal relations.

For the prevention of violence, the imposition of a guarantor appeared necessary in the vast majority of cases. For example, Sebastiano Guazzini writes that 'this caution is never given without a guarantor, indeed a pledge is also included in it, with the principal obliging himself for his not so offending under the obligation of all his goods',[130] as was the practice in almost all regions of Italy. Concerning a suspect person, the Umbrian jurist continues, the application of the caution with a guarantor must be imposed without hesitation, nor can the poverty of the subject be considered a sufficient reason to overlook it. In fact, he adds, the poorer the subjects, the more they are prone to delinquency: 'because men of bad life and condition, the poorer they are, the more prompt they are to commit crimes, since they do not fear the confiscation of goods, which they do not have, and therefore they

[129] Prodi, *Il sacramento del potere*, pp. 273–4, italics mine.

[130] 'nunquam detur ista cautio sine fideiussore, quinimo in ea includatur etiam pignus, cum principalis se obliget non offendere sub obligatione omnium suorum bonorum', Guazzini, *Tractatus de Pace, Treuga, Verbo dato aliqui Principi*, p. 302.

are sent into exile until they find caution'.[131] The guarantee must still be imposed, and the subject sent into exile 'donec cautionem inveniant' (until they find caution), because through exile 'eorum animus flectatur ad pacem, & honeste vivendum' (their spirit is bent towards peace and honest living). Experience shows, Guazzini continues, that if the judge is too cautious in imposing the caution with a guarantor even on the poor, sending them into exile, he will never be able to convert the heart of the felons, as has happened many times in the past, 'especially when the Ecclesiastical State was vexed by an enormous number of banished people'.[132] The guarantor is ultimately an excellent remedy, because the quarrelsome poor man is normally inclined to refrain from offending his adversary out of reverential fear of the 'powerful' who has accepted to act as guarantor.[133]

Imposing a *sicurtà* could, however, prove difficult. Judicial authorities had to contend with endless difficulties in finding suitable people to provide this type of guarantee (real, personal, and spiritual, as seen), as well as frequent resistance from potential guarantors, even when they were close relatives and thus compelled. Complaints and pleas constantly arrived to avoid in every possible way signing the the surety bond in favour of a subject who in many cases was young, violent, quarrelsome, and refractory to any type of containment and discipline. Signing it practically meant decreeing one's ruin, as it was well known that the subject would easily break the *sicurtà*. It was then up to the commissioner or the local judge to evaluate the danger posed by the subject in relation to the seriousness of the crime, his propensity to re-offend, and possibly decide to trust the mere given word *de non offendendo*, an institution provided for and legally regulated, equivalent to the simple oath before the magistrate and before God, specifically designed for noble gentlemen, for whom it would have been dishonourable to submit to the guardianship of another person, or for the poor unable to find a guarantor.[134]

Already during the thirteenth century, exile or banishment increasingly became the response of judicial institutions to the contumacy of offenders: from a sentence for crimes committed, it increasingly became the institutional

[131] 'quia homines malae vitae, & conditionis quanto sunt pauperiores, tanto sunt promptiores ad delinquendum, cum non timeant confiscationem bonorum, quae non habent & propterea mittuntur in exilium donec cautionem inveniant', ibid.

[132] 'maxime quando Status Ecclesiasticus ob ingentem copiam bannitorum vexabatur', ibid.

[133] '& ideo teneo, quod isto casu erit optimum remedium si recipiatur verbum pro isto paupere, & rixoso per aliquem potentem virum, ut in reverentiam illius se abstineat ab offendendo adversarium', ibid.

[134] Op. cit., pp. 254ff.

threat against those guilty of minor offences who refused to appear before the judge to sign a compulsory peace agreement.[135] However, condemning a mere suspect who was unable to sign a *sicurtà* not to harm to exile meant, in fact, swelling the ranks of that very heterogeneous mass of vagabonds, outlaws and criminals who often formed bandit groups, frequently supported and assisted by the nobility, and engaged in theft and all kinds of abuses against the population. Deprived of the entire network of family solidarity that allowed him to procure the means of survival, a poor exile would, in all likelihood, embrace a life of crime and, with equal probability, continue to find no one willing to sign a *sicurtà* on his behalf: the classic snake biting its own tail. It is also for this reason that most pleas for the annulment of exile or banishment were motivated by the achievement of peace with the opposing party rather than the identification of a guarantor. It is also no coincidence that almost always, in the plea, the extreme poverty of the subject was mentioned, along with youth, repentance, and the need to be close to an elderly mother, as elements to be considered in deciding to annul the exile and allow the return to the place of residence.

Roviglieto, *contado* of Foligno: in April 1593, Nardo d'Antonio shot Cecilio Garrone di Francesco with an arquebus; the bullet lodged in the left arm, but the man recovered without any impairments. After a year away from his village, Nardo wanted to reunite with his father, 'and strive to live peacefully and Christianly'.[136] For this reason, 'he appeals to Your Most Illustrious Lordship as a source of mercy to deign to grant him grace to return, considering that he is young',[137] that 'he has never committed another crime and is a family son, and very poor'.[138] Although the plea uses the expression 'se ritrova bannito' (he finds himself banished), it is likely that this was not a banishment sentence imposed at the end of a trial but rather an exile caused by the failure to sign a *sicurtà* not to harm, as practice required in such cases. Strangely, however, the peace obtained from the victim is not mentioned, an indispensable condition – as we know – for the granting of pardon.

[135] See Peter R. Pazzaglini, *The Criminal Ban of the Sienese Commune, 1225-1310* (Milan, 1979); Fabrizio Ricciardelli, *The Politics of Exclusion in Early Renaissance Florence* (Turnhout, 2007); Christine Shaw, *The Politics of Exile in Renaissance Italy* (Cambridge, 2000); Milani, *L'esclusione dal comune*; Glenn Kumhera, *The Benefits of Peace. Private Peace-making in Late Medieval Italy* (Leiden and Boston, 2017), pp. 93–121.

[136] 'et attender' a vivere pacificamente et christianamente', ASR, *Tribunale Criminale del Governatore, Atti di Cancelleria, Lettere*, vol. 44, anno 1594, f. 47.

[137] 'ricorre da Vostra Signoria Illustrissima com'a fonte di misericordia a degnarsi di farli gratia di rimetterlo, mettendoli in consideratione ch'è giovane', ibid.

[138] 'ha commesso mai più altro delitto et è figlio di famiglia, et poverissimo', ibid.

Let's move to Fermo, in the same year. During a brawl, Marco Antonio Leonardi, after chasing and threatening his brother in-law, Giovanni Battista, and armed with a knife, inflicted multiple wounds. As almost always happened, immediately after the incident, the offender fled the Papal States to escape certain imprisonment (pending the identification of a guarantor or the outcome of a trial), but now, once again a year later, considering that the victim had not suffered impairments and had granted him peace, and given that 'he is a youth of 17, going on 18 years, a family son [...] nor is there any information in this Chancellery that he has committed any other crime',[139] and that he is also poor, it is petitioned that 'the trial against him be dropped' and therefore that he be allowed to return to Fermo. The request in favour of Marco Antonio was, apparently, for the termination of an already initiated trial, and in this case we know the outcome of the plea: a settlement of twenty-five scudi and the imposition of a *sicurtà* not to harm, presumably with a guarantor. All the elements lead us to believe that the initial flight may have been caused by the refusal to sign a *sicurtà* or by the awareness of the difficulty in finding a guarantor. In the first case, a pecuniary penalty was generally imposed, half of which would be collected by the Apostolic Chamber and the other half by the offended party.[140]

The line of conduct always seems to be the same. Either by decision of the judge or by the plea of the guilty party, exile constituted the most frequently applied form of temporary sanction. In Todi, in 1585, for a gunshot wound, a man 'begged [the court] and paid the petition which was signed for fifteen scudi, still kept in exile from the city and territory of Todi until he has achieved peace'.[141] One could only hope to be readmitted by accepting a series of conditions (or even just some of these): having spent a certain period of time in exile, paying a composition, accepting *sicurtà* not to harm,

[139] 'è giovane di 17, in 18 anni, figliol di famiglia [...] né di lui s'ha notitia in questa Cancelleria, ch'habbia commesso altro eccesso', op. cit., f. 40.

[140] Thus, for example, the statutes of Rome state: 'Possit etiam quilibet à quacumque persona ex quacumque causa & suspicione securitatem petere, in qua cum idoneis fideiussoribus partes invicem cavere debeant, sub poena arbitrio Senatoris iuxta personarum qualitatem moderanda, pro medietate Camerae Urbis, & pro alia medietate offenso applicanda' ('Any person may also demand bond from any other person for any cause and suspicion, in which the parties must mutually provide bonds with suitable bonds, under a penalty to be moderated at the discretion of the Senator according to the quality of the persons, to be applied half to the Camera of the City and half to the offended party'), *Statuta Almae Urbis Romae*, p. 86.

[141] 'supplicò [la corte] et pagò la supplica che fu signata quindici scudi, servato tamen exilio à Civitate et territorio tudertino donec pacem habuerit', ASR, *Tribunale Criminale del Governatore, Atti di Cancelleria, Lettere*, vol. 42, f. 14 (7 September 1585).

achieving peace (although in this specific case the guilty party was later arrested in Rome and the peace seems to have never been signed).[142] Indeed it is highly probable that, once exiled, the perpetrator of the aggression or murder would continue to commit crimes, even more than before.

Sicurtà not to harm (*sicurtà*) and peace agreement thus appear as conditions, fundamental constraints to which the reintegration of the guilty into the social fabric fractured by criminal events was subordinated, just as the insertion of authority into the balance of a community might have tolerated or sanctioned the behaviour of the guilty party in different ways, without even needing to resort to a notary, or that on the contrary had turned to the judicial authority, local or central, to obtain a form of recognition. If the peace scripts are so numerous in the notarial and non-notarial archives of Italy and if they are so standardised in form and content, it is precisely for this reason. For social actors, making peace was a necessity imposed by political authorities in order to access sovereign pardon and absolution in the forum of conscience, two dimensions that were never to be separated. Giulio di Paolo Nonnio, from Perugia, knew this well when in 1577 he pleaded with Giacomo Boncompagni, at that time General of Santa Chiesa and governor of Fermo, that the graces already granted to the several persons like him implicated in the attempted murder of Alessandro Montesperelli, perpetrated by the criminal gang led by Cesare Montemellini, be extended to him. For having harboured Montemellini and other bandits, Giulio had been condemned *in absentia* to perpetual infamy for rebellion, exile from Perugia and from all the Papal States, and confiscation of his goods. Since Montesperelli had survived the attack and that, also thanks to Boncompagni's intervention, Montemellini had obtained peace from the victim, Giulio asked that all penalties be remitted to him, similar to what had been granted to 'some who were similarly implicated in this matter',[143] 'liberating him broadly in both forums so that for no time in the future may he be bothered in any way or by any means'.[144] It is peculiar that it is written 'per alcun tempo per l'avenire' (for no time in the future), reflecting the awareness of the extreme transience of measures and personal situations, constantly questioned by the evolution of criminal dynamics.

Just as happened with the bulls of Gregory XIII and subsequently of Sixtus V, which have already been mentioned, pardon and internal forum absolution

[142] ibid., above

[143] 'alcuni che furno similmente imputati di questo fatto', op. cit., vol. 41, *filza* 190, f. 19.

[144] 'liberandolo amplamente *nel uno, e, l'altro foro* talmente che per alcun tempo per l'avenire non possi essere molestato per qualsivoglia modo o via di fatto', ibid, italics mine.

went hand in hand, both in the pleas of the condemned and in the practice of concessions, a phenomenon typical of a political context in which authority had the power to govern both dimensions, temporal and spiritual, and in which contravening a signed obligation, even in the civil field, resulted in excommunication.[145] A case rarely remained confined exclusively to one domain; in a civil and patrimonial dispute important elements of assessment for the judges could also come from very different data. In a questionnaire prepared in 1627 in view of the interrogation of the contenders in a civil case in Montemarciano, between Ancona and Senigallia, among the aspects to be investigated was also whether they had 'ever been investigated, prosecuted, imprisoned, condemned and in what penalty for what cause how many times and where and if they had ever incurred any ecclesiastical censure',[146] and also whether they were 'inimici malevoli odiosi' (enemies, malicious, hateful) of their own adversaries and their relatives, if they had 'ever had any litigation and difference'[147] or 'received any displeasure in deeds and words',[148] and even if they were 'accustomed to confess and receive communion every year at Easter and particularly at last Easter, and by which priest, if they were confessed and communicated and in which church and who was present'.[149]

The papal policy made of peace agreements, pardons, remissions, compositions, graces, and absolutions, in a period of great resurgence of banditry, a situation which, according to the common sentiment of the time, required a greater severity, must have seemed incomprehensible to nineteenth-century historiography, as well as to some later historiographers. Precisely on the episode of the attempted murder of Montesperelli, Luigi Bonazzi, a scholar of the history of Perugia, commented as follows:

> Sometimes the exiled nobles dared to come armed into the city. A Francesco Fiumagioli came to kill the brave Captain Camillo Perinelli; a Cesare Montemelini came with 60 exiles to fight Alessandro Montesperelli; Fabrizio Signorelli, at the head of his men, confronted two hundred armed men led by Francesco Ranieri, who was killed in the battle; and many

145 See Fiori, *Espropriare e scomunicare*.

146 'mai stati inquisiti processati carcerati condannati e in qual pena per qual causa quante volte et dove et se mai [fossero] incorsi in censura alcuna ecclesiasticha', ASA, *Governatore di Montemarciano*, year 1627.

147 'mai havuto lite e diferenza alcuna', ibid.

148 'ricevuto [...] dispiacere alcuno in fatti e in parole', ibid.

149 'soliti confessarsi e comunicarsi ogni anno nella Pasqua di Resurrezione et particolarmente nella Pasqua di resurrezione passata, e da qual prete, se [fossero] confessati et communicati e in qual chiesa e chi vi fu presente', ibid.

> killings were committed in Ripa, dragging their victims even from the altars, by the sons and grandsons of Filippo Ghiberti. [...] Opposed to any weapon other than that of their bailiffs, as suitable in the city as inept in the countryside, the papal governors, *rather than fighting the bandits, preferred to come to terms with them*. And in 1583, Gregory XIII pardoned a gang leader of illustrious name, Alfonso Piccolomini, who at twenty-five years old confessed to having committed 370 murders.[150]

Twentieth-century historiography has struggled to move beyond the liberal-positivist interpretation of papal policy against crime as a 'bargaining with bandits', attributing the continued recourse by the popes to instruments of composition and pacification, as well as the numerous acts of clemency that counterbalanced the episodic, exemplary capital sentences, to the lack, or only partial modernisation, of the judicial systems of the state. However, in premodern judicial systems, punitive logic could easily coexist with a different, seemingly contradictory logic, essentially preventive in nature and which – especially in the Papal States – has its roots in the affirmation of the moralising function of the judicial apparatus and in a substantial distrust of the procedural-contentious mechanism, as we will see more clearly below.[151] This logic, underlying the incessant use of *potestas oeconomica*, certainly underwent amplification during the Tridentine and post-Tridentine phases. The fact that authorities immediately proceeded to appraise the goods of suspects and constantly threatened confiscation, even in the surreptitious forms of the *sicurtà* not to harm with the imposition of a guarantee amount (*fideiussione de non offendendo*) or substantial monetary penalties, might suggest

[150] 'talvolta i nobili fuoriusciti ardivano venire in conventicola armata dentro la città. Un Francesco Fiumagioli venne ad uccidervi il prode Capitano Camillo Perinelli; un Cesare Montemelini con 60 fuoriusciti venne a combattervi Alessandro Montesperelli; Fabrizio Signorelli alla testa de' suoi affrontò nelle campagne vicine duecento armati condotti da Francesco Ranieri che rimase ucciso nel combattimento; e molte uccisioni commisero a Ripa, strappando le loro vittime fin dagli altari, i figli e i nipoti di Filippo Ghiberti. [...] Avversi a ogni arma che quella dei loro birri non fosse, tanto opportuna in città quanto inetta in campagna, i governatori pontificii, *anziché combattere i banditi, preferivano di venire a patti con essi*. E perdonato fu da Gregorio XIII nel 1583 un capo di banda d'illustre nome, Alfonso Piccolomini, il quale a venticinque anni confessava d'aver commesso 370 omicidi', Luigi Bonazzi, *Storia di Perugia dalle origini al 1860*, vol. II (Perugia, Tipografia Boncompagni e c., 1879), pp. 262–3, italics mine. On the rebellion of Alfonso Piccolomini see Polverini Fosi, *La società violenta*, pp. 167–85; Giampiero Brunelli, 'Nobili soldati e giustizia nello Stato della Chiesa (1560-1605)', *Roma moderna e contemporanea* V, 1 (1997), pp. 97–115.

[151] Cf. below, Chapter 5.

an exercise of the jurisdictional function marked by sheer fiscal gain, when instead it was a system made of closely interconnected parts whose purpose was to take advantage of social ties or, when necessary, to undo them. That 'privatisation' of the fight against banditry in reality had nothing 'private' about it, as distinguishing the public from the private can prove to be a rather anachronistic operation.[152]

It is then necessary to move beyond modernising schemes and try to understand a model that had its own characteristics. However, this must be done without succumbing to a nonsensical rose-tinted myth, without considering this system – alternative and parallel to that of criminal trials brought to a sentence, to that of a state which, although not yet 'mature', judges and condemns regardless of contexts, cultural and religious constructions, and social ties – as something benign, mild and merciful. On the contrary, it could prove to be a very harsh and suffocating regime of police customs for social actors, the same that made systematic recourse to denunciation under the promise of absolution the main weapon in the fight against religious deviance. It should not be surprising, then, if seemingly very severe sentences were regularly followed by pardon after peace was made between the aggressor and the victim. Still under the pontificate of Gregory XIII, the order came to Todi to pardon a certain Giovanni Antonio. The governor of the city then asked the Chancellor to review the act of condemnation. He resisted strongly and also demanded money for his 'service'. Giovanni Antonio had been 'condemned to the penalty of death, in *crimen laesae maiestatis* and as a rebel regarding the dagger' for having assaulted Giovanni Eusebio Alvi in his home.[153] The guilty party fled, as always happened, and Alvi was persuaded by several people to forgive Giovanni Antonio ('many asked me for peace for the love of God').[154] The peace 'per viver da buon Cristiano' (to live as a good Christian) was celebrated 'in the palace in the presence of the governor, Satiro Borione, Ludovico Sardole, from Todi, Marcello Capitoni from Narni, and Hieronimo, son of Ottavio Corniceo

[152] Giorgio Chittolini, 'Il privato, il pubblico, lo Stato', in *Origini dello Stato. Processi di formazione statale in Italia fra Medioevo ed età moderna*, ed. Giorgio Chittolini, Anthony Molho and Pierangelo Schiera (Bologna, 1994), pp. 553–89. On the emergence of public criminal law as a process of emancipation from a civil law interpreted through a lens of Roman law, see the considerations of Mario Sbriccoli, *Crimen laesae maiestatis: il problema del reato politico alle soglie della scienza penalistica moderna* (Milan, 1974), pp. 6–7.

[153] 'condennato in pena capitis, in crimen laesae maiestatis et ut rebellis per rispetto del pugnale', ASR, *Tribunale Criminale del Governatore, Atti di Cancelleria, Lettere*, vol. 40, *filza* 173, ff. 105r.

[154] 'mi fece da molti domandar la pace per l'amor de Jdio', ibid.

from Santo Camino',[155] that is, the representatives of the small aristocracy of the area, probably also involved in patronage initiatives favouring the pacification of enemies. The governor of Todi read the text of the instrument of peace, which also became a confession:

> Gio. Eusebio Alvi, in past months I came one evening to your house as a friend, and talking with you about many things, without you having reason to guard yourself against me, I struck you in the head with a dagger and you, defending yourself, deprived me of the dagger as you know, and I fled, and knowing I have erred, I ask you to forgive me and make peace for the love of God.[156]

Giovanni Antonio surrendered once peace was achieved and only after receiving assurances about the granting of pardon and that the confession would not be used against him.[157] A capital sentence *in absentia*, even for treason and rebellion, was pardoned based on the victim's forgiveness and the promise to live as a Christian in the future. There is no mention in the document of threats of confiscation, monetary penalties, or the imposition of *sicurtà*, but it is quite possible that the authorities may have used such measures. What is certain is that means of economic and social pressure and references to religious ideals of peace, forgiveness and concord could coexist, in the eyes of men and women of the late sixteenth century, without causing particular difficulty.

For justice in the *Ancien Régime*, re-establishing – illusorily, no doubt – shattered equilibrium was more important than punishment.

5. Peace, kinship, community

Between the 1570s and the 1580s, the Tribunal of the Governor of Rome had to contend with an escalation of violence consisting of murders and armed assaults centred in Sabina: Rieti, but also Aspra, a fiefdom of the Savelli. The

155 'in palazzo in praesentia del governatore, di Satiro Borione, di Ludovico Sardole, da Todi, di Marcello Capitoni da Narni, et di Hieronimo figliolo di Ottavio Corniceo da Santo Camino', ibid.

156 'Gio. Eusebio Alvi alli mesi passati io venni una sera di notte a casa vostra come amico e raggionando con voi di molte cose, senza che voi haveste raggione di guardarvi da me, vi diedi in testa col pugnale e voi difendendovi mi privai del pugnale come sapete et io fugetti et conoscendo di haver fatto error vi prego a perdonarmi e farmi la pace per l'amor d'Iddio', ibid.

157 'Dopo la pace il detto Gio: Antonio se costituì e, fu assoluto non havendoli io contradetto a, niente per haverli data la pace e, il governatore disse che li haveva promesso che la pace che faceva in sua presentia non voleva che li nocesse a niente per la confessione', op. cit., ff. 105^{r-v}.

families involved in the spiral of violence were the Secenari and the Chiavelloni, representatives of the minor aristocracy of Rieti, and also bound by matrimonial ties.[158] In pursuit of their conflict they were capable of mobilising extensive networks of loyal followers and clients, which reached beyond Sabina and as far as Rome. The commissioners sent to the area were primarily tasked with conducting waves of arrests of mere suspects, arrests that could even occur in Rome, where individuals involved in the local feuds often ended up. From Aspra, an appeal was sent to the governor of Rome in March 1576, earnestly requesting that Orazio Basilio, at that moment in the hands of the main criminal tribunal of Rome, be imposed a double *sicurtà* not to harm. The *sicurtà* of his father, normally imposed in such cases, was deemed insufficient, as he 'possesses nothing in the world besides a small house and a small plot of land, which altogether is worth no more than thirty ducats, or slightly less',[159] and furthermore, 'he has to provide dowries for two of his daughters, to whom this property is especially obligated, and has another daughter to marry off, besides the first two'.[160] The future legal inheritance of the offender, and any brothers born hereafter (in case of equal inheritance division), of which they could not be deprived, always had to be counted in the estimate of the assets of offenders to be placed under *sicurtà*, which could render the individual unsuitable to sign the *sicurtà*. In addition to this, the letter's authors stated that Orazio's father, besides being poor, was already 'obligated once before here in Aspra for a *sicurtà* not to harm'.[161] For all these reasons, another *sicurtà* absolutely had to be found, 'so that we are not killed, or forced to become outlaws',[162] because the *sicurtà* of the father alone would have no deterrent effect on Orazio ('it would no more prevent him from doing harm as if it had not been given')[163] It would have been advisable to involve also Giovanni Battista D'Amico, Orazio's uncle, as a guarantor, even though he had previously stated

[158] Among the 'illustrious men' of the city of Rieti, there are accounts of a Patrizio Secenari: born in 1550 and initiated into a military career, he subsequently served Ferdinando I de' Medici; he was the son of Cesare Secenari and Isabella de' Chiavelloni. See Antonio Colarieti, *Degli uomini più distinti di Rieti per scienze, lettere ed arti: cenni biografici* (Rieti, dai Tipi di Salvatore Trinchi, 1860), pp. 141–2.

[159] 'non possede niente al mondo fuore, che un bugio di casa, et un palmo di terreno, quale non vale in tutto trenta ducati, o poco manco', ASR, *Tribunale Criminale del Governatore, Atti di Cancelleria, Lettere*, vol. 40, *filza* 179, f. 13.

[160] 'ha da dar la dote a due sue figliole, alle quali detta robba è specialmente obligata, et ha da maritare un'altra figliola, oltra le due prime', ibid.

[161] 'obligato una altra volta qui in Aspra per *sicurtà* di non offendere', ibid.

[162] 'acciò non siamo ammazzati, ò vero siamo sforzati farci banditi', ibid.

[163] 'non più lo terrà di far male come se non se l'avesse data', ibid.

'that he does not want to provide *sicurtà* for him because he knows who he is, and does not want to be ruined by him one day'.[164]

In those same months, Captain Giovanni Carlo Secenari had been attacked in Rome by a hitman, Bastiano da Santo Giuliano, and killed. Another Secenari, Celio, had been attacked with arquebus shots in Rieti but escaped the ambush. The murder of Giovanni Carlo broke a previously signed *sicurtà* not to harm by the Chiavelloni, their enemies; in fact, it was the second time that the *sicurtà* had been broken. The commissioner had to act decisively to identify all the people involved in the criminal actions, and he did so – in concert with the governor of Rome – first by forcing the *sicurtà* to pay the sum due to the Apostolic Chamber, and proceeding with a series of incarcerations. Bastiano da Santo Giuliano, as the actual executor of the murder, then a certain Policastro da Terni, described as a spy. Shortly after the arquebus shots at Celio Secenari, it was learned that Francesco Chiavelloni had gone to Rome accompanied by the Count of Sciurpa and Policastro da Terni, a journey that, along with other clues, aroused more than a suspicion against them. All these, along with other characters – brothers, receivers, or cohabitants of the suspects – were to be arrested and detained, a necessary measure 'especially where there is a danger of bribery'.[165]

Complicities, connections, criminal plans, escapes and returns intertwined in different places, and it was necessary to 'shed light on this web woven from afar', as, in August 1576, Gianfelice Salvadori, fiscal prosecutor of the Tribunal of the Governor, wrote from Rome to the papal commissioner in Rieti. 'In Rome', Salvadori continued, 'you can place under financial *sicurtà* or under guard depending on how aggravated the individuals are by the evidence, leaving everything to your prudence'.[166] Incarcerations as a preparatory tool for the imposition of *sicurtà* and the execution of confiscations seemed to be the system most used by the Tribunal to try to manage criminal behaviour that was rather difficult to handle.

> When the declarations against the contumacious are given, Your Lordship can inform me, and I will send (if it seems appropriate) a representative to carry out the confiscations. In the meantime, above all, do not fail to enforce the *sicurtà* of the Chiavelloni, as they have been broken twice already, not

[164] 'publicamente che lui non gli vuol far *sicurtà* perché lo cognosce chi è, et non vuol che un dì lo rovini', ibid.

[165] 'massime dove è pericolo di sobornationi', op. cit., f. 32.

[166] 'A Roma potrà rimetter sotto *sicurtà* pecuniarie o di birri secondo le persone saranno più e meno aggravati d'inditij del tutto si rimetta alla prudenza sua', op. cit., ff. 29r–v.

> just once. If they find it difficult to pay, you can send them to Rome under the *sicurtà* for appearing before the Most Reverend Governor, Judge of the case. If necessary, inform me, and I will send a greater number of constables so that the service of our lord [the Governor] can be effected.[167]

The *sicurtà* not to harm with Celio Secenari and his 'designated persons' (a term that usually referred to relatives up to the third degree, but could possibly also include other people belonging to the circle and clientele of the lineage) were quickly signed by the Chiavelloni between August and September 1576. This is confirmed by the fact that, in April 1577, Francesco Chiavelloni wrote to the governor of Rome ('about eight months ago we gave *sicurtà*'[168]) to contest the breadth of the measures imposed on them. The Chiavelloni wanted to be bound by *sicurtà* not to harm only to the Secenari and not also to their 'designated persons', since the opponents had signed *sicurtà* that did not include the Chiavelloni's designated persons. They, therefore, requested that those *sicurtà* be annulled and new ones be signed, so that perfect reciprocity would prevail, as it did not seem fair 'that the Secenari and their relatives live assured, while those of the Chiavelloni, on the contrary, do not'.[169]

We find Francesco Chiavelloni in the prisons of the Tribunal of the Governor in Rome a few years later, in February 1585, most likely not due to the murder of Giovanni Carlo Secenari but for another crime committed subsequently. It was then that the governor of Rieti, Leonardo de Rosello, who had arrived in the city just over a month earlier, wrote to the governor of Rome stating that he had renewed all the *sicurtà* signed under his predecessor, among which was the one, worth 10,000 *scudi*, between Francesco Savarelli and the sons of Matteo Secenari. It might seem contradictory that Francesco Chiavelloni himself had committed to being the *sicurtà* for the sons of Secenari, but in reality, this confirms what is now known about the tying and untying of factional groupings and conflict dynamics: two families could be divided by bloody enmities at certain moments, but at the

[167] 'Quando saranno date le dechiaratorie contro li contumaci Vostra Signoria potrà avisare che Io mandarò (parendoli) un sustituto per effettuar le confiscationi. In tanto sopra tutto non manchi d'astrenger le *sicurtà* delli Chiavelloni sendo già rotte doi volte nonché una, e rendendosi difficile à pagare li potrà mandare à Roma sotto *sicurtà* de comparer avanti al Signor Reverendissimo Governatore Giudice della causa. S'occorrerà avisi che li mandarò maggior numero di birri acciò compitamente possi far il servizio di Nostro Signore', op. cit., f. 29v.

[168] 'circa otto mesi fà habiam data *sicurtà*', op. cit., *filza* 183, f. 213.

[169] 'che i Secernarij et lor parenti vivano assicurati, et quelli de' Chiavelloni al contrario', ibid.

same time the deep bonds, often of affinity due to marriages, that sometimes sealed the peace agreements reached could give rise to alliances and create new fronts of conflict with other families. The problem, Rosello continues, is that Francesco Chiavelloni was, at that moment, imprisoned in Rome, while Savarelli resided permanently in the Eternal City,

> so that I cannot have them renewed as I would like, since Savorella (sic) does not have any close relatives here who can be held accountable for him, and Chiavellone has only one brother, who is being detained because he has to provide *sicurtà* to ensure that the aforementioned Matteo Secenari will observe his exile from the ecclesiastical state during his banishment, and he does not intend to guarantee for his said brother.[170]

The web of cross-vengeances and mutually imposed *sicurtà* not to harm was such that it was sometimes difficult to find a close male relative, residing locally, who could be forced to sign new ones. In this case, if Francesco Chiavelloni was the guarantor for the *sicurtà* signed by the sons of Matteo Secenari, his brother would have had to be the guarantor for Secenari's father: he had, in fact, been incarcerated to force him to provide *sicurtà* ensuring that Matteo Secenari's banishment from the ecclesiastical state would be respected. The authorities, in short, did not go to great lengths, and to obtain the *sicurtà* they imprisoned without any qualms the relatives of criminals, their accomplices, or mere suspects, most of whom had by then made themselves unavailable. Rosello concluded the missive with a noteworthy remark, stating that the *sicurtà* being attempted should be 'in conformity with the old one',[171] and therefore 'secundum ius canonicum' (according to canon law).[172] Normally absent in the correspondence between the Tribunal of the Governor and local officials, this specification suggests that the use of canonical law instruments was possible, with the consequence of involving the sanctions of spiritual justice, such as censures and excommunications, in case of non-compliance.

Precepts, *sicurtà*, fines, seizures and confiscations were, as in civil courts, ordinary tools in the hands of ecclesiastical judges, especially during the

[170] 'di modo che non posso farli renovare come vorrei non havendo il Savorella qui alcun parente prossimo, che si possa astregnere per lui, et il Chiavellone ha un fratello solo, il quale sta retenuto, per haver a dar' *sicurtà*, che Mattheo Secinario sodetto servarà l'essilio dal stato ecclesiastico durante il suo bando, et non intende di promettere per detto suo fratello', ASR, *Tribunale Criminale del Governatore, Atti di Cancelleria, Lettere*, vol. 42, f. 326.

[171] 'conforme alla vecchia', ibid.

[172] ibid.

investigative phase, to put pressure on individuals and family groups to uncover deviant behaviours and solidarity networks. Forced to address the phenomenon of violence perpetrated by ecclesiastics, diocesan tribunals essentially followed the negotiation scheme typical of secular justice, based on the mechanism of supplication–peace–composition–*sicurtà* not to harm, particularly benefiting local oligarchs who possessed the means to bear the costs of peace agreements and compositions and to appeal to Rome (usually to the *Sacra Consulta*), relying on their influence.[173] Inquisitorial tribunals could also permit the release of mere suspects upon payment of a *sicurtà*, an institution whose nature and purposes align perfectly with the *sicurtà* with guarantee (not to harm, for appearing, not to leave one's residence, etc.) used in civil courts.[174] Traces of this can be found in Francisco Peña's commentaries on the famous *Directorium Inquisitorum* by Nicolas Eymerich (fourteenth century), but even the *Sacro Arsenale* by Eliseo Masini, perhaps the most widespread inquisitorial manual intended for the vicars of the Inquisition, dedicates space to the *sicurtà* in the section on the 'Mode of forming Citations, Precepts, Decrees, *Sicurtà*, & other similar things' ('Modo di formare le Citazioni, Precetti, Decreti, *Sicurtà*, & altre cose simili'). Once the accused was cited, once the examination of books and writings in his possession was in all likelihood completed, and once he was imprisoned, 'it is sometimes necessary to release the prisoner from formal imprisonment with *sicurtà* due to illness or another legitimate reason; in such a case, the Inquisitor will record the instrument of it in the process'.[175] The intervention of a third-party *sicurtà* was necessary, and everything leads us to think that, even in this context, individuals could be forced to guarantee the assets of relatives and friends, although the formula 'sponte, & non coactus, fideiussit' (voluntarily, & not coerced, he stood bond) appears in the form used by Masini for the judges' convenience.[176] The obligation that the accused usually assumed with the *sicurtà* was to present himself before the Inquisitor within a certain pre-established time, or as often as deemed necessary by the Inquisitor.

[173] See Pedrini and Dubbini, *Il prezzo del perdono*. On the ecclesiastical criminality see Michele Mancino and Giovanni Romeo, *Clero criminale. L'onore della Chiesa e i delitti degli ecclesiastici nell'Italia della Controriforma* (Rome and Bari, 2014).

[174] On the evolution of the Inquisition courts' procedure see, in general, Andrea Errera, *Processus in causa fidei. L'evoluzione dei manuali inquisitoriali* (Milano, 1998).

[175] 'è necessario tal volta o per infermità, o per altra occasione legittima rilassare il carcerato dalla prigione formale con *sicurtà*; in tal caso l'Inquisitore farà registrar nel processo l'instromento d'essa', Eliseo Masini, *Sacro arsenale, overo Prattica dell'officio della S. Inquisitione ampliata* (in Genova, per Giuseppe Pavoni, 1625), p. 124.

[176] Op. cit., p. 125.

Limiting oneself to reading inquisitorial procedural manuals might make it seem that release during the continuation of the informative process was only provided for health reasons. In civil courts, however, it was rather the imprisonment that was instrumental to the goal, which was the imposition of *sicurtà* with guarantee 'ad futura mala vitanda' (to prevent future evils). It is true, however, that if one moves from doctrine to analysing the concrete cases of those prosecuted by the Roman Inquisition one realises that, in many instances, those accused were burdened with *sicurtà* and then released for reasons other than health: some because influential persons intervened on their behalf, others due to insufficient evidence, others following an abjuration *de levi*, and still others following the conclusion of the process.[177] In many cases, the payment of the surety bond had all the semblance of a composition. The accused knew that at the slightest new suspicion of heterodox readings or behaviours he would also have to answer for the breach of *sicurtà*, a circumstance that would heavily aggravate his position in the eyes of the Inquisitor.

Premodern justice was well aware of the need to consider the decisive role of social, kinship and community ties in the functioning of criminal dynamics, and it sought to intervene in those ties, both in the investigative phase and in the resolution of the crime. As we have already seen, uniting and disuniting, loosening and strengthening, keeping groups in a state of tension and equilibrium were considered more important than punishment. The cohesion of kinship groups was a constant concern for authorities, pursued even through targeted interventions. Between the late Middle Ages and the early modern period, political powers and agents consolidated their tendency to take control of arbitral procedures, making their involvement mandatory for the resolution of conflicts among relatives; for example, in Aragonese Naples, Ferdinand I's two pragmatics on arbitration among relatives date

[177] By way of example, see the case of Giovan Francesco Alois, released on bail in Rome at the end of 1552 and subsequently appearing voluntarily in Naples before the Vicar, Scipione Rebiba, to receive absolution from penances (see Pierroberto Scaramella, *sub voce*, in *Dizionario Storico dell'Inquisizione*, vol. I, pp. 46–7); or the case of Girolamo Donzellini, accused of the escape of Nascimbene Nascimbeni, the student of Giorgio Siculo, to whom in 1578 the Inquisition imposed payment of a bail and abandonment of the medical profession despite having denied all charges (see Anne Jacobson Schutte, *sub voce*, in op. cit., vol. I, pp. 509–10); or again the case of Mosè Belgrado, the Jewish banker tried by the Tribunal of Aquileia and Concordia between 1611 and 1616 along with Leandro Tisanio, a young shoemaker, who was released on bail in Bologna (while Tisanio was sentenced in absentia to major excommunication and confiscation of property), a matter discussed in Pier Cesare Ioly Zorattini's entry, *Ebrei in Italia*, in op. cit., vol. II, p. 524.

back to 1477.[178] Similar measures were numerous, such as the 1558 decree issued by the Council of the municipality of Ancona, later confirmed by a papal brief, 'sopra il smorciamento de ogni lite che potesse nascere ò fosse tra parenti e consanguinei' ('on extinguishing any dispute that might arise or was between relatives and kin'), which committed the authorities to 'making a compromise and election of Arbitrators among relatives'.[179] It was in obedience to this provision that several disputes among relatives and affines ended up before the municipal bodies of Ancona (Elders, Regulators and Predecessors) so that arbitrators could be appointed to resolve them. Among these was the case brought by Tommaso Nappi against his nephew Nappetto, who, contesting its legitimacy, turned to his son-in-law Matteo Brinci as a prosecutor to request that the municipal bodies intervene arbitrarily to ensure peace within the family.[180] Specifically designed to amicably resolve conflicts within kinship groups, especially, but not only, of a civil nature, initiatives like this in subsequent years led to the foundation of arbitral judicial bodies, to be mandatorily appealed to as the first instance for general disputes, not just intra-family ones.[181] Kinship ties needed to be kept under control, both in terms of unity and maintaining peace within them, and in terms of disunion when it could prove useful for combating crime, such as in the case of banditry.

The changing relationships between bandit groups and rural communities was, as Irene Fosi has demonstrated, one of the conditions that, along with a more resolute and effective judicial policy, made it possible to overcome

[178] See Marianna Pignata, *Spazi di giustizia negoziata nel* Regnum *della prima età moderna. I* Commentaria *di Camillo Borrelli* (Napoli, 2018), p. 13.

[179] 'fare tra parenti un compromesso et eletione de Arbitri', ASA, *Comune di Ancona, Conservatori delle leggi-Fascicoli giudiziari*, vols I–II. Depending on the context, the arbitrators tasked with reaching a peace agreement could be elected, designated by the parties as beneficiaries of mutual trust, or the injured party could serve as the arbitrator. Antoine-Marie Graziani noted, for instance, that in Corsica arbitrators were rarely elected. See Graziani, *La violence dans les campagnes corses*, p. 132.

[180] ASA, *Comune di Ancona, Conservatori delle leggi-Fascicoli giudiziari*, vols I–II.

[181] See, further on, the experiments – albeit destined for ephemeral success – of the Congregation of Concord of Bologna, strongly advocated by Archbishop Gabriele Paleotti, and the Tribunal of Concord of Marca, conceived by Governor Filippo Sega, both under the pontificate of Gregory XIII Boncompagni. On the 'necessary arbitration' (*ex necessitate statuti*), i.e., the path, already begun in the communal era, towards the public dimension of the arbitral institution, to be used especially in the context of family communities, see Luciano Martone, *Arbiter-arbitrator. Forme di giustizia privata nell'età del diritto comune* (Naples, 1984), pp. 133–77.

the rampant bandit violence that had characterised previous pontificates, at least starting from the time of Paul IV, during the pontificates of Sixtus V and Clement VIII. The policy of bounties also played a significant role, benefiting anyone who captured or killed a bandit, as did measures aimed at encouraging informers through the promise of monetary rewards. The support and solidarity that bandits often enjoyed, and which the population was unable to deny them due to constant threats, began to crack when communities were subjected to ever increasing and indiscriminate bandit violence.[182]

Any interaction with a bandit was potentially risky. For two cowherds from Tolfa, Giovanni Properzio and Matteo, it was not immediately clear what to do when a certain Olivo, also from Tolfa, who had been sentenced to death for killing Franceschino Romagnolo and was notorious for numerous criminal acts committed with the Guercio di Lanuvio, showed up at their hut. Accepting him would mean becoming accomplices, thus exposing themselves to severe penalties from the authorities. Fully aware of this, the first thing they said to him was: 'Oh Olivo, do not come to us so that you do not make us fall into the hands of the Court';[183] the bandit's reaction to their refusal to shelter and feed him was violent and threatening: 'hearing this, he began to boast, saying that if we did not care to live, he would give us a bullet in the ribs'.[184] On that occasion, the two cowherds decided to make the best of a bad situation by offering him a good meal but resolved that if he came again, they would kill him. Olivo, indeed, returned with the same threatening request, and this time things went differently, as their welcome turned out to be an ambush of the bandit:

> and so, on Thursday evening of the 14th of this month, he returned to our hut and said he wanted to eat. To carry out the plan we had agreed upon, we remained calm and gave him food. At the end of the meal, we said to him, 'Oh Olivo, we told you not to come back because you would cause us to fall into the hands of the Court'. He began to boast, and we reiterated, '[...] do not come here anymore', and he said, 'I want to come'. Jo. Propertio (sic) struck him on the head with an axe, which stunned him, and then I, Matteo, jumped on him and slit his throat, and thus he lay dead outside the hut.[185]

182 See Polverini Fosi, *La società violenta*, pp. 185–91.

183 'Oh Olivo de già no ne venite da noi acciò tu non ci facci mal capitare nelle mani della Corte', ASR, *Tribunale Criminale del Governatore, Registrazioni d'Atti*, vol. 111, f. 2.

184 'sentendo questo ci cominciò a bravare dicendoci che se noi non abbadavamo a vivere che ci havrebbe dato qualche palla nelle coste', ibid.

185 'et così giovedì à sera passata che fu alli 14 di questo lui ritornò, alla nostra capanna et ci disse che voleva mangiare, et noi per far l'effetto tra noi stabilito,

The two beheaded the corpse and, on the advice of two other men, brought the bandit's head to the commissioner of the Tolfa court. Contrary to their expectations, the commissioner was not pleased with what had happened. He told them 'that we could not kill him without his permission or that of the court, furthermore saying that he would make us regret it, and immediately demanded the weapons and belongings we had found on said Olivo'.[186] Giovanni Properzio and Matteo had thought they could keep the bandit's items – the cloak, the leather bag, the dagger, the arquebus – but a dispute arose over the arquebus, as the commissioner claimed it for himself. To gain the upper hand, the commissioner resorted to using the same strong-arm tactics typically employed against criminals:

> He issued me an order that under the penalty of one hundred scudi I should not ask for anything, and with force, he had me imprisoned in solitary confinement. He then turned to me, Matteo, saying, 'I want to examine you', and also had me imprisoned, issuing an order that under the penalty of one hundred scudi I should not speak to anyone.[187]

In response to the commissioner's assertion that the two should not have killed the bandit without the court's express permission, Matteo replied, 'that if I had left to report it to the court, the bandit would have killed me'.[188] The commissioner continued to harass the cowherd until he decided to take him back to prison, where he remained for four hours, and imposed a *sicurtà* of 100 *scudi* for appearing before him; it was then that the two decided to go to Rome, to the Governor, to denounce the mistreatment inflicted by the commissioner, who had also demanded to take the bandit's head for himself.

---

stettemo quieti, et gli dettemo à mangiare et nella fine quasi del mangiare noi gli dissemo Oh Olivo noi te dissemo che tu non ci tornassi perché sarresti causa di farci dare nelle mani della Corte, et lui cominciò a bravare, et noi replicando, [...] non ci venir più et lui disse ce voglio venire, et Jo. Propertio (sic) gli dette una accettata nella testa che io sbalordì, et poi io Mattheo gli saltai adosso et lo scannai, et così morto stette fuori della capanna', ibid.

[186] 'che non lo potevamo ammazzare senza lui né senza licenza della corte, dicendoci inoltre che ce ne voleva far pentire, et subito ci domandò l'arme et le robbe che gli havevamo trovato a detto Olivo', op. cit., ff. 2^{r-v}.

[187] 'lui mi fece un precetto che sotto pena di cento scudi io non dovessi domandar niente, et con impeto mi fece mettere prigione in segreta, et voltossi poi à me Mattheo dicendomi à te, te voglio esaminare, et mi fece mettere anco in prigione, facendomi un precetto che sotto pena di cento scudi io non parlassi a nissuno', op. cit., f. 2^{v}.

[188] 'che quando io mi fusse partito per venirlo a denuntiare alla corte, il bandito mi havrebbe amazzato me', ibid.

For judicial authorities, the main fronts to address were essentially two: the connection between bandits and their communities, and the connection between bandits and their family units. The latter proved to be particularly strong, sometimes unbreakable. From the depositions given by the bandits' family members during the trials, it is evident that they not only 'accepted the situation without regret, merely trying to maintain relations with the outlaw and his companions to provide them with food and assistance, thus putting themselves against the law',[189] but sometimes even 'boasted in front of the court about their contacts with the outlawed relatives'.[190] Aware of the extreme difficulty in breaking the solidarity dictated by blood ties and thus ensuring that relatives voluntarily worked to make criminals abstain from re-offending and abandon their bandit lifestyle, the popes decided to rely on the weapon of economic pressure exerted on those same blood ties.

In other contexts, as well, peace agreements proved to be a fundamental tool in the fight against bandit violence. In the Corsica studied by Antoine-Marie Graziani, peace agreements were not only used to reconcile conflicting families but also to establish a sort of pact between those families and the State, always present – along with representatives of the ecclesiastical hierarchy – behind the signed instruments, to ensure that the expulsion of bandits from the communities was observed. Failure to respect the agreement resulted in the imposition of heavy financial penalties, a threat strong enough to drive families in several instances to kill their own bandits to prevent their return.[191] From this perspective, it is erroneous to consider the 'privatisation' of the fight against banditry as the fundamental limit of papal policy. Rather, it was a cornerstone of a comprehensive strategy to combat deviance, not only criminal but also religious, based on denunciation and the establishment of a policing mechanism managed in a diffuse manner and in constant communication with judicial authorities of the external forum. This is why, in a context such as the Papal States, where the tools and sanctions provided could be either temporal or spiritual, the role of sacramental confession in weaving the plots leading individuals or groups to make peace should not be underestimated, as we will see in more detail below.[192] This pressure, exerted by the ecclesiastical body, added to the economic pressure.

[189] 'accettavano senza rincrescimento la situazione, cercando solo di mantenere i rapporti con chi era bandito e con i suoi compagni, per garantire loro viveri ed assistenza e mettendosi *ipso facto* contro la legge', Polverini Fosi, *La società violenta*, p. 156.

[190] 'come un vanto dinanzi alla stessa corte i contatti avuti con i congiunti colpiti dal bando', ibid.

[191] See Graziani, *La violence dans les campagnes corses*, pp. 127–38.

[192] See below, Chapter 5.

The first to be affected was the father–son relationship, and this was certainly not something new. A long medieval canon law tradition had stipulated, for example, that the penalty of infamy inflicted on a heretic or a felon should also fall on their male descendants up to the second generation, even if innocent, resulting in their ineligibility for public office, which could be remedied through appropriate composition. The same applied to the penalty of confiscation, which affected the children of the condemned.[193] The legal instruments deriving from the exercise of *potestas oeconomica* were firmly anchored in the father–son relationship but in a different way, as we have seen: it was not a penalty that extended to children and potentially grandchildren, but a personal obligation that fathers had to assume for their children. Fathers bore the responsibility for their children's conduct by signing a bond or guarantee.[194] It was also possible that, in the event of the offender's escape, the fathers (or brothers) might be captured and imprisoned to compel them to sign the *sicurtà*, as happened in Cori to Evangelista Pomice and Marsilio Boccabella, respectively the father of Ludovico Paolo Pomice and the brother of Svetonio Boccabella.[195] What was peculiar was that the *sicurtà*, along with the related surety bonds, affected not only the aggressors but also the victims of the criminal action. This essentially constituted the reciprocity of *sicurtà*, a regime that established a sort of triangulation: to the judge who imposed and the subject who – after due pressure – agreed to sign, was added the adversary of the latter, who was required to reciprocate the *sicurtà*. From the authorities' perspective, the intention was perfectly reasonable: to regulate the behaviour of all protagonists of the violent episode and their networks of relationships, preventing the victim and their relatives from retaliating for the offence received; from the families' perspective, the practice was perceived as unjust and severe, as the burden of the *sicurtà*, which was normally referred not only to the individual but to the entire kinship group of the adversary, up to the second or third degree, was added to the aggression suffered.

[193] This was the practice in the Iberian Inquisitions, and theological reflection particularly focused on this data to clarify the distinction between guilt and punishment, that is, the possibility that the latter might not derive from personal will. See Lavenia, *L'infamia e il perdono. Tributi, pene e confessione nella teologia morale della prima età moderna* (Bologna, 2004), p. 133.

[194] In doctrine and criminal practices, the subject who undertakes to guarantee the obligation is called 'mallevadore' (guarantor), but in the documentation that has been consulted, the term '*sicurtà*' is commonly used to indicate both the legal instrument and the person providing the guarantee. See again, as an example, Savelli, *Pratica universale*, pp. 63–6, under the entry 'Carcerati, carceri e catture' ('Prisoners, prisons and arrests'), but also p. 86, 'Confinati' ('Exiled'), p. 227, 'Offese' ('Offences'), and *passim*.

[195] See below, p. 91.

The inevitable differences in class and economic means among the contracting parties confronted the authorities with difficulties, evidenced by the numerous requests for exemption from the obligation to serve as a guarantor or for a downward revision of the amount the court came to establish after a careful inventory of the assets of the offenders and their close relatives. Many of the protestors were fathers, who sought to avoid the financial burden imposed by citing poverty, old age, or other burdens that significantly diminished their solvency, such as a daughter of marriageable age who needed a dowry or legitimate shares to be allocated to close family members, a limit that even judicial authorities could not ignore. Once the possibility of involving the offender's father was discarded, the choice usually fell on the paternal uncle, following a criterion that made agnation the structuring basis of obligations concerning honour and retaliatory mechanisms. In Norcia in 1602, Tarquinio Ranieri and his son Patrizio had to act as guarantors for the sum of 250 *scudi*, for a *sicurtà* for appearing before the governor of Rome as many times as necessary ('as often as requested') imposed on Paolo Antonio Ranieri. Tarquinio is described as the 'grandfather' of Paolo Antonio and deemed suitable as a guarantor, along with his son, because he had previously committed to 500 *scudi* for a *sicurtà* not to harm.[196]

The Bolognese Senate constantly protested to the Roman curia about the use within the legation of a practice that might be considered legitimate for other parts of the state but not for Bologna, which wanted to spread an image of unconditional loyalty to Rome and an absence of violence and conflict, and considered itself endowed with prerogatives that could not be questioned. They contested the very nature of *sicurtà* with guarantee, considered a disguised confiscation (a sanction from which the legation deemed itself exempt), and also contested the principle that fathers should pay for their children's crimes, risking ruin. In 1604, Senator Ottavio Ringhieri, unwilling to sign *sicurtà* for his sons, who had had a conflict with Alessandro Alberini, protested to the point of refusing to accept the order from the auditor of the *Torrone*, Giovan Carlo Cappelli, and demanded that the pope or the cardinal-nephew issue it. Clement VIII, of course, would not hear of it. The *Consulta* gave Ringhieri fifteen days to obey the *Torrone*, but at the same time asked the Advocate of the Poor to intercede so that Alberini would be satisfied with the solution. While Rome and the *Consulta* pressed, the senators sought to buy time in the hope that Ringhieri and Alberini would make peace, in which case Rome would not have the opportunity to humiliate both their representative and the senatorial

[196] ASR, *Tribunale Criminale del Governatore*, *Atti di Cancelleria*, *Lettere*, vol. 49, f. 91.

dignity.[197] Peace was seen as an exit strategy in situations of institutional pressure, exercised not only on individuals and groups but also in the relations between centre and periphery.

Overall, Rome deemed it necessary to proceed without delay in instituting the obligation for fathers to commit financially for their children. In the popes' minds, this was the only way to curb violence, except for adjusting the severity of the measures adopted when the prestige of the person involved or the vehemence of senatorial protests suggested reducing the burden. This happened in the mid-seventeenth century in the dispute between the Malvezzi and Ercolani families when, to obtain a reciprocity of *sicurtà*, the threat of sending an official to oversee the Ercolani assets was made. Count Astorre Ercolani had to provide *sicurtà* for his sons, but they lived far from him, and the Bolognese Senate pointed out that, for this reason, they should be considered 'little observant of authority and paternal respect'.[198] Astorre certainly would not have had the opportunity to control their behaviour, and with this argument, the ambassador appealed to the difference of the Ercolani case from others only apparently similar (Pepoli, Marescotti, Barbazzi), asking the pope not to 'permit such unjust severity to the detriment of this Province's prerogatives and the *ius commune*',[199] also noting that he could achieve 'his intent by other means not as odious as that of fines',[200] and that, 'since the case is so recent, there has not been time to negotiate an adjustment, which with a little time could be brought to fruition',[201] without resorting to such hardship. Bologna thus considered as odious not only the use of *sicurtà* with guarantee but also the sending of an official to oversee assets, which bound the innocent up to the third generation: fathers for sons, brothers for brothers. Count Astorre's resistance managed to prevent the sending of an official to oversee the family's assets but not the reciprocation of the *sicurtà* given by the Malvezzi, to which he ultimately had to submit.[202]

197 ASB, *Ambasciata bolognese a Roma, Registrum*, reg. 13 (the ambassador to the Senate, 11 and 15 December 1604). On the Ringhieri–Alberini case, see Angelozzi and Casanova, *La giustizia criminale*, p. 233.

198 'poco osservanti dell'auttorità, e rispetto paterno', ASB, *Ambasciata bolognese a Roma, Registrum*, reg. 30, f. 290^{v} (the Ambassador to the *Assunti de' Magistrati*, 4 May 1647).

199 'permettere così falso rigore in pregiudicio delle prerogative di cotesta Provincia, e del ius commune', ibid.

200 'il suo intento con altri mezzi non tanto odiosi come quello delle multe', ibid.

201 'per essere tanto fresco il caso non è stato tempo di trattarne di proposito l'aggiustamento, il quale con un poco di tempo potrà maturarsi', ibid.

202 ASB, *Ambasciata bolognese a Roma, Lettere all'Oratore*, reg. 135 (3 July 1647). See Angelozzi and Casanova, *La giustizia criminale*, p. 270.

In other territories of the state, protests were less vehement, and the imposition of *sicurtà* on fathers occurred almost constantly and uniformly. The sense of the traditional agnatic line could also be reversed in some cases, as happened in Perugia in 1618 in the dispute between the Baldeschi and Salvucci families, to which the papal authorities had to dedicate much attention and energy due to its complexity. Following the murder of a member of the Salvucci family, the papal governor of Perugia, Bishop of Caserta Antonio Diaz, initiated the usual investigations not only against a number of men from the Baldeschi family but also against a priest, Don Lorenzo, suspected of complicity with the Baldeschi and of possessing unspecified 'writings' that would prove some connections. The governor ordered Don Lorenzo to be captured in church, an action that required the consent of the Bishop of Perugia, Napoleone Comitoli, and began to target the Baldeschi and Paoli, who were accused of the mortal assault and had meanwhile fled, with a series of incarcerations, and *sicurtà de non ingrediendo* and *de non offendendo*. At the centre of the governor's action were two pairs of father and son from the Baldeschi family (Giulio and his son Galeazzo, Giovanni Battista and his son Pietro), as well as several of their close relatives. After an estimate of the movable and immovable property of Giuseppe Salvucci, a relative of the deceased, the authorities also considered the possibility of placing a bounty on the capture of the Baldeschi, to be entirely financed by Salvucci's personal assets (500 *scudi* dead, 1,500 *scudi* alive).[203]

The grip on families was relentless, prompting Rome to moderate the depth of kinship degrees within which local authorities were authorised to act with incarcerations and *sicurtà*. On 23 June 1618, the governor of Perugia sought clarification from Rome on the recently received order 'not to impose *sicurtà* of close relatives beyond the usual',[204] to understand if it referred 'to the clauses of the instrument'[205] or to 'the degrees of those to be obligated'.[206] A month later, on 16 July , a member of the Baldeschi family, Carlo, appealed to the governor to be freed from the imposed *sicurtà* 'secondo l'ordine della Sacra Consulta' (according to the order of the *Sacred Consulta*) since he was a relative of Giovanni Battista, but only 'in grado assai remoto' (in a very remote degree), and, as often noted in such petitions, because

[203] ASR, *Tribunale Criminale del Governatore, Atti di Cancelleria, Lettere*, vol. 50, fasc. 8, f. 38 (the Governor of Perugia to the Governor of Rome, 10 July 1618).

[204] 'che non si astringhino le sigurtà de prossimi oltre al solito', op. cit., f. 40 (the Governor of Perugia to the Governor of Rome, 23 June 1618).

[205] 'alle clausule dell'instromento', ibid.

[206] 'gradi di quelli che si deveno obbligare', ibid.

his means were 'so poor that without my wife's assets I could not support even a small part of my household'.[207] In any case, contrary to what usually happened, it was Pietro Baldeschi who had to commit, for the considerable sum of 10,000 *scudi*, to ensure that his father, Giovanni Battista, and his uncle, Giulio Baldeschi, would not return to the Papal States and would not harm their adversary, Giuseppe Salvucci. Pietro's commitment was extorted thanks to his imprisonment in the fortress of Ferrara, the city where he was at the time of capture, where he was held for the necessary time under the custody of the castellan, the Perugian Scipione Ansidei. None the less, on 1 August, he was promised that 'by presenting himself before Monsignor Governor of Rome within the current month of August and sending us proof of said presentation, the obligation he made would be annulled and considered not made'.[208] Previously, a petition had reached the Cardinal Legate of Ferrara, Giacomo Serra, requesting that Pietro Baldeschi be allowed to go to Rome, guaranteed by a *sicurtà* for appearing already signed in Perugia, to negotiate new conditions with the governor, 'being very willing to commit and assure the person of said Signor Salvucci not to harm him or have him harmed, as he never had such an intention, and will give every satisfaction',[209] but 'regarding coming and going in the Papal States, it seems harsh that at the request of malevolent people, it could cause his ruin and that of his children'.[210] Baldeschi declared himself willing to sign a *sicurtà* not to harm Salvucci concerning himself but not those for his father and uncle not to return to the Papal States.

No one liked having their wealth and their very lives at the mercy of someone else's conduct, but it was precisely in this attempt to insert public authority into kinship solidarities, especially the most immediate ones, that the salient feature of the papal strategy lay. The fact that, in rare cases where

[207] 'sì povere, che si non fossero i beni di mia moglie non potrei alimentare pure una minima parte della mia casa', op. cit., f. 91 (Pietro Baldeschi to the Governor of Rome, 16 July 1618).

[208] 'costituendose per tutto il presente mese d'Agosto avanti Monsignor Governatore di Roma [e] con mandare à noi fede di detta presentatione il dett'obligo da lui fatto s'intenda annullato, et per non fatto', op. cit., f. 31 (The Cardinal Legate of Ferrara to the Governor of Rome, 1 August, 1618).

[209] 'essendo prontissimo, obligarsi, et assicurare la persona del suddetto Signor Salvucci, di non offenderlo, ne farlo offendere, che mai ha havuto tal animo, et per lui darà ogni sadisfatione', op. cit., f. 70 (Pietro Baldeschi to the Cardinal Legate of Ferrara, undated letter).

[210] 'nel particolare di venire, e andare nello Stato ecclesiastico, pare duro, che a requisitione di malevoli, possa causare la ruina di se, et di suoi figlioli', ibid.

it proved impossible to find a guarantor, judges could be satisfied with the word given to an influential person in the community confirms the underlying philosophy of the system, namely to turn to the judicial power's advantage the bonds primarily of blood, but also those of patronage and friendship.

6. The effectiveness of the system and its pitfalls

So far, the fundamental issue of the effectiveness of a system based more on the application of preventive measures than on those derived from the *ius puniendi* proper to political authority in combating violence and social conflict has been deliberately overlooked. Relatively few trials were brought to sentencing, there were relatively few convictions compared to many precepts, *sicurtà*, pecuniary penalties and reconciliations. What we know is that, if the popes, at least starting from Paul IV Carafa, initiated a large-scale fight against heretical deviance, which within a couple of decades proved to be substantially fruitful, the same did not happen concerning the fight against crime and violence, widespread across all social strata (although it was noble violence that caused the greatest concern). The project of centralising state structures and disciplining individual behaviours, particularly evident from the vast production of normative and doctrinal texts, had to confront objective difficulties in application, which invariably emerge when the historian's gaze shifts from the theoretical plane to the analysis of specific contexts of application. Historiography has long questioned the reasons for the inadequacy of the efforts carried out by the popes to achieve the set goals (and, in this sense, the normative and theoretical scholarship can be considered more a programmatic manifesto than a reflection of reality). The answer that has been given to this question mostly follows the paradigm of incompleteness: the Papal States (though the discussion could easily be extended to other contemporary state realities) was not sufficiently modern, its governing bodies, and particularly the judicial ones, not sufficiently developed in a modern sense, which meant that the repressive systems adopted were not yet sufficiently impersonal.

Was the persistence of private elements in premodern penal systems really the main cause of the failure to achieve satisfactory control over interpersonal violence? We must begin to question the precise meaning of the notions of peace, concord and quiet, identified as the ultimate goal of the political systems, and which invariably emerge both in theoretical and normative literature and in first-hand documentation. Notions that refer to a concept of balance powerfully characterised by precariousness, an ideal of concord that applied to all fields of social life, from armed gangs formed by outlaws and exiles to neighbourhood relations, up to marital and domestic relationships, where similar instruments were used, are far from our modern ideals of impersonal law enforcement and obligatory criminal proceedings. In all these areas, it was perfectly understood that the balances achieved were marked by precariousness.

On 23 June 1594, a series of documents was delivered to the Governor of Rome concerning Giovanni Antonio Zuccone, a Roman, including the testimonies of two women, a surgeon's report and an exile decree. The surgeon had to ascertain (and treat) the head wounds sustained by Zuccone's wife, Giulia Bergetti, from Città di Castello, following a knife attack on her by her husband. But a year earlier, during Lent of 1593, a peace was celebrated between Antonio and Giulia inside the church of San Domenico in Città di Castello. A witness, Cristoforo Dunini, a linen weaver from Città di Castello, interrogated by the court, reported that one day, while inside the church, he was called and detained by a friar Nicola, a Dominican, who told him:'I want you to be a witness to the peace to be made between Giulia and her husband, which is an act of charity'.[211] Cristoforo agreed; the wife and husband were made to kneel before the church altar, and the friar pronounced these words: 'What has been between you, let it pass, and seek no further'.[212] Turning to Zuccone, he said further:'Do you promise before this sacrament not to cause displeasure to Giulia, your wife, and to live in peace with her?'. Zuccone replied, 'I promise never to cause her displeasure nor to offend her, and that I will behave well towards her'.[213] Then, turning to Giulia, the friar said, 'And you do not give cause to your husband to cause you displeasure'.[214] The account of the second witness, Vincenzo di Nicola, confirmed Dunini's version, but added that 'after a few days, I publicly heard that said Giulia's husband had wounded Giulia'.[215]

Twelve days: that was the duration of the peace between Giovanni Antonio and Giulia, celebrated in a church in the presence of a religious figure.

[211] 'voglio che tu sia testimonio alla pace che si deve far tra la Giulia, con suo marito, che è opra di carità'.

[212] 'quel che è stato tra di voi passi, et non si cerchi altro', ASR, *Tribunale Criminale del Governatore*, *Atti di Cancelleria*, *Lettere*, vol. 44, year 1594.

[213] 'prometti tu dinanzi a questo sacramento de non far dispiacere qui alla Giulia tua moglie et di stare in pace con lei', ibid.

[214] 'che prometteva di non farle mai dispiacere ne offenderla et che si saria portato bene di lei, et voltandosi poi alla detta Giulia gli disse, et tu non dar causa a tuo marito che ti habbia da far dispiacere', ibid.

[215] 'de lì poi a certi dì intesi dire publicamente che detto marito della Giulia haveva ferito essa Giulia', ibid.

But it is not the peace itself, and its rapid breakdown, that is the most interesting aspect of the story. At the origin of everything was a complaint, that of Giulia, who had previously turned to the court for repeated mistreatment suffered. She herself recounts it to the judge, after the stabbing incident:

> Being at odds with Giovanni Antonio, my husband, because he left nothing in the house for me, selling everything, and having threatened to kill me, I had him imprisoned, and I wanted *sicurtà* from him that he would not harm me. Since he could not provide it, Monsignor Governor had him exiled. Having several times made me understand that I should have this exile revoked, and I not wanting to do so, yesterday he had Bartolomeo di Baldo call me, saying he wanted to talk to me at the hospital. So I went there to meet him, and he began to ask why I did not want to agree to have the exile lifted. I told him I did not want to consent because I did not want to deal with him anymore as he ruined everything for me. Giovanni Antonio, my husband, then drew a knife used for making shoes and with it gave me two wounds on the head.[216]

Giovanni Antonio, evidently to settle his debts, was squandering the family patrimony, but in response to Giulia's protests, the husband's reaction had been violent and threatening, so much so that it convinced the woman to turn to the judge, who had the man imprisoned to ensure that he would sign the *sicurtà* not to harm with her, which Giulia had requested for her personal protection. Having refused to sign it, Giovanni Antonio was sentenced to five years of exile 'sub poena trirerium' (under penalty of the galleys), from which he sought to escape by asking Giulia (whether personally or through intermediaries is unknown) to agree to its annulment. But the woman no longer wanted anything to do with her husband and made sure not to comply with his request. As a last attempt, therefore, Giovanni Antonio tried to speak personally with Giulia in the hope of convincing

[216] 'essendo stato disparere fra Gio. Antonio mio marito, et me, perché non mi lasciava cosa alcuna in casa, che ogni cosa mi vendeva et havendomi minacciato di volermi ammazzare, lo feci mettere priggione, et io volevo la *sicurtà* da lui, che non mi offendesse, ne trovandola Monsignor Governatore gli ha fatto dare l'essilio, et havendomi più volte fatto intendere, che io gli facesse revocare detto essilio et io non lo volendo fare, hieri mi ha fatto chiamare da Bartolomeo di Baldo che mi voleva parlare lì all'hospitale, così io andai là da lui, quale mi cominciò a dire si perché non volevo consentire, che si cassasse l'essilio, et dicendogli io, che non volevo acconsentire, perché non volevo trattare più con lui, perché ogni cosa mi mandava a male, detto Gio. Antonio mio marito cacciò mano ad un cortello da far pianelle, et con quello me diede due ferite in testa', ibid.

her. It was only at that moment, upon the woman's umpteenth refusal, that Giovanni Antonio – whether acting on impulse or premeditatedly – pulled out a cobbler's knife and struck her on the face and throat.[217]

How, and especially at what moment, does the peace mediated and celebrated in the church by Friar Nicola come into play? It is not clear. According to the deposition of the Dominican friar, it seems that Giovanni Antonio was first imprisoned and then, after a few days, released, 'and he came to St Dominic to ask that I be the cause of making peace with his wife'.[218] We do not know if the release was temporary, but the reason for Giovanni Antonio's request to mobilise the friar is easily understood: if Giulia had granted peace, he could have hoped no longer to be troubled by the court. This detail does not match the woman's deposition, according to which Giovanni Antonio went directly from prison into exile because of his refusal to sign a *sicurtà* not to harm with her. Why did Giulia agree to the peace if she would then persist in her refusal to annul the exile? Why did Giovanni Antonio stab Giulia a few days after the peace was celebrated? Should we perhaps believe that the peace itself was not sufficient to annul the exile sentence? Maybe Giulia had indeed accepted to reconcile, but unlike what her husband hoped, with the intention of giving that peace only religious value, thus continuing to refuse to grant the annulment of the exile in court. A ceremony of reconciliation conducted in a church, in the presence of witnesses, might have had no effect from a judicial point of view, and the actors were perfectly aware of this, knowing how to keep the religious and legal planes distinct and, when necessary, taking advantage of it, using the sacred as a tool of resistance to domestic oppression. Faced with the disciplinary action of the ecclesiastical personnel, one could conform outwardly, only to then not align one's conduct in court with religious precepts.

For those who remained in the community, granting peace to a bandit or an exile, a condition for his return, was in any case a risk. If one refused, out of fear of coming back into contact with one's adversary, sooner or later one would be exposed to his revenge. Giulia had to experience this

[217] On marital violence, see Marco Cavina, *Nozze di sangue. Storia della violenza coniugale* (Rome and Bari, 2011). On marital conflict, see *Coniugi nemici. La separazione in Italia dal XII al XVIII secolo*, ed. Silvana Seidel Menchi and Diego Quaglioni (Bologna, 2000); Cecilia Cristellon, *La carità e l'eros. Il matrimonio, la Chiesa, i suoi giudici nella Venezia del Rinascimento (1420–1545)* (Bologna, 2011).

[218] 'et venne in S. Domenico a ricomandarse che io fusse causa di fare la pace con la sua consorte', ASR, *Tribunale Criminale del Governatore*, *Atti di Cancelleria*, *Lettere*, vol. 44, year 1594.

firsthand, but other evidence tells us that the intentions of those who had been ousted from the community were very often belligerent, vindictive, far from being inclined to forgiveness and peace. From an unknown location, but in all likelihood from the territory of Bracciano, an Orsini possession,[219] on 10 September 1582, Ortensio Polidori wrote a letter to his father in a partly threatening tone in which, after expressing his disappointment for not having received communications from him for some time ('I have not had news from you, but I do not know the cause, perhaps for not having had the opportunity to write to me, well, I excuse you for the past but not for the future'),[220] and besides asking his father for money ('I am in great need because having been imprisoned for a matter I was involved in and having paid several *scudi*, now I find myself without clothing')[221] and advice on whether to break a marriage promise, he demanded to be kept informed of his adversary's intentions:

> I kindly ask you to do me the favour of informing me with one of your letters and advising me of everything, whether my adversary wants to make peace or not. If he does not want to make peace, I will return, and if before I only wounded him, in the future I will kill him. And please, if you care for me, inform me immediately about everything.[222]

Denying peace to a bandit, an exile, or a fugitive meant exposing oneself to their revenge, which could arrive either immediately, with a return as an outlaw to complete the work started with the first offence, or later, once the victim's resistance was overcome and peace granted, as happened to Giulia. No one, after all, could guarantee that even in the case of promptly granting peace, the bandit would return with the best intentions. These were the same fears expressed, if you recall, by Battista di Olivari, from Creda, in the contado of Bologna, regarding the return to the village of Matteino di Nicolò, one

219 The letter is preserved in a file addressed to Paolo Giordano I Orsini, Prince of Bracciano.

220 'io non ho avuta nova di voi ma io non so qual sia la causa forsi per non havere havuta comodità de scriverme, orsù per il passato io ve ametto la scusa ma per lo advenire no', ASR, *Tribunale Criminale del Governatore*, *Atti di Cancelleria*, *Lettere*, vol. 41, f. 11.

221 'ho gran bisogno perché sendo stato pregione per una questione che ho fatta et me ho pagati parechi scuti ora me ritrovo senza vestimenti', ibid.

222 'Ve vo pregare in cortesia che me vogliate far gratia de advisarme con una delle vostre et advisarme del tutto se il mio adversario vol far la pace sibene *se lui non la vol fare io ritornarò et se per prima li ho date le ferite per lo advenire l'ammazarò* et di gratia se me volete bene advisateme subito subito del tutto', ibid, italics mine.

of the signatories of the peace between the Righi of Villa d'Aiano and the Menzani of Montetortore, and consequently among the beneficiaries of the pardons provided.[223] Being forced to choose whether or not to grant peace always entailed the risk of falling victim to revenge. The authorities were well aware of this, and it is for this reason that breaking the peace fell under the category of *crimina atrociora*, those 'reserved cases' of serious crimes against which justice typically acted mercilessly. Criminals knew that killing, wounding, or offending outside of peace could be tolerated to some extent by the authorities, who treated certain motives, especially those related to the defence of honour, with some leniency; but returning to commit a crime after having signed a peace would not be tolerated.

Such an attitude is difficult to comprehend from the viewpoint of modern practices of criminal justice. For the authorities of the time, the pedagogical and edifying function of the measures adopted, aimed at reintegrating the offender into the social fabric after having encumbered the kinship through the *sicurtà*, took on a predominant importance compared to the punitive function, even at the cost of the obvious inefficiency of the system. The tendency was to create an equilibrium in the hope that it would remain intact, but it took little to shatter everything. Peace was something more than an exit strategy from the grip exerted by the authorities through imprisonment, deployment *ad standum*, imposition of *sicurtà* not to harm, or even by exiles wishing to return home. Signing a peace agreement still involved an investment of immaterial resources in the relationships between the aggressor and the victim that it would be wrong to ignore; a moral and religious superstructure that was an integral part of the (fragile) strategy of controlling behaviours, both individual and collective. It is not easy to bring out this aspect from the documentation, either because it is completely absent or because it is overly abundant as it is externally directed, standardised, and detached from reality, as in the case of peace agreements, renunciations and pardons. From the testimony given in 1584 by Michele, however, a Roman described as a 'painter', we can glean something. A Cesari, a wood merchant, accompanied by his brother and other men, went and stood outside his house intending to provoke him ('Oh Michele painter, you are not a man of honour, and I will show you, come down');[224] the men broke into the house through the windows, but

[223] See below, pp. 112–114.

[224] 'o Michel pitore tu non sei homo de onore et te lo farò vedere vien abaso', ASR, *Tribunale Criminale del Governatore, Atti di Cancelleria, Lettere*, vol. 44, year 1594, n. 207, f. 205.

the reaction of Michele's neighbours prevented them from going further in their attempt to attack. Subsequently, Michele declared, two grooms of Cardinal de' Medici (the future Grand Duke Ferdinand I), who were cousins, 'made me make peace',[225] and things quieted down for the moment. But only a few days later, Michele perceived suspicious presences and movements around him ('this Cesari kept spies on me'),[226] and he wanted to get to the bottom of it: 'I caught one of these spies and told him, traitor, why do you pursue me? The spy said that Cesari, the wood merchant, sent him to tell me so'.[227] Michele then decided to immediately return to one of the architects of the peace with Cesari, the groom who went by the name of Titta di Palestrina, to protest: 'I told him that I no longer wanted peace with this Cesari and that he should be warned that *friends do not send spies after one another* and that everyone should guard their own life.'[228] The agreement broke down, and Michele turned to justice, but the threats escalated. The other groom, named Marcantonio, was at that time 'withdrawn from Cardinal de' Medici with four or five others',[229] and one Sunday in August, Michele had to endure an attack in Piazza San Salvatore in Lauro (Rione Ponte) by a squad of ten to twelve people intending to kill him, foiled only thanks to the benevolent intervention of an Antonio Tasso, who made the attackers desist from carrying out their plan. At this point, it became clear to Michele that 'these grooms [are] openly in favour of my said enemies'.[230]

'Friends do not send spies': the phrase is quite eloquent and testifies to a widespread conviction that the transition from enmity to friendship – whether imposed by judicial authorities or spontaneously reached – could not be purely formal, could not turn into mere abstention from aggressions or verbal provocations, but had to translate into behaviours consistent with the state of friendship. There was, after all, a moral, value-based, and religious universe to be respected. Especially since, when Michele stopped and questioned the spy, he not only confessed to being hired by Cesari but

[225] 'mi fecero fare la pace', ibid.

[226] 'questo Cesari mi teneva perseguitato dele spie', ibid.

[227] 'io ne chiapai uno de queste et li dissi traditore perché mi perseguete? Disse detta spia che Cesari mercante di legnia me lo mandava dire', ibid.

[228] 'li disse che io non volevo più pace con questo Cesari et che lo advertisi che *li amici non mandano dreto le spie* et che ognuno si salva', ibid, italics mine.

[229] 'ritirato del Cardenale de Medici con quatro ò cinque', ibid.

[230] 'detti palafrenieri [sono] scopertamente in favore deli detti miei nemici', ibid.

also said 'that this would be a kind of peace to betray me'.[231] Despite the expectations of the subjects involved, peace could in some cases turn into a real trap precisely because of such expectations; it could, in fact, prove to be a suspension of hostilities deliberately aimed at preparing a further attack to be launched in the future. All of this was with the complicity of compliant intermediaries who perhaps – as in the case of the cardinal's grooms – had become credible thanks to their social position.

[231] 'che questo sarà spetia di pace mi cercava a tradire', ibid.

3.

Negotiated justice and centre–periphery relations

1. Vindicatory violence and *lèse-majesté*: the struggle for control over peacekeeping practices

The advent of modernity, both juridical and judicial, has traditionally been identified with initiating the process that made criminal law independent from civil law, to the detriment of the latter, and the concurrent emergence of the public criminal process at the expense of private solutions to conflict resolution. On the *terminus a quo* of this evolution, historiography has not always been in agreement. Some have preferred to relegate the entire pre-revolutionary era to a sort of archaism in which jurists were inclined 'to treat criminal issues [...] with a civil law mentality, as if criminal law were a necessary complement to civil law, a complex of defences prepared to protect particular positions of privilege of individuals or the community.'[1] Others have instead highlighted how much modernity was already present in the criminal doctrine of the fifteenth and sixteenth centuries, which was increasingly forced to address the issue of the public relevance of crimes, the threat they posed to the security and preservation of the state. The transformation, in the direction of an indefinite expansion, of the concept and fields of application of the *crimen laesae maiestatis* was, as Mario Sbriccoli showed almost half a century ago, one of the main instruments – underpinned by an ideology, which may perhaps be seen as the primary force that allowed state jurisdiction to erode fundamental areas of legitimacy from competing jurisdictions, especially feudal ones. It was a process that began in the late Middle Ages and centred the doctrinal reflection and judicial practice on the concept of obedience to the constituted power, both political and religious, supported by a true obsession with betrayal, felony (and heresy, regarding

[1] Giuseppe Bettiol, 'Il problema penale', in Giuseppe Bettiol, *Scritti giuridici*, vol. II (Padova, 1966), p. 623, cited in Mario Sbriccoli, *Crimen laesae maiestatis. Il problema del reato politico alle soglie della scienza penalistica moderna* (Milan, 1974), p. 6, n. 6.

the religious aspect). The first area of application of this system was feudal law: it was the felonious vassal to whom the sovereign applied the penalty of confiscation of assets, both feudal and non-feudal, starting a practice that would be continued in subsequent centuries in the form of confiscation.[2]

The process of centralisation pursued by the popes in the sixteenth century could not but be accompanied by that 'expansion of the majestatic area and the criminal offences', that 'politicisation of many "common" crimes', essentially the application of the *crimen maiestatis* scheme to all crimes to 'instil fear in the citizens and [...] dissuade them from committing any crime',[3] a phenomenon observed throughout early modern Europe. According to most jurists and political thinkers in the service of power, any criminal action was capable of breaking the *pax publica*, understood primarily as the established order and state security. It goes without saying that the articulated manifestations of interpersonal violence were scrutinised by doctrine and classified according to schemes that directly or indirectly placed control over them among the specific competences of sovereign justice. And so it was that not only factional violence but even simple *rixa* (fights) were increasingly conceptualised as potential germs of the dissolution of the political body: the *fractio pacis* (the breaking of a peace agreement), the *quietis publicae turbatio* (disturbing the peace), these can indeed easily lead to tumult and, ultimately, to *seditio* (sedition). Already in the late fifteenth century, the reversal of the trend from late medieval thought (consider Bartolus de Saxoferrato) that managed to contemplate the existence of good factions, a natural defence against a tyrannical government, is clearly visible in the treatise *De factionibus extinguendis* by the Bishop of Bergamo, the Venetian Pietro Barozzi, in which the terms connected to *pars* (group) and *factio* (faction) are all negatively connoted concerning the security of the state: *seditio*, *proditio* (betrayal/treason), *rebellio*, *tumultus*, *coadunatio* (mass gathering).[4] A

2 Cf. Sbriccoli, *Crimen laesae maiestatis*.

3 'dilatazione dell'area maiestatica e delle fattispecie criminose', 'politicizzazione di molti reati "comuni"', 'spaventare i cittadini e [...] dissuaderli dal commettere qualsiasi delitto', i vi, pp. 256–7.

4 Marco Bellabarba, *La giustizia nell'Italia moderna. XVI-XVIII secolo* (Rome and Bari, 2008), p. 59. In the sixteenth century, the possible positive value of the *factio* was already a memory of the past, as also demonstrated by the position taken by the German jurist Konrad Braun (*De seditionibus libri sex, rationibus et exemplis ex omni doctrinarum et authorum genere locupletati*), according to whom it does not only constitute a case of *seditio* but also of *conspiratio*, which contains within it the element of *proditio*: 'propria enim significatione factio semper in malam partem accipitur: est enim factio malorum consensus et conspiratio' ('for in its proper meaning, faction is always taken in a negative sense: it is indeed a consensus

condemnation of the spirit of faction was particularly alive in the years around the turn of the fifteenth and sixteenth centuries, nourished by an aspiration for concord that was both religious and political. In March 1495, Girolamo Savonarola attributed to the intercession of the Virgin the abolition, ordered by the Great Council of Florence, of the 'law of the six beans', an abolition he himself proposed in the Epiphany sermon of that year to allow those condemned by the Signoria for crimes against the state to appeal to the Great Council, which would thus function as a superior tribunal. The 'law of the six beans' had indeed proven to be easily manipulated by the faction in power to strike political opponents, and for this reason, Savonarola, supported by the *piagnone* party, promoted a measure deemed an indispensable piece for the *renovatio* of the republic, part of a broader project of spiritual renewal promoted by the friar from Ferrara.[5]

This expansion of the field of application of *lèse-majesté*, both divine and human, is normally linked to the development of new and more efficient tools for the exercise of the *ius puniendi* of the judicial apparatuses, a direct expression of royal authority. Wielding the spectre of violent and exemplary repression of any crime, modelled on the *crimen maiestatis* scheme, had an essentially dissuasive purpose. But how does the phenomenon we have just described reconcile with the proven persistence (and pervasiveness) of systems of social conflict resolution centred on peace and on legal instruments deriving their legitimacy from the prince's *potestas oeconomica*? How do these two different modes reconcile and intertwine in the concrete solutions adopted to tackle complex and often ruinous dynamics of violence? Historiography has paid little attention to the issue, mostly relegating the pacification procedures – as we have repeatedly verified – to a privatistic, residual and premodern phenomenon, over which public authorities could at most try to impose some form of control but which was nevertheless destined to disappear once the modernisation process was completed. In reality, it was not a linear path, and the definition of the areas of application of the

---

of evildoers and conspiracy'), quoted in Sbriccoli, *Crimen laesae maiestatis*, pp. 301–2. For a detailed analysis of the 'phenomenology of *seditio*', within which jurists have reasoned about *clamores seditiosi*, *quietis publicae turbatio*, *congregatio armatorum*, *factiones* and *partialitates*, *rixa*, etc., see op. cit., pp. 283–306.

[5] See Marco Pellegrini, *Savonarola. Profezie e martirio nell'età delle guerre d'Italia* (Rome, 2020), pp. 139–41. The name of the law refers to the voting procedure used by the *Signoria*: the priors and the gonfalonier of Justice were called to express their opinion on a case by inserting a black bean for yes, or a white bean for no, into a ballot box; with a qualified two-thirds majority, corresponding to six black beans, harsh sentences could be imposed for crimes against the state without the right of appeal for the condemned. I thank Michaela Valente for the suggestion.

crimen maiestatis scheme was the subject of intense and daily confrontation between central judicial bodies, peripheral magistracies, communities and kinship groups, generating a dialectical tension that needs to be thoroughly examined to understand the concrete ways of articulating and exercising power beyond the increasingly solid doctrinal edifices.

It is difficult, but perhaps also pointless, to try to pinpoint once and for all a threshold beyond which violence and revenge became, in the judgement of those exercising power, a threat to the stability of the state and a challenge to the sovereign's legitimate authority. Once the principle was established in the abstract that any crime directly or indirectly threatens public order and peace, the positioning of the line of demarcation between public and private depended on the circumstances and the specific balance of power existing between the centre of power (not necessarily the state) and the specific peripheral territory. Once again, context analysis is of primary importance. In advancing state jurisdiction at the expense of competing ones, public authorities had to take into account not only the resistance posed by traditional magistracies – urban, feudal and communal – which considered themselves legally entitled to intervene to punish or prevent criminal acts stemming from feuds and vendettas, but also the essentially communal and familial nature of the manifestations of violence. Prosecuting and punishing the perpetrator of a single criminal act, even when accomplices were targeted, did not restore an order based on the social balance between families and groups, a balance itself anchored in the respect of certain foundational values, such as honour and prestige, often shared by power apparatuses.

The popes did not rely on *sicurtà* not to harm, which were also extended to the relatives of the offenders, on precepts, bounties, rewards for the capture of bandits, and finally on peace agreements, because they were unable, or did not have the power, to intervene broadly and systematically with coercive instruments; but this was not the only reason. The public or private nature of a phenomenon and, correspondingly, of the instruments deployed to govern it, depended on a very complex series of factors. Moreover, there was a close correspondence between the two levels, because peace understood as an agreement between private individuals, for example, found its deepest legitimacy in being a reflection of public peace, of public quiet, the disturbance of which constituted the gravest of threats to the security of the state, just as the breaking of a peace agreement between private individuals represented the violation of a commitment based on ethical and religious values, an aspect that precisely in the post-Tridentine age underwent some amplification, evidenced by the commitment of ecclesiastical personnel in this field.[6] This explains the severity with which the offence of *fractio pacis* (private) was normally punished. Both violence and peace possessed a character that was at the same time private and public: a homicide, a stabbing, a shooting, a physical assault, these could legitimately remain confined within the kinship group, or – equally legitimately – become an affair of the entire community and its specific magistracies, or – again – justify the intervention of central judicial bodies – an intervention, it should be noted, not always feared and opposed by the former. The contexts just mentioned were not monads, because it was often the families and local powers themselves that sought external solutions. In these cases, it was not necessarily a matter of concessions but of requests to strengthen local conflict resolution systems, needing legitimisation from above.

The tensions that developed between central and local magistracies often revolved around the differentiation between high and low criminality, and it is in these discussions that the role of negotiation and transactional instruments for conflict resolution emerges in all its importance, because the clash did not occur between a local dimension predominantly inclined to such methods and a central dimension inclined instead to rely on coercive solutions. Rather, it was a contest over who should take up the negotiating tools, or at least the tools that seemed likely to effect a solution. The issue was played out on a field of fundamental importance for efforts at state centralisation, in terms of both jurisdiction and fiscality. One of the core issues was the process by which a particular crime was classified as of minor importance (and therefore fully cognisable by peripheral magistracies without any intervention from the central ones) or of serious importance. The strategy used

6 This aspect will be developed in Chapter 5. Here, it is sufficient to recall some studies that have focused on the activity of pacification carried out by the missionary regular clergy in the sixteenth and, especially, the seventeenth century, where the ceremonial aspect was of particular importance: Ottavia Niccoli, *Perdonare. Idee, pratiche, rituali in Italia tra Cinque e Seicento* (Rome and Bari, 2007), pp. 170–85; Ottavia Niccoli, 'Rinuncia, pace, perdono. Rituali di pacificazione della prima età moderna', *Studi Storici* XL, 1 (1999), pp. 219–61; Adriano Prosperi, *Tribunali della coscienza. Inquisitori, confessori, missionari* (Turin, 1996), pp. 642–9; Jennifer D. Selwyn, *A Paradise Inhabited by Devils. The Jesuits' Civilizing Mission in Early Modern Naples* (Aldershot, 2004), pp. 183–209; Paolo Broggio, 'I gesuiti come pacificatori in età moderna: dalle guerre di frontiera nel Nuovo Mondo americano alle lotte fazionarie nell'Europa mediterranea', *Rivista di Storia e Letteratura Religiosa* XXXIX, 2 (2003), pp. 249–89; Paolo Broggio, *Evangelizzare il mondo. Le missioni della Compagnia di Gesù tra Europa e America (secoli XVI-XVII)* (Rome, 2004), pp. 197–243; Paolo Broggio, 'Pratiche e rituali di reintegrazione: la pacificazione dei nemici nella pastorale cattolica in area mediterranea (secoli XVI-XVIII)', *Mediterranea. Ricerche storiche* 61, Agosto 2024, pp. 327–52.

by the pontifical magistracies was not to demand exclusive handling of all criminal matters – nor, for that matter, would they have been able to do so – but to take control of the process of classifying individual crimes. They sought to ensure that all cases reached the central magistracies, regardless of their degree of severity, only to then allow those of minor importance to reverse course, returning to the jurisdiction of local magistracies. The central authority, not the local magistracy, was to decide on the status of the crime. In a sense, it was the establishment of a system of reserved cases based on the distinction – at least theoretically – between high and low criminality, which, however, functioned according to a reverse mechanism compared to what happened in the field of religious crimes, where only those sins that simple confessors equipped with ordinary faculties did not have the power to absolve reached the bishops and inquisitors; higher instances of judgement were reserved for the gravest crimes of faith.[7]

Certainly, this did not occur without hitches, resistance and difficulties of all kinds. It is essentially for this reason that, in the second half of the sixteenth century, the bulk of attempts to create local magistracies characterised by a nature halfway between the secular and the spiritual was concentrated in the Papal States, aimed at the non-contentious, peaceful and conciliatory resolution of minor conflicts. The introduction of such magistracies, as can be easily imagined, provoked conflicts whose deciphering, however, cannot be attributed simply to the paradigm of the resistance of the peripheries against the centralising intents of the sovereign.

2. Neither Marche nor Romagna: the 'exception' of Bologna

On 9 September 1658, one of the meetings of the *Assunteria delle liti e paci* was held in Bologna, a governing body probably established at the beginning of that decade, modelled upon other *assunterie* existing since the first half of the sixteenth century, and aimed at mediating conflicts between noblemen and reaching arbitral solutions. The minutes of the meeting unequivocally explain the motivations behind the establishment of the senatorial body, which were not only to 'procure the quiet of the nobility'[8] but also to 'keep

7 See Elena Brambilla, 'Un percorso segreto e tortuoso. La comparizione spontanea in alcuni recenti studi sul sant'Officio di Aquileia e Concordia', *Società e Storia* 145 (2014), pp. 529–52.

8 'procurar la quiete della nobiltà', ASB, *Assunteria liti e paci*, I, Atti, c. 3v, cited in Niccoli, *Perdonare*, pp. 115–16.

away the prejudices of the City's prerogatives'.[9] In the pacification of enmities among nobles (and not only among nobles), a game was being played that was not only jurisdictional and – as we have seen – fiscal, but also wholly political. There are not many documentary traces of the works carried out by this *assunteria* until the end of the century,[10] but an aspect of certain interest is found precisely in the era when such a body was established in Bologna, clearly an expression of the values and interests of the senatorial nobility but which had to act in concert with the cardinal legate. We are in the mid-seventeenth century, a rather late period compared to the focal years of clashes between the legate and the *Quaranta* regarding the centralisation of criminal justice governance, clashes that also touched on the issue of peace agreements. Even considering the late creation of the *Assunteria delle paci*, it would probably not be an exaggeration to hypothesise that it was a compromise solution, reached only after long negotiations and opposing arguments, between the senatorial claim for local control of conciliation procedures, including for the countryside, and the attempt by the *Tribunale del Torrone* to establish a centralised system that ensured on one hand the achievement of peace agreements following the imposition of a series of restrictive measures, and on the other the channelling of financial proceeds from those same measures to the *Camera Apostolica*.

In the sixteenth century, the clash lasted for decades, at least since the restoration of pontifical authority after the return of the Bentivoglio between 1511 and 1512, and it could never be said to be completely dormant, not even when, during the pontificate of Sixtus V, the bull of 15 March 1589 established once and for all the principle that the Bolognese legation should be considered on a par with all other provinces of the Papal States regarding their competence to impose fines and confiscations, and especially regarding the destination of the related proceeds (including those from monetary compositions) exclusively to the *Camera Apostolica*. Thus, any claim of exemption for Bologna by virtue of ancient privileges, which according to

[9] 'tener lontano i pregiudicij delle prerogative della Città', ibid.

[10] The preserved documentation consists of a register of acts and a bundle of documents. 'Il materiale documentario raccolto a parte mostra come l'Assunteria si impegnò ad appianare molteplici situazioni fra il 1651 e il 1694, sia pure in maniera discontinua e non verbalizzando la propria attività (o comunque non verbalizzare sul registro che ci è rimasto)' ('The separate documentary material shows how the *Assunteria* endeavoured to smooth out multiple situations between 1651 and 1694, albeit in a discontinuous manner and without recording its activity (or at least not recording it in the register that has remained'). Niccoli, *Perdonare*, p. 116.

the political ideology supported by the senatorial class outlined a mixed government in which the power of the legate was accompanied by that of the *Quaranta*, was rejected – a form of government that was supposedly formally established by the chapters signed by Nicholas V in 1447.[11] The Senate reacted to Sixtus's bull of 1589 with dismay: the measure, in fact, 'not only cuts the root of all indulgences and privileges', as the Senate wrote to Cardinal Paleotti on 24 May of the same year, 'but also deprives magistrates and officials of their faculties, and if executed, would reduce us to a state little less than of misery'.[12] Besides the senatorial opposition to the legate's competence to impose confiscation on those condemned to banishment or exile, the *Quaranta* always considered the massive recourse to *sicurtà* not to harm by the officials of the *Torrone*, for crimes that traditionally fell within the jurisdiction of the officials of the *contado* dependent on the commune, as the introduction of a surreptitious form of confiscation, which moreover affected innocent fathers for crimes committed by their sons.

Not long after, the Bolognese had to test the firepower that the Roman popes were able to deploy, combined with the deployment of militias, to maintain their dominion over the legation. In 1512, at the end of the Bentivoglio interlude, Julius II proceeded to absolve the Bolognese from the censures they had incurred, except for those against members of the Bentivoglio family, and to lift the interdict against the city, which had been motivated also by the loyalty that the Bentivoglio Regiment had sworn to the (schismatic) Pisan council in March 1512; a general pardon that corresponded to the restitution to clerics and laypeople of the properties confiscated as a result of the censures and interdict, but which was the prelude to the establishment of a very harsh regime entrusted to the care of the pontiff's nephew, Orlando della Rovere, and Francesco Frescobaldi, who proclaimed himself castellan of the new fortress built on Strada Maggiore. Rewards were promised to anyone who would bring a Bentivoglio to justice, and very heavy contributions were imposed.[13] In such a scenario, it is important not to underestimate the role that censures and excommunications, combined with

[11] Cf. Angela De Benedictis, *Repubblica per contratto. Bologna: una città europea nello Stato della Chiesa* (Bologna, 1995).

[12] 'non solo taglia la radice a tutti gl'indulti et privilegi ma leva le facoltà a magistrati et ufficiali, et esseguendosi ci ridurrebbe in stato poco men che di miseria', ASB, *Senato, Lettere*, series I, reg. 15, the whole letter at ff. 542^{v}–543^{r} (the Senate to the Ambassador, 24 May 1589), also cited in Andrea Gardi, *Lo Stato in provincia. L'amministrazione della Legazione di Bologna durante il regno di Sisto V (1585-1590)* (Bologna, 1994), p. 339.

[13] See De Benedictis, *Repubblica per contratto*, pp. 196–7.

fines and confiscations, played not only in the exceptional circumstances of re-establishing pontifical power over rebellious cities or territories but also in the everyday, as preferential weapons that Rome systematically used to punish those who committed crimes of various seriousness, from open rebellion and *lèse-majesté* to the more common acts of retaliatory violence. It was also through the systematic recourse to the weapons of censure and excommunication, contained in the legal instruments deriving from the economic power of the pope, governors and legates, that the central power managed, albeit with difficulty, to snatch ever more significant slices of jurisdiction from the magistracies dependent on the communes and feudal lords.

The period between the 1560s and the 1580s was the focal moment of the clashes between the Senate and the Tribunal of the *Torrone*, and consequently between the Senate and the popes, regarding the definition of the competence of the officials of the *contado* over minor criminal matters. Faced with repeated Bolognese requests to leave intact the prerogatives of the latter, Rome responded on one hand by stating that such presumed privilege of Bologna would have to be documented, and on the other by reiterating that all criminal matters should pass through the net of the supreme legatine tribunal. The insistent Bolognese requests for a declaration whereby Rome would once and for all establish the distinction between high and low criminal matters availed little; the popes preferred to leave the issue as indeterminate as possible, the only way to avoid unequivocally recognising a precise sphere of competence to local magistracies. Among the cases reserved for the *Torrone* were usually breaches of peace, along with murder, abduction and arson. In November 1555, in response to yet another Bolognese request for a formal papal pronouncement on the extent of the jurisdiction of the officials of the *contado*[14] so that they would not be 'continuously subjected to the discretion which as often as not could cause hatreds and animosities among officials seeing differences made among them',[15] Rome replied that

14 'Al meno Sua Signoria Illustrissima declarasse in quali casi volesse et havessero da procedere, et usare la lor giurisditione eccettuando et nominando o specificando quelli dove non li paresse che si havessero da ingerire come è a dire rapti, incendi o paci rotte che per la nequitia loro et malvagità pareno in certo modo più considerevoli' ('At least His Most Illustrious Lordship should declare in which cases they should proceed and exercise their jurisdiction, excepting and naming or specifying those where it would not seem appropriate for them to intervene, such as abductions, arsons or broken peaces, which due to their wickedness and malice appear somewhat more considerable'), ASB, *Senato*, *Lettere*, series VII, reg. 30 (the Ambassador to the Senate, 6 November 1555).

15 'continuamente sottopposti all'arbitrio il quale bene et spesso potria causare de gli odi et delle malevolentie tra officiali per tempo vedendo esser fatta differentia tra loro', ibid.

such identification was superfluous, because no one intended to question the prerogatives of the officials fixed in the 'pardon'. However, the Bishop of Avignon, Annibale Bozzutti, then prolegate of Bologna, specified to the ambassador that 'it is indeed true that there could arise cases that would need the hand of the vice-legate and the court, to deal with both the nature of the excesses and the weakness of the officials. He wanted the *massari* to make the denunciations to the *Torrone*, not of all indiscriminately, but only of the gravest cases'.[16] A response came from Rome that was largely evasive from the point of view of establishing the general principle: it did not absolutely deny the entirety of the officials' prerogatives but at the same time repeated the strategy of using the community *massari* to bypass the officials of the *contado*, using the presumed weakness of the latter in dealing with 'more heinous crimes' as a shield.

In March of the following year, Bozzutti, still pressed by the Bolognese ambassador, revisited the issue. The ambassador had pointed out to the vice-legate that the pardon signed by the pope exempted peasants and *massari* from bringing cases to the *Torrone*, except for the four reserved cases. This interpretation was confirmed by a letter sent from the legate to the vice-legate, but the prelate responded that, in addition to the letter referenced,

> other letters had been written as well, and that he did not know that in other times, as we claimed, it was customary not to report to the *Torrone* except for serious crimes; on the contrary, in his time, all were reported. Furthermore, it would not be proper otherwise, because it was the duty of the *Torrone* and the superiors to know all the crimes committed to discern which should be left to the officials of the *contado* and which should not. For example, a minor offence, such as a slap, might not be appropriate for an official to handle due to their inexperience and lack of practice. Conversely, a serious crime could be entrusted to a skilled and knowledgeable official, as he claimed to have allowed in his time. He recounted many things against the improper conduct of the officials, specifically noting that he knew that the peasants preferred to go to the *Torrone* rather than to the officials of the *contado*. To this, it was replied that it is typical of the guilty to always avoid the court where they are summoned, etc.[17]

16 'ben vero che potendo nascere delli casi che haverieno bisogno della mano del vicelegato et della corte, sì per la qualità de gli eccessi, come per la debolezza degli officiali voleva che li massari facessero le denoncie al Torrone, et non di tutti indifferentemente, ma solo delli gravissimi', ibid.

17 'ne erano state scritte delle altre, et che non sapeva che per altri tempi come noi allegavamo si fosse usato di non denonciar al Torrone, se non quelli delitti gravi, anzi che al suo tempo si denonciavano tutti; et che altramenti non staria bene, perchè era il dovero che il Torrone et li superiori sapessero tutti li malefici che

The indeterminacy undoubtedly played in favour of Rome's centralising intentions and against the preservation of the officials' prerogatives. The popes did not find it convenient to establish general rules for the division of competences; they preferred to opt for a case-by-case decision system, which inevitably ended up entrusting the judicial bodies dependent on the centre with a decisive role in determining the nature of the case, thus stripping local magistracies of their traditional competences. It is impossible to pinpoint a moment when this solution could be definitively and peacefully accepted. For Rome, it was a continuous reiteration of a directive line that met daily resistance from local judicial bodies, even though, by the end of the sixteenth century, this process could be said to be 'now completed and definitive, despite the protests of the Senate'.[18] This is evidenced by the fact that, even at the end of the seventeenth century, Legate Girolamo Gastaldi found himself having to reiterate once more that the *massari* were obliged to bring all reports to the *Torrone*, regardless of the nature and severity of the crime, which for minor cases 'usually issues a decree *non molestari secuta reconciliatione*'.[19] For peace to culminate in a decree *non molestari* issued by the supreme legatine tribunal, that is, the judiciary's commitment to consider the case closed and thus not prosecute the offender for that same crime in the future, it necessarily had to be signed under the aegis of the *Torrone* and not left to the free initiative of the community magistracies. Some legates, continued Gastaldi in response to a memorial from the community of Vergato sent in March 1683, 'have had these complaints read before them by the head notary of the *Torrone*, who registers them in a notebook, and

si comettevano per discerner qual fosse da lasciar conoscer alli officiali del contà et quali no; perchè potria esser qualche eccesso leggieri, come d'una ceffata, che per la inhabilità et poca pratica dell'officiale, non seria da lassarli conoscer; et per il contrario un grave delitto si potria lassar conoscer ad uno officiale pratico et intelligente, come dice egli al suo tempo di haver lasciato far; et in questa pratica contra il mal proceder delli officiali disse di molte cose, et in specie che sapeva che li contadini andavano molto più volentieri al Torrone che agli officiali del contà; al che si rispose che era proprio del reo di fuggir sempre il foro dove è chiamato ecc.', ASB, *Senato, Lettere*, series VII, reg. 31 (the Ambassador Camillo Paleotti to the Senate, 7 March 1556).

18 'ormai compiuto e definitivo, nonostante le proteste del Senato', Giancarlo Angelozzi, 'Parte I. Gli ordinamenti giudiziari', in Giancarlo Angelozzi and Cesarina Casanova, *La giustizia dei burocrati. La Restaurazione nella Bologna pontificia*, monographic issue of *Bollettino del Museo del Risorgimento* LV (2010), pp. 7–71: p. 9.

19 'è solito fare decreto non molestari secuta reconciliatione', AAV, *Segreteria di Stato, Legazione di Bologna*, vol. 62, cited in Angelozzi and Casanova, *La giustizia criminale*, p. 133.

upon hearing them, the legate writes in the margin of each whether it should proceed or not'.[20] On that occasion, Gastaldi clearly stated that he had always acted in this manner, 'following up only on reports of murders, serious injuries, significant thefts, and insults from which greater crimes could arise; in these cases, a notary and bailiffs were sent to conduct the proceedings'.[21] The control of the *Torrone* over pacification procedures, usually carried out for minor crimes, was thus ensured.

It can be said that, at the beginning of the seventeenth century, the objective of centralising justice procedures in the Bolognese *contado* was essentially achieved through a series of combined strategies, among which stood out the multiplication of the 'cavalcades' of the *sottuditori* and notaries of the *Torrone* and the recourse, always by the officials of the legatine tribunal, to the *massari* of the communities to receive reports of crimes committed. Protests against this practice came not only from the *Quaranta* but also from the communities themselves, which wanted the *massari* not to be forced to bring all cases and complaints to the city but to leave minor crimes, those for which afflictive penalties could not be imposed, fully within the competence of the local officials. Centralising justice did not, therefore, mean limiting recourse to conciliatory solutions of an apparently private nature; it meant, if anything, using those self-same solutions to strip jurisdictional spaces from local magistracies.

Another area of conflict between the legate and the Bolognese Senate, perhaps the one that most engaged the time and energies of the diplomatic representatives active at the curia, was Bologna's claimed exemption from fines and confiscations. The polemic, which lasted for decades, closely touched upon the set of preventive measures linked in various ways to peace, as the *sicurtà* not to harm, widely imposed by the officials of the *Torrone* on occasions of killings, injuries, brawls, beatings and insults, were rightly considered by the *Quaranta* as disguised confiscations, and without a doubt as pecuniary penalties from which Bologna considered itself exempt, with the aggravating factor of indiscriminately affecting innocent people and their families. What is certain is that the method of the oath guaranteed by a *sicurtà* not to harm became the usual way in which the Roman centre related to local political and judicial institutions that were supposed to ensure not only

[20] 'hanno fatto leggere dette querele avanti di sé dal capo notaro del Torrone, che le registra in un quinternetto, e sentendole il legato, fa scrivere al margine di ciascheduna se si deve, o non si deve procedere', ibid.

[21] 'dando seguito solo alle denunce di omicidi, ferimenti, furti rilevanti, insulti dai quali avrebbero potuto nascere delitti maggiori; in questi casi si mandavano notaio e sbirri a fare i processi', Angelozzi and Casanova, *La giustizia criminale*, p. 133.

their loyalty and obedience to the sovereign pope and his representatives but also the maintenance of peace and public order in their territories. The commitment required from the traditionally restless Bolognese nobility, which was not inclined to disciplined behaviour, was thus not generic but in some cases took a very precise form with a guaranteed economic benefit.[22] On the occasion of the killing of Giovanni di Lolo by a group of nobles in a quadrille in 1549, following the death of Pope Paul III Farnese, the senators were asked not only to swear before the vice-legate but also to sign a *sicurtà* of 2,000 *scudi* to further solidify the commitment that no more such episodes would occur. On 16 November 1549, thirty-one senators and several gentlemen swore before the legate, promising 'harmony and concord',[23] while the *sicurtà* not to harm were signed the following month.[24]

The *Torrone* used *sicurtà* and fines extensively, which inevitably raised concerns in the Senate. The fine was triggered in a vast array of cases, even in response to the simple refusal to comply with a precept to provide a *sicurtà* not to harm. In 1566, Ettore Desideri was declared contumacious and sentenced to pay a fine for refusing to sign a *sicurtà* not to harm, and the Senate did not fail to complain about what had happened, 'recognising under such a veil was concealed the confiscation of goods'.[25] At that time, Desideri was engaged in military operations with the Catholic forces in Hungary, and his brother Enea managed to obtain from the *Torrone* a delay in applying the penalty until Ettore's return to Bologna,[26] especially since Ettore was the victim of the violent act and – it was asserted – if he had not already left, he would have willingly consented to the peace agreement. However, the Senate was concerned with the principle, not whether Desideri agreed to pay the fine: the principle that fines or *sicurtà* not to harm that resembled confiscation should not be introduced in Bologna.

Even papal bulls aimed at addressing the scourge of banditry constantly alarmed the Senate, as in the case of Pius V's 1566 ordinance against

22 See in this regard the extensive study by Giancarlo Angelozzi and Cesarina Casanova, *La nobiltà disciplinata. Violenza nobiliare, procedure di giustizia e scienza cavalleresca a Bologna nel XVII secolo* (Bologna, 2003).

23 'buona unione et concordia', ASB, *Senato, Lettere*, series I, reg. 8, f. 426^{v} (the Senate to the Ambassador, 16 November 1549).

24 ASB, *Senato, Lettere*, series VII, reg. 25 (the Ambassador to Giorgio Magiolo and Ludovico De Rossi, 24 December 1549).

25 'conoscendo sotto un tal velo venirsi alla confiscatione di beni', ASB, *Senato, Lettere*, series III, reg. 9 (the Senate to the Ambassador, 14 August 1566).

26 Cf. Angelozzi and Casanova, *La giustizia criminale*, p. 200.

murderers, bandits and troublemakers,[27] which was deemed in several respects to be 'very captious and full of dangers and traps'[28] and therefore requiring clarification from Rome. Pope Ghislieri's intent was particularly centralising. First of all, only the pope could authorise, with a licence or a safe-conduct, the return of a banished murderer to his homeland, even if he had made peace with the relatives of the deceased; retaliations would be severely punished (*lèse-majesté* and confiscation of goods); the same severe penalties would apply to 'all other bandits, seditious persons, rebels, condemned to capital punishment, and troublemakers *who do not want to make peace*';[29] receivers and anyone who collaborated or aided bandits would be condemned for *lèse-majesté* and subjected to confiscation of goods, fiefs and privileges, as well as the destruction of their homes; communities that sheltered bandits or did not make an effort to capture them would be subjected to interdict and heavy fines, while feudal lords would face *latae sententiae* excommunication; absolutions, once granted even by provincial rectors and vicars, would be the exclusive prerogative of the pope. The Senate was concerned, among other things, that the ordinance did not distinguish between voluntary and forced shelter, as well as the fact that it treated all bandits the same and prescribed the same penalties for all, without assessing individual cases.

The issue of criminal absolutions following compositions, for which the achievement of peace was a sine qua non, was equally thorny. Also in September 1566, the ambassador wrote to the Senate expressing great concern over the increasingly widespread practice of sending petitions for absolutions to the Congregation of the *Consulta*, which then returned them to Bologna after evaluating them. The ambassador reported having seen with his own eyes one of these responses from the *Consulta*, where it was written 'Habita pace componat modo suo', that is, 'of the Governor, with the intervention of the Treasurer'. This is very dangerous because:

> introducing this practice places a yoke, an obligation, and a new servitude on this city, as well as instilling a fear and danger that, if continued, could lead to the introduction of the practices of Romagna and the Marca, where

[27] *Ordinatio s.d.n.d. Pij divina providentia pp. V vt eius bullae contra homicidas, bannitos, et alios facinorosos, eorumque receptatores editae singulis annis publice legantur* (Romae, Apud Haeredes Antonij Bladij Impressores Camerales, 1566).

[28] 'molto captiosa et piena di pericoli et lacci', ASB, *Ambasciata bolognese a Roma, Lettere all'Oratore*, reg. 1 (the Ambassador to the Cardinal of Ferrara, 4 September 1566).

[29] 'tutti gli altri banditi, seditiosi, ribelli, dannati in pena capitale, & brigosi, *che non vogliono far pace*', ibid, italics mine.

> compositions are not made and cannot be made without the Treasurers of those places. Consequently, it would also require having a Treasurer here for the Apostolic Chamber. Moreover, it is necessary to consider the damages and inconveniences that those seeking absolution will suffer, especially in non-serious cases where the penalty does not involve capital punishment.[30]

The strategy was clear: taking control of the pacification and composition procedures meant seizing the financial revenues traditionally destined for the Chamber of Bologna. This was a considerable loss, both in jurisdictional and fiscal terms, and particularly intolerable because it aimed to impact even minor criminal matters. The Senate's request, conveyed to the curia and the pope through its ambassador, was to allow all compositions to be decided locally by a superior and deposited with the Chamber of Bologna. Only subsequently, depending on the severity of the crime, could they be referred to the treasurer of the Apostolic Chamber.

3. A civil–ecclesiastical tribunal for peace: the Congregation of Concord of Bologna

In the second half of the sixteenth century, a significant contest was played out over minor criminal matters, at the crossroads between temporal and spiritual, and between retaliatory violence and civil and patrimonial issues. In 1574, Archbishop Gabriele Paleotti obtained from Gregory XIII the licence to establish the *Magistratus et officium concordiae* in Bologna, a judicial body known as the Congregation of Concord (*Congregazione della Concordia*), whose function was to reconcile disputes before the parties turned to the courts. It had its roots in the *Compagnia del Nome di Dio*, founded in 1566 to combat blasphemy and perjury, but which soon took on the task of making peace among members of confraternities before they resorted to official justice. Already in 1569, Pius V had established that, on each instance that anyone accepted or facilitated a reconciliation, they would enjoy forty days

[30] 'introducendosi questo modo si viene a porre a questa città un giogo, un obligo et una servitù nova, et anco un timor et pericolo che continuandosi non s'introduca l'uso della Romagna et della Marca dove le compositioni non si fanno, né far si possono senza li Thesorieri di que' luoghi, et per consequenza di tener anco qui un Thesoriero per la Camera Apostolica, oltra che anco si deve considerar li danni et incomodi che patiranno quei che domandaranno esser assoluti, massime ne' casi non gravi et ne quali non va pena dell'ultimo supplicio', op. cit. (the Ambassador to the Senate, 7 September 1566).

of indulgence.[31] This marks the phase of transition from the *Compagnia del Nome di Dio* to the Congregation of Concord, whose aim was to 'resolve the differences that arise among members of spiritual confraternities; and, since there are many such in this city, many dissensions arise, sometimes causing civil and criminal disputes'.[32] These were the words in July 1570 of the Jesuit Francesco Palmio, brother of the more famous Benedetto, one of Paleotti's closest collaborators, who personally participated in the meetings of the Congregation. 'Since this congregation was established,' Palmio continues, 'the [disputes] and discord have been removed in this easy way, which has given and continues to give much consolation and edification to all those of these companies and to the whole city'.[33]

The judicial nature of the newly established Congregation is not entirely clear today, and probably was not for the actors of the time. The impression is that even Rome did not fully grasp all the implications and potential risks of erecting a true magistracy – albeit an arbitral one, in line with the 'tradition of peaceful composition of disputes within medieval confraternities'[34] – within a confraternal institution. The Orders of the Congregation of Concord date from December 1574, while the following year the governor had the related *Capitoli* printed.[35] The reasons that led Gregory XIII to grant the establishment of an arbitral tribunal in the city of Bologna are explained in the preamble to the *Ordini*, structured on a rhetorical model that would find wide success in the following years, not only in Italy, as we will soon see. Being aware of 'how much damage and danger the controversies of disputes bring about, which are agitated between the parties in the Tribunals',[36] and considering how it has always proven difficult 'troncarle, ò abbreviarle' ('to

[31] See Niccoli, *Perdonare*, p. 154.

[32] 'accordare le differenze che nascono tra persone di confraternite spirituali quali, sì come sono molte in questa città, così vi nascono moltissime dissentioni, che alle volte causavano liti civili et criminali', cited in Paolo Prodi, *Il Cardinale Gabriele Paleotti (1522-1597)*, vol. II (Rome, 1967), p. 33.

[33] 'Dopoi che fu fatta questa congregatione si sono levate le [liti] et discordie con questa via soave che ha dato et dà molta consolatione et edificatione a tutti quelli di dette compagnie et a tutta la città', ibid.

[34] 'tradizione della composizione pacifica delle liti all'interno delle confraternite medievali', op. cit., p. 190.

[35] See *Capitoli et regole sopra l'audire, trattare, et concordare, lite & diferentie per gli huomini della Compagnia del Santissimo Nome di Dio di Bologna* (in Bologna, per Alessandro Benacci, 1575).

[36] 'quanto danno, & pericolo apportano le controversie delle Liti, che si agitano trà le parti ne i Tribunali'.

cut them off, or shorten them') owing to the 'malice and cunning of the interested parties and their supporters',[37] the pope ordered that the members of the Congregation, appointed for this function for four months, meet twice a week to ensure that 'anyone who intends to litigate in court can either obtain justice privately without further contention or withdraw from the dispute if he has no grounds'.[38] The provision of the document from which the creation of the arbitral magistracy derived, if applied literally, could have had disruptive effects on the city's judicial life, in so far as it aimed to inhibit any contentious proceedings unless the path of arbitral conciliation had first been attempted.

> Therefore, it is ordered and expressly prohibited in the name of His Holiness to everyone, regardless of state and condition, who intends to initiate any new civil dispute, whether secular or ecclesiastical, beneficial or spiritual, for any reason and with any person, that they must not summon their adversary to court, nor submit a written petition, nor initiate any process before any tribunal whatsoever, unless the following conditions are first met.[39]

It was particularly the specification 'of any state and condition' ('di qualunque stato, & conditione') that would prove to be the most problematic aspect of the provision, given the importance of the interests involved. Those who turned to the Congregation would have to present, orally or in writing, their request against their adversary, whom the deputies would summon. If the latter refused to appear before the deputies, they would be condemned to a pecuniary penalty, 'to be applied to pious places' ('d'applicarsi à luoghi pii').[40] Even in the case of the adversary's non-appearance, the deputies would still proceed to compose the dispute 'amicably without entering into litigation' ('amorevolmente senza intrare in lite'), and only in the case of no agreement could the plaintiff, after one month from the day of the first request for

[37] 'malitie, & cautele delli interessati, & de loro Fautori', *Ordini della congregatione della concordia. Constituita in Bologna dal santissimo, & beatissimo papa Gregorio 13. Publicata in Bologna alli 24 decemb. & reiterata alli 29 detto l'anno 1574* (in Bologna, per Alessandro Benacci, 1574).

[38] 'ciascuno c'havesse in animo di litigare in iudicio possa, ò conseguire il suo privatamente senz'altra contesa, ò ritirarsi dalla lite non havendo ragione', ibid.

[39] 'Si ordina donque, & espressamente prohibisce in nome di Sua Santità à ciascuno di qualunque stato, & conditione sia, che pretenda voler movere di novo alcuna lite Civile, così profana come Ecclesiastica, beneficiale, ò spirituale, per qual si voglia causa, & con qualonque persona, che non debba convenire l'avversario suo in iuditio, ne dare petitione in iscrito, ò far processo alcuno avanti qualonque Tribunale si sia, se non servate prima l'infrascritte cose', ibid.

[40] 'luoghi pii'('pious places') refers to institutions (and their locations) that, driven by religious and charitable motivations, were engaged in charity and social assistance.

arbitration, 'bring the matter to court at their pleasure and pursue their claim',[41] but not before obtaining from the notary of the Congregation the certificate of attempted arbitration, which the ordinary judges would have to request before agreeing to proceed with a trial. The direction of the Congregation was entrusted to the deputies of the *Compagnia del Nome di Dio*, hierarchically divided by functions, who were to meet at the archbishop's palace three days a week: Tuesday, Thursday and Saturday.

For the initial establishment, the identities of the ten deputies of the Congregation were specified: for the priests, the Prior of San Antonio and the Dean of San Petronio; for the senators, Giulio Bentivoglio and Vincenzo Maria Bargellini; for the doctors, Monterenzio and Gianetto; along with the procurator Stiatico, the notary Filippo Beroaldo, the gentleman knight Cattaneo and the merchant Antonio Maria Scappi. The text of the Chapters faithfully reflects a way of conceiving the arbitral composition of conflicts, thoroughly imbued with religious and pastoral ideals. Even the simple act of gathering in session to hear the petitioners was punctuated by gestures and acts of deep religious significance, such as kneeling, reciting the *Pater Noster*, imposing absolute silence as if it were a mass, invoking the Holy Spirit 'to obtain strength, and the spirit to think, reason and conclude according to the mind and intention of the Company of the Lord'.[42] In addition to the memorials submitted by the petitioners, the deputies were to gather other useful information to bring the litigants to an agreement. The deputies were expected, with God's help, to be 'patient in listening, diligent in examining, and solicitous in conferring, maintaining full charity, and compassionate to the afflicted'.[43] An arbitral task, as neutral and charitable as possible:

> To hear a case without judicial process and strict adherence to the law, but seeking with fairness and pleasantness to induce the parties to *Concordia* with goodness and equity, never letting their opinion be known until they have diligently considered the case and have prepared the parties to be satisfied with what they will judge appropriate.[44]

41 'dedurre in giuditio à suo piacere, & proseguire la sua pretensione', ibid.

42 'per impetrar forza, & spirito di pensar e, ragionare, & concludere cosa che sii secondo la mente, & intentione della Compagnia del Signore', *Capitoli et regole sopra l'audire.*

43 'patienti in ascoltare, diligenti in essaminare, & soleciti in conferire, mantenendosi pieni di charità, & compassionevoli alli afflitti', ibid.

44 'Cognoscendo le cause senza processi, & rigore di ragione, mà de bono & aequo cerchino con equità, & piacevolezza indurre le parti alla Concordia, ne mai si lassino intendere del parer suo, sin che non hanno per buona diligentia fatta già maturato la causa, & disposte le parti di contentarsi di quanto à loro parerà di giudicare', ibid.

The selection of deputies to be assigned to each case had to be made with extreme care; their competences had to be considered, as knowledge of the law and practice in relevant aspects of their life would undoubtedly be helpful. However, it was also emphasised that the true objective of arbitration was not to issue a ruling but to guide the parties towards an agreement.[45] Between 1574 and the early 1578, when the brief establishing the magistracy was issued, there was much discussion in Bologna about both the necessity of an official document conferring solid authority on the magistracy and the advisability of entrusting the pope with the power to appoint the members of the Congregation.[46] Many believed that papal appointment might be effective and beneficial under Gregory XIII but not necessarily under his successors, whose affection for Bologna could not be guaranteed.

In the autumn of 1576, the Senate prepared new chapters for the nascent tribunal, but the founding brief had still not arrived. The ambassador then delivered a draft of the Congregation's chapters, in both the vernacular and Latin, to Giovanni Antonio Facchinetti, bishop of Nicastro (and future Pope Innocent IX), who had been tasked by Pope Boncompagni with preparing the brief, to receive his comments. Facchinetti informed the Senate that it would be better to avoid having the election of deputies left to the pope, since any successor of Boncompagni might have much less interest in the matter as well as little or no knowledge of the people involved; additionally,

45 'Che in ellegere gli Assonti s'habbia avertimento, & riguardo di far elettione di persone intelligenti, et atti in simil cause, come per essempio, in cause mercantili, mercanti, & in cause che havessero bisogno di ventilatione di Instromenti publici, ò processi, altre volte copra ciò fatti si ellegeranno Assonti iurisperiti, & c. quali però nel discorrere le cause, & massime nella Congregatione non disputaranno l'articolo s'è di maggiore, ò nò; mà di discorrerà il fatto tendendo alla concordia, con l'equità con escludendo perciò l'Assonto ad informarsi, qual sia la determinatione della legge, accioche possi co[n] più maturità procedere alla co[n]cordia' ('When selecting the Deputies, attention and consideration must be given to elect individuals who are knowledgeable and suited for such matters. For example, in mercantile cases, merchants should be chosen; and in cases that require the examination of public instruments or processes, jurists may be elected as Deputies, and so on. However, when discussing cases, particularly in the Congregation, they shall not debate whether the matter is of greater or lesser importance; rather, they shall discuss the facts with the aim of reaching concord and fairness. This does not exclude the Deputy from informing himself about the legal determination, so that he may proceed towards concord with greater maturity'), ibid.

46 In March 1576, the ambassador wrote to Senator Cornelio Malvasia that it would be much more prudent to ask the pope to confirm the establishment of the magistracy through a proper brief. ASB, *Ambasciata bolognese a Roma*, *Registrum*, reg. 3 (the Ambassador to Cornelio Malvasia, 10 March 1576).

opponents of the tribunal could send biased reports to Rome, negatively impacting the selection. He also noted that it would be more fitting for Bologna's prerogatives that the appointment be the purview of the local magistrates. The exchange between the ambassador and Facchinetti was particularly interesting, especially when the former, to support the Bolognese position regarding the necessity of papal appointment, pointed out to the prelate that 'men usually do not act except for reward and punishment', suggesting that the prestige conferred by a papal appointment would be the only way to convince people to accept such a position.[47] The prelate responded that a series of incentives could be considered, such as urban exemption, a gift of salt during Easter and Christmas, as well as 'giving them place after the magistrates in public events, a torch for each in the *Corpus Christi* procession, and other such things', along with deprivations and punishments for those who refused.[48] However, the ambassador had to insist, and Facchinetti finally agreed to the request that the officials of the magistracy be chosen by the pope *pro tempore* and not by the Congregation itself, as had been the case up to that point.[49]

In February 1577, Gregory XIII also consented, but there was still no trace of the foundation brief. Correspondence reveals that, as of June, they were still waiting to finalise some wording in the preamble, on which the pope had doubts;[50] by the end of November, after a series of reminders, the ambassador was forced to admit that 'this business brings with it many difficulties'.[51] It was only at the beginning of 1578 that the brief, dated 10 January, was actually published and sent. The document acknowledged a prominent role in the genesis of the Congregation to the *Gonfaloniere* of Bologna, Cardinal Filippo Guastavillani, the pope's maternal nephew, who appears in the text as the guarantor of the city's prerogatives.[52] The document, which did not differ much from the Orders of December 1574, provided for the annulment

[47] 'gli huomini per ordinario non si muovono che per premio et per pena', ibid.

[48] 'dargli luogo doppo li magistrati nelli atti publici, una torza a ciascuno nella processione del Corpus domini et simili altre cose', op. cit. (the Ambassador to the Senate, 13 October, 1576).

[49] Op. cit. (the Ambassador to the Senate, 31 October, 1576).

[50] ASB, *Ambasciata bolognese a Roma, Lettere all'Oratore*, reg. 9 (the Senate to the Ambassador, 29 June 1577).

[51] 'questo negocio porta seco molte difficoltà', ASB, *Ambasciata bolognese a Roma, Registrum*, reg. 4 (the Ambassador to the Senate, 7 December 1577).

[52] On Guastavillani see Giampiero Brunelli, 'Guastavillani, Filippo', in *Dizionario Biografico degli Italiani*, vol. 60 (Rome, 2003), pp. 489–93.

of conflicting statutory norms and stipulated that the Congregation be composed not of ten but twelve members, two for each 'class' (secular clerics; civil and canonical jurists and doctors belonging to the College of Judges; notaries; nobles or citizens of 'good condition'; senators; merchants), and that their mandate should last four months. The procedure was very similar to what was already provided; it confirmed the main characteristic of the new arbitral body, namely to seek to avoid, as far as possible, the initiation of contentious proceedings in ordinary first-instance courts, thus causing considerable harm to ordinary judges and legal procurators.[53]

It might have been precisely for this reason that doubts and confusion about the judicial nature of the Congregation immediately emerged, despite the brief clearly using the term 'magistratus'. Paradoxically, it seems that some of these doubts came from the pope himself, as it is true that, in a letter sent to the *Gonfaloniere* in March 1578, the Bolognese ambassador to Rome reported that Gregory XIII 'abhorred' the idea that the *Concordia* could be considered a magistracy and that the Senate should also oppose such a possibility because it could 'partorire mali effetti'[54] ('produce harmful effects'). In short, the Congregation was born and began to operate amid a thousand doubts about its true nature, along with numerous resistances. By June 1584,

[53] 'Imprimis q[ue] quaecunq[ue] persona Commune, Collegium, Universitas, et alii cuiuscunq[ue] status, gradus, ordinis et conditionis existentes, ta[m] laicis q[uam] clerici sive seculares, sive cuiuscunq[ue] ordinis Regulares Civitates Comitatus, et Districtus Bononien[sis] aut alterius loci, qui aliquam litis intentare voluerit civilium prophanae, ecclesiasticam, mixtam Beneficialem aut spiritualem in dicta Civitate, ac eius Comitatu, districtu, et dioecesi, non possit nec debeat eius adversarium convenire in iudicio, neq[ue] petitionem sua[m] in scriptis porrigere, aut aliquem actum coram quovis ecc[lesiasti]co sive seculari tribunali facere, nisi servatis his, quae his in ordinibus, et statutis continentur, nec aliter, aut quavis alia ratione quod si secus fiat quicunq[ue] actus sit ipso iure et facto nullus, invalidus, nulliusq[ue] roboris vel momenti, etiamsi à neutra partium collitigantium id oppositum fuerit' ('First and foremost, any person, community, college, university and others of whatever status, rank, order and condition, whether laypersons or clerics, secular or of any regular order, cities, counties and districts of Bologna or any other place, who wishes to bring any civil, secular, ecclesiastical, mixed, benefice-related or spiritual lawsuit in the said city, its county, district and diocese, may not and should not summon their adversary to court, nor submit their petition in writing, nor perform any act before any ecclesiastical or secular tribunal, unless they have followed those things which are contained in these orders and statutes. Otherwise, any act done contrary to this shall be null, invalid and of no force or effect by the law itself and in fact, even if none of the litigating parties has raised an objection'), AAV, *Sec. Brev.*, reg. 44, f. 13v.

[54] ASB, *Ambasciata bolognese a Roma, Registrum*, reg. 4, f. 148 (the Ambassador to the *Gonfaloniere*, 8 March 1578).

there was already talk of its 'reform',[55] and the following year, a few months after the death of Pope Boncompagni, it seemed that Sixtus V intended to renew the founding brief of the Congregation.[56] Between 1586 and 1587, there was extensive correspondence between the ambassador and the Senate regarding the renewal of Gregory XIII's brief by his successor and the reform of the *Concordia*, which Cardinal Facchinetti was working on, focusing on limiting its prerogatives.[57] By the end of 1587, after the final touches, the new brief seemed about to be published; in early September, the ambassador sent the draft of the reform brief with Facchinetti's annotations to Bologna, asking for the opinion of the *Quaranta* because, if they agreed, the brief could be 'completed and passed without further delay'.[58]

In April 1588, we have records of the officials chosen by the pope for the four-month term: for the clerics, Antonio Maria Mogli and Vincenzo Ghislieri; for the doctors, Girolamo Fortini (confirmed) and Annibale Castelli; for the senators, Galeazzo Poeti and Mario Casali; for the notaries, Francesco Barbadori (confirmed) and Filippo Beroaldo; for the nobles, Marcello Garzoni and Giovanni Raniero Nascentori; for the merchants, Giovanni Terribilia (confirmed) and Nicolò Buonfiglioli.[59] After this date documentary traces of the Congregation's activities, as instituted by Pope Boncompagni and probably renewed by Sixtus V, become sparse to the point of almost disappearing, at least as far as correspondence is concerned. Until the early seventeenth century, the issue of the feasibility of an arbitral tribunal of first instance reappeared cyclically, especially during the installation of new popes. This was the case shortly after the election of Paul V, when the Bolognese ambassador to Rome wrote to the Senate that nothing harmed Bologna more than disputes and procurators, and thus it was absolutely necessary to revive the Tribunal of Concord.

It seems that the activity of the *Concordia* could survive only sporadically after the death of Gregory XIII. It probably managed, at least for a few years, to curb the rapacity of legal procurators, but the goal of absorbing the entire lower criminal sphere into compositional and arbitral processes proved to

55 Op. cit., reg. 6 (the Ambassador to the *Gonfaloniere*, 6 June 1584).

56 ASB, *Senato, Lettere*, series VII, reg. 58 (the Ambassador to the Senate, 24 August 1585).

57 ASB, *Senato, Lettere*, series VII, reg. 59 (the Ambassador to the Senate, 23 August 1586).

58 'ingrossare et passare senz'altro il breve', op. cit., reg. 60 (the Ambassador to the Senate, 2 September 1587).

59 Op. cit., reg. 61 (Cardinal Montalto to the vice-legate, 23 April 1588).

be an illusion. Over the years, it became clear that the only way to avoid the resistance of judges and procurators, who felt harmed by the possibility that cases could take the path of amicable settlements, was to delineate the operational scope of the Congregation in precise terms. This is evidenced by the fact that, in the early seventeenth century, when discussions resumed about the feasibility of reactivating the *Concordia*, Archbishop Alfonso Paleotti asked the Bolognese ambassador to Rome to try to obtain from Clement VIII not the renewal of Gregory's privilege (an event considered highly improbable) but a privilege allowing the still-existing *Compagnia del Nome di Dio* to handle 'minor' cases, 'of little value, in which the judges and procurators would suffer little loss'.[60] Paleotti had experienced first-hand Rome's ill-disposition during a conversation in Bologna with Clement VIII himself, who responded very clearly to the request to restore Gregory's privilege: 'his holiness refused to hear my arguments, not feeling it right to impede the public tribunals for a month, under the pretext of concord'.[61]

Limiting the *Compagnia*'s scope to 'minor' cases, especially financially, meant making a distinction based primarily on class rather than on the severity of the crimes. This way, those same judges and procurators would suffer no harm, as the Congregation would be limited to addressing the litigiousness of a segment of the population that typically avoided courtrooms due to a lack of means: 'since the poor cannot litigate due to poverty, no harm is done to the tribunals, and His Holiness will be the cause of this good, helping the poor to settle their cases in this Congregation'.[62] One of the premises of the original founding brief, which extended the arbitration obligation to the entire Bolognese population, regardless of state and condition, would thus be undermined. In 1602, Cardinals Domenico Toschi and Camillo Borghese received and examined the memorial sent from Bologna on the matter, to which they responded, again through the ambassador, that there were many difficulties in restoring the Congregation, given that the

60 'di poco valore, nelle quali, li Giudici, e, Procuratori facessero poca perdita', ASB, *Ambasciata bolognese a Roma, Lettere all'Oratore*, reg. 47 (the Archbishop of Bologna to the Ambassador, 31 August, 1602).

61 'la santità sua m'escluse, non sentendo bene, che s'impediscano li tribunali pubblici per un mese, sotto pretesto di concordia', ibid. Pope Aldobrandini stayed in Bologna between 27 November and 1 December 1598, during his return trip to Rome from Ferrara, which had just been annexed to the papal domains following the death without legitimate succession of Alfonso II d'Este. Paleotti had become the city's archbishop on 27 July of the previous year.

62 'non potendo i poveri per la povertà litigare, non si dà danno a, tribunali, e, N.S. sarà causa di questo bene che saranno aiutati concordando i poveri le loro cause in questa Congregatione', ibid.

experience during Boncompagni's pontificate had shown that many of the cases handled had been 'distorted'. The ambassador responded by using Paleotti's argument, suggesting that the *Compagnia* could be entrusted with cases up to a certain limit of composition.[63]

In November 1605, it was the *Gonfaloniere* Girolamo Boncompagni who expressed support for the reconstitution of the *Concordia* based on the model of the magistrature instituted by Gregory XIII, adding, however, that for such a decision, the opinion of the entire *Reggimento* would have to be awaited.[64] Just a couple of months earlier, the ambassador had asked the Senate to try to find a way to overcome the difficulties that had caused the original project to fail, and he had suggested establishing a public register of fideicommissa, given that most disputes arose precisely from these, though he added that the measure would most likely provoke a reaction from the procurators.[65] Cardinal Domenico Toschi, one of the prelates tasked with studying the matter alongside Lucio Machiavelli and Cardinal Borghese, stated that, in his view, disputes should not remain in the *Concordia* Tribunal for more than a month and that it should be monitored to prevent any 'tricks'.[66] In short, there was much opposition both in Bologna and Rome, and the project never took off.

The direction of lay confraternities towards judicial functions of an arbitral nature for conflict resolution cannot, after all, be said to be a specificity of the Papal States given that, only a few years before Paleotti, it had been the Archbishop of Milan, Charles Borromeo, who instituted a Confraternity of *Concordia*, aimed at providing free legal assistance for arbitration and also at raising money to provide economic means to all those who were unable to cover the costs of financial compositions.[67] Roughly in the same years, in

63 ASB, *Ambasciata bolognese a Roma*, *Registrum*, reg. 13 (the Ambassador to the Senate, 23 October 1602).

64 ASB, *Ambasciata bolognese a Roma*, reg. 53 (Girolamo Boncompagni to the Ambassador, 9 November 1605).

65 On the reasons for conflicts arising from fideicommissa, see Stefano Calonaci, 'Non solo onore: vertenze patrimoniali e arbitrato mediceo nell'Italia del Seicento', in *Stringere la pace. Teorie e pratiche della conciliazione nell'Europa moderna (secoli XV-XVIII)*, eds. Paolo Broggio and Maria Pia Paoli (Rome, 2011), pp. 107–34.

66 ASB, *Ambasciata bolognese a Roma*, *Registrum*, reg. 14, f. 37 (the Ambassador to the Senate, 21 September 1605).

67 See cf. Angelo Turchini, '"A beneficio pubblico e onor di Dio". Povertà e carità nella legislazione e nella pastorale della chiesa milanese', in *La città e i poveri: Milano e le terre lombarde dal Rinascimento all'età spagnola*, ed. Danilo Zardin (Milan, 1995), pp. 191–252; John Bossy, *Peace in the Post-Reformation. The Birkbeck Lectures, 1995* (Cambridge, 1998), p. 14.

Spanish Sicily, specifically in Palermo, the *Compagnia di Santa Maria della Consolazione*, or *Compagnia della Pace*, was founded, having exactly the same aims because – as the text of the Constitutions stated – complaints and trials 'have little of the Christian' ('sentono poco del Cristiano') in so far as they 'contain infamy' ('contengono infamia').[68] The Palermo *Compagnia* did not function as a true arbitral tribunal, but the 'peace policies' concluded thanks to the intervention of its peacemakers were signed 'in the name and with the authority of the government';[69] the policy constituted the certificate, legally recognised by the political power, of the peace achieved, necessary for obtaining grace. In the major cities, not only in Sicily but throughout the peninsula, institutions of this type emerged, a phenomenon undoubtedly favoured by the Counter-Reformation climate. A true genre emerged within pastoral preceptive literature, forming an ideal type, that of the pacificator, parallel to that of the arbiter/arbitrator, especially in closed and circumscribed contexts such as seminaries, colleges, universities and schools of doctrine, particularly exposed to conflict and litigiousness.[70] It is no coincidence that the primitive constitutions of the Bolognese Congregation made explicit reference to conflicts 'among members of spiritual confraternities'.[71]

The results were rarely up to expectations, precisely because of the strong resistance that these hybrid magistratures, religious and secular at the same time, a product of extending to the whole of society a model originally conceived to regulate the life of Christian confraternities, had to face. Resistance from judges and legal procurators, as mentioned, who had a specific interest in profiting from the proliferation and prolongation of disputes, as even Archbishop Gabriele Paleotti himself understood.[72] But – and here lies

[68] Cited in Bruno Pomara Saverino, *Bandolerismo, violencia y justicia en la Sicilia barroca* (Madrid, 2011), p. 136.

[69] 'in nome e coll'autorità del governo', ibid.

[70] On the general question, see Jonathan Davies, 'Violence and Italian Universities during the Renaissance', *Renaissance Studies* 27, 4 (2013), pp. 504–16.

[71] 'tra persone di confraternite spirituali', Prodi, *Il Cardinale Gabriele Paleotti*, vol. II, p. 33.

[72] 'La Congregatione della Concordia instituita dal nostro sommo pontefice et che apporta infinita utilità a tutta la cittade, havrà anch'essa da essere a cuore a V.S.R. ma che in tutti li luochi, et occasioni la favorischi gagliardamente et farsi intendere da procuratori che con loro vie indirette non cerchino sturbarla' ('The Congregation of *Concordia*, instituted by our supreme pontiff and bringing infinite benefits to the entire city, should also be of concern to Your Most Reverend Lordship, ensuring that in all places and occasions it is vigorously supported and making it known to procurators that with their indirect ways, they should not seek to disturb it'), memoir sent by Paleotti in 1577 to the Governor Giovanni Battista Castagna, cited in op. cit., p. 191, footnote n. 29.

the seemingly paradoxical element – Rome's attitude was not at all uniform. The paradox lies in the fact that if, in Counter-Reformation Europe, arbitration, as we will see later,[73] rose to an ideal of reference for a conciliatory and Christianly inspired justice that the faithful should prefer to contentious justice, deemed socially, economically, and spiritually harmful, in the case of the Papal States it was precisely the curial bodies, and the popes themselves, who paid particular attention to the functioning mechanisms of these magistratures established within lay congregations, and possibly to limit or even – in fact – prohibit them.

Paolo Prodi, noting how the Bolognese magistrature did not survive the Boncompagni pontificate, wrote that 'Sixtus V was not the pope suited to favour the formation of autonomous jurisdictions (even if devoid of any coercive power), not dependent on his governors'[74] – an observation that perfectly captures the political–institutional implications of creating arbitral bodies but does not reach the point of identifying the true stakes, which were not only of a jurisdictional but also a financial nature. It was one thing, in fact, to offer free legal aid or economically help the indigent so they could resolve their disputes still going through local magistratures; quite another thing to foresee a system that formally inhibited access to the normal judicial paths leading to financial compositions, a financial flow that, as seen, was being directed towards the coffers of the *Camera Apostolica* thanks to the projects of judicial centralisation. Since the late Middle Ages, municipal statutes had, after all, provided for facilitated loan grants to help the poor face the expenses for compositions, both civil and criminal. In Bologna, the same *Concordia* Congregation had among its tasks that of noting 'all the pious and miserable causes in which the Company will provide legal aid and expenses before any tribunal, according to the form of the Decree made for this by the Company',[75] but there was also a *Monte della Concordia*, erected by Paul III Farnese in 1543, one of the public loan institutions whose administration was entrusted to a college of creditors, later merged in the late seventeenth century into the *Monte Secondo Clemente privilegiato e francabile*.[76] The privilege that Gregory XIII had granted to the Congregation of

73 See below, Chapter 5.

74 Prodi, *Il Cardinale Gabriele Paleotti*, vol. II, p. 191.

75 *Capitoli et regole sopra l'audire.*

76 'Sono in detta città il Monte della Concordia, Monte Maggiore, Monte Abondanza, fruttano chi sei, chi cinque, e chi 4 per cento l'anno; sono stati eretti in diversi tempi, & hanno assignationi per pagar i frutti sopra li Dacij, & altri introiti sicuri. Il detto Monte della Concordia fù eretto da papa Paolo Terzo per la somma de ducati 440V. di Camera da dieci giulij l'uno, e d'annua rendita alla ragione di

Concord – perhaps not entirely consciously and thoughtfully, given his reaction, just two months after the brief's publication, to the never-extinguished request for recognition of the organism's properly judicial nature – consisted in inhibiting the action of ordinary magistratures until the attempt at conciliation was made, and was thus exceptional and could potentially interfere in the relations between the Roman curia and episcopates. How would such a magistrature fit into the logic of jurisdictional competences? Would the 'reformed' Congregation be subject to visitation by the archbishop like all other lay confraternities, according to the Tridentine dictate?[77] What effects would such a *ius visitandi* have on its properly judicial, albeit arbitral, action? Would the Congregation effectively position itself as an extension of episcopal justice, given that it claimed competence in inhibiting both secular and ecclesiastical, benefice, and spiritual causes, and given the prominent role played by Paleotti in its founding? An ecclesiastical court capable of interfering not only with legatine justice but also with senatorial/communal justice? It is no coincidence that the Congregation, as conceived in the 1570s, functioned for only a short time; nor, after all, did the activities of other Bolognese tribunals suffer significant setbacks during that brief period of operation. The experiment, ultimately, would never be proposed again in that form.

---

otto per cento l'anno, e poi da Papa Sisto Quinto ridotta alla ragione di sei, & accresciuto d'altri 250V. annui, e queste rendite per la loro pontualità sono meritamente riputate fra le migliori d'Italia' ('In said city, the *Monte della Concordia*, *Monte Maggiore* and *Monte Abondanza* yield six, five and four per cent annually, respectively. They were established at different times and have assignments to pay the interest from the Dacij and other secure revenues. The aforementioned *Monte della Concordia* was established by Pope Paul III for the sum of 4,400 ducats of Camera, each worth ten *giulii*, with an annual yield at the rate of eight per cent per year, which was later reduced to six per cent by Pope Sixtus V, and increased by another 2,500 annual ducats. These incomes, due to their punctuality, are deservedly regarded among the best in Italy'), *Il negotiante, di Gio: Domenico Peri Genovese, parte seconda, dedicata al Clarissimo Signore Gio: Pace Castelli* (Venetia, presso Gio: Giacomo Herz, 1672), p. 50.

[77] *Concilium tridentinum*, *Sessio* XXII, *Canon* VIII (17 settembre 1562). 'Episcopi etiam tamquam Sedis Apostolicae delegati in casibus a iure concessis omnium piarum dispositionum tam in ultima voluntate quam inter vivos sint executores habeant ius visitandi hospitalia collegia quaecumque ac confraternitates laicorum etiam quas scholas sive quocumque alio nomine vocant non tamen quae sub regum immediata protectione sunt sine eorum licentia' ('Bishops, as delegates of the Apostolic See in cases granted by law, shall be executors of all pious dispositions both in the last will and inter vivos, and shall have the right to visit hospitals, colleges, and any confraternities of laypeople, even those called schools or by any other name, except those under the immediate protection of kings without their permission').

4. Finances for peace: the threat of fines and confiscations

The interception of petty criminals by the Tribunal of the *Torrone* through the recruitment of community *massari*, to the detriment of the *contado* officials, was, as we have seen, the main path that Rome took to undermine the communal and feudal magistracies in the Bolognese legation and to centralise the administration of justice. The issue of the salary to be paid to the officials, and to the legate himself, was crucial; an insufficient salary effectively encouraged the improper use of justice procedures, consisting of the abuse of monetary compositions, as Ambassador Aldrovandi pointed out in a letter to the *Gonfaloniere* in January 1559. Seen from the periphery, the centralisation strategy could only cause harm: if the *contado* officials were not bypassed by the *massari*, 'the innocent would pay nothing and the delinquents would be punished according to the laws and statutes of the city; if the condemnations went to the Chamber, then a decent salary could be paid to the auditor and the notaries'.[78] In this way, the auditor of the vice-legate would judge only summary cases, while those 'di gran discussione' ('requiring extensive discussion') would go to the *Rota*; thus, the cases would not go on 'forever as the procurators, who are leeches of that city, seek to make them, creating fifteen or twenty heads out of one case to obtain fifteen or twenty fees, of which it is known that the vice-legates, or governors, have taken a share'.[79] With an adequate salary for the legate, the 'arbitrary power that allowed the banished to be easily acquitted for money, which in the past has caused many homicides' would also disappear;[80] 'this absolving all sorts of crimes for money', Aldrovandi continues, 'has so many inconveniences of one kind and another in the city and its *contado*'.[81]

Recent historiography has clearly shown that the advancement of inquisitorial and *ex officio* procedures embodied by the central magistrates did not

78 'li innocenti non pagarebbono cosa alcuna et li delinquenti verriano puniti secondo la forma delle leggi e statuti della città; se le condennationi andassero alla Camera, et di quelle si potria poi pagar un sallario honesto come ho detto di sopra all'auditore et alli nottari', ASB, *Senato, Lettere*, series VII, reg. 10 (Aldrovandi to the *Gonfaloniere*, undated letter).

79 'immortali come cercano di far li procuratori che sono sanguisughe di quella città e di una causa sola non si gli faria quindici o venti capi come si fa dalla banda de vicelegati per haver quindici o venti propine delle quali si sa che li vicelegati, o governatori sono stati alla parte', ibid.

80 'l'arbitrio per il che li banditi non potriano esser così facilmente assoluti per danari, il che per lo adietro ha causato di molti homicidi', ibid.

81 'questo assolver tutte le sorte de malefitii per danari ha causato tanti et tanti inconvenienti che si sono fatti nella città et suo contado', ibid.

coincide, as traditionally believed, with the progressive retreat and final fading out of conciliation procedures, the so-called community justice. The proceedings initiated by a *massaro*'s complaint were moments when defendants and victims, their families and relatives, the entire community appeared before the *Torrone* notaries to explain the circumstances of the crime, to stage (and mediate) feelings of revenge and various needs under the guidance of the magistrate, who ended up guiding the parties towards a peace, perhaps preceded by the removal of the offender from the community.[82] From this perspective, it now seems certain that no opposition exists between hegemonic justice and community justice, since in a large number of cases the judicial institutions themselves shaped their procedures on a conciliatory and arbitral model, contrary to a common historiographical sense that led us to consider the inquisitorial process model as the only characteristic of judicial modernity. However, in premodern criminal justice, peace was central in another sense as well. There is a much less 'peaceful' and much more conflictual aspect of the phenomenon, in which peace was at the centre of a very tough and prolonged clash between legatine justice and local magistracies, in so far as the generalised and indiscriminate imposition of fines and confiscations in the form of *sicurtà* not to harm created a system of prevention/oppression that pivoted precisely on peace and its potential breach. This system played a significant role in the process of centralising justice in the Papal States starting from the mid-sixteenth century.

The Bolognese Senate was constantly forced to intervene to try to curb the conduct of the *Torrone*, which systematically violated the city's prerogatives through the imposition of fines and precepts. In particular, what the Senate found unacceptable was both the imposition of fines for sentences other than capital ones and the obligation for the offender's relatives to purchase the confiscated goods. Fines could only be imposed 'by the disposition of the common laws or the city's statutes, and not by the provisions made by the legates and governors',[83] commented the Bolognese ambassador to Rome in a missive addressed to the *Gonfaloniere* in October 1576. In January of the following year, a man was injured and – although he was the victim of the attack – cited by the *Torrone* auditor to reciprocate the *sicurtà* imposed to the assailant. Upon his refusal, the injured man was ordered to pay the

[82] See Colin S. Rose, 'Violence and the Centralization of Criminal Justice in Early Modern Bologna', in *Violence and Justice in Bologna, 1250-1700*, ed. Sarah Rubin Blanshei (Lanham, Boulder, New York and London, 2018), pp. 101–22.

[83] 'per la dispositione delle leggi comuni o delli statuti della città, et non per le provvisioni che fanno li legati et governatori', ASB, *Ambasciata bolognese a Roma, Registrum*, reg. 3 (the Ambassador to the *Gonfaloniere*, 27 October 1576).

fine resulting from the failure to observe the precept, to which the Senate protested, reminding once again that in Bologna fines could only be imposed in cases of capital convictions. In July, the *Gonfaloniere* warned the ambassador about the behaviour of the *Torrone* auditor, who continued to demand the collection of fines and confiscations even for non-capital crimes and for amounts below 2,000 *scudi*, the limit established in previous agreements between the Senate and the Pope. The introduction of pecuniary penalties in the realm of petty crime represented a huge threat to Bologna's prerogatives:

> because ordinarily confiscations are only carried out in capital cases, such as homicides, while pecuniary condemnations are imposed for any minor offence, such as assaults, injuries and similar occasions; *and in consequence of wanting to collect these penalties the situation of those who commit lesser crimes would be made worse*. The treasury is not deprived of income; because the delinquents are always under obligation, and they must either pay or go to God, otherwise they would be imprisoned, and if they want to return, they must settle with the treasury.[84]

In most cases, as has been shown, behind a pecuniary penalty there was the imposition of a *sicurtà* not to harm, and the horizon of a *sicurtà* was represented by a peace, which individuals were encouraged to sign in the hope of avoiding the actual collection of the surety bond. The problem is that often *sicurtà* and fines were conflated, and it is not by chance that on numerous occasions the *Quaranta* complained that *sicurtà* not to harm were in reality disguised confiscations and fines. The situation was further aggravated by the behaviour of individual auditors, sub-auditors or even simple notaries, who could distort the system's functioning and turn it to Rome's advantage. This could happen if the *Torrone* officials demanded that the *sicurtà*, which would eventually end up in the coffers of the Apostolic Chamber, be collected before the breach of the *sicurtà*, i.e., at the very moment of its signing. Juridical treatises are rather vague on this point, not defining in detail when the *sicurtà* not to harm should be paid; however, since it is a *sicurtà*, i.e., a guarantee of another's obligation, it follows that the amount should only be collected if the guaranteed party failed to fulfil the assumed obligation.

[84] 'perchè ordinariamente le confiscationi non si fanno, se non in le cause capitali, et d'homicidii, et le condennationi pecuniarie si fanno per ogni semplice delitto, et per insulti, feriti et simili occasioni; *et volendo riscoter queste pene, saria voler far di peggior conditione, quelli che facessero minori delitti*, né per questo viene deluso il fisco; perchè li delinquenti sempre restano obligati, et bisogna che paghino, o che si vadino con Dio, altrimenti sariano messi prigioni, et volendo ritornar bisogna che sieno d'accordo col fisco', ASB, *Ambasciata bolognese a Roma, Lettere all'Oratore*, reg. 9 (the *Gonfaloniere* to the Ambassador, 13 July 1577), italics mine.

Based on documentary evidence, it is legitimate to hypothesise that on certain occasions the pontifical tribunals did not respect the normal procedure but demanded the immediate payment of the sum of money. Moreover, compared to a proper fine, the *sicurtà* not to harm also affected the victims of the offence and their relatives, creating a deterrence system perceived by the population as unfair and particularly oppressive.

In Bologna, this practice aroused lively protests from the Senate, but evidence from other areas of the Papal States suggests that it was not an uncommon practice and that it was not only the courts directly dependent on Rome that adopted it. The decisive action of the legate and the Tribunal of the *Torrone* on petty crime was also joined by the actions of the curial congregations, especially the *Consulta*, the supreme administrative and judicial body conceived by Paul IV and only officially established, by Sixtus V, in 1588. The *Consulta* was very attentive to ensuring that the traditional channels used in the periphery for peace agreements and compositions were increasingly dominated by the centre. In early November 1579, the *Gonfaloniere* wrote a response letter to the ambassador in Rome, who had previously informed him of a memorial sent to the Sacred *Consulta* by a Bolognese woman to report an unusual incident. Her husband had been killed, and she was willing to make peace with the murderer and his family; however, she was told – though it was not clear by whom – that this peace should not follow the traditional channels, namely the *Anziani Consoli*, members of the Senate. The problem was that this peace had already been concluded through the *Anziani*, and thus the *Gonfaloniere* wrote to the ambassador that the only thing he could do was personally order the *Anziani* notaries to keep the peace secret and not to let any related documents leak out,[85] and also to ask the woman herself to avoid spreading the news to Rome.[86] Bologna's request, to be conveyed to the *Consulta*, was to allow the Senate to follow the ancient customs in matters of peace; at the end of the same month, the *Gonfaloniere* transmitted the peace agreement signed by the woman to the ambassador, emphasising that it was in accordance with the statutes, but Cardinal-Nephew Filippo Boncompagni ordered that the peace agreement be annulled. The legate then executed the Roman order by issuing a decree annulling the peace, not without triggering the predictable protests from the *Anziani*.[87]

A simple peace agreement, one of many, became an exemplary case in so far as a curial body had been officially called to rule on its validity. A

[85] Op. cit., reg. 12 (the *Gonfaloniere* to the Ambassador, 7 November 1579).

[86] ibid. (the *Gonfaloniere* to the Ambassador, 14 November 1579).

[87] ibid. (the *Gonfaloniere* to the Ambassador, 28 November 1579).

clear and strong message needed to be sent to Bologna: Rome, through its judicial bodies operating locally, could not be excluded from any conciliation procedure.

5. Legates and governors dealing with local jurisdictions

The process of judicial centralisation at the expense of competing jurisdictions was not straightforward; it necessarily developed through constant negotiation with the peripheries, often coming to a halt and sometimes regressing. This is true for both the municipal magistracies, which characterised the central–northern possessions of the Papal States, and the feudal courts, which were prevalent especially in the Patrimony, in Sabina and in the southern provinces of Campagna and Marittima. There is also an additional and fundamental limitation to the judicial centralisation policy pursued between the sixteenth and seventeenth centuries, namely nepotism, which only increased and reinforced the forum prerogatives in the feudal possessions of the papal families (Aldobrandini, Borghese, Barberini, Pamphili, Chigi), prerogatives that added to those already granted to the families of the ancient Roman aristocracy.[88] In the modern era, moreover, it was not only the state that centralised. Like the popes, the feudal lords also sought to impose a hierarchy, and undertook a process of reorganisation and imposition of close surveillance on the activities of judicial officers scattered throughout their territories. The Papal States configured themselves as a truly multicentric reality.[89]

[88] On the governance of justice in the feudal domains of the Colonna in the eighteenth century, see David Armando, *Barone, vassalli e governo pontificio. Gli stati dei Colonna nel Settecento* (Rome, 2018), pp. 189–288.

[89] On the case of the Borghese domains, see Bertrand Forclaz, *La famille Borghese et ses fiefs. L'autorité négociée dans l'État pontifical d'Ancien Régime* (Rome, 2006). 'Les Borghese mettent en oeuvre une hiérarchisation de leurs territoires, organisent les fiefs de Sabine en "États", promulguent des édits valables dans tous leurs fiefs, font parvenir à leurs représentants des instructions, envoient des "visiteurs" dans les fiefs. Cette politique "centralisatrice", qui fait écho aux efforts des autorités romaines, représente en réalité un dessein poursuivi par tous les pouvoirs à l'époque moderne – les feudataires, l'autorité ecclésiastique, les monarchies – et de fait, il existe une pluralité de "centres"' ('The Borghese implement a hierarchy of their territories, organise the fiefs of Sabina into "States", promulgate edicts valid in all their fiefs, send instructions to their representatives, and dispatch "visitors" to the fiefs. This "centralising" policy, which echoes the efforts of the Roman authorities, actually represents a design pursued by all powers in

Social actors willingly turned to the courts, contrary to a historiographical tradition – culminating in the teachings of Mario Sbriccoli – that has considered the resort to official justice as a phenomenon of 'interim and last resort'.[90] In the criminal sphere, in cases of insults, assaults or even murders, the first instance to which people turned was represented by the seigniorial courts or the officials dependent on the municipality. Throughout the modern age, numerous were the petitions from the enfeoffed communities to the lord to appoint a specific governor residing locally, an unequivocal sign that being judged by foreign tribunals was perceived as a strong diminishment of the community's prestige and as a harmful interruption of the chain of ties and solidarity binding the offender to their human and social context.[91] The fruitful contribution of legal anthropology has ensured that, in recent decades, particular attention has been paid to the 'uses' of justice, the role of resorting to courts within the framework of the web of reciprocal relationships among social actors, the objectives of the petitioners, the degrees of tolerance of violence and vengeful mechanisms by the authorities, according to a bottom-up approach. From this perspective, it can certainly be affirmed that resorting to the judge for the resolution of a conflict constituted the first part of a close negotiation among social actors, communities of belonging and judicial personnel.[92] The methods of composition and arbitration have mostly appeared to scholars as the culmination of the strategies implemented by the petitioners, necessarily placed outside the courtrooms and therefore shielded from their coercive power (hence the recourse to the categories of 'extra-justice' or, more recently, 'infra-justice'), to which they arrived after trying to strengthen their position *vis-à-vis* their adversaries precisely through official justice. The predominant focus on the resort to

the modern era – the feudal lords, the ecclesiastical authority, the monarchies – and indeed, there exists a plurality of "centers"' (p. 88).

90 See Andrea Zorzi, 'L'egemonia del penale in Mario Sbriccoli', in *Penale, giustizia, potere. Metodi, ricerche, storiografie. Per ricordare Mario Sbriccoli*, ed. Luigi Lacchè, Carlotta Latini, Paolo Marchetti and Massimo Meccarelli (Macerata, 2007), pp. 155–78.

91 Angelantonio Spagnoletti, 'Giudici e governatori regi nelle università meridionali (XVIII secolo)', *Archivio Storico delle Province Napoletane* CV (1987), pp. 415–54.

92 On reciprocity, see, for example, Natalie Zemon Davis, *The Gift in Sixteenth Century France* (Oxford, 2000). On procedures and practices of justice according to a non-teleological approach focused on the conceptions of social actors, see the issue of *Quaderni Storici* on 'Procedure di giustizia' (vol. 34, no. 101/2, 1999), ed. Renata Ago and Simona Cerutti. Simona Cerutti's study *Giustizia sommaria, Pratiche e ideali di giustizia in una società di Ancien Régime (Torino XVIII secolo)* (Milan, 2003), is specifically dedicated to procedures.

justice by actors, however, has ended up overshadowing the capacity of judicial apparatuses to move *ex officio* to implement conflict resolution strategies none the less supported by instruments that were, at least apparently, conciliatory. The objective of peaceful and transactional conflict resolution was not an exclusive prerogative of the actors; it constituted the juridical–cultural horizon within which the judicial power itself also moved.

If one takes this view, it will be better understood why central authorities attempted to create, either anew or through a reconversion of existing institutions, peripheral magistracies directly dependent on the governors with the task of 'occupying' the field of conciliation. The experiment of the Congregation of Concord in Bologna, which was not particularly successful, has been analysed, but elsewhere in the Papal States the objective of establishing central control over peace-making procedures led, significantly in the same years, to similar attempts that sometimes encountered resistance from local powers. From a reference contained in a letter from the Bolognese ambassador in Rome to the *Gonfaloniere* dated 7 September 1605, we know, for example, that in Perugia there was a judicial body with purposes very similar to the Bolognese Congregation, as the Perugian constitutions had been handed over to Rome, to Lucio Machiavelli, to use as a model to try to reform the constitutions of the Bolognese *Concordia*.[93] What is certain, however, is that in 1575, shortly after his appointment as Governor of the Marca, Filippo Sega (who simultaneously became the bishop of Ripatransone, an important seat near Ascoli Piceno) issued a series of provisions related to justice, among which stands out the establishment, by ordinance dated 29 June, not of a centralised concord tribunal, based in Macerata, but rather of a network of arbitration courts scattered throughout the Marca territory.[94]

This was clearly a measure modelled on the Congregation of Concord in Bologna, from which it borrowed – albeit on a reduced scale – its operational mechanism. The intent, declared in the *Proemium* of the document establishing these tribunals, was to meet the needs of a population forced to bear the high costs of ordinary justice to resolve their disputes, those cases for

[93] ASB, *Ambasciata Bolognese a Roma*, *Registrum*, reg. 14, f. 31 (the Ambassador to the *Gonfaloniere*, 7 September, 1605).

[94] Sega was appointed Governor of the Marca in January 1575 and bishop of Ripatransone in May of the same year. He held the highest governmental office of the Marca until 1577; see *Legati e Governatori dello Stato pontificio (1550-1809)*, ed. Christoph Weber (Rome, 1994), p. 286. On 3 October 1578 he was promoted to the diocese of Piacenza, although he left its care to a vicar. See Vincenzo Lavenia, 'Sega, Filippo', in *Dizionario Biografico degli Italiani*, vol. 91 (Rome, 2018), pp. 724–7.

which the people of Sega's jurisdiction 'every day must come here and there to the courts, consuming themselves without often being able, out of exhaustion and inability, to reach a conclusion',[95] a reality of fact but also a *topos* of much political, legal and moral literature of the time. To this end, the new governor provided to 'establish and appoint for all the Cities, Lands and Castles of his government a new Tribunal, consisting of four more expert men, to be called the Tribunal of the Elected to Concord, in which His Most Reverend Lordship orders and commands that they must proceed with the authority, terms, methods and chapters below'.[96] Each court, composed precisely of four 'expert' men, endowed with 'ample authority to proceed in disputes and differences',[97] was to compose the latter 'summarily without judicial procedure and without any sort of writing, even by royal hand, considering only the truth of the matter, taking extra-judicially the information without forming an examination, and as they shall best see fit'.[98] Governor Sega's project appears as a sort of secularisation of a model originally conceived as proper to pastoral and ecclesiastical justice. As in Bologna, the Elected officials, in office for one year, were to meet three times a week, on Monday, Wednesday and Friday, but in the *Palazzo dei Priori* of the individual places, the heart of local municipal power, 'in the room usually convened by the Council'.[99] The beginning of each session was to be announced to the community through the sound of the municipal bell, or the blast of a trumpet, by the announcement of the bailiff or 'in another way that will be judged more appropriate'.[100]

To the Elected officials, the petitioner would present a petition 'either verbally or in writing in the vernacular only, and not in any other way',[101]

[95] 'tutto dì convengono hor quà, hor là per le Corti andar consumandosi senza molte volte per istracchezza, & impotenza loro venire a fine', *Tribunale della concordia, eretto nuovamente per tutti i luoghi della provincia da Monsig. Filippo Sega Vescovo della Ripatransona Governatore della Marca a beneficio d'essa* (Macerata, appresso Sebastiano Martellini, 1575) (BMF, 2M9 / 14860).

[96] 'erigere & diputare per tutte le Città, Terre & Castelli del suo governo un nuovo Tribunale, che sia di quattro huomini più esperti, & si chiami il Tribunale degli eletti alla Concordia, nel quale Sua Sig. Reverendissima ordina, & commanda, si debba procedere con l'auttorità, termini, modi, & capitoli infrascritti', ibid.

[97] 'ampla facultà di procedere nelle liti, & differentie', ibid.

[98] 'sommariamente senza tela giudiciaria, & senza alcuna sorte di scrittura, etiam manu regia attesa solo la verità del fatto pigliando extragiudicialmente l'informationi senza formar essamine, & come meglio parrà à essi', ibid.

[99] 'nella stanza solita congregarvisi il Conseglio', ibid.

[100] 'in altro modo, che sarà giudicato più opportuno', ibid.

[101] 'in voce, o in iscrittura volgare solamente, & non in altro modo', ibid.

and if the defendant became contumacious after the citation, which the tribunal could eventually reiterate, he could 'be fined by said Judges with those pecuniary penalties that they deem appropriate [...] to be applied to pious places'.[102] The tribunal's task was to bring the litigants to an agreement, in which case 'each of said Elected officials separately, and by himself alone, shall have full authority to sentence, decide, and definitively resolve, as if the vote and opinion of his Colleagues concurred, and they were all together in sentencing'.[103] If, however, it proved impossible to reconcile the litigants, the Elected officials were to 'summarily [...] fully inform themselves of the merits of the case, and, also using the judgement and opinion of other Experts, resolve to decide it',[104] reaching a sentence, 'even if there is no consent of the parties',[105] unanimously or by a majority of three out of four. This was an element of significant differentiation from the functioning of the Congregation of *Concordia* in Bologna; by virtue of this rule, the Marchigian *Concordia* tribunals could raise the arbitration bar a little higher, imposing an award on the parties.

While the term of office for the Elected officials, as mentioned, was one year, their authority for each case lasted one month; for this purpose, and for greater certainty, it was prescribed that the notary precisely indicate the date of the first appearance in the records. Once this period had elapsed without a solution, the case remained without judgement, and the litigants had no recourse but to 'bring the judgement before their ordinary judges'.[106] Cases resolved through agreement between the parties were to be considered unappealable, while those resolved by award (due to lack of agreement) could be appealed within the normally prescribed terms. The appeal was to be addressed directly to the Tribunal of the Governor of the Marca; the appellant had to 'bring a copy of the sentence to be given to him free of charge by the notary of said Elected officials',[107] an essential requirement, as he could neither 'first summon him in another Tribunal, nor attempt to

[102] 'da detti Giudici esser multato in quelle pene pecuniarie, che à loro pareranno convenienti [...] da applicarsi a' i luoghi pii', ibid.

[103] 'ciascuno di detti Eletti disgiuntamente, & solo per se stesso habbia piena auttorità di sententiare, decidere, & terminare diffinitivamente, come se vi concorresse il voto, & parere di suoi Colleghi, & fussero tutti insieme à sententiare', ibid.

[104] 'con sommarietà [...] appieno informarsi delli meriti della causa, &, servendosi anco del giuditio, & parere d'altri Periti, risolversi alla decisione di essa', ibid.

[105] 'quantunque non vi sia il consenso delle parti', ibid.

[106] 'muovere il giudizio innanti i loro giudici ordinarii', ibid.

[107] 'portarsi copia della sententia da darsegli gratis dal notaro di detti Eletti', ibid.

obtain commission, letters or other writings or orders from His Most Reverend Lordship against said Adversary, unless he has fully informed His Lordship of said sentence with the merits of the case, and if done otherwise, he wishes and declares that whatever is done shall be null and void'.[108]

The most interesting aspect is contained in this paragraph of the document establishing the Marchigian *Concordia* tribunals:

> That any person of any state, rank or condition who wishes to initiate and newly engage in any civil litigation or judgement against anyone, and of any importance, cannot summon the Adversary in any other Tribunal than that of the said Elected officials. And the ordinary Judges cannot hear anyone who would go before them for the cause of litigation, if they do not first have proof that they have been to the Tribunal of the said Elected officials, and that the litigation has remained pending due to expired jurisdiction [...] or they truly do not have a particular commission from His Most Reverend Lordship.[109]

Just as in Bologna – this was the novelty, the disruptive force, but at the same time the seed of the failure of such initiatives – it was stipulated that, for certain types of dispute, the first instance of judgement had to be obligatorily that of arbitration and conciliation, excluding ordinary judges. The Elected officials, as we have seen, were none the less endowed with the authority to issue an award in case of failure to reach an agreement, but it was to them that one had to turn before embarking on the path of an ordinary trial. Although the procedure and criteria for the selection of the Elected officials were not specified in the decree establishing the courts, it is presumed that the prerogative fell upon the same priors of the different communities. Nevertheless, their authority, by virtue of the establishing act, emanated from the highest representative of papal power, which thus insinuated itself into local contexts traditionally dominated by magistracies dependent on the municipalities and

108 'prima convenirlo in altro Tribunale, né tam poco tentare di cavare commissione, lettere, né altre scritture, ò ordini da sua Signoria Reverendissima contra d'esso Avversario, se non haverà pienamente informato esso Monsignore di detta sententia con i meriti della causa, & facendosi altramente, vole, & dichiara, che sia Irrito, & nullo ciò che si farà', ibid.

109 'Che qualunque persona di qualsivoglia stato, grado, ò conditione vorà però principiare, & muovere nuovamente lite, & giuditio alcuno civile contra chi si sia, & di qualsivoglia importanza, non possa convenire l'Avversario in altro Tribunale, che in quello di detti Eletti. Et i Giudici ordinarii non possano ascoltare alcuno, che per causa di lite andasse innanti a loro, se prima no[n] haveranno fede che si sia stato al Tribunal di detti Eletti, & che la lite sia rimas[t]a pendente per la spirata giurisditione [...] ò veramente non ne haveranno particolar commissione da Sua Signoria Reverendissima', ibid.

communities. The two safeguard clauses that concluded the document did little to dispel the doubts and suspicions of the communities regarding the establishment of the courts:

> That everything which is done before the said Elected, both verbally and in writing, may not cause or bring any prejudice in the judgement that may later be made before the Ordinaries.
>
> That the time of the month given to the said Elected may not be counted as part of the term within which any case must be expedited before the Ordinaries, so that in no way may it be alleged therefore as a cause of peremption or abandonment of the cases.[110]

The summary procedure and arbitration, aimed at concluding peace agreements, clearly became, in the intentions of the papal power, a tool for eroding competing jurisdictions. Filippo Sega, the creator of this widespread arbitral judicial system, remained in office for only a couple of years, and after his departure from the Marche, it became necessary to consult the communities to ascertain their opinion on the advisability of continuing the experience of the tribunals of concord. In March 1579, under the government of Niccolò Aragonia (Bishop of Ascoli Piceno), the *gonfalonier* and the priors of the Municipality of Jesi – a few years before the city and its surrounding area were transformed into a governorship by Sixtus V – communicated to Pietro Filoteri, chancellor and syndic of the Papal Province based in Macerata, their firm decision not to seek the establishment of a tribunal of concord, citing as their reason the existence in that territory of another magistracy endowed with papal authority and operating according to summary procedure 'fin' à un certo segno' ('to a certain extent'), likely referring to the scope of the composition:

> It has recently been resolved that, as the tribunal of the Consuls of Summary Law with the authority of the Supreme Pontiffs to hear and decide cases to a certain extent is already present here, our community does not intend to establish or desire any other tribunal.[111]

[110] 'Che tutto quello, che si farà innanti à detti Eletti tanto in voce, quanto in iscritto, non possa cagionare, né apportar pregiuditio alcuno nel giuditio, che poi si facesse innanti à gli Ordinari. Che il tempo del mese dato à i detti Eletti non possa computarsi à conto del termine, frà il quale alcuna causa si havesse à spedire innanti à gli Ordinarii si, che si possa in alcun modo perciò allegare peremptione, ò desertione delle cause', ibid.

[111] 'si è ultimamente risoluto che essendo qui il tribunale delli Consoli de Jure summario con autorità de sommi Pontifici di conoscere, et decidere le cause fin' à un certo segno, la nostra comunità non intende di erigere qui, o desiderar' alcun'altro

The priors of Osimo, on their part, always responded to Filoteri – perhaps in an attempt to buy time – that 'for the next post we will inform Your Lordship of what we need regarding the distribution for the new impositions, and also the Tribunal of Concord',[112] while those of Morrovalle informed the government of Macerata that the General Council of the community had 'resolved, for universal good, that every possible effort be made for the said Tribunal of Concord, established during the time of the Most Blessed Monsignor Sega, to continue to operate in our land'.[113] The governance of hatred at the local level through non-contentious methods was evidently becoming a rather delicate matter in terms of the relationships between local communities and papal government bodies. The response from the communities was not uniform, as can be seen. For some, it was necessary to reaffirm their capability to ensure peace and order at the local level on their own, without external interference, even through compositions and transactions. Certainly, the imposition of *sicurtà* and peace by the justice bodies dependent on the province was not a welcome prospect for the communities, which, while striving to project to Rome an image of peaceful and Christian-inspired disposition towards pacification by the local populations within the framework of traditional community mediation tools, in fact used methods not so different. In July of the same year, the priors and consuls of Offida reassured Filoteri about the outcome of some brawls that had occurred in the communities, for the resolution of which they had promptly intervened ('we did not fail to make provision that the new brawlers reconcile, as they have reconciled, and yesterday the peace agreements were stipulated');[114] moreover, 'since the incident happened suddenly, with little harm, and among relatives', the priors asked the authorities of the Province to 'show clemency to these brawlers in the

tribunale', ASM, *Governatore Generale della Marca di Ancona*, no. 1144 (Jesi, 18 March 1579). For the judicial resolution methods of a feud that occurred in Jesi a few years earlier, see Diego Pedrini, Lucia Dubbini, '1563: una faida a Jesi', *Proposte & Ricerche* 80 (2018), pp. 127–51.

112 'per la futura posta daremo avviso a V.S. di quanto ci occorre intorno al ripartimento per le nuove importioni, et anco al tribunale della Concordia', ASM, *Governatore Generale della Marca di Ancona*, n. 1144 (Osimo, 17 March 1579).

113 'resoluto, per bene universale, che si facesse ogni opera pussibile, che detto Tribunal della Concordia già al tempo del Monsignore Beatissimo, Sega, e resto, sia ancora per l'advenire exercitato nella nostra terra', ibid (Morro de Valle, 8 March 1579), italics mine.

114 'non siamo mancati far provisione che li nuovi rissanti si pacifichino, come se sono pacificati e hieri forno stipulate le paci', ibid.

petitions they will submit, having reconciled amicably for the love of God and our Community'.[115]

The community of Offida felt called upon, in a certain sense, to guarantee before the provincial government the validity of the peace agreements concluded locally, in so far as these constituted, as we know, the condition for the granting of pardon or commutation of penalties. We find ourselves in the territory of Ascoli, one of the areas most closely monitored by papal authorities due to the particular inclination of the population towards violence and insubordination.[116] At that time, Offida must have felt rather besieged by the governor's initiatives aimed at making the control of local conflicts efficient, constant and, above all, centralised, both in the town and in other centres of the area. Due to some violence and tensions that occurred in Ripa (Ripatransone) and Montefiore (Montefiore dell'Aso), the governor indeed tried to station a constable and a certain number of bailiffs in Offida, whose maintenance would burden the municipal coffers. The priors and consuls then addressed Filoteri to protest to the governor; they requested to 'not be burdened in any way', 'fearing we would be prejudiced by having to contribute to their damages by making us pay and contribute to them'.[117] It must not have been the first time that Rome tried to impose the control of the district on the main municipality as, in the letter, the priors refer to an appeal to the pontiff 'from whom it was granted that in the future we should no longer be burdened by the tribulations of Ripa, which, if necessary, we will send'.[118]

The peace agreements, as well as the *sicurtà*, were integral parts, if not at the very centre, of the power struggle between the papal authority and local powers over the control of the instruments used to govern hatred and social conflict. If Rome repeatedly intervened to affirm the necessity of applying the papal constitutions on public order as faithfully as possible, recommending to local governments that 'for the future – as stated in one of these instructions

[115] 'usar clemenza à questi rissanti nelle suppliche che daranno, sendosi pacificati amorevolmente per amor d'Iddio, et di questa nostra Comunità', ibid (Offida, 7 July 1579).

[116] On the factional struggles and the massive political exodus, which were linked with banditry and plagued the Ascoli area starting from the mid-sixteenth century, see Irene Polverini Fosi, *La società violenta. Il banditismo dello Stato pontificio nella seconda metà del Cinquecento* (Rome, 1985), pp. 54-63.

[117] 'dubitando noi non esser pregiudicati d'accontribuire alli loro danni de farci pagare et concorrere ad essi', ASM, *Governatore Generale della Marca di Ancona*, n. 1144 (Offida, 17 March 1579).

[118] ibid.

sent to papal representatives in the Marca – they should never come to composition or commutation of ordinary penalties in the cases included in these Constitutions, without having given notice and waited for the order from here',[119] this does not mean that the central government wanted to enhance coercive and afflictive tools at the expense of transactional ones, but rather that it considered it of primary importance to assert firm central control over locally managed transactional procedures. An example from the territory of Ascoli will help us better understand this dynamic of continuous negotiation between the local papal government and communities.

Montefiore, a small town near Ripatransone and about fifty kilometres from Ascoli, was at that time the scene of numerous acts of violence caused by longstanding enmities. The Governor of the March had sent a commissioner, Giovanni Corona, to remove the families involved in the feuds and to compel 'those who own houses outside'[120] and who 'non sono interessati' ('are not involved') to provide *sicurtà* not to harm. The documents do not specify this, but the direct reference to 'houses' suggests that it was not so much about *sicurtà* not to harm, but rather about guarantees ensuring the obligation not to harbour those who had been exiled or banned. The priors of Montefiore judged the request to be unfair and unusual, not conforming to the letter of commission received from the governor. The pontifical authorities continued the practice of targeting extensive networks of community members according to a system of concentric circles based on kinship ties, regardless of their involvement in the dynamics of violence and revenge. Moreover, the letter continued, it was unclear why the commissioner intended to adopt different measures in Montefiore compared to what had been done in Ripatransone, 'where he ordered that only those who are involved and have houses outside the town should provide them'. The priors asked Pietro Filoteri 'not to compel those who are not involved to provide these *sicurtà* for houses outside nor to compel them to pay a penalty for not having provided them within the term of their bans';[121] instead, it would have been more appropriate for only 'those who have houses outside and are involved'[122] to be required to provide *sicurtà*

[119] 'per l'avvenire non venghino mai a composizione o commutazione di pena ordinaria ne i casi compresi da esse Costituzioni, senza haverne dato avviso et aspettare l'ordine di qua', cited in Polverini Fosi, *La società violenta*, p. 55.

[120] 'quelli che possedono le case fuori', ASM, *Governatore Generale della Marca di Ancona*, n. 1144 (Montefiore, 23 March 1579).

[121] 'che non vogli astrengere quelli che non sono interessati a dare queste sigurtà per le case de fuori ne meno astrengerli a pagar pena per non haverle date sin hora nel termine de suoi banni', ibid.

[122] 'quelli tali che hanno le case fuora e sono interessati', ibid.

not to harm, in addition to 'paying the travel expenses of the Commissioner and obtaining from His Most Reverend Lordship the letters desired according to the memorandum we sent for the service of the Peace'.[123] The community of Montefiore thus asked the Governor of the Marche to adhere to an approach that allowed for local management of peacekeeping procedures, but still with a form of recognition and legitimation from above. The alternative, which the priors intended to avoid, was a commissioner acting in a burdensome manner and enforcing peace through the usual highly coercive methods.

The distinction is not to be found in the presence or absence of coercion in the process leading to peace, as even locally managed systems were not less coercive than centrally managed ones, but rather in the processes of political and legal legitimation to which that same coercion was directed.[124] The assertion that community judicial systems were characterised by the horizontality of procedures and solutions adopted, and were 'allergic' to the imposing interventions of central power in governing local conflicts, needs to be nuanced. The idea of communities being closed in on themselves, jealous of their conflict resolution systems considered more equitable, and resistant to the intervention of judicial bodies, becomes even weaker when considering that, in peripheral rural communities subjected to feudal lordships, the demand for justice was strong, and the exercise of jurisdiction by the lord was favourably perceived by social actors. Whether it concerned fiefs of ancient imperial investiture or recent enfeoffments by regional Italian princes, feudal justice operated in both civil and criminal fields with relative autonomy and not always in competition and rivalry with princely justice. In general, it can be said that regional states were indeed willing to delegate the administration of justice to feudal lords in remote, inaccessible and difficult-to-reach areas. Therefore, the relationships between feudal powers and central powers, which sometimes – but not always – reserved rights of avocation and appeal for cases initiated within the feudal domain, remain to be assessed on a case-by-case basis, based on a continuous process of political negotiation.[125]

[123] 'pagare il viatico del Commissario et ottenere da Sua Signoria Reverendissima le lettere che desidero secondo il memoriale ve mandamo per servizio delle Paci', ibid.

[124] See Gian Maria Varanini, 'Legittimità implicita dei poteri nell'Italia centro-settentrionale del tardo medioevo. La tradizione cittadina e gli Stati regionali', in *La légitimité implicite*, vol. II, ed. Jean-Philippe Genet (Rome and Paris, 2015), pp. 223–39; Andrea Zorzi, *La giustizia*, in op. cit., pp. 337–50.

[125] See Stefano Calonaci, *Lo spirito del dominio. Giustizia e giurisdizioni feudali nell'Italia moderna (secoli XVI-XVIII)* (Rome, 2017), pp. 93–100.

In the communal era, the expansion of the criminal sphere, the consequent recourse to *ex officio* procedure, and the very high rate of contumacy were parts of a process of political legitimation that marked the transition from the *podestà* regime to the popular regime and made use of procedures of grace and reduction and cancellation of penalties as mechanisms for the social reintegration of the offender.[126] With the transition to seigniorial regimes and the formation of regional states, this essentially negotiable legal and judicial system, although centred on the *ex officio* procedure, neither regressed nor disappeared, but had to adapt to the new institutional context and make changes on multiple levels. The pontifical power, in the late sixteenth century, was in need of legitimation as it was new, but above all external to local political and judicial institutions. To achieve this goal, the strategy used was essentially the same: to intervene in the *ex officio* procedure and the systematic use of contumacy and banishment so that papal power could assume the role of the great peacemaker, dispensing grace and readmitting the guilty into the social fabric. The signing of peace became the primary condition imposed on the banned offender to return to their community, with the dual purpose of reaffirming the full legitimacy of the penal action – since the conviction had already been issued – and simultaneously recognising the operation of traditional conflict resolution systems.[127]

In the late sixteenth century, the goal of communities was not to operate with the greatest possible autonomy to quell conflicts and feuds, as it is often the case that they themselves requested the pacifying intervention of external authority, a direct emanation of pontifical power, especially when conflicts involved multiple communities. The background of the protest by the priors of Montefiore regarding the method adopted by the Governor of the Marche is enlightening from this perspective. From correspondence

[126] See Andrea Zorzi, 'Negoziazione penale, legittimazione giuridica e poteri urbani nell'Italia comunale', in *Criminalità e giustizia in Germania e in Italia. Pratiche giudiziarie e linguaggi giuridici tra tardo medioevo ed età moderna / Kriminalität und Justiz in Deutschland und Italien. Rechtspraktiken und gerichtliche Diskurse in Spätmittelalter und Früher Neuzeit*, ed. Marco Bellabarba, Gerd Schwerhoff and Andrea Zorzi (Bologna, 2001), p. 22.

[127] Often, once a sentence of banishment had already been pronounced, following a peace agreement with the victim's family, the courts allowed the return of the condemned individual, provided they imposed a pecuniary sanction and a symbolic penalty (such as, for example, an oath in a church or in front of a devotional object or image). This practice is attested, for instance, in the Venetian area, as referenced in Claudio Povolo, *L'intrigo dell'onore. Poteri e istituzioni nella Repubblica di Venezia tra Cinque e Seicento* (Sommacampagna, 1997), p. 137.

exchanged in early February 1579, only a month and a half earlier, it is learned that Montefiore had asked Offida to appoint and send two 'ambassadors' to Macerata to negotiate peace between Valentino, Aurelio and Cesare Egidi on one side, and the Lauri family on the other. The priors of Offida decided to ask Filoteri to assume this responsibility on their behalf, and the priors of Montefiore did the same, with a letter sent at the same time: 'we pray that you willingly take on this burden of such a holy work that besides earning a reward from the Divine Majesty of God, we will remain perpetually obliged to you'.[128] For peace negotiations, the two communities relied entirely on the syndic and chancellor of the Province and a person, Catalli, in whom both placed their trust. The priors of Offida asked Filoteri to 'negotiate whatever [Catalli] exposes to you as the desire of the Community of Montefiore and ours, using our usual diligence to complete the business, for which we will be most grateful'.[129]

Negotiating peace or a truce meant not only mediating between the conflicting parties but also seeking a balance between private interests and public authority, a constant, looming and threatening presence. To put 'brains to the test', conditions were imposed, interdicts and excommunications were threatened, and monetary sanctions were applied:

> We have received the summary of the impositions, which were to have put the minds to the test, and we fear not going for absolution and encountering the interdict, because we find that in all four payments we are extremely burdened. Therefore, we await your opinion before decreeing the vote of our Community, which Your Lordship will write back to us upon the return of Messer Costanzo.[130]

Something, however, must have gone wrong if, in the month of July, Offida found itself compelled to protest against the governor of the province's intention to install a constable and bailiffs to contain the disorders

[128] 'la pregamo se degni pigliare volentieri questo peso de si opera santa che oltre ne haverrà premio dalla Divina Maestà de Idio, noi le ne restaremo con perpetuo obligo', ASM, *Governatore Generale della Marca di Ancona*, n. 1144 (Montefiore, 3 February 1579).

[129] 'negotiare quanto da esso [Catalli] vi verrà esposto essere dessiderio della Comunità di Montefiore, e nostro, usando ogni nostra solita diligenza per compimento del negotio, che ne sarà gratissimo', ibid (Offida, 3 February 1579).

[130] 'Havemo recevuto il sommario dell'impositioni quale è haver messo i cervelli a partito, e dubitiamo non andar per l'assolutione e ritrovar l'interdetto, per che troviamo ch'in tutti quattro li pagamenti siamo gravatissimi, però aspettiamo il vostro parere prima che decretiamo il voto della nostra Comunità, il qual parere V.S. ce lo riscriverà alla tornata di messer Costanzo', ibid.

afflicting those territories. Perhaps the peace agreements had not been finalised, or they had not been able, as often happened, to stop the violence. The fact remains that the dynamics triggered by the use of compositional tools were not progressively limited and delegitimised by Rome; on the contrary, they were valued, albeit accompanied by a desire for control. The tools used by local justice were essentially the same as those used by sovereign justice; Rome's intervention varied according to the conditions of the territory in question. From the enfeoffed lands of Lazio, but often also from Umbria, appeals and requests for pardon following a conviction issued by a local auditor reached Rome. These requests were subject to the condition of obtaining peace from the opposing party. In 1585, in Sacrofano, an Orsini fief, Antonio, known as Stangone, pleaded for pardon before the governor of Rome after the auditor of the local feudal court had sentenced him to death for the killing of Tommaso Ciferto. This had occurred over matters of honour and within the context of a complex group dynamic that Stangone detailed. The peace reached with the relatives of the deceased was the basis of his request for the auditor to annul the sentence:

> Because, Most Excellent Lord, as you know, peace has followed, and he [Stangone], worn out by the long years of exile with much suffering and the loss of his aforementioned brother who was killed, desires to return to a better life and to make arrangements for marrying off his poor sister whom he has, and to completely abandon his life of crime. Therefore, he appeals to Your Most Illustrious Excellency, begging that you pardon him for these crimes and homicide, and instruct your Auditor to annul all proceedings, complaints and condemnations formed and issued against him, and that he be no longer harassed for this reason, and that he may freely go about your state without being molested.[131]

Petitions were appeals aimed at bypassing the jurisdictional authority – be it a legate or a peripheral governor, feudal court, communal court or even an apostolic commissioner – that had issued the condemnation. The cases are

[131] 'Perché Eccellentissimo Signor come lei sa è seguitane la pace, et egli [Stangone] macerato dal lungo esilio di tanti anni con molto patere con perdita di detto suo fratello ammazzato desidera redursi, à, miglior vita, et dare opera di maritare una sua povera sorella che egli ha, et in tutto distogliersi dal mal vivere. Però ricorre à Vostra Eccellenza Illustrissima supplicandola si degni perdonargli detti delitti et homicidio, e, commetter al suo Auditore che cassi ogni processo, querela, et condennatione contra esso formata, e, data, et che per tal causa non sia più molestato, et che possa repraticare liberamente per tutto il suo stato senza esser molestato', ASR, *Tribunale Criminale del Governatore, Atti di Cancelleria, Lettere*, vol. 42, f. 299.

numerous, and the structure of these documents is more or less always the same. In Perugia, in 1577, the apostolic commissioner Jacopo Panico had condemned Giulio di Paolo Nonnio to exile and perpetual infamy for harbouring bandits and attempting to murder a certain Alessandro; following the peace between Giulio and his victim, a petition was made to the powerful son of the pope, Giacomo Boncompagni, then governor of Fermo, to intercede with the pontiff to 'remit all penalties and prejudice of said sentence and process, and generally any guilt that he may have committed in this matter, freeing him fully in both civil and ecclesiastical courts so that in the future he may not be harassed in any way or by any means'. As can be seen, the penalties imposed were both temporal and spiritual, which contributed to giving an even fuller meaning to the peace imposed as a condition for the granting of sovereign pardon, since the forgiveness of enemies was, as is well known, the condition for the granting of absolution from censures and excommunications.

Peace could be the condition locally achieved for obtaining a centrally granted pardon, but at the same time the outcome of a centrally managed forceful action aimed at stopping a spiral of violence. Especially in the territories immediately subject to the central authority, commissioners could be sent (or called) to intervene with local courts that were unable to pacify warring families and factions, imposing 'their' peace under threat of military intervention and financially burdening the affected communities' coffers. This meant taking control of the situation and, through executors, managing peace and truce negotiations, effectively stripping the courts of their authority. To restore order in a bloody conflict, Commissioner Candido Zitelli arrived in October 1579 in Capranica and Sutri, two territories subject to the Sacred *Consulta*, spending eleven days to 'hold councils at both courts, create syndics and procurators for both courts, and draw up the chapters included in the instrument'.[132] The conflict had evidently erupted between the two communities, and in the face of the deadlock, the commissioner's intervention must have seemed the only way to achieve a cessation of hostilities. Finding a point of agreement was not a simple operation, however, and required good mediation skills. 'After discussing it with them several times',[133] wrote Zitelli to the governor of Rome, 'the instrument of the truce was finally drawn up to the satisfaction and agreement of both parties':[134]

[132] 'far celebrare li consegli all'una et l'altra Corta, far creare li sindici et procuratori a tutti dui le Corta et far li capitoli compresi nel istromento', op. cit., vol. 41, *filza* 190, f. 39r.

[133] 'Discorsoli più volte fra di loro', ibid.

[134] 'finalmente forno fatti l'istromento della tregua con sodisfatione et concordia d'una parte et l'altra', ibid.

the truce had been reached, but one must wonder through what means of persuasion and at what cost to the communities. First and foremost, the commissioner ordered that the financial burden of the intervention, corresponding to the provision to be paid to the executors, should be borne equally by the two courts, 'because nothing was attended to but their peace'[135] and 'if Your Most Illustrious Lordship had not sent me here, they would have killed each other like dogs'.[136] The court of Capranica, 'having understood this reasoning',[137] obeyed Zitelli's order, but once the executors arrived in Sutri, they had to confront the refusal of the other court to pay its share, both that destined for the executors and that destined for the commissioner himself and the notary. The tone of the missive addressed to the governor is between annoyed and discouraged:

> I cannot leave from here because I am attending to the resolution of other cases, and it seems to me that it is a mechanical art to go and litigate such provisions, which they should handle on their own without others having to ask them. *I have brought them to peace without calling in the armies of soldiers as Our Lord would command.*[138]

The alternative to the cessation of hostilities and the achievement of peace was, in short, the dispatch of the army by the pontifical commissioner. Communities knew very well that finding a point of agreement meant, first and foremost, averting sanctions and extremely harsh coercive actions from the central authorities. And even when such actions occurred, the outcome would still be a peace, though celebrated after arrests, violence and summary condemnations, under the strict supervision of soldiers. The commissioners of the governor of Rome arrived, endowed with extensive inspection powers, even in territories not immediately subject. In 1585, in Carpineto Romano, a fief of the Caetani of Segni-Valmontone but which would pass to the Aldobrandini within a few years, Commissioner Favenzio Gandolfo was sent to conduct thorough investigations into a series of violent acts and serious incidents of harbouring bandits. Initially, witnesses were questioned about a priest, Lorenzo Porta, who was known to have visited another priest

135 'perché non s'è atteso ad altro che alla quiete loro', ibid.

136 'se Vostra Signoria Illustrissima non me mandava qua si sarriano ammazzati come cani', op. cit., f. 39^{v}.

137 'fattasi capace di questa ragione', op. cit., f. 39^{r}.

138 'Io non posso lassare qui perché attendo al espeditione del altre cause et poi me pare che sia arte mecanica per andare a litigar simil provisioni che doveriano farlo da loro senza che altri gli l'adimandi, *che li ho messi in pace senza chiamare l'eserciti delli soldati sicome comandaria Nostro Signore*', op. cit., f. 39^{v}, italics mine.

two years earlier, who lived near Carpineto in the company of seventeen to eighteen bandits. Gandolfo summoned Priest Lorenzo to appear, intending to prosecute him if he did not appear and, in any case, to detain him in prison once the interrogation was over. At the same time, the commissioner gathered evidence against an apothecary, Giovanni Lucido, because he was the uncle of a certain Nardarello, who was currently imprisoned in Rome. It was necessary to determine whether Nardarello had indeed gone to his house after a crime known as the 'powder incident', which had been followed by a peace agreement, and to verify whether 'said Giovanni Lucido is aware of the crime of the said powder and perhaps the said *sicurtà* has also been broken';[139] at the same time, the judge in Rome was to interrogate Nardarello to find out whether 'he alone or in the company of other armed men was harboured by said uncle after the powder incident'.[140] No evidence was found to confirm the suspicion that the arquebus shot against Ascanio Cantelli had been fired by Giovanni Farinaccio. But, as had happened with Commissioner Zitelli in Capranica and Sutri, it was the issues related to provisions and travel expenses that raised concerns for Commissioner Gandolfo:

> I inform you that we might encounter difficulties in raising funds for our expenses here and for the travel allowances because they are all poor people. It appears that those who remained have cleared out everything, and moreover, the patent I have does not seem too clear because it states that I should conduct the process up to the sentence exclusive, and then it says that the travel expenses are to be paid every time delinquents are found and indicted for such crimes. If I cannot declare them delinquents, I cannot do anything on this matter, and to say every time that delinquents and indicted persons are found is a confusing statement. You know how difficult it is to collect these payments if they are not very clear, in addition to many other difficulties that arise. Therefore, if you deem it appropriate, I would suggest sending a declaration stating that I can be paid from the goods of the indicted even if they are not yet condemned, as has always been done in the past, as you have seen in all the other patents. Otherwise, it will either be impossible to collect, or if collected by force, it would lead to litigation in Rome, which would not honour anyone.[141]

139 'detto Giovan Lucido sia consapevole del delitto della detta polvere e forse sia anco rotta la detta *sicurtà*', op. cit., vol. 42, f. 22^{v}.

140 'solo overo in compagnia di altri armati è stato ricettato da detto suo zio dopo il delitto della polvere', ibid.

141 'vi aviso che potrebbe essere che havessimo difficultà in far dinari e per le spese nostre qua, e per li viatici perché son tutti poveracci e s'intende che chi è restato ha sgombrato ogni cosa e tanto più che la patente che io ho non par troppo chiara

The remuneration of commissioners and other accompanying officials weighed heavily on the communities where they were sent. These communities were often poor or rendered semi-deserted by the preventive flight of the main suspects. In this case, Gandolfo highlighted a contradiction in the letter patent, which stated that the commissioner could carry out the processes but without issuing the sentence, and that travel expenses were due whenever 'delinquents and suspects' were found. However, as the commissioner implied, one is considered a delinquent only after the sentence. For this reason, the commissioner asked the governor of Rome for an official clarification, hoping that it would be possible to 'be paid from the goods of the suspects even if they are not yet condemned, as has always been done in the past'.[142]

perché dice che io faccia il processo usque ad sententiam exclusive, e poi dice che le spese di viatici si pagano ogni volta saranno trovati dellinquenti, et inditiati di tali delitti, e se io non li posso fare dellinquenti non posso far cosa alcuna per questo capo, et a dir ogni volta che saranno trovati dellinquenti et inditiati per una cosa confuso e questi pagamenti se non son più che chiari sapete quanta difficultà si ha a riscoterli oltre molte altre difficultà che ne nascano e però se vi pare a proposito consideraria me ne mandassero una declaratoria la quale fosse che mi possa far pagare delli beni delli inditiati seben non sono condannati ancora, si come si è fatto sempre per il passato come havete visto in tutte l'altre patenti, altrimenti o non si potrà riscotere, ò riscotendosi per forza si litigarebbe poi in Roma con poco honore di tutti', op. cit., ff. 22v–23r.

142 'far pagare delli beni delli inditiati seben non sono condannati ancora, si come si è fatto sempre per il passato', op. cit., f. 23r.

4.

A European culture of social containment through conciliation

1. Bi-confessionality, social peace and arbitral justice: the monarchy of France

The presence of a significant Huguenot minority and the bloody civil war that erupted from the early 1560s made France an extraordinarily important laboratory for the development of the concepts of concord and peace. The intense theoretical reflection on religious concord was not detached from the practices aimed at overcoming interconfessional conflict, which in the context of communities could arise from other factors (personal and family enmities, hatred, vengeance). The 1973 essay by Natalie Zemon Davis on the rites of violence in religious conflict in France undoubtedly marked a historiographical turning point, not least by her ability to graft the anthropological perspective onto the historical data of 'crowd violence'.[1] Just as it is possible to write a history of violence, even in its ritual and performative dimension, one can attempt to write a history of peace and the search for peaceful coexistence in contexts of bi-confessionality. The challenge, as in the analysis of conflict and explosions of violence, lies in evaluating the degree of impact of religious motivation in the search for concord, assuming it is possible to fully separate it from social factors.

The theoretical reflection on religious concord took its cue from the reflection on social concord, a common heritage, as has been seen, of Renaissance political thought, as well as from Erasmus-inspired Christian irenicism. Some prominent figures of French culture in the 1550s and 1560s have left testimonies of great interest. Consider, for example, François Bauduin and his idealisation of Emperor Constantine and the *Respublica Christiana* as models of peaceful coexistence based both on the observance of the law and the constant pursuit of action founded on moderation, the absence of

[1] See Natalie Zemon Davis, 'The Rites of Violence: Religious Riot in Sixteenth-Century France', *Past & Present* 59 (1973), pp. 51–91.

excessive rigour and repression as a tool to be adopted only in extreme cases.[2] Even in the writings of a less influential author than Bauduin, such as Louis Le Roy, religious conflict, an ineliminable element of history, is directly connected to imperfect human nature, which drives people to inconsistency, to obey feelings of malice and selfishness, preventing them from enjoying the perfection inherent in Christianity. For Le Roy, internal struggles, seditions and external wars are nothing more than the direct consequence of the diversion from the original state of perfection of the evangelical message; this necessitates a work of correcting abuses – that is, a profound reform of the Church, albeit in a prudent form, since reforms themselves are often capable of generating discontent and seditions.[3]

Sedition and heresy, social conflict, and religious division: all these phenomena stem from a common root, which lies in the prevalence of passions over human thoughts and actions. They are different aspects of the same problem, aspects that influence each other. In many of these authors, the ideal remains religious concord, not tolerance; not the acceptance of the coexistence of multiple confessions, but the pursuit of confessional unity understood as conciliation and recomposition. However, the history of philosophical and juridical ideas alone does not capture the complexity of social and political relations that have been shaped and sedimented in various local contexts over time.

Is it possible to draw a parallel between the search for peace, concord and friendship in the religious field and the governance of interpersonal violence driven by non-confessional motivations? Partially, yes, because the agencies involved were often the same. Olivier Christin has shown how the city constituted the central place for both the struggle between confessions and the search for peaceful coexistence. The *bailliages* played a central role in interpreting the pacification agreements signed at the general level (such as the one of Amboise in 1563); in some cases, the magistrates advocated a restrictive interpretation of these agreements which, while helping to curb violence against members of the confessional minority, were used by magistrates as tools of coercion and persecution against them, which could lead to further

2 See Mario Turchetti, *Concordia o tolleranza? François Bauduin (1520-1573) e i 'moyenneurs'* (Genève, 1984), p. 112.

3 Loys Le Roy, *Des differens et troubles advenans entre les hommes par la diversité des Religions* (à Paris, de l'Imprimerie de Frederic Morel, Rue S. Iean de Beauvais, au Franc Meurier, 1562). See Luigi Magno, 'Apologie étatique et concorde religieuse. Sur quelques pamphlets de Loys Le Roy', *Krypton. Identità, potere, rappresentazioni* 1 (2013), available online at http://193.205.139.95/ojs/index.php/krypton/article/view/452/449

eruptions of violence.[4] In other cases, it was possible to achieve a situation of real bi-confessionality, but what certainly stands out is, on the one hand, the possibility for a magistrate to manipulate a peace agreement – whether religious or civil – to exert pressure on social actors or entire categories, and on the other hand, the use, not only in theory but also in judicial practice, of terms and concepts (peace, friendship, concord) identical to those usually employed to describe interpersonal relations in mono-confessional contexts.[5]

Sometimes the documentation shows members of minorities being very cautious in taking advantage of the favourable conditions contained in the pacification edicts, given the presence of deep-seated hatreds of different kinds that undermined the mutual trust essential for peace to function. Religious hatred and social hatred were indissolubly linked, and it is extremely difficult to think of separating them clearly. The pacification edicts had to be applied in each specific context, and central to this process was the action of commissioners specifically appointed and sent from the centre to the most remote peripheries to re-establish peaceful coexistence within communities; an action that, however, exclusively benefitted the Catholic majority. The use of the pact, the oath not to use (or resume using) violence against one's

4 See Olivier Christin, *La paix de religion. L'autonomisation de la raison politique au XVIe siècle* (Paris, 1997), pp. 80–3.

5 'Certes, le biconfessionnalité locale et "l'amitié voisinale" paraissent parfois relever davantage du pragmatisme et de la prudence politiques que de l'adhésion consciente aux idéaux de la tolérance et de la paix civile, car la menace d'une intervention militaire de l'empereur ou du roi de France n'est jamais absente des esprits, mais, dans le contexte général de renforcement des identités confessionnelles qui est celui de la seconde moitié du XVIe siècle, elles représentent déjà, en dépit de leurs incertitudes et de leurs ambigüités, un espace important de liberté relative et d'expérimentation des formes de coexistence. Elles démontrent que, en l'absence de tout rapprochement doctrinal, voire de toute sympathie pour l'autre confession, des accords ponctuels, politiques et juridiques, peuvent être conclus et durer, et que ces accords peuvent parfois suffire à enrayer les débordements violents, les émotions, les meurtres' ('Certainly, local bi-confessionality and "neighbourly friendship" sometimes seem to derive more from political pragmatism and prudence than from conscious adherence to the ideals of tolerance and civil peace, as the threat of military intervention by the emperor or the king of France is never absent from minds. However, in the general context of strengthening confessional identities in the second half of the sixteenth century, they already represent, despite their uncertainties and ambiguities, an important space of relative freedom and experimentation with forms of coexistence. They demonstrate that, in the absence of any doctrinal rapprochement or even any sympathy for the other confession, specific political and legal agreements can be concluded and sustained, and that these agreements can sometimes suffice to curb violent outbursts, emotions and murders'), in op. cit., p. 83.

neighbour, similar to private peace acts, was very frequent in various regions of France following the publication of the pacification edicts, but in contexts of multi-confessional coexistence, the indispensable higher reference, typically religious, that usually underpinned the agreements became an almost insurmountable obstacle. It was impossible to resort to objects of devotion, typically saints or the Virgin, and for this reason the commissioners were forced to secularise the form and contents of the pacts: one was called to swear on the preservation of the common good, or on the observance of the edicts, under threat of severe judicial consequences; the protagonists were no longer clerics but royal officers and magistrates. No reference to the sacred, then, in an era when a political oath was inconceivable without it.[6] Jérémie Foa has well described the precariousness of the balances that could be achieved, given a context in which the peace agreements signed were marked by great mutual distrust.[7]

6 With the Reformation and the consequent birth of territorial churches, we move to the phase of sworn professions of faith. 'Ciò che caratterizza appunto la professione di fede rispetto al credo è il giuramento: mentre il giuramento politico si ideologizza [...] riempiendosi del contenuto teologico e sacrale prima riservato alla sfera ecclesiastica, la adesione di fede si politicizza riempiendosi dei contenuti di appartenenza tipici della realtà secolare' ('What characterises the profession of faith compared to the creed is precisely the oath: while the political oath becomes ideologised [...] filling itself with the theological and sacred content previously reserved for the ecclesiastical sphere, adherence of faith becomes politicised, filling itself with the contents of belonging typical of secular reality'), Paolo Prodi, *Il sacramento del potere. Il giuramento politico nella storia costituzionale dell'Occidente* (Bologna, 1982), p. 283.

7 'Par leurs tâtonnements entre formes de cohésion liées à l'individu, au groupe, à la religion, au gage mutuel, au judiciaire et finalement à la monarchie, les serments impulsés par les commissaires, souvent repris ultérieurement par les habitants, illustrent la difficulté des contemporains à penser ce qu'est une "communauté d'habitants qui n'est plus soudée par les mêmes liens religieux, par le recours aux mêmes saints patrons, aux mêmes rites et aux mêmes cérémonies". Plusieurs signes convergents montrent qu'en plusieurs endroits, ni les promesses d'oubli, ni les serments de sauvegarde ne suffisent à convaincre les habitants et encore moins les commissaires que la paix sera préservée après leur départ. Qu'est-ce qui garantit que le calme se perpétuera en leur absence?' ('Through their groping between forms of cohesion linked to the individual, the group, religion, mutual surety, judicial means, and finally the monarchy, the oaths driven by the commissioners, often later taken up by the inhabitants, illustrate the difficulty contemporaries faced in conceiving what a "community of inhabitants that is no longer bound by the same religious ties, the same patron saints, the same rites, and the same ceremonies" is. Several converging signs show that in many places, neither promises of oblivion nor oaths of safeguard suffice to convince the inhabitants, and even less the commissioners, that peace will be preserved after their

At the interconfessional level, religious conflicts were compounded by those stemming from personal animosities and vendettas, which were settled through arbitration within the community or by appealing to seigniorial justice. At the intraconfessional level, however, the Consistory had jurisdiction over the Huguenot field, regularly performing its arbitral function in resolving interpersonal conflicts, absorbing a portion of local cases.[8] Indeed, it could be argued that, in many cases, religious conflict between individuals or, more often, between families constituted more of an epiphenomenon than the real substance of violent episodes, which were fundamentally based on economic or prestige issues.[9] The modalities of translating religious conflict into the realm of criminal judicial conflict must be established on a case-by-case basis, as no generalisation is possible. Gregory Hanlon observed, on the one hand, that a substantial number of peace agreements were jointly signed by Catholics and Huguenots, and on the other, that most of the individuals involved in the cases belonged to the local elite. This would demonstrate that, in seventeenth-century Layrac, violence was more an expression of social integration than of marginality and exclusion. Following the Edict of Nantes in 1598, a specific magistracy, the *Chambre de l'Édit*, was created in Paris by Henry IV of Navarre to regulate relations between Catholics and Huguenots. In other areas of France, other special courts, composed of magistrates from both confessions, were established in local parliaments (Grenoble, Bordeaux, Rouen, Toulouse). These tribunals had jurisdiction over various types of crime, including offences, assaults, violence, injuries and even killings. By exercising control over the conduct of lower officials administering justice at the local level to prevent abuses against the Huguenot minority, the *Chambre de l'Édit* functioned as an appellate body from which both exemplary punishment for the perpetrators of violence (including abusive officials) and the arbitral resolution of minor disputes were expected. The problem lies in the fact that, in seventeenth-century France, resorting to violence was legitimised not only by the defence of one's honour, and thus one's social status, but also by the defence of one's community from the penetration of heresy.[10]

departure. What guarantees that calm will persist in their absence?'), Jérémie Foa, *Le tombeau de la paix. Une histoire des édits de pacification (1560-1572)* (Limoges, 2015), p. 363.

8 See Gregory Hanlon, *Confession and Community in Seventeenth Century France. Catholic and Protestant Coexistence in Aquitaine* (Philadelphia, 1993), pp. 73 ss.

9 See Stuart Carroll, 'The Peace in the Feud in Sixteenth- and Seventeenth-Century France, *Past & Present* 178, 1 (2003), pp. 74–115.

10 See Diane C. Margolf, *Religion and Royal Justice in Early Modern France. The Paris Chambre de l'Edit, 1598-1665* (Kirksville, 2003), pp. 148 ss.

In the field of justice governance, sixteenth and seventeenth-century France was fully integrated into a broader European panorama in which a combined juridical and moral culture of mediation and arbitral dispute resolution was given considerable reflective space. The image of a France, tested by the late sixteenth-century civil wars, that by the time of Henry IV had initiated a grand process of centralisation not only of the administrative and governmental apparatus but also of the judicial apparatus, culminating in the long reign of Louis XIV, has undoubtedly overshadowed a practice of arbitral mediation of social conflicts perfectly embedded in royal legislation, and thus anticipated, encouraged and regulated.[11] It is no coincidence that the peak of such regulation occurred precisely in the late seventeenth century, during the mature phase of the Sun King's reign, when the judicial delegations to the feudal aristocracy underwent a certain amplification, especially in contexts of extraordinary conflicts and violence, including religious ones. This was a sign of the strength rather than weakness of a state apparatus that managed to incorporate the arbitral procedures traditionally governed by feudal lords holding (venal) offices, subjecting them to control.

For the mid-sixteenth century, we have a precious and extraordinary testimony in the form of the diary of Gilles Picot, lord of Gouberville and Mesnil-au-Valle, and lieutenant of the waters and forests of the viscounty of Valognes in Normandy. The account offers a wealth of details that allows us to reconstruct the reality and daily activities of a feudal lord, although not among the richest and most influential in the Kingdom, in which arbitration and peace-making are well present and assume significant importance. The high frequency of the verb *accorder* within the diary indicates to what extent the feudal lords (not all in the same way, of course) conceived their role also as one of social mediation, and to what extent the subjects looked to them as natural arbiters of disputes. Often, it was a matter of reconciling people over small economic issues, but there are also references to delicate situations of violence and conflict where mediation frequently failed, an aspect that other types of sources deliberately omit. In early March 1556, on Ash Wednesday, Picot gathered at his residence the parish priest of Bretteville, Clément Rouxel, Jean Fournel and Guillaume Potet to reconcile the parish priest of Tourlaville with his brother and Jean Fournel, 'which we could not do because

[11] See Eric Wenzel, 'La paix par la justice. Les modes alternatifs de règlement des conflits dans la France d'Ancien Régime', in *Stringere la pace. Teorie e pratiche della conciliazione nell'Europa moderna (secoli XV-XVIII)*, ed. Paolo Broggio and Maria Pia Paoli (Rome, 2010), pp. 509–19.

of the obstinacy of the parties'.[12] The conflict was rooted in economic issues, but the major public order problems caused by the Parmentier family in the region during those years gave Gilles de Gouberville the opportunity to deal with conflicts arising from assaults, property destruction and even murders. The excesses committed by Rouland le Parmentier and his sons Jean and Thomas led to the intervention of Monsieur de Bordeaux, a counsellor in the *Parlement* of Normandy, and Monsieur Bigot, the Attorney General of the same *parlement*, to gather information about their conduct. In August 1558, Jean and Thomas, in conflict with the lord of Coqueville for having destroyed his property, murdered the sergeant Guillaume Chandeleur, who had been appointed by Coqueville to demand they cease their excesses. Anne, Coqueville's widow, abandoned by the entire community and tired of the violence perpetrated by the family, then turned to Gouberville to mediate and resolve the conflict. However, the meetings he organised in September and November of the same year yielded no results, given the Parmentiers' refusal to accept conditions deemed too onerous. It was a refusal that cost them their lives, as the *Parlement* of Rouen sentenced Thomas and Jean to death, while their father, Rouland, was spared but fined. The interesting aspect is that the conflict did not end with the sentences, because only the quantification and acceptance of reparation, and the consequent peace, could put a lasting end to the clashes. Negotiations between Coqueville's widow and Rouland continued through Gouberville's good offices, but again, no satisfactory result was reached: Rouland, a Huguenot, was killed in 1562 by a Catholic, while at the end of the same year Anne revoked Gouberville's mandate to continue the negotiations, deciding to take the matter to the viscount court of Valognes.[13]

Diaries represent a source of great importance due to their ability to reveal the extreme flexibility of the conciliatory and arbitrative activities carried out by prominent members of the community. In addition to the role of feudal lords, the role of the parish clergy was crucial. Some parish priests have also left us diaries, through which it is possible to grasp the complex motivations driving them, the evolution of the strategies they employed over time, the types of relationship existing between the parish priests and the litigants, and those among the litigants themselves, who were immersed in familial, kinship and patronage networks. An exceptional case, for example, is that of Hugues Aulanier (1601–91), the parish priest of Brignon (in the

12 'ce que ne fisme pour l'ostination des partyes', in 'Le journal du Sire de Gouberville', *Mémoires de la Société des Antiquaires de Normandie*, vol. XXXI (Caen, Rouen and Paris, 1892), p. 335.

13 See Carroll, *The Peace in the Feud*, pp. 103–4.

Velay region), whose extensive diary was closely analysed by Anne Bonzon in her recent book.[14] In France, the mediating role of the feudal aristocracy never waned, and ecclesiastical authorities moved in the same direction in the seventeenth century, without the centralising king *par excellence*, Louis XIV, viewing this phenomenon as an obstacle to the affirmation of his prestige and power. At the very moment when the *Ordonnance criminelle* of 26 August 1670, a major reform of criminal procedure desired by the Sun King, was promulgated by the *Parlement* of Paris, openly providing for alternative outcomes to convictions in trials, several French bishops intervened – following the decision made during the General Assembly of the Clergy on 17 November 1670 to distribute Alexandre de La Roche's book in all dioceses, which will be discussed shortly[15] – to reaffirm the obligation of

[14] See Anne Bonzon, *La paix au village. Clergé paroissial et règlement des conflits dans la France d'Ancien Régime* (Paris, 2022), pp. 54–84.

[15] 'Monseigneur de Meaux, a dit, qu'une compagnie de Paris pleine de charité, lui avoit mis en main, un petit livre intitulé, l'*Arbitre charitable*, pour faciliter l'accord des procez et querelles, suivant l'Edit du Roy Henry IV du 10 Mars 1610 et les Edits de nostre Monarque à present regnant contre les Duels, que ce livre avoit deja produit de tres bons effets, et qu'on en esperoit encore plus de fruits, s'il plaisoit à l'Assemblée de l'appuyer de son Authorité: il a ajouté que la mesme compagnie procuroit des remedes, pour les pauvres gens et leur bestiaux, qui avoit esté éprouvez en divers lieux avec succez, suivant l'attestation des Messeigneurs les Prelats, qui en avoit pris pour leurs Dioceses. L'Assemblée a loüé le zele et la charité de ladite compagnie, et l'a exorté de faire envoyer dans les Provinces, de ces livres de l'Arbitre charitable et de ses remedes, et a invité Messeigneurs les Evesques d'en prendre pour leur Dioceses, et d'établir dans leur Paroisses des Confrairies de saint Charles Borromeé pour l'execution des oeuvres de charité' ('Monseigneur de Meaux said that a charitable company in Paris had handed him a small book entitled the *Arbitre charitable* to facilitate the settlement of lawsuits and quarrels, following the Edict of King Henry IV of 10 March 1610, and the Edicts of our present Monarch against duels. He noted that this book had already produced very good effects and that even more benefits were expected if the Assembly pleased to support it with its authority. He added that the same company was providing remedies for the poor and their livestock, which had been successfully tested in various places, according to the testimony of the Prelates who had adopted them for their Dioceses. The Assembly praised the zeal and charity of the said company and exhorted it to send copies of the *Arbitre charitable* and its remedies to the Provinces. It also invited the Bishops to take them for their Dioceses and to establish in their Parishes the Confraternities of Saint Charles Borromeo for the execution of charitable works'), *Procez pour s'en garantir, et les terminer promptement, avec l'Instruction du Feu Seigneur Grangier Evesque de Treguier, à ses Curéz et Missionnaires, pour l'accord des procez, et querelles, et empêcher les Duels, dont la pluspart dans les Provinces viennent des querelles animées, qui naissent des procez immortels qui sont parmy la noblesse; pour*

parish priests to engage in arbitral mediation in conflicts.[16] This obligation was reiterated, this time by the state, in 1695. For example, in 1671 in Angers, Bishop Henri Arnauld, brother of Antoine Arnaud and very close to the Jansenist cause, published a *Mandement* urging priests to perform their duties fervently both in assisting the poor and the sick and in intervening in contexts dominated by judicial processes that fuelled hatred, as those in such situations 'can hardly be on the path to their salvation':

> the parties which are animated against each other, far from seeking the truth, they instead try to corrupt it, as passion and vengeance typically erupt between those who litigate. The Demon, unable to tolerate the fear of God in the heart of man, has often made it yield to the fear of losing a lawsuit. It is not just that the Pastor should allow hatred and animosity to speak alone in such encounters, and that the voice of peace should not be heard among the flock. Nature alone inspires us to call for peace between those who make war on each other, Ecclesiastical and Civil laws command it, and Charity makes necessary for all Christians, and even more so for the Curates, what nature and laws require from the duty of all men.[17]

The measures immediately following the Assembly's recommendation aimed to spread the action of social containment through mediation, and addressed all social categories: the nobility, in terms of limiting duels, and at the opposite end, the indigent classes. This is evidenced by the fact that arbitral solutions aimed at limiting lawsuits went hand in hand with assistance

à quoy remedier, suivant les saintes intentions de Sa Majesté, Edits et Ordonnances de nos Rois, l'Assemblé generale du Clergé de France l'an 1670, exorta tous les Prelats d'establir des Assemblées dans leurs Paroisses, pour accorder lesd. procez et querelles, BNF, D 9378.

16 See Bonzon, *La paix au village*.

17 'des parties animées l'une contre l'autre, bien loin de rechercher la verité, ne tâchent au contraire qu'à la corrompre, que la passion et la vengeance éclattent ordinairement entre ceux qui plaident, et que le Demon ne pouvant souffrir la crainte de Dieu dans le coeur de l'homme, l'a fait souvent ceder à celle de la perte d'un procès. Il n'est pas juste que le Pasteur souffre que la haîne et l'animosité parle seule en ces rencontres, et la voix de la paix ne se fasse point entendre parmi le oüailles. La nature seule nous inspire de la rappeler entre ceux qui se font la guerre, les loix Ecclesiastiques et Civiles nous l'ordonnent, et la Charité la rend necessaire à tous les Chrestiens, et à plus forte raison aux Curez, ce que la nature et les loix, exigent du devoir de tous les hommes', *Mandement de Monseigneur l'Evesque d'Angers, pour l'accord des proces, et des querelles, et pour establir dans son Diocese, la distribution des remedes pour les Pauvres de la Campagne, suivant la deliberation de la derniere Assemblée generale du Clergé, du 17 novembre 1670*, BNF, E 2400, p. 3.

to the poor and the sick and the fight against begging. The notion of charity encompassed both the governance of begging and the governance of social hatred.[18] Arbitral methods were precisely embedded in a specific logic of relations that were intended to be harmonious between the rich and the poor: royal edicts would 'prevent the rich from oppressing the poor through lawsuits, and prevent the poor from unjustly suing the rich'.[19] Following the examples of Emperor Trajan, Charlemagne, Saint Louis, and Henry IV, who, according to the document, had the merit of abolishing 'chicanery', ecclesiastical authorities acknowledged the establishment throughout France of local assemblies dedicated to the arbitral resolution of ongoing lawsuits, presided over by bishops and feudal lords, without distinction between civil and ecclesiastical jurisdiction: in Paris, the Duke of Luynes; in Lyon, Aix-en-Provence, Avignon, Marseille, Toulon, Senez, Sisteren and other places, the bishops and archbishops; in Brittany, Pierre Le Gouvello, lord of Kériolet, president of the *Parlement* and head of the assembly established in his hometown; in the Charente-Maritime, Claude d'Assigné, Marquis of Carnavalet, Governor of the stronghold of Hiers-Brouage. All followed the example of Armand de Bourbon, first Prince of Conti, who first adopted such a policy in his possessions. Even Balthasar Grangier de Liverdis, bishop of Tréguier in Brittany, founded several 'charitable assemblies' in his diocese and recommended to parish priests and missionaries that they pacify the faithful engaged in lawsuits because 'lawsuits are a fatal nursery and second source of all kinds of evils for the body and soul, hatreds, enmities, revenges, the ruin of families and so on'.[20] Engaging in lawsuits means being contentious, a condition incompatible with that of a good Christian, which ceases only when one amicably agrees with one's enemies. A person engaged in a lawsuit could not even receive priestly ordination because initiating a lawsuit means offending God.[21]

The distinction between civil and ecclesiastical spheres became difficult to draw as the higher ecclesiastical benefices were accessed by the high feudal aristocracy; consequently, the lord/bishop often had to govern concurrently

[18] *Remedes pour les pauvres gens de la campagne. Et l'accord des procès et des querelles*, BNF, RP 688.

[19] 'empêché les riches d'opprimer les pauvres par les procés, et empêché les pauvres d'en faire de mauvais aux riches', *Procez pour s'en garantir, et les terminer promptement …*

[20] 'le procez estant une pepiniere funeste et seconde de toute sorte de maux pour le corps, et pour l'ame, haines, inimitiez, vengeances, ruïne des familles, et c. en viennent', ibid.

[21] ibid.

the episcopal and seigniorial courts even within different territories. Consider the case of François de Harlay de Champvallon, archbishop of Rouen and primate of Normandy, who was also the feudal lord of Dieppe (also in Normandy) and in 1659 published an *Ordonnance ... pour maintenir la paix dans son diocese* following various disturbances caused by conflicts within the Catholic camp between the Jesuits (and their supporters) and the Jansenists. Champvallon, a fervent Gallican, supporter of Mazarin's religious policy and also of the repeal of the Edict of Nantes, resolved to adopt the measure, as he realised that in his flock 'they give each other names of Sect and party among Catholics; they call each other Jansenist and Semipelagian, with bitterness that breaks the holiest friendships [...]; they defame each other; they slander each other; and by an unfortunate emulation that they believe to be for the glory of God'.[22] A strong reference to Saint Augustine, a doctrinal authority capable of garnering favour from all conflicting parties, whose conception of peace strongly recalled that of justice, which in this case could only be ensured by strict adherence to the bulls issued on the matter by Innocent X and Alexander VII. To ensure peace in the diocese, Champvallon thus prohibited everyone from using the terms 'Jansenist' and 'Semipelagian' as accusations against their opponents, words that evoke schism and factional spirit, and also from 'defaming each other on indiscreet suspicions and mistrusts, completely contrary to divine peace'.[23]

The project was both political and religious. The abolition of 'chicanery', exactly the expression used, a phenomenon 'that consumes the lives and goods of most men in France', would bring benefits in all fields: the nobility 'would serve in the Armies, with more assiduity, and in greater numbers'; commerce 'would be more flourishing'; the peasants, less ill and engaged in lawsuits, would have their land 'mieux labourée' ('better tilled') and would be able to pay 'more easily the rent, the *taille* and the *gabelle*'.[24] Compared to

22 'on se donne des noms de Secte et de party entre des Catholiques; on se traitte de Ianseniste et de Semipelagien, avec des aigreurs qui rompent les amitiés les plus saintes [...]; on se diffame; on se calonnie; et par une malheureuse émulation que l'on estime estre pour la gloire de Dieu', *Ordonnance de Monseigneur l'Illustrissime et Religiosissime Archevesque de Roüen Primat de Normandie, pour maintenir la Paix dans son diocese* (à Rouen, par L. Maurry Imp. Ord. De l'Archevesche, 1659).

23 'se diffamer les uns les autres sur des soupçons et des deffiances indiscretes, et tout à fait ennemies de la divine paix', ibid.

24 'plus aisement la Ferme, la Taille et la Gabelle', *Pour etablir dans toutes les Paroisses du Royaume, sans qu'il en couste rien à personne, l'accord des procez et des querelles, et la distribution des remedes pour les pauvres gens de la campagne, suivant l'Evangile, les Ordonnances de nos Roys, l'Arresté des Evesque des dernieres Etats de Languedoc. Et la deliberation de la derniere Assemblée generale du Clergé de France,*

the confraternal model introduced a century earlier in Italy by Borromeo in Milan or by Paleotti in Bologna, the context of the late seventeenth-century French measures is that of a state taking control of both charitable and welfare activities and the fight against the corruption of magistrates and lawyers, and obliging clergy, feudal lords and all holders of bureaucratic offices to implement initiatives aimed at combating both begging and social conflict.[25]

In the territories of the French monarchy, the pursuit of social peace also relied on the arbitral role of the clergy, especially the secular clergy, constantly urged in this direction by both ecclesiastical and civil authorities. However, one should not believe that the ecclesiastics held a sort of monopoly in the arbitral field. An interpretation entirely based on religious aspects, for instance, led John Bossy to read in the passage contained in Jean Bodin's *Six livres de la République* about intermediary bodies an indirect reference, as far as pacifications and 'moral tradition' are concerned, to confraternities, although he acknowledges that 'Bodin's account of fraternity does not explicitly require unity of faith among participants'.[26] In reality, the chapter *Des Corps et Colleges, Estats et Communautés* (Book III, Chapter VII) is inextricably linked to another central issue in the thought of the great French jurist on the state, that of the family (Book I, Chapter VI).[27] '[...] a Commonweale can no more be without a Familie', writes Bodin, 'than a Citie without houses, or a house without a foundation';[28] it is precisely on this ground that Bodin sites the issue of violence and revenge. Associative

du 17. Novembre 1670. qui a exorté tous les Evesques du Royaume, sur la remontrance de M. L'Evesque de Meaux, à établir dans leur Dioceses ces deux actions de charité. Après l'attestation des Seigneurs Evesques qui l'avoient dé-ja fait, que cela produisoit de grands biens, au spirituel, & au temporel, in *Remedes pour les pauvres de la campagne, & pour leurs bestiaux, qui coûtent peu* (à Paris, chez Denys Langlois, 1672), p. 20.

25 See *Justice et religion. Regards croisés: histoire et droit,* Actes du colloque international de l'Université d'Avignon et des Pays de Vaucluse (13 octobre 2008), ed. Eric Wenzel (Avignon, 2010).

26 John Bossy, *Peace in the Post-Reformation. The Birkbeck Lectures* (Cambridge, 1998), p. 34.

27 See Anna Becker, *Gendering the Renaissance Commonwealth* (Cambridge, 2020), pp. 106–44.

28 *The six bookes of a commonweale. Written by I. Bodin, a famous Lawyer, and a man of great Experience in matters of State, out of the French and Latin copies, done into English, by Richard Knolles* (London, Impensis G. Bishop, 1606), p. 46; original edition: 'La Republique ne peut estre sans famille, non plus que la ville sans maison, ou la maison sans fondement', *Les Six Livres de la Republique par I. Bodin Angevin* (à Lyon, par Iacques du Puy Iuré à l'Université de Paris, 1580), p. 47.

life begins when heads of families are compelled, out of necessity, to negotiate with each other on an equal footing, thereby renouncing the authority they naturally enjoy within their respective families. At that moment, they leave the family to enter the city; they cease to deal with domestic affairs to address public issues; they stop being lords and heads to become citizens. Before then, 'there was no city, no citizens, no form of Republic among men, each head of a family was sovereign in his house, having the power of life and death over the wife and children'.[29] And what armed the heads of families against each other if not 'force, violence, ambition, avarice, revenge'?[30] At that point, it became necessary to elect, among the winners of these primordial wars that had enslaved the vanquished, the one who would be 'chef et capitaine' ('chief and captain'), legitimised to command both the winners, who would be loyal to him as subjects, and the vanquished, who would remain slaves. It is precisely force and violence that gave rise to the social contract by which men renounce their absolute freedom and give birth to the state, whose task is precisely to limit the recourse to violence.[31]

29 *The six bookes of a commonweale*, p. 47; 'il y eust ny cité, ny citoyens, ny forme aucune de Republique entre les hommes, chacun chef de famille estoit souverain en sa maison, ayant puissance de la vie et de la mort sur la femme, et sur les enfans', *Les Six Livres de la Republique*, ibid.

30 *The six bookes of a commonweale*, ibid; 'la force, la violence, l'ambition, l'avarice, la vengeance', *Les Six Livres de la Republique*, ibid.

31 'Then that full and entire libertie by nature given to every man, to live as himselfe best pleased, was altogether taken from the vanquishe, and in the vanquishers themselves in some measure also diminished, in regard of the conquerour; for that now it concerned everie man in privat to yeeld his obedience chiefe soveraigne; and he that would not abate any thing of his libertie, to live under the lawes and commaundement of another, lost all. So the word of Lord and Servant, of Prince and Subiect, before unknown unto the world, were first brought into use. Yea Reason, and the verie light of nature, leadeth us to beleeve very force and violence to have given course and beginning unto Commonweals. And albeit that there were no reason therefore, it shall be hereafter declared by the undoubted testimonies of the most credible historiographers, that is to say, of Thucydides, Plutarch, Caesar, and also by the laws of Solon, That the first men that bare rule, had no greater honour and vertue, than to kill, massacre and rob men, or to bring them in slaverie. [...] And thus much concerning the beginning of Commonweals, which may serve to manifest the definition of a Citisen, by us before set down, to be true, which is no other thing to say, but A free subiect holding of soveraigntie of another man. A free subiect', *The six bookes of a commonweale*, pp. 47–8; 'Alors la pleine et entiere liberté, que chacun avoit de vivre à son plaisir, sans estre commandé de personne, fut tournee en pure servitude, et du tout ostee aux vaincus: et diminuee pour le regard des vainqueurs, en ce qu'ils prestoyent obeïssance à leur chef souverain, et celuy qui ne vouloit quitter

Compared to the family, a natural community, the bodies are civil communities; all together they are parts of a whole, constituted by the state, which, being endowed with sovereign power, could live without intermediary bodies, but not without families, as natural communities. '[...] the beginnings of all civill societies are derived from a familie';[32] as society grew and became more complex, families felt the need to associate in larger community organizations, so that it seemed to be but one family. In this primordial society, however, quarrels and disputes early manifested in the form of the law of the strongest, since 'the first sort of men was most given to rapine, murther and theft, delighting in nothing more, not accounting any honour greater than to robbe and kill, and to oppresse the weaker sort as slaves'[33]. These are the conditions that led the first men to unite: 'This license and impunitie of robbing and reaving, constrained men which as yet had no Princes nor Magistrats, to ioyne themselves in societie and amitie for the defence of one another, and to make Communities and Fraternities'.[34] And it is in this way, through the development and strengthening of bonds of friendship, that civil concord and peace could be guaranteed.

In the face of attacks from external enemies, the different kinships and communities united and elected a leader to whom they conferred sovereign authority. These communities and bodies, founded on the sworn friendship of their members, where they met and ate together, were not only tolerated

quelque chose de sa liberté, pour vivre sous les loix et commandements d'autruy, la perdoit du tout. Ainsi le mot de seigneur, et de serviteur, de Prince et de subiect auparavant incongnus, furent mis en usage. La raison et lumiere naturelle nous conduit à cela, de croire che la force et violence a donné source et origine aux Republiques. Et quand la raison n'y seroit point, il sera monstré cy apres par le tesmoignage indubitable des plus veritables historiens, c'est à sçavoir de Thucydide, Plutarque, César, et mesmes des loix de Solon, que les premiers hommes n'avoyent point d'honneur, et de vertu plus grande que de tuer, massacrer, voler, ou asservir les hommes. [...] Voila l'origine des Republiques, qui peut esclaircir la definition de Citoyen, qui n'est autre chose que le franc subiect, tenant de la souveraineté d'autruy', *Les Six Livres de la Republique*, pp. 47–8.

32 *The six bookes of a commonweale*, p. 361; 'L'origine des corps et colleges est venue de la famille', *Les Six Livres de la Republique*, p. 330.

33 *The six bookes of a commonweale*, p. 362; 'le plus grand poinct d'honneur et de vertu qui fust entre les premieres hommes [...] estoit de massacrer, tuer, ruïner les hommes, ou les rendre esclaves', *Les Six Livres de la Republique*, p. 330.

34 *The six bookes of a commonweale*, p. 362; 'Cette licence et impunité de voler, contraignit les hommes qui n'avoyent encore Princes et Magistrats, de se joindre par amitié, pour la defense les uns des autres, et faire communautés et confrairies', *Les Six Livres de la Republique*, p. 331.

by princes in antiquity but sometimes their creation was even ordered, as Lycurgus did in Sparta. In ancient Rome, they were called *sodalitia*, whose members '[had] no judges but themselves, if any difference or strife chaunced to fall out amongst them, being such companions and fellowes; as knowing that amitie and friendship was the onely foundation of all humane and civill societie'.[35] Friendship/amity is much more suitable than justice for the maintenance of social harmony,

> for that iustice never flexible, but alwayes keeping the uprightnesse of it selfe, by iust iudgement well endeth suits; but not hatred, making oft times of friends foes: wheras amitie and friendship, which is by company nourished, yeelding of the right of it selfe, best establisheth the true natural iustice, and plucketh up all controversies by the root, with great quietnesse and love reconciling subiects among themselves, together with the Commonweale. Now the principall end & scope of all laws, both divine and humane, is to keep and maintaine the love of men one towards another amongst themselves, and them altogether in their dutie towards God; which cannot better be done, than by ordinarie and orderly conversing and combining of men themselves together'.[36]

The sodalities can certainly be religious ones, but, in Bodin's thought, the discourse is of a general nature and concerns all intermediary bodies, which among their functions included that of regulating and containing internal conflicts through autonomous resolution methods. Here emerges again the theme of 'informal' peace procedures aimed at preserving friendship, by definition preferable to justice, as the only ones capable of bringing about the 'true' natural justice on earth, which is embodied in the love between citizens accustomed to mutual frequentation and union, and between them and God, whereas lawsuits only fuel hatreds and enmities. There is no contradiction, therefore, between a sovereignty entirely concentrated in the State, personified by the sovereign, as conceived by Bodin, and the existence of autonomous jurisdictional spheres derived from intermediary bodies that satisfy primordial needs for socialisation and mutual aid.

35 *The six bookes of a commonweale*, p. 363; 'n'avoyent autres iuges qu'eux mesmes, s'il y avoit quelque different entre les compagnons associés, congnoissant que l'amitié est le seul fondament de toute societé', *Les Six Livres de la Republique*, p. 332.

36 *The six bookes of a commonweale*, pp. 363–4; 'fait bien souvent les amis ennemis: et l'amitié cedant de son droit, establit la vraye iustice naturelle: attendu que le seul but de toutes les loix divines et humaines, est d'entretenir l'amour entre les hommes, et des hommes envers Dieu, ce qui ne se peut mieux faire que par frequentation et union ordinaire', *Les Six Livres de la Republique*, p. 332.

It would indeed be quite paradoxical to speak of a 'weak' statehood in reference to the reign of Louis XIV. Clearly, it is not a weak statehood that favours arbitral solutions; rather, it is necessary to avoid thinking in terms of the strength or weakness of state apparatus when dealing with peace and arbitration. Negotiated and arbitral procedures were neither a monopoly of ecclesiastical personnel nor a treatment reserved for an aristocratic class still too attached to the methods of private revenge. As mentioned, in the late seventeenth century, there was a concentration of measures, both state and ecclesiastical, aimed at strengthening state control over arbitral procedures to contain social conflict within a national reality that was intended to be rigidly mono-confessional. The *Ordonnance* of 1670 provided, for trials involving minor offences (serious crimes were excluded), various alternative outcomes to the issuance of a conviction sentence: an agreement between the parties, which could result in a homologation sentence or a waiver; the 'jugement en l'état', an abbreviated procedure following an admission of guilt (a kind of plea bargaining).[37] The path of alternative procedures had been laid out several decades earlier by royal ordinances aimed at prohibiting duels, starting with that of Henry IV in April 1602, followed by another of the same nature in 1610, and constantly renewed by subsequent sovereigns up to the famous 'edict on duels' of 1679.[38] However, the content of these provisions shows that the objective was not only to regulate the behaviour of the nobility.

The action was conceived on a broad scale. In 1673, there was an initiative by the King's Attorney General (*Procureur Général*) in the *Parlement* of Paris aimed at ending 'à l'amiable' ('amicably') pending trials before the King's Council (*Conseil du Roy*) between the correcting counsellors and auditors on one side, and the presidents and *maîtres* on the other, all belonging to the *Chambre des Comptes*, trials that risked 'greatly delaying the King's service'[39] and also undermining 'unity in all orders'.[40] Also from the late seventeenth century is a *Projet d'Edit, ou d'Ordonnance pour faire terminer un grand nombre de procès à l'amiable*, designed to 'encourage all kinds of people to

37 See Wenzel, *La paix par la justice*.

38 See *Edit du Roy portant reglement general sur les duels, donné en Saint Germain en Laye au mois d'Aoust 1679, registré en Parlement le I jour de Septembre de la mesme année, avec le nouveau reglement des Messieurs les Mareschaux de France sur le mesme sujet* (à Paris, par les Imprimeurs du Roy, 1679).

39 'beaucoup retarder le service du Roy', *Sur ce qui a esté remontré par le Procureur General du Roy* ... (de l'Imprimerie de Louis Sevestre, seul imprimeur pour la Chambre des Comptes, ruë Saint Jacques, 1700).

40 'l'union dans tous les ordres', ibid.

choose arbitrators to settle their existing and future disputes'[41] in all categories of offences, 'except for those that concern the King's domain and public causes'.[42] The decisions of the arbitrators could not be appealed, while arbitration could be imposed for certain matters and certain categories of people: 'between fathers, mothers, children, fathers-in-law, mothers-in-law and sons-in-law, grandparents, brothers and sisters, brothers-in-law, uncles and nephews, children of brothers and sisters and between associates'.[43]

On the social front, on the one hand the aim was to encourage all classes to resort to feudal justice, preferably functioning according to arbitral criteria, and on the other, to develop confraternal initiatives on the Borromean model that fulfilled a broadly assistance function and also provided social mediation for the lower social classes. In 1699, there was an appeal to Louis XIV drafted by François Vigneron, lord of Heucqueville, royal councillor, and president of the *baillage* of Beauvais, in which the stereotypical image of ordinary justice blocked by the excessive number of trials, resulting both from a natural tendency to litigiousness on the part of the people and from the corruption of judges and lawyers, serves to exalt justice based on arbitration. After 'the great things that all of Europe has seen so gloriously executed by Your Majesty, after having completely subdued all your external enemies, after having overcome their resistance to accepting peace',[44] to pacify the kingdom internally, to 'heal this mortal wound, which is insidiously undermining us',[45] the only way is recourse to arbitrators, because 'it is not subject to all the judicial formalities that are full of pitfalls and surprises, which entail great delays, and cost the parties infinitely'.[46]

41 'exciter toutes sortes de personnes à choisir des arbitres pour faire regler leurs differents nés et à naître', *Projet d'Edit, ou d'Ordonnance pour faire terminer un grand nombre de procés à l'amiable*, BNF, Rz 2567.

42 'hormis de celles qui concernent le domaine du Roy et des causes publiques', ibid.

43 'entre peres, meres, enfans, beauperes, belle-meres, et gendres, ayeul et ayeule, frere et soeur, beaufreres, oncles et neveux, enfans de freres et de soeurs et entre associés', ibid.

44 'les grandes choses que toute l'Europe a vû executer si glorieusement a Vôtre Majesté, après avoir entierement reduit tous ses ennemis au dehors, après avoir vaincu leur resistance à accepter la paix', *Discours, où l'on propose un moïen facile pour empêcher la plûpart des procès dans leur naissance, où pour les faire régler sans frais et un peu de temps*, BNF, Rz 2566, p. 15.

45 'guerir cette playe mortelle, qui nous mine insensiblement', ibid.

46 'elle n'est pas sujette à toutes les formalités judiciaires qui sont pleines d'embûches et de surprises, qui emportent des grands delais, et coutent infiniment aux parties', op. cit., p. 18.

The attack on ordinary judges is frontal, and arbitration is presented not as a class attribute but as a remedy useful for everyone: arbitration saves the nation from the hands 'of these inferior Ministers of Justice who, like insects of the earth, are formed only from corruption, who regard us as their prey, and do not let go until they have completely exhausted us';[47] it spares 'in the course of a case a thousand troubles and a thousand sorrows, often even more unbearable than the loss of property',[48] it is far from the suspicion of favouritism, because the arbitrators are chosen by the parties; it softens 'all the bitterness that trials leave in the mind';[49] it is the salvation of the poor and the oppressed, 'against the influence and power of the rich',[50] it is 'always enlightened, always just, prompt and disinterested, it saves souls and property, and gives us peace, what is more useful, what is more desirable'.[51] Vigneron then makes a specific request to the sovereign that he should:

> renew the old Ordonnances on arbitrators, and if anything is lacking, you can increase their power, you can make them compulsory among close relatives and in certain matters, without the ordinary judges being able to take cognisance of them. You can even show your courtiers how pleasing to you is the conduct of those who choose this way, and the desire they will have to please Your Majesty, combined with their own interests, will easily lead them to take this path. They will seek only to escape the troubles in which they find themselves due to lawsuits; all your people will unfailingly follow their example, the novelty that has its charms will attract them, and in a very short time, the success of your enterprise will be seen.[52]

47 'de ces Ministres inferieurs de la Justice qui semblables aux Insectes de la terre ne se forment que de corruption, qui nous regardent comme leur proye, et ne nous quittent qu'après nous avoir tout-à-fait épuisés', ibid.

48 'dans le cours d'une affaire mille peines et mille chagrins, souvent encore plus insupportables que la perte du bien', ibid.

49 'toute l'aigreur que les procés laissent dans les esprit', ibid.

50 'contre le crédit et la puissance des riches', op. cit., p. 19.

51 'toûjours éclairée, toûjours juste, prompte et disinteressée, elle sauve les ames et les biens, et nous donne la paix, qu'y a-t-il de plus utile qu'y a-t-il de plus désirable', ibid.

52 'renouveller les anciennes Ordonnances des arbitres, et s'il y manque quelque chose, vous pouvés augmenter leur pouvoir, vous pouvés les rendre forcés entre les proches et en de certaines matieres, sans que les Juges ordinaires en puissent prendre connoissance, vous pouvés même témoigner à vos courtisans combien le procedé de ceux qui choisiront cette voye vous est agréable, et l'envie qu'ils auront de plaire à Vôtre Majesté jointe à leurs propres interêts, leur fera prendre aisément ce parti, ils ne chercheront qu'à sortir des embarras où ils se trouvent par les procés, tous vos peuples suivront infailliblement leur exemple, la nouveauté

And an amicable solution can – even according to the aristocrat – be imposed. Men sometimes refuse to accept arbitration for fear of appearing uncertain about their righteousness, of appearing fearful of a judge's decision; for this reason, they need a push: they 'sometimes want to be compelled to do well', 'want to be encouraged by the prospect of a reward that touches them'. Therefore, a system of incentives, rewards, but also punishments must be devised:

> but if Your Majesty promises some honour or profit to the one who proposes arbitration, if she threatens some penalty to those who refuse it, if she absolutely forbids her Judges to contravene the Ordinances she will make on this subject, this Tribunal will be eagerly sought after without fear of giving any advantageous suspicion to the other party, without fear of being poorly heard by the Judges.[53]

Arbitrators chosen by the parties, but also selected by the sovereign himself, 'persons truly animated by the zeal for justice, distinguished by their positions, by their capability, by their prudence, and by the esteem they have acquired in the world'; magistrates, inspired by the methods always used by the parochial clergy and the regulars on mission, whom the people would look to as

> angels favourable to our wishes, sent by the Almighty to announce peace to men of good will, to deliver by your authority all those whom lawsuits hold captive in their chains, to destroy by the torch of truth the empire of malice and chicanery, to exterminate by the sword of your justice falsehood and iniquity.[54]

At least two strands can be identified in French public discourse of the sixteenth and seventeenth centuries: one concerning noble honour and non-violent ways to preserve it in case of received insult, and the other on the

qui à ses charmes les y attirera, et l'on voira en très peu de temps le succés de vôtre entreprise', op. cit., pp. 19–20.

53 'mais si Vôtre Majesté promet quelque honneur ou quelque profit à celuy qui proposera l'arbitrage, si elle menace de quelque peine ceux qui le refuseront, si elle deffend absolument à ses Juges de contrevenir aux Ordonnances qu'elle fera sur ce sujet, on reclamera tout d'un coup ce Tribunal sans craindre de donner aucun soupçon avantageux a sa partie, sans craindre d'être mal écouté par le Juges', op. cit., p. 21.

54 'des Anges propices à nos voeux, Envoyés du Tout-puissant pour annoncer la paix aux hommes de bonne volonté, pour délivrer par vôtre autorité tous ceux que les procés tiennent captifs dans leurs fers, pour détruire par le flambeau de la verité l'Empire de la malice et de la chicane, pour exterminer par le glève de vôtre justice le mensonge et l'iniquité', op. cit., p. 22.

preferability of arbitral methods of dispute resolution over resorting to courts of justice. The antiduelling literature certainly includes the *Chrestienne confutation du poinct d'honneur sur lequel la noblesse fonde aujourd'hui ses querelles et monomachies*, published in 1568 by the Franciscan theologian – of aristocratic birth – Christophe de Cheffontaines. An anti-Protestant controversialist who personally experienced the rigours of the Roman Inquisition (some of his works were condemned *donec corrigatur*), he was the general minister of the order between 1571 and 1579, later auxiliary bishop of Sens. During the religious conflicts in France, Cheffontaines composed a work based on a background that was broadly philosophical and literary, but especially scriptural and theological, and which aimed to dismantle the entrenched belief that the only way for a gentleman to avenge an offence and maintain his honour was through duelling.

The second strand includes other moral works whose purpose was to exalt arbitral methods and discourage recourse to justice, a theme so recurrent that it became a stereotype, blending religious motivations with civil and political ones. Even the *Dictionaire general et curieux* compiled by jurist and lexicographer César de Rochefort reflects this genuine 'Christian disdain' for resorting to ordinary justice under the entry 'Process': 'Whoever wants to maintain a reasonably Christian conscience should never approach a lawsuit except with leaden steps, and leave it, if possible, with the wings of an eagle'. The lawsuit is the negation of Christian principles, 'born of chaos and night, it is nothing but confusion and darkness, a mixture of all evils'. 'Lord, deliver us from lawsuits', exclaims Rochefort, and 'from the devouring flames of hatred and animosity that follow Chicanery', which tear priests from their altars, merchants from their trades, farmers from their lands and Christians from the sacraments, with their hearts poisoned by anger, wishing for others' ruin through 'its subtleties'. The theme of courtrooms as something to be scrupulously avoided if one wishes to maintain peace with others and oneself becomes a highly successful and long-lasting topos. In 1765, a small book, *L'ami de la concorde, ou essai sur les motifs d'eviter les procès, et sur les moyens d'en tarir la source*, by an anonymous parliamentary lawyer, immediately clarifies what is meant by 'way of justice':

> Resorting to judges to resolve disputes is called the way of Justice; however, this does not mean it is more just to proceed this way than to conclude through arbitration or a settlement: for on the contrary, it is infinitely more in accordance with Divine law and therefore more just, and moreover more useful, to avoid this path and to seek peace, even at the risk of some loss, than to litigate and become entangled in the consequences to which all lawsuits lead, which are equally contrary to charity and self-love.[55]

[55] 'On appelle le recours aux Juges, pour terminer les différens, la voye de la Justice; ce n'est pas qu'il soit plus juste de se pourvoir par cette voye, que de finir par un

A few years earlier, the preferability of arbitration had also been clearly expressed in Montesquieu's *Esprit des lois*, albeit based on non-religious premises: to prevent aristocratic families from becoming disunited, it is necessary to ensure that there are no excessive wealth disparities between them and that personal differences do not become, due to the intervention of the courts, differences between families.[56] However, for more than two centuries, a Christianised moral conception of justice had been making its way into French culture. In 1574, the jurist Jean Figon published a poem in verse, *Le Moyen d'éviter procès, faict pour l'utilité des marchans, et autres negociateurs*, focused more on civil proceedings but still aimed at spreading a culture of mediation.[57] Similarly in verse is the *Eridographie, contenant la description de proces, qui le nourrit, et que fault il avoir pour l'eviter*, by the learned Toulousian Antoine Noguier, published more than twenty years earlier, in 1552.[58] But the most significant and well-known work is undoubtedly the *Arbitre charitable, pour eviter les procez et les querelles, ou du moins pour les terminer promptement*, published in Paris in 1668 by the prior of Saint Pierre, Alexandre de La Roche. The General Assembly of the Clergy in 1670 then ordered it, as previously mentioned, to be disseminated in all dioceses and parishes of France. Openly inspired by the conflict resolution efforts undertaken within his feudal possessions by Armand de Bourbon, the first Prince of Conti, La Roche composed a sort of manifesto of a conception of justice understood as systematic recourse to the amicable and arbitral resolution of conflicts,

arbitrage ou une transaction: car au contraire il est infinement plus conforme à la loi Divine et par conséquent plus juste, et d'ailleurs plus utile aussi d'éviter cette voye, et de rechercher la paix, au péril même de quelque perte, que de plaider et s'engager dans les suites où conduisent tous les procès, qui sont également contraires à la charité, et à l'amour propre', *L'ami de la concorde, ou essai sur les motifs d'éviter les procès, et sur les moyens d'en tarir la source, par un avocat au Parlement* (à Londres, [s.e.], 1765), pp. 3–4.

56 'Quand les lois ont égalisé les familles, il leur reste à maintenir l'union entre elles. Les différends des nobles doivent être promptement décidés: sans cela, les contestations entre les personnes deviennent contestations entre les familles. Des arbitres peuvent terminer les procès, ou les empêcher de naître', *OEuvres de Montesquieu, avec les remarques des divers commentateurs, et des notes inédites, seule édition complète, dirigée par M. Collin de Plancy* (Paris, Louis Duprat Duverger Editeur, 1823), p. 32.

57 *Le Moyen d'eviter proces, faict pour l'utilité des marchans, et autres negociateurs, par M. Jean Figon de Montelimar Docteur és Droictz* (à Lyon, par Paul Favre, 1574).

58 *L'eridographie, contenant la description de proces, qui le nourrit, et que fault il avoir pour l'eviter, par Antoine Noguier Tolosain* (imprimé à Tolose par Guyon Boudeville, iuré de ladite Ville et Université d'icelle, aux depends de Henry Dugua, habitant dudit Tolose, avec privilege du Roy pour six ans, 1552).

centred on intermediary bodies. It is difficult not to see in this political–religious programme the full adherence to the tendencies expressed by the *dévot* party and the *Compagnie du Saint-Sacrement*, tendencies that were both anti-Protestant and anti-absolutist, which Louis XIII first and Louis XIV later continued to suppress throughout their reigns.[59]

All of society would have been affected by this 'corporative' justice reform proposal, which aimed to 'prevent Duels' ('empescher les Duels') and 'abolish Chicanery' ('abolir la Chicane') through mediators and arbitrators. The wise emperors and sovereign predecessors of Louis XIV, argues La Roche, had realised, based on experience, that 'if there were intermediaries and common friends, [...] the one who desires peace would first give his word, and the other would have difficulty refusing it, out of respect and deference for the Mediator'.[60] The invitation is therefore directed to the king, called to adhere to a higher-profile model of justice, who in turn should ensure that all royal personnel, both ecclesiastical and civil, followed his directives: provincial governors, bishops, parish priests.

The work revolves around the five archetypal dispensers of good justice, depicted in the beautiful engravings that accompany the text: King Louis XIV, Saint Augustine, Saint Ivo Hélory – a French priest who lived in the second half of the thirteenth century and was known for his advocacy for the poor in trials – provincial governors and feudal lords, and finally lawyers and prosecutors, despite the latter's poor reputation at the time, as previously noted. Civil and ecclesiastical authorities were to deploy a whole range of instruments to facilitate the arbitral resolution of disputes that would otherwise clog the courts and continue to fuel animosities: public hearings, advocacy for the poor, charitable prosecutors, parish assemblies, confraternities.[61] For La Roche, the lawsuit is nothing but the manifestation of that 'esprit de chicane' that paralysed the functioning of the judicial machine. Addressing the French bishops, the prior focuses on chicanery, a veritable plague

[59] See Alain Tallon, *La Compagnie du Saint-Sacrement, 1629-1667. Spiritualité et société* (Paris, 1990); and especially Bonzon, *La paix au village*, pp. 113–45.

[60] 's'il y avoit des Entremetteurs et des amis communs, [...] celuy qui desire la Paix donneroit d'abord sa parole, et que l'autre auroit peine à la refuser, à cause du respect et de la déference qu'il auroit pour le Mediateur', [Alexandre de La Roche], *L'arbitre charitable pour eviter les procez et les querelles; ou du moins pour les terminer promptement, sans peine & sans frais ...* (à Paris, chez Laurens Ravenau, 1668), *Epistre*.

[61] See Jean-Pierre Gutton, 'L'assistance judiciaire dans la France de l'Ancien Régime', in *Mélanges offerts au professeur Maurice Gresset. Des institutions et des hommes*, ed. François Lassus, Paul Delsalle, Corinne Marchal and François Vion-Delphin (Besançon, 2007), pp.101–11.

> which ruins the body and soul, temporal and spiritual goods, destroys families, causes a languishing life at the doors of Palaces and Tribunals, and finally produces these irreconcilable hatreds and animosities, these blasphemies, despair and fatal revenges, which are the prolific and unfortunate source of hundreds of millions of mortal sins that Christians commit today in France. [...] Confessors can tell you about the hatred litigants bear against each other, their desires for vengeance, and the unfortunate fruits that this produces, including staying away from the Sacraments and not wanting to approach them during the lawsuit, of which we will report deplorable examples hereafter.[62]

The obligation for bishops, parish priests and missionaries to intervene to prevent individuals in conflict from resorting to the courts, and to end ongoing lawsuits by pushing the parties towards an arbitral agreement, offering themselves as mediators, is modelled on the functioning of the Christian communities of the early Church and reinforced by precise dictates derived from the Gospel, councils and even the legislation of the Most Christian Kings of France. The conviction that drives the Prior is that lawsuits do nothing but fuel hatreds instead of healing them. Many French bishops were accustomed to holding public hearings twice a week for one hour, where everyone was admitted without distinction of class, personally resolving conflicts. In the case of lawsuits,

> he would have the parties agree on arbitrators in his presence and sign a compromise, which he would send to the arbitrators with a request to expedite the matters of the said parties and come back to inform him (within the time he specified) whether they had reached an agreement and who was responsible for any delays. His secretary kept a register of all these compromises, and the said parties, especially the poor, were instructed to come and complain if their adversaries did not faithfully execute what they had promised.[63]

[62] 'qui ruine le corps et l'ame, les biens temporels et spirituels, qui détruit les familles, qui fait mener une vie languissante aux portes des Palais et Tribunaux, et enfin qui produit ces haines et hanimositez irreconciliables, ces blasphemes, desespoirs, et ces vengeances funestes, qui sont la source feconde et mal-heureuse, de cent et cent millions de pechez mortels, que les Chretiens aujourd'hui commettent en France. [...] Les confesseurs vous peuvent dire la haine des Plaideurs les uns contre les autres, leur desirs de vengeance, & les fruits mal-heureux que cela produit, jusques à s'éloigner des Sacremens, et n'en vouloir point approcher pendant le procez, dont nous rapporterons cy-apres des exemples deplorables', [Alexandre de La Roche], *L'arbitre charitable*, p. 5.

[63] 'il faisoit aux parties convenir d'Arbitres en sa presence, et signer un compromis, qu'il envoyoit aux Arbitres, avec prière d'expedier lesdites parties, et luy venir dire (dans le temps qu'il limitoit) s'ils estoient d'accord, et à qui il avoit tenu. Son

This was a custom that, according to the author, the bishops had inaugurated in imitation of what the Prince of Conti was doing in his possessions, where he operated as a feudal judge. Compared to the traditional role of the clergy in mediating conflicts, in France, the connection between episcopal justice and feudal justice became deep and, in a certain sense, unprecedented, at least compared to other contexts such as Italy. The most interesting aspect of this small book lies not so much in its doctrinal references but probably in the political–religious proposal it interprets. The Augustinian and Augustinian-inspired influence of *L'Arbitre charitable* was correctly highlighted by Stuart Carroll, who also emphasised its distance from contemporary Italian treatises on noble honour and against duelling, which were deeply influenced by humanistic ideals.[64] However, the absolute peculiarity of the work by the Prior of Saint Pierre must be sought elsewhere. It should be sought in its envisioning of a French monarchy – structured between the ecclesiastical hierarchy and the bureaucratic-administrative apparatus of the State – entirely moulded on arbitral functioning criteria concerning conflict containment. It should be sought in its foundation on a political ideal that we might define as both Gallican and anti-absolutist, clearly evident in its proposal to strengthen the jurisdictional prerogatives of both seigneurial and ecclesiastical authorities. It was episcopal hierarchy, integral to the state apparatus, which, according to La Roche, should have adopted arbitral dispute resolution systems borrowed from those used by the sovereign and feudal lords of France, despite an at least apparent ecclesiastical primacy in the field of social containment.

Could the choice of Armand de Bourbon-Conti as the ideal model of arbitral justice be considered coincidental? Certainly not. We are not dealing with just any high aristocrat, but with someone who had led the parliamentary *Fronde* starting in 1649. Although defeated and reconciled with Cardinal Mazarin and Louis XIV, the figure of the Prince of Conti was well-suited to embody the ideal of the good feudal lord inspired by divine law, constantly committed to ensuring the well-being of his vassals and who would accept anything except the renunciation of his delegations in favour of royal jurisdiction. La Roche attributes these words to him:

> A nobleman must believe himself more obliged than any other Christian, since by his vocation he is primarily the man of his neighbour, being made

---

Secretaire faisoit registre de tous ces compromis, et lesdites parties avoient ordre, sur tout les pauvres, de se venir plaindre, si leurs adversaires n'executoient pas de bonne foy ce qu'ils avoient promis', op. cit., p. 22.

64 See Stuart Carroll, 'Peace-Making in Early Modern Europe: Towards a Comparative History, in *Stringere la pace*, pp. 75–92.

solely for him; to relieve him in his needs, to console him in his afflictions, to correct him in his failings, to render him justice, to pull him out of oppression, to protect him from violence.[65]

The predominant character of La Roche's work is pragmatism, not sophisticated theoretical-doctrinal elaboration. He provides very precise instructions regarding the selection of arbitrators, the conduct of mediators, the relationships between the former and the latter, and a series of other issues and difficulties that arbitral activity might encounter. The arbitrators should be persons 'of recognised probity and capacity',[66] armed above all with a 'principle of charity' ('principe de charité'), and with the indispensable 'patience to listen to the long complaints of the parties, which seemingly have nothing to do with the substance of the matter, and yet, [...] often decide it'.[67] The distinction between mediator and arbitrator must be well-defined; the mediator is the bishop, the feudal lord, the parish priest, the governor, the embodiment of authority that helps the parties choose the arbitrators from among trusted individuals. The choice of the arbitrator must be free, just as must be the choice of the confessor or the doctor. La Roche then goes on to illustrate a series of examples of measures adopted at different levels for the establishment of this practice of arbitral conflict resolution and also the reasons for its failure to be implemented throughout France. In 1610, Henry IV, with the support of the first chancellor Sillery, had ordered that in each court and jurisdiction of the Kingdom an assembly of consultants, charitable arbitrators, procurators and lawyers be established to assist the poor in their disputes, especially when they were victims of oppression by the rich. However, apart from the *Parlement* of Provence and in other isolated cases (such as the parish of Saint-Sulpice in Paris), the sovereign's order remained a dead letter.

The work concludes with the reproduction of forms for agreements according to a typological classification: compromise, citation of arbitration among equals, citation of arbitration by a noble against an inferior, citation of arbitration by an inferior against a noble, as well as models of arbitral resolution in civil or commercial cases.

[65] 'Un grand doit s'y croire plus obligé qu'un autre Chrétien, puisque par sa vocation il est principalement l'homme du prochain, n'estant fait que pour luy; pour le soulager en ses besoins, le consoler dans ses afflictions, le corriger dans ses manquemens, luy rendre justice, le tirer de l'oppression, le garentir de la violence', [Alexandre de la Roche], *L'arbitre charitable*, p. 39.

[66] 'de probité et capacité reconnuë', op. cit., p. 59.

[67] 'patience d'écouter les longues plaintes des parties, qui en apparence ne font rien au fonds de l'affaire, et neantmoins, [...] souvent le décident', ibid.

2. Protection of honour and 'Christian Revenge': a Hispanic culture of peace-making

Historiography, especially that from the Anglo-Saxon tradition, has provided evaluations that even contrast sharply on violence, crime and justice in modern Spain, at least partly marred by the stereotypes of the Black Legend. An example is the work of Michael Weisser, who described a Spanish culture as reactionary, dominated by violence, and particularly repressive (consider the treatment of religious minorities and the actions of the Inquisition), contrasted with a particularly tolerant ('careless') justice system towards crime, given the low number of sentences issued compared to the trials conducted.[68] In response to the actual decrease in trials in the higher courts, Richard Kagan proposed the hypothesis of a progressive shift of jurisdictional competencies towards lower courts concerning violent crimes,[69] while the work of Tomás Mantecón Movellán focused on the increasingly consistent recourse to informal mediation procedures during the modern age, refuting the assumption of the necessary advancement of state justice and adopting the paradigm of social discipline and the 'civilisation of violence'.[70]

In 1961, the legal historian Francisco Tomás y Valiente, in an essay that soon became an essential reference, analysed the mechanism of the granting of forgiveness by the victim of a crime within the Castilian judicial system of the early modern age.[71] The analysis did not limit itself to the letter of the law and the interpretations gradually provided by doctrine, but extended to

68 See Michael Weisser, 'Crime and Punishment in Early Modern Spain', in *Crime and the Law. The Social History of Crime in Western Europe since 1500*, ed. Vic A. C. Gatrell, Bruce Lenman and Geoffrey Parker (London, 1980), pp. 76–96.

69 See Richard L. Kagan, *Lawsuits and Litigants in Castile, 1500-1700* (Chapel Hill, 1981), pp. 210–35.

70 See Tomás Mantecón Movellán, 'El peso de la infrajusticialidad en el control del crimen durante la Edad Moderna, *Estudis* 28 (2002), pp. 43–75; Tomás Mantecón Movellán, 'Territorio, poderes y actitudes ante el crimen en la moderna Cantabria rural', in *Monarquía, imperio y pueblos en España*, ed. Pablo Fernández Albaladejo (Alicante, 1997), pp. 757–70; Tomás Mantecón Movellán, 'Popular Culture and the Arbitration of Disputes. Northern Spain in the Eighteenth Century', in *Crime, Punishment, and Reform in Europe*, ed. Louis A. Knafla (Westport and London, 2003), pp. 39–55; Tomás Mantecón Movellán, 'The Patterns of Violence in Early Modern Spain', *The Journal of the Historical Society* VII, 2 (2007), pp. 229–64.

71 See Francisco Tomás y Valiente, 'El perdón de la parte ofendida en el derecho penal castellano (siglos XVI, XVII y XVIII)', *Anuario de Historia del Derecho Español* XXXI (1961), pp. 55–114.

understanding the practices of forgiveness, and by publishing in the appendix a substantial series of *apartamiento* writings, i.e., acts of forgiveness and renunciation. Among Tomás y Valiente's merits is undoubtedly having clearly demonstrated that, in the vast majority of cases, forgiveness had a 'price', albeit carefully concealed in the records. Philip II's *Pragmática* of 1566 (P. 7, 1, 22) incorporated the Roman law principle that everyone has the right to redeem their own blood ('Because it is a fair and just thing that every man can redeem his blood'),[72] in other words to seek the forgiveness of the offended person (or the relatives of the person killed in the case of murder) to avoid for oneself the capital or corporal punishment. The *avenencia*, the agreement between the offender and the offended (or the offended's relatives), if it occurred before the sentence was pronounced, did not necessarily terminate the trial, as the judge still had the option to proceed *ex officio*, but it was a necessary condition for obtaining royal clemency. Subsequent restrictions provided by doctrine allowed the crown to maintain the sentence of galley slavery even in cases of forgiveness and *avenencia*, as well as to establish a series of exceptions to the rule.[73]

Perhaps the most interesting aspect of the phenomenon lies precisely in the concealment of the economic transaction underlying the *avenencia*, motivated by the content of the *Pragmática* itself: it was indeed stipulated that only a forgiveness 'por precio' ('for a price') could be used by the judge as a confession of the accused. The granting of forgiveness responded to multiple interests. In the case of women whose husbands had been killed, financial compensation could resolve or alleviate the material difficulties arising from the loss, especially in the presence of minor children; it could also restore neighbourly and familial relationships disturbed in the frequent cases where the murder had been perpetrated by relatives or members of the community. The reference to living in peace and the religious justification of the act were recurring elements. The widow of Miguel Martínez, murdered on 20 October 1624, in Moretón, Navarra, forgave the perpetrators of the murder, relatives of the victim, and renounced the criminal case against them both because of the family connection and 'por servir a Dios' ('for serving God'). Catalina de Mazcarelle, widow of Pedro da Pena El Joven, killed by his father and brothers at the height of a quarrel in Coto da Pena de Lugo, Galicia, granted forgiveness to her father-in-law and brothers-in-law

72 'porque guisada cosa es e derecha, que todo ome pueda redimir su sangre'.

73 1) When the accused had already been forgiven by the victim or pardoned by the sovereign for another crime; 2) In the presence of aggravating circumstances, such as cruelty or committing the crime in a sacred place; 3) The enormity of the crime. See op. cit., pp. 86–7.

'For certain amounts of *maravedís*, goods and other things that the supplicants have given to the aforementioned [the woman and her children] for their remedy and by reason of the said death',[74] even taking care, in the text of the notarial act drawn up seven months later, to exonerate the husband's aggressors. However, many times these pardons were not able to stop the spiral of violence between individuals and kinship groups that had caused the murder.

Social actors had rather limited freedom of action both in seeking the agreement, for which it was necessary to employ mediators and comply with a series of constraints arising from social and familial balances, and in drafting the *apartamiento* act, which had to necessarily follow pre-established models that had become increasingly standardised over time, and which was subject to careful scrutiny by both jurists serving the court and theologians, to ensure it appeared as 'a perfect analogy of the grace of the king and the pardon of Christ',[75] and that forgiveness had not been granted under the influence of venal interest, received threats or fear of retaliation. The reality was quite different, though. The personal conditions of the victim significantly influenced the decision to grant forgiveness, far beyond the desire to conform to the evangelical precept. A young man from Madrid, Blas de Méndez, in 1629 forgave Bartolomé Villora, his brother's murderer, because of his young age and 'for that reason of their poverty, and [because of] the uncertainty of the costs and expenses of justice'.[76] Villora's pardon came a few months later. The reading of the *apartamiento* acts alone, as well as of the *chartae pacis in general*, proves misleading once again.

The *apartamiento* was required to fit into a well-oiled and meticulously regulated system, which was that of granting royal clemency: by obtaining forgiveness from his victim, the guilty/penitent asked to be pardoned by the sovereign and absolved by God; at the same time, the sovereign granted

[74] 'por ciertas cantidades de maravedís, bienes y otras cosas que los suplicantes han dado a los susodichos para su remedio y por raçón de la dicha muerte', cited in Tomás A. Mantecón Movellán, *La acción de justicia en la España Moderna: una justicia dialogada, para procurar paz*, in *Stringere la pace*, p. 347.

[75] 'une analogie parfaite de la grâce du roi et du pardon du Christ', Olivier Caporossi, 'Les madrilènes face à la violence: la pratique du pardon privé au XVIIe siècle', *Hispania Sacra* LX (2008), pp. 231–66: p. 240. On crime and royal justice in Madrid in the seventeenth century, see also, by the same author, the more extensive *Exercer la justice du roi à Madrid. La juridiction royale d'une ville de cour pendant le règne de Philippe IV (1621-1665)* (Bordeaux, 2020).

[76] 'por esa razón de su pobreza, y [por] la incertidumbre de las costas y gastos de justicia', cited in Mantecón Movellán, *La acción de justicia en la España Moderna*, p. 349.

his pardon not to everyone indiscriminately but to those cases previously selected by the *Cámara de Castilla*, in imitation of Christ and to ensure divine protection for the monarchy; this often happened on Good Friday. The ritual phrase pronounced by the sovereign was: 'I forgive you, so that God may forgive me'.[77] The religious significance and justification of the entire system were profound, to the point that most moral theologians dealt extensively with the issue, partly because a doctrinal response (both theological and legal) had to be given to a reality well present in the social fabric: the legitimisation of revenge practices and private violence to protect one's honour and that of one's family – response that had to maintain a precarious balance between justification, tolerance and attempts at correction.[78]

The private and intimate dimension of a granted pardon pales in comparison to its enormous public significance, concerning both kinship and the community of belonging, and political and ecclesiastical power. Forgiving did not mean giving up reparation, which remained due by the offender (and which consisted, as seen, in a 'price' to be paid to the victim or their family, thereby guaranteeing their subsistence).[79] The pardon negotiated in private and the request for grace gave the sovereign the opportunity to show the other face of royal power, a counterbalance to the ferocious capital executions; in this mechanism, religious power was perfectly integrated, both because pardons were obtained in the confessional (forgiving is an obligation for Christians and also a condition for absolution), and because the entire system was framed within the economy of salvation: individual, collective and of the state apparatus, in terms of its sacrality.

The Second Scholasticism had perfectly focused on the problem: honour and reputation are goods that a man has the right to defend, just like material ones; being the master of these goods, a man also has the right to renounce

[77] 'Yo os perdono, porque Dios me perdone'.

[78] See Paolo Broggio, 'Justice, vengeance et légitime défense dans les traités juridiques et théologico-moraux de l'époque moderne', in *La vengeance en Europe (XIIe-XVIIIe siècle)*, ed. Claude Gauvard and Andrea Zorzi (Paris, 2015), pp. 269–85.

[79] Thus expressed the Augustinian friar Juan Enríquez de Zúñiga: 'aunque el hombre ofendido está obligado a perdonar la injuria, no está obligado a perdonar la satisfacción de la injuria: y assí puede responder que perdona la injuria pero no la satisfacción' ('Although the offended man is obliged to forgive the injury, he is not obliged to forgive the satisfaction of the injury: thus he can respond that he forgives the injury but not the satisfaction'), *Compendio de casos morales* (Sevilla, 1634), cited in Caporossi, *Les madrilènes face à la violence*, p. 239.

them, forgiving his enemies in obedience to the word of God.[80] If the objective, at least officially, was to break the chain of violence, it is also undeniable that reaffirming the principle whereby he who redeems his blood can 'corrupt' his victim to obtain forgiveness means maintaining intact – at the root – the culture of hatred and revenge, leaving the survival of the guilty to the uncertainty of the process and the decision of the sovereign. If Christianity has managed to incorporate the death penalty by shifting attention from the salvation of the body to the salvation of the soul of the condemned,[81] a similar and specular process has taken place for forgiveness and peace, which ascended from the private to the public in a symbolic symmetry of great significance. The preservation of friendship relationships (and client relationships, in the case of unequal relationships), the maintenance of peace, were at stake in a process of integrating Christian forgiveness within the judicial framework, on which personal salvation depended. It was not only an expression of a power of grace that is a direct consequence of the divine derivation of the sovereign's power to administer justice, but a way to relate divine justice, sovereign justice and the justice of remissions and peace agreements. This undeniable symbolic parallelism should not be underestimated, referring to three levels, from top to bottom: the divine, universal forgiveness that God granted to men through the sacrifice of Christ, the sovereign forgiveness, and the individual, private forgiveness granted by the victim to those who sought pardon, a condition of possibility for sovereign forgiveness.[82]

In the economy of forgiveness and salvation, everyone was included, regardless of social class. If the sovereign himself did not escape the control over his conscience (and therefore over his actions) exercised by confessors

[80] See for example Domingo de Soto, *De iustitia et iure* (book V, *quaestio* V).

[81] The mandatory reference is to the fascinating fresco by Adriano Prosperi, *Delitto e perdono. La pena di morte nell'orizzonte mentale dell'Europa cristiana, XIV-XVIII secolo* (Turin, 2013).

[82] Underestimation that seems to occur in Adriano Prosperi who, in relation to the powers of grace, emphasised the strengthening, between the late Middle Ages and the beginning of the modern age, of the image of the sovereign as the representative of God and executor of His justice in the hegemonic forms of inquisitorial procedure, increasingly removed from the corruption of communal systems, 'all the more decisively as the intervention of written rules and personnel authorised by central powers came to replace the direct entrustment of the judging function to God Himself through the forms of ordeal' ('tanto più decisamente quanto più l'intervento di regole scritte e di personale autorizzato da poteri centrali venne prendendo il posto occupato dall'affidamento diretto della funzione giudicante a Dio stesso attraverso le forme dell'ordalia'), Adriano Prosperi, *Giustizia bendata. Percorsi storici di un'immagine* (Turin, 2008), p. 89.

and *ad hoc* bodies composed of moralists,[83] at the very opposite end of the social hierarchy, a true alternative jurisdiction was ideally offered even before it became fact. It represented a scaled-down mirror of an ideal society where conflicts had to be overcome through agreements, settlements, renunciations, forgiveness and compensations, and above all without trials. This alternative jurisdiction was constituted by brotherhoods, to which individual members had the duty to turn in case of conflicts (especially following insults and other morally illicit behaviours such as concubinage, blasphemy and failure to observe sacramental obligations) before resorting to any other judicial instrument, as trials are useless and costly, while the intervention of mediators guarantees the exercise of restorative justice (mainly in terms of honour), capable of satisfying the parties, avoiding the radicalisation of clashes, and thus ensuring lasting peace. Not accepting the solution proposed by the chapter of the brotherhood and bringing the conflict outside its perimeter was behaviour harshly sanctioned: a scandal and a grave offence to the entire institution, which stood midway between the civil and the ecclesiastical and was jealous of its image of strict observance of moral precepts, concord and internal cohesion. A system that certainly could not rely solely on the voluntarism of individuals and that made the institutionalisation of fraternal correction one of its operational pillars. The brotherhood indeed relied on the action of the *celadores*, carefully chosen people, appointed annually by the superior, who had the task of overseeing the behaviours, both private and public, of the brothers, even using informers, and bringing transgressions to the attention of the leadership.[84]

These are ideal models that certainly, in concrete reality, were never able to fully absorb community conflict, even that of 'low intensity', on which the councils (rural or even urban) and local courts continued to play an important if not predominant role, albeit in connection with other instances of social containment. None the less, what remains interesting are the reference ideals and this insistence on honour and the need for the reparation of the debt of honour, far from being the exclusive prerogative of the aristocratic classes, although it was precisely on noble honour and the attempts to redefine it in the perspective of recourse to revenge and duelling that philosophers, writers and moralists focused their attention, as is well known.

[83] See now the extensive and solid study by Nicole Reinhardt, *Voices of Conscience. Royal Confessors and Political Counsel in Seventeenth-Century Spain and France* (Oxford, 2016).

[84] See Tomás A. Mantecón Movellán, *Contrarreforma y religiosidad popular en Cantabria. Las cofradías religiosas* (Santander, 1990), pp. 106–23.

In the Spain of the Golden Age, the issue of peace and the peaceful resolution of disputes arising within the nobility did not take the form, as it did in the Italian peninsula, of a 'manual' for the nobility on the most effective way to compose chivalric disputes without bloodshed, safeguarding the reputation and honour of the offended. Different paths were preferred to reshape the noble ideology based on the changing needs of the general political framework, dominated by the absolutist designs of the Habsburgs. Consider the case of Jerónimo de Urrea, an Aragonese soldier and writer who held positions precisely in Italy, that Italy which in the early sixteenth century was the cradle of duelling.[85] Author of epic poems and chivalric novels (as well as translator into Castilian of Ludovico Ariosto's *Orlando Furioso*), with the *Diálogo* Urrea aimed, as many contemporary works did, to continue the flourishing tradition of Italian duelling literature represented by Girolamo Muzio or Giovanni Battista Possevino to instil in the nobility the conviction that true honour does not depend on others' opinions and does not consist in resorting to violence in case of receiving an offence: honour corresponds to the Aristotelian understanding of virtue, and the most honourable action imaginable is the forgiveness of one's enemies. However, despite the declared intentions, the *Diálogo* presented itself as a copious chronicle of famous chivalric challenges that only perpetuated the noble ideology based on the 'mystique' of duelling.

A different discourse applies to the work of Artal de Alagón, III Count of Sástago, Viceroy of Aragon from 1575 to 1588 but also a Franciscan tertiary,[86] which can be considered an example of the attempt to bend noble ideology to evangelical dictates precisely concerning the most sensitive point in the framework of noble behaviours: the obligation to respond with violence to verbal or physical offences received. Yet, it is still the genuine expression of a noble mentality that could not entirely reject the recourse to private violence for the defence of honour. At the end of his treatise, Alagón indeed affirmed:

[85] Gerónimo Borao, *Noticia de Don Gerónimo de Urrea y de su novela caballeresca inédita'Don Clarisel de las Flores'* (Zaragoza, Establecimiento Tipográfico de Calisto Ariño, 1866); Carlos Clavería, *Le Chevalier Deliberé de Olivier de la Marcha y sus versiones españolas del siglo XVI* (Zaragoza, 1950); Maxime Chevalier, *L'Arioste en Espagne (1530-1650). Recherches sur l'influence Roland furieux'* (Bordeaux, 1966); Pierre Geneste, *Le capitaine poéte aragonais Jerónimo de Urrea. Sa vie et son oeuvre. Ou, chevalerie et Renaissance dans l'Espagne du XVIe siècle* (Paris, 1978).

[86] See Josefina Mateu Ibars, 'Don Artal de Alagón, Conde de Sástago, Virrey de Aragón (1575-1588): algunas notas sobre su alcurnia y gobierno (el pleito sobre Virrey extranjero y disposiciones contra el bandolerismo)', in *Estudios dedicados a la memoria del profesor Luis Miguel Díaz de Salazar Fernández*, ed. María Rosa Ayerbe Iríbar, vol. I (*Estudios histórico-jurídicos*) (País Vasco, 1993), pp. 431–46.

> I do not intend to condemn all individual combats, nor to discourage men from preserving their honour and not responding, and fighting for the honour of God and their own in the manner that is proper and in cases where it is lawful to do so. On the contrary, I would rather encourage them and instil in them the spirit for it, as I understand that there is more need for this than for cooling their blood, which is already so cold that it is pitiful to see how much substantial valour has fallen in men, in whom it should be very whole, seeing how they let serious matters pass unnoticed and the little regard they have for them and for that in which nobility consists, behaving out of weakness and little valour in dealing with sad matters. And for these I say (which are those being discussed today) that one should not immediately come to blows, nor should they want to deal with things of such little importance by them, not doing so for those that are of great importance, such as the defence of the Christian Religion and the Faith that is owed to God and the Kings, which, above not losing it, it is well to lose one's life if it cannot be defended otherwise, for with this, one's own honour will be preserved.[87]

The Spanish legal framework of the sixteenth century is clear regarding the absolute unlawfulness of resorting to duels, whether judicial or private in a chivalric manner, since only the sovereign, and consequently the judicial authority, holds the right to punish injuries perpetrated against third parties. Canon law also had soon to conform to the conciliar dictates.[88] However,

87 'Yo no pretendo condenar todos los combates particulares, ni dessanimar a los hombres a conservar su honra, y a no responder, y bolver por la de Dios, y por la propia, de la manera que se deve, y en los casos en que es lícito el hazerlo, antes querría animarlos, y ponerles brío para ello, de que entiendo ay más necessidad que no de enfriarles la sangre, que lo está tanto, que es lástima ver quan caído está el valor sustancial en los hombres, en quien havria de estar muy entero, por ver como se les passan por alto las cosas graves, y el poco caso que hazen dellas, y de aquello en que consiste la nobleza, haziendose por floxedad y poco valor al trato de cosas tristes, y por estas digo (que son las que oy se tratan) que no se ha de venir luego a las manos, ni se ha de querer llevar por ellas cosas de tan poca importancia, no lo haziendo por las que son de mucha, como lo son la defensa de la Religión Christiana, y de la Fé que a Dios y a los Reyes se deve, que sobre no perderla, es bien perder la vida, si de otra manera no se puede defender, que con esto se conservará la propia honra', *Concordia de las leyes divinas y humanas, y desengaño de la iniqua ley de la vengança, compuesta por Don Artal de Alagón Conde de Sástago, religioso de la tercera regla del Señor San Francisco, y a petición de Don Martin de Alagón su hijo, de la Cámara del Príncipe nuestro Señor* (Madrid, por Luys Sánchez, 1593), ff. 126^{r-v}. See also Scott K. Taylor, *Honor and Violence in Golden Age Spain* (New Haven and London, 2008), pp. 28–9.

88 See Taylor, *Honor and Violence*, pp. 70–1. On the conciliar prohibition see Giancarlo Angelozzi, *La proibizione del duello: Chiesa e ideologia nobiliare*, in *Il concilio di Trento e il moderno*, ed. Paolo Prodi and Wolfgang Reinhard (Bologna, 1996), pp. 271–308.

compared to the Italian area, in that same Spain of Philip II, which hastened, despite difficulties, to apply the Tridentine decrees,[89] jurists and theologians chose different means and editorial outlets to disseminate the reasons that made peace preferable to resorting to violence and to provide concrete indications of the most suitable procedures for resolving private enmities. Regarding the kingdoms of the Spanish monarchy, the issue of peace and the rejection of vengeance must be sought in the folds of a non-uniform and non-specific treatise literature.

A few years after the Bolognese Fabio Albergati in Rome, a nobleman, political writer, curia man and diplomat, published his treatise on the 'modo di ridurre a pace le inimicitie private' ('way to bring private enmities to peace'), dedicating great attention to the properly political aspects of noble disputes and the unlawful resort to duels, Artal de Alagón decided to frame his discourse according to a scheme that well illustrates the great distance between the juridical–philosophical–moral culture of Spain and the contemporary literary output of Italian scholars, at least concerning the redefinition of noble ideology. At the centre of everything stands God and the evangelical teaching: man, created in the image and likeness of the Almighty, desirous of glory, greatness and nobility by virtue of his divine descent, is none the less driven to violence and revenge because of original sin. For this reason, the only possible foundation of fame and nobility must be divine law, particularly the love of God and love of neighbour, two fundamental Christian precepts.

The second book of the treatise is entirely dedicated to the duty of knowledge and love towards God and the observance of the Decalogue, which man, and even more so the nobleman, is bound to; the third and final book, however, addresses the question of 'verdadera nobleza' (true nobility), a condition that, according to the author, can only be achieved within the 'Christian family'. At the base of Alagón's reasoning is, naturally, the conception of the natural and necessary inequality among individuals: men are not all equal, and certain families, based on clear and shared requirements, have the right to excel over others. The key, therefore, lies in redefining these requirements by reshaping them according to the observance of divine law.[90]

[89] On the complex issues arising from the application of the Council in the territories under the Spanish monarchy, see Ignasi Fernández Terricabras, *Felipe II y el clero secular. La aplicación del Concilio de Trento* (Madrid, 2000). See also Agostino Borromeo, 'Felipe II y la tradición regalista de la Corona española', in *Felipe II (1527-1598). Europa y la Monarquía Católica*, vol. III, ed. José Martínez Millán (Madrid, 1998), pp. 111–37.

[90] See also in this regard the contribution of the Franciscan Antonio de Solís concerning the satisfaction and happiness derived from belonging to a social rank,

Very interesting, from this perspective, is the enumeration of the criteria on which it is possible to determine the greater or lesser degree of 'worldly' nobility of a family: the first is 'descending from a very noble lineage and ancient estate';[91] the second is having 'maintained that nobility of lineage with illustrious and worthy deeds';[92] the third is 'the bond of male succession, excluding women';[93] the fourth, finally, is that a family 'does not mix with infamous people, nor contrary to their nobility, as we now say in these times, that our children should not marry Jews, nor descendants of Moors'.[94] According to Alagón, these criteria can be transposed to the spiritual plane. Regarding the antiquity of the family, indeed, the 'Christian family' can boast absolute supremacy over all others, since 'our head is Christ, who is the second person of the Holy Trinity', and all those who profess his faith can claim to be descendants of Jesus.[95] But it is not enough to 'naturally' descend from Jesus to be part of his family: the only true criterion of belonging – and thus of true nobility – is the imitation of Christ, especially in his most profound teaching: the forgiveness of enemies. In this perfect parallel – which comes to permeation – between worldly nobility and spiritual nobility, the aspect of masculinity also assumes considerable significance:

> The third thing we proposed that could tarnish a lineage was not having ties, and for this reason, those who wished to preserve their family and estate linked it and created entails, linking them to a male, due to the great danger of the family name ending if a woman were to succeed: instead, it must always go from man to man, that is to say, it must be preserved with manly deeds, and not effeminate ones, because with a woman entering it, which is weakness, it runs a great risk of becoming debased.[96]

---

and the cause of dissatisfaction (which leads to social disorder) identified in ambition and greed. See Adolfo Carrasco Martínez, *Sangre, honor y privilegio. La nobleza española bajo los Austrias* (Barcelona, 2000), p. 17.

91 'proceder de nobilíssima cepa, y antiguo solar', Alagón, *Concordia de las leyes divinas*, f. 94$^{r.}$

92 'averse conservado en essa nobleza de su cepa, con obras ilustres, y dignas de tal linage', ibid.

93 'el vínculo de sucessión de varones, excluyendo a las mugeres', op. cit., f. 94$^{v.}$

94 'no se mezcle con gente infame, ni contraria a su nobleza, como agora en estos tiempos dezimos, que no se han de casar nuestros hijos, con Iudios, ni con decendientes de Moros', Alagón, *Concordia de las leyes divinas*, ff. 94$^{r-v.}$

95 'nuestra cabeça es Christo, que es la segunda persona de la Santíssima Trinidad', ibid.

96 'Lo tercero que propusimos que podía macular à un linage, era no aver vínculos, y por esto los que dessearon conservar su familia y estado, la vincularon y hizieron mayorazgos, vinculandolos a varon, por el peligro grande que corre de acabarse

At stake, therefore, is the definition of true nobility, a constant and almost insistent theme in the moral–religious publications of these years. True nobility and true honour depend not on the changing opinion of the common people but on the observance of divine laws, to which political authorities themselves are obliged to conform. God has given man only two laws: 'The one that related directly to God, which was that of obedience, in commanding him not to eat from the forbidden tree. And the other that, being human, he should show it by not wanting for another what he would not want for himself';[97] even if man, with Adam, disobeyed the first law, he maintained the second and taught it to his descendants, because it is only on this basis – charity, the absence of a spirit of revenge and cruelty towards others – that social relationships can arise and be preserved. It is for this reason, continues Alagón, that the main political institutions in history have prohibited revenge. The duel is a form of revenge that cannot be admitted: neither as a tool for proving the truth, according to the model of the ordeal duel, nor as a means of obtaining satisfaction in the case of an offence received, because, in such a case

> it would mean dismantling the whole machinery of the world, and the peaceful state of it, and encroaching on the jurisdiction of God, to whom belong the lives of men, and who alone, along with His ministers, has the authority to dispose of them: and thus no one can make honour out of what is treachery, just as it would be treason to rise against the King, usurping the dominion he has over his subjects, and what is proper to his royal dignity. Whoever did so would be deemed a traitor, and would lose nobility and its privileges.[98]

---

el nombre de la familia, sucediendo muger: sino que ha de yr siempre de varón en varón, es saber, que se ha de conservar con obras varoniles, y no afeminadas, porque entrando muger en ella, que es flaqueza, corre gran peligro de bastardear', op. cit., f. $101^{r.}$ On honour and gender in the Hispanic world see Shifra Armon, *Masculine Virtue in Early Modern Spain* (London and New York, 2016); Grace E. Coolidge, 'Contested Masculinity: Noblemen and Their Mistresses in Early Modern Spain', in *Contested Spaces of Nobility in Early Modern Europe*, ed. Matthew P. Romaniello and Charles Lipp (London and New York, 2001), pp. 61–84.

97 'La una que directamente tenía respeto a Dios, que fue la de la obediencia, en mandarle que no comiesse del fruto del árbol vedado. Y la otra de que siendo hombre humano, lo mostrasse con no querer para otro lo que no quisiesse para si', Alagón, *Concordia de las leyes divinas*, ff. 111^{r-v}.

98 'sería descomponer a toda la máquina del mundo, y al pacífico estado dél, y tocar en la jurisdición de Dios, cuyas son las vidas de los hombres, y quien solo y a sus ministros toca el disponer dellas: y assí no puede hazer nadie honra de lo que es alevosía, que sí lo sería levantarse contra el Rey, usurpándole el dominio que

But, as we have seen, Alagón does not hesitate – immediately afterwards – to introduce distinctions that greatly undermine the value of the principles so peremptorily stated. Condemning revenge does not, in fact, mean condemning all possible forms that challenges between private individuals may take, and above all, it does not mean instilling in the nobility a fatal tendency towards submissiveness. A vigorous response to a defamatory action against oneself remains, for Alagón, a duty for the noble, and the most recommended mode is hand-to-hand combat, in which not only physical strength but also the courage and 'spirit' of the nobleman are measured. The latter must at least know how to assess the severity of the offence received and thus avoid coming to blows – or to the sword – for matters of little importance.

Almost half a century later, in 1640, in a significantly different political and cultural climate, Juan Antonio Lozano, an obscure Aragonese parish priest, published a small treatise in Zaragoza titled *Destierro y azote del libro del duelo. Dedicado a Christo crucificado por amor de enemigos.*[99] Lozano's work presents itself as a memorandum addressed to Philip IV only two years after the convocation, by the royal favourite the Count-Duke of Olivares, of a *Junta* expressly tasked with devising measures to reform the 'ley del duelo' and curb the proliferation of this form of dispute resolution among nobles. Olivares himself had proposed a series of measures aimed at an internal reform of the laws governing the chivalric duel, a reform essentially based on the acceptance of the principle that a noble cannot in any way shirk the obligation to demonstrate his courage, the foundation of the code of honour.[100] Olivares was convinced that, if a law imposed the penalty of infamy on the one hand on those who offended someone in a place where the latter could not respond, and on the other hand on those who did not respond to an offence received, the spiral of violence would automatically cease: it was necessary to give members of the aristocratic class the opportunity to defend their honour by manifesting their courage, and the law should sanction not the duel itself but, rather, cowardly actions.[101]

---

tiene sobre sus vasallos, y lo que es propio de su dignidad real, y el que lo hiziesse quedaría dado por traydor, y perdería la nobleza y privilegios della', op. cit., ff. 125^{v}–126^{r}.

99 Juan Antonio Lozano, *Destierro y azote del libro del duelo. Dedicado a Christo crucificado, por amor de enemigos. Por el Doctor Juan Antonio Lozano de Ibdes, Colegial del Complutense Theólogo de S. Martín, y S. Emerenciana; y cura de la Mata de los Olmos. En forma vulgar y predicable* (en Zaragoza, por Christóval de la Torre, 1640).

100 *Discurso en orden a reformar la Ley del Duelo*, BNE, Ms. 5791.

101 See Claude Chauchadis, 'Noblesse, pouvoir et duel: les débats autour du discours d'Olivares contre la loi du duel (1638)', in *Pouvoir et société dans l'Espagne*

Juan Antonio Lozano's treatise is as diametrically opposed as one can imagine to the proposal of Olivares. For Lozano, the 'libro del duelo', the code of honour that imposes armed combat on nobles to redress an offence received, is the work of the devil, and combating it simply means engaging in a battle between good and evil. The bold wager is to completely overturn the belief that honour rests on the demonstration of courage and chivalric (and thus warrior) valour; honour, as Alagón had already written at the end of the sixteenth century and as other contemporary authors had also written, consists in virtue – a virtue shaped by the imitation of Christ, who died on the cross out of love for his enemies.[102] Posed in these terms, revenge became a central issue for the Catholic soteriological system. Christ saved man from sin by forgiving his enemies; therefore, the primary obligation of a Christian must be to endure and forgive offences received. Indeed, God 'permits offences so that forgiveness may be glorified'.[103] The code of conduct that imposes revenge is the result of the devil's presence in the world, acting to stimulate self-love and thus undermine the evangelical teaching of love for one's enemies and forgiveness. It is clear that instilling such a model of behaviour in the nobility means decisively challenging its ideological foundations.

The radical nature of the message is entirely contained in the form that Lozano's treatise takes: it is not a matter of mediating between noble ideology and the needs for the complete and firm imposition of the monopoly on the use of violence by public powers through the use of religious terms and concepts; we are faced with something quite different, namely the attempt to subject political conduct to evangelical dictates. Lozano's work is in fact halfway between the homiletic genre and that of arbitrism, which was flourishing at the time. The arguments used by the Aragonese priest are first and foremost, if not exclusively, religious, and only secondarily do they touch the political sphere. But when this happens, it is in an absolutely incisive manner, in the conviction that the political–judicial order must necessarily conform to the spiritual order:

> I note in passing that even if judges do not punish someone who has injured their enemy because they have said or done some great injury in words or deeds, one should not imagine that it is permissible to do either.

moderne. Hommage à Bartolomé Bennassar, ed. Jean-Pierre Amalric (Toulouse, 1993), pp. 77–7. See also the *Opinion* drafted by the *letrado* Juan Bautista Larrea, analysed by Paola Volpini, *Lo spazio politico del* letrado. *Juan Bautista Larrea magistrato e giurista nella monarchia di Filippo IV* (Bologna, 2004), pp. 275–9.

102 Lozano, *Destierro y azote del libro del Duelo*, pp. 12–13.

103 'permite las ofensas para que seglorifique el perdonar', op. cit., p. 41.

> For judges also permit many sins, such as dishonest acts in public houses. Furthermore, as we will prove below, judges should, in conscience, punish certain things that they do not currently punish, and additional judges should be appointed if those that exist are insufficient to remedy the many rotten members that arise in the Republic. Some laws of infamy, which the world regards as opposed to the humble and virtuous disciples of Christ who suffer without seeking revenge, should be abolished. The truths of Christ, contrary to those of the world, should be valued and followed.[104]

Without considering – adds Lozano – that if the law must conform to natural reason, what is closer to natural reason than love, concord and the principle that one cannot desire for others what one does not desire for oneself?[105] The harshly critical judgement towards legislation that does not reward, but rather punishes, those who align their behaviour with the evangelical dictate of forgiving received offences, and probably the implicit reference to the recent proposal by the Count-Duke of Olivares aimed at introducing laws that sanction conduct deemed cowardly according to the parameters of noble ideology, are very clear.

Lozano's proposed solution operates on two levels: the first is eminently spiritual, consisting of the personal conversion of the Christian; the second is political, aiming to profoundly reform social behaviours through the proper (from a Christian viewpoint) functioning of political and judicial institutions. True honour, Christian honour, is nothing but the reward of virtue, the only thing that truly matters. It is not that he denies the legitimacy of the rigidly estate-based structure of *Ancien Régime* society, but the demonstration of Christian virtues in his discourse becomes an element so powerful that it relegates the uncontested and unquestionable supremacy of the aristocracy to the

[104] 'Advierto de passo, que aunque los Iuezes no castiguen al que hirió a su enemigo, porque le dixo, o hizo alguna grande injuria de palabra, ò obras; no se ha de imaginar por esso, que se pueda hazer lo uno, o lo otro. Porque los Iuezes también permiten muchos pecados, como los actos deshonestos en las casas públicas. A mas, que abaxo provaremos, que deven en conciencia los iuezes castigar algunas cosas que no castigan, y que se ha de añadir iuezes si no bastan los que ay, para remedio de tantos miembros podridos, como se levantan en la República, y que deven quitarse algunas leyes de infamia, reputadas por el mundo contra los humildes y virtuosos discípulos de Christo, que padecen sin vengarse, y que se deven estimar y seguir las verdades, que son las de Christo, contrarias a las del mundo', op. cit., pp. 16–17.

[105] 'Si hombre es racional, y no hay cosa mas conforme a razón natural, que el amor y concordia, pues su principio es, lo que quieres para ti has de querer para el otro, no havrá mayor irracional, que el que va contra el amor y concordia, deshaziendo lo que la naturaleza haze, y por quien Dios padece', op. cit., pp. 81–2.

background: in the eyes of God, 'only he who is not a servant of sin is noble'.[106] It is therefore about re-founding the concept of nobility in a Christian manner. The nobleman should indeed draw inspiration from the virtue demonstrated by his illustrious predecessors, and one who 'glories only in the lineage of his parents, shows that he is devoid of virtue'.[107] Being offended or injured is not a dishonour, whereas offending and committing violence is. Forgiveness is thus the most honourable act that exists; and, expressly recalling Seneca, Lozano states that the Christian cannot cease to benefit someone because of the ingratitude of the beneficiary, for it is not even lawful to take revenge on ingratitude. One must, in fact, continue to benefit the ungrateful to make them grateful, since the enemy is more easily won over with kindness than with violence; the result will be the humiliation of the enemy and therefore the almost certain cessation of the dispute (including judicial disputes). Overcome evil with good (Rom 12:21).

In Lozano's discourse, the individual level intersects deeply with the social and political levels. Social harmony is derived from the behaviours of individuals; these behaviours must then be adequately directed, acting also on the character and temperament of individuals (anger is the fruit of fear, and indeed – Lozano explains – the most choleric people are usually the most timid and cowardly), according to an ideal model of true holiness whose attainment would avoid most 'voluntary' civil and criminal cases.[108] The reference to anger is of great importance in the context of regulating the duel, as psychological elements served the noble class, especially in the second half of the sixteenth century, to continue to assert – despite canonical prohibitions – the legitimacy of the 'question/fight', that violent confrontation that can follow an insult and is provoked by a fit of anger from the offended party. This was referenced by Pope Gregory XIII himself in the bull *Firmum ita*, of November 1582, which stated that 'under this our sanction we do not wish to include those who in a sudden brawl arising in a moment of furious anger have appointed a certain place for such combat, even if they have met there for the purpose of fighting and have fought'.[109] This served in general, even after Clement VIII's bull *Illius vices*, to justify the resort to arms on the simple basis that for

[106] 'aquel sólo es noble, que no es siervo del pecado', op. cit., p. 53.

[107] 'se gloria sólamente en la casta de sus padres, da a entender, que está vacío de virtud', ibid.

[108] Op. cit., p. 92.

[109] 'sub hac nostra sanctione nolumus comprehendi, qui in rixa de improviso nata statim in ipso iracundiae furore, certum aliquem locum ad huiusmodi certamen condixerint, etiam si ibi confligendi causa tum convenerint, et inter eos sit pugnatum', cited in Giancarlo Angelozzi and Cesarina Casanova, *La nobiltà disciplinata*.

a proper duel (definitively prohibited) to be configured, a prior agreement between the parties on the place and time of the violent confrontation was necessary. Therefore, other and more informal forms of spontaneous brawl were excluded from the prohibition, which the nobleman was in fact obliged to engage in if he wanted to avoid the mark of infamy for having renounced the defence of his own honour.[110]

Juan Antonio Lozano, much less inclined than the Italian professors of honour to indulge in the more impermeable aspects of noble ideology, became a proponent of a project of radical reform of the existing system starting from the inner depths of individuals. For him, anger is not the natural and inevitable consequence of the violent action received; it is not the driving force of a reaction – the 'question' – that the noble must demonstrate he can complete if he wants to defend his good name. There is no concession on his part to these 'worldly laws' of honour: affirming that avenging received offences is lawful corresponds, for Lozano, to heresy, a manifest error of faith, which should be dealt with by the tribunal of the Holy Office. Just as for the Holy Scriptures, vengeance must be left to God ('Mihi vindicta', Rom 12:19),[111] in the political order it is the judges who must avenge

Violenza nobiliare, procedure di giustizia e scienza cavalleresca a Bologna nel XVII secolo (Bologna, 2003), p. 273.

110 Michel Nassiet notes how the emphasis in late sixteenth- and seventeenth-century petitions for clemency on psychological or emotional impulses in explaining the causes of violence has led historians to underestimate the real motivations behind feuds, which are greatly dependent on kinship ties: 'Killing in self defence thus became the only remissible crime, and as a consequence supplicants had to prove that the homicide was the result of fortuitous circumstance or fit of passion, either caused by fear or induced by drunkenness. As a result, studies that place blind trust in pardon tales seriously overestimated the role played by emotion and passionate impulses as a cause of violence', Michel Nassiet, 'Vengeance in Sixteenth and Seventeenth-Century France', in *Cultures of Violence. Interpersonal Violence in Historical Perspective*, ed. Stuart Carroll (Houndsmill and New York, 2007), pp. 117–18.

111 'Si fieri potest, quod ex vobis est, cum omnibus hominibus pacem habentes: non fieri vosmetipsos defendentes carissimi, sed date locum irae. Scriptum est enim: Mihi vindicta: ego retribuam, dicit Dominus. Sed si esurierit inimicus tuus, ciba illum: si sitit, potum da illi: hoc enim faciens, carbones ignis congeres super caput ejus. Noli vinci a malo, sed vince in bono malum' ('If it be possible, as much as lieth in you, live peaceably with all men. Dearly beloved, avenge not yourselves, but rather give place unto wrath: for it is written, Vengeance is mine; I will repay, saith the Lord. Therefore if thine enemy hunger, feed him; if he thirst, give him drink: for in so doing thou shalt heap coals of fire on his head. Be not overcome of evil, but overcome evil with good').

injuries, pursuing and severely punishing crimes against persons. From an eminently spiritual discourse, as we can see, it transitions to a strictly political reasoning, with very precise indications – after all, it is a memorandum addressed to Philip IV – about the attention that rulers must pay in choosing those appointed to the administration of justice. This is precisely the dominant stylistic feature in Lozano's treatise, that of a cleric-preacher who takes on the role of an arbitrator to try to influence the political decisions of the crown.[112] The sovereign must surround himself with evangelical preachers who always show him the right path (even if uncomfortable and difficult to follow) rather than flatterers and sycophants. For Lozano, advisor and preacher must merge into a single figure; only in this way can there be a guarantee of perfect coherence between political action and divine law.[113]

Judges must be just, God-fearing, ready to punish bad behaviour and reward righteous conduct; it is the prince's fault if those chosen to administer justice are unfit individuals who prefer to protect the interests of the powerful. This concept contains another peculiar element of Lozano's treatise, also found in much contemporary literature: justice must protect the weakest, the 'poorest'; when there is doubt about whom to favour between a rich and a poor person, the judge must presume that the right lies with the poor; this is a notion we have already found in Alexandre de la Roche and aligns with the widespread perception of courtrooms: a space where the rich had the opportunity to oppress the poor and, thus, a true 'public evil'.[114] State justice becomes, in the discourse of the Aragonese priest, a central and knotty issue, which is both complex and ambiguous. Indeed, Lozano does not advocate for the systematic recourse to justice by those who have suffered an offence that somehow damaged their honour. If, as seen, bearing insults and repelling 'pleytos' (litigations) is a specifically Christian (and honourable) virtue, it is nevertheless the State, in the person of the sovereign, that must simultaneously reward this virtuous behaviour (and therefore not declare it infamous) and preserve the worldly honour of the offended by ordering its judges to harshly punish the offender.[115]

[112] See the extensive study on the political role of royal preachers during the reign of Philip IV by Fernando Negredo del Cerro, *Los predicadores de Felipe IV. Corte, intrigas y religión en la España del Siglo de Oro* (Madrid, 2006).

[113] Lozano, *Destierro y azote del libro del duelo*, pp. 188–9. On the royal preacher as a royal advisor, see also, regarding the many figures from various religious orders who played an important role in the political decisions of Philip IV, Negredo del Cerro, *Los predicadores de Felipe IV*, pp. 79–210.

[114] See Kagan, *Lawsuits and litigants in Castile*, p. 17.

[115] See Lozano, *Destierro y azote del libro del Duelo*, pp. 133–4.

The monarchy must ensure that the offended, the weak, the 'poor', have the option to resort to judges to see their enemy (the powerful, the 'rich') punished and to recover the honour that was taken from them, because 'closing this path is opening ways to hell, giving place to vengeance'.[116] It is about instilling in subjects the trust in a justice that must become an instrument capable of restoring honour: there is nothing worse for the stability of a Republic than a judge who mocks an offended person for having turned to him for justice and to regain their reputation. The increased state repression of crimes against individuals and their honour,[117] loudly demanded by Lozano, should not be seen as a wish for the proliferation of cases but rather as a request for increased efficiency of the justice apparatus in punishing the guilty in cases of complaints by the injured party and also in the initiation of proceedings *ex officio*. It is due to the inactivity and tolerance of judges towards crimes related to honour, Lozano concludes, that the scourge of duelling and, more generally, of revenge is still so present in Spanish society.[118] An individual will be much better able to endure insults, and therefore – eventually – avoid litigation, if they know that there is a state apparatus ready to punish them.[119]

Lozano's work appears very distant from the Italian anti-duelling literature of various figures such as Fabio Albergati, Camillo Baldi, Berlingiero Gessi, Giovanni Battista Olevano and Francesco Birago, an authentic expression of a noble culture that, although undergoing redefinition, was far from desiring such a strong reinforcement of the state judicial apparatus for the repression of crimes against honour. Albergati, for example, indicated 'private peace' as the best tool for resolving disputes and achieving social concord; the judge's action was considered less profitable in this sense, as it was not capable, according to the Bolognese noble, of restoring damaged honour.[120] There is

[116] 'el cerrar este camino, es abrir senderos para el infierno, dando lugar a venganças', ibid.

[117] In this sense, by 'libro del duelo' Lozano means not so much the duel itself but rather the more general recourse to forms of private revenge.

[118] See Claude Chauchadis, *La loi du duel. Le code du point d'honneur dans l'Espagne des XVIe-XVIIe siècles* (Toulouse, 1997), pp. 167–71.

[119] On the sovereign as an indispensable mediator for overcoming revenge systems (especially in the case of *riepto*, a sort of primitive version of the Spanish duel), see Francisco Tomás y Valiente, *El derecho penal de la Monarquía absoluta* (Madrid, 1969).

[120] 'se bene [i giudici] castigano con rigorosa pena nella robba, o nella vita l'ingiuriante: tuttavia non provedendo all'honore dell'ingiuriato; anzi molte volte sforzandolo a ingiusta pace, senza dichiarare che l'ingiuriante sia infame, et privo d'honore, et che l'offeso resti senza alcuna macchia, rimane quella falsa opinione

no space, instead, in the *Destierro y azote* for what constitutes one of the central cores of peace treatises in the Italian area, namely the description of ways to make peace in a chivalrous and Christian manner through the figure of the 'mediator'. This silence is all the more strange given Lozano's personality: originating from Ibdes, a remote rural locality in Aragon halfway between Zaragoza and Sigüenza, he was indeed a theologian educated in one of the lesser colleges of the prestigious University of Alcalá de Henares (the college of San Martín and Santa Emerenciana, also called 'Teólogo de Aragón'), but he was also a preacher and parish priest of another small and obscure rural community in Lower Aragon, La Mata de los Olmos. Preaching, both learned and popular, was traditionally linked precisely to private peace agreements, to the informal resolution of disputes between individuals or families. It is also significant that the chapters corresponding to 'remedio para amar enemigos' ('remedy to love enemies') and 'remedio para hazer amigo al enemigo' ('remedy to make a friend of the enemy') are entirely dedicated not to mediation techniques for achieving peaceful reconciliation while preserving the honour of the people involved in the conflict, but to the exposition of an infallible inner remedy for reaching a spiritual dimension capable of preventing individuals from quarrelsome and vengeful behaviours: the practice of frequent communion, which Lozano calls 'remedio eucharístico' ('Eucharistic remedy'). The principle of efficacy of this remedy is of a spiritual-sacramental type, as, through communion, the faithful participate directly in the body and blood of the Saviour, who died for the love of his enemies:

> God wanted to teach us to love our enemies, not being content with dying for love of them once on the Cross, but also dying anew every day many times, mysteriously through this Sacrament. For by the power of the Priest's words, He would place Himself in the Sacrament, with His

nel volgo accesa, et pare tacitamente dal Principe confermata, non cercando di correggerla, et rimuoverla: cioè, che l'ingiuriato sia d'honor privo, et che l'ingiuriante dell'ingiuria fatta riporti honore' ('Even though [the judges] rigorously punish the offender with fines or even capital punishment, they do not address the honour of the injured party; indeed, often forcing them into an unjust peace without declaring that the offender is infamous and devoid of honour, and that the offended remains without any stain. This leaves that false opinion inflamed among the populace, and it seems tacitly confirmed by the Prince, who does not seek to correct and remove it: namely, that the injured party is devoid of honour, and that the offender gains honour from the offence committed'), *Trattato di Fabio Albergati, Gentilhuomo bolognese, del modo di ridurre a Pace l'inimicitie private* (Roma, per Francesco Zannetti, 1583), p. 121.

> body separate from His blood, if they were not together, as they are now. And He is not content with always dying mystically for us, but He wants to invite us with His Flesh and Blood so that by His death, we may live.[121]

It is within a spiritual tradition that can be traced back to the successful *Guía de pecadores* by Luis de Granada – and probably even earlier – that a treatise like that of Juan Antonio Lozano fits, representing a unique work in the Spanish baroque literature for being entirely dedicated to the problem of duelling. However, it appears much less original when placed within a pastoral horizon – composed of printed sermons, popular preaching, manuals for penitents and confessors – aimed at the internalisation by the faithful of individual behaviour models that served as an antidote to the natural predisposition to violence.[122] In the Spanish homiletics of the *Siglo de Oro*, it is not so much the conciliar prohibition of duelling or the papal interventions in this regard that are emphatically highlighted; rather, the focus of the message that Spanish preachers directed at the nobility is the evangelical law of forgiving enemies and the prospect of eternal damnation that befalls those who do not respect this mandate. The fear of God and the infernal punishments for those who stain themselves with the crime of revenge must prevail over the fear of social sanctions that befall those who do not act according to the code of noble honour.

The positions expressed in the theological–moral treatises of the Spanish area on the topic of the legality of duelling and the defence of honour through the use of violence appear much more complex. Here, the distinctions are far more numerous and primarily relate to the social status of the individuals, as for many theologians the duty to respond to an offence belongs exclusively to nobles and soldiers, due to their role in war, while religious figures, literati,

[121] 'Quiso Dios enseñarnos a amar enemigos, no contentándose con morir por amor de ellos una vez en la Cruz; si tembién muriendo de nuevo cada día muchas, mysteriosamente por este Sacramento. Pues por la fuerça de las palabras del Sacerdote, se pusiera en el Sacramento, apartado el cuerpo de la sangre, sino estuviera junto con ella/o, como aora está. Y no se contenta con estar siempre muriendo místicamente por nosotros, sino que quiere convidarnos con su Carne, y Sangre, para que muriendo el, vivamos nosotros', Lozano, *Destierro y azote*, pp. 221–2.

[122] John Bossy has reconstructed a very fascinating picture of European history between the late Middle Ages and the early modern period by focusing his attention on the social history of Christian sacraments, seen as prisms through which to study the transition from a world dominated by communal dimensions and conflicts to a world increasingly individualised and tendentially 'disciplined'. See John Bossy, *Christianity in the West 1400-1700* (Oxford, 1985), Italian translation: *L'Occidente cristiano. 1400-1700* (Turin, 2001); John Bossy, *Dalla comunità all'individuo. Per una storia sociale dei sacramenti nell'Europa moderna* (Turin, 1998).

jurists, doctors, etc., are authorised to flee without risking the loss of honour. On the other hand, an important element of evaluation must be the 'direction of intention' behind the violent reaction to the offence received, as it is acceptable if it can be interpreted not as revenge but as legitimate defence – that is, as a legitimately violent action aimed at recovering the honour tarnished by the insult. Francisco de Vitoria held this view in his famous *De iure belli*, as did Pedro de Navarra and Martín de Azpilcueta, known as Doctor Navarrus, who goes so far as to support the legality of a violent response to an offence received, even culminating in the killing of the aggressor. The issue of *restitutio*, central to the legal and theological regulation of theft and fraud, also explodes in the casuistry of the late sixteenth and the seventeenth centuries concerning the realm of intangible goods, such as honour and reputation (but also consider the restitution of the conjugal debt and the contribution to this field by the Jesuit Tomás Sánchez).

The somewhat extreme position of Navarrus is not shared by all: the Dominican Pedro de Ledesma, for example, does not accept this subtle distinction between revenge and the recovery of honour based on the direction of intention, nor the distinction between an immediate violent response to an offence and a delayed action, accepting the former and condemning the latter; and Ledesma is one of the rare Spanish theologians to make a precise reference to the evangelical precept of 'turning the other cheek', whereas, as seen, Lozano indicated bearing insults as the most Christian of virtues to which the faithful should conform their behaviour. In the conceptual labyrinths of the casuist, in any case, the absolute prohibition of responding to violence with violence is often circumvented by considerations that draw their legitimacy from the dominant social mentality and the social extraction of the theologians, themselves very often belonging to noble houses or in any case strongly influenced by those values. Ledesma, in particular, to the question 'if it is lawful to wound someone who threatens with a stick in hand or raising a hand to give a slap, so that the injured party may defend their honour, not being able to defend it in any other convenient way', responds in this way:[123]

> To this difficulty, I say first, that without a doubt it is lawful in defence of honour to wound and kill when it cannot be defended in any other way. This is the common opinion of all the Doctors [...]. The reason is:

[123] 'si es lícito herir al que amenaza con un palo en la mano o levantando la mano para dar un bofetón, para que assí defienda el injuriado su honra, no pudiendo de otra manera commodamente defenderla', Pedro de Ledesma, *Secunda parte de la Summa, en la qual se summa y cifra todo lo moral, y casos de consciencia que no pertenecen a los sacramentos* (Salamanca, en casa de Antonio Ramírez, 1605), p. 672.

> because although life is a higher-order good [compared to honour], as is well known, the one who intends to take honour has placed their life at stake and put it in that danger. Therefore, the harm must be attributed to themselves. Consequently, a nobleman or knight is not obliged to flee in order not to kill the one who attacks him.[124]

An interesting discrepancy can thus be seen between the severe doctrine proposed from the pulpits and that practised instead in the secrecy of the confessional, the latter being much more flexible in accommodating the needs of the aristocratic classes. This aspect did not escape the criticism of Pascal in his *Provinciales*, given the virulence with which he attacked Jesuit casuistry (Hurtado de Mendoza, Tomás Sánchez, Manuel Sa, etc.), which, precisely on the basis of the direction of intention, had come to consider even homicide lawful if committed in defence of one's honour.[125] A noteworthy aspect is none the less the fact that many Spanish moralists indicate recourse to public justice as the only way out of the impasse of the difficulty in reconciling the law of duelling and the evangelical law. This stands in contrast to a noble ideology

[124] 'A esta difficultad, digo lo primero, que sin duda es lícito en defensión de la honra, herir y matar quando no se puede defender de otra manera. Esta es commún sentencia de todos los Doctores [...]. La razón es: porqué aunque la vida sea bien de más excelente orden [than honour], como es cosa notoria: pero el que pretende quitar la honra puso la vida al tablero, y la pusso a esse peligro. Por lo qual a si mismo se ha de imputar el daño. De lo qual se sigue, que un hombre noble o caballero no está obligado a huyr, por no matar al que le acomete', ibid.

[125] After quoting a passage from the work of Diego Hurtado de Mendoza, which authorised duelling when it was the only way to defend one's property, Pascal writes: 'J'admirai sur ce passage, de voir que la piété du Roi emploi sa puissance à deffendre et à abolir le duel dans ses Etats, et que la piété des Jésuites occupe leur subtilité à le permettre et à l'autoriser dans l'Eglise', [Blaise Pascal], *Les provinciales, ou les lettres écrites par Louis de Montalte à un provincial de ses amis et au RR. PP. Jésuites* (à Cologne, chez Henry Schouten, 1738), pp. 105–9: p. 106; English edition: 'I was struck, on hearing these passages, with the reflection that while the piety of the king appears in his exerting all his power to prohibit the practice of duelling in the State, the piety of the Jesuits is shown in their employing all their ingenuity to tolerate and sanction it in the Church', *The Provincial Letters of Blaise Pascal, a new translation with historical introduction and notes by Rev. Thomas McCrie* (New York, published by Hurd and Houghton, 1866), p. 236. Pascal's indignation reaches its peak when he exposes the position of Tomás Sánchez and Doctor Navarrus (who was not a Jesuit), as they allowed a Christian not only to accept a duel if challenged but also to challenge an opponent to a duel, to secretly kill a false accuser and his witnesses, as well as the corrupt judge who favours him, all the while being careful to 'direct one's intention well'.

that considered an appeal to a public justice body as an odious act of cowardice on the part of the offended.[126] Yet, here too, contradictions and ambiguities abound, because, while on the one hand some Spanish theologians sought to show the utmost respect for civil laws, indicating the tribunal, a traditional guarantor of social peace, and the penal sanctions consequent to the trial as a bulwark against the spread of violence,[127] on the other hand the judicial route to a dispute, the recourse to a tribunal, even in relation to other matters, remained anchored to a morally negative judgement tending to favour solutions of a transactional and informal type. The Dominican Bartolomé de Medina writes in his *Breve Istruttione de' confessori* that absolution should be granted only with great prudence to those penitents who had revealed in confession that they had forgiven in their hearts the author of a wrong suffered but had none the less resorted to justice. In this case, the confessor should carefully examine the penitent, because

> Although this may be said with the mouth, he should none the less examine his heart well, because the ordinary rule is that resentment and the desire for revenge always remain in the heart, not well recognised by him, for which it is not compatible that there be true forgiveness before God. Therefore, he should be admonished to leave the complaint and be spoken to, in imitation of Christ, who forgave His enemies and prayed for them, as did other Saints. And as we have said above, he should not be absolved until he has truly removed hatred from his heart.[128]

The Spanish moralists generally failed to reject completely the codes of noble conduct, which were so deeply rooted in the mentality of the time, and they sought a difficult and unstable compromise. Particularly with the Dominican Domingo Báñez, a system began to emerge that would allow a Christian to avoid a duel while maintaining his honour: this would be possible

[126] See José Antonio Maravall, *Potere, onore, élites nella Spagna del Secolo d'Oro* (Bologna, 1984), p. 150; original edition: *Poder, honor y élites en el siglo XVII* (Madrid, 1979).

[127] See Chauchadis, *La loi du duel*, p. 178.

[128] 'quantunque ciò si dica ben con la bocca, nondimeno essamini bene il cor suo, perché la regola ordinaria è che sempre nel cuore resta rancore, & desiderio di vendetta, non ben conosciuta da lui, per lo quale non si compatisce, che sia vero perdono appresso a Dio; & così l'ammonisca, che lasci la querela, & gli parli, a imitation di Christo, che perdonò a' suoi nemici, & pregò per loro, & d'altri Santi. Et come habbiamo detto di sopra non si deve assolvere fin tanto che non ha levato veramente l'odio dal suo cuore', Bartolomé de Medina, *Breve Istruttione de' confessori come si debba amministrare il Sacramento della Penitentia* ... (in Venetia, appresso Bernardo Basa, 1594), cc. 77^v–78^r.

by refusing the duel explicitly in the name of faith and simultaneously declaring a readiness to respond to any aggression from that moment on. The answer lay, therefore, in taking time, not entirely discarding the possibility of resorting to arms but refusing, at least at that moment, to do so. The Franciscan Enrique de Villalobos, drawing precisely from Báñez, wrote:

> But it will then be lawful for the provoked Christian to say in defence of his honour to the one who challenges him: 'Wherever you attack me, I am a man who knows how to defend himself, and you will not boast of it'. And if the enemy says: 'I want to have a few words with you in private', he may say: 'I do not wish to hear them now, and be careful of what you do, for if you attack me, you will regret it'. He is not obliged to stay at home, and if he meets him and the other draws his weapon, he may do what he can to defend himself, as Báñez says.[129]

It is precisely in this conceptualisation of a 'Christian duel in the Spanish manner' that the Spanish specificity of a body of literature resides. Although it does not directly address peace and the most effective systems for resolving chivalric disputes without resorting to violence, it nevertheless moves in the direction of peace. The defence of a Spanish specificity concerning the violent response to an insult received deserves particular attention. Already in the mid-sixteenth century, Domingo de Soto claimed in a very particular way for the Spanish the right even to kill in response to an attack carried out with a stick, considered particularly dishonourable. This view was confirmed by the Augustinian Pedro de Aragón and the Jesuit Gabriel Vázquez. Refusing to respond violently to a blow from a stick equates to a complete loss of consideration in the eyes of people, particularly in Spain.[130] But the same Spanish specificity, according to other authors, would be the origin of the great consonance between the law of honour and the evangelical law visible in the practices already in use on the Iberian Peninsula, and in Castile in particular.

[129] 'Mas será entonces lícito al Christiano provocado, dezir en defensa de su honra, al que le desafía: "Donde quiera que me acometiéredes, soy hombre que sabré defenderme, y no os yréis alabando dello". Y si dixesse el enemigo: "quiéroos dos palabras a parte", podrá dezir: "no os las quiero oyr ahora, y mirad lo que hazéis, que si me acometéys, os pesará". Y no está obligado a no salir de casa, y si el le topare, y echare mano, podrá hazer lo que pudiere para defenderse, como dice Báñez', Enrique de Villalobos, *Suma de teología moral y canónica* (Salamanca, 1622), p. 186.

[130] 'Praesertim in Hispania ubi tam atrox illa injuria reputatur' ('Especially in Spain where that injury [the blow with a stick] is considered so atrocious'), Domingo de Soto, *De Iustitia et Iure*, t. III, book V, *quaestio* 1, cited in Chauchadis, *La loi du duel*, p. 177.

The Jesuit Pedro Hurtado de Mendoza is one of the most accomplished theorists of this kind of marriage between evangelical and canonical law and the law of duelling. Starting from legitimate defence as the keystone of this conceptual structure that would make duelling lawful under certain circumstances (for example, in the case where duelling was the only way to prove one's innocence in the face of an unjust and defamatory accusation), Hurtado de Mendoza identifies two possible ways of responding to an insult, verbal or physical: the first is recourse to justice, the other is recourse to the 'iudicium peritorum legum duelli christiani' ('judgement of experts in the laws of the Christian duel'). But what does the Christian duel consist of? And who are these experts in the law of the Christian duel? They are intermediaries who must be present at the meeting in the designated place for the duel to ensure it leads to peace while ensuring that the honour of both parties remains intact. Hurtado de Mendoza provides a concrete example: two challengers go to the field chosen for the duel, both accompanied by sponsors of clear nobility and fame; one of the sponsors loudly proclaims that the first who dares to assert that the offended person did not repel the violent action as a gentleman is obliged to do is a liar and that he would support this with a sword in hand. The same exact formula should be followed by the sponsor of the other party; in this way, the duel would be avoided while preserving the honour of both. Hurtado de Mendoza's conclusion is that the duel is not necessary to preserve the integrity of honour, not only according to evangelical and canonical law but also according to the same law of duelling in force in Spain: 'From which I conclude that the challenge to a duel is not necessary to preserve the integrity of honour, not only according to the law of Christ but also according to the law of duelling, as it prevails among our Spaniards'.[131] For him, the Spanish duel is thus already Christian in itself, containing those characteristics that prevent violent confrontation and possibly killing, because it cares for the preservation of the noblemen's honour, an honour founded on reputation.

[131] 'E quibus concludo provocationem ad certamen non esse necessariam ad conservandam integritatem honoris, non solum ex lege Christi, sed neque ex lege duelli, ut viget apud nostros hispanos', Pedro Hurtado de Mendoza, *Scholasticae et morales disputationes*, Salmanticae, Iacinthum Taberniel, 1631, vol. II, p. 1452, cited in Chauchadis, *La loi du duel*, p. 193.

3. King's peace and legal instruments for crime prevention: the English case

Since the Middle Ages, the English crown aimed to construct a complex and extensive institutional structure to ensure the King's peace, or *Pax regis*: the peace of the sovereign, a concept typical of Anglo-Saxon common law that broadly indicated the maintenance of public order. Peace and order became a true political obsession during the late Elizabethan period and the early years of the reign of James I, a peace to be achieved through an extensive judicial system capable not only of ensuring the observance of laws but also of governing the territory.[132] Among the peculiarities of the English context, there has always been, on the one hand, the marked preponderance of the sovereign's laws over subordinate normative systems (communal and feudal), much more so than in continental Europe, and on the other, the traditional use, at the lower end of this branching pyramid, of Parish constables, or Petty constables, officials chosen from within the communities but unpaid, tasked with transmitting detailed reports, precepts, warrants and summonses to the High constables, who would then forward them to the Justices of the Peace, the Quarter Sessions or the Assizes, for the continuation of proceedings against suspects. At the top of the hierarchy of English courts was, in theory, the Court of King's Bench, the only one of the three common law courts at Westminster with criminal jurisdiction, which was unlimited. It had the right to take over criminal cases from lower courts but in practice did not deal with high-profile crimes, instead focusing on transgressions (assaults and brawls) committed by yeomen or members of the gentry. Between 1540 and 1640, the King's Bench was rivalled by the Star Chamber, an innovation introduced by the Tudor dynasty, essentially the King's Council acting as a court. Competent in judging any violation of the King's peace (brawls, riots, assaults, acts of intimidation, but also fraud, counterfeiting, perjury and other offences that other courts could not handle), it was quite popular because it seemed to guarantee speed and flexibility in judgement. It was a much used court, but also abused; it was abolished in 1641 by the Long Parliament, and its competencies were transferred to the King's Bench.

The answer to social conflict through arbitration or mediation instruments could come about, as one might imagine, especially at the base of this pyramid, both through the Petty constables, who belonged to the communities and thus knew their dynamics well, and the Assizes or the Justices of

[132] See Steve Hindle, *The State and Social Change in Early Modern England, 1550-1640* (Houndmills, 2002), p. 94.

the Peace, whose personnel had the advantage of being perceived as outsiders to local conflicts. By the mid-sixteenth century, England was divided into six 'circuits'; two judges of the Assizes were to traverse it twice a year, in summer and winter. Their authority derived from the 'commission' they received each time they set out to travel the circuit. By intercepting cases arising at the local level, they performed an important function of linking the centre to the peripheries and controlling the governance of the territories. They were itinerant judges, whose arrival represented a very important moment in the life of the communities. Their activity was characterised by a deliberate formal ritual to give the population a solemn image of central power, but the same local elite thus had, twice a year, the opportunity to meet and settle pending issues.[133] The arrival of the judges in the community was therefore comparable to the arrival of the bishop or his vicar during pastoral visits or the arrival of an itinerant preacher: a moment when life stopped to witness an event of extraordinary socialisation and ritual, where the moral contents of the disseminated messages, verbal and non-verbal, were massive, the mix of sacred and profane profound and systematic, and the register of the instruments enacted fluctuated between persuasion and coercion.[134]

The very presence of clerics and the delivery of sermons during the Assizes underscored the profoundly sacred character of the entire English justice machinery in the modern era. It was a machinery that the Puritan minister Samuel Ward, a renowned preacher and anti-Catholic and anti-Spanish polemicist, compared to a clock in which all the individual gears, from the largest to the smallest, from the most important to the least important, must work in unison to ensure the observance of the law, which is also God's law. In his sermon delivered in 1620 on the occasion of the Assizes of Bury St Edmunds in Suffolk, the Justices of the Peace, as well as all the courts and officials tasked with maintaining the King's Justice, became for Ward instruments

[133] See James A. Sharpe, *Crime in Early Modern England 1550-1750* (London and New York, 1984), pp. 23–4.

[134] 'The rituals of legal process repeatedly emphasized the foundation of the criminal law in morality and religion: the splendid processions of officials to and from court, the stylized confrontations between defendants and jurors, the gruesome spectacles of public punishments; all these provided eloquent lessons for the populace. The intimate interweaving of criminal law and morality found expression not only in legal ceremonies, but also in contemporary sermons, literature, and legal dicta. The ingrained awareness of the link between good order and good conscience can even be traced in early modern epitaphs. [...] *The definition of the common law as common justice and the identification of both with divine notions of virtue infused the legal and social structures of Early Modern England*', Cynthia B. Herrup, *The Common Peace. Participation and the Criminal Law in Seventeenth-century England* (Cambridge, 1987), p. 194, italics mine.

of Jethro, the father-in-law of Moses, who as mentioned in Exodus advised the legislator of Israel to delegate the powers of judgement and governance to a hierarchy of capable men, so that these could judge ordinary crimes; the most serious and difficult cases were to be reserved for Moses.[135] For the efficient

[135] 'The next day Moses sat in judgement for the people, who waited about him from morning until evening. When his father-in-law saw all that he was doing for the people, he inquired, "What sort of thing is this that you are doing for the people? Why do you sit alone while all the people have to stand about you from morning till evening?" Moses answered his father-in-law, "The people come to me to consult God. Whenever they have a disagreement, they come to me to have me settle the matter between them and make known to them God's decisions and regulations". "You are not acting wisely", his father-in-law replied. "You will surely wear yourself out, and not only yourself but also these people with you. The task is too heavy for you; you cannot do it alone. Now, listen to me, and I will give you some advice, that God may be with you. Act as the people's representative before God, bringing to him whatever they have to say. Enlighten them in regard to the decisions and regulations, showing them how they are to live and what they are to do. But you should also look among all the people for able and God-fearing men, trustworthy men who hate dishonest gain, and set them as officers over groups of thousands, of hundreds, of fifties and of tens. Let these men render decisions for the people in all ordinary cases. More important cases they should refer to you, but all the lesser cases they can settle themselves. Thus, your burden will be lightened, since they will bear it with you. If you do this, when God gives you orders you will be able to stand the strain, and all these people will go home satisfied". Moses followed the advice of his father-in-law and did all that he had suggested. He picked out able men from all Israel and put them in charge of the people as officers over groups of thousands, of hundreds, of fifties and of tens. They rendered decisions for the people in all ordinary cases. The more difficult cases they referred to Moses, but all the lesser cases they settled themselves. Then Moses bade farewell to his father-in-law, who went off to his own country', Exodus 18:13–27 ('Altero autem die sedit Moyses, ut iudicaret populum, qui assistebat Moysi de mane usque ad vesperam. Quod cum vidisset socer eius, omnia scilicet, quae agebat in populo, ait: "Quid est hoc, quod facis in plebe? Cur solus sedes, et omnis populus praestolatur de mane usque ad vesperam?" Cui respondit Moyses: "Venit ad me populus quaerens sententiam Dei. Cumque acciderit eis aliqua disceptatio, veniunt ad me, ut iudicem inter eos et ostendam praecepta Dei et leges eius". At ille: "Non bonam, inquit, rem facis. Consumeris et tu et populus iste, qui tecum est. Ultra vires tuas est negotium; solus illud non poteris sustinere. Sed audi verba mea atque consilia, et erit Deus tecum: Esto tu populo in his, quae ad Deum pertinent, ut referas causas ad Deum ostendasque populo praecepta et leges viamque, per quam ingredi debeant, et opus, quod facere debeant. Provide autem de omni plebe viros strenuos et timentes Deum, in quibus sit veritas, et qui oderint avaritiam, et constitue ex eis tribunos et centuriones et quinquagenarios et decanos, qui iudicent populum omni tempore. Quidquid autem maius fuerit, referant ad te, et ipsi minora tantummodo iudicent; leviusque sit tibi, partito cum aliis onere. Si hoc feceris, implebis imperium Dei et praecepta eius poteris

functioning of the judicial machinery, however, the last of the Petty officers is, for Ward, as important as the Star Chamber, the last of the parish priests as important as the bishop:

> What can the Superior doe, if the Inferiour informe not: what can the eye doe, if the hand and foot be crooked and unserviceable: yea, not onely if such as be organs of Justice, such as have places of Iudicature. But if the media and spectacles of the sense will yeeld a false report, how shall the common sense make a right iudgement? If Pleaders and Attourneyes will colour and gloze, if the Clarkes and Pen-men make false records, may not any of these disturb or pervert Iustice? If the least finger or toe of this body be distorted, I meane Iaylor or Sargent or any other that should execute Iustice, be remisse and slacke, then must the Dutch-mans proverb be veryfied, Looke what the bell is without the clapper, such are good lawes and iudgements without due execution.[136]

The climate of the civil war and religious dissent, certainly not resolved by the establishment of the Cromwellian regime, brought the issue of unity, peace and concord, in both religious matters and interpersonal relationships, to the forefront of public discourse. Just after the Restoration, in 1663, before the Assizes gathered in Dorchester, in the county of Dorset, Henry Glover reminded others that the office of the magistrate is directly delegated by God, and that if the Christian must leave vengeance to God, the magistrate is the one who, by administering justice, enacts divine vengeance.[137] The only permissible vengeance is therefore judicial, which is inflicted on behalf of God and cannot be followed by any other form of private vengeance; killing a wrongdoer after he has been judged by the magistrate represents a

---

sustentare, et omnis hic populus revertetur ad loca sua cum pace". Quibus auditis, Moyses fecit omnia, quae ille suggesserat; et, electis viris strenuis de cuncto Israel, constituit eos principes populi, tribunos et centuriones et quinquagenarios et decanos, qui iudicabant plebem omni tempore. Quidquid autem gravius erat, referebant ad eum, faciliora tantummodo iudicantes. Dimisitque socerum suum, qui reversus abiit in terram suam').

136 *Jethro's Justice of Peace. A Sermon Preached at a Generall Assises Held at Bury St. Edmunds, for the Countie of Suffolke, by Samuel Ward Batchelour of Divinitie* (London, Augustine Mathewes, 1621), pp. 56–7.

137 'And thus you see how the Magistrate comes to be a *Revenger*; God hath put him into his own seat, and put his own sword into his hand, to execute that Vengeance which before he executed himself', *ΕΧΔΙΧΗΣΙΣ or a Discourse of Vengeance. Delivered in a Sermon Preached at Dorchester, at the Assises holden there for the County of Dorset, March 4 1663, by Henry Glover Rector of Shroton* (London, printed for Henry Brome, 1664), p. 8, italics in the original.

serious crime that must be punished severely. As an instrument of God, the magistrate must also not be guided by passion and partiality, but only by piety and compassion. Similarly, the good Christian who has been wronged, especially if the offence is minor, must arm himself with patience, meekness and a spirit of endurance, preparing himself for forgiveness and reconciliation, because resorting to a court for minor wrongs is a sign of lingering resentment. Thomas Goodwin senior, one of the most influential Puritan theologians and preachers of the time, had also insisted on the twofold duty of reconciliation that burdens the Christian, with God and with his neighbour, during the height of the civil war.[138]

By the end of the sixteenth century, the Assizes had secured a monopoly over trials for the most serious crimes (felonies). Previously, many of these cases could be judged by the Quarter Sessions, but in 1590 the reform of the Commissions of the Peace initiated by Sir Christopher Wray (Lord Chief Justice of the Queen's Bench) conferred upon the Assizes the monopoly on high crimes: the 'difficult cases' intercepted by the Justices of the Peace had to be mandatorily transferred to the Assizes, although jurisprudence allowed them ('out of sessions') to manage the initial phase of the proceeding, especially in the investigative process and preventive detention, as unequivocally stated by the jurist Michael Dalton.[139] The 'difficult cases' – the resonance with the biblical passage relating to Jethro is significant ('The more difficult cases they referred to Moses, but all the lesser cases they settled themselves') –

[138] *Christ the Universall Peace-maker. Or, The Reconciliation of All the People of God Notwithstanding all their Differences, Enmities, by Thomas Goodwin, B.D.* (London, printed by J. G. for R. Dawlman, 1651). Close to Goodwin's religious positions was the preacher Jeremiah Burroughs, one of the main supporters of the congregationalist system, who published *Irenicum, to the Lovers of Truth and Peace. Heart-Divisions opened in the Causes and Evils of them: with Cautions that we may not be hurt by them, And Endeavours to heal them*, by Jeremiah Burroughs (London, printed for R. Dawlman, 1653).

[139] 'The Justices of Peace may inquire of Petty Treason, as of Felony: And out of their Sessions, every Justice of Peace may deal with the Offenders therein, as in case of Felony, by Examination of the Offenders, by taking Information against them, and binding over the Informers to the General Gaol-delivery, and committing the Offenders to the Gaol', *The Country Justice. Containing the Practice of the Justices of the Peace out of their Sessions. Gathered for the better help of Such Justices of Peace, as have not been much conversant in the Study of the laws of this Realm. By Michael Dalton of Lincoln's-Inn, Esq., and one of the Masters in Chancery* (London, printed by William Rawlins and Samuel Roycroft, 1690), p. 339. Sharing the same view: Willian Sheppard, *The Whole Office of the Country Justice of Peace, wherein is plainly set down all their Power and Duty both in, and out of the Quarter Sessions* (London, printed for W. Lee, D. Pakeman, G. Bedell, 1656), p. 37.

were crimes punishable by death, such as murder, petty treason (offences against a person of higher rank), grand larceny, arson, rape and witchcraft. The Quarter Sessions, which met four times a year, and the Petty Sessions, presided over by the Justices of the Peace and usually meeting every month, were thus left with the management of minor crimes and conflicts related to land ownership, hereditary transmissions, the application of Poor Laws and so forth. These were the fundamental agencies responsible for the daily governance of the counties, a system that particularly relied on the involvement (also, if not especially, in judicial proceedings as witnesses, sureties, etc.) of property owners within the community who had a primary interest in ensuring that the law was fully respected and, consequently, that peace was preserved. The very perception of legality and morality among property owners could influence the concrete application of the laws; an application characterised by great flexibility, in contrast to legislation that, rooted in divine law, seemed fixed and immobile.

Never as in the turbulent seventeenth century did peace in the Church become in England a perfect metaphor for peace in the political body, two entities so fused in political and religious discourse as to seem almost indistinct. Sermons provide vivid testimony to this, whether those delivered before judicial bodies, as in the cases just evoked of Samuel Ward or Henry Glover, or those delivered on the occasion of meetings of Parliament or within churches at moments of particular significance. Shortly before Oliver Cromwell's death, two sermons, later printed, were delivered a year apart by Edward Reynolds, soon to be appointed Bishop of Norwich, on the occasion of two distinct parliamentary sittings. At the centre of the preacher's discourse was the duty of fraternal reconciliation that falls on the Christian; the duty of unity, concord and peace. To do this, Reynolds built his discourse around two passages from Saint Paul's Letter to the Philippians (Phil. 3:15–16[140] for the sermon of 27 January 1657, and Phil. 2:1–2[141] for the sermon of 4 February 1658, although the same theme is addressed by Paul

[140] 'Let us, then, who are "perfectly mature" adopt this attitude. And if you have a different attitude, this too God will reveal to you. Only, with regard to what we have attained, continue on the same course' ('Quicumque ergo perfecti, hoc sentiamus; et si quid aliter sapitis, et hoc vobis Deus revelabit; verumtamen, ad quod pervenimus, in eodem ambulemus').

[141] 'If there is any encouragement in Christ, any solace in love, any participation in the Spirit, any compassion and mercy, complete my joy by being of the same mind, with the same love, united in heart, thinking one thing' ('Si qua ergo consolatio in Christo, si quod solacium cari tatis, si qua communio spiritus, si quae viscera et miserationes, implete gaudium meum, ut idem sapiatis, eandem caritatem habentes, unanimes, id ipsum sapientes').

in Rom. 15:1–6), and around two concepts of ancient philosophy, 'omonoia' (concord) and *phronesis/autophronesis* (wisdom or prudence).

A Christian must strive to ensure that there are no irreparable breaches in the edifice of the Church, constituted by heresy ('which untieth the bond of Faith') and schism ('which breaketh the bond of love'),[142] and to do this, he must adopt the same attitudes that Paul of Tarsus proposed to the inhabitants of Philippi as a break from the dominant values in the Greek world: prudence, meekness, gentleness, moderation, humility, the absence of aggressiveness and the spirit of anathema and the rejection of 'cavillosity' (here returns the theme of chicane/chicanery), attitudes that alone can guarantee the preservation of friendship. The parallel with the civil sphere is more implicit than explicit but absolutely clear, especially considering the historical moment in which the sermon arises, that of a kingdom first torn apart by civil war and then held together by a highly repressive regime. The diversity of opinions and judgements is inevitable for Reynolds, but it is essential to know how to govern it so that everyone can move in the same direction, all towards the same goal.[143] The unity of the Church and the resolution of internal doctrinal conflicts, especially between Presbyterians and Anglicans, became a central theme of open reflection in seventeenth-century England, much more so than in the Catholic sphere, which was equally crossed by internal conflicts.[144] Conflicts must be pacified and resolved, and this is possible only if 'mature' individuals (in the sense of strong in faith) know how to relate in the right way to their weaker brothers in faith, following the outline of chapter 14 of the Letter to the Romans:

142 *The substance of two sermons one touching composing of controversies. Another touching unity of judgement and love amongst brethren. Preached in two honourable conventions of Parliament. The former, Jan. 27. 1657. The other, Feb. 4. 1658. By Edward Reynolds, D.D.* (London, printed by Tho. Radcliffe for George Thomason at the Sign of the Rose and Crown in St Pauls Church-yard, 1659), pp. 1–2.

143 'Let the *piety* of our lives in walking by the same *rule* of Faith and love, the *unity* of our judgement, the *concord* of our affections, the *concurrence* of our *ends*, our consent and delight in the same truth (all which are intimated in the words τό άυτό φρονείν)', op. cit., pp. 5–6, italics in the original.

144 Along the same lines, the Scottish Presbyterian John Dury in his writing: *A peace-maker without Partiality and Hypocrisie. Or, the Gospel-way to make up the present breaches of Brotherhood, and heale the divisions, whereby some of the reforming Professors and Ministers of this Kingdome at this time, sadly dishonour their profession, mainely obstruct our Reformation, utterly destroy the safe constitution both of Church and State ... All written upon severall occasions and at severall times by Mr. John Dury, one of the Assembly of Divines & c.* (London, printed by R. Cotes for John Ballamy, 1648).

> So then what ever be the *differences* amongst true believers, who agree in the great things of Gods Kingdom, the *strong* ought not *to despise* the weak, nor the *weak to judge* the strong, neither ought to hurt, grieve, wound, offend the hearts of one another, in as much as we are all *fellow servants* to one common Lord, who will judge us all, and in as much as we are *owned by that Lord*, and accepted, the weak as well the strong, who doth not so much value us by the degrees of our *knowledge*, as by the sincerity of our *love*, who doth not reap any benefit by the differences of our services, but is pleased and glorified by the uprightness of our hearts, yea possibly is more pleased with the *conscionable tendernesse* of the weak brother that errs, then with the *confident* and inexpedient *liberty* of the strong brother who doth not erre.[145]

The strong and the weak in faith become an all too evident metaphor for the differences in rank within English society. Absolute uniformity of opinions is impossible, but conflicts can be smoothed out if one can distinguish between the *fundamentalia fidei*, on which unanimity of judgement is necessary (under penalty of the collapse of the entire edifice), and the *adiaphora*, the matters of lesser importance:

> there can be *no Syncretisme* or Accommodation in case of differences, where the differences are *against the foundations* of Faith, Worship, Obedience, and Holiness, there can be *no agreement between light and darkness, Christ and Belial, damnable Heresies*, and the Doctrine according unto Godliness [...]. Hereticks are to be admonished, and in case of pertinacy to be rejected. [...] in differences of inferior nature, which do not touch the Essentials, and Vitals of Religion, *mutuall tolerance*, *meekness*, and tenderness is to be used, *as amongst brethren*, and fellow members.[146]

The distinction is rooted in Cynic and Stoic thought and, as is known, represented one of the cornerstones of seventeenth-century irenicism;[147] we can find it translated and reproduced in the English judicial system in the different treatment reserved for felony crimes (equivalent to *atrociora et graviora crimina*), which required exemplary trials and punishments (in most cases the death penalty) to the extent that the offender, through his act, placed himself

145 *The substance of two sermons one touching composing of controversies*, section II, pp. 12–13, italics in the original.

146 ibid., op. cit., pp. 21–3, italics in the original.

147 See Alexandra Walsham, *Charitable Hatred. Tolerance and Intolerance in England, 1500-1700* (Manchester, 2006). For more in general, see Benjamin Kaplan, *Divided by Faith. Religious Conflict and the Practice of Toleration in Early Modern Europe* (Cambridge, MA, 2007).

outside and against the community, compared to breaches of the peace, minor crimes to be resolved through arbitration and mediation.[148]

The process of reaction to the criminal act, and the treatment of its perpetrator, was defined immediately. When a crime occurred, a number of individuals – relatives, friends, or neighbours of the victim, possibly but not necessarily assisted by the Constables – would move pre-emptively to conduct informal investigations and isolate the suspect from the rest of the community. Once arrested, the perpetrator was brought before a Justice of the Peace for interrogation; the magistrate could independently decide whether to proceed with arbitration between the parties, not proceed at all, or refer the perpetrator to a trial before the Assizes or the Quarter Sessions. Certainly, the social context and the initiative of the various individuals involved had a significant weight in the Justice's decision: it was, in effect, a participatory process. The outcome of the proceeding was determined by the social status of the perpetrator: the line between what was tolerable and intolerable was dictated not only by the nature of the infraction but also by the social context. In any case, for less serious crimes – that is, not felonies, but such as trespassing, which were considered crimes even when they did not generate violence and brawls – convictions were not systematically reached, not only at the level of the Justices of the Peace: in Essex, for example, out of seventy-six cases brought before the Quarter Sessions, fourteen ended with an order of restitution, six were punished with a fine, seven with a dismissal (ignoramus), and one with a peace order. Thus, convictions were reached in about half of the cases.[149]

Alongside the common law courts, there were also canon law courts, such as the consistory courts. They had competencies in resolving conflicts that had a predominantly moral profile, concerning marriage, wills, tithes, but also defamation and slander, an area in which ecclesiastical courts competed with civil ones and where one perceives the great importance that social actors attributed to reputation and fame, their own or that of their family members, especially women, and the frequent recourse to the court to defend them. In

[148] Another example of a sermon where peace, unity and concord become the keystone of both the ecclesiastical and political edifice comes from the preacher John Jones: *The Conquest of the Saints. Or, a short Treatise of Concord and Peace: Wherein is shewed the necessity of Unity and Peace, without which neither Church nor Common-wealth can stand. Preached by John Jones Master of Arts, late Minister at St Michael Bashenshaw in London, and now published for the common good* (London, printed by G. M. for William Jones, 1634).

[149] See James A. Sharpe, *Crime in Seventeenth-Century England. A County Study* (Cambridge, 1983), p. 74.

the transition between the late Middle Ages and the sixteenth century, it is noted that defamation cases increasingly concerned sexual behaviour rather than crimes such as murder and theft, which became the purview of secular courts. It is also noted that, in consistory courts, the most encouraged mode of resolution was conciliatory. As Ralph Houlbrooke highlighted, 'it was the duty of the ecclesiastical judge to encourage the peaceful settlement of most types of dispute by compromise or arbitration'.[150] Although arbitration was not always effective,[151] ecclesiastical courts were indispensable tools available to the elders of various communities for the preservation of morality, in their ability to sanction transgressions and mediate in conflicts most amenable to transactional solutions.[152]

Early modern England is probably the clearest example of a reality where community justice was deeply intertwined with hegemonic justice, if we continue to use this distinction. The power to enforce the law and punish those who refused to submit to such a command was not the exclusive prerogative of judicial personnel. The class of property owners held real power within the local judicial machinery; besides judges and judicial staff, a large number of people had the opportunity to participate in the process, and, where a broadly agreed-upon resolution could not be reached, suspects were generally not arrested, charged, convicted or punished.[153] As in any other European context of the time, a part of the conflict was certainly managed through completely informal procedures of which little or no documentary trace remains. However, the English judicial system was conceived in such a way that there was an intimate connection between properly judicial instruments and community reconciliation instruments, where the former often served to transform seemingly negotiable solutions into coercive ones, as has been observed in the contemporary Italian reality.

[150] Ralph Houlbrooke, *Church Courts and the People during the English Reformation. 1520-1570* (Oxford, 1979), p. 43

[151] See *Justice and Conciliation in a Tudor Church Court. Depositions from EDC 2/6, Deposition Book of the Consistory Court of Chester, September 1558-March 1559*, ed. E. Kate Jarman (Bristol, 2012), pp. XXXIX–XL.

[152] See, for example, Martin Ingram, *Church Courts. Sex and Marriage in England, 1570-1640* (Cambridge, 1987).

[153] See Herrup, *The Common Peace*, p. 195. 'The people who controlled the legal system were in some sense representatives of their communities. The obligation to participate in prosecutions went deep into the ranks of propertied society, assuring not only the involvement of a fair number of persons but also their interest in upholding deference to the law', ibid.

Even in territories subject to the English crown, and perhaps even more so than elsewhere, peace was a powerful rhetorical device whose use went hand in hand with the stigmatisation of litigiousness, which was associated with the morally reprehensible 'esprit de chicane' we have already encountered in France, and with the indication of recourse to arbitration and mediation as part of the duty of charity. At the same time, however, political and judicial power widely resorted to indirect coercion instruments.[154] In comparison to the Italian reality, English practice also featured the centrality of instruments very similar to the *sicurtà di non offendere*. In the Anglo-Saxon common law tradition, these were called binding over instruments, where the use of the verb 'to bind' is particularly evocative of their functioning; they allowed the integration of public authority into seemingly spontaneous and informal pacification processes, and this integration was not merely a result of the early modern age. They belonged to the ancient Anglo-Saxon legal tradition and were embedded in the sureties (or warrants) of peace and the sureties (or warrants) of good behaviour, the acceptance of which by the offender was necessary for the sovereign's grant of pardon. Their first formalisation dates back to the Justices of the Peace Act of 1361, but they have continued to function effectively up to the present day.[155]

In his criminal practice, published in 1618 and widely disseminated at the time, the aforementioned Michael Dalton, a lawyer and jurist trained at Cambridge and active during the reigns of Elizabeth I and James I, meticulously describes all the cases, depending on the quality of the person subject

[154] Such instruments are akin to what, in modern legal terminology, albeit with reference to the civil and commercial sphere, are referred to as 'means of inducing performance' (in our case, inducing abstention from performing a certain act), which rely on the threat of sanction. Perhaps even more closely, they resemble the 'penal remedies and penances [...] to prevent crimes' contained in the current Code of Canon Law (can. 1312, § 3), to which penal precepts are connected.

[155] 'Both the massive growth of civil litigation and extensive popular participation in the criminal and administrative aspects of the legal system suggest a general familiarity with, and desire to use, judicial structures and processes. Striking demonstration of such popular legalism is provided by the widespread practice of appearing before magistrates to swear the peace, to request that an opponent be bound over. Binding over refers to a magistrate's power to bind an individual in a fixed sum, or recognizance, and for a fixed period, to keep the peace and/or to be of good behaviour irrespective of conviction for a criminal offence. If the person bound over was subsequently found to have breached the peace and/or failed to be of good behaviour during that period, he or she was liable to have the recognizance "estreated" or forfeited to the crown. The practice has underpinned the structures of authority in English society for almost ten centuries', Hindle, *The State and Social Change*, p. 97.

to the measure, in which the sureties of peace could be imposed by the Justices of the Peace in their activities 'out of their sessions'. A high aristocrat could not be subjected to a surety by a Justice, as a promise 'upon his Honour' (the English equivalent of the *verbo dato de non offendendo*) was sufficient for him; if someone wanted to obtain such a measure against a Lord (Peer of the Realm), they would have to go through the Court of Chancery (a court of equity that usually did not operate based on common law), which could issue a *subpoena* (a common law institution) binding the high aristocrat to keep the peace.[156] Knights and any other layperson below the rank of Baron or Peer could be subjected to a surety of peace by the Justices of the Peace. Dalton cites a particular case that occurred in Surrey: a surety had been issued during a Session against Sir Nicholas Stoughton, who was himself a Justice of the Peace (and also a member of the House of Commons); the measure was contested by Stoughton on the principle that a Justice cannot issue measures against his peer. However, the King's Bench reaffirmed the measure, clarifying in its motivations that while it is true that Justices are peers among themselves, it is equally true that the Sessions collectively constitute a court whose authority is superior to that of its individual members.[157]

The issue of rank was central, and the range of relationships that could be covered by such measures was very broad and emanated not only from the Justices of the Peace. For example, a wife could request a Justice to issue a warrant to seek sureties against her husband if she felt threatened with mistreatment, injury or even death, just as the Justice himself could do so on his own initiative against the violent husband; the woman, however, also had the option of turning to the Chancery, which could issue a *supplicavit*, an act whose function was to protect against retaliation someone who had requested the issuance of a surety against another. These were preventive measures aimed at

[156] In the Anglo-Saxon legal tradition, a subpoena is a measure intended to compel a person to testify (*subpoena ad testificandum*) or to produce evidence (*subpoena duces tecum*), with the notice that non-compliance entails a sanction.

[157] 'Sir Nicholas Stoughton in Surrey, was, upon the Complaint of one Gilham required in Sessions to give Sureties for the Good-behaviour for a sufficient cause; be refuted; the Sessions committed him until, & c. he gave Sureties: And afterwards complaint was made hereof in the King's Bench, and he was compelled there to give Sureties, notwithstanding it was objected that the Justices of the Peace were all of equal power: But it was answered by the Court, That the Sessions made a Court, which Court might require Sureties for the Peace or Good-behaviour of any one Justice of Peace', *The Country Justice. Containing the Practice of the Justices of the Peace out of their Sessions. Gathered for the better help of Such Justices of Peace, as have not been much conversant in the Study of the laws of this Realm. By Michael Dalton of Lincoln's-Inn, Esq., and one of the Masters in Chancery* (London, printed by William Rawlins and Samuel Roycroft, 1690), p. 268.

preventing the breach of the King's peace, or preventing it from being broken again after a generally minor criminal event had already occurred.

In 1728, Joseph Shaw, a London jurist educated at Oxford, published another successful criminal practice manual dedicated to the activities of the Justices of the Peace, in which the author carefully defines both the types of behaviours liable for surety and the circumstances in which these behaviours could occur. The surety was a measure applied in cases of Breaches of the Peace, such as assaults, battery, threats, forgery, imprisonment without warrant, pushing someone into water, etc., and for these behaviours 'a man may be bound to keep the Peace, and be indicted and fined'. The surety of the peace was 'the acknowledging of a recognisance to the King, taken by a competent Judge of Record for the keeping of the Peace', that is, the certification of the commitment made before the sovereign, guaranteed by a monetary surety bond, not to break the peace in the future. It thus required the intervention of a third party, who would act as a guarantor of the commitment made, under penalty of payment of a certain sum of money. To obtain a surety against someone, one had to swear (take an oath) to be in a state of serious and real danger resulting from the threats or offences received from the person against whom the measure was requested:

> When the Peace is granted, upon Request, there must be an Oath made by the Party desiring it, That it stands in Fear of his Life, or some bodily Hurt, or the Firing of his House by him against whom he desires it, or by his Procurement; and that he desires the Peace against him, not out of Malice or Hatred, but out of very Fear from his threatening to do it, or procuring it to be done, or otherwise.[158]

The Justice was not obliged to issue the measure but could, at their discretion, agree to do so if they deemed the petitioner reliable and the conditions met.[159] The refusal of the surety would automatically trigger a proceeding and incarceration. The Justices 'out of the session', in their daily contact with social reality, were at the forefront in the use of such instruments, as William Lambarde, a well-known scholar and jurist of the Elizabethan age, had shown well a few years before Dalton.[160] They positioned themselves as 'paternal guides' of

[158] *The Practical Justice of Peace: or, a Treatise shewing the present Power and Authority of that Officer, in all the Branches of his Duty ... by Joseph Shaw of the Middle Temple Esq.*, vol. I (in the Savoy [London], Printed by Henry Lintot, 1744), p. 714.

[159] 'The Justice may not bind to the Good Behavior, nor commit to Prison, for refusal to give Surety upon a general Accusation, without some Particulars', ibid.

[160] *Eirenarcha, or, of the Office of the Iustices of Peace, in Foure Bookes ... , first collected by William Lambarde of Lincolns Inne Gent* (London, Printed for the Companie of Stationers, 1619), pp. 72ff.

the communities in which they lived, and thus were they generally perceived; a paternalism that was essentially based on the work of arbitrating and resolving disputes. In the eighteenth century, Baronet John Eardly-Wilmot, a judge and politician from Derbyshire, described the duties of the Justice of the Peace in this way:

> The most important part of their duties was their residence in the various places in the county where they lived and where they were enabled to act as friends of the poor and heal disputes as arbitrators and referees. In cases of assault, differences between masters and servants, and cases of trespass, their interposition was most constant and useful.[161]

In the communities, the Justices performed tasks that were not solely jurisdictional. In their balancing of legal and extra-legal tools, judicial-coercive methods and negotiation-persuasive methods, they were seen by community members as both judges and paternal guides, 'a fatherly ruler preserving the peace of England's green fields by beneficent guidance'.[162] One of the most interesting aspects of the English case lies in the fact that a significant part of the mediation and arbitration activity, which in other contexts has not left documentary traces as it did not produce written records or initiate judicial proceedings, surfaces thanks to the diaries in which the Justices of the Peace recorded all the warrants issued. At the beginning of the nineteenth century, for instance, Sir Samuel Whitbread documented in his diaries a series of conflicts he had been called to resolve, from which it is inferred that only in very few cases were both parties willing to appear before the judge, and thus the only way to do so was to issue a warrant against the recalcitrant party. It was the parties who turned to him, not the other way around, and only very rarely did both request his arbitration. The most recurring situation thus saw a complainant approaching the Justice to request that a warrant be issued against their aggressor. Only in a small fraction of cases was a dossier produced to be sent to the Quarter Sessions. In eighteenth-century Wiltshire, the warrant issued by the Justice alone was often sufficient to resolve the conflict without initiating a proceeding.[163]

161 Cited in Norma Landau, *The Justices of the Peace, 1679-1760* (Berkeley, Los Angeles and London, 1984), pp. 173–4.

162 Op. cit., p. 174.

163 'these justices settled the disputes of their neighbours – sometimes by the exaction of a fine, but most frequently by reconciling the disputants. Indeed, the diary of the Wiltshire justice reveals that the issue of a warrant was sometimes in itself sufficient to produce concord among disputants', op. cit., p. 192.

The central point of the system is the relationship between the number of warrants issued and the number of recognisances to keep the peace, an institution of Anglo-Saxon common law through which the Justice compels two subjects to pay a certain sum of money in case of non-compliance with the obligation signed and to appear before a court, specifically the Quarter Sessions.[164] In England, the use of preventive measures similar to the *cautiones de non offendendo*, as a preferential (and sufficient in itself) means to maintaining peace, seems to undergo a substantial amplification in the transition to the post-Restoration period. If in the Elizabethan age (the evidence left by Lambarde is important from this point of view) and in the first half of the seventeenth century a significant number of people against whom a warrant had been issued were affected by a recognisance (a quarter, in some cases even half), in the late seventeenth and the eighteenth centuries there is a marked decrease in this proportion (10%, on average). As Norma Landau observed, this means that, in the eighteenth century much more than in the past, the vast majority of cases did not reach the Quarter Sessions, being resolved at the level of the Justices of the Peace by the warrant alone:

> By substituting mediation for reliance upon the recognizance, eighteenth-century rural justices were increasing the extra-legal component of their authority emphasized in the label 'paternal ruler'. They had replaced a legal instrument which forwarded disputants to the court of Quarter Sessions with the practice of mediation, and mediation neither sent disputants to another tribunal nor produced a legal document which subjected disputants to the rules of law.[165]

If some doubt can be raised, in light of the historiographical debate following the publication of Landau's book regarding the use of the term 'extra-legal', the evidence of a practice of mediation and paternalistic management of communities that intensifies as we move further into the eighteenth century must make us seriously reconsider the validity of certain assumptions still too automatically applied to explain the evolution of

[164] 'Every Recognisance must have these Things in it: the Time of making it, the Justice's Name before whom, the Names of the Persons bound, with the Additions of their Places of Habitation, Trade, & c., the Sum they are bound him. It must be made to the King, and in his own name; if for the Peace, to appear to the next Sessions of the Peace; if for Felony, at the next Gaol delivery; and it should be in Latin, and wrote on Parchment, but being on Paper it is good in Law. The Condition usually is, to keep the Peace or Good Behavior against all Men, and especially [specific person] till the next Sessions, and then to appear, & c. this is the best Form', *The Practical Justice of peace*, vol. II, p. 91.

[165] Landau, *The Justices of the Peace*, pp. 193–4.

judicial practices in modern Europe. Once again, peace and mediation – far from being spontaneous phenomena resulting from the internalisation of behavioural paradigms, perhaps borrowed from Christian morality – are not mere residues and it is not certain that they tended to disappear everywhere. Instead, they may have been encouraged by a strong state apparatus that was aware of the great benefits that could result from reducing the pressure on judicial bodies. A clogged and slow justice system risked becoming increasingly less fair. Proposals for reform were not lacking, even in the English monarchy, aimed precisely at preventing trivial causes from going through all the stages of the judicial process, significantly slowing down the entire apparatus.[166]

[166] See, for example, [William Leach], *A Preservative Against the major part of Trials and Non-suits in triviall Causes. And many other unnecessary charges about other things in further order to the regulation of the unnecessary charges in the proceedings in Law, and for saving to the people of this Nation every year hereafter a considerable part of three millions of money formerly unlawfully extracted from them by Monopolizers about the Law written, proposed, and tendered to the same consideration as were many former Propositions, by W.L. of the Middle Temple* (London, British Museum, 1650).

5.

The peace of Christians

'Don't you think it's a disgrace, and a sure sign of poor education, to be forced to rely on an extraneous justice – that of masters or judges – for want of a sense of justice of one's own?'

'The greatest disgrace possible,' he said. 'And yet, is it really any more disgraceful, would you say, than the person who in addition to spending the greater part of his life in the law courts as defendant or plaintiff, is also convinced, such is his ignorance of what is good, that his cleverness at committing crimes, and his subsequent ability to use every evasion and loophole to escape conviction and avoid paying the penalty, is actually a matter for self-congratulation? And all for the sake of what is trivial and of no importance, because he does not realise how much finer and better it is to see to it that his life does not depend on finding a juror who is half-asleep.'

'You're right', he said. 'That is worse than the previous example.'

Plato, *The Republic*, Book 3, 405a–c[1]

1. Christian culture and secular justice between repression and reconciliation

In the evolution of the concepts and concrete methods of governing human justice in Western European societies, Christian thought, including its Judaic roots, has played a decisive role. The debate on such a complex and profound topic is so vast that any attempt at synthesis proves impossible.[2]

1 Plato, *The Republic*, edited by G. R. F. Ferrari, translated by Tom Griffith, 'Cambridge Texts in the History of Political Thought', eds. Raymond Geuss and Quentin Skinner, Cambridge, Cambridge University Press, 2000, pp. 96–7.

2 A good observatory, albeit partial, on this debate is offered by the various discussion interventions prompted by the publication of Paolo Prodi's volume, *Una storia della giustizia. Dal pluralismo dei fori al moderno dualismo tra coscienza e diritto* (Bologna, 2000). Among these, it is certainly worth noting Adriano Prosperi,

However, there seems to be no doubt about one central idea developed by European culture. Human justice has been imagined as a reflection of divine justice, ever since Paul of Tarsus established once and for all the nature of the relationship between the sacred and secular power in Christianity ('Let every person be subordinate to the higher authorities, for there is no authority except from God, and those that exist have been established by God', Rom. 13:1–4).[3] In early medieval judicial practice, the request for God's intervention in resolving doubtful judicial cases took the form of the ordeal, which survived until the Church itself banned it as blasphemous at the beginning of the thirteenth century.[4] It was between the eleventh and thirteenth centuries that the fundamental transition towards modern European legal and judicial systems occurred: on the one hand, the recovery and victory of Roman law as common law over customary laws, and on the other hand, the transfer of the divinely derived jurisdictional function from the figure of the emperor to that of the sovereigns. Even before the legislative function, the sovereign was recognised with the power to administer justice on behalf of God; it was a true delegation because judging was considered an intrinsically divine function. Judges were in turn delegated by the sovereign based on this primordial mandate.[5] Simultaneously, theology and the ecclesiastical apparatus had undergone, since the early centuries, a process of juridicisation that had fundamental consequences on the conception of the law court: it was particularly Cyprian who defined the bishop as 'iudex a Deo datus' ('judge given by God').[6]

From the perspective of political organisms, the issue is not only ideological; it does not reflect exclusively on images, symbolic and allegorical representations aimed at spreading certain conceptions and behaviour models to the subjects. Even on a much more concrete level, theology and canon law effected that turning point that led to the birth of the process understood

---

'Una discussione con Paolo Prodi', *Storica* 17 (2000), pp. 85–100; Mario Montorzi, *La giustizia di Paolo Prodi: note di lettura*, in the same issue, pp. 101–13; Mariuccia Salvati, 'Una storia della giustizia', *Passato e Presente* XIX, 53 (2001), pp. 153–64.

3 'Omnis anima potestatibus sublimioribus subdita sit non est enim potestas nisi a Deo quae autem sunt a Deo ordinatae sunt'.

4 See Finbarr McAuley, 'Canon Law and the End of the Ordeal', *Oxford Journal of Legal Studies* 26, 3 (2006), pp. 473–513.

5 Evolution outlined in Adriano Prosperi, *Giustizia bendata. Percorsi storici di un'immagine* (Torino, 2008), pp. 81–131. See also Diego Quaglioni, *La giustizia nel Medioevo e nella prima età moderna* (Bologna, 2004).

6 See Prodi, *Una storia della giustizia* [2015], p. 31.

as inquisition. The judge was recognised with a function no longer of mediation between the parties but of seeking the truth through *inquisitio*: at the centre of the new procedure was the secret investigation of the accused, initiated *ex officio* and not at the request of a party, which had to occur without external interference. To conduct the investigation, the judge used the instrument of torture and, once reaching the truth, even based on simple 'indubitable indications', issued a sentence.[7] Having established the principle that only in the Kingdom of Heaven can true justice reign, the sovereign's justice conformed to concepts of the divine one, attempting to imitate it: the first inquisitor was God himself in the act of questioning Adam, as many authors wrote. The objective of the sovereign's justice, exercised according to the inquisitorial method, was to limit as much as possible the recourse to private vengeance and ensure peace among the subjects. In the rhetoric of power, this severe, expeditious justice, which everyone could not but fear, was thought to protect individuals, primarily from others' vengeance, in a world dominated by factional divisions and private wars.

However, there exists a concept of justice that is not alternative but parallel to the one just described and which, although well represented at the level of practice, has left less evident traces in literature, treatises and iconography, dominated by a prevailing narrative more concerned with showing the double-sided nature, both terrible and merciful, of sovereign justice as the severe and unappealable punishment of the criminal and as the arbitrary annulment of punishment based on an act of magnanimity by the sovereign. It is the justice of remissions and arbitrations, of pardons and compensations, practices – widely diffused and persistent – normally defined by scholars as 'customary', thus presumably in conflict with the affirmation of common law, and yet, in various writings from the late medieval and early modern periods, often indicated as *preferable* to courts and trials. We will need to examine carefully this attitude of distrust and suspicion towards the judicial path for resolving interpersonal conflicts, as it was far from being merely the result of a sentiment of distrust harboured by subordinate classes or local communities towards hegemonic classes or central powers, or a mere denunciation of the corruption of judges and lawyers. It constituted a precise strand of Western European thought, whose religious derivation is equally profound. It is no coincidence that the genre perhaps most engaged in spreading this idea of justice was homiletics, as we will see shortly.

7 See Marco Bellabarba, *La giustizia nell'Italia moderna* (Rome and Bari, 2008), p. 133; see in general Mario Sbriccoli, *Storia del diritto penale e della giustizia: scritti editi e inediti, 1972-2007*, vol. I (Milan, 2009), pp. 130–5.

Distrust towards the category of judges and lawyers is recurrent in the Bible, in both the Old and New Testaments. In the book of the prophet Amos, the condemnation of the corruption of judges is vibrant, as, in the times of the reign of Jeroboam II, they had turned into oppressors of the poor (Amos 5:10–15);[8] Zephaniah compared the judges to 'wolves of the night that have had no bones to gnaw by morning' (Zeph. 3:3), while for Isaiah the return to the perfection of the past was possible only if the judges and counsellors returned to be as they were at the beginning (Isa. 1:26).[9] A constant concern for justice administered with equity runs through the books of the prophets, as well as the Pentateuch, but one must arrive at the Gospels to trace a different declination of the same theme, destined for a great subterranean fortune. Both Luke and Matthew express a very precise precept, a consequence of a different way of understanding justice compared to that of the Scribes and Pharisees, according to which the Christian must reconcile with his adversary before bringing him before a judge:

> If you are to go with your opponent before a magistrate, make an effort to settle the matter on the way; otherwise your opponent will turn you over to the judge, and the judge hand you over to the constable, and the constable throw you into prison. I say to you, you will not be released until you have paid the last penny. (Luke 12:58–9)

8 'They hate him who reproves at the gate and abhor him who speaks the truth. Therefore, because you have trampled upon the weak and exacted of them levies of grain, though you have built houses of hewn stone, you shall not live in them! Though you have planted choice vineyards, you shall not drink their wine! Yes, I know how many are your crimes, how grievous your sins: Oppressing the just, accepting bribes, repelling the needy at the gate! Therefore the prudent man is silent at this time, for it is an evil time. Seek good and not evil, that you may live; Then truly will the LORD, the God of hosts, be with you as you claim! Hate evil and love good, and let justice prevail at the gate; Then it may be that the LORD, the God of hosts, will have pity on the remnant of Joseph' ('Odio habuerunt corripientem in porta et loquentem perfecte abominati sunt. Idcirco, pro eo quod conculcastis pauperem et portionem frumenti abstulistis ab eo, domos quadro lapide aedificastis et non habitabitis in eis, vineas plantastis amantissimas et non bibetis vinum earum. Quia cognovi multa scelera vestra et fortia peccata vestra, opprimentes iustum, accipientes munus et pauperes deprimentes in porta. Ideo prudens in tempore illo tacet, quia tempus malum est. Quaerite bonum et non malum, ut vivatis, ita ut sit Dominus, Deus exercituum, vobiscum, sicut dixistis. Odite malum et diligite bonum et constituite in porta iudicium, si forte misereatur Dominus, Deus exercituum, reliquiis Ioseph').

9 'I will restore your judges as at first, and your counsellors as in the beginning; After that you shall be called city of justice, faithful city' ('Et restituam iudices tuos, ut fuerunt prius, et consiliarios tuos sicut antiquitus; post haec vocaberis Civitas iustitiae, Urbs fidelis').

> Settle with your opponent quickly while on the way to court with him. Otherwise your opponent will hand you over to the judge, and the judge will hand you over to the guard, and you will be thrown into prison. Amen, I say to you, you will not be released until you have paid the last penny. (Matt. 5:25–6)

Here, the ecclesiological question plays a decisive role. Since the origins of Christianity, the ecclesia, the assembly of believers, has posed itself as 'a place by its nature alternative to political power'.[10] In contrast to the pagan world, Judaeo-Christian culture established the separation between State and Church, a separation that did not contradict the Pauline conception of the divine derivation of political power. In the progressive and consequent distinction between sin as a lack towards God and towards other men, and the crime as disobedience to the law, the assembly has a central role in so far as it holds the power to remit sins but also to resolve internal disputes among its members. The levels are different but closely intertwined, as Paolo Prodi has lucidly highlighted, and the result was the creation of a penitential forum 'that becomes an alternative to human justice',[11] an alternative structure to political justice deriving from the need to make the Church an open community, solely based on the baptismal bond, in opposition to sects. The passages from the Gospels of Luke and Matthew just mentioned should then be read in intimate connection with that of Matthew on fraternal correction (*correctio fraterna*) or evangelical denunciation (*denunciatio evangelica*):

> If your brother sins (against you), go and tell him his fault between you and him alone. If he listens to you, you have won over your brother. If he does not listen, take one or two others along with you, so that every fact may be established on the testimony of two or three witnesses. If he refuses to listen to them, tell the church. If he refuses to listen even to the church, then treat him as you would a Gentile or a tax collector. (Matt. 18:15–17)

It is precisely based on the 'continuous call to sin, mercy and forgiveness that pervades all New Testament writings [that] the assembly of disciples is given the power to interpret and concretise divine forgiveness with the establishment of a forum that becomes an alternative to human justice'.[12] It is not a question, continues Prodi,

10 'il luogo per natura sua alternativo al potere politico', Prodi, *Una storia della giustizia*, p. 26.

11 'che diviene alternativo alla giustizia umana', op. cit., p. 27.

12 'richiamo continuo al peccato, alla misericordia e al perdono che pervade tutti gli scritti neotestamentari [che] viene data all'assemblea dei discepoli il potere

of the presence of a dual system of norms within the New Testament Christian community (on one side, the relationship with God, and on the other, interpersonal relationships; on one side, ethical norms, and on the other, legal norms), but rather the establishment of an alternative structure to political justice, as evidenced by the verses of Matthew immediately following those mentioned: 'Amen, I say to you, whatever you bind on earth shall be bound in heaven, and whatever you loose on earth shall be loosed in heaven' (Matt. 18:18–19).[13]

As an open and non-sectarian community, the Church had to immediately address the issue of excluding those who are in sin, thereby identifying the line of demarcation between orthodoxy and heterodoxy. However, the system of correcting faults that required secret correction to precede denunciation to ecclesiastical hierarchies remained in place. Paolo Prodi also reminds us how, in the evolution of confession from a complex penitential system to a sacrament, which led to its transformation into a tribunal of conscience (with the confessor becoming a judge who enquires about sins and pronounces, with the 'ego te absolvo', a definitive sentence effective in itself regardless of the purification path undertaken), the precept of evangelical denunciation weighed heavily. This precept, in the twelfth century, transformed into *denunciatio judicialis* or *canonica*: the obligation for the faithful to report to the Church, but only after confidential and private admonition, the author of a public sin.[14] Confidential and private amendment was recognised as valid and practicable only for hidden sins, as its objective was, as much as possible, to protect the reputation of the guilty. However, it was deemed useless for public sins since the sinner's reputation was already compromised.[15]

di interpretare e concretare il perdono divino con la costituzione di un foro che diviene alternativo alla giustizia umana', Prodi, *Una storia della giustizia*, p. 27.

13 'della presenza di un doppio sistema di norme all'interno della comunità cristiana neotestamentaria (da una parte il rapporto con Dio e dall'altra parte i rapporti interpersonali, da una parte le norme etiche e dall'altra le norme giuridiche) ma della costituzione di una struttura alternativa rispetto alla giustizia politica, come testimoniano i versetti di Matteo immediatamente successivi a quelli riportati: "vi assicuro che tutto quello che voi avrete proibito sulla terra sarà proibito anche in cielo; e tutto quello che voi permetterete sulla terra sarà permesso anche in cielo" (Matteo, 18:18–19)', op. cit., p. 28.

14 See op. cit., p. 70.

15 Indispensable on the subject is the study by Piero Bellini, *'Denunciatio evangelica' e'Denunciatio judicialis privata': un capitolo di storia disciplinare della Chiesa* (Milan, 1986). On the emergence of jurisdiction over secret and occult sins as a fundamental junction in the construction of the bond of obedience and the

Moreover, the need to suppress heretical dissent led to a weakening of the reserved corrective action, favouring procedural action: the hidden sinner became, according to the evolving system of censures, a contumacious person who evaded the justice of the external forum. A society that, after the year 1000, had been transforming and becoming increasingly complex, needed to provide satisfaction systems – integral to the new sacrament of confession in their forms of punishment – that allowed certain categories of individuals (merchants, soldiers, etc.) to continue their activities. It also required mechanisms (tariffed) to commute or anticipate the penalties of Purgatory, an intermediate state between eternal salvation and damnation, arising from individual judgement after death.

A heated debate also developed on the interpretation of the letter of the Gospel passage, particularly regarding the individual or communal nature of sin: in the phrase 'Si autem peccaverit in te frater tuus', did 'in te' mean 'in your presence' or 'against you'? Did it apply only to sins committed against an individual or those against the entire community? What is certain is that '*correctio* increasingly became a mechanism applied in relations between members of "closed" and hierarchical communities: confraternities, universities, religious orders'.[16] The significant influence that the passage from Matthew's Gospel had on the history of the relationship between internal forum and contentious external forum in the repression of hidden crimes, particularly heresy, has been the subject of numerous studies providing very different, even diametrically opposed, interpretations and responses over the past decades.[17] Much less attention, however, has been paid to the relationship between the precept of fraternal correction and the resolution of interpersonal conflict, given that the closed and hierarchical communities

political subject, see Jacques Chiffoleau, *La Chiesa, il segreto e l'obbedienza. La costruzione del soggetto politico nel medioevo* (Bologna, 2010).

[16] 'la *correctio* divenne sempre più un meccanismo applicato nei rapporti tra i membri di comunità "chiuse" e gerarchiche: confraternite, università, ordini religiosi', Vincenzo Lavenia, *L'infamia e il perdono. Tributi, pene e confessione nella teologia morale della prima età moderna* (Bologna, 2004), p. 110. From the same author see also 'Assolvere o infamare. Eresia occulta, correzione fraterna e segreto sacramentale', *Storica* 20–1 (2001), pp. 89–154. On the same topic see Stefania Pastore, 'A proposito di Matteo 18, 15. *Correctio fraterna* e Inquisizione nella Spagna del Cinquecento', Rivista Storica Italiana 113 (2001), pp. 323–68.

[17] See especially Adriano Prosperi, *Tribunali della coscienza. Inquisitori, confessori, missionari* (Torino, 1996); Prodi, *Una storia della giustizia*; Elena Brambilla, *Alle origini del Sant'Uffizio. Penitenza, confessione e giustizia spirituale dal medioevo al XVI secolo* (Bologna, 2000); Giovanni Romeo, *Ricerche su confessione dei peccati e inquisizione nell'Italia del Cinquecento* (Reggio Calabria, 2006).

previously mentioned, which statutorily provided for informal and non-contentious mechanisms for resolving disputes between members, and even between members and outsiders, were conceived as a small-scale reproduction of a Christian society whose judicial mechanisms were to be inspired by the precept of charity and aimed at peace and concord. Sixteenth-century moral theology was unanimous in considering the system of correction as an obligation for the Christian precisely in all those cases where the crime/sin did not endanger the common good (primarily heresy and high treason), and minor interpersonal violence fell exactly into this category.[18]

What occurred was a legal, theological and cultural distancing of penitential practice from the resolution of community conflicts, but this link was never completely severed. The subsequent process of individualisation and psychologisation of sacramental confession, with a progressive shift of focus from the act to the sinful intention/disposition of the soul, and from interpersonal hatred to sins of a sexual nature, reached full completion in the Tridentine and post-Tridentine era. However, this did not prevent confessors from continuing to intervene in family and community conflict dynamics, although in different ways than in the past. John Bossy wrote that 'where the medieval Church promoted penance as a means of removing social hostility, the counter-reformation Church objected to social hostility because it prevented people going to confession'.[19] We will need to verify to what extent this suggestive statement is acceptable; the fact remains that the Church could never lower its attention to social conflict. If commerce and war posed pressing problems of conscience, issues related to kinship, alliance, friendship, honour, and thus peaceful coexistence among Christians continued to represent a primary field of reflection from which a course of action, often not univocal, derived. The Church's attitude was not one of irreducible opposition to violence and conflict; the ecclesiastical culture was extremely porous concerning deeply rooted socio-political dynamics and a value system over which it had little intervention capability and from which it could never completely distance itself.

Theology eventually left open spaces for negotiation with groups and social actors, who certainly did not remain inert to the programmatic disciplining

[18] See for example Bartolomé de Medina in his *Breve instruction de como se ha de administrar el Sacramento de la Penitencia, dividida en dos libros [...] En la qual se contiene todo lo que ha de saber, y hazer el sabio Confessor, para curar almas, y todo lo que deve hazer el penitente para conseguir el fructo de tan admirable medicina* (impresso en Barcelona, en la Imprenta de Gabriel Graells y Giraldo Dotil, 1604), ff. 92^{r-v}.

[19] John Bossy, 'The Social History of Confession in the Age of the Reformation', *Transactions of the Royal Historical Society* Vol. 25 (1975), pp. 21–38: p. 31.

action carried out by the institutions of church and state. Manifestations of hatred needed to be governed, and in governing them, certain aspects could not be ignored. The complete eradication of conflict is a goal beyond the reach of any agency of acculturation, partly because – an aspect too often overlooked – it can be useful to those same agencies. Consider the correlation between the state of enmity and reports to the Inquisition courts for heresy or other crimes related to morality, especially sexual morality, which the Church none the less benefited from, even if sometimes these reports proved unfounded or false.[20] Also, consider the 'consumption of devotions', a field where congregations and devotional associations, mostly composed of laypeople and only partly controlled by ecclesiastical hierarchies, played a significant role in translating social hierarchies and prestige politics, inherently filled with tensions and conflicts, to the level of ritual and ceremonial. Thus, there were spaces of tolerance but also of legitimisation.[21]

Since the early centuries of its existence, the Church had to confront the issue of its relationships with a world made of social connections, of 'flesh and blood',[22] of kinships and factional and clan aggregations, where enmity and conflict were a physiological and omnipresent phenomenon. While

[20] See, for example, Sergio Pagano, *Paesi infetti. Magia, eresia e faide familiari nel tortonese durante il secolo XVI* (Roma, [2003]). On the Roman context, Irene Fosi writes:'C'era poi chi era stato ingiustamente accusato per ignoranza e, molto spesso, per cattiva disposizione di "inimici, emoli e curiosi", il più delle volte annidati fra gli stessi parenti' ('There were also those who were unjustly accused due to ignorance and, very often, due to the ill disposition of "enemies, rivals and busybodies", most often nestled among the same relatives', and further: 'Si suggeriva anche di tenere opportunamente conto dei "memoriali ciechi", delle denunzie anonime che, pur dettate spesso da rancori personali, potevano servire a individuare e punire gli autori di gravi misfatti' ('It was also suggested to appropriately take into account the "blind memorials", anonymous denunciations that, although often dictated by personal grudges, could serve to identify and punish the perpetrators of serious misdeeds'), Irene Fosi, *La giustizia del papa. Sudditi e tribunali nello Stato pontificio in età moderna* (Rome and Bari, 2007), respectively p. 30 and p. 159. On the territories of the Spanish monarchy, see Jaime Contreras, *Sotos contra Riquelmes. Regidores, inquisidores y criptojudíos* (Madrid, 2013), 1st edn: Anaya, 1992.

[21] See Angelo Torre, 'Il consumo di devozioni: rituali e potere nelle campagne piemontesi nella prima metà del Settecento', *Quaderni Storici* 58, 1 (1985), pp. 181–223; Angelo Torre, *Il consumo di devozioni. Religione e comunità nelle campagne dell'* Ancien Régime (Venice, 1995).

[22] See John Bossy, 'Blood and Baptism: Kinship, Community and Christianity in Western Europe from the Fourteenth to the Seventeenth Centuries', in *Sanctity and Secularity. The Church and the World*, ed. D. Baker (Oxford, 1973), pp. 129–43.

historiography has deepened, and largely clarified, the change in the relationship between the Church and social ties of kinship and friendship concerning the administration of marriage, baptism and the celebration of Mass from the Middle Ages to the modern age, less investigated is the attitude that matured in Christian culture regarding the use of judicial instruments of the external forum, both ecclesiastical and secular, concerning the repression of hate crimes and the containment of social conflict.

At first glance, the meaning of the precept of the *denunciatio evangelica* expressed in Matt. 18:15–17 is different from the duty of reconciliation with one's adversary contained in Matt. 5:25–6 and Luke 12:58–9. In the latter case, the reference is to the justice of the traditional Jewish world, to which the Christian should look with a certain degree of caution and suspicion, for reasons already highlighted; in the former case, however, we are faced with the founding act of a forum of judgement distinct from the external one, concerning hidden sins. But in the patristic tradition, a comprehensive, combined interpretation of different places in Scripture emerged that could touch on issues representing the core of a Christian vision of civil coexistence: bonds of friendship, the emergence of enmity, and ways to overcome conflict and interpersonal violence. The homilies of Saint John Chrysostom on the Gospel of Matthew are a guide of great utility in this sense, also for their attempt to provide an explanation of the emergence of enmity and properly Christian ways to overcome it. Conflict, Chrysostom explains in Homily 16, often arises from actions and especially words that are commonly considered minor offences. Why does Jesus state that anyone who utters an insult deserves very severe penalties (Matt. 5:22)? Because even a small offence can generate anger and a desire for revenge. From a small offence to murder, the step can be brief; insults destroy the bond of charity, which is the greatest good of a community, the most sacred of bonds. Paul of Tarsus recommends reconciling with one's enemy before the sun sets (Eph. 4:26) because hatred must be extinguished immediately, not given the chance to mature and rekindle.[23] It is a precept that directly continues the teaching of Jesus expressed in the Sermon on the Mount and taken up by Matthew and Luke: one must not delay reconciliation with one's adversary; one must avoid bringing a brother before the judge, as the effects of a trial can be very damaging.

Jesus's precept of forgiving enemies and the duty of reconciliation was potentially disruptive in a world accustomed to the law of retaliation, just as it would, in the following centuries, encounter many difficulties in coexisting with a culture of revenge that permeated European society and institutions and

[23] 'Be angry but do not sin; do not let the sun set on your anger' ('Irascimini et nolite peccare; sol non occidat super iracundiam vestram').

never entirely subsided. For Jesus, the one who offends us is not a criminal deserving of punishment but a person sick with hatred who must be healed, paradoxically precisely by the person he has offended. The latter, in fact, must seek out his offender and reconcile with him before risking ending up before a judge, as, once in court, one is no longer master of oneself: 'before thou art come to the doors of the court; before thou standest at the bar and art come to be thenceforth under the sway of him that judgeth. Since, before entering in, thou hast all in thine own control; but if thou set thy foot on that threshold, thou wilt not by ever so earnest efforts be able to arrange thy matters at thy will, having come under the constraint of another'.[24] It is better to be willing to give up some of our rights than to risk losing our freedom. Some think that Jesus intended to allude to the devil when he speaks of the adversary, meaning that making an agreement with him actually means refusing to have anything to do with him, which would no longer be possible after death; in reality, Chrysostom asserts, Jesus refers precisely to civil courts. Agreement, reconciliation, benefits the victim to the extent that it avoids submitting to the power of judges and the hatred of trials, and it benefits the offender to the extent that the disconcerting gesture of the victim can heal him from the disease of hatred, thus leading to his conversion. All these precepts concern less serious offences, as evil must be treated before it can reveal itself in its irreparable outcome, that is, murder.

This line of thought, that of Chrysostom, firmly rooted in Christ's preaching and echoed in much sixteenth-century spiritual literature, was instrumental in various ways in projects of Church and religious life reform. It is significant to trace the same theme in the 1537 treatise *Del perdonare* (On Forgiveness) by Tullio Crispolti, a figure of some prominence in the milieu of Italian Evangelism, fully integrated into the spiritual circle animated in Verona by Bishop Gian Matteo Giberti, which included figures like Marcantonio Flaminio, Gasparo Contarini, the Capuchin Giovanni Da Fano and the Erasmian Johann van Kampen. Predominant in these discussions was – as is well known – the issue of the relationship between human works, divine grace and eternal salvation, which would soon monopolise reflections around the *Beneficio di Cristo* (Benefit of Christ), projecting onto devotional practices with a robust communal dimension, within which the ideal of frequent confession and the deliberate use of the instrument of fraternal

[24] *The Homilies of St. John Chrysostom on the Gospel of St. Matthew*, ed. Philip Schaff, vol. X (*St. Chrysostom: Homilies on the Gospel of Saint Matthew*) (Edinburgh, T&T Clarc), 1888 (Homily 16:13).

correction assumed a very significant role.[25] Towards those who offend us, we must not feel hatred or a desire for revenge but compassion, 'knowing that only by having offended have they done as much harm to themselves as no enemy could desire, and that for this reason, it falls to us to be solicitous to remove them from that evil and not do them worse'.[26]

Living in peace, maintaining intact Christian friendships through the exercise of charity, privately correcting a brother who errs and has wronged us to prevent a public correction or trial from scandalising the community and humiliating the offender: these are all behaviours aimed at preventing more serious violence, and the link between the precept of reconciliation and the precept of fraternal correction is evident. The one who offends someone is a victim as much as his own victim: he is a victim of the hatred he harbours in his heart, and intervention is needed to heal him. Indeed, God seeks the good of both the offended and the offender, but the latter is more a victim than the former because he has been overcome by his anger and succumbed to evil; Jesus wants his salvation, not his punishment. That is why Jesus commands the victim of the offence, free from that disease of the soul, to seek out the one who has offended him, not the other way around. But all this has meaning only if the one who has offended us is a Christian brother; this precept does not apply to pagans and infidels. The brother who sins must be admonished in secret, as it is presumed that he will be more willing to be corrected if such correction comes from his victim and is done secretly. Only if he persists can third-party intervention be sought: a couple of witnesses, or the entire community, according to a precise gradation of corrective intervention. The failure of all these attempts decrees the incurability of the offender's disease and his downgrade to the level of pagans and tax collectors.

That the practice of fraternal correction later increasingly restricted itself to the realm of hidden sins, particularly heresy, does not contradict the fact that it is part of a series of precepts originating from the need to contain conflict, enmity, the culture of hatred and revenge, through transactional and non-contentious means. And the subsequent verses of Matthew 18 are nothing

[25] See Paolo Salvetto, *Tullio Crispoldi nella crisi religiosa del Cinquecento. Le difficili 'pratiche del viver christiano'* (Brescia, 2009), pp. 114–26.

[26] 'sapendo che solo per haverne offeso han fatto tanto male a se stessi quanto a niuno inimico potria desiderar, et che per questo a noi tocca di esser solleciti di levarli di quel male et di non far loro peggio', *Alcune ragioni del perdonare, raccolte per Tullio Crispoldo da Riete* (in *Vinegia*, per Stephano da Sabbio, 1539), unnumbered pages. On Tullio Crispolti from Rieti and his treatise, see also Ottavia Niccoli, *Perdonare. Idee, pratiche, rituali in Italia tra Cinque e Seicento* (Rome and Bari, 2007), pp. 138–41.

but a celebration of the sacredness of friendship understood in a Christian sense, of the union that must prevail among brothers, of forgiveness.[27] Strong friendship, the one that does not break at the first accident, is friendship in Christ. Not an external and human union but an internal and divine union; not a friendship founded on mutual interest and the satisfaction of earthly and transient needs, as such bonds easily transform into mortal enmities.

Already in the time of Chrysostom, who insisted on the literal meaning of the relevant Gospel passages, the precept of reconciliation with one's adversary was subject to anagogical readings. Augustine, for example, identified the adversary with whom one must come to terms before he hands us over to the judge with the word of God. When one wants to sin, the adversary of the will is the word of God; we must seek it to avoid sinning, to find an agreement with it, long before the day of individual judgement, whose arrival we cannot foresee.[28] And, with a reference to Ezekiel 3:18, Augustine also recalls how compelling the obligation for the Christian to admonish a sinning brother is, regardless of whether the former is righteous or wicked, because, in the act of correction, it is God's law that operates, not the individual Christian, who becomes a mere instrument; just as we must joyfully accept someone admonishing us that we are acting against Christ's teaching. In such cases, we perceive the one correcting us as an adversary, but in reality, it is God Himself operating through him, and for this reason, seeking agreement means seeking it with the one admonishing us but also, and above all, with God Himself and His law.[29] The law is our adversary, with which

[27] '"Amen, I say to you, whatever you bind on earth shall be bound in heaven, and whatever you loose on earth shall be loosed in heaven. Again, (amen,) I say to you, if two of you agree on earth about anything for which they are to pray, it shall be granted to them by my heavenly Father. For where two or three are gathered together in my name, there am I in the midst of them." Then Peter approaching asked him, "Lord, if my brother sins against me, how often must I forgive him? As many as seven times?" Jesus answered, "I say to you, not seven times but seventy-seven times"', ('"Amen dico vobis: Quaecumque alligaveritis super terram, erunt ligata in caelo; et, quaecumque solveritis super terram, erunt soluta in caelo. Iterum dico vobis: Si duo ex vobis consenserint super terram de omni re, quamcumque petierint, fiet illis a Patre meo, qui in caelis est. Ubi enim sunt duo vel tres congregati in nomine meo, ibi sum in medio eorum." Tunc accedens Petrus dixit ei: "Domine, quotiens peccabit in me frater meus, et dimittam ei? Usque septies?". Dicit illi Iesus: "Non dico tibi usque septies sed usque septuagies septies"'), Matt. 18:18–22.

[28] St Augustine, *Sermons*, vol. III/4 (94a–147a on the New Testament), translation and notes Edmund Hill O.P., editor John E. Rotelle O.S.A. (New York, 1992), *sermon* 109, 2–3, pp. 133–4.

[29] Op. cit., vol. III/10 (341–400), *sermon* 387, pp. 397–400.

we must make peace before arriving at the divine tribunal. *Correctio* and reconciliation appear as closely linked.

The evangelical precept of reaching an agreement with one's adversary before bringing him before the judge was precisely received in this way in moral and catechetical literature, as well as in Christian homiletics, without thereby undermining its literal meaning. On the contrary, the anagogical reading only reinforced that parallelism between human justice and divine justice upon which the entire Christian conception of justice was based: just as the remission of guilt in the confessional through contrition/attrition, and the execution of *satisfactio* as part of the sacrament of penance, were not able to completely extinguish divine vindicative justice, from which descends a punishment to be expiated in Purgatory, similarly, the agreement with the offended party and the *restitutio*/reparation (*ex iustitia commutativa*) do not protect the guilty party from punishment *ex iustitia vindicativa*.[30] One could even hypothesise a specular relationship between indulgence and tariffed transaction with the offended party (where possible) to the extent that both are able to impact the severity of the penalty inflicted: by God in the first case, by the earthly judge in the second.

The same indication is given by St Paul in the first letter to the Corinthians, chapter 6, where he deems it inconceivable that a Christian would prefer to submit his disputes to pagan judges rather than to the arbitration of Christian brothers:

> How can any one of you with a case against another dare to bring it to the unjust for judgement instead of to the holy ones? Do you not know that the holy ones will judge the world? If the world is to be judged by you, are you unqualified for the lowest law courts? Do you not know that we will judge angels? Then why not everyday matters? If, therefore, you have courts for everyday matters, do you seat as judges people of no standing in the church? I say this to shame you. Can it be that there is not one among you wise enough to be able to settle a case between brothers? But rather

[30] Thus, Luis de Molina in *De iustitia et iure, Disputatio* 715 (*Discrimen inter restitutionem, & satisfactionem, & num pro iniuria & offensa, sumptis praecisè, à damno dato, restitutio debeatur?*), nos 3–4, on which see Maria Sole Testuzza, 'Rimediare al male con il bene. La giustizia e il perdono della vittima nell'età della Controriforma: tra Restitutio, Satisfactio/Satispassio e Potestas in se ipsum', *Vergentis* 4 (2017), pp. 267–95: p. 279. Regarding the theological construction of Purgatory, which made the practice of indulgences possible and constituted one of the major points of conflict with the Reformed world, the obligatory reference is Jacques Le Goff, *La naissance du Purgatoire* (Paris, 1981). On the Italian echoes of this conflict, and in particular on the case of Francesco Spiera, see Adriano Prosperi, *L'eresia del Libro Grande. Storia di Giorgio Siculo e la sua setta* (Milano, 2000), pp. 104ff.

brother goes to court against brother, and that before unbelievers? Now indeed (then) it is, in any case, a failure on your part that you have lawsuits against one another. Why not rather put up with injustice? Why not rather let yourselves be cheated? Instead, you inflict injustice and cheat, and this to brothers. Do you not know that the unjust will not inherit the kingdom of God? Do not be deceived; neither fornicators nor idolaters nor adulterers nor boy prostitutes nor practising homosexuals nor thieves nor the greedy nor drunkards nor slanderers nor robbers will inherit the kingdom of God. That is what some of you used to be; but now you have had yourselves washed, you were sanctified, you were justified in the name of the Lord Jesus Christ and in the Spirit of our God.[31]

The progressive Christianisation of the Roman imperial structure and the subsequent emergence of power and jurisdictional structures openly conceived as direct derivations of the power of the Christian God, aimed at ensuring peace by judging sins/crimes, eliminated the main premise of Pauline argumentation, since secular courts could no longer be considered akin to pagan ones. Nevertheless, the combined disposition of various passages denotes an attitude towards the apparatus of justice that can be considered typical of Christian culture, especially concerning the disputes that Paul defines as 'saecularia iudicia', an expression that refers to that everyday litigiousness ('lower lawcourts') which could arise from various motivations and cannot be confined exclusively to civil and commercial cases. Yet theft, unpaid debts, unfulfilled contracts, slander and defamatory injury could well generate hatred and lead to episodes of violence, and the fatal outcome of murder was not such an improbable eventuality.

[31] 'Audet aliquis vestrum habens negotium adversus alterum iu dicari apud iniquos et non apud sanctos? An nescitis quoniam sancti de mundo iudicabunt? Et si in vobis iudicabitur mundus, indigni estis minimis iudiciis? Nescitis quoniam angelos iudicabimus, quanto magis saecularia? Saecularia igitur iudicia si habueritis, contemptibiles, qui sunt in ecclesia, illos constituite ad iudicandum? Ad verecundiam vestram dico! Sic non est inter vos sapiens quisquam, qui possit iudicare inter fratrem suum? Sed frater cum fratre iudicio contendit, et hoc apud infideles? Iam quidem omnino defectio est vobis, quod iudicia habetis inter vosmetipsos! Quare non magis iniuriam accipitis, quare non magis fraudem patimini? Sed vos iniuriam facitis et fraudatis, et hoc fratribus! An nescitis quia iniqui regnum Dei non possidebunt? Nolite errare: neque fornicarii neque idolis servientes neque adulteri neque molles neque masculorum concubitores neque fures neque avari, non ebriosi, non maledici, non rapaces regnum Dei possidebunt. Et haec quidam fuistis. Sed abluti estis, sed sanctificati estis, sed iustificati estis in nomine Domini Iesu Christi et in Spiritu Dei nostri!', 1 Cor. 6:1–11.

The Pauline dictum, based on Christ's teaching as testified by Matthew and Luke, opened a fundamental path for the birth of a line of thought that centred on the preference for arbitration (among 'brothers') over judgement as the outcome of a judicial proceeding, all of this in parallel – and without contradiction – with the subsequent vigorous development of canon law, episcopal courts and, later, even inquisitorial ones.[32] What is expressed in the gospels is not so much a distrust of secular justice, courtrooms and judges as potentially corrupt or biased, nor of external forum justice *per se*, but rather of the mechanism of the judicial process if used to contain ordinary conflict, to heal the state of enmity. It is considered as not necessarily the most suitable instrument for achieving justice and asserting one's rights for types of crimes that do not harm the established order and the bond of loyalty that binds subjects to power. Often, the court case is won not by those who are right but by those who know how best to exploit legal loopholes, who have better dialectical skills, who can afford the best lawyers – all behaviours that certainly violate the Christian precepts of charity and justice.

A conflict of any nature, even religious, can be more easily resolved if one avoids entering into a contentious and forensic dynamic, provided one maintains a meek and moderate spirit. Among others, Augustine explains this very well in the midst of the anti-Donatist struggle, a moment that paradoxically marked a change in the Bishop of Hippo's attitude towards heretics in the direction of adopting repressive methods.[33] In the polemic engaged against Cresconius, a grammarian and rhetorician who had intervened in defence of Petilianus, Bishop of Cirta in Numidia, Saint Augustine writes:

> Also, you criticise that effort to strive for the truth – because we often wanted to discuss it with you, so that, once the error was removed, fraternal charity would rejoice in the bond of peace – by labelling it with the negative name of contentiousness and hostility. Would it not be better, I ask you, that the cause of truth and unity be addressed among bishops with peaceful words and in more tranquil settings, rather than litigated in a court by bishops through lawyers? What was done by the supporters of Primian, your bishop of Carthage, against Maximian and those who

[32] See Luca Loschiavo, 'Non est inter vos sapiens quisquam, qui possit iudicare inter fratrem suum? Processo e giustizia nel primo cristianesimo dalle origini al vescovo Ambrogio', in *Ravenna Capitale. Giudizi, giudici e norme processuali in Occidente nei secoli IV-VIII*, vol. I (Saggi), ed. Gisella Bassanelli Sommariva (Santarcangelo di Romagna, 2015), pp. 67–106. More extensively, see Luca Loschiavo, *L'età del passaggio. All'alba del diritto comune europeo (secoli III-VII)* (Turin, 2019), pp. 61–113.

[33] Cf. Geoffrey G. Willis, *St. Augustine and the Donatist Controversy* (London, 1950).

> were condemned with him in the council of Bagai, before the legate at Carthage and before four or more proconsuls. Surely, in a debate, precautions must be taken to prevent it from escalating into a quarrel, and such precautions can and should be maintained by those who are restrained and gentle. But when the dispute is brought to the forum with lawyers contending on both sides, then it is, without a doubt, already a litigation. Nor do I criticise your people for this if they were compelled by necessity to seek counsel, rather than by a love of litigation. However, I urge you – a man endowed with good sense – to consider, to understand, and to realise that those who did not avoid, but instead undertook and pursued, the noise of the forum and the legal disputes in which they aimed to convict and expel those they had already condemned in council, could have much more easily debated peacefully with us. They preferred to cover a weak case with excuses rather than to settle it through discussion.[34]

A reasonable agreement is far better than a trial, an adage destined to have great resonance in subsequent centuries, up to recent times, when the process of state formation and the imposition of its jurisdiction could well be said to be completed. This is not only evident in religious literature, as the maxim attributed to Honoré de Balzac and placed in the epigraph of this volume demonstrates. To reach an agreement, it is necessary to free oneself from hatred, resentment and the desire for revenge, and to arm oneself with reasonableness. Entering into a contentious dynamic means exposing oneself to the temptation of sin. Therefore, it is better to reach an agreement before going to court, as advised by Luke and Matthew, also because no one can be

[34] 'Illud etiam, quod studium pro veritate certandi, quia saepe voluimos conferre cum vestris, ut errore sublato fraterna caritas pacis vinculo laetaretur, contentionis et animositatis vitioso nomine reprehendis: nonne melius, obsecro te, causa veritatis et unitatis pacificis verbis et pacatioribus locis inter episcopos ageretur, quam in foro ab episcopis per advocatos litigaretur? Quod a partibus Primiani Carthaginiensis episcopi vestri adversus Maximianum et adversus eos, qui cum illo Bagaiensi concilio damnati sunt, apud legatum Carthaginis et apud quattuor vel amplius proconsules factum est. Certe in collatione disputationis hoc cavendum est, ne prorumpatur in litem, et caveri a modestis et mitibus et potest et solet; cum vero advocatis utrinque luctantibus in foro controversia vertitur, iam procul dubio litigatur. Neque hoc in vestris reprehendo, si ad hoc non amore litigandi, sed consulendi necessitate compulsi sunt; verumtamen admoneo te bono ingenio praeditum virum, ut advertas, ut sentias, ut intellegas eos, qui forensem strepitum et iudiciaria iurgia, quibus accusatos convincerent et expellerent quos in concilio iam damnaverant, non declinaverunt, sed susceperunt exercuerunt, multo nobiscum facilius pacifice conferre potuisse, nisi mallent causam malam cooperire excusatione quam disputatione finire', Augustine of Hippo, *Contra Cresconium Grammaticum Donatistam Libri Quatuor*, IV, §3 (my translation).

sure of emerging unscathed from a judicial proceeding. Indeed, one goes to the judge to win against the opposing party, but one can easily end up losing, and thus being sentenced to prison. Furthermore, the trial can become an instrument of oppression of the poor and the weaker individuals. This opened up what we might call an intermediate ground between the penitential internal forum and the contentious external forum, in which negotiation tools – a natural extension of fraternal correction – represent the prevalent method for containing conflict within the community, without the *a priori* exclusion of the intervention of external forum instruments. This is also because it would be difficult to confine enmity to the territory of notorious sins, as the confessor can investigate the inner – and hidden – conscience of the penitent, where hatred, resentment and the desire for revenge are cultivated.

It could be said that the Church intended to establish, from ancient times, a specific jurisdiction over hatred, to some extent alternative to the ordinary mechanisms of judgement and punishment of the guilty, which centred on the sacrament of penance and necessarily also on that distinction, introduced by Augustine and later incorporated into Gratian's *Decretum*, between venial sins, the faults to which all cannot but fall, and grave sins or crimes, for which one is 'accusatione et damnatione dignissimum' ('worthy of accusation and condemnation').[35] A jurisdiction that entailed the keeping of a true and proper account of the 'enemies' by parish priests was finally made possible by the application of the decree *Omnis utriusque sexus* of the Fourth Lateran Council (1215), which imposed on all the faithful the obligation of confession to their 'own priest' at least once a year and the impossibility for the confessor to grant absolution to those who refused to forgive and make peace with their enemies. However, the relationship between the Church and the world, between the Church and society, between the Church and family groups did not end here, as the evocative pages of John Bossy have shown us. The history of the medieval Church is the history of an institution for which 'the admission of a variety of forms of the extended kin-group, natural and artificial, as constituent elements in its life became fundamental'.[36] Penance was just one piece of a sacramental edifice aimed at maintaining peace

[35] In the *Tractatus in Johannis evangelium* Augustine established that candidates for the priesthood do not need to be without sin, but they must not have committed 'crimes', 'such as, murder, adultery, any uncleanness of fornication, theft, fraud, sacrilege, and others of that sort' ('sicuti est homicidium, adulterium, aliqua immunditia fornicationis, furtum, fraus, sacrilegium, et caetera huiusmodi'), *Nicene and Post-Nicene Fathers*, ed. Philip Schaf, vol. VII (*Homilies on the Gospel of John; Homilies on the First Epistle of John; Soliloquies*) (Grand Rapids, 1979), p. 382.

[36] John Bossy, *Blood and Baptism*, pp.129–30.

in a world dominated by feuds: marriage, in its role as a contract between two hostile groups mediated by intermediaries and sealed with a ritual of peace;[37] baptism, which 'brings into play the bonds of existing kinship, and creates new ones',[38] especially through godparenthood and the creation of spiritual kinship, aimed at extending natural kinship relations to broaden networks of friendship.[39] The primary task of the parish priest was always to calm conflicts and pacify feuds; the establishment of formal, predominantly horizontal relationships, constituted and cemented by sacramental and cult practices, served exactly this purpose.

Regarding the judicial realm more specifically, from the earliest centuries, Christian thought contributed to delineating an idea of earthly justice intimately connected with the concepts of charity and mercy. Augustine, although not dedicating any specific work to the theme, made his contribution from his concrete experience as an ecclesiastical judge in times marked by great conflicts. As Bishop of Hippo, he had to deal with delicate issues, including the treatment to be reserved for the *mangones*, slave traders, against whom a law issued by Emperor Honorius had prescribed punishment and perpetual banishment or death. In his correspondence with Alipius, Augustine declares that he intends to use the imperial legislation but does not want to apply it in its extreme form, as punishments and capital punishment are legitimate deterrent tools and therefore dissuasive, but their execution is useless in so far as the criminal, by dying, would no longer have the possibility of repenting.[40] According to Augustine, the ultimate aim of the law lies in the cessation of injustice and, at the same time, in the amendment of the criminal's behaviour, whereas the execution of a particularly severe punishment can trigger reprisals and vendettas, thereby perpetuating evil.[41] The fear of punishment for breaking the law is a necessary but not

[37] The definition is taken from John K. Campbell, *Honour, Family and Patronage. A Study of Institutions and Moral Values in a Greek Mountain Community* (Oxford, 1964).

[38] Bossy, *Blood and Baptism*, p. 132.

[39] See Guido Alfani, *Fathers and Godfathers. Spiritual Kinship in Early-Modern Italy* (London, 2009), original edition: *Padri, padrini, patroni. La parentela spirituale nella storia* (Venice, 2006).

[40] See Aldo Andrea Cassi, *La Giustizia in S. Agostino. Itinerari agostiniani del* quartus fluvius *dell'Eden* (Milan, 2013); Aldo Andrea Cassi, 'Agostino contro i mercanti di schiavi: *Ius gladii, ungulae carnificis* e funzione della pena', *Etica & Politica / Ethics & Politics* XVI, 1 (2014), pp. 457–71.

[41] 'In no way, then, do we approve of the sins that we want to be corrected, nor do we want the wrongdoing to go unpunished because we find it pleasing. Rather,

sufficient element, as the penalty must also have a preventive function, and the only way to prevent further crimes is to make the transition from fear of punishment to love of good: 'Not because those who avoid sin out of fear are to be pronounced good; for no one is good who is good out of fear of punishment, but out of love of justice' (*Epistle* 153, 6:16). The *ius puniendi* is necessary and forms the basis of the legitimacy of political authority, but it alone is not enough; an openness to mercy is needed, which is not at all in contradiction with the penalty. The criminal must, in essence, convert to good based on an inner conviction and not merely the fear of punishment. This is also why Augustine exhorts Donatus, proconsul of Africa, to punish the Donatists but not to kill them, even going so far as to say that he would not hesitate to refrain from denouncing them before courts that applied the death penalty (*Epistle* 100, §2).

A double parallelism can be seen in Augustine's conception of justice, destined to become one of the salient features of Christian thought *tout court*. The dimension of forgiveness and reconciliation involves not only the higher authority, which can pardon a penalty through the granting of grace, but also the lower, meaning the criminal who, to avoid returning to crime, must undertake a path of conversion to good, just as the victim of the crime must forgive their enemy in obedience to the evangelical precept. God is not willing to forgive those who do not forgive.[42] The other parallelism is between crime and sin from the perspective of repentance and its absolution, with a clear reference to the distinction between attrition and contrition, a distinction which Christian moral theology has continued to discuss for centuries.[43] The fear of punishment acts extrinsically on the ability to commit evil, not on the will; to act on the will, an intervention on the interiority is

having compassion for the person and detesting the sin or crime, the more we are displeased by the sin the less we want the sinful person to perish without having been corrected', Augustine of Hippo, *Letters 100-155*, II/2, translation and notes by Roland Teske, S.J., ed. Boniface Ramsey (New York, 2003), *Letter* 153, 1.3, p. 392 ('Nullo modo ergo culpas quas corrigi volumus, approbamus, nec quod perperam committitur, ideo volumus impunitum esse, quia placet; sed hominem miserantes, facinus autem seu flagitium detestantes, quanto magis nobis displicet vitium, tanto minus volumus inemendatum interire vitiosum').

42 'If you forgive others their transgressions, your heavenly Father will forgive you. But if you do not forgive others, neither will your Father forgive your transgressions' ('Si enim dimiseritis hominibus peccata eorum, dimittet et vobis Pater vester caelestis; si autem non dimiseritis hominibus, nec Pater vester dimittet peccata vestra'), *Mt* 6:14–15, but also *Col* 3:13; *Ef* 4:32; *Mk* 11:25.

43 See Pietro Stella, 'Attrizione e contrizione in età moderna: l'importanza storica di una disputa irrisolta', *Annali di Scienze Religiose* 3 (1998), pp. 151–72.

needed, which ultimately is *sub specie Dei*.[44] Additionally, the convergence – recently emphasised by Katherine L. Jansen – between a penitential practice gradually increasingly centred on the examination of conscience and the circumstances of sin, which the confessor was called to investigate like a real judge, and peace agreements that similarly 'spelled out the circumstances of the crimes committed and relieved both the victim and perpetrator of guilt, allowing forgiveness and reconciliation to take place between adversarial parties', should not be underestimated.[45]

The two dimensions, of the trial and of the agreement (perhaps reached through the intervention of arbitrators, the 'witnesses' of the passage from the Gospel of Matthew), are therefore not only perfectly compatible but co-essential to the proper functioning of justice. Hegemonic justice and negotiated justice, to use the expressions coined by Mario Sbriccoli, are perfectly inscribed within the Christian structure of criminal justice. Just as the sinner must seek reconciliation with God before the universal judgement, before it is too late, the *litigiousus* must seek agreement with his adversary before taking him to court, but this does not negate the legitimacy, necessity and irreplaceability of the latter's existence; nor does it negate that the criminal/sinner can be urged, if not in fact forced, to seek an agreement, just as it does not negate that pardons can be 'tariffed', exactly like indulgences. Early modern judicial practice perfectly reflects the theoretical assumption just outlined, since the imposition of a penalty despite the achievement of peace (or the signing of a renunciation) represents a rather frequent occurrence, although more typical of conflicts among the lower classes.[46]

The relationship between *restitutio* and *satisfactio/satispassio* (punishment) in relation to absolution was a focal point of Catholic moral theology from the sixteenth century, giving rise to lively debates. The tendency, especially in the practice of sacramental confession, was to give less and less social relevance to the element of *satisfactio*: Cardinal De Vio had already written that satisfactions should be 'medicinal' and not vindictive. Monetary compensations towards the offended parties were the means by which the faithful could align their conscience, just as alms were the means by which those who received illicit or dubious gains could 'restore the stolen goods' without knowing exactly to whom to restore them. In this way, a state of

44 See Cassi, *Agostino contro i mercanti di schiavi*, p. 470.

45 Katherine L. Jansen, *Peace and Penance in Late Medieval Italy* (Princeton and Oxford, 2018), p. 211.

46 See Claudio Povolo, *L'intrigo dell'onore. Poteri e istituzioni nella Repubblica di Venezia tra Cinque e Seicento* (Sommacampagna, 1997), p. 137.

horizontal justice was restored, but the question of the vertical relationship between the penitent and God or the State remained open.

Satisfaction as an afflictive element was the exclusive competence of the confessor/judge, but while the penalties inflicted by the confessor were increasingly spiritual-medicinal in nature, Catholic moral theology increasingly entrusted the task of punishing the guilty to the sentences of public magistrates, assigning a significant role to the injured party in the penitential/procedural mechanism. In his *De iustitia et iure*, Luis de Molina clarified that a transaction (at a fair price) capable of stopping a trial, where there was no specific prohibition by positive law, was always lawful but might still not be deemed sufficient by the injured party. In this case, as well as when the crime had caused damage, the trial became inevitable, and the forgiveness already granted by the victim, while capable of extinguishing the hatred held in their heart, would need to be supplemented by the *satisfactio/satispassio* legitimately inflicted by virtue of the imposition of the penalty.[47]

Low crimes, within the perimeter of which homicide fell, were still deeply linked in the late sixteenth century to systems of initiating trials at the request of the injured party, especially if issues of honour were involved. But what was the contribution of Christian culture in outlining the appropriateness of resorting to a court of external forum in cases of offences, insults, beatings, assaults, wounds and killings?

2. Judicial litigiousness as an illness to be cured

The reality of the excessive power or corruption of judges is a common theme in the literary genre of *specula principum*, where the ideal sovereign is always vigilant, judicious in the selection of judges, and ready to intervene in case of abuses. We owe to Rodolfo De Mattei a brief essay on that fracture line between 'politicians' and 'jurists' which began to deepen in correlation with the explosion of treatises on the *Reason of State*.[48] It was a true disdain, harboured by political writers, towards jurists, who were seen as petty, dry and captious interpreters of the laws, incapable of reaching the higher principles of moral philosophy and aspiring to equity; people who thrive on disputes, the true pestilence of the century. Traces of this polemic, which had already begun with Humanism, can be found – with slightly different

47 See Testuzza, *Rimediare al male con il bene*.

48 See Rodolfo De Mattei, 'La vertenza tra "filosofi politici" e "legisti"', in Rodolfo De Mattei, *Il pensiero politico italiano nell'età della Controriforma*, vol. I (Milan and Naples, 1982), pp. 164–87.

nuances – in authors such as Ludovico Zuccolo, Fabio Albergati, Traiano Boccalini, Giovanni Antonio Palazzo, Scipione Ammirato and Virgilio Malvezzi. Alongside the exaltation of ancient times for having few laws and much virtue, there is a sharp critique of the present, plagued instead by the multiplication of laws and, above all, by the malice of the ever-increasing number of practical jurists, always ready to cite authorities and interpret them by distorting their meaning just to win cases and enrich themselves.

> Among so many interpreters and glossators who, with sophistries, twist and distort the intentions of the Legislator, the guilty always find some hiding place to shield themselves from the sword of justice amidst the infinity of counsels, treatises and readings; or they do not fear it, seeing it has lost its edge and point in the great disputes that the Legists have among themselves with a thousand doctrines, opinions and decisions, each one contrary to the other.[49]

The critique of the corruption of judges, the mismanagement of justice, and the entire prevailing legal system, 'overabundant and confused, [...] far from the primitive simplicity of customs',[50] as well as the attack on the practical knowledge of jurists, emerged precisely at the height of the legal profession's prominence within the socio-political fabric of seventeenth-century states. The two strands invoked so far – the religious distrust of courts of law and the secular derision of jurists – are not perfectly superimposable but share an important aspect: the judicial process, if used to handle minor crimes and the ordinary and unavoidable social litigiousness, becomes a useless and counterproductive tool as it tends to foment and simultaneously submit to an *esprit de chicane* that concerns not only the proverbial pettifoggers ('causidici e legulei') but also – and this is the most interesting aspect – the litigants themselves. The process does not cure but, rather, perpetuates hatred. What needs to be restored is friendship, and only an agreement can do this, as both the recourse to the process and its outcome are expressions of revenge

[49] 'Tra tanti interpreti e glossatori che vanno con fanfaluche stirando e stravolgendo i sentimenti del Legislatore, al reo si scopre sempre qualche ripostiglio da nascondersi dalla spada della giustizia tra la infinità de' consigli, de' trattati e delle letture; o pur non la teme, vedendola aver perduto il taglio e la punta nelle gran contese che fanno tra di loro i Leggisti con mille dottrine e pareri e decisioni, l'una contraria all'altra', Ludovico Zuccolo, *Considerazioni politiche e morali sopra cento oracoli d'illustri personaggi antichi* (Venezia, Presso N. Ginami, 1621), p. 371, cited in De Mattei, *La vertenza tra'filosofi politici' e'legisti'*, p. 171, n. 32.

[50] 'sovrabbondante e confuso, [...] lontano dalla primitiva semplicità dei costumi', Italo Birocchi, *Alla ricerca dell'ordine. Fonti e cultura giuridica nell'età moderna* (Turin, 2002), p. 275.

rather than justice. From this perspective, even the numerous memorials, signed or anonymous, which flowed into the chanceries of Italian states especially in the first half of the seventeenth century to expose distortions, evils, excesses and deficiencies in the governance of justice, assume new tones. These writings cannot be collectively reduced to a generic denunciation of judicial corruption. In the *Discorso sopra il buon governo di Roma*, for example, beyond the observation of excessive rigour, often bordering on cruelty, with which criminal justice was mostly administered by the courts, the anonymous author was perfectly aware of the need to distinguish between serious crimes (against God), for which severe measures must be taken, and lesser crimes (against men), 'quarrels and resentments deriving from anger, such as blows and insulting words even among the lowest people and women',[51] for which it is useless to burden the already overworked courts, to the benefit of the pockets of lawyers and prosecutors, always ready to alter facts to gain from cases. In these cases, clemency is preferable.

When the tearing apart of political order is not at stake, a notion that, as is known, has a sacred connotation (not by chance the memorial speaks of crimes 'against God' to indicate the *crimina atrociora*), contentious justice is useless as it cannot cure the evil at its root and can even be counterproductive. This was certainly not a new concept. In Italian communal society, relationships between individuals – especially those of the military aristocracy – were invariably read, in the various testimonies available, through the dichotomous pair friendship/enmity, where the latter term inexorably prevailed over the former. An example comes from Boncompagno da Signa's *Amicitia*, dating to the early thirteenth century, a work that, as has been written, deals with the opposite of friendship, namely hatred, the fundamentally imprudent nature of man, and the utilitarian, if not opportunistic, root of friendship.[52] More optimistic, however, was Albertanus of Brescia, a jurist and literatus, who in the *Liber consolationis et consilii*, written in 1246, a few decades later than Boncompagno's work, offers readers not only a thorough examination of the mechanisms of conflict but also a vivid testimony to the centrality of *consilium* (counsel) in choosing strategies to resolve it, within

[51] 'risse e risentimenti d'ira per leggierissimi che siano, come di pugni, di parole ingiuriose etiandio tra gente infima e donnicciuole', cited in Fosi, *La giustizia del papa*, p. 170. The anonymous memoir is found in BC, ms. 2097, cc. 253^{r}–290^{v}.

[52] See Jean-Claude Maire Vigueur, *Cavalieri e cittadini. Guerra, conflitti e società nell'Italia comunale* (Bologna, 2004), pp. 399–400. See also Boncompagno da Signa, *L'assedio di Ancona. Liber de obsidione Ancone*, ed. Paolo Garbini (Rome, 1999).

which revenge and pacification appear as options to be carefully evaluated.[53] Revisiting concepts fully expressed in the *De amore et dilectione Dei et proximi et aliarum rerum et de forma vitae* (1238),[54] in the dialogue between Melibeo, the perfect embodiment of the knight, and his wife Prudenzia, a wrong suffered by the former at the hands of three enemies who entered his house to insult and beat the women of his family is narrated. The council, gathered in the knight's house, deliberates, with the majority in favour of a vengeful response to the serious wrong suffered, but Prudenzia intervenes, trying to convince Melibeo not to follow the council's outcome, primarily because in this field it is not prudent to trust certain categories of people (youths, flatterers, false friends) whom he had made the mistake of convening, but also because revenge is dangerous if certain conditions (wealth, military power, size and cohesion of lineage) are not met.

To Melibeo's arguments about the need to punish crimes, also to prevent their proliferation, Prudenzia replies that the proper revenge is public, guaranteed by recourse to courts, to 'judges, who have command and jurisdiction',[55] who have the precise duty to punish wrongdoers, because 'the judge who does not chastise the sinner commands to sin. Therefore, the judge must take revenge by punishing men corporeally and pecuniarily'.[56] However, Melibeo counters that the judicial revenge does not satisfy him:'such revenge displeases me; because they would care little about a bad name and the loss of money. But they would care about the person: and I, who am pure and clean, could not live without dishonour and shame for the injury done to me and my daughter, receiving judicial revenge'.[57] The outcome of a judicial process, although

[53] See Andrea Zorzi, 'Consigliare alla vendetta, consigliare alla giustizia. Pratiche e culture politiche nell'Italia comunale', *Archivio Storico Italiano* 170, 2 (2012), pp. 263–84.

[54] The vernacular translation of three works by Albertanus, published by Bastiano de' Rossi in 1610 by the Giunti press, is used here. Albertanus of Brescia, *Tre trattati d'Albertano Giudice da Brescia. Il primo della dilezion d'Iddio, e del prossimo, e della forma dell'onesta vita. Il secondo della consolazione, e de' Consigli. Il terzo delle sei maniere del parlare, scritti da lui in lingua latina dall'Anno 1235, infino all'Anno 1246 e traslatati ne' medesimi tempi, in volgar fiorentino* (Firenze, appresso i Giunti, 1610), pp. 92ff.

[55] 'giudici, che hanno imperio, e giurisdizione', op. cit., p. 171.

[56] 'lo giudice, che non gastiga lo peccatore, comanda di peccare. Dunque lo giudice dee far vendetta, punendo gli huomini corporalmente, e pecunialmente', ibid.

[57] 'cotal vendetta mi dispiace; perocché del mal nome, e del perdimento della pecunia, poco curerebbono. Ma della persona si curerebbono: e io, che son netto, e mondo, per l'ingiuria fatta a me, e alla mia figliuola, senza disonore, e vituperio vivere non potrei, ricevendo vendetta giudiciale', op. cit., p. 172.

favourable, would not be able to recover for Melibeo either the offended honour or the financial losses suffered. Prudenzia's proposed solution, which will later be accepted by Melibeo, is the path of negotiation and peace, the only one capable of curing the evil at its root, an evil in which everyone recognised the seed of the dissolution of the communal regime. To Melibeo's doubt about the concrete possibility of resorting to reconciliation ('How can I reconcile with my enemies: they started the discord, they do not ask for concord'),[58] Prudenzia responds that the Christian must first ask for peace from his enemy, forgiving the received injury, to overcome evil with good: the Franciscan influence, as well as that of Seneca's thought, is immediately perceptible in the pages of the *Liber consolationis et consilii*. Recourse to courts, the search for public revenge, appears as one of the possible options, to be carefully evaluated along with others, not accepted unquestionably as the only one, while the path of reconciliation, forgiveness and peace is for Albertanus the preferable one, although much more difficult to undertake as it implies a *conversio* of the aggressor.[59]

The mechanisms of the process are judged to be lacking in virtue, incompatible with *pietas*, with the sentiment of charity and ultimately incompatible with individual salvation. It is a negative conception of procedural mechanisms that has given rise to specific terms. In the early modern age, in the French language, as already noted, the term 'chicane' indicated the 'difficulty raised to complicate a judicial matter';[60] and also the verb 'chicaner', first attested in 1460 and of uncertain etymology, which from the meaning of 'poursuivre en justice' ('pursue in justice') (*Grand Testament* by François Villon, 1460) passes to that of 'raise difficulties to complicate a judicial matter' (*Thresor de la langue françoyse* by Jean Nicot, 1606),[61] and according to this latter meaning was used by ecclesiastical apparatuses to encourage arbitration solutions. From the late seventeenth century, the term was borrowed by the English language, in its variant chicanery, where it assumed a different nuance, mostly disconnected from the court, indicating discourses or behaviours aimed at deception or fraud. The Italian equivalent is the verb 'cavillare' (from the Latin 'cavillus', jest or joke), in its meaning of 'inventing false reasons that appear to be true'[62] (*Dizionario della lingua italiana* by

58 'Come mi posso io riconciliare alli miei nimici: elli fenno lo 'ncominciamento della discordia, la concordia non dimandano', op. cit., p. 179.

59 See Maire Vigueur, *Cavalieri et cittadini*, p. 403.

60 'difficulté qu'on suscite pour embrouiller une affaire judiciaire'.

61 'soulever des difficultés pour embrouiller une affaire judiciaire'.

62 'inventar ragioni false che abbiano sembianza di verità'.

Niccolò Tommaseo, Bernardo Bellini, 1861) with specific reference to court matters and, in particular, to pettifoggers.

One might object that the phenomenon should be limited to civil cases, as in the modern age the field of criminal law was already fully conquered by the inquisitorial process and *ex officio* procedures, leaving very little room for the initiative of the parties. But this is a perspective illusion, as it has been widely documented that even in criminal law the margin of action left to the parties remained significant. Base crimes are rather intertwined with civil ones; often verbal or physical violence stemmed from episodes of encroachment, unreturned loans, insults to honour and reputation, precedence disregarded, broken marriage promises, unpaid dowries, provocations of all kinds. Serious injury and even homicide were by no means exceptions but rather recurring eventualities, for which conciliatory and arbitration mechanisms were set in motion, involving compensations (monetary) and peace agreements, celebrated with massive recourse to religious symbolism. It is the modern distinction between civil and criminal that is poorly suited to representing the reality of pre-modern justice. A man who mortally wounds another man to defend his honour, or because he was provoked, is not considered at first glance a dangerous threat to social order, an enemy to be isolated and excluded from the community like a heretic, a thief, a fraudster or a recidivist murderer. This man is, rather, a brother who has erred and must be recovered, creating bonds both familial and communal (also more or less compelling and pivoting on the threat of sanction, as has been seen), as well as devotional.

What the Church sought to implement was an attempt to Christianise the law courts and the recourse to tribunals, following a very long tradition of mistrust towards judges and lawyers that had its roots in classical culture. It is precisely from Plato's *Republic*, and the conception of justice that derives from it, that the treatise on the uses and abuses of law and justice by the Flemish lawyer Andreas Bouwens originates. Bouwens, a native of Leuven, entered the service of the Prince-Archbishop of Liège.[63] Dedicated to the Bishop of Roermond, Andreas Creusen, and commissioned by the jurist Jean de Chokier de Surlet, a disciple of Justus Lipsius, the *Iuris iustitiaeque usus et abusus* is conceived as an examination, also aimed at the training of preachers, of the characteristics of the court and the trial from the perspective of the idea of justice and what those who turn to it must do to save

63 *Iuris iustitiaeque usus et abusus: exemplis et documentis ex omni aevo demonstrati per Andream Bouwens I. C. Mosae Trajectinum. Opus non tantùm Synedris, omnibusque Nomothetis, sed & concionatoribus utilissimum* (Leodii, ex Officina Typographica Henrici & Ioannis Mathiae Hoviorum, 1655).

their souls (verse 15, chapter 30 of Ecclesiasticus, 'Salus animae in sanctitate iustitiae', referring to the sound education of children, stands as an epigraph on the title page of the work).[64] The opening of the first chapter, as mentioned, takes its cue from the Platonic concept of the cessation of disputes and controversies at the moment of the establishment of the perfect political regime, one in which the communion of goods prevails. But this – Bouwens argues – has not happened and cannot happen, and the only way to extinguish litigiousness, thus guaranteeing peace and prosperity to the city, is to be inspired by the ideal of justice:

> But apart from the fact that such a Republic can indeed be imagined but not established, the most excellent remedy for all disputes and litigations is given by Justice, which is the Peace of the peoples, the safeguard of the Homeland, the immunity of the Plebs, the bulwark of nations, the care of the sick, the joy of men, the serenity of the sea, the fertility of the land, the solace of the poor, the inheritance of the children, and for those who cultivate it, the hope of future blessedness.[65]

The court, a place where the law should be spoken and applied according to criteria of equity, can instead become a place where injustice is not only present but grows, proliferates and strengthens; it can become a place where one enters smiling and returns home sad and suffering; a place whose frequentation leads the Christian to sin, to pursue personal gain at the expense of others and the common good; a place where disputes multiply instead of being resolved:

> A small dispute gives birth to a larger one: and with the convoluted root of litigation intertwining within the court's confines, it is difficult to completely eradicate its remnants, preventing new offshoots from emerging, which will create a new root of the dispute. After one or more judgements and numerous court orders, these offshoots often sprout, producing a tangled progeny.[66]

64 'Health of the soul in holiness of justice, is better than all gold and silver: and a sound body, than immense revenues' ('Salus animae in sanctitate iustitiae et melior omni auro et argento et corpus validum quam census inmensus').

65 'Sed praeterquam quod talis Respublica quidem fingi possit, non autem constitui, remedium praestantissimum omnium controversiarum ac litium datur Iustitia, quae Pax est populorum, tutamen Patriae, immunitas Plebis, munimentum gentium, cura languorum, gaudium hominum, serenitas maris, terrae foecunditas, solatium pauperum, haereditas filiorum, et illam colenti spes futurae beatitudinis', *Iuris iustitiaeque usus et abusus*, pp. 1–2.

66 'Liticula liti agnascitur: et litigii sinuosi multiplici radice intra ambitum fori confibrati, difficile est stirpitus reliquias elidere, ne subnascantur stolones, stirpem litis

It is necessary, therefore, for those who operate in the court (judges, lawyers, but also litigants) to be inspired by justice, conform to Christian precepts and avoid using its mechanisms to gain illicit advantages, oppress the weaker and perpetuate injustices. A significant part of the work is dedicated to illustrating the virtues that judges, prosecutors and lawyers must possess, but the aspect that interests us the most concerns the judgement Bouwens expresses about the contentious process itself, a judgement that could only be founded on concepts and precepts borrowed from the Holy Scriptures. Indeed, it is to the aforementioned passage of the First Letter of Paul to the Corinthians (1 Cor 6:1–11) that the Flemish jurist refers to explain that, for the Christian, 'litigare in iudicio' (to litigate in court) is prohibited only 'coram iudice infideli' (before an infidel judge). The process is not inherently evil but should be avoided if possible. Why? 'For not everyone is suited for such contention, both for the sake of honesty: for it is an honour for a man to avoid strife: and for the preservation of peace [for every judgment is a provocation of the heart]'.[67] Here the reference is twofold: on one hand, the Book of Proverbs (20:3), which openly states that it is a glory for a man to avoid strife; on the other, Saint John Chrysostom's commentary on the Gospel of Matthew, where he affirms that the process leads to 'irritatio cordis' (provocation of the heart).

What, then, makes the process unchristian? It is the 'strepitus fori' (clamour of the forum), the publicity, when used to gain illicit advantage, going against the truth. Thomas Aquinas had clearly highlighted this in his commentary on the Epistle to the Romans, explaining the use of the term 'contention' in verse 29 of chapter 1: 'Est autem contentio impugnatio veritatis cum confidentia clamoris' ('But contention is the assault on truth with the confidence of clamour').[68] These themes permeated part of the European legal–moral thought in the modern age. In the Catholic world, the influence of Tacitism and Senecanism, which found in Justus Lipsius one of its highest representatives – not coincidentally Bouwens's main point of reference – was

facturi, qui post unam alteramque unam et multas sententias, arrestaque Curiae, pullolos saepè emittunt, nodosamque sobolem', op. cit., p. 4.

67 'Ideo quia non omnibus expedit talis contentio, tum propter honestatem: honor est enim homini, qui se separat à contentione: tum propter pacis conservationem [omne enim iudicium irritatio cordis est]', p. 12.

68 Thomas Aquinas, *Pauline Commentaries*, *Commentary on Romans*, C.1, L.8 (1:26–32), available online at https://aquinas.cc/la/en/~Rom.C1.L8.n158.3 (accessed 26 October 2024).

decisive.[69] An iconographic source of great interest also comes from the Flemish area, a series of eight engravings made in 1597 by Hendrick Goltzius (later reworked and reproduced by Philipp and his son Theodoor Galle, also renowned Flemish engravers) on the theme of the abuse of trials (*Litis abusus*).[70] The main subject of these images is neither the judges nor the lawyers nor the practical jurists; at the centre of the iconographic programme is the litigious person, who appeals to justice and who, because of the trials, is impoverished not only materially but also physically and psychologically. Usually associated with civil disputes, the meaning of the iconographic programme in these engravings can also apply to the low-level criminal cases that occupied much of the courts' energy between the late Middle Ages and the early modern period, often originating from hostilities generated by property or inheritance disputes, without excluding *a priori* significant acts of violence within its scope. Perfectly in line with the literary trend of denouncing recourse to justice analysed in these pages, Goltzius's engravings depict litigiousness as the evil to be eradicated, something monstrous in itself; turning to the judge to resolve a conflict essentially means yielding to a Luciferian temptation and condemning one's soul to eternal damnation.[71]

The captions accompanying the engravings summarise the main themes evoked: on one hand, the negative feelings that lead to judicial litigiousness; on the other, the disastrous consequences of trials for the litigants. The cycle opens with greed, represented by the figures of 'mine' and 'yours', violently driving out love, concord, peace and fear of God (Figure 1); the fourth engraving represents the qualities that the litigator must pledge to bear the weight of a trial, which are patience, impudence and also a good amount of money (Figure 2). The trial is a path fraught with difficulties, and its outcome depends on the wisdom of the judge one encounters, and it also represents an unnecessary risk to be taken. In the series of eight engravings, the image of the trial as a monster with an animal head (probably a wolf), hands shaped like hooks and legs depicted as large wooden screws, similar to those of presses, emphasising the act of pressing or squeezing, recurs twice (Figure 3).

[69] See Santo Burgio, *In publicis malis. Saggi sulla constantia in Giusto Lipsio* (Soveria Mannelli, 2009).

[70] See *Hendrick Goltzius (1558–1617). Mythos, Macht und Menschlichkeit*, ed. Norbert Michels (Petersberg, 2017).

[71] See Alain Wijffels, 'Lawyers and Litigants: The Corrupting Appeal and Effects of Civil Litigation in Hendrick Goltzius' *Litis Abusus*', in *The Art of Law. Artistic Representations and Iconography of Law and Justice in Context, from the Middle Ages to the First World War*, ed. Stefan Huygebaert, Georges Martyn, Vanessa Paumen, Eric Bousmar and Xavier Rousseaux (New York, 2018), pp. 181–99.

Figure 1. Hendrick Goltzius, *Litis abusus* (1597). Engraving no. 1 (British Museum, London, inv. 1986,1004.19). © The Trustees of the British Museum.

The captions are complemented by a robust apparatus of biblical citations, both Old and New Testament, modulated according to the predominant symbols in each engraving, emphasising the solid Christian foundation of the radically negative view of judicial litigiousness that Goltzius's iconography intends to propose.

For the initial engraving (Figure 1), for example, 1 Cor. 10:24 is cited ('No one should seek his own advantage, but that of his neighbour'), Phil. 2:21 ('For they all seek their own interests, not those of Jesus Christ'), Matt. 24:12 ('and because of the increase of evildoing, the love of many will grow cold'); (Figure 2), Isa. 59:8 ('The way of peace they know not, and there is nothing that is right in their paths; Their ways they have made crooked, whoever treads them knows no peace'), and Ecclesiasticus 1:28 ('For he that is without fear, cannot be justified: for the wrath of his high spirits is his ruin'). A reference to Matt. 5:25 is, of course, included in the eighth engraving (Figure 4), depicting the fruits of a trial: *conscientia mala* and *paupertas*, in the form of two flames emerging from a hole dug by two women in the middle of a square. Behind one of the women lies the lifeless *litigator*, from whose mouth a small human figure emerges, promptly captured by the monster/trial, this time in the guise of a winged devil.

What unfolds before our eyes is, indeed, an attempt to Christianise the contentious judicial forum that impacts the entire Catholic world. Moving from Flanders to Spanish Italy, for example, one encounters a unique work, precisely titled *Foro christiano*, composed in the late sixteenth century by the lawyer Rocco Gambacorta, a native of Messina but a citizen of Palermo (and he practised law in the capital of the Sicilian viceroyalty).[72] The aim is not only to provide guidelines to prevent private individuals from taking their cases to court and initiating trials, or to make proper use of contentious justice, but also to outline a sort of perfect society, harmoniously structured, which pivoted on one hand on the sound legal education of young people destined for the liberal professions and on a Christian-inspired forensic deontology, and on the other on the necessary difference in judicial treatment depending on the age, condition and social class of the litigants. The

[72] *Iesus Mariae Filius. Foro Christiano. Nel quale si tratta come deveno osservarsi l'humane leggi conforme alle divine. Diviso in cinque parti, secondo le convenienti età dell'huomo, Adolescenza, Gioventù, Virilità, Vecchiezza, & Decrepità. Confirmandosi con l'autorità della Sacra Scrittura, Dottori Catholici, & detti di persone Savie del mondo. Accioche honeste e Christiane sieno tutte l'attioni de gli huomini in quel che può lor' occorrere per farsi un Sacro Senato, Santo Giuditio, giusto negotio, & honesto essercitio. Composto per Rocco Gambacorta Dottore nativo della Città di Messina, & Cittadino Palermitano* (in Palermo, appresso Gio. Francisco Carrara, 1594).

Figure 2. Hendrick Goltzius, *Litis abusus* (1597). Engraving no. 4 (British Museum, London, inv. 1986,1004.22). © The Trustees of the British Museum.

Figure 3. Hendrick Goltzius, *Litis abusus* (1597). Engraving no. 3 (British Museum, London, inv. 1986,1004.21). © The Trustees of the British Museum.

Figure 4. Hendrick Goltzius, *Litis abusus* (1597). Engraving no. 8 (British Museum, London, inv. 1986,1004.26). © The Trustees of the British Museum.

division of the work follows the succession of the different phases of a man's life: adolescence, youth, manhood, old age, decrepitude. After clarifying that lawyers must proceed in the cause with a spirit of justice and without resorting to slander against the opposing party, nor initiate criminal or civil disputes on their own initiative, Gambacorta centres the reflection on the act itself of administering justice, which, to be Christianly inspired, must be animated by compassion, 'each one lamenting human frailty and misery [...] not rushing into it with a fierce spirit, rejoicing in the harm and punishment of others'.[73] In this way, one enters a territory that belongs to conscience, as the Sicilian lawyer himself specifies:

> But since, in all that is dealt with in the present chapter, the end with good or bad intention in the person executing the mandate is considered: with many considerations and qualities (without departing from our order), we will refer to that Modern and copious Theologian in the treatise de finibus humanorum actuum, explaining the following chapter, cum minister, with many necessary requisites in the forum of conscience, and penitential, which can be seen there as they are useful for everyone to know.[74]

The reference to Martín de Azpilcueta, known as Doctor Navarrus, the foremost representative of Iberian moral theology, is significant in itself. But from the realm of conscience to outward acts, the step is immediate, and compassion, for Gambacorta – supported in this assertion by a substantial series of authorities, ranging from the Holy Scripture and theology to Latin writers – must be the guiding star of any act of justice, because 'he who goes forth ready and willingly to punish the delinquents, from being a Minister of Justice becomes a murderer: lacking the compassionate quality of mercy which is a part of Justice'.[75] Compassion, mercy, charity: qualities and attitudes that, according to the Catholic culture of the Counter-Reformation, must permeate not only the sphere of punishment but the entire field of criminal justice, reaching even the most hidden intentions of those who

[73] Op. cit., f. 125^{v}.

[74] 'Ma poiché di tutto quel che si tratta nel presente capitolo, il fine con la buona, ò mala intentione ne l'huomo ch'esseguisce il mandato si considera: con molte considerationi, e qualità (non ci appartando del nostro ordine) ne remetteremo a quel Moderno e copioso Theologo nel trattato de finibus humanorum actuum, dichiarando il seguente capitolo, cum minister, con molti requisiti necessarij nel foro della conscienza, & penitenziale quali ivi si ponno vedere essendo à tutti utili à sapere', op. cit., ff. 125^{v}–126^{r}.

[75] 'colui quale và pronto, e volintieri à castigar li delinquenti, di Ministro di Giustizia diventa homicida: mancandoli la qualità compassionevole della misericordia qual'è parte di Giustizia', op. cit., f. 126^{r}.

administer it (the judge) and those who seek it (the litigants).[76] Addressing the judges, and following Augustine, Seneca and Ovid, Gambacorta concludes that 'justice [...] without tempering it with mercy becomes bad',[77] but later similar observations are dedicated also to the plaintiff, the defendant, the sureties and the relatives of the accused.

The relatives and friends of an accused person have a specific Christian obligation of help and support towards him, which is not limited to providing money but may even mean giving their own lives. This obligation, derived from the precept of charity, is realised by accepting to act as surety; if the 'pleggiaria' (a term used in Sicily to indicate the surety) proves too burdensome for a single person, 'seeing the friend and relative in tribulation, the relatives and friends should gather together, so that all gathered together can easily do that work which one alone could not do'.[78] By introducing, for the Christian, a duty of aid towards others through the assumption of surety, the Catholic legal–moral culture was embedding itself, legitimising them, in the heart of the mechanisms that allowed political power to harness the spaces of action of social actors and thereby contain conflict.

Moreover, the clear assertion of the necessity to abstain from disputes could not be missed, as it is a Christian obligation for both the plaintiff and the defendant, based on many of the previously cited texts of Holy Scripture, but not only on these. It primarily draws on the Sermon on the Mount, reported in the Gospels of Matthew and Luke, chapter 20 of Proverbs, the Pauline epistles, but also John Chrysostom or Augustine's sermon 109, where the Christian was admonished about the necessity of reconciling quickly with the word of God given the uncertainty of the moment of individual judgement,[79]

[76] See in general *Misericordie. Conversioni sotto il patibolo tra Medioevo ed età moderna*, ed. Adriano Prosperi (Pisa, 2007).

[77] 'la giustizia [...] senza temperarla con la misericordia diventa cattiva', *Iesus Mariae Filius. Foro Christiano*, f. 126ᵛ.

[78] 'vedendo l'amico, & parente tribulato devino congregarsi li parenti, & amici, acciò facilmente tutti congregati facciano quell'opera, quale non potria fare un solo', *Op. cit.*, f. 316ᵛ.

[79] 'Such is the road on which we have set out. What are we going to do with that adversary, that is the word of God? Agree with it; after all you don't know when you're going to reach the end of the road. When the road ends, there remains the judge, and the officer, and the prison. But if you have kept on the right side of your adversary, and have been in agreement with him, then instead of a judge you will find a Father, instead of a ferocious officer, an angel to carry you up to Abraham's bosom, instead of prison, paradise. How quickly you have changed everything on the road, because you have reached agreement with your adversary', Augustine of Hippo, *Sermons*, vol. III/4, *Sermo* 109, §4., p. 134 ('Quid

demonstrating that literal interpretation and anagogical interpretation of the verses of Matthew and Luke continued to coexist peacefully. The plaintiff and the defendant are, above all else, brothers 'under the same God (and under the peaceful Christian banner)';[80] precisely for this reason, Jesus orders reconciliation with one's brother before bringing him before a judge.

The process leads to the 'irritatio cordis, & cogitationum malarum' (Chrysostom), and thus to enmity:

> Since it is impossible for the world to be free of disputes and differences, it is better for the parties themselves to settle them between each other (without waiting for a judge's sentence) before they reach an agreement: this results in common benefit. [...] For this reason, all divine and human laws persuade, and often compel, the parties to reach an agreement, which emulates the Catholic and Imperial Majesty of Emperor Charles V, who ordered in the Kingdom that the cases of related persons be compromised. No sentence can ever be so favourable that it is not said by everyone that *a lean agreement is better than a fat sentence*, as is commonly heard. The outcome of a lawsuit is doubtful and uncertain. Therefore, whoever does not want to be deceived settles quickly.[81]

The intellectual roots of the preferability of agreements over trials are deep, and this culture of transaction and amicable composition was also invigorated by European Christian Humanism, especially in its legal aspect.[82]

---

facturi sumus cum adversario illo, id est, cum sermone Dei? Concorda cum illo. Nescis enim quando via finiatur. Cum via finita fuerit, iudex restat, et minister, et carcer. At si servaveris adversario tuo bonam voluntatem, et cum eo consenseris; pro iudice invenies patrem, pro ministro saevo angelum tollentem in sinum Abrahae, pro carcere paradisum. Quam cito in via cuncta mutasti, quia tuo adversario consensisti!').

80 'sotto l'istesso Iddio (& il vessillo Christiano pacifico essendo)', *Iesus Mariae Filius. Foro Christiano*, f. 321^{v}.

81 'Non potendo farsi nel mondo non accaschino liti, & differenze, sarà meglio quelle accommodarle le proprie parti tra loro (non aspettando sentenza di Giudice) innanzi s'accorderanno: questo rivertendo in commune beneficio. [...] Per questo tutte le leggi divine, & humane persuadino, & spesso forzano le parti che si accordano, quali imitando la Catholica, e Cesarea Maestà di Re Carlo Quinto Imperadore ordinò nel Regno le cause delle persone congiunte si compromettessero. Mai può essere tanta la sententia favorevole, che non si dica per tutti *meglio accordio magro che sentenza grassa*, & come si sente in ogni luogo dire. Dubius, & incertus est litis eventus. Per questo chi non se vuole ingannare tosto s'accorda', op. cit., ff. 322^{r-v}, italics mine.

82 In citing the proverb 'better a lean agreement than a fat sentence', Gambacorta references André Tiraqueau, one of the foremost representatives of French legal

Gambacorta admits that sometimes the process is inevitable. These are the 'legitimate causes', to which he dedicates a specific paragraph, situations in which 'it is necessary to litigate and have in that case the sentence and determination from the Judge',[83] but the Christian 'must always have the intention ready to settle, with all his interest to avoid the troubles, dangers and inconveniences that disputes bring with them'.[84] Moreover, it is not enough to outwardly agree if there is no true intention: how many times does the pursuit of agreement with the help of arbitrators and notaries turn out to be mere façade if greed or the desire for revenge resides in people's hearts? Often, brothers divided over a contested inheritance (Luke 12:13–16) go to the notary 'with simulation', to 'show the world that they are just',[85] but 'in the end, they never reach any true conclusion'.[86] Even in cases of offences, insults and violence, to reconcile two brothers a judge is not needed, but rather piety, 'thus the mind with the right intention wants to correspond with actions, and in this way I desire that everyone seeks to agree, not with mere words, but with deeds'.[87]

The Church's action in this field derived its *raison d'être* from the awareness of the need to Christianise practices of justice that massively resorted to both the contentious forum and transactional and compositional tools, whose

humanism, and a key figure in the mid-sixteenth century for those dedicated to harmonising local rights and customs with the *ius commune* (with a strong preference for the former, to whose knowledge and dissemination he devoted much of his work). Among his numerous treatises, particularly noteworthy is *Andreas Tiraquellus De poenis legum, ac consuetudinum, statutorumque temperandis, aut etiam remittendis, & id quibus quotque ex causis. Accessit rerum, verborum, & sentientiarum insignium locupletissimus index* (Lugduni, Ad Salamandrae, apud Claudium Sennetonium, 1559). For Tiraqueau's contribution to the definitions of nobility, see Claudio Donati, *L'idea di nobiltà in Italia (secoli XIV-XVIII)* (Rome and Bari, 1988), pp. 114–17. For a general overview, see Giovanni Rossi, *Incunaboli della modernità. Scienza giuridica e cultura umanistica in André Tiraqueau (1488-1558)* (Turin, 2008).

83 'è necessario litigare, & havere in quella causa la sentenza, & determinatione dal Giudice', *Iesus Mariae Filius. Foro Christiano*, f. 322^{v}.

84 'deve havere sempre l'intentione pronta ad accordarsi, con ogni suo interesse per levarsi de' travagli pericoli, & incommodità quali portano seco le questioni', op. cit., ff. 322^{v}–323^{r}.

85 'mostrare al mondo che sono giusti', op. cit., f. 323^{r}.

86 'nella fine mai venno ad alcuna conclusione vera', ibid.

87 'così l'animo con la giusta intentione vuole corrispondere con l'opere, & di questo modo desidero ch'ogn'uno cerchi d'accordarsi, non con sole parole, mà con effetti', ibid.

use was often, if not always, inspired by reasons and motives far removed from the imperatives of Christian morality. For this reason, the implementation of transaction procedures could not, in any way, be separated, in the concerns of jurists and moralists, from attention to the inner dimension. For Gambacorta, punishment, even very severe, must be reserved for public and heinous crimes, directed both at God and at others, for which no accuser is provided. These are the crimes that offend God and undermine the foundations on which the political and social order rests; also due to their public dimension, in punishing them judges do not act at the request of a party but *ex officio*. They do not concern the relations between Christian brothers, which can find a solution away from indiscreet eyes, *sine strepitu ac figura iudicii*, but rather the public good and the established order itself.

3. Confession and moral theology

In which cases should the confessor deny or defer absolution? This is a central issue for moral theology, whose resolution has enormous consequences not only on the level of the individual salvation of the sinner but also on social discipline and the systems for intercepting religious deviance. The mechanism of the *spontanea comparitio* of the penitent before the external forum judge, bishop or inquisitor was based precisely on the deferral of absolution;[88] based on this practice, Charles Borromeo could establish a powerful system for controlling behaviours and, above all, religious orthodoxy in the Milan of his day.[89] Among the cases in which the confessor had to deny or defer absolution was the state of enmity, as forgiving one's enemies represents an obligation for the Christian. By forgiving, the Christian imitates Jesus, who with his sacrifice forgave the sins of all humanity, and he does so not for his own merits 'but only for the grace and benignity of our Lord'.[90] On the obligation of the confessor to defer absolution to the penitent if he refused to forgive his enemy (and therefore to abandon the hatred towards him both in the intimacy of his conscience and in outward behaviour), sixteenth- and seventeenth-century moral theology was called

[88] See Brambilla, *Alle origini del Sant'Uffizio*; Adriano Prosperi, 'L'Inquisitore come confessore', in *Disciplina dell'anima, disciplina del corpo e disciplina della società tra medioevo ed età moderna*, ed. Paolo Prodi (Bologna, 1994), pp. 187–224, and, with greater amplitude, Adriano Prosperi, *Tribunali della coscienza*, pp. 465–84.

[89] See Wietse De Boer, *The Conquest of the Soul: Confession, Discipline, and Public Order in Counter-Reformation Milan* (Leiden and Boston, 2001).

[90] 'ma sol per gratia & benignità del Signor nostro', *Alcune ragioni del perdonare*.

to provide answers. In the *Breve instruction de como se ha de administrar el Sacramento de la Penitencia*, perhaps the most widespread manual for confessors in seventeenth-century Catholic Europe, the Dominican Bartolomé de Medina includes among the cases in which the confessor must not grant absolution that in which the penitent 'holds hatred and enmity formed against his neighbour',[91] and it should not be granted until he 'quits such hatred and reconciles with his neighbour and restores speech to him if he has taken it away'.[92] The level becomes immediately twofold: the internal level of conscience and the external signs necessary so that the entire community becomes aware of the reconciliation between enemies. To grant absolution, the penitent must abandon inner hatred. But is it equally necessary for him to offer external signs of abandoning rancour? To resume associating with his enemy and speak to him? Thomas Aquinas addressed the problem in the *Secunda Secundae*, in the part relating to the object of charity (Question 25, article 9), concluding that, since signs of benevolence derive from inner affection and are proportionate to it, a general obligation of charity exists for the Christian (as when praying for the faithful or the people) regarding both the disposition of mind and external signs. As for individual cases, i.e., specific persons, the obligation is not absolute, depending on the state of necessity of the person with whom we are at enmity:

> it is not necessary for salvation that we show our enemies suchlike favours and signs of love, except as regards being ready in our minds, for instance to come to their assistance in a case of urgency, according to Prov. 25,21: 'If thy enemy be hungry, give him to eat; if he thirst, give him [...] drink'. Outside cases of necessity, to show suchlike favours to an enemy belongs to the perfection of charity, whereby we not only beware, as in duty bound, of being overcome by evil, but also wish to overcome evil by good [Rom. 12,21], which belongs to perfection: for then we not only beware of being drawn into hatred on account of the hurt done to us, but purpose to induce our enemy to love us on account of our kindliness.[93]

91 'tiene odio y enemistad formada contra su proximo', Medina, *Breve instruction de como se ha de administrar el Sacramento de la Penitencia*, f. 54^{v}.

92 'quite el tal odio, y se reconcilie con su proximo, y le restituya la habla si se la tiene quitada', ibid.

93 *The Summa Theologiæ of St. Thomas Aquinas*, second and revised edition, literally translated by Fathers of the English Dominican Province, *IIa-IIae, quaestio* 25, art. 9 (London, 1920; Online Edition 2017) ('Et talia beneficia vel dilectionis signa inimici exhibere non est de necessitate salutis, nisi secundum preparationem animi, ut scilicet subveniatur eis in articulo necessitatis: secundum illud Proverb. 25. Si esurierit inimicus tuus, ciba illum, si sitit, da illi potum. Sed

Together with Matthew 5, the epistle of Saint Paul to the Romans (12:14–21) is the cornerstone upon which Catholic theology has built its reflections on revenge, hatred, forgiveness, charity and justice. The Christian must not avenge the injury received but must leave vengeance to God; giving outward signs of *dilectio* to one's enemy is not an obligation but belongs to religious perfection, meaning taking a further step in obedience to the precept of not being overcome by evil: it means overcoming evil with good. From this, we understand why Catholic moral theology has particularly focused on two mirror issues: on the one hand, whether *dilectio proximi*, to be expressed through acts of benevolence, also involves an inner obligation to abandon hatred;[94] on the other hand, the identification of circumstances in which the abandonment of hatred in one's heart is not sufficient for the confessor to grant absolution. This is the keystone of the system by which penance could well represent, even in early modern times, a tool in the hands of the ecclesiastical body to achieve reconciliations between individuals and family groups. Although in different ways compared to the past, in the post-Tridentine age confession continued to be a fundamental instrument for controlling social conflict. It was not only – as hypothesised by John Bossy regarding the penitential practice up to the late Middle Ages, with very strong community connotations – about pacifying enemies in order to allow the faithful to approach confession (inhibited in case of enmity if reconciliation was refused), but also about continuing to use confession, albeit in the new forms it was gradually assuming (individualisation, psychologisation, internalisation), to mend fractures and interpersonal conflicts precisely from the dimension of the inner forum. The confessor moved from the soul's hatred towards the cure of social hatred.

Ludovico Carbone from Costacciaro, author of a treatise dedicated to the pacification of enemies, whose peculiarity lies in the perspective halfway

---

quod praeter articulum necessitatis huiusmodi beneficia aliquis inimicis exhibeat, pertinet ad perfectionem charitatis: per quam aliquis non solum cavet vinci à malo, quod necessitatis est, sed etiam vult in bono vincere malum, quod est etiam perfectionis: dum scilicet non solum cavet propter iniuriam sibi illatam detrahi ad odium, sed etiam propter sua beneficia intendit inimicum pertrahere ad suum amorem', *S. Thomae Aquinatis Secunda Secundae partis Summae Theologicae Sancti Thomae Aquinatis. De virtutibus omnis et vitiis in speciali*, Antverpiae, ex Officina Christophori Plantini, 1569, p. 82).

94 See Santo Burgio, 'Teologie del negozio. *Amor sui e dilectio proximi* nel probabilismo di Tommaso Tamburini S.I.', in *Stringere la pace. Teorie e pratiche della conciliazione nell'Europa moderna (secoli XV-XVIII)*, ed. Paolo Broggio and Maria Pia Paoli (Rome, 2010), pp. 411–28.

between theology and law, not surprisingly devotes several paragraphs to the issue of the obligation of outward signs of friendship and renewed concord.[95] Without particular originality, Carbone collects and systematises the doctrine on this point, starting from the Thomistic distinction between general signs and particular signs of reconciliation: the former are obligatory, the latter optional, unless certain circumstances exist. He highlights as a very serious abuse the fact that some confessors consider that, for absolution, it is sufficient 'solum deponere odium' ('merely to lay aside hatred'), and therefore 'it is not necessary to declare it with outward signs',[96] then reviews the cases in which the penitent is obliged to ask for forgiveness from their adversary or to take the first step towards resolving the dissension, since 'reconciliatio interior non sufficit' ('inner reconciliation is not sufficient').[97] For example, when the adversary is in conditions of necessity, either bodily or spiritual, or when the refusal of outward reconciliation generates an imminent danger of mortal sin, in relations between members of the same family, even religious (or lay congregation), and in general when the refusal to grant such signs is capable of causing scandal in the community. Nor, moreover, can it be left to the penitent's discretion to determine whether the outward signs offered by the adversary are sufficient to accept reconciliation.[98]

To strengthen the argument for the necessity of outward reconciliation, Carbone resorts to Luke 17:3–4 ('Take heed to yourselves. If thy brother sin against thee, reprove him: and if he do penance, forgive him. And if he sin against thee seven times in a day, and seven times in a day be converted unto thee, saying: I repent: forgive him'), carefully analysing, based on the

95 Born in Costacciaro, near Gubbio, in 1532, he likely received his first education from the Conventual Franciscans in his hometown before benefiting from the educational opportunities offered by nearby Gubbio at the time when the diocese was led by Marcello Cervini (the future Pope Marcellus II). Part of his educational journey was also influenced by the Jesuits, particularly Claudio Acquaviva, who became the General of the order in 1581. He was a *Magister Sacrae Theologiae* and a prolific writer in fields ranging from theology to philosophy, from rhetoric to catechesis. See Euro Puletti, *Ludovico Carbone da Costacciaro. Vita, pensiero ed opere* (Gualdo Tadino, 2013).

96 'necessarium non esse id declarare signis externis', *De pacificatione et dilectione inimicorum iniuriamque remissione. Tractatio admodum utilis Remp. Et curam animarum gerentibus, concionatoribus, pacificatoribus, armatis, alijsqu. Viris, ut ex indice capitum cognoscere licet, cum apendice, de amore et concordia fraterna. Auctore Ludovico Carbone* (Florentiae, apud Bartholomaeum Sermatellium, 1583), p. 153.

97 Op. cit., p. 154.

98 Op. cit., p. 155.

available doctrine, the meaning of the evangelical precept.[99] In dwelling on the 'Paenitet me' contained in the passage, Carbone firmly rejects any interpretation – including that of Cardinal De Vio – tending to equate repentance with simple remorse rather than with the detestation of the sin committed and satisfaction, supported in this latter sense also by non-Christian authors like Cicero and Terence. Moreover, Carbone adds, 'for the opinion of Luther and his followers, who consider penance to be solely a new life, is completely false'.[100] And to the matter of restitution (of honour, reputation, in case of harm done and even murder, in the form of compensation for expenses incurred by the family of the deceased for any care before death or lost earnings), Carbone dedicates several chapters of his work.[101]

For all these reasons, sacramental confession could not but be at the centre of the mechanisms of informal dispute resolution. This is further demonstrated by Bartolomé de Medina, who, addressing the same topic, also reviews the circumstances in which the Christian is obliged to give outward signs of reconciliation and focuses on the heart of the problem from the outset. For the founder of probabilism, this obligation arises primarily when:

> he who has wronged you asks for forgiveness in the forum they call of conscience, the offended will be obliged in the same forum of conscience, which is solely for God, not to deny forgiveness and to reconcile with him, because by denying it you cause scandal, and provoke hatred against yourself.[102]

It is from the internal forum that confessors are called to weave a network of mutual obligations of forgiveness and reconciliation, which must then correspond to the necessary outward manifestations. If the perpetrator, faced with the possibility of not being granted absolution, declares *in foro*

[99] 'Attendite vobis! Si peccaverit frater tuus, increpa illum et, si paenitentiam egerit, dimitte illi; et si septies in die peccaverit in te et septies conversus fuerit ad te dicens: "Paenitet me", dimittes illi'.

[100] 'nam falsas prorsus est Lutheri, & sectatorum opinio, qui poenitentiam, solam vitam novam esse arbitrantur', *De pacificatione et dilectione inimicorum*, p. 157.

[101] See Vincenzo Lavenia, *Restituire, condonare. Lessico giuridico, confessione e pratiche sociali nella prima età moderna*, in *Grazia e giustizia. Figure della clemenza fra tardo medioevo ed età contemporanea*, ed. Karl Härter and Cecilia Nubola (Bologna, 2011), pp. 389–411.

[102] 'el que contra vos erró os pide perdon en el foro que llaman de la consciencia, obligado será el offendido en el mismo foro de la consciencia, que es solamente para con Dios, a no le negar perdon y reconciliarse con el, por que negando se le escandalizays, y procurays a odio contra vos', *Breve instruction de como se ha de administrar el Sacramento de la Penitencia*, f. 54^{v}.

conscientiae the intention to ask for forgiveness from their victim, the latter cannot refuse, also *in foro conscientiae*, to grant it. This, of course, could occur more easily if the confessor was the same for both parties in conflict. In this latter circumstance, the confessor could act as a true mediator between the parties and, compared to any mediator, he could wield a far more convincing weapon: the power to deny or defer absolution, with all the serious canonical consequences that this could entail (censures and excommunications). The willingness to reconcile must obviously be mutual, because – returning to Carbone – he who 'has inflicted injury, by the Lord's precept is obliged to approach the brother to seek outward reconciliation, about which there is no doubt concerning the internal',[103] but the brother 'who was treated injuriously, must give signs of a reconciled spirit',[104] because 'if someone stubbornly denies the pursuit, saying that Christ does not obligate the offended but the offender, it is indeed a ridiculous evasion'.[105]

Outward reconciliation is a consequence of the inner one and is also necessary in other cases, where the lack of a return to a visible state of concord is capable of causing scandal, harmful to the entire community:

> Outward reconciliation is also necessary between very close persons such as husband and wife, between parents and children, between brother and sister, and between superiors and inferiors. Likewise, among those whose hatreds and factions are expected to result in deaths, scandals and dissensions. Similarly, between neighbours who are very close or beneficiaries of the same Church, because here too, there will be scandal if they persist for a long time without speaking to each other.[106]

Even Martín de Azpilcueta, always within the framework of Thomistic doctrine, is very clear in asserting that, although the Christian is obliged

[103] 'iniuriam irrogavit, ex dominico praecepto tenetur adire fratrem ad petendam reconciliationem externam, qui de interna nulla est dubitatio', *De pacificatione et dilectione inimicorum*, p. 162.

[104] 'qui fuit iniuriosè tractatus, debet dare signa conciliati animi', ibid.

[105] 'si quis pervicaciter consecutionem neget, dicendo Christus non obligare offensum, sed offendentem, ridicula sanè est Evasio', ibid.

[106] 'Tambien es necessario la reconciliacion exterior entre personas muy conjuntas como es marido y muger, entre padres y hijos entre hermano y hermana, y entre superiores y inferiores. Assi mismo entre aquellos por cuyos odios, y vandos se esperan muertes, escandalos y dessensiones. Assi mismo entre vezinos muy allegados o beneficiados de una misma Iglesia, porque aqui tambien abra escandalo si perseveran mucho tiempo sin hablarse', *Breve instruction de como se ha de administrar el Sacramento de la Penitencia*, ff. 54^{v}–55^{r}.

'to cast out of the heart hatred and bad rancour'[107] stemming from an offence received, he is under no obligation to either abandon the 'good rancour born of anger, with which one desires that the crime be punished by justice'[108] or to outwardly reconcile with his enemy, that is, to 'receive him into conversation and friendship'[109] unless 'en tiempo de necesidad' (in time of necessity).[110] It is under those circumstances of necessity that moral theology has been able to investigate to configure the confessional as a place where penitents could be urged or, more accurately, compelled to reconcile, not only in conscience but also by showing outward signs of inner reconciliation.

The distinction made by Navarrus between 'rancor bueno' ('good rancour'), born of anger, which leads the victim to achieve a just end, namely the intervention of justice and the imposition of a penalty, and 'rancor malo' ('bad rancour'), born of sloth, which can lead to private vengeance, is important. The intervention of justice was in no way excluded, as the pages of Luis de Molina, already examined, clearly show; 'public' process and 'private' peace were non-self-excluding paths that had various points of contact and exchange, with the Church maintaining the preference, primarily moral, for transactional and informal solutions for certain types of crime, specific categories of subjects and under certain circumstances. The relationship between these two paths was, moreover, meticulously regulated by theology and canon law; Carbone himself preliminarily clarifies that law and punishment are necessary because – as the maxim derived from Horace's epistles reminds us – noble souls hate sin out of love for the good, but evil men hate sin out of fear of punishment ('Oderunt peccare boni, virtutis amore; Oderunt peccare mali, formidine poenae').

Marc'Antonio Savelli, in the late seventeenth century, seems to be more prudent in regarding the obligation for the Christian to ensure that outward signs of reconciliation correspond with the abandonment of hatred expressed in internal forum. The Tuscan jurist first asserts rather

107 'echar del corazón el odio, y rancor malo', *Manual de confessores y penitentes, que contiene quasi todas las dudas que en las confessiones suelen occurrir delos peccados, absoluciones, restituciones, censuras, & irregularidades [...] compuesto por el Doctor Martin de Azpilcueta Navarro, Cathedratico jubilado de prima en Canones* (impresso en Valladolid, por Francisco Fernandez de Cordova impressor de la Magestad Real, 1570), p. 142.

108 'rancor bueno hijo de la ira, con que quiere, que por justicia se castigue el delito', ibid.

109 'recebirlo a su conversación y amistad', ibid.

110 ibid.

confidently that 'external peace is not necessary in the forum of conscience, it being sufficient for the salvation of the soul to inwardly forgive every offence, injury and rancour';[111] therefore, if the offended person forgives his adversary in his heart but still intends to 'pursue justice' ('proseguire per giustizia'), he should be absolved by the confessor. Indeed, as noted by the Valencian jurist Lorenzo Mateu y Sanz, to whom Savelli expressly refers, when inner hatred is avoided, it is still meritorious 'to pursue justice', if not even an obligation.[112] But, he adds, 'it is to be noted in this particular, that it is difficult to find a case where one abandons hatred against an enemy while wanting to pursue him in court',[113] also because it is not uncommon 'for the denial of external peace to be intended to cause serious harm to the enemy, such as forcing him to exile from his homeland, suffer confiscation of goods, or other notable damages, which peace could easily prevent'.[114] It does not correspond to evangelical precepts to strive to inflict significant damage on one's enemy: if one does so, it means that there is still hatred in the penitent's heart. Savelli does not provide a definitive answer on the matter, but concludes that perhaps the most 'true and sure in conscience' ('vera, e sicura in coscienza') opinion is that denying peace can be a sign of merit 'when the public good requires it, and it is done with this sole intent',[115] but adding that it is also true that 'forgiving

[111] 'la pace esteriore non è necessaria in foro di coscienza, bastando per salute dell'anima rimetter interiormente ogni offesa, ingiuria, e rancore', *Pratica universale del Dottor Marc'Antonio Savelli, Auditore della Rota Criminale di Firenze, compendiosamente estratta per alfabetto dalle principali Leggi, Bandi, Statuti, Ordini, e Consuetudini, massime Criminali, e miste, che si osservano nelli Stati del Serenissimo Gran Duca di Toscana* ... , tomo VII (in Parma, per gli Eredi di Paolo Monti all'Insegna della Fede, 1733), p. 240.

[112] See *Laurentii Matthaeu et Sanz, Tractatus de re criminali, sive controversiarum usufrequentium in causis criminalibus, cum earum decisionibus, tam in aula suprema ac Hispana criminum, quam in summo senatu novi orbis, Editio prima, cum triplici indice controversiarum, jurium, ac rerum locupletissimo* (Lugduni, sumpt. Claudij Bourgeat, sub signo Mercurij Galli, 1676).

[113] 'è [...] d'avvertire in questo particolare, che difficilmente si può dar il caso, che uno deponga l'odio contro del nemico, mentre vuol proseguirgli contro in giudizio', *Pratica universale del Dottor Marc'Antonio Savelli*, p. 240.

[114] 'col denegar la pace esteriormente, e per instromento al nemico, s'intendesse di cagionargli danno grave, come se per non haver la pace fusse necessitato ad esiliar dalla patria, patir confiscatione di beni, ò altri danni notabili, alli quali con la pace potesse facilmente ovviare', ibid.

[115] 'quando il bene pubblico richiedesse così, e si facesse con questo solo intento', ibid.

the enemy for the injuries is the most meritorious and excellent virtue that can exist in a Christian'.[116]

Long before Savelli, another jurist – the Umbrian Sebastiano Guazzini, whom we have already encountered – had questioned the same issue by reviewing the opinions for and against the possibility of the confessor absolving a penitent who refused to give outward signs of reconciliation with the enemy, while declaring to have abandoned hatred in his heart. Starting very cautiously from the traditional cornerstone constituted by the doctrine of Thomas and passing through the commentary on that specific part of the *Summa* composed by Cardinal De Vio, Guazzini finally unhesitatingly adopts the opinion of the Portuguese Luis de Beja Perestrelo,[117] a leading theologian in the Bologna of Paleotti, who 'with very solid foundations concludes for the negative side of this issue',[118] that is, that the confessor cannot absolve in the case of refusal of external pacification. Although Claro wrote that the decision should be left to the discretion of individual bishops, continues Guazzini, 'I firmly believe that there is no way to depart from this opinion of Ludovic,[119] which is founded on good reasons drawn from Sacred Scripture. And because it is undoubtedly safer, and when it comes to the salvation of the soul, that opinion should be embraced'.[120] Also because, he concludes, preventing a person from benefiting from the effects of peace would be contrary to evangelical precepts.[121] And the

[116] 'il rimettere all'inimico l'ingiurie è la più meritoria, ed eccellente virtù, che si possa dare in un cristiano', ibid.

[117] *Responsiones casuum conscientiae. Qui omnibus curatis, ac poenitentiarijs singulis Mensibus, coram Illustriss. ac Reverendiss. Card. Paleoto Archiepiscopo Bonon. proponuntur. Per admodum R.P. Ludovicum de Beia Palaestrelum, Lusitanum, Ordinis Eremitarum, Theologum* (Bergomi, Typis Comini Venturae, 1588), pp. 22–32 (Congregation IV, Weekday V, March 16, first case).

[118] 'per solidissima fundamenta concludit pro ista parte negative', *Sebastiani Guazzini I.C. de Civitate Castelli nuper Supremi Tribunalis Illustriss. et Reverendiss. D. Auditoris Camerae Locumtenentis Criminalis, & Causarum Criminalium Advocati in Urbe primarij. Tractatus de Pace, Treuga, Verbo dato aliqui Principi, vel alteri personae nobili, & de cautione de non offendendo per Quaestiones divisus. Omnibus Iudicibus, Advocatis, et aliis in Foro versantibus, nedum utilis, sed per quam necessarius ...* (Romae, ex Typographia Guillelmi Guacciotti, 1610), p. 5.

[119] Luis de Beja Perestrelo.

[120] 'sed ego omnino credo quod nullo modo sit recedendum ab ista opinione Ludovic. quae est fundata super bonis rationibus desumptis ex Sacra Scriptura. & quia etiam sine dubio est tutior, & quando agitur de salute animae illa opinio sit amplectenda', *Sebastiani Guazzini I.C. de Civitate Castelli*, ibid.

[121] The doctrinal discussion is well analysed in Niccoli, *Perdonare*, pp. 162ff, where, however, the author erroneously attributes to Guazzini an opinion in line with the

effects of peace were constituted by the annulment of the ban or the reduction of punishment, as has been seen.

For his part, Carbone from Costacciaro pays particular attention to the relationship between criminal action and satisfaction/restoration towards the victim. If the renunciation (with or without compensation) by the plaintiff does not exclude the possibility of the judge proceeding against the offender, according to Guazzini, the doctrine is also unanimous in considering that no judge, neither superior nor inferior, can annul or reduce the penalty to the offender before the injured party has forgiven the received injury.[122] Although the power to pardon the penalty based on the renunciation of the injured party is not within the remit of inferior judges but belongs only to the superior judge, that is, the instance from which the law itself emanates (the prince), these passages show that a significant manoeuvring space was nevertheless left to agreements between the parties. The strengthening of political power and the legislative and jurisdictional functions emanating from the sovereign triggered a reaction from moralists, and in particular from probabilists, who began to increasingly emphasise the 'peculiarities of the internal forum compared to the external forum, both ecclesiastical and civil',[123] towards the stabilisation of that dualism between conscience and law, between *culpa theologica* and *culpa juridica*, on which historiography has long reflected. However, it was a dualism that was osmotic, as Paolo Prodi taught us: defining, for example, restitution more and more as a duty of conscience does not mean excluding in principle the connection between the internal forum and the external forum.

The sacrament of penance was the fulcrum of a system of governance of social conflict that could take on very different faces, depending on the period and contingencies. In Borromean Milan, the almost police-like control of the frequency of sacraments by the faithful necessarily involved the issue of hatreds and enmities. On Easter Monday, just after the liturgical period in which the Christian was required to fulfil the obligation of annual confession, it was announced to the non-compliant faithful that they had a week to comply with the canonical norms and thus finally approach the confessional. In most cases, this meant that they would have a week to abandon hatreds and reconcile their conflicts not only – as just illustrated – in the intimacy of their

---

rigid separation between the forum of conscience and outward signs of reconciliation, typical of the thought of Thomas de Vio (Cajetan).

122 'Quando is, qui laesus est, non dum remisit actionem iniuniarum, nullus iudex sive inferior, sive supremus debet absolvere reum, aut poenam relaxare', *De pacificatione et dilectione inimicorum*, p. 268.

123 Miriam Turrini, *La coscienza e le leggi. Morale e diritto nei testi per la confessione della prima Età moderna* (Bologna, 1991), p. 304.

own conscience but also in their relationships with their enemies, to whom they had to show evident signs of reconciliation. This did not happen through generic admonitions but through the much more feared publication of actual proscription lists: at the end of the week after Easter, the list of those who had not communicated and not confessed, drawn from parish registers and confession certificates, was made public, and an interdict was immediately imposed on these people, except for granting an additional week for the recalcitrant to regularise their position. The interdict entailed the prohibition of entering the church and exclusion from burial in consecrated ground.[124]

The project of policing customs and beliefs implemented by the Archbishop of Milan in the second half of the sixteenth century was, at least in its intentions, an exceptional experience in the history of the Counter-Reformation, the actual results of which are still the subject of historiographical discussion, but the mechanism of deferring absolution could function even in less coercive contexts, less bureaucratically organised, and with less stringent regulations than Borromean Milan. The gradual affirmation of the penitential style introduced by the new sixteenth-century religious orders, and especially the Jesuits, increasingly oriented towards spiritual direction and the frequentation of confession and communion, within which the public nature of satisfaction was increasingly given less legitimacy,[125] although fitting poorly with the practice of accounting for those who had confessed and communicated at the parish level, capable of triggering the sanctioning mechanisms just illustrated, it is also true that the casuistry of conscience continued to consider as an integral part of the requirements for granting absolution the outward manifestation of the abandonment of hatred. These are signals that legitimately lead us to believe that, in the post-Tridentine era, the confessional could continue to be a fundamental centre for reconciling conflicting social relations for which the ecclesiastical personnel, both secular and regular, sought remedy.

One of the effects of this transformation of the penitential forum, specifically regarding the abandonment of hatreds and enmities, was probably

[124] See De Boer, *The Conquest of the Soul*, pp. 198–206.

[125] Lavenia, *Assolvere o infamare*. In the seventeenth century, as is well known, the practice of frequent communion was violently opposed by the rigorist front, particularly by the French Jansenists. One of the works that marked the *querelle* was indeed written on this subject by Antoine Arnauld, *De la fréquente communion. Ou les sentimens des Pères, des Papes, & des Conciles, touchant l'usage des Sacremens de Pénitence & d'Eucharistie, sont fidèlement exposez. Pour servir d'adresse aux personnes qui pensent sérieusement à se convertir à Dieu, & aux Pasteurs & Confesseurs zélés pour le bien des âmes. Par M. Antoine Arnauld, Prêtre, Docteur en Théologie de la Maison, de Sorbonne* (à Paris, chez Pierre le Petit, [1643] 1683).

the amplification of the collective character of rites and ceremonies of reconciliation. As the element of individual public satisfaction gradually lost value in post-Tridentine theological–moral doctrine and penitential practice, the peace ceremonies staged chorally within the pastoral care of the people may have represented a useful compensation, a way to neutralise the more humiliating and socially indigestible aspects of individual satisfactions.[126] This evolution is clearly evident in the transition from the missionary practices of the immediately post-Tridentine period to those of the full Baroque, when the standardised ritual and spectacular aspect of functions aimed at the pacification of enemies only diluted the reference to the concreteness of the reconstitution of social relationships fractured by hatred, in favour of an indistinct staging of the Christian obligation to forgive enemies. The rapprochement and physical contact, the exchange of signs of peace, were shown in these missions of the mid-seventeenth century more as signs of the success of the performative action of the missionary-preacher, more as tangible proof of his persuasive abilities, than as signs of achieved reconciliation.[127] Even at the level of iconographic representations, a certain rarefaction of the theme of the embrace or kiss of peace can be noted: present, though not particularly recurring, in paintings, frescoes and pictorial cycles in central and northern Italy until the fifteenth century, the *osculum pacis* ended up disappearing in the figurative arts of the sixteenth and seventeenth centuries. In the late Middle Ages, the sign of the reconciliation of enemies could be included within an *ex-voto* to Saint Francis, such as in the scene of reconciliation between the knights Joan de Tolsà and Joan de Marrodes, which took place in Ferrara in 1432 and was depicted by Antonio Orsini from Venice (Figure 6), or given under the aegis of a female figure (Figure 5) or the angel of peace (Figures 7, 8, 9); this is a theme particularly attested in the Umbrian area and in some cases linked to moments of particular social tension, such as that which gave rise, in 1399, to the penitential movement of the *Bianchi* (flagellants).[128] In the full and late Baroque, however, in the very few available examples, the tutelary deity is always the Virgin Mediatrix, and the exchanged signs between the enemies are usually not represented. In one case, that of the eighteenth-century *Madonna della Pace*, from the Benevento area, by Paolo De Matteis, the depiction of the two men – probably faction

[126] See Kiril Petkov, *The Kiss of Peace. Ritual, Self, and Society in the High and Late Medieval West* (Leiden and Boston, 2003).

[127] See Niccoli, *Perdonare*, pp. 179–85.

[128] See Stefania Giraudo, 'La devozione dei Bianchi del 1399: analisi politica di un movimento di pacificazione', *Reti Medievali Rivista* 14, 1 (2013), pp. 167–95.

leaders – making peace is perceptibly archaising, with a marked popular, as well as devotional, characterisation; in the austere climate of the Counter-Reformation, the kiss gave way to the handshake (Figure 10).[129]

In the early modern age, the iconography of the *Madonna della Pace* is only indirectly connected to private reconciliations. Devotions to the *Madonna della Pace* still practised today, perhaps organised in confraternities, retain a very faded direct connection with the overcoming of individual (or familial) conflicts. In Giugliano, near Naples, the related festival, culminating in the ceremony of the 'flight' of the angel, embodied by a child suspended at great height between buildings supported by a cable, is celebrated every year – apparently since the fifteenth century – at Pentecost, but its origins are rather uncertain; tradition speaks of an image of the Virgin coming from Byzantium that arrived in the Campanian locality transported by angels was found at sea by sailors, or was discovered by peasants in the surrounding countryside. The title could be due to an episode of family pacification that took place at an unspecified period, but there are also other hypotheses.[130] The same applies to the Confraternity of Santa Maria della Pace in Taranto, founded in the late seventeenth century due to the miraculous discovery of a Byzantine icon of the Queen of Peace.

Peace and universal brotherhood gradually became generic symbols, increasingly detached from the concreteness of social relations. It is probably for this reason that in early modern iconography the depiction of the faithful making peace and exchanging the *signum* tends to disappear and the function of intercession in the pacification of interpersonal conflicts is

[129] See Sergio Marinelli, 'La pacificazione, non la vendetta', *Acta Histriae* 25, 1 (2017), pp. 109–19. Throughout the early modern age, the kiss, along with the 'hand-touching' and the 'embracing', continued to be considered by jurists as proof of the existence of a regularly and effectively concluded peace, an element that was necessary to ascertain in order to open a judicial proceeding for breach of peace (see Daniele Edigati, *La pace nel processo criminale. Il caso toscano in età moderna,* in *Stringere la pace*, pp. 369–409: p. 385). A study of the persistence of the kiss between the sixteenth and eighteenth centuries in the conclusion of peace agreements signed in Italy, beyond the edifying ceremonies of missionary pastoral care, remains to be done, but it is reasonable to hypothesise some regional variability in this area.

[130] See *Memorie istoriche della terra di Giugliano raccolte, e date alla luce dal Reverendo D. Agostino Basile, dedicate all'Eccellentissimo Signore D. Andrea Colonna, Principe di Stigliano, ed Alliano, Marchese di Castel Nuovo, utile Signore di detta terra* (in Napoli, nella Stamperia Simoniana, 1800), pp. 295–300.

Figure 5. Giovanni di Corraduccio, known as Giovanni Mazzaforte (? – c.1440), *Allegory of Concord*, fresco. Orfini Podestà Palace (Loggia), Foligno, Perugia.

entirely absorbed by the cult of Mary, Mediatrix of Graces.[131] The decline of the *osculum pacis* in iconography paralleled the marginalisation of the exchange of the kiss in marriage ceremonies. Until the sixteenth century, the kiss was a fundamental part of the rites accompanying the exchange of matrimonial promises, precisely in its symbolic meaning as a sign of peace, and thus of agreement (also, if not especially, economic) between families.[132] With the Tridentine reform decrees, however, the rite reflected a changed

[131] See, as another example, the history of the Venetian Congregation of *Santa Maria della Pace*, connected to the veneration of the Marian image present in the chapel adjacent to the cloister of the church of *SS. Giovanni e Paolo*, belonging to the Dominicans. Since the fifteenth century, the icon has been invoked to request Mary's intercession in the pacification of conflicts between families, but no space was ever given to the iconographic representation of those being reconciled. See Deborah Walberg, 'Tradition and Propaganda in the Venetian Madonna della Pace', *Ikon* 9 (2016), pp. 269–82.

[132] The 'baciatico' indicated, in the Middle Ages, the right of the bride-to-be to receive a donation from the groom, with precise guarantees in case of the future husband's premature death. On marriage as a community rite of alliance and reconciliation between families, see John Bossy, *Christianity in the West 1400-1700* (Oxford, 1987), pp. 19–26.

Figure 6. Antonio di Cristoforo Orsini da Venezia († 1483), *Ex voto to Saint Francis of Assisi*, Musée des Arts Décoratifs, Paris. © MAD, Paris / Jean Tholance.

conception of the marital bond and the criteria for proving its existence, no longer centred on the varied community management, from below, of marriage itself, but instead on sacralisation, individualisation and uniformisation of practices, under the rigid control of ecclesiastical hierarchies[133].

4. To preach peace through agreement

The theme of forgiving enemies and seeking peace is certainly one of the most recurring in Christian preaching. It was so during the centuries of the Middle Ages, particularly marked by feuds and private wars; it continued in the early modern era, when measures to delimit and contain the recourse to private violence were unable to immediately produce that disciplining of individual behaviours theoretically considered essential for the affirmation and consolidation of powers, especially that of the state, over the territory. In a world dominated by violence, ecclesiastics – and preachers in particular – played a crucial role in the work of pacification. A group of French bishops initiated

[133] See Giovanni Tamassia, 'Osculum interveniens. Contributo alla storia dei riti nuziali', *Rivista Storica Italiana* II, 2 (1885), pp. 241–64; Piero Rasi, *La conclusione del matrimonio nella dottrina prima del Concilio di Trento* (Naples, 1958), p. 265; *Matrimoni in dubbio. Unioni controverse e nozze clandestine in Italia dal XIV al XVIII secolo*, ed. Silvana Seidel Menchi and Diego Quaglioni (Bologna, 2001); Daniela Lombardi, *Storia del matrimonio. Dal Medioevo a oggi* (Bologna, 2008), pp. 27–8.

the movement of the Peace and Truce of God (*Pax Dei*) between the tenth and eleventh centuries to protect churches, ecclesiastical personnel and the poor from the harassment of feudal lords, leading to the celebration of Peace Councils (the first at Charroux in 989); the territorial peaces (*Landfrieden*) that followed in the Holy Roman Empire from the eleventh century until the end of the fifteenth century, which required the renunciation of feuds and armed violence for a determined period, were inspired by the *Pax Dei*. In Italy, the preaching of peace was a cornerstone of the charism underlying the founding of mendicant orders and their action in the territory. Francis of Assisi not only made reconciliation between warring parties one of the most recurring themes of his preaching and teaching, but also personally intervened to reconcile enemies, as when he invited the bishop and the *Podestà* of Assisi, who were in conflict, to meet and sing together parts of the *Canticle of Brother Sun*, adjusted to contain references to the forgiveness of enemies.[134]

Figure 7. Bartolomeo di Tommaso (c.1408–54), *Angel of Peace and Concord Between Soldiers*, fresco. Sanctuary of the Madonna of Grace, Rasiglia, Perugia.

In the 'Alleluia Movement' (or 'Great Devotion') that developed in 1233 in much of central and northern Italy through the initiative of an itinerant preacher, but was quickly monopolised by Dominicans and Franciscans, the vigorous anti-heretical and moralising action on customs – which also led to several condemnations to the stake – was accompanied by an equally vigorous push for pacification. The history of the Movement is the history of preachers who transform into *podestas*, and *podestas* who transform into preachers, 'at a time of redefining the forms and gestures of oratorical practice, both secular and ecclesiastical, especially when it concerns urban governance'.[135] The political significance of the 1233 pacification campaign is thus evident:

[134] See Rosa Maria Dessì, 'Pratiques de la parole de paix dans l'histoire de l'Italie urbaine', in *Prêcher la paix et discipliner la société. Italie, France, Angleterre (XIIIe-XVe siècle)*, ed. Rosa Maria Dessì. (Turnhout, 2005), p. 245–78.

[135] 'à une époque de redéfinition des formes et des gestes de la pratique oratoire, laïque et ecclésiastique, en particulier lorsque celle-ci concerne le gouvernement urbain', op. cit., p. 247.

Figure 8. Umbrian school, *Angel of Peace and Madonna with Child*, fresco, 15th century. Church of Sant'Alò, Terni.

the action to recompose the balance in a social fabric torn by continuous violence, which aimed at conquering urban power, went hand in hand with the consolidation of the alliance between the power of the Papacy, local episcopates and popular-oriented ruling classes in the anti-heretical struggle. As the movement wound down, Pope Gregory IX reiterated on several occasions that continuous disorder and violence undermined the rights of the churches and favoured the spread of heresy. This meant ensuring that the ruling classes, by accepting to limit their internal conflicts, subjected themselves to forms of control from Rome precisely with a view to combating heresies and moralising customs, giving unprecedented space to the action of the Inquisition led by Dominican and Franciscan friars.[136]

[136] See Andrea Piazza, 'Stratégies de la parole: paix et hérétiques en Italie dans les Registres de Grégoire IX', in op. cit., pp. 103–22.

Figure 9. Umbrian school, *Angel of Peace*, fresco, 15th century. Church of Santa Maria del Monumento, Terni.

In subsequent centuries, the preaching of peace remained an indispensable task for all clergy, from bishops to parish priests, from Lenten preachers to court preachers, to itinerant friars, and, in the post-Tridentine era, to the new figure of the popular missionary.[137] The homiletic genre cannot be historically analysed in isolation both from the context of production and 'consumption' of sermons and from other genres, particularly theological – and theological–moral – rhetorical, catechetical, spiritual and even juridical, as well as from other ecclesiastical instruments of discipline, such as ecclesiastical justice, auricular confession and the institution of lay confraternities. It is not so much the obvious call, contained in the sermons, to the obligation for Christians to forgive their enemies and to recompose the bonds of friendship deteriorated or erased by hatred that is interesting, but rather the idea of justice, and the articulation between the contentious forum and the sacramental forum, in order to contain social conflict, that emerges from the vast printed production of moral reasonings and sermons. In the act of communicating the contents of the faith and behavioural models, what image did the ecclesiastical hierarchy intend to transmit to the faithful regarding courtroom justice and, conversely, the 'informal' means of overcoming hatred and interpersonal violence? How could the discourses produced by ecclesiastical hierarchies for the containment or overcoming of conflict be functional to the pursuit of other crucial objectives such as the control of heretical deviations and matrimonial and sexual behaviours?

It is, then, of particular interest to verify how, in the modern era, those Gospel passages, along with their exegetical and theological framework, which we have placed as the religious foundation of a conception of justice not exclusively based on repressive judiciary means, were used in preaching. In printed collections of sermons, as well as in spiritual works and moral reasonings, it is quite common to encounter commentary on Matt. 5:25–6,

[137] See Adriano Prosperi, 'Il missionario', in *L'uomo barocco*, ed. Rosario Villari (Rome and Bari, 1991), pp. 179–218.

and it could not be otherwise since that passage is part of the Sermon on the Mount and, in particular, of the Beatitudes, one of the cornerstones of Christ's preaching, which both Christian morality and spirituality have largely inspired. In general, it can be said that in these writings the Augustinian, and thus anagogical, exegesis that we have already had occasion to mention is accompanied by the literal one. Starting from the reflection on prison, the obligation of reconciliation with the adversary, the satisfaction due to him, the forgiveness of the offended and the expiation of the penalty become the perfect metaphor for the sacrament of penance. In homiletics, the image of the prison one risks ending up in if unable to come to terms with one's adversary takes on different meanings. The Sicilian Jesuit Giulio Cesare Mazzarino, a famous preacher in Borromean Milan,[138] compares it now to a labyrinth from which it seems impossible to escape except at the cost of a thousand hardships and sufferings, now to a closed corral, now to those circuses in which one is forced to fight against wild animals 'because prisoners are disposed to be torn apart by the cruel bites of notaries, attorneys and lawyers',[139] and now to Purgatory, 'because in both places one purges, in one the committed crimes and in the other at least the presumed ones, and suffering is more satispassion than satisfaction'. But the prison is much worse than Purgatory:

> Certainly, if one were in prison as one is in purgatory, one would suffer willingly only for the pains and not for the faults, one would praise the equity of the master who here holds just and loving souls, and one would not condemn the justice of the judge, who is spurred on by angry and hateful men, and if messengers of heavenly comforts came, and not envoys of infernal despair.[140]

138 See Flavio Rurale, 'Mazzarino, Giulio Cesare', in *Dizionario Biografico degli Italiani*, vol. 72 (Roma, 2008), pp. 528–31.

139 'perché i prigionieri sono disposti ad essere co' ispietati morsi di notai, procuratori, e avvocati laceri', Giulio Cesare Mazzarino, *De' ragionamenti su'l sermone del Signore in Monte ..., parte quarta. Nella quale si spiega l'ottava beatitudine delle persecutioni, et si và innanzi al rimanente del Sermone* (in Bologna, per gli heredi di Gio. Rossi, 1618), p. 614.

140 'Si per certo, se nel carcere si stesse come nel purgatorio volentieri, si patisse solamente per le pene non per le colpe, si lodasse l'equità del padrone che qui trattiene anime giuste e amanti, e non si condannasse la giustitia del giudice, da rei huomini d'ira e d'odio stimolati, ci capitassero nuntij di celesti conforti, e non messi d'infernali disperationi', ibid.

Figure 10. Paolo De Matteis (1662–1728), *Madonna of peace, oil on canvas*. Museum of Sannio, Benevento.

In the metaphor, a powerful image of an earthly justice system emerges, frankly infernal, dominated not only by unjust judges and rapacious lawyers but also by contenders full of hatred and rancour. The Jesuit's conclusion can only be one: 'Now I resolve that it is necessary to say that this is the greatest punishment, whatever it may be, since Christ, instead of saying hell, said prison'.[141] This implies specific obligations for the Christian, namely satisfaction and reconciliation with the adversary aimed at the restoration of friendship, regardless of the initiation of a contentious mechanism, which is not excluded in principle. Satisfaction, in fact, 'can be either free, by voluntarily paying and satisfying, or declared and determined by the judge; of the former it says, "Be agreeable with your adversary", and of the latter (which should rather be called *satispassio*), "lest he hand you over to the judge"; the former belongs to commutative justice, and the latter to vindictive justice'.[142]

What lesson can be drawn for Mazzarino, then, from this passage of the Sermon on the Mount? Just as one should not delay reconciliation with God because there will come a time when it will be too late to do so, one should not delay reconciliation with one's adversary; the judge is Christ, 'who says, "What you did for one of the least of these brothers and sisters of mine, you did for me"',[143] the adversary is the person we have offended and who turns to the judge for justice, the executor minister is the devil, 'prisoner of the infernal prison, where anyone who is enclosed will never be able to leave, because they will never be able to fully pay the infinite debt'.[144] For this reason, 'we are shown that the restitution of reputation, property or other damages done, and the due satisfaction should not be delayed, because while what is owed to our neighbour is delayed, the injustice of the injury or damage continues, and every hour the guilt grows'.[145] Satisfaction and the resolve not to commit other sins/crimes in the future, as necessary components of the sacrament of

[141] 'Ora io mi risolvo ch'è forza dire, che sia questa pena massima, qualunque essa sia, poiché Cristo invece di dire inferno, disse carcere', ibid.

[142] 'può essere ò libera con pagare e sodisfare volontariamente, o dal giudice dichiarata e determinata; di quella dice Esto consentiens adversario, e di questa (che piuttosto si doverebbe chiamare satispassione) Ne forte tradat te iudici; quella alla commutativa, e questa alla vendicativa giustizia s'appartiene', ivi op. cit., p. 615.

[143] 'che dice Quod uni ex minimis meis mihi fecistis', ibid.

[144] 'prigioniere dell'infernale carcere, onde chi ci è racchiuso mai non potrà uscirne, perché mai non fornirà di pagare intieramente il debito che è infinito', ibid.

[145] 'ci si dimostra che la restitutione della fama, della roba, o d'altro danno fatto, e la dovuta soddisfattione non si dee tardare, perché mentre si differisce quella che al prossimo si dee, l'ingiustitia dell'ingiuria, ò del danno continua, e più ogni ora con la colpa s'aggrava', ibid.

penance, become necessary components for any type of judgement, including contentious ones. Without satisfaction, there is no true justice, as the mere fulfilment of vindictive (or corrective) justice does not repair the wrong, nor does it restore the balance that has been broken. Moreover, the fact that a punitive component is necessary in confession is demonstrated by the fact – continues Mazzarino – that 'in every civil reconciliation, whether private or public, some form of satisfaction is always involved'.[146]

The theologians engaged in those same years in the drafting of treatises *De iustitia et iure* constructed a juridical–theological edifice in which the internal forum and the external forum were conceived in an almost unitary manner. The Jesuit Luis de Molina, precisely starting from the evangelical precept of reconciliation with one's enemy, recognised as natural law the possibility of the offended party forgiving the wrong suffered by accepting fair compensation, without depriving the same offended party of the possibility to demand, none the less, the conduct of a trial against the offender and the imposition of a penalty.[147] The *satisfactio* and *compensatio*, where applicable, were thus considered acts capable of stopping a judgement, without compromising the possibility of pursuing vindictive justice, just as the remission of sin in confession by virtue of the contrition/attrition of the penitent does not shield from the potential expiation required after death (Purgatory). In Catholic theology, the progressive transformation of confession into a tribunal (of conscience), which reached a moment of completion with the creation of the modern Inquisition and the need to stop the spread of heretical ideas, is part of a global redefinition of justice that made the mirroring between the internal forum and the external forum the basis of their functioning mechanisms, provided they did not concern hidden sins.[148]

It is only in this way that the concern expressed for the non-proliferation of hatred, a phenomenon that by definition resides halfway between the interiority of conscience and the exteriority of human actions, becomes intelligible to us. It is only in this way that we can understand why in moral theology and homiletics the precept of reconciliation with the adversary constantly intersects with that of fraternal correction. If the adversary being discussed is the one who has offended us, in the request for reconciliation what is done is to remind him of what the Word of God is; that is, to correct him. If instead we are the offenders, we will be obliged to accept reconciliation

[146] 'che in ogni civile riconciliatione privata o pubblica che sia, sempre qualche soddisfattione ci si vede intervenire', ivi op. cit., p. 622.

[147] See Testuzza, *Rimediare al male con il bene*, pp. 276–84.

[148] See Prosperi, *Tribunali della coscienza*.

as a necessary act of submission to the law of God. People are merely instruments used by God to restore justice, and if we are admonished by a person who appears to us as a sinner, we must accept the admonition in any case, because at that moment it is not the person acting, but God himself. 'It is not men who speak on these occasions, but God himself, as Saint Paul says, who speaks to men through men, to sanctify some through charity, and others through humility',[149] was a frequent assertion from the pulpit in the second half of the seventeenth century, on the third Tuesday of Lent, by Guillaume de Saint Martin, pastor of the church of the Sainte Chapelle in Paris and royal preacher, precisely when commenting on the obligation of the evangelical *denunciatio* (Matt. 18:15). This would also be emphasised, with extreme clarity, by the Jesuit Paolo Segneri senior, almost a century after Mazzarino:

> Consider how this precept says 'your Adversary', not because he wishes you harm (for in that case, he would be called an enemy) but because he contradicts your incorrect desires, performing for you the same office that the Angel did for the inconsiderate Balaam when he said: 'I have come to oppose you because your path is a reckless one, contrary to mine'.[150] Sometimes this adversary wants to draw you away from the evil into which you are rushing; at other times, he wants to incite you to the good to which you are reluctant. Thus, in both cases, he always opposes you and is always your Adversary, adversatur tibi. But what? Will you hold any ill will against him for this? On the contrary, you should love him all the more for this. A Friend who opposes is better than an Enemy who flatters.[151]

[149] 'Ce ne sont pas les hommes qui parlent en ces occasions, mais Dieu mesme, comme dit Saint Paul, qui parle aux hommes par les hommes, pour santifier le uns par la charité, et les autres par l'humilité', *Sermons pour tous les jours du Caresme, preschez par M.re Guillaume de S. Martin, Prestre, Docteur en Théologie, Conseiller, Aumosnier, et Predicateur ordinaire du Roy, et Curé de l'Eglise de la basse Sainte Chapelle de Paris, tome premier* (à Paris, chez Edme Couterot; 1683), p. 455.

[150] The reference is to Num. 22:23–4: 'The ass seeing the angel standing in the way, with a drawn sword, turned herself out of the way, and went into the field. And when Balaam beat her, and had a mind to bring her again to the way' ('Cernens asina angelum Domini stantem in via, evaginato gladio in manu sua, avertit se de itinere et ibat per agrum. Quam cum verberaret Balaam et vellet ad semitam reducere, stetit angelus Domini in angustiis duarum maceriarum, quibus vineae cingebantur') and to Num. 22:32: 'And the angel said to him: Why beatest thou thy ass these three times? I am come to withstand thee, because thy way is perverse, and contrary to me' ('Cui angelus Domini: Cur, inquit, tertio verberas asinam tuam? Ego veni, ut adversarer tibi, quia perversa est via tua mihique contraria').

[151] 'Considera come questo dettame si dice Avversario tuo, non perch'egli voglia il tuo male (giacché il tal caso si sarebbe detto nimico) ma perché contraddice alle tue voglie scorrette, facendo con esso te quell'ufficio, che fece l'Angelo con

And it is the same Saint Martin who emphasises that, for the moral policing of a society, it is necessary first and foremost that every Christian feels obligated to tell the truth to a brother who sins, and who perhaps has inflicted a wrong on us, as it is 'necessary for the glory of God and the public good';[152] consequently 'the laws have even instituted public censors to have oversight of the lives of men, to remind them of their duty, and to reprimand their vices'.[153] A particularly noteworthy aspect lies in the fact that, in Saint Martin's reconstruction, this system based on denunciation, and thus on a potentially non-contentious resolution of conflicts, originated in the civil order and then passed to the ecclesiastical order, and not vice versa:

> which passed from the civil and political state into the Christian and Ecclesiastical Republic, where we see in fact that the Son of God not only instituted public censors in the person of Preachers and Apostolic Men, but also as many private censors as there are Christians obligated to the precept of fraternal correction.[154]

Every Christian, in their own small way, must assume the functions of a censor of others' behaviour, a tangible sign not of hatred but of the love we have for our neighbour, even if they are our adversary, since in this way we preserve them from eternal damnation. The intimate connection between the precept of reconciliation with one's adversaries and the precept of fraternal correction thus appears in all its clarity and sheds new light on

---

l'inconsiderato Balamo, quando egli disse: Ego veni, ut adversarer tibi, quia perversa est via tua, mihique contraria.130 Alle volte questo avversario ti vuole ritrar dal male, in cui tu trascorri; e alle volte ti vuole incitare al bene, a cui sei ritroso. Però nell'un caso, e nell'altro ti avversa sempre, e così sempre è Avversario, adversatur tibi. Ma che? Per questo gli vorrai male alcuno? Anzi per questo lo devi amar maggiormente. Meglio è un Amico che avversa, che non è un Nimico che adula', *La manna dell'anima, overo esercizio facile insieme, e fruttuoso, per chi desidera in qualche modo attender all'Orazione, proposto dal Padre Paolo Segneri della Compagnia di Giesù, per tutti i giorni dell'anno*, in *Opere del Padre Paolo Segneri della Compagnia di Giesù distribuite in quattro tomi*, tomo I (in Venezia, presso Paolo Baglioni, 1716), p. 325.

152 'necessaire pour la gloire de Dieu et le bien publique', *Sermons pour tous les jours du Caresme*, p. 457.

153 'les loix ont institué mesme des censeurs publics pour avoir inspection sur la vie des hommes, pour les avertir de leur devoir, reprendre leurs vices', ibid.

154 'ce qui a passé de l'estat civil et politique dans la Republique Chrestienne et Ecclesiastique, où nous voyons en effet que le Fils de Dieu n'a pas seulement institué des censeurs publiques en la personne des Predicateurs et des Hommes Apostoliques, mais autant de censeurs particuliers qu'il y a de Chrestiens obligez au precepte de la correction fraternelle', ibid.

the central role of sacramental confession in the judicial mechanisms of governing violence and social conflict, which, in addition to being linked to significant fiscal matters, were characterised by the continual oscillation between conciliatory and transactional methods and coercive methods. We know, in fact, how often acts of grace and clemency related to the issue of the *restitutio famae* (restitution of honour/reputation) were subjected to the payment of a sum of money. An oscillation between the forum of conscience and the contentious forum was made possible by the theological–legal ambiguity of the statute of *iniuria*: from what degree of severity of the offence should the justice of the external forum intervene? To what extent could (or should) everything be halted at the composition, managed by a mediator perhaps assisted by the same confessor who had directed the penitent to an agreement with their adversary? And was it really a matter of the intensity of the inflicted offence, or should the gravity be measured according to other parameters?

These are issues that, developed and gradually refined by theologians and jurists, also needed to be brought to the knowledge of the faithful, who had to know how to behave in certain circumstances. Preaching and catechesis thus became privileged tools for disseminating behavioural norms that went beyond the precept of forgiveness and the re-establishment of bonds of peace and friendship. The message had to be calibrated to the occasion and the audience, but the issue of recomposing the social fabric was too important to be left to chance. Through *exempla* and continuous references to Scripture and a theology adapted to the audience, preachers insisted on the necessity of repentance and the remission of sins, trying to exploit the secrecy of the entire process. In the mid-sixteenth century, Cornelio Musso, one of the most prominent prelates of the Tridentine Church, referred to the conversion of King David, which occurred through the Lord's intervention thanks to a sermon 'not public, but private [...] which penetrated the heart from the ear [...], impressed upon the spirit like a thorn in a foot, like a stick in an eye'.[155] If, previously,

> he was hiding first the adultery, then the homicide to avoid being disgraced in the Kingdom, later pierced inside by this stimulus that did not let him rest day or night, that accused him, condemned him, made him

[155] 'non publica, ma privata [...] che dall'orecchio penetrò al cuore [...], gli s'impresse nello spirito, come una spina in un pie', com'uno stecco in un'occhio', *Il terzo libro delle prediche del Reverendissimo Mons. Cornelio Musso, Vescovo di Bitonto, con due tavole, l'una delle prediche, l'altra delle cose più notabili* (in Vinegia, appresso Gabriel Giolito De' Ferrari, 1572), p. 100.

see hell open; at last, he opened his mouth, and exaggerating the case as much as he could against himself, he confessed simply to the holy priest and obtained the remission of his sins.[156]

One must always come to terms with one's enemy because one's enemy is the Word of God, 'which always says the opposite of what you would like'.[157] They must reconcile with their own conscience as soon as possible to avoid living constantly tormented by remorse, and when it is too late to remedy the sins committed, that same conscience will condemn us to perpetual hell. In line with this, in the mid-seventeenth century the Capuchin François de Toulouse, superior of the mission of Vigan in the Cévennes, a region in France traditionally with a high concentration of Huguenots, in the seventh sermon of those composing the usual cycle that took place during the mission, warned the faithful of the necessity of reconciling with their enemy to prevent the enemy from harming them, using 'the power of justice to take revenge'[158] or attacking them 'with an authority which we cannot resist'.[159] But there is a far more formidable enemy, Toulouse continued, which is a guilty conscience, a sort of domestic enemy that ceaselessly torments the sinner, and on this aspect, he focused most of his sermon. Francesco Panigarola, Bishop of Asti and Observant Franciscan, delved into the details of the behaviours a Christian must adopt in the case of wrongs committed or suffered. In one of his Lenten sermons held in Saint Peter's, Rome, in 1577, Panigarola stated that if you are the one causing the offence 'you must humble yourself and ask for peace';[160] if you are the victim of an injury you

[156] 'andava ascondendo hora l'adulterio, hora l'homicidio per non essere infamato nel Regno, trafitto poi tutto di dentro da questo stimolo che no'l lasciava posare né dì, né notte, che l'accusava, che lo condannava, che gli faceva veder l'inferno aperto; all'ultimo aprì la bocca, et essagerando il caso quanto più puoté contra di se stesso, si confessò semplicemente al santo sacerdote, et ottenne la remission de' suoi peccati', ibid.

[157] 'che dice sempre il contrario di quel che voi vorreste', ibid.

[158] 'le pouvoir de la justice pour se vanger', *Le missionnaire apostolique ou sermons utiles à ceux qui s'employent aux missions, pour retirer les hommes du peché, et les porter à la Penitence. Par le R.P. François de Thoulouse, Superieur des Capucins de la Mission du Vigan, dans les Sevenes, tome sixième, des vertus et des vices*, à Paris, chez Denys Thierry, 1671, p. 149.

[159] 'par une authorité à laquelle nous ne sçaurions resister', ibid.

[160] 'tu dei humiliarti, e chiederli la pace', *Prediche quadragesimali del Reverendiss. Monsig. Panigarola Vescovo d'Asti, dell'Ordine di S. Francesco de' Minori Osservanti, predicate da lui in S. Pietro di Roma l'anno 1577* (in Venetia, appresso gli heredi di Marchiò Sessa, 1600), p. 33.

must consider that your enemy, by offending you, has done three things: offended God, filled you with rancour and caused you harm. How should you behave in this case? You must hate the sin of your enemy with all your heart, but not the person of the enemy; you must transform the rancour he has instilled in you so that you can remain 'free of all hatred' ('netto d'ogni odio'); as for the fact that your enemy has 'taken your health, honour, property or child',[161] if the harm is present 'you can appeal to Reason and seek to recover it'.[162] but if the harm is past:

> I say whether you can compensate yourself or not: if you can compensate yourself, I do not prevent you from appealing to the judge; with charity none the less, and without rancour; I do say, however, that if you simply forgive, it is an act of perfection: but if the damage cannot be compensated, and he humbles himself before you, he has killed your son, and he would compensate if he could, but he cannot, and he asks for peace; what should you do? I say that you are obliged to forgive him; and I don't know how it is safe to say, I have forgiven him, let Justice now proceed; because this rarely happens without harbouring hatred, and also the servant in the Gospel left it to Justice: and as it was none the less said to him, 'You should have had mercy on your fellow servant', but I will not delve into that for now: as a testimony of good will, Christ says, 'Do good and to those who cannot do it, add what cannot be hindered. Pray for those who persecute you'.[163]

Recourse to the judge is not excluded in principle, but under specific conditions. First, if there is a concrete possibility of restitution, and in any case, if one approaches the process with a spirit of charity and without rancour; if restitution is not practicable and the wrongdoer humbles himself and asks for forgiveness, on one hand, we are obliged to grant forgiveness, and on the other hand, we are not authorised – once granted – still to seek the judge's

[161] 'tolto ò la sanità, ò l'honore, ò la robba, ò il figlio', ivi op. cit., p. 34.

[162] 'tu puoi ricorrere alla Ragione, e cercar di rihaverti', ibid.

[163] 'dico se puoi ricompensarti, ò nò: se puoi ricompensarti, non t'impedisco, che non ricorri al giudice; con charità nondimeno, e senza rancore; dico bene, che se tu lo rimetti semplicemente è opra di perfettione: ma se'l danno non è possibile che se ricompensi, e ch'egli te se humilia, t'ha ucciso il figlio, & egli lo ricompensarebbe, se potesse, non può, e ti chiede la pace; quà che dei fare? Dico che sei obligato a perdonargli; e non sò come sia sicuro il dire, io gli ho perdonato, faccia hora la Giustitia; perché difficilmente accade questo senza haver odio, et anco il servo del Vangelo lasciava fare alla Giustitia: e come a lui nondimeno fu detto. *Oportet te misereri conservi tui*, ma a questo io non v'entro per hora: in testimonio della buona volontà dice Christo. *Benefacite* & a quello, che non può fare, aggionge quello, che non può esser impedito. *Orate pro persequentibus vos*', ibid.

intervention to impose a punitive sentence *ex iustitia vindicativa*, 'because this rarely happens without harbouring hatred'.[164] By resorting to justice, we would behave like the servant mentioned in Matt. 18:32–5, who, after being forgiven (and forgiven his debt) by his master for unrepaid money, refuses to forgive the debt owed to him by his peer, handing him over to the judge and having him thrown into prison.[165] If we are not willing to forgive our enemy, neither will God be willing to forgive us.

In early modern homiletics, commentary on the Gospel passages regarding the obligation to forgive and reconcile with one's enemies is always accompanied by specific considerations regarding the governance of passions. This was certainly not a novelty: in the sermons of Saint John Chrysostom on the Gospel of Matthew, the theme is recurrent, in the conviction that distinguishing between useful and lawful passions and destructive and deadly passions is essential precisely to prevent the violence of murder:

> *He that is angry with his brother without a cause shall be in danger of the judgement*: so He speaks.
>
> Thus He hath not altogether taken the thing away: first, because it is not possible, being a man, to be freed from passions: we may indeed get the dominion over them, but to be altogether without them is out of the question.
>
> Next, because this passion is even useful, if we know how to use it at the suitable time. See, for instance, what great good was wrought by that anger of Paul, which he felt against the Corinthians, on that well-known occasion; and how, as it delivered them from a grievous pest, so by the same means again he recovered the people of the Galatians likewise, which had fallen aside; and others too beside these.[166]

[164] 'perché difficilmente accade questo senza haver odio', ibid.

[165] 'His master summoned him and said to him, "You wicked servant! I forgave you your entire debt because you begged me to. Should you not have had pity on your fellow servant, as I had pity on you?". Then in anger his master handed him over to the torturers until he should pay back the whole debt. So will my heavenly Father do to you, unless each of you forgives his brother from his heart' ('Tunc vocavit illum dominus suus et ait alii: "Serve nequam, omne debitum illud dimisi tibi, quoniam rogasti me; non oportuit et te misereri conservi tui, sicut et ego tui misertus sum?". Et iratus dominus eius tradidit eum tortoribus, quoadusque redderet universum debitum. Sic et Pater meus caelestis faciet vobis, si non remiseritis unusquisque fratri suo de cordibus vestris') (Matt. 18:32–5).

[166] *The homilies of St. John Chrysostom, Archbishop of Constantinople, of the Gospel of St. Matthew, translated with notes and indices*, part I, Hom. I–XXV (Oxford, John Henry Parker J.G.F. and J. Rivington, 1893), p. 240.

Anger is illicit if we use it for revenge, to seek justice on our own, and one of the ways to prevent a natural passion such as anger from turning into revenge is to accelerate the process of reconciliation with one's enemy as much as possible. By focusing on controlling passions and omitting detailed references to the nature of the offences, both given and received, homiletics and catechetical literature managed to neutralise the substance of conflict in a society that, on the other hand, continued to legitimise revenge, especially for the defence of personal and family honour.

In his *Quaeresimale* (Third Sermon, on the Friday after Ash Wednesday), Paolo Segneri presents revenge as something completely separate from judicial mechanisms, as a passion that must be kept under the strict control of rational capacities. Segneri acknowledges that, when talking about revenge, one refers to 'a passion so fierce that it does not value reasons, does not want advice, does not yield to prayers, and, like an enraged asp, scorns listening so as not to stop biting',[167] and reassures his audience by making it clear that it is not his intention to diminish the faults of those who have offended, insulted, or struck the present, thus deserving a response equal to the offence received; 'I myself', continues Segneri, 'would like to be the first to incite your hatred against them, and would wish them much more harm than you perhaps would know how to inflict on them, if it were lawful'.[168] But the preacher's sole interest is the material and spiritual good of the faithful, and revenge is to be abandoned not only because Christ commands it, but also because it only brings disasters to those who carry it out.

The aim is not so much to eradicate anger definitively but to temper it with the use of prudence, and this can only be achieved by avoiding acting immediately on the impulse of passion. The reference, again, is to Ephesians 4:26–7 ('Be angry: and sin not. Let not the sun go down upon your anger. Give not place to the devil'). Anger 'is the most precipitous affection of all [...] Whoever acts, carried away by it, never acts with prudence, but with temerity. It imagines all difficulties as easy, all dangers as certain, all events as favourable, and does not consider how often it has happened that one who

[167] 'una passione sì fiera che non apprezza ragioni, non vuol consigli, non si arrende a preghiere, e, qual aspido inferocito, sdegna di udire per non lasciare di mordere', *Quaresimale del Padre Paolo Segneri della Compagnia di Gesù*, vol. I (Milano, per Giovanni Silvestri, 1827), p. 48.

[168] ' io stesso vorrei essere il primo ad irritare il vostro odio contro di loro, e vorrei loro pregare, se fosse lecito, assai più male di quello che forse voi non sapreste loro recare', ibid.

trusted to remain the victor fell defeated'.[169] Therefore, we must ensure that the sun (the sun of reason, according to Thomas's interpretation) does not set on our anger, as Paul teaches; we must avoid acting immediately, impulsively, and wait to fully understand the situation and conditions, convincing ourselves that revenge is nothing but the beginning of an uninterrupted series of sufferings. Taking revenge is like 'cutting off the head of the hydra' ('recidere il capo all'idra').[170]

In seventeenth-century France, it was also a preacher, the Oratorian Jean-François Senault, a direct disciple of Pierre de Bérulle, who delved into the profound meaning of passions, their personal, social, religious and political significance, and how to govern them, through the publication of a work specifically dedicated to this, *De l'usage des passions*, first printed in Paris in 1641. For Senault, passions are 'both the seeds of vices and virtues',[171] but

> we are no longer in that happy state of innocence, where our Passions awaited the order of Reason, and where they did not arise without having obtained its consent. They are unfaithful and no longer recognise the voice of their Sovereign; they obey the first who commands them and just as soon take the side of a Tyrant as that of their legitimate Prince.[172]

Passions are not inherently evil, and in this he is undoubtedly indebted to a tradition of thought that, starting with Juan Luis Vivès (*De Anima et Vita*, 1538), conceived them not merely as functions of the sensitive soul, in the line that stretches from Stoicism to Saint Thomas, but as fully human, necessary for the realisation of man's ultimate end and also the foundation of any moral discipline.[173] According to the French Oratorian, however, it

[169] 'è la più precipitosa affezione che sia fra tutte [...] Chi opera, trasportato da essa, non opera mai con prudenza, ma con temerità. Si finge agevoli tutte le difficoltà, sicuri tutti i pericoli, favorevoli tutti gli eventi, e non considera quante volte è avvenuto che cada vinto chi si fidava di rimaner vincitore', ibid.

[170] ibid.

[171] 'aussi bien les semences des vices et des vertus', Jean-François Senault, *De l'usage des passions* (Leiden, chez Jean Elsevier, 1658), p. 142.

[172] 'nous ne sommes plus en cet heureux estat de l'innocence, où nos Passions attendoient l'ordre de la Raison, & où elles ne s'ellevoient point qu'elles n'en eussent obtenu le congé, elles sont infidelles, & ne recognoissans plus la voix de leur Souveraine, elles obeïssent au premier qui leur commande, & prennent aussi-tost le party d'un Tyran que celuy de leur Prince légitime', ibid.

[173] See Marina Mestre Zaragozá, 'La théorie des passions de Juan Luis Vivès', in *Les passions à l'âge classique*, ed. Pierre-François Moreau (Paris, 2006), pp. 29–44.

is essential to be aware that the transition from good to evil, from virtue to vice, can be immediate and difficult to control:

> The same desires that elevate us to heaven attach us to the earth, what Nature has given us to set us free throws us into prison and binds us in chains; the same hope that flatters us deceives us; and the hope that should soften our past misfortunes brings us new ones; the same anger that drives the courageous to battle animates the cowards to revenge, and that which is noble in war becomes cruel in peace.[174]

Who, after all, if not the preachers, could be so deeply and subtly interested in the issue of passions and their proper control and use? Eloquence – a central discipline in Renaissance and Baroque culture, also thanks to the revival of Aristotelian *Rhetoric*[175] – is aimed at stirring not only the intellect but also the 'senses' and the 'affections'; to use a modern word, emotions:

> Orators who wish to capture the soul through the senses combine beautiful words with sound reasoning, flatter the ear to touch the heart, and employ all figures of speech to stir the affections. They attack both parts that make up man, using the weaker to conquer the stronger, and just as the Demon lost man through the woman, they win Reason through Passion.[176]

It is for this reason that, according to Senault, preachers had over time acquired an enormous, perhaps excessive, influence over people, particularly over those who govern ('it seemed that the hearts of Princes were in the hands of Orators, and that Monarchy had become a slave to Eloquence'),[177]

174 'Les mesmes desirs qui nous ellevent au ciel, nous attachent a la terre, ce que la Nature nous a donné pour nous mettre en liberté, nous iette dans la prison, & nous engage dans les fers; La mesme esperance qui nous flate, nous abuse; & celle qui doit adoucir nos mal-heurs passez, nous en procure de nouveau; La mesme cholere qui porte le courageux au combat, anime les lasches à la vengeance, & celle qui est genereuse à la guerre, devient cruelle dans la Paix', Senault, *De l'usage des passions*, pp. 142–3.

175 See Marc Fumaroli, *L'âge de l'éloquence. Rhétorique et'Res literaria' de la Renaissance au seuil de l'époque classique* (Genève, 2002).

176 'les Orateurs qui veulent prendre l'ame par le sens, ioignent les belles paroles aux bonnes raisons, flatent l'oreille pour toucher le coeur, & employent toutes les figures pour esmouvoir les affections. Ils attaquent les deux parties qui composent l'homme, il se servent de la plus foible pour emporter la plus forte, & comme le Demon perdit l'homme par le moyen de la femme, ils gagnent la Raison par le moyen de la Passion', Senault, *De l'usage des passions*, p. 183.

177 'il sembloit que le coeur des Princes fut entre les mains des Orateurs, & que la Monarchie fust devenüe esclave de l'Eloquence', ivi op. cit., p. 184.

causing enormous damage to republics: 'by too often arousing the movements of the lower part of the soul, they ruined the Empire of the higher part, and could neither heal the wounds they had opened nor extinguish the flames they had kindled'.[178]

By relating, in ecclesiastical discourse, revenge to human passions, the hierarchies were able to carve out a privileged ground for action in controlling social conflict. Beyond preaching, catechesis, the reform of sacramental practices, and the dissemination of a culture of forgiveness and reconciliation that paid particular attention to the noble class (treatises, education in seminaries for nobles, theatre, etc.), the Church could act undisturbed in a space – the forum of conscience – that lay between the external manifestations of violence and the intimate, hidden sphere: the sphere of passions and feelings. When theologians sought to precisely delineate, in the ways of resolving conflict, the realms of competence between public, external action and informal, secret action, they were not compromising with longstanding community customs but rather reaffirming a traditional sphere of intervention for the ecclesiastical hierarchies in the mechanisms of violence.

It was essential to convey to the faithful a precise idea of the action of justice, according to which contentious proceedings were to be avoided as much as possible for all those crimes of hatred that originated or maintained states of enmity between individuals. This was not a residual effect of medieval legal institutions impacting an evolving judicial reality but the very essence of the functioning mechanisms of pre-modern justice. Only with the Enlightenment would those mechanisms be radically challenged, legally, theologically and culturally.

[178] 'pour avoir trop souvent excité les mouvemens de la partie inferieure de l'ame, ils ruinerent l'Empire de la superieure, & ne pûrent guerir les playes qu'ils avoient ouvertes, ny esteindre les flammes qu'ils avoient allumées', ibid.

Conclusions

The prevalent focus on the emergence of the public and mandatory criminal trial within the judicial institutions of Western Europe from the Middle Ages to the early modern era has overshadowed parallel developments, which have generally been portrayed as contradictory and dissonant or, at best, minor; residues of the past, as has often been noted in these pages. New investigative methodologies have instead shown that the paths traced by law and the mechanisms for sanctioning crime and resolving conflicts were not linear, were not necessarily oriented towards progress and institutional strengthening, and also how arbitrary it can be to draw an abstract line of demarcation between modernity and archaism. About twenty years ago, Simona Cerutti and Renata Ago brought to the attention of the scientific community the issue of judicial procedure, too often neglected by a historiography traditionally much more focused on social conflict and the institutional control exercised over it.[1] A few years later Simona Cerutti, in particular, would dedicate a research project to the topic, centred on the spread of summary procedure in eighteenth-century Turin, aiming to investigate the 'demand for justice formulated by men and women to a wide range of legal institutions'[2] and the 'ways in which these different institutions acted in response to these demands and to those formulated by their own members'.[3] The success of the summary procedure in commercial disputes is a story that can open up highly interesting perspectives on conceptions of justice from a viewpoint that rejects folkloric readings and socio-historical approaches that are scarcely, or not at all, interested in the doctrinal and intellectual dimension.

In eighteenth-century Turin, within a few decades, the ordinary procedure replaced the summary one, characterised by brevity and speed, simplicity

[1] See Renata Ago, Simona Cerutti, 'Premessa', *Quaderni Storici* (*Procedure di giustizia*), 34, 101/2 (1999), pp. 307–14.

[2] 'domanda di giustizia formulata da uomini e donne a un'ampia gamma di istituzioni legali', Simona Cerutti, *Giustizia sommaria. Pratiche e ideali di giustizia in una società di Ancien Régime (Torino, XVIII secolo)* (Milan, 2003), p. 12.

[3] 'modi in cui queste diverse istituzioni agivano rispondendo a queste domande e a quelle formulate dai loro stessi membri', ibid.

and low cost, inspired by the ideals of natural law and the concept of *aequitas* (equity), far from the specialised domain of legal professionals. The history of the summary procedure traced by Cerutti intertwines, at least in part, with that of peace and pacification procedures. A polysemic term that does not refer only to issues of judicial procedure, peace was nevertheless connected to an ideal of speed and brevity, rejection of quibbles, capable of defining not only the aspirations of social actors but also the concrete methods of governing crime and conflict by public authorities. When the Roman pontiffs, starting from the mid-sixteenth century, established that to eradicate the plague of banditry, vendettas and factional violence, it was necessary to proceed 'summarily' ('procedatur summarie, simpliciter, & de plano sine strepitu, & figura judicii'),[4] inviting the population to denounce and promising absolutions from censures and interdicts to those who collaborated, they expressed a concept that remained mostly unnoticed, namely that speed responded not only to the needs of subordinate classes who had to deal daily with the obscure technicalities of the ordinary process, with the 'high' knowledge of prosecutors and judges, with grammars and conceptions of justice perceived as distant and not 'fair' according to the principles of natural law, but also to those of legal institutions that, using a procedural tool normally conceived for civil and property disputes,[5] aimed to insert themselves, through a continuous process of adaptation to power relations and a series of socially shared ideals, into mechanisms of regulation of interpersonal violence that already existed. Forum of conscience and external forum acted in concert, as the ban was evidently configured as a civil excommunication and, therefore, peace as an absolution from excommunication;[6] it is no coincidence that the two measures were usually imposed together.

This 'summarie et executive' mode had deep connections with peace and did not exclusively characterise the interventions of central powers in exceptional circumstances, where it was urgent to restore order. In the action

4 See above, p. 103.

5 In the statutory legislation of the early modern period, the matters for which summary procedure was admissible were specified. In the statutes of Rome under Gregory XIII, 'summary causes' were defined as all those 'in quibus de summa infra ducatorum auri vigintiquinque, vel de re valorem praedictum non excedente, agitur' ('in which the amount in question is less than twenty-five gold ducats, or involves a matter not exceeding the aforementioned value'), *Statuta Almae Urbis Romae Auctoritate Gregorii Papae XIII, a Senatu Populoq. Rom. Reformata, & Edita* (Romae, in Aedibus Populi Romani, 1590), p. 41. For cases of a non-property or civil nature, the amount referred to the sum of the composition.

6 See Antonio Pertile, *Storia del diritto italiano. Dalla caduta dell'Impero Romano alla codificazione*, vol. V (Turin, Unione Tipografico-Editrice, 1892), pp. 309–41.

strategy of the judicial powers of the Papal States, peace was central not only in the phase following the issuance of the sentence, when the condemned person had the opportunity to escape punishment 'by paying for forgiveness', provided they had obtained peace from the offended party.[7] The papal power could act 'sine processu ex justa suspicione', to use the expression of Giovan Domenico Rainaldi, resorting to crime prevention tools rooted in the *potestas oeconomica* of the pope's representatives, typically sureties with guarantors, fines, and confiscations; peace in this case had the effect of liberation from the corresponding financial obligations. In both cases, the entire system was aimed at achieving peace, the true keystone of the judicial systems of the *Ancien Régime*. Behind transactive and consensual institutions, ultimately there hid a particular type of summary procedure that fully revealed its coercive face both when social actors accessed it and when those same actors failed to comply with the signed pact, the sacred as well as legal nature of which were revealed to the maximum degree in the case of solemn peace agreements signed in front of representatives of the ecclesiastical hierarchy.

It is a story with long roots, that of the use of tools for the prevention of crime and violence, founded in oaths, pecuniary penalties and confiscations, capable of targeting not only the guilty but also their kinship networks, usually privileging agnatic lines.[8] Peace was indissolubly linked to these tools, to the point that it was sometimes difficult to distinguish between a peace and a *sicurtà di non offendere* (not to harm), especially from an intrinsic point of view.[9] This is an important element of differentiation between the speed of transactional and pacification procedures and that typical of the summary procedure in the commercial field, which, according to Simona Cerutti, would have contributed to enhancing an individual conception of judicial responsibility, given that – as stated also by Samuel Pufendorf – a father cannot commit himself for his

7 With reference to episcopal justice, see Diego Pedrini and Lucia Dubbini, *Il prezzo del perdono. Il Tribunale episcopale di Jesi in età moderna (1530-1730)* (Fermo, 2020).

8 Christiane Klapisch-Zuber provides a clear and highly interesting picture of the Florentine judicial arsenal during the years straddling the fourteenth and fifteenth centuries. See Christiane Klapisch-Zuber, *Retour à la Cité. Les magnats de Florence (1340-1440)* (Paris, 2006), pp. 145–92. But even in the late thirteenth century, imposed peace agreements, complete with the intervention of *sicurtà* not to harm, were commonplace, as attested by several studies, including most recently Katherine L. Jansen, *Peace and Penance in Late Medieval Italy* (Princeton and Oxford, 2018), p. 137 ff.

9 For late medieval France, the relationship between peace and *asseurement* has been illustrated in Claude Gauvard, *'De Grâce especial'. Crime, État et société en France à la fin du Moyen Âge* (Paris, 1991), pp. 779–88.

son through an oath. This is exactly what had happened in the sixteenth and seventeenth centuries, when fathers were forced to sign *cautiones de non offendendo* for sons involved in episodes of violence.[10]

The attitude of public authorities and legal doctrine towards institutions such as peace and arbitration has been the subject of refined analyses which, however, have had the limitation of categorising these latter somewhat too rigidly as forms of 'private justice', albeit subjected to a process of progressive publicisation. This has resulted in a certain inability to understand to what extent, between the late Middle Ages and the early modern period, those same public authorities were able to combine the apparently informal ways of resolving social conflict with the affirmation of *iurisdictio*. They succeeded by increasingly imposing their presence and protection on those same tools, through surveillance over the notary system, the selection and operation of *amicabiles compositores*, the access mechanisms to arbitration, sureties and peace agreements, and especially through the severe sanction of oath-breaking, an event with high destabilising potential in what was in all respects a 'sworn society' ('società giurata') and in a period when the imposition of the oath was conceived as a 'prerogative of sovereignty' ('prerogativa della sovranità').[11]

The 'tendency to exalt arbitration as a typical manifestation of freedom and rejection of forensic mediation' is not typical,[12] as Luciano Martone hypothesised, only of the mature phase of the process of consolidation of state structures, a moment when corrosive Enlightenment criticism attacked ministerial arbitrariness and the apparatus of the state, but crosses the thought and judicial practices of the West precisely thanks to the diffusion of the concept, with very strong Christian connotations, and the legal tool of peace, without coming into conflict with the progressive affirmation of public jurisdictional structures.

The terrain is constantly on the borderline between civil and criminal matters. The stigmatisation, supported by powerful religious arguments, of *litis abusus* did not only concern civil disputes, even in cases of assaults, wounds and insults, which often resulted in killings; the authorities pushed towards compositional solutions, according to a non-punitive perspective, in various ways: through pre- or para-judicial pressure, in a context of triggering

[10] See Cerutti, *Giustizia sommaria*, p. 76.

[11] Paolo Prodi, *Il sacramento del potere. Il giuramento politico nella storia costituzionale dell'Occidente* (Bologna, 1992), p. 231.

[12] 'tendenza ad esaltare l'arbitrato quale tipica manifestazione di libertà e di rifiuto della mediazione forense', Luciano Martone, *Arbiter-arbitrator. Forme di giustizia privata nell'età del diritto comune* (Naples, 1984), p. XIV.

the *ex officio* procedure, aimed at forcing the contenders (and their kin) to sign sureties or make peace; through pushing for procedural outcomes other than the sentence of condemnation; finally, through the mechanism of banishment for contumacy and later reintegration of the offender. Peace, despite everything, was not mere fiction; it was not the cynical masking of coercion by means of the benign face of concepts such as forgiveness, love for one's neighbour, concord and friendship. Social actors, although most of the time forced to enter into a transaction with their adversaries, attributed real value to the promise, regardless of the fact that breaking that promise was the rule. The concepts of grace, mercy and peace that permeated images of justice from the Middle Ages onwards and that invaded the practices of criminal justice, as highlighted by Adriano Prosperi on several occasions,[13] did not only concern the sovereign exercise of the power to condemn and pardon, but were realised in a dynamic parallelism between high and low, where the bottom of the social hierarchy was called to share the same ideals of granting forgiveness periodically enacted by the sovereign.[14] All this mobilised the powerful machine of juridical–theological thought, which aimed at focusing on the issue, far from marginal, of the necessity to correspond to the forgiveness of the offence received, matured in the depths of conscience, with external signs of reconciliation. A ground of conjunction between internal and external forum, between persuasion and repression, which had enormous consequences on the concrete practice of governing interpersonal hatred.

On these bases, a flourishing tradition of thought developed in medieval and early modern European societies, aiming to highlight the limits, and even the dangers, of contentious justice to the full advantage of arbitral, transactional and contractual justice, which had as a reflection the creation of precise legal tools halfway between judicial coercion and arbitral conciliation, such as the *asseurements* in France and the sureties (or warrants) of good behaviour in England. In Christian culture (and not only there, as the same phenomenon is observed in the Jewish context as well),[15] turning to a judge signifies a display of enmity towards the one who has wronged us. Without this causing the slightest embarrassment or opposition from the established powers, in various kinds of discursive practices, the process and

[13] See especially Adriano Prosperi, *Giustizia bendata. Percorsi storici di un'immagine* (Turin, 2008); Adriano Prosperi, *Delitto e perdono. La pena di morte nell'orizzonte mentale dell'Europa cristiana, XIV-XVIII secolo* (Turin, 2013).

[14] See Ottavia Niccoli, *Perdonare. Idee, pratiche, rituali in Italia tra Cinque e Seicento* (Rome and Bari, 2007).

[15] See Stuart Carroll, *Enmity and Violence in Early Modern Europe* (Cambidge, 2023), p. 151.

the courts were portrayed as places to be avoided as much as possible, and also as places of perdition from the perspective of Christian morality, while chicanery (*esprit de chicane*) was seen as ruinous of a healthy social balance. In this field, the rigid – and modernising – distinctions between high and low criminal, as well as between the areas of justice and law (civil, criminal, commercial, canonical/spiritual), do not allow us to fully understand all the implications of practices widely used by actors and equally widely proposed (and imposed) by apparatuses. The path of distinction between high and low criminal was uneven from both a geographical and chronological point of view. Still in France in the second half of the eighteenth century, a large number of *graviora crimina* (thefts, serious wounds, homicides) were resolved through arbitrations and mediations; much depended on the motives for the crime, as judicial and social tolerance towards those committed for the defence of honour was still quite high.[16]

In early modern Europe, peace appears more as a sort of litmus test of the persistence and degree of institutional legitimisation of retaliatory systems than as a sign of an increasingly effective work of civilising customs and disciplining behaviours. Even an institution such as the Church, usually considered one of the main agents of social discipline, merely adapted to the culture of revenge cultivated by the aristocracy and beyond. Claiming ecclesiastical immunity, which made the right of asylum possible, meant on the one hand encouraging crime, and on the other offering the parties involved the opportunity to pursue negotiations that could potentially lead to peace agreements. The Catholic Reformation, as recently emphasised by Anne Bonzon,[17] certainly pursued a broad programme of pacifying society through the discipline of the internal forum and the actions of the parish and regular/missionary clergy. However, the role of the latter must be carefully analysed in all its complexity and also in its contradictions. As has been observed, religious culture was by no means alien to the culture of revenge, and the points of contact between the Church and violence were far from limited to the issue of confessional conflicts.[18] Ultimately, peace is not an indicator of the decline of violence but rather a reflection of the pervasiveness of retaliatory violence.

[16] See Nicole Castan, 'The Arbitration of Disputes under the "Ancien Régime"', in *Disputes and Settlements. Law and Human Relations in the West*, ed. John Bossy (Cambridge, 1983), pp. 219–60.

[17] See Anne Bonzon, *La paix au village. Clergé paroissial et règlement des conflits dans la France d'Ancien Régime* (Paris, 2022), p. 294.

[18] See Carroll, *Enmity and Violence*, pp. 56–9.

Bibliography

Primary material

Manuscript sources

Archivio Apostolico Vaticano (Vatican City)

Armadio V, t. 44, n. 242, f. 33 (*Breve di Gregorio XIII a favore di cardinali deputati ad assolvere e comporre in materia di banditi*).
Armadio V, Misc., t. X, n. 208, f. 101 (*Indulto di Gregorio XIII nel quale si dà per un anno la facoltà alli confessori di poter assolvere dalle censure quelli che haveranno conversato con banditi*).
Secretaria Brevium, reg. 44, f. 13*v*.
Segreteria di Stato, Legazione di Bologna, vol. 62.

Archivio di Stato di Ancona

Governatore di Montemarciano, year 1627.
Comune di Ancona, Conservatori delle leggi-Fascicoli giudiziari, vols I–II.

Archivio di Stato di Bologna

Ambasciata Bolognese a Roma, reg. 53.
Ambasciata Bolognese a Roma, Lettere all'Oratore, reg. 1, 9, 12, 47, 135.
Ambasciata Bolognese a Roma, Registrum, reg. 3, 4, 13, 14, 30.
Assunteria liti e paci, I, *Atti*.
Senato, Lettere, series I, reg. 8, 11, 15.
Senato, Lettere, series III, reg. 9, 10.
Senato, Lettere, series VII, reg. 10, 25, 30, 31, 40, 58, 59.
Tribunale Criminale del Torrone, Registri, vol. 886.

Archivio di Stato di Macerata

Curia Generale della Marca di Ancona, vol. 391, 397, 423,
Governatore Generale della Marca di Ancona, no. 1144.

Archivio di Stato di Perugia

Governo Pontificio, Sezione I, Classe I, nos 1, 3.

Archivio di Stato di Roma

Tribunale Criminale del Governatore, Atti di Cancelleria, Lettere, vols 40, 41, 42, 43, 44, 45, 47, 49, 50.
Tribunale Criminale del Governatore, Registrazioni di Atti, vols 67, 68, 111.

Biblioteca Casanatense (Rome)

Manuscript n. 2097 (*Discorso sopra il buon governo di Roma*).

Biblioteca Nacional de España (Madrid)

Manuscript n. 5791 (*Discurso en orden a reformar la Ley del Duelo*).

Primary printed sources

[Alagón, Artal de], *Concordia de las leyes divinas y humanas, y desengaño de la iniqua ley de la vengança, compuesta por Don Artal de Alagón Conde de Sástago, religioso de la tercera regla del Señor San Francisco, y a petición de Don Martin de Alagón su hijo, de la Cámara del Príncipe nuestro Señor* (Madrid, por Luys Sánchez, 1593).
[Albergati, Fabio], *Trattato di Fabio Albergati, Gentilhuomo bolognese, del modo di ridurre a Pace l'inimicitie private (Roma, per Francesco Zannetti, 1583)*
[Albertanus of Brescia], *Tre trattati d'Albertano Giudice da Brescia. Il primo della dilezion d'Iddio, e del prossimo, e della forma dell'onesta vita. Il secondo della consolazione, e de' Consigli. Il terzo delle sei maniere del parlare, scritti da lui in lingua latina dall'Anno 1235, infino all'Anno 1246 e traslatati ne' medesimi tempi, in volgar fiorentino* (Firenze, appresso i Giunti, 1610).
L'ami de la concorde, ou essai sur les motifs d'éviter les procès, et sur les moyens d'en tarir la source, par un avocat au Parlement (à Londres, [s.n.], 1765), pp. 3–4.
[Aristotle], *The Nicomachean Ethics of Aristotle*, translated by F. H. Peters (London 1884).
[Arnauld, Antoine], *De la fréquente communion. Ou les sentimens des Pères, des Papes, & des Conciles, touchant l'usage des Sacremens de Pénitence & d'Eucharistie, sont fidèlement exposez. Pour servir d'adresse aux personnes qui pensent sérieusement à se convertir à Dieu, & aux Pasteurs & Confesseurs zélés pour le bien des âmes. Par M. Antoine Arnauld, Prêtre, Docteur en Théologie de la Maison, de Sorbonne* (à Paris, chez Pierre le Petit, [1643] 1683).
Augustine of Hippo, *Sermons*, translation and notes Edmund Hill O.P., editor John E. Rotelle O.S.A. (New York, 1992).

Augustine of Hippo, *Contra Cresconium Grammaticum Donatistam Libri Quatuor*, available online at https://www.augustinus.it/latino/contro_cresconio/index2.htm

Augustine of Hippo, *Letters 100-155*, II/2, translation and notes by Roland Teske, S.J., ed. Boniface Ramsey (New York, 2003).

[Azpilcueta, Martín de (Doctor Navarrus)], *Manual de confessores y penitentes, que contiene quasi todas las dudas que en las confessiones suelen occurrir delos peccados, absoluciones, restituciones, censuras, & irregularidades [...] compuesto por el Doctor Martin de Azpilcueta Navarro, Cathedratico jubilado de prima en Canones* (impresso en Valladolid, por Francisco Fernandez de Cordova impressor de la Magestad Real, 1570).

[Bartoli, Daniello], *La ricreazione del savio in discorso con la natura e con Dio, del padre Daniello Bartoli della Compagnia di Gesù*, vol. I (Venezia, dalla Tipografia di Giuseppe Gattei, 1831).

[Basile, Agostino], *Memorie istoriche della terra di Giugliano raccolte, e date alla luce dal Reverendo D. Agostino Basile, dedicate all'Eccellentissimo Signore D. Andrea Colonna, Principe di Stigliano, ed Alliano, Marchese di Castel Nuovo, utile Signore di detta terra* (in Napoli, nella Stamperia Simoniana, 1800).

Beccaria, Cesare, *Dei delitti e delle pene, nuova edizione corretta e accresciuta* (Harlem and Paris, Dal Molini Librajo rue du Jardinet près la rue du Paon, 1780). English edition: *An Essay on Crimes & Punishments, translated from the Italian with a Commentary, attributed to M. de Voltaire* (Philadelphia, William P. Farrand and Co., 1809).

[Bodin, Jean], *Les Six Livres de la Republique par I. Bodin Angevin* (à Lyon, par Iacques du Puy Iuré à l'Université de Paris, 1580); *The six bookes of a commonweale. Written by I. Bodin, a famous Lawyer, and a man of great Experience in matters of State, out of the French and Latin copies, done into English, by Richard Knolles* (London, Impensis G. Bishop, 1606).

Boncompagno da Signa, *L'assedio di Ancona. Liber de obsidione Ancone*, ed. Paolo Garbini (Rome, 1999).

[Bouwens, Andreas], *Iuris iustitiaeque usus et abusus: exemplis et documentis ex omni aevo demonstrati per Andream Bouwens I. C. Mosae Trajectinum. Opus non tantùm Synedris, omnibusque Nomothetis, sed & concionatoribus utilissimum* (Leodii, ex Officina Typographica Henrici & Ioannis Mathiae Hoviorum, 1655).

Bullarum privilegiorum ac diplomatum Romanorum Pontificum amplissima collectio cui accessere Pontificum omnium Vitae, Notae, & Indices opportuni. Opera et studio Caroli Cocquelines, tomus tertius, par tertia (ab Eugenio IV ad Leonem X, scilicet ab anno 1431 ad 1521), (Romae, typis et sumptibus Hieronymi Mainardi, 1743).

[Burroughs, Jeremiah], *Irenicum, to the Lovers of Truth and Peace. Heart-Divisions opened in the Causes and Evils of them: with Cautions that we may not be hurt by them, And Endeavours to heal them, by Jeremiah Burroughs* (London, printed for Robert Dawlman, 1653).

[Cantini, Lorenzo], *Legislazione toscana raccolta e illustrata dal dottore Lorenzo Cantini socio di varie accademie*, vol. II (Florence, nella Stamperia Albizziniana da S. Maria in Campo per Pietro Fantosini e figlio, 1801)

[Carbone, Ludovico], *De pacificatione et dilectione inimicorum iniuriamque remissione. Tractatio admodum utilis Remp. Et curam animarum gerentibus, concionatoribus, pacificatoribus, armatis, alijsqu. Viris, ut ex indice capitum cognoscere licet, cum apendice, de amore et concordia fraterna. Auctore Ludovico Carbone* (Florentiae, apud Bartholomaeum Sermatellium, 1583).

Capitoli et regole sopra l'audire, trattare, et concordare, lite & diferentie per gli huomini della Compagnia del Santissimo Nome di Dio di Bologna (in Bologna, per Alessandro Benacci, 1575).

Cavallo, Pietro, *Resolutionum criminalium ... centuriae duae* (Venetiis, apud Bertanos, 1644).

Contra homicidas, Brigosos, Duellantes, & alia gravia crimina patrantes, Bannitosque, & eorum complices, receptatores, & fautores, in *Bullarum privilegiorum ac diplomatum*, tomus quartus, pars prima (ab Hadriano VI ad Paulum IV, scilicet ab Anno 1521 ad 1599) (Romae, typis et sumptibus Hieronymi Mainardi, 1745).

[Crispolti, Tullio], *Alcune ragioni del perdonare, raccolte per Tullio Crispoldo da Riete* (in Vinegia, per Stephano da Sabbio, 1539).

[Dalton, Michael], *The Country Justice. Containing the Practice of the Justices of the Peace out of their Sessions. Gathered for the better help of Such Justices of Peace, as have not been much conversant in the Study of the laws of this Realm. By Michael Dalton of Lincoln's-Inn, Esq., and one of the Masters in Chancery* (London, printed by William Rawlins and Samuel Roycroft, 1690).

De Luca, Giovanni Battista, *Il dottor volgare, ovvero il compendio di tutta la legge civile, canonica, feudale, e municipale, nelle cose più ricevute in pratica*, vol. IV (Colonia [Köln], a spese di Modesto Fenzo Stampatore in Venezia, 1740).

[Dury, John], *A peacemaker without Partiality and Hypocrisie. Or, the Gospel-way to make up the present breaches of Brotherhood, and heale the divisions, whereby some of the reforming Professors and Ministers of this Kingdome at this time, sadly dishonour their profession, mainely obstruct our Reformation, utterly destroy the safe constitution both of Church and State ... All written upon severall occasions and at severall times by Mr. John Dury, one of the Assembly of Divines & c.* (London, printed by R. Cotes for John Ballamy, 1648).

Edit du Roy portant reglement general sur les duels, donné en Saint Germain en Laye au mois d'Aoust 1679, registré en Parlement le I jour de Septembre de la mesme année, avec le nouveau reglement des Messieurs les Mareschaux de France sur le mesme sujet (à Paris, par les Imprimeurs du Roy, 1679).

[Ercolani, Francesco], *Tractatus Francisci Herculani Perusini Iureconsulti & Equitis Lauretani. De Cautione de non offendendo* (Venetiis, apud Io. Andream Valvassorem cognomine Guadagninum, 1569).

[Farinacci, Prospero], *Prosperi Farinacii Iurisconsulti Romani Praxis et Theoricae Criminalis Amplissimae, Pars Tertia* (Prodit e Collegio Paltheniano, quod est in nobili Francofurto, 1605).

[Farinacci, Prospero], *Prosperi Farinacii I.C. Romani Responsorum Criminalium Liber secundus ...* (Lugduni, sumptibus Horatii Cardon, 1616).

[Figon, Jean], *Le Moyen d'eviter proces, faict pour l'utilité des marchans, et autres negociateurs, par M. Jean Figon de Montelimar Docteur és Droictz* (à Lyon, par Paul Favre, 1574).

[François de Toulouse], *Le missionnaire apostolique ou sermons utiles à ceux qui s'employent aux missions, pour retirer les hommes du peché, et les porter à la Penitence. Par le R.P. François de Thoulouse, Superieur des Capucins de la Mission du Vigan, dans les Sevenes, tome sixième, des vertus et des vices*, à Paris, chez Denys Thierry, 1671.

[Gambacorta, Rocco], *Iesus Mariae Filius. Foro Christiano. Nel quale si tratta come deveno osservarsi l'humane leggi conforme alle divine. Diviso in cinque parti, secondo le convenienti età dell'huomo, Adolescenza, Gioventù, Virilità, Vecchiezza, & Decrepità. Confirmandosi con l'autorità della Sacra Scrittura, Dottori Catholici, & detti di persone Savie del mondo. Accioche honeste e Christiane sieno tutte l'attioni de gli huomini in quel che può lor' occorrere per farsi un Sacro Senato, Santo Giuditio, giusto negotio, & honesto essercitio. Composto per Rocco Gambacorta Dottore nativo della Città di Messina, & Cittadino Palermitano* (in Palermo, appresso Gio. Francisco Carrara, 1594).

[Glover, Henry], *ΕΧΔΙΧΗΣΙΣ or a Discourse of Vengeance. Delivered in a Sermon Preached at Dorchester, at the Assises holden there for the County of Dorset, March 4 1663, by Henry Glover Rector of Shroton* (London, printed for Henry Brome, 1664).

[Goodwin, Thomas], *Christ the Universall Peace-maker. Or, The Reconciliation of All the People of God Notwithstanding all their Differences, Enmities, by Thomas Goodwin, B.D.* (London, printed by J. G. for R. Dawlman, 1651).

[Grangier de Liverdis, Balthasar], *Procez pour s'en garantir, et les terminer promptement, avec l'Instruction du Feu Seigneur Grangier Evesque de Treguier, à ses Curéz et Missionnaires, pour l'accord des procez, et querelles, et empêcher les Duels, dont la pluspart dans les Provinces viennent des querelles animées, qui naissent des procez immortels qui sont parmy la noblesse; pour à quoy remedier, suivant les saintes intentions de Sa Majesté, Edits et

Ordonnances de nos Rois, l'Assemblé generale du Clergé de France l'an 1670, exorta tous les Prelats d'establir des Assemblées dans leurs Paroisses, pour accorder lesd. procez et querelles (Paris, s.n., 1682)

[Guazzini, Sebastiano], *Sebastiani Guazzini I.C. de Civitate Castelli nuper Supremi Tribunalis Illustriss. et Reverendiss. D. Auditoris Camerae Locumtenentis Criminalis, & Causarum Criminalium Advocati in Urbe primarij. Tractatus de Pace, Treuga, Verbo dato aliqui Principi, vel alteri personae nobili, & de cautione de non offendendo per Quaestiones divisus. Omnibus Iudicibus, Advocatis, et aliis in Foro versantibus, nedum utilis, sed per quam necessarius* ... (Romae, ex Typographia Guillelmi Guacciotti, 1610).

[Guazzini, Sebastiano], *Sebastiani Guazzini Jurisconsulti & in Curia Romana advocati, ac Petri Pauli Guazzini [...] Opera omnia juridica et moralia* (Coloniae Allobrogum, sumptibus Marci-Michaelis Bousquet & Sociorum, 1738).

[Guicciardini, Francesco], *Opere inedite di Francesco Guicciardini illustrate da Giuseppe Canestrini e pubblicate per cura dei conti Piero e Luigi Guicciardini*, vol. VIII (Firenze, presso M. Cellini e Comp., 1866).

Guidicini, Giuseppe di Giovanni Battista, *I Riformatori dello stato di libertà della città di Bologna dal 1394 al 1797* (Bologna, 1876).

[Harlay de Champvallon, Francois de], *Ordonnance de Monseigneur l'Illustrissime et Religiosissime Archevesque de Roüen Primat de Normandie, pour maintenir la Paix dans son diocese* (à Rouen, par L. Maurry Imp. Ord. De l'Archevesche, 1659).

[Heucqueville, Vigneron], *Discours, où l'on propose un moïen facile pour empêcher la plûpart des procès dans leur naissance, où pour les faire régler sans frais et un peu de temps*, s.l., s.n, 1699.

De homicidis aliisque reis poenae capitalis vel sanguinis, etiam non condemnatis vel in contumaciam condemnatis, et infra sex menses non sponte se in carceribus constitutis non audiendis, appellationibusque condemnatorum in poenam fisco et Camerae Apostolicae applicatam non admittendis, nisi facto deposito. Ac de poenis fractae pacis vel treguae, et allegatione novae causae vel minoritatis, et legitimae filiorum confiscatione, in *Bullarum, diplomatum et privilegiorum sanctorum romanorum pontificum taurinensis edito, locupletior facta collectione novissima plurium brevium epistolarum decretorum actor umque S. Sedis a S. Leone Magno usque ad praesens* ... , vol. VII (Augustae Taurinorum, Seb. Franco et Henrico Dalmazzo editoribus, 1862).

Hurtado de Mendoza, Pedro, *Scholasticae et morales disputationes* (Salmanticae, Iacinthum Taberniel, 1631).

[John Chrysostom], *The Homilies of St. John Chrysostom on the Gospel of St. Matthew*, ed. Philip Schaff, vol. X (*St. Chrysostom: Homilies on the Gospel of Saint Matthew*) (Edinburgh, T&T Clarc), 1888.

[John Chrysostom], *The homilies of St. John Chrysostom, Archbishop of Constantinople, on the Gospel of St. Matthew, translated with notes and indices*, part I, Hom. I–XXV (Oxford, John Henry Parker-J.G.F. and J. Rivington, 1893).

[Jones, John], *The Conquest of the Saints. Or, a short Treatise of Concord and Peace: Wherein is shewed the necessity of Unity and Peace, without which neither Church nor Common-wealth can stand. Preached by John Jones Master of Arts, late Minister at St Michael Bashenshaw in London, and now published for the common good* (London, printed by G. M. for William Jones, 1634).

Justinian I (Roman Emperor), *Le pandette di Giustiniano riordinate da R.G. Pothier*, vol. VI (in Venezia, co' tipi di Antonio Bazzarini, e C., 1835).

[Lambarde, William], *Eirenarcha, or, of the Office of the Iustices of Peace, in Foure Bookes ... , first collected by William Lambarde of Lincolns Inne Gent* (London, Printed for the Companie of Stationers, 1619).

[Leach, William], *A Preservative Against the major part of Trials and Non-suits in triviall Causes. And many other unnecessary charges about other things in further order to the regulation of the unnecessary charges in the proceedings in Law, and for saving to the people of this Nation every year hereafter a considerable part of three millions of money formerly unlawfully extracted from them by Monopolizers about the Law written, proposed, and tendered to the same consideration as were many former Propositions, by W.L. of the Middle Temple* (London, British Museum, 1650).

Ledesma, Pedro de, *Secunda parte de la Summa, en la qual se summa y cifra todo lo moral, y casos de consciencia que no pertenecen a los sacramentos* (Salamanca, en casa de Antonio Ramírez, 1605).

Le Roy, Loys, *Des differens et troubles advenans entre les hommes par la diversité des Religions* (à Paris, de l'Imprimerie de Frederic Morel, Rue S. Iean de Beauvais, au Franc Meurier, 1562).

Locke, John, *Two Treatises of Government* (London, Whitmore and Fenn-C. Brown, 1821).

[Lozano, Juan Antonio], *Destierro y azote del libro del duelo. Dedicado a Christo crucificado, por amor de enemigos. Por el Doctor Juan Antonio Lozano de Ibdes, Colegial del Complutense Theólogo de S. Martín, y S. Emerenciana; y cura de la Mata de los Olmos. En forma vulgar y predicable* (en Zaragoza, por Christóval de la Torre, 1640).

[Machiavelli, Niccolò], *Opere istoriche e politiche di Niccolò Machiavelli, Segretario e Cittadino fiorentino*, vol. I (Filadelfia, nella Stemperia delle Provincie Unite, 1818).

Machiavelli, Niccolò, *Florentine Histories*, a new translation by Laura F. Banfield and Harvey C. Mansfield Jr (Princeton, 1988).

Machiavelli, Niccolò, *Discourses on Livy*, translated by Harvey C. Mansfield and Nathan Tarcov (Chicago and London, 1996).

Mandement de Monseigneur l'Evesque d'Angers, pour l'accord des proces, et des querelles, et pour establir dans son Diocese, la distribution des remedes pour les Pauvres de la Campagne, suivant la deliberation de la derniere Assemblée generale du Clergé, du 17 novembre 1670, s.l, s.n.

Masini, Eliseo, *Sacro arsenale, overo Prattica dell'officio della S. Inquisitione ampliata* (in Genova, per Giuseppe Pavoni, 1625).

[Mateu y Sanz, Lorenzo], *Laurentii Matthaeu et Sanz, Tractatus de re criminali, sive controversiarum usufrequentium in causis criminalibus, cum earum decisionibus, tam in aula suprema ac Hispana criminum, quam in summo senatu novi orbis, Editio prima, cum triplici indice controversiarum, jurium, ac rerum locupletissimo* (Lugduni, sumpt. Claudij Bourgeat, sub signo Mercurij Galli, 1676).

Mazzarino, Giulio Cesare, *De' ragionamenti su'l sermone del Signore in Monte ..., parte quarta. Nella quale si spiega l'ottava beatitudine delle persecutioni, et si và innanzi al rimanente del Sermone* (in Bologna, per gli heredi di Gio. Rossi, 1618).

Medina, Bartolomé de, *Breve Istruttione de' confessori come si debba amministrare il Sacramento della Penitentia ...* (in Venetia, appresso Bernardo Basa, 1594).

Medina, Bartolomé de, *Breve instruction de como se ha de administrar el Sacramento de la Penitencia, dividida en dos libros [...] En la qual se contiene todo lo que ha de saber, y hazer el sabio Confessor, para curar almas, y todo lo que deve hazer el penitente para conseguir el fructo de tan admirable medicina* (impresso en Barcelona, en la Imprenta de Gabriel Graells y Giraldo Dotil, 1604).

[Montesquieu (Charles-Louis de Secondat, baron of La Brède and of Montesquieu)], *OEuvres de Montesquieu, avec les remarques des divers commentateurs, et des notes inédites, seule édition complète, dirigée par M. Collin de Plancy* (Paris, Louis Duprat Duverger Editeur, 1823).

[Moroni, Nicolò], *Tractatus aureus, de Fide, Treugua, & pace. Clarissimi Iuriconsulti D. Nicolai Moroni Patricij Gualdensis. In quo omnia fère continentur, quae in civilibus & criminalibus iudicijs frequentius in controversiam venire solent ...* (Venetiis, apud Damianum Zenarum, 1574) (first edition 1570).

Muratori, Ludovico Antonio, *Introduzione alle paci private, composta, e dedicata, all'Altezza Serenissima di Rinaldo I, Duca di Modena, Reggio & c.* (in Modena, per Bartolomeo Soliani Stamp. Ducale, 1708).

[Musso, Cornelio], *Il terzo libro delle prediche del Reverendissimo Mons. Cornelio Musso, Vescovo di Bitonto, con due tavole, l'una delle prediche, l'altra delle cose più notabili* (in Vinegia, appresso Gabriel Giolito De' Ferrari, 1572).

[Noguier, Antoine], *L'eridographie, contenant la description de proces, qui le nourrit, et que fault il avoir pour l'eviter, par Antoine Noguier Tolosain* (imprimé à Tolose par Guyon Boudeville, iuré de ladite Ville et Université d'icelle, aux depends de Henry Dugua, habitant dudit Tolose, avec privilege du Roy pour six ans, 1552).

Ordinatio s.d.n.d. Pij divina providentia pp. V vt eius bullae contra homicidas, bannitos, et alios facinorosos, eorumque receptatores editae singulis annis publice legantur (Romae, apud Haeredes Antonij Bladij Impressores Camerales, 1566).

Ordine et declaratione ducale contra coloro che romperanno le paci e le tregue, in *Gride ducali, provisioni, gratie et ragioni della città di Modona* (Modena, 1575).

Ordini della congregatione della concordia. Constituita in Bologna dal santissimo, & beatissimo papa Gregorio 13. Publicata in Bologna alli 24 decemb. & reiterata alli 29 detto l'anno 1574 (in Bologna, per Alessandro Benacci, 1574).

Ordini, e Consuetudini, massime Criminali, e miste, che si osservano nelli Stati del Serenissimo Gran Duca di Toscana ... , tomo VII (in Parma, per gli Eredi di Paolo Monti all'Insegna della Fede, 1733).

[Paleotti, Gabriele], *Responsiones casuum conscientiae. Qui omnibus curatis, ac poenitentiarijs singulis Mensibus, coram Illustriss. ac Reverendiss. Card. Paleoto Archiepiscopo Bonon. proponuntur. Per admodum R.P. Ludovicum de Beia Palaestrelum, Lusitanum, Ordinis Eremitarum, Theologum* (Bergomi, Typis Comini Venturae, 1588).

[Panigarola, Francesco], *Prediche quadragesimali del Reverendiss. Monsig. Panigarola Vescovo d'Asti, dell'Ordine di S. Francesco de' Minori Osservanti, predicate da lui in S. Pietro di Roma l'anno 1577* (in Venetia, appresso gli heredi di Marchiò Sessa, 1600).

Patrizi, Francesco, *De Regno et regis institutione libri IX. Ad Alphonsum Aragonium inclitum ac celeberrimum Calabriae Ducem scripti* (Argentinae, Impensis Lazari Zetzeneri, 1594).

[Pascal, Blaise], *Les provinciales, ou les lettres écrites par Louis de Montalte à un provincial de ses amis et au RR. PP. Jésuites* (à Cologne, chez Henry Schouten, 1738). English edition: *The Provincial Letters of Blaise Pascal, a new translation with historical introduction and notes by Rev. Thomas McCrie* (New York, published by Hurd and Houghton, 1866).

[Peri, Domenico], *Il negotiante, di Gio: Domenico Peri Genovese, parte seconda, dedicata al Clarissimo Signore Gio: Pace Castelli* (Venetia, presso Gio: Giacomo Herz, 1672).

[Picot, Gilles (Lord of Gouberville)], *Le journal du Sire de Gouberville*, in *Mémoires de la Société des Antiquaires de Normandie*, vol. XXXI (Caen, Rouen and Paris, 1892).

Plato, *The Republic*, edited by G. R. F. Ferrari, translated by Tom Griffith, 'Cambridge Texts in the History of Political Thought', eds Raymond Geuss and Quentin Skinner, (Cambridge, 2000).

Pour etablir dans toutes les Paroisses du Royaume, sans qu'il en couste rien à personne, l'accord des procez et des querelles, et la distribution des remedes pour les pauvres gens de la campagne, suivant l'Evangile, les Ordonnances de nos Roys, l'Arresté des Evesque des dernieres Etats de Languedoc. Et la deliberation de la derniere Assemblée generale du Clergé de France, du 17. Novembre 1670. qui a exorté tous les Evesques du Royaume, sur la remontrance de M. L'Evesque de Meaux, à établir dans leur Dioceses ces deux actions de charité. Après l'attestation des Seigneurs Evesques qui l'avoient dé-ja fait, que cela produisoit de grands biens, au spirituel, & au temporel, in *Remedes pour les pauvres de la campagne, & pour leurs bestiaux, qui coûtent peu* (à Paris, chez Denys Langlois, 1672).

Projet d'Edit, ou d'Ordonnance pour faire terminer un grand nombre de procés à l'amiable, s.l, s.n.

[Rainaldi, Giovan Domenico], *Syntaxis rerum criminalium, cum adnotationibus ad bannimenta generalia civitatis, et legationis bononiae* (Romae, Ex Typographia Dominici Antonij Herculis, 1688).

[Rainaldi, Giovanni Domenico], *Jo. Dominici Raynaldi, Sacrosanctae Basilicae Principis Apostolorum de Urbe canonici, Observationum criminalium, civilium, & mixtarum, liber primus, in quo rariores quaestiones in foris tum ecclesiasticis tum saecularibus disceptari solitae, & ad regimen politicum accommodatae, plenèdiscutiuntur ... cum additionibus, ac suppletionibus seorsim anteà impressis, congruis nunc locis distributis ... necnon votis ejusdem authoris noviter emanatis* (Venetiis, apud Paulum Balleonium, 1699).

Remedes pour les pauvres gens de la campagne. Et l'accord des procès et des querelles, s.l., s.n.

[Reynolds, Edward], *The substance of two sermons one touching composing of controversies. Another touching unity of judgement and love amongst brethren. Preached in two honourable conventions of Parliament. The former, Jan. 27. 1657. The other, Feb. 4. 1658. By Edward Reynolds, D.D.* (London, printed by Tho. Radcliffe for George Thomason at the Sign of the Rose and Crown in St. Pauls Church-yard, 1659).

[Roche, Alexandre de la], *L'arbitre charitable pour eviter les procez et les querelles; ou du moins pour les terminer promptement, sans peine & sans frais* ... (à Paris, chez Laurens Ravenau, 1668).

Rousseau, Jean-Jacques, *Du contrat social* (Paris, 2001). English edition: *The social contract: or, principles of political law. Also, a project for perpetual peace, by Jean-Jacques Rousseau, citizen of Geneva* (New York, Peter Eckler, 1893).

[Saavedra Fajardo, Diego de], *Idea de un principe politico christiano, representada en cien empresas, dedicada al Principe de las Españas, nuestro Señor, por Diego de Saavedra Fajardo* (en Amberes, en casa de Ieronymo y Iuan Bapt. Verdussen, 1655).

[Saint Martin, Guillaume de], *Sermons pour tous les jours du Caresme, preschez par M.re Guillaume de S. Martin, Prestre, Docteur en Théologie, Conseiller, Aumosnier, et Predicateur ordinaire du Roy, et Curé de l'Eglise de la basse Sainte Chapelle de Paris, tome premier* (à Paris, chez Edme Couterot, 1683).

[Savelli, Marco Antonio], *Pratica universale del dottor Marc'Antonio Savelli, Auditore della Rota Criminale di Firenze, compendiosamente estratta per alfabetto dalle principali leggi, bandi, statuti, ordini, e Consuetudini, massime criminali, e miste, che si osservano nelli Stati del Serenissimo Gran Duca di Toscana* (Venice, presso Paolo Baglioni, 1697).

Schaf, Philip (ed.), *Nicene and Post-Nicene Fathers*, vol. VII (*Homilies on the Gospel of John; Homilies on the First Epistle of John; Soliloquies*) (Grand Rapids, 1979).

[Segneri, Paolo (sr.)], *La manna dell'anima, overo esercizio facile insieme, e fruttuoso, per chi desidera in qualche modo attender all'Orazione, proposto dal Padre Paolo Segneri della Compagnia di Giesù, per tutti i giorni dell'anno*, in *Opere del Padre Paolo Segneri della Compagnia di Giesù distribuite in quattro tomi*, tomo I (in Venezia, presso Paolo Baglioni, 1716).

[Segneri, Paolo (sr.)], *Quaresimale del Padre Paolo Segneri della Compagnia di Gesù*, vol. I (Milano, per Giovanni Silvestri, 1827).

Senault, Jean-François, *De l'usage des passions* (Leiden, chez Jean Elsevier, 1658).

Seneca, Lucius Annaeus, *Anger, Mercy, Revenge*, translation by Robert A. Kaster and Martha C. Nussbaum (Chicago, 2010).

[Shaw, Joseph], *The Practical Justice of Peace: or, a Treatise shewing the present Power and Authority of that Officer, in all the Branches of his Duty ... by Joseph Shaw of the Middle Temple Esq.*, vol. I (in the Savoy [London], Printed by Henry Lintot, 1744).

Sheppard, William, *The Whole Office of the Country Justice of Peace, wherein is plainly set down all their Power and Duty both in, and out of the Quarter Sessions* (London, printed for W. Lee, D. Pakeman, G. Bedell, 1656).

S.D.N. Sixti papae V absolutio et gratia generalis iis, qui aut cum bannitis versati fuerint, aut iisdem auxilium praestiterint concessa (Romae, apud haeredes Antonij Bladij Impressores Camerales, 1586).

Statuta Almae Urbis Romae Auctoritate Gregorii Papae XIII, a Senatu Populoq. Rom. Reformata, & Edita (Romae, in Aedibus Populi Romani, 1590).

Statuta urbis Ferrariae nuper reformata (Ferrariae, Giovan Battista Pigna, 1567).

Sur ce qui a esté remontré par le Procureur General du Roy ... (de l'Imprimerie de Louis Sevestre, seul imprimeur pour la Chambre des Comptes, ruë Saint Jacques, 1700).

[Tiraqueau, André], *Andreas Tiraquellus De poenis legum, ac consuetudinum, statutorumque temperandis, aut etiam remittendis, & id quibus quotque ex causis. Accessit rerum, verborum, & sententiarum insignium locupletissimus index* (Lugduni, Ad Salamandrae, apud Claudium Sennetonium, 1559).

[Thomas Aquinas], *S. Thomae Aquinatis Secunda Secundae partis Summae Theologicae Sancti Thomae Aquinatis. De virtutibus omnis et vitiis in speciali*, (Antverpiae, ex Officina Christophori Plantini, 1569).

[Thomas Aquinas], *The Summa Theologiæ of St. Thomas Aquinas*, second and revised edition, literally translated by Fathers of the English Dominican Province (London, 1920; available online at https://www.newadvent.org/summa (2017)).

Thomas Aquinas, *Pauline Commentaries, Commentary on Romans*, available online at https://aquinas.cc/la/en/~Rom.C1.L8.n158.3

Tribunale della concordia, eretto nuovamente per tutti i luoghi della provincia da Monsig. Filippo Sega Vescovo della Ripatransona Governatore della Marca a beneficio d'essa (Macerata, appresso Sebastiano Martellini, 1575).

[Vannozzi, Bonifacio], *Della suppellettile degli avvertimenti politici, morali, et christiani di Mons. Bonifatio Vannozzi, Dottor Pistoiese, & Protonotario Apostolico*, vol. III (in Bologna, appresso gli Heredi di Giovanni Rossi, 1613).

Villalobos, Enrique de, *Suma de teología moral y canónica* (Salamanca, Diego de Cossío, 1622).

[Volpelli, Ottaviano], *Octaviani Vulpelli a Sancto Angelo Metaurense Tractatus de Pace, Indutiis, et Promissionibus de non offendendo. In quo Sex, & centum quaestiones ad forensem praxim pertinentes, examinantur* ... (Venetijs, ex Typographia Guerraea, 1573).

[Ward, Samuel], *Jethro's Justice of Peace. A Sermon Preached at a Generall Assises Held at Bury St. Edmunds, for the Countie of Suffolke, by Samuel Ward Batchelour of Divinitie* (London, Augustine Mathewes, 1621).

Zuccolo, Ludovico, *Considerazioni politiche e morali sopra cento oracoli d'illustri personaggi antichi* (Venezia, Presso M. Ginami, 1621).

Zuccolo, Ludovico, *Il Molino o vero della amicizia scambievole fra' cittadini*, in Zuccolo, Ludovico, *Dialoghi* (in Venetia, appresso Marco Ginami, 1625).

Secondary sources

Ago, Renata, 'Gli storici italiani e le fortune dell'antropologia. Il dibattito sulla storia sociale in Italia', in *Orientamenti marxisti e studi antropologici italiani. Problemi e dibattiti* (Milan, 1980), pp. 223–9.

Ago, Renata and Cerutti, Simona (eds), *Procedure di giustizia*, *Quaderni Storici*, vol. 34, no. 101/2, 1999, monographic issue.

Albera, Dionigi, Blok, Anton and Bromberger, Christian (eds), *L'anthropologie de la Méditerranée* (Cahors, 2001).

Alessi, Giorgia, 'Giustizia pubblica, private vendette. Riflessioni intorno alla stagione dell'infragiustizia', *Storica* 39 (2007), pp. 91–118.

Alfani, Guido, *Fathers and Godfathers. Spiritual Kinship in Early-Modern Italy* (London, 2009).

Alsworth Ross, Edward, *Social Control. A Survey of the Foundations of Order* (New York and London, 1901).

Althoff, Gerd, *Spielregeln der Politik im Mittelalter. Kommunikation in Frieden und Fehde* (Darmstadt, 1997).

Angelozzi, Giancarlo, 'La proibizione del duello: Chiesa e ideologia nobiliare', in Prodi, Paolo and Reinhard, Wolfgang (eds), *Il concilio di Trento e il moderno* (Bologna, 1996), pp. 271–308.

Angelozzi, Giancarlo and Casanova, Cesarina, *La nobiltà disciplinata. Violenza nobiliare, procedure di giustizia e scienza cavalleresca a Bologna nel XVII secolo* (Bologna, 2003).

Angelozzi, Giancarlo and Casanova, Cesarina, *La giustizia criminale in una città di antico regime. Il tribunale del Torrone di Bologna (secc. XVI–XVII)* (Bologna, 2008).

Angelozzi, Giancarlo and Casanova, Cesarina, *La giustizia criminale a Bologna nel XVIII secolo e le riforme di Benedetto XIV* (Bologna, 2010).

Angelozzi, Giancarlo and Casanova, Cesarina, 'La giustizia dei burocrati. La Restaurazione nella Bologna pontificia', *Bollettino del Museo del Risorgimento* LV (2010), monographic issue.

Angiolini, Franco, 'La società', in Greco, Gaetano and Rosa, Mario (eds), *Storia degli antichi stati italiani* (Rome and Bari, 1997), pp. 297–74.

Antichi, Valerio, 'Giustizia consuetudinaria e giustizia d'apparato nello Stato pontificio: la *ruptura pacis* (1550-1600)', in Broggio, Paolo and Paoli, Maria Pia (eds), *Stringere la pace. Teorie e pratiche della conciliazione nell'Europa moderna (secoli XV–XVIII)* (Rome, 2011), pp. 229–75.

Armando, David, *Baroni, vassalli e governo pontificio. Gli stati dei Colonna nel Settecento* (Rome, 2018).

Armon, Shifra, *Masculine Virtue in Early Modern Spain* (London and New York, 2016)

Artifoni, Enrico, 'Boncompagno da Signa, i maestri di retorica e le città comunali nella prima metà del Duecento', in Baldini, Massimo (ed.), *Il pensiero e l'opera di Boncompagno da Signa.* Atti del convegno nazionale (Signa, 23–4 febbraio 2001) (Signa, 2002), pp. 23–36.

Artifoni, Enrico, 'I governi di "popolo" e le istituzioni comunali nella seconda metà del secolo XIII', *Reti Medievali* 4, 2 (2003). Available online at http://www.rmojs.unina.it/index.php/rm/article/view/urn%3Anbn%3Ait%3Aunina-3304/5085

Baja Guarienti, Carlo, *Il bandito e il governatore. Domenico d'Amorotto e Francesco Guicciardini nell'età delle guerre d'Italia* (Rome, 2014).

Battaglia, Felice, *Francesco Patrizi politico senese del Quattrocento, Annuario della Regia Università di Pisa*, 1933/4.

Becker, Anna, *Gendering the Renaissance Commonwealth* (Cambridge, 2020).

Bellabarba, Marco, *La giustizia ai confini. Il Principato vescovile di Trento agli inizi dell'età moderna* (Bologna, 1996).

Bellabarba, Marco, *La giustizia nell'Italia moderna* (Rome and Bari, 2008).

Bellini, Piero, *'Denunciatio evangelica' e 'Denunciatio judicialis privata': un capitolo di storia disciplinare della Chiesa* (Milan, 1986).

Benigno, Francesco, 'Conflitto politico e conflitto sociale nell'Italia spagnola', in Musi, Aurelio (ed.), *Nel sistema imperiale. L'Italia spagnola* (Naples, 1994), pp. 115–46.

Benigno, Francesco, 'Ancora lo "stato moderno" in alcune recenti sintesi storiografiche', *Storica* VIII, 23 (2002), pp. 119–43.

Benigno, Francesco, *Parole nel tempo. Un lessico per pensare la storia* (Rome, 2013).

Benigno, Francesco, 'Stato moderno', in Benigno, Francesco, *Parole nel tempo. Un lessico per pensare la storia* (Rome, 2013), pp. 163–84.

Berengo, Marino, *L'Europa delle città. Il volto della società urbana europea tra Medioevo ed Età moderna* (Turin, 1999).

Berni, Stefano and Cosi, Giovanni, *Fare giustizia. Due scritti sulla vendetta* (Milan, 2014).

Bettiol, Giuseppe, *Il problema penale*, in Bettiol, Giuseppe, *Scritti giuridici*, vol. II (Padova, 1966).

Bianco, Furio, *1511. La'crudel zobia grassa'. Rivolte contadine e faide nobiliari nel Friuli tra '400 e '500* (Pordenone, 1995).

Bien, Günther, *La filosofia politica di Aristotele* (Bologna, 1985).

Biferali, Fabrizio, 'Serbelloni, Gabriele (Gabrio)', in *Dizionario Biografico degli Italiani*, vol. 92, (Rome, 2018), pp. 66–8.

Birocchi, Italo, *Alla ricerca dell'ordine. Fonti e cultura giuridica nell'età moderna* (Turin, 2002).

Bonazzi, Luigi, *Storia di Perugia dalle origini al 1860*, vol. II (Perugia, Tipografia Boncompagni e c., 1879).

Bonzon, Anne, *La paix au village. Clergé paroissial et règlement des conflits dans la France d'Ancien Régime* (Paris, 2022).

Borao, Gerónimo, *Noticia de Don Gerónimo de Urrea y de su novela caballeresca inédita'Don Clarisel de las Flores'* (Zaragoza, 1866).

Borromeo, Agostino, 'Felipe II y la tradición regalista de la Corona española', in Martínez Millán, José (ed.), *Felipe II (1527-1598). Europa y la Monarquía Católica*, vol. III (Madrid, 1998), pp. 111–37.

Bouchard, Marco and Mierolo, Giovanni, *Offesa e riparazione. Per una nuova giustizia attraverso la mediazione* (Milan, 2005).

Bossy, John, 'Blood and Baptism: Kinship, Community and Christianity in Western Europe from the Fourteenth to the Seventeenth Centuries', in Baker, D. (ed.), *Sanctity and Secularity. The Church and the World* (Oxford, 1973), pp. 129–43.

Bossy, John, 'The Social History of Confession in the Age of the Reformation', *Transactions of the Royal Historical Society* 25 (1975), pp. 21–8.

Bossy, John, *Christianity in the West 1400-1700* (Oxford, 1985).

Bossy, John, *Dalla comunità all'individuo. Per una storia sociale dei sacramenti nell'Europa moderna* (Turin, 1998).

Bossy, John, *Peace in the Post-Reformation. The Birkbeck Lectures* (Cambridge, 1998).

Brambilla, Elena, *Alle origini del sant'Uffizio. Penitenza, confessione e giustizia spirituale dal medioevo al XVI secolo* (Bologna, 2000).

Brambilla, Elena, 'Un percorso segreto e tortuoso. La comparizione spontanea in alcuni recenti studi sul sant'Officio di Aquileia e Concordia', *Società e Storia* 145 (2014), pp. 529–52.

Broggio, Paolo, 'I gesuiti come pacificatori in età moderna: dalle guerre di frontiera nel Nuovo Mondo americano alle lotte fazionarie nell'Europa mediterranea', *Rivista di Storia e Letteratura Religiosa* XXXIX, 2 (2003), pp. 249–89.

Broggio, Paolo, *Evangelizzare il mondo. Le missioni della Compagnia di Gesù tra Europa e America (secoli XVI-XVII)* (Rome, 2004).

Broggio, Paolo, 'Justice, vengeance et légitime défense dans les traités juridiques et théologico-moraux de l'époque moderne', in Gauvard, Claude and Zorzi, Andrea, *La vengeance en Europe (XIIe-XVIIIe siècle)* (Paris, 2015), pp. 269–85.

Broggio, Paolo, 'Pratiche e rituali di reintegrazione: la pacificazione dei nemici nella pastorale cattolica in area mediterranea (secoli XVI-XVIII)', *Mediterranea. Ricerche storiche* 61, August 2024, pp. 327–52.

Broggio, Paolo and Paoli, Maria Pia, 'Introduzione', in Broggio, Paolo and Paoli, Maria Pia (eds), *Stringere la pace. Teorie e pratiche della conciliazione nell'Europa moderna* (Rome, 2011), pp. 9–28.

Brunelli, Giampiero, 'Nobili soldati e giustizia nello Stato della Chiesa (1560-1605)', *Roma moderna e contemporanea* V, 1 (1997), pp. 97–115.

Brunelli, Giampiero, 'Guastavillani, Filippo', in *Dizionario Biografico degli Italiani*, vol. 60 (Rome, 2003), pp. 489–93.

Brunelli, Giampiero, *Il Sacro Consiglio di Paolo IV* (Rome, 2011).

Brunner, Otto, *Land und Herrschaft. Grundfragen der territorialen Verfassungsgeschichte Südostdeutschlands im Mittelalter* (Baden bei Wien, 1939).

Burgio, Santo, *Appartenenza e negozio. La crisi della teologia barocca* (Soveria Mannelli, 2004).

Burgio, Santo, In publicis malis. *Saggi sulla* constantia *in Giusto Lipsio* (Soveria Mannelli, 2009).

Burgio, Santo, 'Teologie del negozio. *Amor sui* e *dilectio proximi* nel probabilismo di Tommaso Tamburini S.I.', in Broggio, Paolo and Paoli, Maria Pia (eds), *Stringere la pace. Teorie e pratiche della conciliazione nell'Europa moderna (secoli XV-XVIII)* (Rome, 2010), pp. 411–28.

Calasso, Francesco, 'Iurisdictio' nel diritto comune classico, *Annali di storia del diritto* IX (1965), pp. 89–110.

Calonaci, Stefano, 'Non solo onore: vertenze patrimoniali e arbitrato mediceo nell'Italia del Seicento', in Broggio, Paolo and Paoli, Maria Pia (eds), *Stringere la pace. Teorie e pratiche della conciliazione nell'Europa moderna (secoli XV-XVIII)* (Rome, 2011), pp. 107–34.

Calonaci, Stefano, *Lo spirito del dominio. Giustizia e giurisdizioni feudali nell'Italia moderna (secoli XVI-XVIII)* (Rome, 2017).

Campbell, John K., *Honour, Family and Patronage. A Study of Institutions and Moral Values in a Greek Mountain Community* (Oxford, 1964).

Caporossi, Olivier, 'Les madrilènes face à la violence: la pratique du pardon privé au XVIIe siècle', *Hispania Sacra* LX (2008), pp. 231–66.

Caporossi, Olivier, *Exercer la justice du roi à Madrid. La juridiction royale d'une ville de cour pendant le règne de Philippe IV (1621-1665)* (Bordeaux, 2020).

Caravale, Mario and Caracciolo, Alberto, *Lo Stato pontificio. Da Martino V a Pio IX*, 'Storia d'Italia' directed by Giuseppe Galasso, vol. XIV (Turin, 1991).

Carrasco, Martínez Adolfo, *Sangre, honor y privilegio. La nobleza española bajo los Austrias* (Barcelona, 2000).

Carroll, Stuart, 'The Peace in the Feud in Sixteenth- and Seventeenth-Century France', *Past & Present* 178, 1 (2003), pp. 74–115.

Carroll, Stuart, 'Introduction', in Id (ed.), *Cultures of Violence. Interpersonal Violence in Historical Perspective* (Houndsmill and New York, 2007), pp. 1–43.

Carroll, Stuart, 'Peace-Making in Early Modern Europe: Towards a Comparative History', in *Stringere la pace. Teorie e pratiche della conciliazione nell'Europa moderna* (Rome, 2011), pp. 75–92.

Carroll, Stuart, 'From Feud to Enmity', *Acta Histriae* 25, 2 (2017), pp. 433–44.

Carroll, Stuart, *Enmity and Violence in Early Modern Europe* (Cambridge, 2023).

Casanova, Cesarina, *Comunità e governo pontificio in Romagna in età moderna* (Bologna, 1981).

Casey, James, *The History of the Family. New perspectives on the Past* (Oxford, 1989).

Cassi, Aldo Andrea, *La Giustizia in S. Agostino. Itinerari agostiniani del* quartus fluvius *dell'Eden* (Milan, 2013).

Cassi, Aldo Andrea, 'Agostino contro i mercanti di schiavi: *Ius gladii, ungulae carnificis* e funzione della pena', *Etica & Politica / Ethics & Politics* XVI, 1 (2014), pp. 457–71.

Castan, Nicole, *Justice et répression en Languedoc à l'époque des Lumières* (Paris, 1980).

Castan, Nicole, *Les criminels de Languedoc. Les exigences d'ordre et les voies du ressentiment dans une société prérévolutionnaire (1750-1790)* (Toulouse, 1980).

Castan, Nicole, 'The Arbitration of Disputes under the "Ancien Régime"', in Bossy, John (ed), *Disputes and Settlements. Law and Human Relations in the West* (Cambridge, 1983), pp. 219–60.

Cavina, Marco, *Nozze di sangue. Storia della violenza coniugale* (Rome and Bari, 2011).

Cerutti, Simona, *Giustizia sommaria. Pratiche e ideali di giustizia in una società di Ancien Régime (Torino, XVIII secolo)* (Milan, 2003).

Chauchadis, Claude, 'Noblesse, pouvoir et duel: les débats autour du discours d'Olivares contre la loi du duel (1638)', in Amalric, Jean-Pierre (ed.), *Pouvoir et société dans l'Espagne moderne. Hommage à Bartolomé Bennassar* (Toulouse, 1993), pp. 77–87.

Chauchadis, Claude, *La loi du duel. Le code du point d'honneur dans l'Espagne des XVIe-XVIIe siècles* (Toulouse, 1997).

Chevalier, Maxime, *L'Arioste en Espagne (1530-1650). Recherches sur l'influence Roland furieux'* (Bordeaux, 1966).

Chiffoleau, Jacques, *La Chiesa, il segreto e l'obbedienza. La costruzione del soggetto politico nel medioevo* (Bologna, 2010).

Chittolini, Giorgio, 'Ricerche sull'ordinamento territoriale del Dominio fiorentino agli inizi del secolo XV', in Chittolini, Giorgio, *La formazione dello stato regionale e le istituzioni del contado. Secoli XIV e XV* (Turin, 1979), pp. 292–351.

Chittolini, Giorgio, 'Il privato, il pubblico, lo Stato', in Chittolini, Giorgio, Molho, Anthony and Schiera, Pierangelo (eds), *Origini dello Stato. Processi di formazione statale in Italia fra Medioevo ed età moderna* (Bologna, 1994), pp. 553–89.

Christin, Olivier, *La paix de religion. L'autonomisation de la raison politique au XVIe siècle* (Paris, 1997).

Clavería, Carlos, *Le Chevalier Deliberé de Olivier de la Marcha y sus versiones españolas del siglo XVI* (Zaragoza, 1950).

Cicerchia, Andrea, *Giuristi al servizio del papa. Il tribunale dell'auditor Camerae nella giustizia pontificia di età moderna* (Vatican City, 2016).

Clavero, Bartolomé, *Antidora. Antropología católica de la economía moderna* (Milan, 1991).

Colarieti, Antonio, *Degli uomini più distinti di Rieti per scienze, lettere ed arti: cenni biografici* (Rieti, dai Tipi di Salvatore Trinchi, 1860).

Contreras, Jaime, *Sotos contra Riquelmes. Regidores, inquisidores y criptojudíos* (Madrid, 2013; 1st edition: Anaya, 1992).

Coolidge, Grace E., 'Contested Masculinity: Noblemen and Their Mistresses in Early Modern Spain', in Romaniello, Matthew P. and Lipp, Charles (eds), *Contested Spaces of Nobility in Early Modern Europe* (London and New York, 2001), pp. 61–84.

Cooney, Mark, *Warriors and Peacemakers. How Third Parties Shape Violence* (New York, 1998).

Cristellon, Cecilia, *La carità e l'eros. Il matrimonio, la Chiesa, i suoi giudici nella Venezia del Rinascimento (1420-1545)* (Bologna, 2011).

Cummins, Stephen and Kounine, Laura, 'Introduction: Confronting Conflict in Early Modern Europe', in Cummins, Stephen and Kounine, Laura, *Cultures of Conflict Resolution in Early Modern Europe* (Farnham and Burlington, 2016).

Dani, Alessandro, *Giovanni Battista De Luca divulgatore del diritto. Una vicenda di impegno civile nella Roma barocca* (Rome, 2012).

Dani, Alessandro, 'Gli statuti comunali nello Stato della Chiesa in Antico Regime: qualche annotazione e considerazione', *Historia et ius* 2 (2012), paper 6, available online at http://www.historiaetius.eu/uploads/5/9/4/8/5948821/dani.pdf

Davies, Jonathan, 'Violence and Italian Universities during the Renaissance', *Renaissance Studies* 27, 4 (2013), pp. 504–16.

Davies, Wendy and Fouracre, Paul (eds), *The Settlement of Disputes in Early Medieval Europe,* (Cambridge, 1986).

De Benedictis, Angela, *Repubblica per contratto. Bologna: una città europea nello Stato della Chiesa* (Bologna, 1985).

Delille, Gérard, *Le maire et le prieur. Pouvoir central et pouvoir local en Méditerranée occidentale (XVe-XVIIIe siècle)* (Rome and Paris, 2003).

De Boer, Wietse, *The Conquest of the Soul: Confession, Discipline, and Public Order in Counter-Reformation Milan* (Leiden and Boston, 2001).

De Mattei, Rodolfo, *Il pensiero politico italiano nell'età della Controriforma*, vol. I (Milan and Naples, 1982).

Del Re, Niccolò, 'Prospero Farinacci giureconsulto romano (1544-1618)', *Archivio della Società Romana di Storia Patria* 98 (1975), pp. 135–220.

Dessì, Rosa Maria, 'Pratiques de la parole de paix dans l'histoire de l'Italie urbaine', in Dessì, Rosa Maria (ed.), *Prêcher la paix et discipliner la société. Italie, France, Angleterre, XIIIe-XVe siècle* (Turnhout, 2005), pp. 245–78.

Di Fiore, Giacomo, 'E tutti piansero. Perdonismo e impunità criminale tra Cinquecento e Settecento', in Razzotti, Bernardo (ed.), *Filosofia Storiografia Letteratura. Studi in onore di Mario Agrimi* (Lanciano, 2001), pp. 685–718.

Di Rovasenda, Enrico, 'L'amicizia nel Commento di Tommaso d'Aquino all'Etica a Nicomaco di Aristotele e nella *Summa Theologiae*', in *Il concetto di amicizia nella storia della cultura europea / Der Begriff Freundschaft in der Geschichte der Europäische Kultur.* Atti del XXII Convegno Internazionale di Studi Italo-Tedeschi (Merano, 9–11 maggio 1994) (Merano, 1995), pp. 538–43.

Di Simplicio, Oscar, *Le rivolte contadine in Europa. I grandi movimenti che scuotono le campagne nell'epoca moderna* (Rome, 1986).

Di Sivo, Michele, 'Le costituzioni e i bandi di Sisto V: l'amministrazione della giustizia tra accentramento e crisi dello Stato pontificio', *Archivi per la Storia* IV (1991), pp. 137–48.

Di Sivo, Michele, 'Il tribunale criminale capitolino nei secoli XVI-XVII: note da un lavoro in corso', *Roma moderna e contemporanea* 3 (1995), pp. 201–16.

Donati, Claudio, *L'idea di nobiltà in Italia. Secoli XIV-XVIII* (Rome and Bari, 1988).

Edigati, Daniele, *Una vita nelle istituzioni. Marc'Antonio Savelli giurista e cancelliere tra Stato pontificio e Toscana medicea* (Pisa, 2005).

Edigati, Daniele, 'Le annotazioni agli statuti come genere di letteratura giuridica nell'età del diritto comune', *Archivio Storico Italiano* 170, 4 (2012), pp. 653–704.

Edigati, Daniele, 'La pace nel processo criminale. Il caso toscano in età moderna', in Broggio, Paolo and Paoli, Maria Pia (eds), *Stringere la pace. Teorie e pratiche della conciliazione nell'Europa moderna (secoli XV-XVIII)* (Roma, 2011), pp. 369–409.

Ehrlich, Eugen, *Grundlegung der Soziologie des Rechts* (München and Leipzig, 1913).

Elias, Norbert, *Über den Prozeß der Zivilisation*, 2 vols (Basel, 1939). English edition: *The Civilizing Process*, vol. I: *The History of Manners*, vol. II: *State Formation and Civilization* (Oxford, 1969 and 1982).

Errera, Andrea, 'Processus in causa fidei', *L'evoluzione dei manuali inquisitoriali* (Milano, 1998).

Evangelisti, Claudia, 'Angela Vallerani, vedova (1559-1600 ca.)', in Niccoli, Ottavia (ed.), *Rinascimento al femminile* (Rome and Bari, 1998) (1st edition 1991), pp. 197–236.

Evangelisti, Claudia, *Roffeno: ricerche su una comunità montana di fine Cinquecento* (Verona, 2010).

Evans Pritchard, Edward E., *The Nuer. A Description of the Modes of Livelihood and Political Institutions of a Nilotic People* (Oxford, 1940).

Fasano Guarini, Elena, 'Gli statuti delle città soggette a Firenze tra Quattrocento e Cinquecento: riforme locali e interventi centrali', in Chittolini, Giorgio and Willoweit, Dietmar (eds), *Statuti città territori in Italia e Germania tra medioevo ed età moderna* (Bologna, 1991), pp. 69–124.

Fasano Guarini, Elena, 'Produzione di leggi e disciplinamento nella Toscana granducale tra Cinque e Seicento (spunti di ricerca)', in *Disciplina dell'anima, disciplina del corpo e disciplina della società tra medioevo ed età moderna*, ed. Paolo Prodi (Bologna, 1994), pp. 659–90, republished in Fasano Guarini, Elena, *L'Italia moderna e la Toscana dei principi. Discussioni e ricerche storiche* (Florence, 2008), pp. 105–24.

Fasano Guarini, Elena, 'Geographies of Power: The Territorial State in Early Modern Italy', in Martin, John J. (ed.), *The Renaissance. Italy and Abroad* (London, 2003), pp. 89–104.

Fernández Terricabras, Ignasi, *Felipe II y el clero secular. La aplicación del Concilio de Trento* (Madrid, 2000).

Ferrone, Vincenzo, *La società giusta ed equa. Repubblicanesimo e diritti dell'uomo in Gaetano Filangieri* (Rome and Bari, 2008).

Fiori, Antonia, *Espropriare e scomunicare. L''executio parata' delle obbligazioni camerali (secoli XIV-XIX)* (Naples, 2018).

Fiume, Giovanna (ed.), *Onore e storia nelle società mediterranee* (Palermo, 1989).

Foa, Anna, 'Castellari (Castellaro), Bernardino (Bernardino della Barba)', in *Dizionario Biografico degli Italiani*, vol. 21 (Rome, 1978), pp. 652–6.

Foa, Jérémie, *Le tombeau de la paix. Une histoire des édits de pacification (1560-1572)* (Limoges, 2015).

Forclaz, Bertrand, *La famille Borghese et ses fiefs. L'autorité négociée dans l'État pontifical d'Ancien Régime* (Rome, 2006).

Forzati, Francesco, 'Il diritto penale dell'obbedienza fra fondamento etico-religioso dell'offesa e funzione potestativa della pena', *Archivio Penale* 3 (2017).

Fosi, Irene, *La giustizia del papa. Sudditi e tribunali nello Stato pontificio in età moderna* (Rome and Bari, 2007).

Fosi, Irene, *La società violenta. Il banditismo dello Stato pontificio nella seconda metà del Cinquecento* (Rome, 1985).

Fossier, Arnaud, 'L'exemple ou la norme? De l'art d'administrer par formulaire (XIIIe-XIVe)', in Giavarini, Laurence (ed.), *Pouvoir des formes, écriture des normes. Brièveté et normativité (Moyen Âge/Temps Modernes)* (Dijon, 2017), pp. 21–40.

Fossier, Arnaud, Petitjean, Johann and Revest, Clémence (eds), *Écritures grises. Les instruments de travail des administrations (XIIe-XVIIe s.)* (Paris, 2019).

Foucault, Michel, *Discipline and Punish: The Birth of the Prison* (London, 1978).

Foucault, Michel, *The History of Sexuality*, vol. 1 (*An Introduction*) (New York, 1980).

Fumaroli, Marc, *L'âge de l'éloquence. Rhétorique et'Res literaria' de la Renaissance au seuil de l'époque classique* (Genève, 2002).

Gaeta, Franco (ed.), *Il vescovo Pietro Barozzi e il trattato 'De Factionibus Extinguendis'* (Florence, 1958).

Gaille, Marie, *Machiavelli on Freedom and Civil Conflict. An Historical and Medical Approach to Political Thinking* (Leiden and Boston, 2018).

Gardi, Andrea, *Lo Stato in provincia. L'amministrazione della Legazione di Bologna durante il regno di Sisto V (1585-1590)* (Bologna, 1994).

Gatti, Tancredi, *L'imputabilità, i moventi del reato e la prevenzione criminale negli statuti italiani dei sec. XII-XVI* (Padua, 1933).

Gauvard, Claude, *'De Grâce especial'. Crime, État et société en France à la fin du Moyen Âge* (Paris, 1991).

Geneste, Pierre, *Le capitaine poéte aragonais Jerónimo de Urrea. Sa vie et son oeuvre. Ou, chevalerie et Renaissance dans l'Espagne du XVIe siècle* (Paris, 1978).

Gentile, Marco, 'Giustizia, protezione, amicizia: note sul dominio dei Rossi nel Parmense all'inizio del Quattrocento', *Reti Medievali Rivista* V, 1 (2004), available online at http://www.rmoa.unina.it/2275/1/gentile.pdf

Gentile, Marco, 'La vendetta di sangue come rituale. Qualche osservazione sulla Lombardia fra Quattro e Cinquecento', in Salvestrini, Francesco, Varanini, Gian Maria and Zangarini, Anna (eds), *La morte e i suoi riti in Italia tra Medioevo e prima Età moderna* (Florence, 2007), pp. 209–41.

Gentile, Marco, *Fazioni al governo. Politica e società a Parma nel Quattrocento* (Rome, 2009).

Giannini, Massimo C., 'Odescalchi, Paolo', in *Dizionario Biografico degli Italiani*, vol. 79 (Roma, 2013), available online at https://www.treccani.it/enciclopedia/paolo-odescalchi_(Dizionario-Biografico)

Ginzburg, Carlo, 'Una testimonianza inedita su Ludovico Zuccolo', *Rivista Storica Italiana* LXXIX, fasc. IV (1967), pp. 1122–8.

Ginzburg, Carlo, *Nondimanco. Machiavelli, Pascal* (Milan, 2018).

Ginzburg, Carlo, 'Gabriele Pedullà e la carta della Cina', *Storica* 72 (2018), pp. 193–8.

Ginzburg, Carlo and Biasiori, Lucio (eds), *A Historical Approach to Casuistry. Norms and Exceptions in a Comparative Perspective* (London, Oxford, New York, New Delhi and Sidney, 2018).

Giraudo, Stefania, 'La devozione dei Bianchi del 1399: analisi politica di un movimento di pacificazione', *Reti Medievali Rivista* 14, 1 (2013), pp. 167–95.

Giuliani, Marzia, 'Il segretario e l'arte del 'particolarizzamento'. Bonifacio Vannozzi e le corti di Torino, Roma e Firenze', in Geremicca, Antonio and Miesse, Hélène (eds), *Essere uomini di 'lettere'. Segretari e politica culturale nel Cinquecento* (Florence, 2016), pp. 189–99.

Guarisco, Gabriele, *Il conflitto attraverso le norme. Gestione e risoluzione delle dispute a Parma nel XIII secolo* (Bologna, 2005).

Gluckman, Max, 'The Peace in the Feud', *Past & Present* 8 (1955), pp. 1–14.

Gluckman, Max, *Politics, Law and Ritual in Tribal Society* (Oxford, 1965).

Gratteri, Nicola and Nicaso, Antonio, *Fratelli di sangue. Storie, boss e affari della 'ndrangheta, la mafia più potente del mondo* (Milan, 2006).

Graziani, Antoine-Marie, *La violence dans les campagnes corses du XVIe au XVIIIe siècle* (Ajaccio, 2011).

Grendi, Edoardo, 'Introduzione all'analisi storica delle comunità liguri: Cervo in età moderna', in *Studi di micro-analisi storica (Piemonte-Liguria secoli XVI-XVIII), Miscellanea Storica Ligure* VII, 2 (1977), pp. 135–211.

Grendi, Edoardo, 'Il sistema politico di una comunità ligure: Cervo fra Cinquecento e Seicento', *Quaderni storici* XVI, 46 (1981), pp. 92–129.

Grendi, Edoardo, 'Premessa', in *Quaderni Storici* (monographic issue on *Fonti criminali e storia sociale*) 66 (1987), pp. 695–700.

Grendi, Edoardo, 'Stato e comunità nel Seicento genovese', in *Studi in memoria di Giovanni Tarello*, vol. I (*Saggi storici*) (Milan, 1990), pp. 243–82.

Grendi, Edoardo, 'Sulla 'storia criminale': risposta a Mario Sbriccoli', *Quaderni Storici* 73 (1990), pp. 269–75.

Grossi, Paolo, *L'ordine giuridico medievale* (Rome–Bari, 1995).

Gutton, Jean-Pierre, *L'assistance judiciaire dans la France de l'Ancien Régime*, in Lassus, François, Delsalle, Paul., Marchal, Corinne and Vion-Delphin, François (eds), *Mélanges offerts au professeur Maurice Gresset. Des institutions et des hommes* (Besançon, 2007), pp.101–11.

Hanlon, Gregory, *Confession and Community in Seventeenth Century France. Catholic and Protestant Coexistence in Aquitaine* (Philadelphia, 1993).

Härter, Karl and Nubola, Cecilia (eds), *Grazia e giustizia. Figure della clemenza fra tardo medioevo ed età contemporanea* (Bologna, 2011).

Herrup, Cynthia B., *The Common Peace. Participation and the Criminal Law in Seventeenth-century England* (Cambridge, 1987).

Hespanha, António M., *La gracia del derecho. Economía de la cultura en la edad moderna* (Madrid, 1993).

Houlbrooke, Ralph, *Church Courts and the People during the English Reformation. 1520-1570* (Oxford, 1979).

Hindle, Steve, *The State and Social Change in Early Modern England, 1550-1640* (Houndmills, 2002).

Ingram, Martin, *Church Courts. Sex and Marriage in England, 1570-1640* (Cambridge, 1987).

Ingrasci, Ombretta, ''Ndrangheta Women in Contemporary Italy: Between Change and Continuity', in Serenata, Nicoletta (ed.), *The 'Ndrangheta and Sacra Corona Unita. The History, Organization and Operations of Two Unknown Mafia Groups* (Cham, Heidelberg, New York, Dordrecht and London, 2014), pp. 63-80.

Ioly Zorattini, Pier Cesare, 'Ebrei in Italia', in *Dizionario Storico dell'Inquisizione*, ed. A. Prosperi, vol. II (Pisa, 2010), p. 523–6.

Jacobson Schutte, Anne, 'Donzellini, Girolamo', in *Dizionario Storico dell'Inquisizione*, ed. A. Prosperi, vol. I (Pisa, 2010), pp. 509–10.

Jansen, Katherine L., *Peace and Penance in Late Medieval Italy* (Princeton and Oxford, 2018).

Jarman, E. Kate M. (ed.), *Justice and Conciliation in a Tudor Church Court. Depositions from EDC 2/6, Deposition Book of the Consistory Court of Chester, September 1558-March 1559* (Bristol, 2012).

Kagan, Richard L., *Lawsuits and Litigants in Castile, 1500-1700* (Chapel Hill, 1981).

Kaplan, Benjamin, *Divided by Faith. Religious Conflict and the Practice of Toleration in Early Modern Europe* (Cambridge, MA, 2007).

Klapisch-Zuber, Christiane, *Retour à la Cité. Les magnats de Florence (1340-1440)* (Paris, 2006).

Kostoris, Roberto E. (ed.), *Percorsi giuridici della postmodernità* (Bologna, 2017).

Kumhera, Glenn, *The Benefits of Peace. Private Peacemaking in Late Medieval Italy* (Leiden and Boston, 2017).

Landau, Norma, *The Justices of the Peace, 1679-1760* (Berkeley, Los Angeles and London, 1984).

Lavenia, Vincenzo, 'Assolvere o infamare. Eresia occulta, correzione fraterna e segreto sacramentale', *Storica* 20–1 (2001), pp. 89–154.

Lavenia, Vincenzo, *L'infamia e il perdono. Tributi, pene e confessione nella teologia morale della prima età moderna* (Bologna, 2004).

Lavenia, Vincenzo, 'Restituire, condonare. Lessico giuridico, confessione e pratiche sociali nella prima età moderna', in Härter, Karl and Nubola, Cecilia (eds), *Grazia e giustizia. Figure della clemenza fra tardo medioevo ed età contemporanea* (Bologna, 2011), pp. 389–411.

Lavenia, Vincenzo, 'Sega, Filippo', in *Dizionario Biografico degli Italiani*, vol. 91 (Rome, 2018), pp. 724–7.

Lecomte, Louis-Henry, *Napoléon et le monde dramatique. Étude nouvelle sur des documents inédits* (Paris, 1912).

Le Goff, Jacques, *La naissance du Purgatoire* (Paris, 1981).

Levi, Giovanni, *L'eredità immateriale. Carriera di un esorcista nel Piemonte del Seicento* (Turin, 1985).

Levi, Giovanni, 'Reciprocidad Mediterránea', *Hispania* 60, 204 (2000), pp. 103–26.

Levi, Giovanni, 'Aequitas *vs.* fairness. *Reciprocità ed equità fra età moderna ed età contemporanea*', *Rivista di Storia Economica* XIX, 2 (2003), pp. 195–204.

Lombardi, Daniela, *Storia del matrimonio. Dal Medioevo a oggi* (Bologna, 2008).

Lombardini, Sandro, 'Rivolte e ribellismo contadino nel Monregalese del Seicento: ipotesi di ricerca', *Bollettino storico-bibliografico subalpino* 80 (1982), pp. 645–57.

Lombardini, Sandro, 'Le premesse ecologiche di una rivoluzione contadina. Agricoltura e demografia nel Monregalese all'epoca delle Guerre del sale', *Bollettino della Società per gli studi storici, archeologici ed artistici della Provincia di Cuneo* 89 (1983), 2, pp. 107–89.

Loschiavo, Luca, 'Non est inter vos sapiens quisquam, qui possit iudicare inter fratrem suum? Processo e giustizia nel primo cristianesimo dalle origini al vescovo Ambrogio', in Bassanelli Sommariva, Gisella (ed.), *Ravenna Capitale. Giudizi, giudici e norme processuali in Occidente nei secoli IV-VIII*, vol. I (Saggi) (Santarcangelo di Romagna, 2015), pp. 67–106.

Loschiavo, Luca, *L'età del passaggio. All'alba del diritto comune europeo (secoli III-VII)* (Turin, 2019).

McAuley, Finbarr, 'Canon Law and the End of the Ordeal', in *Oxford Journal of Legal Studies*, 26, 3 (2006), pp. 473-513.

Magno, Luigi, 'Apologie étatique et concorde religieuse. Sur quelques pamphlets de Loys Le Roy', *Krypton. Identità, potere, rappresentazioni* 1 (2013), available online at http://193.205.139.95/ojs/index.php/krypton/article/view/452/449

Maire Vigueur, Jean-Claude, *Cavaliers et citoyens. Guerre, conflits et société dans l'Italie communale, XIIe-XIIIe siècles* (Paris, 2004).

Mancino Michele and Romeo, Giovanni, *Clero criminale. L'onore della Chiesa e i delitti degli ecclesiastici nell'Italia della Controriforma* (Rome and Bari, 2014).

Mannori, Luca, *Il sovrano tutore. Pluralismo istituzionale e accentramento amministrativo nel Principato dei Medici (secc. XVI-XVII)* (Milan, 1994).

Mannori, Luca (ed.), *Comunità e poteri centrali negli Antichi Stati Italiani. Alle origini dei controlli amministrativi* (Naples, 1997).

Mannozzi, Grazia, *La giustizia senza spada. Uno studio comparato su giustizia riparativa e mediazione penale* (Milan, 2003).

Mantecón Movellán, Tomás A., *Contrarreforma y religiosidad popular en Cantabria. Las cofradías religiosas* (Santander, 1990).

Mantecón Movellán, Tomás A., 'Territorio, poderes y actitudes ante el crimen en la moderna Cantabria rural', in Fernández Albaladejo, Pablo (ed.), *Monarquía, imperio y pueblos en España* (Alicante, 1997), pp. 757–70.

Mantecón Movellán, Tomás A., 'El peso de la infrajusticialidad en el control del crimen durante la Edad Moderna', *Estudis* 28 (2002), pp. 43–75

Mantecón Movellán, Tomás A., 'Popular Culture and the Arbitration of Disputes. Northern Spain in the Eighteenth Century', in Knafla, Louis A. (ed.), *Crime, Punishment, and Reform in Europe* (Westport and London, 2003), pp. 39–55.

Mantecón Movellán, Tomás A., 'The Patterns of Violence in Early Modern Spain', *The Journal of the Historical Society* VII, 2 (2007), pp. 229–64.

Mantecón Movellán, Tomás A., 'La acción de justicia en la España Moderna: una justicia dialogada, para procurar paz', in Broggio, Paolo and Paoli,

Maria Pia (eds), *Stringere la pace. Teorie e pratiche della conciliazione nell'Europa moderna (secoli XV-XVIII)* (Rome, 2011), pp. 333–67.

Maravall, José Antonio, *Poder, honor y élites en el siglo XVII* (Madrid, 1979).

Maravall, José Antonio, 'Saavedra Fajardo: moral de acomodación y carácter conflictivo de la libertad', in Maravall, José Antonio, *Estudios de historia del pensamiento español*, serie tercera (Madrid, 1984), pp. 223–54.

Marcarelli, Michelangelo, 'Pratiche di giustizia in età moderna: riti di pacificazione e mediazione nella Terraferma veneta', in Chiodi, Giovanni and Povolo, Claudio (eds), *L'amministrazione della giustizia penale nella Repubblica di Venezia, secoli XVI-XVIII*, vol. II (*Retoriche, stereotipi, prassi*) (Sommacampagna, 2004), pp. 259–309.

Margolf, Diane C., *Religion and Royal Justice in Early Modern France. The Paris Chambre de l'Edit, 1598-1665* (Kirksville, 2003).

Marinelli, Sergio, 'La pacificazione, non la vendetta', *Acta Histriae* 25, 1 (2017), pp. 109–19.

Martone, Luciano, *Arbiter-arbitrator. Forme di giustizia privata nell'età del diritto comune* (Naples, 1984).

Mateu Ibars, Josefina, 'Don Artal de Alagón, Conde de Sástago, Virrey de Aragón (1575-1588): algunas notas sobre su alcurnia y gobierno (el pleito sobre Virrey extranjero y disposiciones contra el bandolerismo)', in Ayerbe Iríbar, María Rosa (ed.), *Estudios dedicados a la memoria del profesor Luis Miguel Díaz de Salazar Fernández*, vol. I (*Estudios histórico-jurídicos*) (País Vasco, 1993), pp. 431–46.

Mauss, Marcel, 'Essai sur le don. Forme et raison de l'échange dans les sociétés archaïques', *L'Année Sociologique*, 1923–4.

Mazzacane, Aldo, 'Claro, Giulio', in *Dizionario Biografico degli Italiani*, vol. 26 (Rome, 1982), pp. 141–6.

Mazzacane, Aldo, 'De Luca, Giovanni Battista', in *Dizionario Biografico degli Italiani*, vol. 38 (Rome, 1990), pp. 340–7.

Mazzacane, Aldo, 'Farinacci, Prospero', in *Dizionario Biografico degli Italiani*, vol. 45 (Rome, 1995), pp. 1–5.

Mazzone, Umberto, '"Evellant vicia ... aedificent virtutes": il cardinal legato come elemento di disciplinamento nello Stato della Chiesa', in Prodi, Paolo (ed.), *Disciplina dell'anima, disciplina del corpo e disciplina della società tra medioevo ed età moderna* (Bologna, 1994), pp. 691–731.

Menzinger, Sara, *Giuristi e politica nei comuni di Popolo. Siena, Perugia e Bologna, tre governi a confronto* (Rome, 2006).

Menzinger, Sara and Vallerani, Massimo, 'Giuristi e città: fiscalità, giustizia e cultura giuridica tra XII e XIII secolo. Ipotesi e percorsi di ricerca', in Caciorgna, Maria Teresa, Carocci, Sandro and Zorzi, Andrea (eds), *I comuni di Jean-Claude Maire Vigueur. Percorsi storiografici* (Rome, 2014), pp. 201–34.

Mestre Zaragozá, Marina, 'La théorie des passions de Juan Luis Vivès', in Moreau, Pierre-François (ed.), *Les passions à l'âge classique* (Paris, 2006), pp. 29–44.

Michels, Norbert (ed.), *Hendrick Goltzius (1558-1617). Mythos, Macht und Menschlichkeit* (Petersberg, 2017).

Miglietti, Sara, 'Amitié, harmonie et paix politique chez Aristote et Jean Bodin', *Astérion. Philosophie, histoire des idées, pensée politique* 7 (2010), available online at https://journals.openedition.org/asterion/1660

Milani, Giuliano, *L'esclusione dal comune. Conflitti e bandi politici a Bologna e in altre città italiane tra XII e XIV secolo* (Rome, 2003).

Muir, Edward, *Mad Blood Stirring. Vendetta in Renaissance Italy* (Baltimore and London, 1998).

Mario Montorzi, 'La giustizia di Paolo Prodi: note di lettura', *Storica* 17 (2000), pp. 101–13.

Musin, Aude, 'Le droit de vengeance et son déclin dans les Pays-Bas (XIVe-XVIe siècles)', *Krypton. Identità, potere, rappresentazioni* V–VI (2015), avialable online at http://romatrepress.uniroma3.it/wp-content/uploads/2019/05/Le-droit-de-vengeance-et-son-d%C3%A9clin-dans-les-Pays-Bas-XIVe-XVIe-si%C3%A8cles.pdf

Musin, Aude, *Sociabilité urbaine et criminalisation étatique. La justice namuroise face à la violence de 1360 à 1555* (Turnhout, 2017).

Nassiet, Michel, 'Vengeance in Sixteenth and Seventeenth-Century France', in Carroll, Stuart (ed.), *Cultures of Violence. Interpersonal Violence in Historical Perspective* (Houndsmill and New York, 2007), pp. 117–28.

Negredo del Cerro, Fernando, *Los predicadores de Felipe IV. Corte, intrigas y religión en la España del Siglo de Oro* (Madrid, 2006).

Niccoli, Ottavia, 'Rinuncia, pace, perdono. rituali di pacificazione della prima età moderna', *Studi Storici* 40, 1 (1999), pp. 219–61.

Niccoli, Ottavia, 'Giustizia, pace, perdono. A proposito di un libro di John Bossy', *Storica* 25–6 (2003), pp. 195–207.

Niccoli, Ottavia, *Perdonare. Idee, pratiche, rituali in Italia tra Cinque e Seicento* (Rome and Bari, 2007).

Nubola, Cecilia and Würgler, Andreas (eds), *Suppliche e* gravamina. *Politica, amministrazione, giustizia negli Stati italiani e nel Sacro Romano Impero (secc. XIV-XVIII)* (Bologna, 2002).

Olivari, Michele, 'Lettura "politica" dei resoconti missionari di Pedro de León, gesuita andaluso (1580-1620)', *Rivista di Storia e Letteratura Religiosa* XXII, 3 (1986), pp. 475–91.

Padoa Schioppa, Antonio, 'Delitto e pace privata nel pensiero dei legisti bolognesi. Brevi note', *Studia Gratiana* 20 (1976), pp. 271–86.

Pagano, Sergio, *Paesi infetti. Magia, eresia e faide familiari nel tortonese durante il secolo XVI* (Rome, 2003).

Paoli, Letizia, *Fratelli di mafia. Cosa Nostra e 'Ndrangheta* (Bologna, 2000).

Pastore, Alessandro, 'Inquisitori, confessori, missionari', *Rivista Storica Italiana* CX (1998), pp. 666–86.

Pastore, Stefania, 'A proposito di Matteo 18, 15. *Correctio fraterna* e Inquisizione nella Spagna del Cinquecento', *Rivista Storica Italiana* 113 (2001), pp. 323–68.

Pazzaglini, Peter R., *The Criminal Ban of the Sienese Commune, 1225-1310* (Milan, 1979).

Pedrini, Diego and Dubbini, Lucia, '1563: una faida a Jesi', *Proposte & Ricerche* 80 (2018), pp. 127–51.

Pedrini, Diego and Dubbini, Lucia, *Il prezzo del perdono. Il Tribunale episcopale di Jesi in età moderna (1530-1730)* (Fermo, 2020).

Pedullà, Gabriele, *Machiavelli in tumulto. Conquista, cittadinanza e conflitto nei'Discorsi sopra la prima deca di Tito Livio'* (Rome, 2011).

Pedullà, Gabriele, *Machiavelli in Tumult. The Discourses on Livy and the Origins of Political Conflictualism* (Cambridge, 2018).

Pedullà, Gabriele, 'Machiavelli secondo Carlo Ginzburg', *Storica* 71 (2018), pp. 9–86.

Pellegrini, Marco, *Savonarola. Profezie e martirio nell'età delle guerre d'Italia* (Rome, 2020).

Peristiany, John G. (ed.), *Honour and Shame. The Values of Mediterranean Society* (Chicago, 1966).

Peristiany, John G. and Pitt-Rivers, Julian (eds), *Honor and Grace in Anthropology* (Cambridge, 1991).

Petkov, Kiril, *The Kiss of Peace. Ritual, Self, and Society in the High and Late Medieval West* (Boston, 2003).

Piano Mortari, Vincenzo, *Gli inizi del diritto moderno in Europa* (Napoli, 1980).

Piazza, Andrea, 'Stratégies de la parole: paix et hérétiques en Italie dans les Registres de Grégoire IX', in Dessì, Rosa Maria (ed.), *Prêcher la paix et discipliner la société. Italie, France, Angleterre (XIIIe-XVe siècle)* (Turnhout, 2005), pp. 103–22.

Piccialuti, Maura, 'I controlli del Buon Governo sulle comunità negli anni del Prefetto Giuseppe Renato Imperiali (1701-1737)', in Mannori, Luca (ed.), *Comunità e poteri centrali negli Antichi Stati Italiani. Alle origini dei controlli amministrativi* (Naples, 1997), pp. 183–209.

Pignata, Marianna, *Spazi di giustizia negoziata nel* Regnum *della prima età moderna. I* Commentaria *di Camillo Borrelli* (Naples, 2018).

Pissavino, Paolo, 'Il *De officiis* del Della Casa e alcuni raffronti metodologici', in Mozzarelli, Cesare (ed.), *'Famiglia' del principe e famiglia aristocratica* (Rome, 1989), pp. 51–145.

Piva, Franco, 'Le cadre historique et normatif du théâtre français sous le Consulat et l'Empire', *Studi Francesi* 191, LXVII, II (2020) (De Santis, Vincenzo, Perazzolo, Paola and Piva, Franco (eds), 'Théâtre, identité, et politique culturelle sous le Consulat et l'Empire') pp. 258–68.

Pizzolato, Luigi Franco, 'L'amicizia in S. Agostino e il "Laelius" di Cicerone', *Vigiliae Christianae* 28 (1974), pp. 203–15.

Poloni, Alma, 'Il comune di popolo e le sue istituzioni tra Due e Trecento. Alcune riflessioni a partire dalla storiografia dell'ultimo quindicennio', *Reti Medievali Rivista* 13, 1 (2012), pp. 3–25.

Pomara, Saverino Bruno, *Bandolerismo, violencia y justicia en la Sicilia barroca* (Madrid, 2011).

Porret, Michel, 'Lumières et droit de punir: l'impossible vengeance', in Gauvard, Claude and Zorzi, Andrea (eds), *La vengeance en Europe, XIIe-XVIIIe siècle* (Paris, 2015), pp. 307–17.

Povolo, Claudio, *L'intrigo dell'onore. Poteri e istituzioni nella Repubblica di Venezia tra Cinque e Seicento* (Sommacampagna, 1997).

Puletti, Euro, *Ludovico Carbone da Costacciaro. Vita, pensiero ed opere* (Gualdo Tadino, 2013).

Prodi, Paolo, *Il Cardinale Gabriele Paleotti (1522-1597)*, vol. II (Rome, 1967).

Prodi, Paolo, *Il sovrano pontefice. Un corpo e due anime: la monarchia papale nella prima età moderna* (Bologna, 1982).

Prodi, Paolo, *Il sacramento del potere. Il giuramento politico nella storia costituzionale dell'Occidente* (Bologna, 1992).

Prodi, Paolo (ed.), *Disciplina dell'anima, disciplina del corpo e disciplina della società tra medioevo ed età moderna* (Bologna, 1994).

Prodi, Paolo, *Una storia della giustizia. Dal pluralismo dei fori al moderno dualismo tra coscienza e diritto* (Bologna, 2000).

Prosperi, Adriano, 'Il missionario', in Villari, Rosario (ed.), *L'uomo barocco* (Rome and Bari, 1991), pp. 179–18.

Prosperi, Adriano, 'L'Inquisitore come confessore', in Prodi, Paolo (ed.), *Disciplina dell'anima, disciplina del corpo e disciplina della società tra medioevo ed età moderna* (Bologna, 1994), pp. 187–24.

Prosperi, Adriano, *Tribunali della coscienza. Inquisitori, confessori, missionari* (Turin, 1996).

Prosperi, Adriano, *L'eresia del Libro Grande. Storia di Giorgio Siculo e la sua setta* (Milano, 2000).

Prosperi, Adriano, 'Una discussione con Paolo Prodi', *Storica* 17 (2000), pp. 85–100.

Prosperi, Adriano (ed.), *Misericordie. Conversioni sotto il patibolo tra Medioevo ed età moderna* (Pisa, 2007).

Prosperi, Adriano, *Giustizia bendata. Percorsi storici di un'immagine* (Torino, 2008).

Prosperi, Adriano, *Delitto e perdono. La pena di morte nell'orizzonte mentale dell'Europa cristiana, XIV-XVIII secolo* (Turin, 2013).

Quaglioni, Diego, *La giustizia nel Medioevo e nella prima età moderna* (Bologna, 2004).

Raggio, Osvaldo, 'La politica nella parentela. Conflitti locali e commissari in Liguria orientale (secoli XVI-XVII)', *Quaderni Storici* XXI, 63 (1986) (Lombardini, Sandro, Raggio, Osvaldo and Torre, Angelo (eds), *Conflitti locali e idiomi politici*, monographic issue), pp. 721–57.

Raggio, Osvaldo, *Faide e parentele. Lo stato genovese visto dalla Fontanabuona* (Turin, 1990).

Rasi, Piero, *La conclusione del matrimonio nella dottrina prima del Concilio di Trento* (Naples, 1958).

Raviola, Blythe Alice, *Giovanni Botero. Un profilo fra storia e storiografia* (Milano, 2020).

Reinhardt, Nicole, *Voices of Conscience. Royal Confessors and Political Counsel in Seventeenth-Century Spain and France* (Oxford, 2016).

Ricciardelli, Fabrizio, *The Politics of Exclusion in Early Renaissance Florence* (Turnhout, 2007).

Roberts, Simon, *Order and Dispute. An Introduction to Legal Anthropology* (London, 1979).

Romeo, Giovanni, *Ricerche su confessione dei peccati e inquisizione nell'Italia del Cinquecento* (Reggio Calabria, 1997).

Rose, Colin S., 'Violence and the Centralization of Criminal Justice in Early Modern Bologna', in Rubin Blanshei, Sarah (ed.), *Violence and Justice in Bologna, 1250-1700* (Lanham, Boulder, New York and London, 2018), pp. 101–22.

Rossi, Giovanni, *Incunaboli della modernità. Scienza giuridica e cultura umanistica in André Tiraqueau (1488-1558)* (Turin, 2008).

Rossi, Maria Clara, 'Polisemia di un concetto: la pace nel basso medioevo. Note di lettura', *Quaderni di storia religiosa* 12 (2005) (Rossi, Maria Clara (ed.), *La pace tra realtà e utopia*, monographic issue), pp. 9–45.

Rousseaux, Xavier, 'La violence dans les sociétés pré-modernes: sources, méthodes et interprétations. Nivelles, une cité brabançonne à travers cinq siècles', in Musin, Aude, Rousseaux, Xavier and Vesentini, Frédéric (eds), *Violence, conciliation et répression. Recherches sur l'histoire du crime, de l'Antiquité au XXIe siècle* (Louvain-la-Neuve, 2008), pp. 263–88.

Rovigo, Vito, 'Le paci private: motivazioni religiose nelle fonti veronesi del Quattrocento', *Quaderni di storia religiosa* 12 (2005) (Rossi, Maria Clara (ed.), *La pace tra realtà e utopia*, monographic issue), pp. 201–33.

Rurale, Flavio, 'Clemente VIII, i gesuiti e la controversia giurisdizionale milanese', in Signorotto, Gianvittorio and Visceglia, Maria Antonietta (eds), *La corte di Roma tra Cinque e Seicento.'Teatro' della politica europea* (Rome, 1998), pp. 323–66.

Rurale, Flavio, 'Mazzarino, Giulio Cesare', in *Dizionario Biografico degli Italiani*, vol. 72 (Rome, 2008), pp. 528–31.

Salvati, Mariuccia, 'Una storia della giustizia', *Passato e Presente* XIX, 53 (2001), pp. 153–64.

Salvetto, Paolo, *Tullio Crispoldi nella crisi religiosa del Cinquecento. Le difficili 'pratiche del viver christiano'* (Brescia, 2009).

Savelli, Rodolfo, 'Tribunali, "decisiones" e giuristi: una proposta di ritorno alle fonti', in Chittolini, Giorgio, Molho, Anthony and Schiera, Pierangelo (eds), *Origini dello Stato. Processi di formazione statale in Italia tra medioevo ed età moderna* (Bologna, 1994), pp. 397–421.

Saviano, Roberto, *Gomorra. Viaggio nell'impero economico e nel sogno di dominio della camorra* (Milan, 2015).

Sbriccoli, Mario, *L'interpretazione dello statuto. Contributo allo studio della funzione dei giuristi nell'età comunale* (Milan, 1969).

Sbriccoli, Mario, Crimen laesae maiestatis. *Il problema del reato politico alle soglie della scienza penalistica moderna* (Milan, 1974).

Sbriccoli, Mario, 'Fonti giudiziarie e fonti giuridiche: riflessioni sulla fase attuale degli studi di storia del crimine e della giustizia criminale', *Studi Storici* 29 (1988), pp. 491–501.

Sbriccoli, Mario, 'Giustizia negoziata, giustizia egemonica. Riflessioni su una nuova fase degli studi di storia della giustizia criminale', in Bellabarba, Marco, Schwerhoff, Gerd and Zorzi, Andrea (eds), *Criminalità e giustizia in Germania e in Italia. Pratiche giudiziarie e linguaggi giuridici tra tardo medioevo ed età moderna / Kriminalität und Justiz in Deutschland und Italien. Rechtspraktiken und gerichtliche Diskurse in Spätmittelalter und Früher Neuzeit*, (Bologna, 2001), pp. 345–64.

Sbriccoli, Mario, *Storia del diritto penale e della giustizia: scritti editi e inediti, 1972-2007*, vol. I (Milan, 2009).

Scaramella, Pierroberto, 'Alois, Giovanni Francesco', in Prosperi, Adriano (ed.), *Dizionario Storico dell'Inquisizione*, vol. I (Pisa, 2010), pp. 46–7.

Schiera, Pierangelo, 'L'amicizia politica in Francesco Patrizi, senese', in Angelini, Giovanna and Tesoro, Marina (eds), *De amicitia. Scritti dedicati a Arturo Colombo* (Milan, 2007), pp. 61–72.

Schneider, Reinhard, 'Politische Freundschaft', in *Il concetto di amicizia nella storia della cultura europea / Der Begriff Freundschaft in der Geschichte der Europäische Kultur*, Atti del XXII Convegno Internazionale di Studi Italo-Tedeschi (Merano, 9-11 maggio 1994) (Merano, 1995), pp. 372–94.

Seidel Menchi, Silvana and Quaglioni, Diego (eds), *Coniugi nemici. La separazione in Italia dal XII al XVIII secolo* (Bologna, 2000).

Seidel Menchi, Silvana and Quaglioni, Diego (eds), *Matrimoni in dubbio. Unioni controverse e nozze clandestine in Italia dal XIV al XVIII secolo* (Bologna, 2001).

Selwyn, Jennifer D., *A Paradise Inhabited by Devils. The Jesuits' Civilizing Mission in Early Modern Naples* (Aldershot, 2004).

Sharpe, James A., *Crime in Early Modern England 1550-1750* (London and New York, 1984).

Shaw, Christine, *The Politics of Exile in Renaissance Italy* (Cambridge, 2000).

Sinclair, Thomas A., *A History of Greek Political Thought* (London, 1952).

Signorotto, Gianvittorio (ed.), 'L'Italia degli Austrias. Monarchia cattolica e domini italiani nei secoli XVI e XVII', *Cheiron*, fasc. 17–18 (1993), monographic issue.

Smail, Daniel L., *The Consumption of Justice. Emotions, Publicity and Legal Culture in Marseille, 1264-1423* (Ithaca and London, 2003).

Smail, Daniel L. and Gibson Kelly, Lyn (eds), *Vengeance in Medieval Europe. A Reader* (Toronto, 2009).

Spagnoletti, Angelantonio, 'Giudici e governatori regi nelle università meridionali (XVIII secolo)', *Archivio Storico delle Province Napoletane* CV (1987), pp. 415–54.

Spierenburg, Pieter, 'Social Control and History: An Introduction', in Roodenburg, Herman and Spierenburg, Pieter (eds), *Social Control in Europe*, vol. I (*1500-1800*) (Columbus, 2004), pp. 1–21.

Spierenburg, Pieter, 'Violence: Reflections about a Word', in Body-Gendrot, Sophie and Spierenburg, Pieter (eds), *Violence in Europe. Historical and Contemporary Perspectives* (New York, 2009), pp. 13–25.

Sousa Santos, Boaventura de, *Law Against Law. Legal Reasoning in Pasargada Law* (New Haven and London, 1974).

Sousa Santos, Boaventura de, *Toward a New Legal Common Sense. Law, Globalization, and Emancipation* (London, 2002).

Stella, Pietro, 'Attrizione e contrizione in età moderna: l'importanza storica di una disputa irrisolta', *Annali di Scienze Religiose* 3 (1998), pp. 151–72.

Tallon, Alain, *La Compagnie du Saint-Sacrement, 1629-1667. Spiritualité et société* (Paris, 1990).

Tamassia, Giovanni, 'Osculum interveniens. Contributo alla storia dei riti nuziali', *Rivista Storica Italiana* II, 2 (1885), pp. 241–64

Tavilla, Carmelo Elio, 'Paci, feudalità e pubblici poteri nell'esperienza del Ducato estense', in Cavina, Marco (ed.), *Duelli, faide e rappacificazioni. Elaborazioni concettuali, esperienze storiche* (Milan, 2001), pp. 290–1.

Taylor, Scott K., *Honor and Violence in Golden Age Spain* (New Haven and London, 2008).

Tedeschi, John, 'Guazzini, Sebastiano', in Prosperi, Adriano (ed.), *Dizionario Storico dell'Inquisizione*, vol. II (Pisa, 2010), pp. 740–1.

Testuzza, Maria Sole, 'Rimediare al male con il bene. La giustizia e il perdono della vittima nell'età della Controriforma: tra Restitutio, Satisfactio/ Satispassio e Potestas *in se ipsum*', *Vergentis*, 4 (2017), pp. 267–95.

Thermes, Diana, 'L'amicizia cosmica e cosmopolitica di Jean Bodin', in Angelini, Giovanna and Tesoro, Marina (eds), *De amicitia. Scritti dedicati a Arturo Colombo* (Milan, 2007), pp. 73–82.

Tocci, Giovanni, *Le comunità in età moderna. Problemi storiografici e prospettive di ricerca* (Rome, 1997).

Torre, Angelo, 'Faide, fazioni e partiti, ovvero la ridefinizione della politica nei feudi imperiali delle Langhe tra Sei e Settecento', *Quaderni Storici* 63 (1986), pp. 775–810.

Thomas, Yan (ed.), *L'exception dans tous ses états* (Paris, 2007).

Thomas, Yan, 'Fictio legis. L'empire de la fiction romaine et ses limites médiévales', *Droits* 21 (1995), republished as *Les opérations du droit* (Paris, 2011).

Thomson, Edward P., *Società patrizia, cultura plebea. Otto saggi di antropologia storica sull'Inghilterra del Settecento* (Turin, 1981).

Tocci, Giovanni, *Le comunità in età moderna. Problemi storiografici e prospettive di ricerca* (Rome, 1997).

Tomás y Valiente, Francisco, 'El perdón de la parte ofendida en el derecho penal castellano (siglos XVI, XVII y XVIII)', *Anuario de Historia del Derecho Español* XXXI (1961), pp. 55–114.

Tomás y Valiente, Francisco, *El derecho penal de la Monarquía absoluta* (Madrid, 1969).

Torre, Angelo, 'Il consumo di devozioni: rituali e potere nelle campagne piemontesi nella prima metà del Settecento', *Quaderni Storici* 58, 1 (1985), pp. 181–223.

Torre, Angelo, 'Faida, fazioni e partiti: la ridefinizione della politica nei feudi imperiali delle Langhe tra Sei e Settecento', *Quaderni Storici* 63 (1986), pp. 775–810.

Torre, Angelo, 'Antropologia sociale e ricerca storica', in Rossi, Pietro (ed.), *La storiografia contemporanea. Indirizzi e problemi* (Milan, 1987), pp. 206–39.

Torre, Angelo, *Il consumo di devozioni. Religione e comunità nelle campagne dell'*Ancien Régime (Venice, 1995).

Turchetti, Mario, *Concordia o tolleranza? François Bauduin (1520-1573) e i 'moyenneurs'* (Geneva, 1984).

Turchini, Angelo, '"A beneficio pubblico e onor di Dio". Povertà e carità nella legislazione e nella pastorale della chiesa milanese', in Zardin, Danilo (ed.), *La città e i poveri: Milano e le terre lombarde dal Rinascimento all'età spagnola* (Milan, 1995), pp. 191–252.

Turrini, Miriam, *La coscienza e le leggi. Morale e diritto nei testi per la confessione della prima Età moderna* (Bologna, 1991).

Vallerani, Massimo, *La giustizia pubblica medievale* (Bologna, 2005).

Vallerani, Massimo (ed.), *Sistemi d'eccezione*, *Quaderni Storici* XLIV, 2 (2009), monographic issue.

Varanini, Gian Maria, 'Legittimità implicita dei poteri nell'Italia centro-settentrionale del tardo medioevo. La tradizione cittadina e gli Stati regionali', in Genet, Jean-Philippe (ed.), *La légitimité implicite*, vol. II, (Rome and Paris, 2015), pp. 223–39.

Verga, Marcello, *Storie d'Europa. Secoli XVIII-XXI* (Rome, 2004).

Viggiano, Alfredo, *Governanti e governati. Legittimità del potere ed esercizio dell'autorità nello Stato veneto della prima età moderna* (Treviso, 1993).

Viggiano, Alfredo, 'Giustizia, disciplina, ordine pubblico', in Cozzi, Gaetano (ed.), *Storia di Venezia dalle origini alla caduta della Serenissima*, vol. VI (*Dal Rinascimento al barocco*) (Rome, 1994), pp. 825–57.

Villari, Rosario, *Politica barocca. Inquietudini, mutamento e prudenza* (Rome and Bari, 2010).

Volpini, Paola, *Lo spazio politico del* letrado. *Juan Bautista Larrea magistrato e giurista nella monarchia di Filippo IV* (Bologna, 2004).

Walberg, Deborah, 'Tradition and Propaganda in the Venetian Madonna della Pace', *Ikon* 9 (2016), pp. 269–82.

Walsham, Alexandra, *Charitable Hatred. Tolerance and Intolerance in England, 1500-1700* (Manchester, 2006).

Wangerin, Laura E., *Kingship and Justice in the Ottonian Empire* (Ann Arbor, 2019).

Warren Sabean, David, Teuscher, Simon and Mathieu, Jon (eds), *Kinship in Europe. Approaches to Long-term Developments (1300-1900)* (New York and Oxford, 2007).

Weber, Christoph (ed.), *Legati e governatori dello Stato pontificio (1550-1809)* (Rome, 1994).

Weisser, Michael, 'Crime and Punishment in Early Modern Spain', in Gatrell, Vic A. C., Lenman, Bruce and Parker, Geoffrey (eds), *Crime and the Law. The Social History of Crime in Western Europe since 1500* (London, 1980), pp. 76–96.

Wenzel, Eric, *La paix par la justice. Les modes alternatifs de règlement des conflits dans la France d'Ancien Régime*, in Broggio, Paolo and Paoli, Maria Pia (eds), *Stringere la pace. Teorie e pratiche della conciliazione nell'Europa moderna* (Rome, 2009), pp. 509–19.

Wenzel, Eric (ed.), *Justice et religion. Regards croisés: histoire et droit,* Actes du colloque international de l'Université d'Avignon et des Pays de Vaucluse (1-3 octobre 2008) (Avignon, 2010).

Wickham, Chris, *Courts and Conflict in Twelfth-Century Tuscany* (Oxford, 2003).

Willis, Geoffrey G., *St. Augustine and the Donatist Controversy* (London, 1950).

Wijffels, Alain, 'Lawyers and Litigants: The Corrupting Appeal and Effects of Civil Litigation in Hendrick Goltzius' *Litis Abusus*', in Huygebaert,

Stefan, Martyn, Georges, Paumen, Vanessa, Bousmar, Eric and Rousseaux, Xavier (eds), *The Art of Law. Artistic Representations and Iconography of Law and Justice in Context, from the Middle Ages to the First World War* (New York, 2018), pp. 181–99.

Zanetti, Gianfrancesco, *La nozione di giustizia in Aristotele* (Bologna, 1993).

Zemon Davis, Natalie, 'The Rites of Violence: Religious Riot in Sixteenth-Century France', *Past & Present* 59 (1973), pp. 51–91.

Zemon Davis, Natalie, *Fiction in the Archives. Pardon Tales and Their Tellers in sixteenth-century France* (Stanford, 1987).

Zemon Davis, Natalie, *The Gift in Sixteenth Century France* (Oxford, 2000).

Zorzi, Andrea, 'Politica e giustizia a Firenze al tempo degli Ordinamenti antimagnatizi', in Arrighi, Vanna (ed.), *Ordinamenti di giustizia fiorentini. Studi in occasione del VII centenario* (Florence, 1995), pp. 107–47.

Zorzi, Andrea, 'Negoziazione penale, legittimazione giuridica e poteri urbani nell'Italia comunale', in Bellabarba, Marco, Schwerhoff, Gerd and Zorzi, Andrea (eds), *Criminalità e giustizia in Germania e in Italia. Pratiche giudiziarie e linguaggi giuridici tra tardo medioevo ed età moderna / Kriminalität und Justiz in Deutschland und Italien. Rechtspraktiken und gerichtliche Diskurse in Spätmittelalter und Früher Neuzeit* (Bologna, 2001), pp. 13–34.

Zorzi, Andrea, 'L'egemonia del penale in Mario Sbriccoli', in Lacchè, Luigi, Latini, Carlotta, Marchetti, Paolo and Meccarelli, Massimo (eds), *Penale, giustizia, potere. Metodi, ricerche, storiografie. Per ricordare Mario Sbriccoli* (Macerata, 2007), pp. 155–78.

Zorzi, Andrea, 'I conflitti dell'Italia comunale. Riflessioni sullo stato degli studi e sulle prospettive di ricerca, in Zorzi, Andrea (ed.), *Conflitti, paci e vendette nell'Italia comunale* (Florence, 2009), pp. 7–41.

Zorzi, Andrea, 'Consigliare alla vendetta, consigliare alla giustizia. Pratiche e culture politiche nell'Italia comunale', *Archivio Storico Italiano* 170, 2 (2012), pp. 263–84.

Index of Names

Index of Places

Index of Subjects

Printed and bound by CPI Group (UK) Ltd, Croydon, CR0 4YY

13/09/2026

14961005-0008